TRAVELER

japan

japan

by Perrin Lindelauf & Nicholas Bornoff
photography by Ken Shimizu

National Geographic
Washington, D.C.

CONTENTS

Pages 2–3: Tea pickers in springtime at the foot of Mount Fuji
Opposite: The temple of Senso-ji, in Tokyo, welcomes all travelers.

TRAVELING WITH EYES OPEN

Alert travelers go with a purpose and leave with a benefit. If you travel responsibly, you can help support wildlife conservation, historic preservation, and cultural enrichment in the places you visit. You can enrich your own travel experience as well.

To be a geo-savvy traveler:

- Recognize that your presence has an impact on the places you visit.

- Spend your time and money in ways that sustain local character. (Besides, it's more interesting that way.)

- Value the destination's natural and cultural heritage.

- Respect the local customs and traditions.

- Express appreciation to local people about things you find interesting and unique to the place: its nature and scenery, music and food, historic villages and buildings.

- Vote with your wallet: Support the people who support the place, patronizing businesses that make an effort to celebrate and protect what's special there. Seek out local shops, restaurants, and inns. Use tour operators who love their home—who love taking care of it and showing it off. Avoid businesses that detract from the character of the place.

- Enrich yourself, taking home memories and stories to tell, knowing that you have contributed to the preservation and enhancement of the destination.

That is the type of travel now called geotourism, defined as "tourism that sustains or enhances the geographical character of a place—its environment, culture, aesthetics, heritage, and the well-being of its residents." To learn more, visit National Geographic's Center for Sustainable Destinations at *travel.nationalgeographic.com/travel/geotourism.*

ABOUT THE AUTHORS & THE PHOTOGRAPHER

Perrin Lindelauf was born in the Canadian Rockies and came to Japan in 2005 after studying English literature, philosophy, and languages at the University of British Columbia. During his time in Japan, he has traveled to all of its corners, hunting for little-known treasures and historical oddities. He has gotten a little lost in mountains all over the archipelago, gotten naked with strangers more times than he can count, and eaten everything from fermented sushi to live minnows. He researched and revised the previous edition of this book and has edited several other guides in the Traveler series. He currently splits his time between Kyoto, Tokyo, and Vancouver.

Born in London of Anglo-French parentage, **Nicholas Bornoff** was educated in both France and the United Kingdom. He worked as film critic for the *Japan Times* and wrote about contemporary Japanese arts and society for magazines such as the *Far Eastern Economic Review, Asian Advertising & Marketing*, and the *Tokyo Journal*. In addition to researching the first three editions of this book, Bornoff published the nonfiction survey *Pink Samurai: Love, Marriage & Sex in Contemporary Japan* to critical acclaim in 1991. He died in 2010.

Ken Shimizu is a freelance photographer based in Tokyo, whose clients include *National Geographic Japan* and A.F.P. He has a master's degree in visual communication from Ohio University.

Charting Your Trip

Japan may be a narrow archipelago, but its geographical and cultural variety is vast. From snowy volcanoes to lush subtropical atolls, from pulsing mega-cities to the still of Zen gardens, there's a side of Japan for everyone. Tokyo, Earth's most populous metropolis; Kyoto, cultural capital for a thousand years; snowcapped Mount Fuji; somber memorials in Hiroshima; a Buddhist bell rung in a mountain temple: The essential Japanese experiences could fill a lifetime.

The Japanese archipelago runs 1,860 miles (2,994 km) southwest from the chilly island of Hokkaido off eastern Siberia to the subtropical islets of Okinawa near Taiwan. Honshu (the "main island") is home to many large cities and ancient historical sites, while the smaller islands of Shikoku, Kyushu, and Hokkaido are relatively rural. Well-maintained roads vein the mountainous terrain, yet rail is the most popular form of transit. The Shinkansen or "bullet train" links nearly all Japan, and at a top speed of 186 miles an hour (300 kph) it covers the 320 miles (515 km) between Tokyo and Kyoto in just 2.5 hours. On the Shinkansen, nearly anywhere is within a half-day's travel. The train is affordable if you buy the Japan Rail Pass (japanrailpass .net) at a travel agent before you leave for Japan: This allows unlimited travel for one to three weeks on JR lines (US$380–$810). If you count time spent reaching airports, the Shinkansen is as fast and as cheap as flying within the main island of Honshu, but trips to the southernmost or northernmost islands are faster and cheaper by plane, outside holiday seasons. If you prefer to fly, All Nippon Airways (ANA, ana .co.jp) and Japan Airlines (JAL, jal.co.jp) are the two national carriers. Newer low-cost carriers such as Peach Airlines (flypeach.com) offer cheaper, less-convenient flights.

The countryside has scenic roads for driving or cycling enthusiasts, but most expressways are expensive, elevated concrete half-pipes with no views. Gas and car rental prices make road trips best for groups, but highway buses are cheaper than trains if you have time. JR Highway Bus runs almost everywhere, and a variety of smaller firms such as Willer Express (willerexpress.com) and Sakura Kanko offer better prices, more leg room, or free Wi-Fi and power outlets. Most bus websites are only in Japanese so travel agents are the easiest way to book tickets. For shorter distances, nearly every city has a punctual, convenient subway or train system, and buses run to remote villages. Taxis are plentiful in towns and cities, typically charging about ¥620 ($6) for two km and ¥260 ($2.50) for each

Sushi adds color to tables worldwide.

additional kilometer. Bicycle rental is a good transit alternative in most midsize towns, and drivers are used to sharing the road with cyclists.

How to Visit: If You Have One Week

In planning a Japan trip, variety is key. Many visitors are overwhelmed by the pace of the big cities or quickly tire of temples, so the ideal one-week trip is a sampler of activities. After arriving at Tokyo's Narita or Haneda Airport, spend **Day 1** visiting the Tokyo National Museum, then head to Asakusa, the capital's oldest district and home of Tokyo Skytree. For nightlife, explore Kabuki-cho or Roppongi. On **Day 2** wake early for sushi breakfast at Tsukiji Central Fish Market, then shop in glitzy Omotesando, and explore the subcultures of Akihabara's Electric Town. On **Day 3** take a day trip to Kamakura for Buddhist and samurai history, or to the lakes at the base of iconic Mount Fuji.

NOT TO BE MISSED:

Plunging into the hectic, electric metropolis of Tokyo 63

Climbing sacred Mount Fuji 122

A visit to Gion in Kyoto, Japan's main Geisha district 210–211

The quiet grace of an exquisite tea ceremony 227

Eating your heart out in lively, hedonistic Osaka 245–250

Experiencing the life of a monk on Mount Koya 257

Shedding stress at an *onsen*, a hot-spring resort 322

   The second half of the trip should be spent around Kyoto, the ancient capital, 320 miles (515 km) southwest. Take the Shinkansen (2.5 hr.) or night bus (8 hr.) and spend **Day 4** in the Higashiyama district, making sure to see Fushimi Inari Shrine, the great temple Kiyomizu-dera, and Nanzen-ji's beautiful Zen gardens. End the day wandering around Gion, trying to spot a geisha among the cobbled lanes and teahouses.

   On **Day 5** beat the crowds to Kinkaku-ji, the Golden Pavilion, then take the bus to the Arashiyama district, notable for the gardens of Tenryu-ji and Okochi Sanso, as well as the Bamboo Grove. In the evening watch a traditional arts performance or head to Osaka for its wild nightlife and exquisite restaurants. **Day 6** can be spent on any number of excellent day trips from Kyoto or Osaka, including venerable Nara city (25 miles/ 40 km, 45 minutes by train from Kyoto), which has some of the oldest wooden temples in the world; Hiroshima (236 miles/380 km, 100 minutes by Shinkansen) is a sobering reflection on war; and Mount Koya (68 miles/110 km, 2.5 hours by train) is a mountain

Visitor Information

The Japan National Tourism Organization (*www.jnto.go.jp*) covers all major tourist sites and offers emergency information. As the most popular destinations, Tokyo (*gotokyo.org*) and Kyoto (*kyoto.travel*) have excellent online introductions to their sights. Tourist information booths can be found in all airports, in most Shinkansen stations, and in smaller train stations serving rural tourist areas. Individual cities have English tourism websites, listing *anaba* (secret spots).

   Local publications are the best way to learn about events and the countless festivals occurring year-round: The *Japan Times* (*japantimes.co.jp*) is Japan's only native English newspaper and lists major cultural events. In Tokyo, the monthly *Tokyo Journal* (*tokyo-journal.com*) and free biweekly *Metropolis* (*metropolisjapan.com*) cover Tokyo's restaurant and nightlife scene. Kyoto's cultural highlights and Osaka's party lifestyle are detailed in *Kansai Scene* (*kansaiscene.com*), a free monthly.

Currency

The Yen (¥)—pronounced "en"—comes in six coins: an aluminum ¥1, a light copper ¥5 with a hole, a dark copper ¥10, a nickel ¥50 with a hole, a nickel ¥100, and a light copper ¥500, and in bills of ¥1,000, ¥2,000, ¥5,000, and ¥10,000. The yen is presently even with the U.S. penny, with ¥100 nearly $1. Japan is a cash-based society: There's no debit card system, and credit cards are only used for large purchases, expensive restaurants, and hotels. Be sure to carry cash, but be warned: ATMs shut down with banks during national holidays!

Admission Costs

The $–$$$$$ scale used in this guidebook delineates entry fees:

    $ = Up to $5
    $$ = $5–$9
    $$$ = $10–$15
    $$$$ = $16–$25
    $$$$$ = Over $25

monastery where you can retreat in quiet contemplation with trainee Buddhist monks.

Before returning to Tokyo, you *must* stay in an *onsen* (hot spring) resort. Favorites include Kinosaki (99 miles/160 km, 2.5 hours by train from Kyoto), a town on the Sea of Japan, famous for crab and its public baths; Yuzawa Onsen (124 miles/200 km, 80 minutes by train from Tokyo), great for snowy slopes and an après-ski soak; and Kawayu Onsen (161 miles/260 km, 4 hours by train or bus from Kyoto), where hot water bubbles up from under the river and you can dig your own bath.

If You Have More Time

With more than a week, it's possible to visit the beautiful countryside. Many tourists attempt to "do Japan" by train in a blazing three-week trip, but it is better to deeply explore a limited area.

An extra week allows for time in the Japan Alps, a north–south range between Tokyo and Kyoto. You'll find stunning hikes out of Kamikochi and timeless mountain towns such as Takayama. For scenery and excellent onsen, the Tohoku region, north of Tokyo, rivals the Japan Alps.

Farther afield, the island of Shikoku preserves old Japan. Despite being linked to the mainland in the 1990s with three massive bridges, rugged Shikoku has largely defied the breakneck modernization of Honshu. A Buddhist pilgrimage route established 1,200 years ago begins in Tokushima city, follows the coast, and is popular with walkers, soul searchers, and bus pilgrims (see p. 293). Shikoku's Yoshino River also has the best rafting in Japan, but if thrills aren't your thing, Kochi city, on the Pacific coast, is renowned as a chilled-out surfers' paradise. The islands of the Inland Sea,

What to Pack

Traveling light is easy in Japan, but as shoes must come off in restaurants, temples, hotels, and homes, be sure to bring comfortable slip-ons and hole-free socks. The Japanese are appearance-conscious, so pack good clothes for going out. Shorts are worn only by boys, but you'll be forgiven in August. A handkerchief is useful as public toilets often lack paper towels and you'll want to mop sweat like a local during summer. For electronics,

Japan uses two parallel-blade plugs, like North America, but three-prong devices need an adapter. Voltage is lower (100V), so some devices may not work. Wi-Fi is more and more common, especially at hotels, Starbucks, and McDonald's. To avoid roaming charges on your cell phone, consider renting a SIM card from Softbank at your airport of arrival. Most importantly, bring little gifts from home for the people you meet during your trip.

Three thousand people cross at every light change in Shibuya Crossing, Tokyo.

between Honshu and Shikoku, are worth visiting for their excellent art museums. The southernmost large island, Kyushu, sits closest to the Asian mainland. Nagasaki, victim of the second A-bomb, was once the only trade port for foreign vessels, and its surviving historical districts reflect old ties with distant nations. Nowadays it is Fukuoka that welcomes most travelers: Ferries connect with the continent, and lively street food stalls feed all comers. Kyushu's active tectonics make for stunning scenery at the massive Mount Aso supercaldera, while Sakurajima, a volcanic island offshore, regularly belches ash on Kagoshima city. Geothermic activity blesses the onsen town of Beppu, where water bubbles up in vibrant colors and you can bathe in steaming-hot sand. Kumamoto is notable for its reconstructed castle, and the towns of Saga Prefecture have a rich history of ceramic crafts.

The farthest ends of Japan, Okinawa and Hokkaido, are both natural refuges for stressed-out city-folk. Okinawa, once a separate kingdom, has a laid-back islander culture, turbulent history, and strong American influence. There's fine underwater life off Miyako island and Iriomote island's jungle-carpeted mountains are laced with trails and rivers for kayaking. Northernmost Hokkaido island has rolling farmland around mountain ranges that draw hikers and skiers. Sapporo, the prefectural capital, is famous for its Snow Festival and beer, and the rest of Hokkaido abounds with parks. Popular Mount Niseko, southwest of Sapporo, has deep, powder snow, and volcanic Daisetsuzan National Park offers visitors some of Japan's finest wilderness. ∎

When to Go

In spring the *sakura* (cherry trees) explode in pink from late March. A *hanami* (cherry blossom party) is a must-do, but hotels fill quickly in April. *Tsuyu*, the short rainy season in June and July, is intense and humid. Fall is milder and the foliage is stunning. Winters are cold and wet, but mountains along the Sea of Japan receive huge snowfalls to the delight of skiers and the country's *onsen* (hot springs) fill with flesh. Avoid the national holidays of Golden Week (April 29–May 5), O-Bon (the 2nd week of August), and the week around New Year, as prices soar and crowds hit critical mass.

History & Culture

Japanese parasol of waxed paper
and bamboo
Opposite: A *maiko* prepares for
her life as a geisha.

Japan Today

Self-identity sits awkwardly with the Japanese. After a long history of cultural isolation, followed by half a century as an aggressor in the Pacific, Japan has recently struggled to explain its rich culture, customs, and mind-set; the cherry trees, electronics, ninja, and karaoke machines the outside world knows never quite capture the essence of the people.

"We Japanese," they'll begin, "don't dance. We worship our ancestors but aren't very religious. We eat rice and fish, and most of us can't drink. We are shy, respect our elders, and maintain harmony over everything else." This, too, misses the mark. The myth of a pure people, descended from the sun goddess and unmixed with other nations, combined with mono-ethnic Japan's 1.2 percent foreign population, has led many Japanese to believe in and propagate that cultural edifice, the homogenous but misleading "we."

Much of Japan's refracted sense of self-identity came about through its historical interactions with the West. American gunboat diplomacy ended Japan's long isolation in the 19th century. At the time, the concept of a universally held Japanese culture served as a bulwark against the tidal wave of modernizing Western technology and thinking. The same fears—that Japan is losing its language, dress, mind-set, and cuisine—motivate the arguments about orthodox culture today, but the homogeneity of the past has broken down, rendering the phrase "we Japanese" as intangible as "we Americans." Technology, globalization, the income gap between pre- and post-economic bubble generations: The factors for increasing cultural diversity are many. Modern Japan could just as easily be described as a nation of brazen iconoclasts, of dancers and the deeply devout, of burger eaters and boozers. So, visitors should take such sweeping pronouncements with a grain of salt. There are many generalities to be made about modern Japan, but the reality of its culture is more dazzlingly diverse than the traditionalists dare admit.

> **Much of Japan's refracted sense of self-identity came about through its historical interactions with the West.**

Economy

Japan's economic miracle, emerging from the advantages of cheap labor and a weak yen during the postwar period, saw exports increase rapidly from inexpensive tin toys to quality goods. Transistor radios paved the way for cameras, electrical appliances, ships, steel, color televisions, and cars. With a phenomenal growth rate of 11 percent, Japan was already the world's second largest economy outside the Iron Curtain by 1967.

By devaluing the yen, accepting wage cuts, and redoubling their effort, the Japanese softened the impact of the oil crisis of 1973. Exports soared, pushing up a trade surplus that had started five years before. In 1979 the second oil crisis was dealt with in a similar way.

Tokyo Skytree: At 2,080 feet (634 m), Tokyo's new broadcast tower on the Sumida River is the tallest tower and second tallest building in the world.

During the 1980s, Japan's economy surpassed even that of the United States. Its formidable wealth was sustained by booming domestic financial and consumer markets, low interest rates, and soaring real estate values in what was later dubbed the "Bubble Economy." A huge overseas trade imbalance, however, prompted international currency markets to force up the yen/dollar exchange rate in 1985. *Endaka*—the high value yen—slowed exports and economic performance at home, but doubled the value of national savings and generated a spending spree on overseas property markets. The bubble continued to inflate.

In 1990 the value of Japan's overseas holdings plummeted; its stock market lost almost half its value. In 1991 beleaguered Japanese banks raised interest rates to cover the loss—only exacerbating the growing problem of bad loans. The bubble burst. Japan's subsequent economic recovery was increasingly hampered by recession in the Asia-Pacific region because of its enormous investments in the area. As bad loans accumulated, bankruptcy became rife among the largest financial institutions during the 1990s.

The subsequent "Lost Decade" saw deflation, recession, and high unemployment, particularly among university graduates, but for most the standard of living remained as comfortable, if not as luxurious. In the 2010s, a strong yen due to the turbulent global economy crippled exports, and companies were forced to move more operations overseas. The 2011 Great East Japan Earthquake also caused energy shortages that pinched businesses and forced radical energy-saving measures and the implementation of alternative-shift schedules to accommodate the demand for electricity. These factors have impeded the economy's recovery, but hopes are that the large infrastructure investments for the 2020 Tokyo Olympics will be the final push in Japan's economic revival.

A Japanese bride wears her horn-hiding hat; the groom's belly cushion exaggerates his wealth.

The World of Work

The Japanese work ethic is legendary. The salaryman (male office worker) traditionally commutes for an average of two hours and spends up to ten hours in the office, six days a week. O.L.s (office ladies) work eight hours a day. When the office closes, the salaryman is expected to join coworkers for a drink, using alcohol an as excuse to express opinions about work that can't be said during the day. His children will be asleep when he gets home; he spends only Sunday with them—if he can stay awake. He is entitled to two weeks' paid holiday a year, but corporate loyalty reduces this to around four days. Until the mid-1990s, the salaryman was employed for life, ascending the corporate hierarchy with age. If the middle management responsibilities of his 40s did not result in *karoshi*—dropping dead from overwork—he went on to senior management and retirement at 60.

Although still common, this traditional work model has come under heavy social and economic pressure since the Bubble Economy burst. Promotion is based increasingly on ability; head-hunting and job changing are becoming more common. Japan's targeted 40-hour workweek has gotten closer as a somewhat toothless law limiting overtime to 45 hours a month has been passed. The energy crisis and economic downturn have also forced many companies to send their staff home early rather than lay them off, but overtime, once a matter of course and unpaid, is now work taken home.

The smaller the company, the greater the likelihood of long hours. Many small businesses are subcontractors for larger firms, and competition remains sharp even during a recession: If one firm cannot meet low prices and hard deadlines, another is ready and willing. Some run sweatshops with foreign labor, much of it illegal.

Unemployment, which still stood at 2.5 percent in 1991, shot up in the Lost Decade. Even today, the life employment system—though declining—keeps Japan's unemployment at an enviably low rate, between 4 and 5 percent, although this figure conceals a large number of young people working part-time and the estimated one million *hikikomori* recluses (see p. 217) who have retreated from the pressures of society completely.

Men & Women

The relationship between Japanese men and women is currently at a crossroads. Today's elders were typically married off by arrangement, and marriages survived due to the social stigma of divorce and a lot of patience. Modern generations have largely chosen for themselves, but the mating dance has been difficult. Long work hours and the general habit of keeping to friends of one's own gender severely limits the opportunities to meet a prospective partner; in addition, despite the adoption of marriage-for-love, Japanese men generally remain shy about pursuing a love interest: The new term "herbivore males" describes this lack of interest in sex or power. Blame has been attributed to comic-book fantasies, a societal ambivalence to prostitution, and profuse pornography.

Most Japanese women have stuck to the equally passive "wait and hope" method, but recent stopgap measures, such as singles' parties, have improved the situation somewhat. A sense of impending deadline, usually experienced around the age of 28, leads to many rushed marriages, and the divorce rate has climbed accordingly to 35 percent.

The Devil in the Details of *Tsunokakushi*

The traditional white paper hats that many Japanese brides wear are called *tsunokakushi*, literally "horn hiders." The custom comes from the legendary difficulty of marrying off daughters who were born as grouchy ogresses, complete with horns. The family of the bride would hide her horns with this hat to make sure the arranged marriage went through.

The honeymoon period was over once the horns came out, and the newlywed husband would then lament not realizing that he had been married off to an ogress. As sexist as this may now sound, Japanese women usually join in the tongue-in-cheek fun of tsunokakushi, warning, "That's right, I do have horns, so watch out!"

Those young Japanese who do manage to get married today face a society vastly different from that of their parents. The traditional salaryman, burdened with overtime, stumbled home late. Modern Japanese women, now more independent, better educated, and more likely to make a decent salary, are turned off by men who aren't willing to help raise children or share housework. The combination of fatigue, lack of privacy, and poor understanding of contraceptive alternatives has also rendered many marriages sexless and spouses more sibling-partners than lovers.

These troubles aside, members of the nearly invisible LGBTQ community have a much harder time finding social acceptance. Despite a well-documented history of gay relationships between monks, samurai and their apprentices, even about well-known warlord Oda Nobunaga (see p. 38) and his page Mori Ranmaru, many Japanese do not believe that homosexuality exists in Japan. Many heterosexual marriages are made to conceal true orientations and outing oneself is rare, except for a few celebrities. The use of cross-dressing characters on variety shows for a cheap laugh can't help either.

Home & Family

The old *ie* (household) system, male-dominated and based on seniority, was banned by the constitution in 1946—a factor contributing to mass urban migration prompted by job opportunities. Traditionally, three generations lived under one roof, an extended family pattern now seen only in rural areas; more than 66 percent of the population lives in towns, where the nuclear family is the norm.

However, a falling birthrate poses the growing problem of a graying society. With care for the elderly woefully inadequate, extended households within the same building are increasing again. But with their own apartments, the generations enjoy greater privacy and independence.

Home for the average one-child urban family is 2LDK—two bedrooms, living/dining/kitchen in one. Because of the lack of living space, the majority of Japanese—especially men—seek entertainment outside the home.

> **Those young Japanese who do manage to get married today face a society vastly different from that of their parents.**

The meek salaryman who bows at work but lords over his own family is increasingly rare as the traditional housewife has headed into the workforce and has less time to wait upon him. The image of an obedient housewife kneeling at the door and asking, "Would you like a bath or dinner first, dear?" is laughably outdated. Traditionally women have ruled the roost, managing expenses, savings, investment, house repairs, and children's education. Wage-slaving husbands have often seen only a tiny bit of their salaries, handed over as *kozukai* (his allowance), while the purse strings remain tightly tied. This arrangement is also in flux among the younger generation: More men take active roles with the kids, cook, and participate in money discussions.

Upbringing & Education: Westerners are often said to grow out of the strictures of childhood into the relative freedom of adulthood, while in Japan the reverse is the case. Japanese children are generally indulged to a greater degree than their Western counterparts. Spanking is frowned upon; a naughty child is usually threatened with either maternal abandonment or ridicule by others.

Japan's future will rely heavily on a well-educated workforce and an edge in electronics.

The vise starts tightening outside the home. During six years of elementary, three of junior high, and three of high school, the pressures to conform to rules and group restraints tend to override individual aspirations. The *jiken jigoku* (examination hell) period before university entrance exams is notorious, leaving teens with about five hours' sleep a night. With at least double the homework of U.S. counterparts, children enroll in *juku* (cram schools) for up to three hours after school. The educational Cold War has only gotten worse, with heavy cramming to pass entrance exams to good junior high schools, elementary schools, and even kindergartens. Private "escalator schools" circumvent this problem: After passing an entrance exam, wealthy scions join elementary schools connected to good universities and no further entrance exams are required. Convenient for wealthy families, the system's academic value is dubious as it's nearly impossible to flunk out.

Many Westerners have a misconceived awe for Japanese education, assuming that it underlies the country's economic success. In fact, although the form changed to follow American patterns during the Occupation (1945–1952), the rote memorization demanded by exams is only now beginning to change toward active, student-centered learning. Failure to be admitted to the desired university causes great anguish in parents and pupils alike; those redoubling their efforts to succeed by studying at full-time cram schools outside the state education system are known as *ronin* (masterless samurai).

Previously, prospective employers chose fresh university graduates based on the reputation of their alma mater rather than on grade point average, so once a student made it into a famous university he no longer had to study. Merely attending some classes and submitting substandard work was often enough to graduate, so for most students university life was four years of bliss where they were free to develop neglected social skills and rest their burned-out brains. This worked when companies would hire and fully train new lifetime employees, but the collapse of lifetime employment has led to shorter training and more pressure on universities to prepare students for the world of work.

(continued on p. 24)

Food & Drink

When it comes to Japan's soft power, cuisine is king. The number of Americans without passing familiarity with dishes such as sushi, ramen, and teriyaki chicken is smaller and smaller each year. Beyond these common dishes, Japanese cuisine is amazingly diverse.

Cold buckwheat noodles: Even the simplest Japanese cuisine delights the taste buds and the eyes.

The Japanese pursue their cuisine with passion. It is no wonder that a nation obsessed with eating out and striving for the very best should be host to ever increasing numbers of Michelin-starred restaurants and have created the globally popular *Iron Chef* cook-off TV show.

The foundation of Japanese cuisine is rice, so much so that *gohan* means both "meal" and "rice." The Japanese primarily eat *japonica*, a sticky, short-grain, slightly sweet variety, as well as *mochi*, a glutinous variety used to make rice cakes. As *hakumai* (white rice), japonica is milled to less than fifty percent of its original size and is prized for its firm texture and sweetness. Brown rice, or *genmai*, is popular with the health-conscious, but it is generally disliked for being too hard. Rice is usually eaten plain, but it is sometimes covered with raw fish or beef in a casual *donburi*. Putting soy sauce on Japanese

rice is not only disrespectful to its delicate flavor and your cook's abilities, it is the behavior of a naughty Japanese toddler. You have been warned.

After rice, pride of place goes to the humble soybean and its many uses. Tofu is either soft, fried in oil, or fried and then dried. Miso, the ubiquitous fermented soybean paste, is used to make soup or as a glaze, and *natto,* the sticky, stinky, fermented beans famous for turning off most foreign visitors, are eaten daily for their healthy probiotic cocktail and ostensible flavor. Most important is *shoyu* (soy sauce), which, along with *dashi* (fish or seaweed soup stock), *mirin* (sweetened rice wine), and saké, make up the essential flavor combinations of Japanese food. Indeed, "teriyaki sauce" does not exist in Japan, as it is a simple mix of soy sauce, saké (or mirin), and sugar that anyone can make.

Noodles round out the carbohydrates. Two wheat-based noodles, thick *udon* and very thin *somen,* are typically eaten in a light fish stock with vegetables. *Soba,* a buckwheat noodle, is frequently eaten chilled with a dipping sauce in the summer. Originally a Chinese dish, ramen wheat noodles are a national obsession, with hundreds of noodle joints in each large city and soup stocks ranging from a light salt or soy sauce base to the heavy "liquid pig" *tonkotsu* (pork bone) broths.

Legumes, Fruit & Vegetables

One reason for Japanese longevity is the large amount of vegetables, typically boiled or pickled, that are served in traditional dishes. Indeed, the average traditional dish is heavily weighted toward rice and vegetables, with meat or fish providing a tasty garnish. Along with common carrots, onions, and the like, giant radishes, bamboo shoots, baby ferns, and lotus or burdock root stand out as typical of Japan's cuisine. *Shun,* roughly translated as "perfect seasonality" or "being just ripe," is the quality that Japanese chefs consider essential in their produce, which also explains some of the crazy prices for pristine cantaloupes and $100 a cap *matsutake* mushrooms.

Most internationally popular fruit is consumed in Japan, but some unusual produce is worth looking out for. The *yuzu* (like a citron) has an excellent fragrance and is also put in the bath in winter for its smell; the *sudachi* (similar to a lime) is great in drinks, and the *biwa* (loquat) is delicate and wonderful when in season. *Kaki* (persimmons) are popular too; in winter keep your eyes open for dried and sugared *shibugaki* (astringent persimmons).

Other than the important soy bean, the *azuki* is the most common legume. A small red bean, it is boiled with sugar for sweets such as *yokan* or added to rice for *sekihan,* a dish eaten on special days.

Seafood

Although the Japanese diet has incorporated more meat since the war, seafood is a regular part of a meal. Ideally, seafood is fresh enough

---

EXPERIENCE: Eat Deadly Fugu!

Puffer fish, blowfish, balloonfish, swellfish, or culinary death wish: Whatever you call it, *fugu,* the deadly winter fish, is Japan's most infamous dish.

Innocuously plump in display tanks, fugu's appearance belies the fatal neurotoxins concentrated in its liver, ovaries, and spines. Only licensed chefs are permitted to serve it, as training is required to remove the toxic organs and avoid contaminating the rest of the fish.

Despite the dangers, deaths are extremely rare and are usually the result of preparing self-caught fugu at home or of intentionally eating the liver at a restaurant willing to break the law to serve wealthy foodies—the organ is said to be the most delicious. Even with the death rate as low as three fatalities per year,

why even risk it? First, eating fugu is the culinary equivalent of skydiving. Second, the Japanese consider it a delicacy, a very special (and typically expensive) treat, although most foreigners can really only remember the iron taste of fear the first time they try it. While the chefs remove the toxic parts, some diners still experience a thrilling and psychosomatic tingling of the lips. Last, you'll be able to tell friends back home that you ate the deadly fugu and lived to tell the tale! Good places to try fugu include:

Tokyo: Fugu Fukuji *(tel 03/5148-2922; 3-11-13 Ginza, Chuo-ku)* puts on a real budget-breaking feast.

Osaka: Zuboraya *(tel 06/6211-0181; 1-6-10 Dotombori, Chuo-ku)* serves cheaper farmed fugu year-round.

to be enjoyed raw—in slices as *sashimi* or on rice as *sushi*—but grilled and broiled fish are daily mainstays. Although *maguro* (tuna) in sushi or sashimi is the most iconic, a huge variety of seafood is eaten: Whatever doesn't taste good raw (such as *saba*, or mackerel) or is slightly less than fresh gets grilled. Cooking in a hot pot with mirin can also cut the fishy flavor and transform an unusual sea creature into a delicacy. Octopus, sea urchin, a host of shellfish, and *unagi* (eel) are all popular.

Meat

Formerly forbidden by Buddhist precepts, meat is on the fast track to pass fish in the hearts of young Japanese. Although popular, meat is usually sliced thin and boiled with vegetables in *sukiyaki* or served in minute steaks: It rarely outweighs the meal's vegetable component. As with other ingredients, quality is emphasized over volume. While Kobe beef is the most famous dish internationally, a more typical meal would be *tonkatsu,* a breaded pork cutlet adopted during Japan's craze for all things Western in the late 19th century.

Offal, or *horumon* (literally "ditch food"), was once considered only fit for Korean immigrants, who would eat something that the Japanese threw out. Although this attitude is largely a thing of the past and barbecue restaurants serve everything from second stomach to aorta, the name has stuck.

Sweets

Traditional sweets are based around azuki beans boiled with sugar, and glutinous mochi rice, which is pounded into cakes. Such sweets are intended to offset the bitterness of strong tea, rather than be eaten as dessert, which essentially doesn't exist in traditional cuisine. Sadly, most Western desserts are adapted to the Japanese palate: Low in sugar and fat, they tend to be a bit predictable and bland, though it is possible to stumble across a baker hell-bent on making authentic French pastry, whether or not it sells.

Tea & Saké

When it comes to beverages, tea is drunk before or after meals, and coffee is widely popular for break time. The full range of experiences, between the highest quality and the most convenient, are no better seen than in tea and coffee. On the one hand, coffee

---

Dinner Manners

Although the Japanese are very forgiving, it is possible to offend at meals. Foremost, chopsticks should never be stuck vertically into food nor be used to pass food from chopsticks to chopsticks. Both of these gestures are associated with funerals. Always place your chopsticks on the small rest provided. To pass food, place it on a small plate with the reverse ends of your chopsticks. Disposable chopsticks shouldn't be rubbed together after breaking them apart: This implies that they are cheap and splinters have to be rubbed off, which reflects poorly upon your host. Above all, do your best with chopsticks—no spearing!—and your hosts will shower you with praise, as they don't believe foreigners can use them. Likewise, beginning the meal with *"itadakimasu"* ("I humbly receive") and ending with *"gochisosama"* ("thanks for the meal") scores major guest points.

A common faux pas is pouring your own drinks. This implies that the host isn't looking after you and didn't notice your glass was empty. The host will fill your glass while you lift it from the table with both hands. To reciprocate, lift the bottle with both hands, even if it is small.

Lastly, the number one no-no is blowing your nose. Dab and sniff like the locals, or excuse yourself.

Sushi chefs serve seafood delights to Tokyo residents at counters like these throughout the city.

addiction grips Japan nearly as tightly as it does the West, and excellent cafés abound. *Matcha*, powdered green tea, and *sencha*, the whole leaf variety, both have complex tea ceremonies built up around their consumption, involving codes of behavior, complementary works of art, and appropriate setting. On the other hand, both coffee and tea are overwhelmingly consumed out of plastic bottles from the 5 million vending machines across the nation. Here's a challenge: At any point during your trip to Japan, spin in a circle and see how many vending machines you can count. Needless to say, these beverages aren't great, but they go down well on a hot summer day or a cold winter evening.

Saké refers to all Japanese alcohol; the fermented rice known abroad by the same name is also called *nihonshu* (15–18 percent alcohol) and is served hot or cold in little cups. In Japan's chilly winters, hot saké is a real pick-me-up. *Shochu* is a liquor distilled from sweet potatoes, barley, or rice, and the better varieties resemble whisky or vodka. Another easy drink to try is *umeshu*, a sweet plum liqueur.

All of these drinks, however, pale before domestic beer. Most popular are big-name lagers by Asahi, Sapporo and Kirin, but watch out for *happoshu* and "third beer": These cheap, reduced-malt brews are cut with grain alcohol and will leave you much the worse after a night out. Also beware "all-free" beer, as it has no calories, no alcohol, and no flavor. Fortunately, *jibiru* (craft beer) is gradually gaining popularity, so there's more to try beyond the big brands.

Vegetarian, Vegan, Gluten Free

While the Japanese have traditionally eaten little meat, avoiding fish is tricky. Unless a soup stock is made with *konbu* (kelp), you can assume that the base is bonito, shellfish, or chicken. *Shojin-ryori*, the traditional temple cuisine, is vegan-friendly, but hard to find and pricey. It is better to specifically seek out restaurants in large cities that cater to vegetarians and vegans, or eat Indian food, which usually has several veggie options.

The Japanese happily eat gluten, even whole blocks of pure wheat gluten, called *namafu*, and the gluten-free diet has no traction here. To go gluten free, you'll need to avoid soy sauce, tempura breading, and all noodles, but more than that, you'll need to explain why you can't consume the all-important soy sauce, a significant language and culture problem.

Leisure & Recreation

When they find the time, Japanese take leisure very seriously. Traditional pursuits such as the tea ceremony, flower arrangement, and calligraphy remain just as popular as video games, comics, and online surfing. Nearly everyone learns some form of martial arts at school, but the big sports nowadays are decidedly Western. Baseball enjoys a fanatic following, and soccer has exploded in popularity with the successes of both national teams and the co-hosting of the 2002 World Cup. Eating out is a national passion: Japanese women tend to be more gregarious, shopping and hitting cafés with friends, while men are more likely to engage in solo pursuits, playing video games or reading comics.

Language & Writing

The origin of the Japanese language is unknown. Possibly related to the Ural-Altaic group, which includes Finnish, Mongolian, Turkish, and Korean, it is grammatically similar to Korean but shares almost no words. Despite Japan's adoption of many aspects of Chinese culture, including writing, the language is unrelated to Chinese. It may go back to Japan's early inhabitants, such as the Ainu, but beyond a few words and place-names, the Ainu language appears unrelated. There is evidence of a distant relationship with Austronesian languages, such as those of Malaysia, Indonesia, and the Philippines, mainly through similarities in vowel sounds.

A Latin-sounding A-E-I-O-U syllabary makes picking up a few words of Japanese easy, but learning to speak well is another matter. Instead of the subject-verb-object sentence order of most European languages, Japanese places the object first and the verb, which incorporates the subject, last. Speech is divided into familiar, informal, formal, and humble forms; men and women express themselves using different personal pronouns and synonyms appropriate to the context.

Japanese uses three character sets simultaneously. *Kanji,* or Chinese characters, were imported during the fifth century; of purely Japanese origin, the phonetic *hiragana* and

Western sports, such as soccer, inspire fanatical support in Japan.

katakana syllabaries were adopted during the eighth century. Very simply, kanji characters are used for nouns, hiragana for turning them into adjectives and verbs, and katakana for rendering words of foreign origin. Widely used in contexts such as advertising, *romaji* (the Roman alphabet) is virtually a fourth character set. There are simply too many homophones to make a single phonetic script viable (for instance, unless shown with a kanji character, *suru* could mean to do, print, rub, squander money, or pick a pocket).

Japanese Homes

First-time visitors to Japanese homes are often struck by the difference in lifestyle from the West. First, shoes must be taken off in a little foyer. Shoes would quickly destroy the tatami—thick, densely woven rush mats—so shoes inside are traditionally taboo, even in homes without tatami. The open layout of traditional homes is divided by walls of *fusuma,* sliding doors made of thick paper stretched on a wooden frame. They also have shoji, wooden grids covered in thin white paper that slide open behind windows.

Many homes have Western beds, but the traditional bedroom is nearly bare. Stored away in a closet during the daytime, the futon mattresses and bedding are laid out on the floor at night. Chairs are now common in the dining area, but especially in a tatami room you will be entertained at a low table while seated on cushions on the floor. The traditional Japanese home is built for airflow in the summer: Come winter, people resort to warming their feet and arms under a *kotatsu*—a table with a skirt of quilting and an electric heater inside—but as this leaves one's head and back cold, modern homes typically rely on heated flooring or vented heat to the sacrifice of the pleasant familial mood of a shared kotatsu.

The bath *(ofuro)* is a deep cube in which you soak, but only once you're squeaky clean. Soap yourself first and rinse off using a tap, a shower, or water drawn from the bath in a bucket. Never wash in the bath; others will relax in the water after you.

The Western toilet is common, as is the "washlet," with a heated seat, bidet, and anti-odor function. Increasingly rare, the squat toilet can still be found in train stations.

Religion

It is facetiously said that the Japanese are born Shintoist, marry Christian, and are buried Buddhist. Although Buddhism and Shinto have countless devotees, Japan

---

Basic Japanese Terms

The most immediately important words are for the bathrooms, and although you'll usually see the men's and women's symbols or some variant in English, some traditional hotels and classy restaurants use only the Chinese characters: 男 is "man" (gents) and 女 is "woman" (ladies).

In Japan, a few pleasantries go a long way. Master these before tackling the Language Guide (see p. 359).

Kon'nichi wa	Hello
Sayonara	Good-bye
Sumimasen	Excuse me
Gomen'nasai	I'm sorry
Arigatou	Thank you

Several common suffixes are used throughout this book:

-ji or -dera (temple) as in Hongan-ji or Kiyomizu-dera
-jinja or -gu (shrine) as in Inari-jinja
-jo (castle) as in Matsumoto-jo
-ko (lake) as in Ashino-ko
-san or -dake (mountain) as in Fuji-san or Tsurugi-dake
-kawa or -gawa (river) as in Sumida-gawa, Shira-kawa
-dori (street) as in Omotesando-dori
-koen (park) as in Yoyogi-koen

is increasingly secular, and, for many, observances are a matter of form. More than 90 percent of Japanese practice both Shinto, for the rites of baptism and marriage, and Buddhism, mainly reserved for memorial ceremonies. Christianity is practiced by a minority, but ersatz Christian weddings held in chapel-shaped hotel halls and presided over by foreign English teachers in priestly garb are de rigueur.

Shinto: Shinto (the Way of the Gods) is the name given to various animistic belief systems of prehistoric origin that worship *kami*, the deities in all things. According to Shinto creation myths, the Japanese and their emperors descended from the gods. Many Shinto variants are based on the belief that all people become kami after death, so a large part of Shinto practice is ancestor worship. Very few entertain truly animist beliefs today, but Shinto thrives as a matter of ceremony and superstition. Colorful *matsuri* (festivals) remain popular, and some 70 million people visit shrines during New Year's celebrations.

Confucianism: The code of ethics of the Chinese sage Confucius (551–479 B.C.) preaches humility, frugality, generosity, and temperance. Founded on filial piety, respect for the aged, and observance of tradition, it was applied to governmental principles in Japan from around the seventh century, but had little direct influence until after 1333, when new Chinese forms were adopted and adapted by the samurai. Confucianism served to reinforce social hierarchy and loyalty to feudal lords and/or the emperor, according to the swing of the pendulum of power.

Country of Endless Surprises

Each country has its own peculiarities and Japan is no exception, with striking differences that pop up at unexpected moments. Here's a checklist of things to take in stride—or even seek out—as a worldly traveler.

1. Waking in a peaceful, tiny village to a municipal loudspeaker blasting the "It's now 6 a.m.!" song.
2. Realizing that the local delicacy is still alive, or at least not quite dead.
3. Finding your every purchase triple-wrapped and double-bagged.
4. Spotting ubiquitous surgical masks come pollen season and head-to-toe swaddling on overheating, sunburn-conscious ladies in the summer.
5. Witnessing rebellious teens riding tiny scooters, gunning their little engines just to annoy the neighbors.
6. Passing by someone in a cosplay (costume play) outfit, any time of day or night.
7. Being physically jammed into the train by a white-gloved station attendant during rush hour (see sidebar p. 88).
8. Getting a warm, wet surprise on a Japanese washlet toilet (see Travelwise p. 358).
9. Hearing "Auld Lang Syne," a "Japanese song about fireflies" in shops every evening at closing time.
10. Striking up a conversation in the nude at an *onsen* (hot spring; see sidebar p. 322).
11. Watching young women on the subway putting on makeup and fake lashes, and then shaving off their eyebrows, oblivious to all other passengers.
12. Joining excited spectators who are throwing cushions into the ring to register their delight at a sumo wrestling upset (see sidebar p. 99).

A woman in traditional aristocratic pilgrim costume prays at Kumano Hongu Taisha, Tanabe, Wakayama Prefecture.

It also dictated the *ie* system, a patriarchal hierarchy in the household (see p. 18). Confucianism, with its emphasis on conformity, bolstered strict government control between 1603 and 1868 and was more recently exploited by nationalists. It is still taught in Japanese schools, as conformity remains a virtue, corporate loyalty overrides family life, and society remains hierarchical. The Japanese love of social harmony and avoidance of confrontation are also legacies of Confucianism.

Buddhism: Holding that the remedy for the pain of existence lies in meditation, the elimination of desire, and awareness of the transience of life, the teachings of the Buddha (Enlightened One) made their way from India to Japan via China and Korea. Brought by Korean emissaries in the mid-sixth century A.D., Mahayana Buddhism was decreed a state religion by Prince Shotoku in 593. During ensuing centuries, the Buddhist influence increased as various sects evolved.

The most internationally recognizable form of Japanese Buddhism, Zen was introduced from China during the Kamakura period (1185–1333). It discards scriptures and doctrine, believing that enlightenment is attainable only through individual effort, special meditation *(zazen),* and abstinence. Zen was favored by the samurai and has had a profound and enduring influence on the architecture, arts, and culture of Japan.

Christianity: Christianity was brought to Japan by Portuguese and Spanish friars, notably the Jesuit St. Francis Xavier, in the mid-16th century. It made headway, especially in Kyushu, but its spread posed a political threat to the shoguns (military governors) who, fearful of European colonialism, repressed it ruthlessly. With the closure of the country to outsiders in 1635, Christians went underground, emerging from hiding when the shogunate fell in 1868. Today about 2.4 million Christians practice in about 9,000 churches throughout Japan. ■

The Land

Forests cover nearly 60 percent of Japan's islands. Japanese cedar *(Cryptomeria)* and species of maple, beech, and magnolia are cultivated over most of the country. Chinquapin (chestnut), oak, and beech occur mainly in the forests of Honshu, with fir and silver fir in the Siberian climate of Hokkaido.

The vegetation in Kyushu and Okinawa takes a more tropical turn, boasting several species of palm and flowers that north of Tokyo could bloom only in a hothouse. Trees admired for their glorious spring blossoms, especially plum and

Japanese maple in fall, when much of Japan becomes a riot of red leaf

cherry, are found throughout the country. Azaleas, hydrangeas, and irises blossom during early summer, and red maples and chrysanthemums show their colors in the fall.

Many animals found in Honshu, Shikoku, and Kyushu are species also found elsewhere in the Northern Hemisphere. They include black bears, ferrets, wild boar, and the *tanuki* (raccoon dog), as well as birds such as pheasants, hawks, ducks, and cranes. Unique to Japan is the giant salamander, as well as the Japanese macaque—ubiquitous except on Hokkaido. The cicadas stand out among the insects for their diverse, incredibly loud shrieks. As the various species emerge at different times over the summer, each new call signals another step closer to the fall. Animals in chilly Hokkaido include sables and red foxes, as well as the brown bear. Some 6 feet (2 m) tall and 880 pounds (400 kg) in weight, it is about twice the size of its Honshu counterpart. Okinawa also has unique species of its own, such as the Iriomote wildcat, Amami hare, and habu viper.

> **Trees admired for their glorious spring blossoms, especially plum and cherry, are found throughout the country.**

A broad variety of sealife can be found along the Japanese archipelago. The Kuroshio current brings warm water up the coasts, carrying a host of fish to northern feeding grounds and heating the coast enough to allow soft coral reefs to grow. Everything from northernly king crab to fluorescent squid and the rare Okinawan dugong frequents Japan's waters.

Frequently forced out of their natural habitats by urbanization, Japan's wildlife populations have been steadily declining. Conservation measures adopted by the Environment Ministry in the 1980s protect 136 endangered species, but the Iriomote wildcat may soon go the way of the Japanese river otter, declared extinct in 2012.

Rural Japan has become increasingly developed, but past the bedroom towns of the major cities, the landscape is divided into rice fields and uninhabited mountains. Fear of landslides has often limited development of the steep interior. On flatlands, rice terraces are plentiful; much of the rest is managed forest, largely hay fever–inducing Japanese cedar plantations.

Resources

Up to the mid-20th century, Japan was mainly agricultural, but after World War II farming declined dramatically with the mass migration from the countryside. Nowadays manufacturing and construction account for about a third of national industry, and booming retail and service industries account for some three-fifths.

Today, with their livelihoods increasingly threatened by imports, farmers are major recipients of government subsidies. Rice, the national staple for centuries, is overproduced due to efficient modern techniques—the excess is seen as a backup plan for calamity, rather than waste. A traditional fondness for soybean products means that Japan imports more than 11 times the soybeans it produces. Eggs, poultry, and most vegetables are domestically produced, but 60 percent of the country's fruit is imported.

Three-quarters of Japan's dairy products come from Hokkaido; the rest are imported. Hokkaido also produces a substantial amount of wheat, about one-tenth of the total consumed. The world's largest per capita consumer of seafood supplies half of its demand with imports; Japan also imports half its meat, especially beef. Increased imports are often an indication of a change in consumer tastes, but for Japan, imports are simply cheaper.

Japan's notorious extravagance with wood and pulp products for everything ranging from houses to books—and a tendency for shops to wrap almost everything—is fueled by imports, notably from nations little concerned with the impact of deforestation on the global environment. Fully 72 percent of Japan's wood is imported.

A major steel producer, Japan has to import iron. Having very few energy resources, its industry is highly dependent on overseas sources, especially for oil. Since the 2011 Fukushima meltdown, there has been intense public pressure on the government and major energy companies to shift away from potentially disastrous nuclear energy, formerly the panacea to all of Japan's energy problems.

Manners & Behavior

In Japan, harmony, achieved through conformity and consensus, is a primary social concern; private cares are masked with public smiles, and the individual is obliged to conform to the outlook of the group.

The Japanese abhor being conspicuous and are usually reluctant to air personal opinions. In Japan, the vague and understated always trumps the forthright. Outspokenness is considered to be plain bad manners, and conversations find participants bending over backward to agree with each other.

Decisions are nearly always reached through consensus; in corporate contexts, the process can take some time. This underlies the cultural difficulties sometimes encountered by foreigners doing business in Japan and accounts for Japanese politicians sometimes being viewed as somewhat inarticulate abroad. That's the common view, anyway.

A quick look around reveals plenty of exceptions: punks revving motorbike engines just to irritate passersby; outspoken, opinionated old women holding forth about everything from public morality to the issues of the day; open weeping and rage in the wake of the Great East Japan Earthquake; even the bold, "to hell with bureaucratic consensus" stance of former prime minister Junichiro Koizumi, which won him much popular acclaim and the admiration of a grateful nation.

Still, this small, crowded country functions thanks in large part to the concerted effort of most of its citizens not to upset the apple cart.

The futuristic Series N700A Shinkansen rests in the old-world hub of Tokyo Station. The famous bullet train stitches Japan's archipelago together socially and economically.

Japan's Cities

The first impression of the Japanese landscape is that it is overwhelmingly urban and crowded. "Japan is a small country," the locals apologize, yet the urban proportion of the population is about two-thirds, lower than the North American average. Why then the intense crowds of Japan's major urban centers? With a median age of 46.5 years, Japan has one of the oldest population in the world, the oldest members of which retire to the ancestral country home. The younger generations flock to cities, but unlike other nationalities that move to the closest urban center to find work, the Japanese pile into a handful of megacities, leaving the capitals of rural prefectures underpopulated and quiet.

The reasons are part cultural, part historical. Near the end of the 19th century, the Meiji government moved to Tokyo and forced several industry-leading companies to relocate there as well so that they could be better regulated or manipulated. More fundamentally, however, the importance of face-to-face business meetings, necessitates that many businesses set up close to major partners. More than a quarter of Japan's 127 million people have crammed into the Greater Tokyo Metropolitan Area.

Where urban life goes, concrete follows. Japan's love affair with reinforced concrete stems from the postwar reconstruction era: Concrete was cheap and resistant to both earthquakes and fire, a lesson learned when Tokyo's wooden homes were torched during Allied firebombing. Little thought was given to design in the race to rebuild, and many provincial cities are marred with ugly, featureless cubes. In the intervening years, lavish pork-barrel spending has gone to firms close to the government, resulting in concrete breakwaters, concrete banks and beds for even the tiniest creeks, and concrete plasters retaining slopes stripped of their trees and never replanted. ■

History of Japan

Stone implements found in Japan show people lived there before the Ice Age, when the islands were linked to the Asian mainland. However, the earliest recognizable culture is known as Jomon, after the method used for decorating pottery and figurines.

Prehistory

Jomon means "straw rope," and the era, which lasted from 10,000 B.C. to 300 B.C., gets its name from the use of rope to imprint wet clay. The origins of the Jomon people are disputed, but we know they were hunter-gatherers and fishermen; among them were the ancestors of the Ainu, a people of prehistoric Siberian origin now living on Hokkaido. In the millennium after 500 B.C., mainland migrants gradually pushed these tribes to the far north and came to outnumber them ten to one.

Meaning "early spring," the Yayoi period (300 B.C.–A.D. 300) is the era of the most important mass migrations, mainly of Koreans arriving in northern Kyushu. The Koreans brought iron and bronze and, most importantly, the cultivation of rice to Japan. The arrival of agriculture early in the Yayoi era greatly shaped Japan. As farming spread, land ownership became the basis of status in the community; these changes in social structure paved the way for the feudal systems that would dominate in the future.

> **The Koreans brought iron and bronze and, most importantly, the cultivation of rice to Japan.**

Early Japan

Kofun (300–552): During the *Kofun* ("old tomb") period, rice cultivation was concentrated in the region that is now Kansai—probably the country described in fourth-century Chinese records as Yamato, ruled by Queen Himiko, a female shaman. The numerous burial mounds, some of enormous size, found on Honshu and Kyushu indicate that the Kofun era saw tribal headmen replaced by powerful chieftains able to raise large workforces from their sizable domains.

Some of the larger burial mounds, typically shaped like a keyhole and surrounded by a moat, have yielded sophisticated artifacts, including *haniwa* (clay representations of animals, objects, and humans), bronze mirrors, armor, swords, and jewelry. The largest of all Kofun tombs, near Osaka, is thought to contain the remains of the fifth-century emperor Nintoku. To this day, however, the excavation of imperial tombs is forbidden.

Asuka (552–710): Named after Yamato's first capital, thought to be in the south of present-day Osaka and Nara Prefectures, the Asuka period witnessed the accelerated adoption of Chinese culture. Introduced by visiting Korean statesmen during the mid-sixth century, Buddhism brought with it a cultural package including administration and bureaucracy, medicine, geomancy (like the Chinese feng shui, a belief in lucky and unlucky cardinal points), Confucianism, and writing.

Shirakawa-go's World Heritage site, with its *gassho-zukuri*-style (prayer hands) farmhouses

The process intensified under the scholarly and devout Shotoku Taishi (574–622), prince regent of the ruling Soga family. His active exchanges with China prompted major political, educational, and ethical reforms—including Japan's first constitution, based on Confucian principles—and also brought more sophisticated architecture, sculpture, painting, music, and poetry. Shotoku sponsored the building of many temples in the Asuka area, including Horyu-ji (see pp. 240–243).

Fierce rivalries followed Shotoku's death; the Soga clan grew greedy and sought to usurp the imperial line, forcing rival clans to assassinate key Soga members in 645 and drive the clan from power. Japan lost its foothold in Korea following a sea battle in 663, but exchanges with China continued. The new capital, Fujiwara, the first of three emulations of the great Chinese city of Ch'ang-an, was built south of Asuka in 694.

The Taika (Great Change) Reform, which was implemented by those who seized power from the Soga, furthered the centralization of imperial power that the Soga had begun. Independent landowners were enlisted as local government officials as their lands were nationalized and new taxes began to flow through the central government.

Nara (710–794): Heijo, a new, larger capital, was established just west of what is now Nara in 710 (see pp. 234–239). In the eighth century, greater unification was achieved through a new network of main roads connecting provincial capitals. This helped consolidate central government power. Buddhism made substantial headway under the pious Emperor Shomu (R.724–749), who built temples and monasteries—among them Nara's great Todai-ji—in each province of his realm.

> **Centralized government came under threat from both Buddhist clergy and clans who controlled outlying districts.**

Centralized government came under threat from both Buddhist clergy and clans who controlled outlying districts. Prominent in the labyrinth of intrigue was the Fujiwara family, which rose through astute marriages it arranged for its daughters. Koken, daughter of Shomu by a Fujiwara consort, succeeded him as empress in 749. Koken later had an affair with a powerful Buddhist priest and tried to make him emperor—a failing that is thought to have prompted the banning of women from imperial succession for almost a thousand years. To sever the influence of the Buddhist priesthood over the state, the capital was moved again in 784 to Nagaoka, southwest of what is now Kyoto.

Heian (794–1185): It is believed that several deaths in his family or a flood spurred the emperor Kammu to move the capital again in 794, to a site ten miles (16 km) northeast of Nagaoka. Heian-kyo—the capital of peace and tranquillity (later to become Kyoto)—was the grandest of all the copies of Ch'ang-an. The era was dominated by the Fujiwara family, which reached its zenith with Michinaga (966–1028), who married four daughters into the imperial line and successively placed two nephews and three grandsons on the throne.

New Buddhist sects—Tendai and Shingon—were imported from China with state support to reduce the power of the temples of Nara. Studious, ascetic Tendai became the state sect, and esoteric Shingon entranced the aristocracy with its mysterious rituals.

The Age of the Samurai

In ancient Japan, clan chieftains kept a tenuous hold on territories threatened by brigands, bands of warrior monks, and desperadoes of every description. Having had to raise armies to protect themselves (often from each other), some chieftains became immensely powerful—the forerunners of the great feudal lords.

During the peaceful Heian era (794–1185), conflicts dwindled. But in the 12th century the fierce Gempei War broke out between the Taira and Minamoto clans. The glorification of the warrior ensued, and the protagonists have been enshrined ever since as the first samurai. The great hero Minamoto Yoshitsune, who finally crushed the Taira in 1185, became a samurai paragon, but it was his half brother Yoritomo who established the samurai as the ruling caste for the next 700 years.

The Kamakura period saw the establishment of Bushido (the Way of the Warrior)—the samurai code of ethics, conduct, and strategy. Bushido dictated upholding the clan's honor even at the cost of individual annihilation, figuratively and literally. Glorifying self-sacrifice, it decreed absolute loyalty to the feudal lord. Atonement for any misconduct shaming the clan, which included defeat, demanded *seppuku* (or *harakiri*), a gruesome ritual of self-disembowelment. As various *daimyo* (feudal samurai lords) fought for influence, three leaders arose and brought the country under a central government: Oda Nobunaga (1534–1582), Toyotomi Hideyoshi (1536–1598), and Tokugawa Ieyasu (1543–1616). Although Nobunaga's adoption of firearms introduced by the Portuguese changed the style of warfare forever, the samurai never lost their reverence for the sword. During the 15th century, samurai were attracted to Zen Buddhism for its austerity and self-discipline, and founded the principles of swordsmanship, archery, and martial arts on its concepts.

In the 17th century, Confucian-inspired revisions of samurai codes permeated society with the introduction of a caste system headed by

The samurai spirit lives on in the Sennin Gyoretsu Festival at Tosho-gu.

a military aristocracy. To ensure their loyalty, daimyo were obliged to divide their time between Edo and their fiefdoms on alternate years, leaving their families behind in the capital as virtual hostages. Even without wars to fight, the samurai held power until ousted in 1867.

The samurai manifested a brutality that has faded in the light of popular culture. If slighted by a commoner, they were free to test their swords upon them with impunity. Their regard for womenfolk was also low: Considering women merely housemaids and breeding stock, many instead took their young apprentices as lovers for "mutually ennobling" pederasty.

The samurai era saw the creation of castle cities, the Noh theater, the Zen garden, and the tea ceremony. Many shogun or daimyo were great patrons of the arts. The 17th-century master swordsman Miyamoto Musashi was also a philosopher, writer, and painter. The samurai legacy finds modern echoes in the national characteristics of forbearance and stoicism.

Exchanges with China dwindled with the collapse of the T'ang dynasty in 907. Japanese culture now developed on its own. The arts reached new heights during the Heian period; literature flourished with diaries and the earliest novels in the world, notably the female courtier Murasaki Shikibu's *Tale of Genji*. Splendidly dressed courtiers enlivened their languid existence with lavish ceremonies and the avid pursuit of the arts.

While the Fujiwara were going soft and sinking into succession squabbles, the new samurai class was on the rise. Led by able administrators and comprised of their body-guards and the soldiers pacifying the countryside, the samurai—particularly the Taira (aka Heike) and Minamoto (aka Genji) clans—began to butt into matters of imperial succession. Rival factions of the Fujiwara clan supporting different claims to the throne pitted the Taira and Minamoto against each other, and while the Taira were initially victorious,

The early medieval Tsurugaoka Hachiman-gu shrine in Kamakura was built in 1063.

the Minamoto took their revenge during the ensuing Gempei War. The army raised by Minamoto Yoritomo (1147–1199) drove the Taira from the capital in 1180 and crushed them at the sea battle of Dan-no-ura in 1185. Among those who perished was the seven-year-old emperor Antoku.

Medieval Period

Kamakura (1185–1333):
Having vanquished the Taira, Yoritomo was the most powerful man in the nation. Receiving the title of *shogun* (generalissimo) from emperor Go-Toba in 1192, he established a new military capital in Kamakura, southwest of present-day Tokyo. The object was to keep the emperor apart from the affairs of state as a divine figurehead in Kyoto. As

> **In the late 13th century, the Mongol emperor Kublai Khan, whose empire embraced all Asia, turned his attentions to Japan.**

shogun, Yoritomo headed a military government known as the *bakufu* (shogunate). Consisting of provincial governors served by *bushi* (warriors), it was a military dictatorship. When Yoritomo died in 1199, power was taken by his wife's family—the equally ruthless Hojo clan. The Hojo established a branch of the bakufu in Kyoto, tightening their grip on the imperial court. Resistance from the court and its allies was crushed during the Jokyu War of 1221, and the Hojo gained direct control over the imperial line.

In the late 13th century, the Mongol emperor Kublai Khan, whose empire embraced all Asia, turned his attentions to Japan. His fleet reached Hakata, Kyushu, in 1274, but it was repelled, thanks largely to a storm at sea. In 1281 Kublai Khan redoubled his efforts with a massive armada of more than a thousand ships and 140,000 men. The Japanese held out under the assault for two months, when a second typhoon destroyed much of the invading fleet. The Japanese called these fortuitous storms *kamikaze*—the wind of the gods—the name adopted by suicide pilots during World War II.

The Hojo, bankrupted by the preparations for the Mongol Wars, lost popular support. They were driven from Kyoto in 1333 by an army raised by the exiled emperor Godaigo, who exploited growing discontent to restore his power.

Although it was intensely militaristic, the Kamakura era produced many fine temples and outstanding works of art. Great castles such as those of Osaka and Himeji were built; swords and armor were exquisitely fashioned. The age saw the establishment of new Buddhist sects: the populist Jodo (Pure Land) and Nichiren sects, which opened Buddhism up to the common man with simple prayers, and Zen, which would exert a lasting influence on culture and the arts.

Japan's Hidden Christians

Following the Shimabara massacre (1637–1638), Japan's surviving Catholics practiced in secret, in fear for their lives. Statues of the bodhisattva Kannon were worshipped as Mary, prayers were chanted in the intonation of sutras to mask their content, and teachings were passed down orally. In the 234 years before Christianity could be practiced openly again, the absence of priests also caused some confusion, such as the worship of St. Francis Xavier, to creep into their practice. Most Christians gave up unorthodox beliefs when foreign priests returned in the late 1800s, but tiny communities in Nagasaki's Goto Islands still carry on the faith of the hidden Christians. Their fate, and that of the missionaries who led them, was dramatized in the 2016 Martin Scorsese movie *Silence* (see sidebar p. 330).

Muromachi & the Ashikaga Shogunate (1333–1573): A poor politician, Emperor Godaigo levied taxes to support his lavish lifestyle; his brief reign ended when the shogun Ashikaga Takauji (1305–1358) sent him back into exile. The military government moved to the Muromachi district of Kyoto. When Godaigo set up a rival government, known as the Southern Court, in the mountains of Yoshino, south of Nara, Takauji founded the Northern Court in 1336 with hand-picked emperors. The rival courts continued for more than 50 years until reunited by the shogun Ashikaga Yoshimitsu (1358–1408) in 1392. Maybe the greatest of the Ashikaga shoguns, Yoshimitsu increased financial and cultural assets in Japan by accelerating trade with China. He also nurtured Noh theater (see pp. 53–55).

Culture flourished during the Muromachi period. Chinese art, especially ceramics and painting, was widely collected. The greatest cultural innovations emerged from Zen Buddhism, which was increasingly adopted by the samurai. For all its strife, the Muromachi was an era of progress. Ports and castle towns thrived; farming and industry prospered.

By the reign of the decadent Yoshimasa (1436–1490), the eighth Ashikaga shogun, the country was falling apart. Provincial warlords came to the fore, and feudal clans such as the Hosokawa undermined the government; many regions became virtually autonomous. Fanned by a dispute over Yoshimasa's succession, conflict culminated in the Onin War (1467–1477), during which Kyoto burned. This inconclusive war heralded the Sengoku Jidai—the century-long era of warring states. The enfeebled Ashikaga shoguns remained in Kyoto despite their successive domination by other clans, a situation remedied only with the arrival of Oda Nobunaga (1534–1582), a unifying leader. Nobunaga began his sudden rise to power by crushing the Inagawa clan's bid to invade Kyoto in 1560. Eight years later he invaded the city himself, temporarily restoring power to the Ashikaga shogun Yoshiaki before removing him and closing down the dynasty in 1573.

Christianity & the Edo Period

The Christian Century: Three Portuguese sailors from a vessel run aground on Tanegashima, Kyushu, in 1543 were the first Europeans in Japan. Merchants paved the way for Portuguese and Spanish missionaries, notably St. Francis Xavier, who landed in Kyushu in 1549. By 1600, they had converted 150,000 Japanese. Initially welcomed as a buffer between state and Buddhist sects, Christians were soon seen as a threat. Over the next century, clampdowns escalated. Foreigners were expelled and during the Shimabara Rebellion (1637–1638), 37,000 people, mainly Christians, were massacred (see sidebar above).

Azuchi-Momoyama (1573–1603): Nobunaga incorporated 3,000 musketeers into his army to wipe out the troops of warlord Takeda Katsuyori at Nagashino in 1575. After building a colossal castle at Azuchi, Nobunaga controlled most of the country until 1582, when, betrayed by one of his own generals and ambushed in Kyoto, he committed *seppuku*, the Japanese ritual suicide by disembowelment.

Nobunaga's avenger and former general, Toyotomi Hideyoshi (1536–1598), conquered eastern Japan in 1590. To secure dominion over the entire country, he conducted a land survey to streamline taxation and forbade peasants to carry arms. Hideyoshi was fond of the arts. The Kano school of painting burgeoned under his patronage, and the aesthetic pursuit of the tea ceremony flourished during his reign— but he was as ruthless as any military despot. In 1592 Hideyoshi staged a rash invasion of Korea. Undaunted by its failure, he launched a second attempt in 1598; interrupted

Osaka-jo in Chuo-ku: The castle played a major role in the unification of Japan in the 16th century.

by his death, it was abandoned. Before he died, Hideyoshi entrusted guardianship of his son, Hideyori, to Tokugawa Ieyasu (1543–1616), a trusted ally. Territorial rivalry raged again after Hideyoshi's death. Wanting a unified Japan for himself, Ieyasu crushed all foes, including Hideyori's followers. He won the Battle of Sekigahara on October 20, 1600, and founded the military dynasty that was to rule the country for 268 years.

Edo Period (1603–1868): Ieyasu considered Kyoto to be a powerless imperial realm and sought a spot for a new, unassailable military capital. He chose the old outpost of Edo, near Kamakura; this was a strategic base with access to the rest of

A changing Japan is shown in this 1864 image contrasting protests with samurai warfare.

the country and was suitable as a port. Having proclaimed himself shogun of Japan, in 1603 he founded Edo (later renamed Tokyo) as the new capital city.

The last of the regime's foes, Toyotomi Hideyoshi's son Hideyori, committed seppuku after a yearlong siege of Osaka Castle in 1615. Ieyasu died the following year. His legacy of laws governing society and national administration secured unprecedented stability.

A social hierarchy placed samurai at the top, followed by farmers, artisans, and merchants. Actors, artists, entertainers, and licensed prostitutes were classless. Beneath them were social outcasts and criminals. From Edo, the shogun ruled over a country of fiefdoms governed by the *daimyo* (feudal samurai lords) in his service.

In 1635, two years before the Shimabara massacre, no citizen was allowed out of or back into Japan—on pain of death. The only visitors were Chinese; the only Europeans allowed to trade were the Dutch, landing only at the tiny island of Dejima in Nagasaki Bay.

The Rise of the Townsman: With a population of more than a million by the middle of the 18th century, Edo was the largest city on Earth. Commerce, considered beneath the dignity of the ruling caste, was the preserve of merchants, and merchant princes came to outnumber samurai with comparable wealth. As money swung the balance of power, the bakufu hit back at intervals with Confucian reforms decreeing sumptuary laws.

Edo's famous Yoshiwara (red-light district) moved east after the great Meireki fire of 1657. By the prosperous Genroku era (1688–1704), the heyday of Edo, the pleasure quarters in major cities were flourishing as the *ukiyo*–the Floating World. The home of geisha and courtesans, it formed the hub of an entire popular culture, including fashion, literature, Kabuki theater (see p. 54), and graphic art.

The Black Ships: A four-year famine culminated in insurrection in Osaka in 1837. Similar rioting had once been easily quashed, but the bakufu, by now impoverished and politically diminished, barely won the day, foreshadowing its coming collapse.

During the 1840s, the United States twice made vain requests for a Japanese port of call on the long trade route between Shanghai and California. In 1853 Commodore Matthew Perry steamed into Edo Bay with his four heavily armed paddle frigates, which the Japanese refer to as the "black ships." His tone was cordial but the message clear: Swords and rusty muskets would be no match for modern weapons. After the Kanagawa Treaty between the U.S. and Japan was signed on Perry's return a year later, treaty ports (open to foreign trade) were established in 1859 and the doors of the country creaked open.

These so-called unequal treaties negotiated at gunpoint opened ports for trade, set low tariffs on foreign goods, and allowed Americans to live in Japanese ports outside local law, but most importantly, they smashed the policy of seclusion and crushed national pride. Both the bakufu and foreigners were on the receiving end of an enraged populace crying *sonno joi*: "Revere the emperor, expel the barbarian!" As civil unrest escalated all over Japan, the great southwestern clans of Satsuma, Tosa, and Choshu united with rebellious members of the court to overthrow the old samurai regime and restore the emperor to power. Following a coup d'état with comparatively little bloodshed, the Tokugawa shogunate fell in 1867. The last shogun, Yoshinobu, staged a futile attempt to attack Kyoto, but following the defeat of his samurai troops, Edo was captured by the armies of the clan alliance.

Enlightenment & a National Identity

Meiji (1868–1912): In April 1868 the 16-year-old emperor Mutsuhito (posthumously known as emperor Meiji) moved from Kyoto to Edo, which was renamed Tokyo—the Eastern Capital. The new era was called the Meiji (Enlightenment), and the return of imperial rule is known as the Meiji Restoration. The new Meiji rulers, mainly Satsuma and Choshu clansmen, instituted rapid and radical changes in order to catch up with the West and avoid being colonized. Abolishing the old samurai caste system and prohibiting the carrying of swords, they adopted the solar calendar and introduced compulsory education and military service. As American and European merchants, missionaries, and advisers flocked into Japan, legions of young Japanese went abroad to learn about Western civilization.

> In 1853 Commodore Matthew Perry steamed into Edo Bay with his four heavily armed paddle frigates, which the Japanese refer to as the "black ships."

Following construction of a railroad between Tokyo and Yokohama in 1872, Tokyo and other cities began sprouting Western-style buildings. Modernization hurtled ahead with mining operations, heavy industry, and factories; mass production turned textiles into a major export. In 1873 a criminal code of French origin was adopted, along with German systems of administration. Western dress became usual working-day attire for men in corporate and government offices.

Satsuma clansman Saigo Takamori, one of the architects of the Meiji Restoration, feared that Westernization was undermining Japan. Heading 20,000 ex-samurai, Saigo fought a losing battle against Imperial forces in Kyushu during the Satsuma Rebellion in 1877; when defeated, he committed suicide.

Rifts within the government led to the establishment of party politics. Government leader Okubo Toshimichi was assassinated in 1881, and Ito Hirobumi became Japan's first prime minister in 1885. The Meiji Constitution he drafted was approved by the emperor in 1889, setting up a system of government that survived until 1945.

The emperor was revered as the paramount figure of the era, although his real power was debatable. A legacy from the Edo period, nationalist ideology was revived and became a basis for emperor worship. The amalgamation of diverse animist beliefs into Shinto, the official national religion, was designed to eliminate Buddhist political influence and succeeded in severely curtailing Buddhism after 1870. Affirming the divine lineage of the emperor and the Japanese, seventh-century Shinto myths were taught as historical truth in schools—with dire consequences in the next century.

Expansion: Colonial expansion was one of the hallmarks of industrialized nations in the late 19th century, so Japan turned to empire-building. China eyed Korea, but the Japanese invaded first in 1894. Losing the ensuing Sino-Japanese War, China was forced to cede Taiwan and the Liaodang Peninsula on the mainland to Japan. Germany, France, and Russia, however, prevented Japan from claiming its gains on the Chinese mainland.

In 1900, Japan's vital role in releasing several thousand foreign hostages in Beijing during the Boxer Rebellion enhanced its status in the West. Wary of Germany's colonial maneuvers, the British sought a strong Pacific ally; the Anglo-Japanese Alliance was signed in 1902. In 1904, Japan went to war with Russia over the control of Korea and astonished the world when its British-trained navy annihilated the Russian fleet. Deadlocked on land, the Russo-Japanese War ended with the intervention of Theodore Roosevelt and the signing of the Portsmouth Treaty in 1905.

The Japanese tightened their grip on Korea, forcing the king's abdication and installing Ito Hirobumi as governor. Following the latter's assassination by a Korean patriot in 1909, Japan annexed the country in 1910, causing a century of resentment.

With the death of the emperor in 1912, a momentous era came to an end. During the Meiji period, Western culture had a deep impact on Japanese artistic and literary trends, sometimes to the detriment of traditional arts. The zeal for modernism caused many samurai castles to be destroyed. Endorsed by imperial approval, Kabuki became respectable and Western-style drama took root.

Emperor Hirohito of Japan wearing ceremonial robes for his coronation in 1928

Taisho (1912–1926): Taisho means "Great Righteousness," but, being mentally impaired, the Taisho emperor was unable to make public appearances. Crown Prince Hirohito (1901–1989) became regent in 1921.

Japan sided with the Allies in World War I and seized East Asian and Pacific territories from Germany, including Changdong in China. In 1920, Japan joined the League of Nations, and in 1922 the Washington Naval Conference accorded greater power to the Japanese in the Pacific, against British objections. The Anglo-Japanese Alliance was dissolved, but friendship between the two nations was undented.

Democratic aspirations and imported ideologies colored Japanese politics during the 1920s, a time of great socio-political ferment. Japan witnessed the introduction of a wealth of political concepts from overseas, including social-ism, communism, labor unions, campaigns for women's suffrage, and student movements. Despite the gap between urban rich and rural poor, the early Taisho period is still regarded as a golden age of emerging democracy—until tolerance was swamped by rising nationalism.

> Colonial expansion was one of the hallmarks of industrialized nations in the late 19th century, so Japan turned to empire-building.

World War I triggered an industrial boom, but recession and inflation followed. Cheaper rice was imported, sparking anger among farmers and leading to civil unrest, which culminated in the Rice Riots of 1918. The Taisho governments never lived up to their liberal ideals. Those calling the tune belonged to the same oligarchy that had ruled during the Meiji period: a conservative aristocracy, nationalistic politicians, and big business, which thrived on militarization.

Calamity struck in 1923: The Great Kanto Earthquake reduced Tokyo and Yoko-hama to rubble, killing 140,000 citizens. Some three million homes were destroyed. The impact on the economy was equally catastrophic.

The Taisho emperor died in 1925. The year brought good news with the right to vote for all men over 25, and bad news with the imposition by nationalists of the Peace Preservation Law. This spawned the increasingly virulent repression of commu-nists and dissidents and a special police division to deal with "dangerous thoughts."

Taisho was at the same time an age of intense intellectual activity, producing legions of new writers and thinkers. *Moga* (modern girl) and *mobo* (modern boy) reveled in the Roaring Twenties. Western trends and fashions made deeper inroads—but not for long. Much as in Weimar Germany, the party was to end with the rise of ultranationalism.

The Shaping of Modern Japan

Showa (1926–1989): Crown Prince Hirohito became emperor in 1926. The era was called Showa, meaning "Enlightened Harmony," something that would be a long time coming. The country instead sank into what the Japanese now call *kurai tanima*—the dark valley.

The economic afflictions of the Taisho era worsened with the Wall Street Crash of 1929. Japanese exports plummeted; unemployment soared. A growing number of nationalists advocated exerting greater control in Asia. Now that the voices of liberals had been silenced in crackdowns, this notion met with little opposition. Out in the hungry countryside, rightist societies, militaristic youth groups, and patriotic farmers' associations proliferated as ultranationalism rapidly gained ground.

During an international conference held in London in 1930, Japanese government representatives signed a treaty reducing Japan's armaments, but it infuriated army chiefs of staff and was nullified in Japan. Prime minister Hamaguchi Osachi was assassinated by a right-wing fanatic the same year.

In 1931 the Japanese army staged the sabotage of a railroad under its protection in Guangdong, China. The fabrication provided a pretext to attack Chinese troops and overrun Manchuria, which fell under Japanese rule as Manchukuo. Condemned globally, the action was also opposed by Japanese prime minister Inukai Tsuyoshi, who was murdered in 1932. Faced with international opprobrium, Japan withdrew from the League of Nations in 1933. Ultranationalism and isolationism intensified. Efforts were made to purge Japan of foreign concepts, which led to nationalistic Meiji-era emperor worship, historical disinformation promulgated through education (mythical emperors and warriors were presented as fact), and the glorification of the Japanese race.

> **Faced with international opprobrium, Japan withdrew from the League of Nations in 1933. Ultranationalism and isolationism intensified.**

The Pacific War: In 1936, Japan signed the Anti-Comintern Pact, allying it to Fascist Italy and Nazi Germany. Its aggression in China reached a climax in 1937 with the taking of Nanking (Nanjing), during which some 200,000 civilians were savagely massacred and an estimated 20,000 girls and women were gang-raped to death. One of the most horrific acts of war in recorded history, the Rape of Nanking is still denied by nationalists and some prominent Japanese politicians. The military forced the government to pass the National Mobilization Law, putting the nation's resources at the ready for war beyond China. Prince Konoe, the prime minister from 1937, tried to rein in the military leaders but was ousted with his cabinet in 1941. The government was taken over by the military, with Gen. Tojo Hideki as prime minister. The United States reacted to Japan's aggression in China by ceasing the supply of raw materials, freezing Japanese assets in U.S. territory, and imposing an oil embargo. Retaliating with a surprise attack on Pearl Harbor on December 7, 1941, Japan plunged blindly into war. Its fierce expansionism, nobly dressed up as the foundation of a Greater East Asia Co-Prosperity Sphere, wrought some of the worst atrocities in the history of world colonialism.

By 1942, Japan had invaded most of Southeast Asia. The same year, its navy was battered in the Battle of Midway, which drove the Japanese military to send young men on mainly futile suicide missions as kamikaze pilots. As civilians and soldiers almost starved, the war effort pressed on relentlessly. In March 1945, a three-day incendiary bombing of Tokyo left more than 100,000 dead and 700,000 homes destroyed; the attack was repeated around Japan. In April the Allies invaded Okinawa, where more than 200,000 died, half of them civilians. The Potsdam Declaration in July, calling for Japan's unconditional surrender, was ignored. On August 6 the U.S. dropped an atomic bomb on Hiroshima (see sidebar opposite). Three days later, another atomic bomb was dropped on Nagasaki. A week after this, the emperor, apparently taking his own initiative against hard-line opposition, stunned the people of Japan by announcing the inevitability of capitulation. In September, Japanese officials signed the surrender before Gen. Douglas MacArthur, who headed the U.S. occupation forces landing in Japan. With more than 2 million dead and 13 million homeless, Japan was broken, having lost all its overseas territories.

The Occupation: Tokyo citizens came out of hiding when they realized that the carnage predicted by militarists was not going to happen. General MacArthur was respected as Supreme Commander of the Allied Powers (SCAP), even by the Japanese. In 1946 the International Military Tribunal for the Far East (IMTFE) jailed 25 former militarists for war crimes; seven were executed two years later, including Tojo Hideki. Some 4,000 war criminals were simultaneously tried by IMTFE tribunals around the Pacific.

With the exception of Okinawa (which reverted to Japan by popular vote in 1972), the U.S. occupation forces left Japan to the Japanese. Having abolished the armed forces and purged the government of militarists, the Occupation authorities administered on the basis of mutual cooperation. In 1946 they drafted a new American-style democratic constitution that remains in force today. Emphasizing individual fulfillment and egalitarianism, it announced land reforms, the emancipation of women, and a new education system. Most importantly, Article 9 forbids the development of a military and any future belligerent acts, a clause inspired not so much by Japanese contrition as by the Occupation's desire to keep modern Japan toothless.

In 1951, Prime Minister Yoshida Shigeru (1878–1967) signed a treaty with 48 nations at the San Francisco Peace Conference. The Occupation ended the next year. At the end

The Atomic Bomb

On August 6 and 9, 1945, Japan suffered history's only military uses of the atomic bomb. The Allies were concerned that a land invasion would prove too costly, as Japanese forces had fought to the death at Okinawa. So began a devastating fire-bombing campaign on major cities. When the Japanese government ignored the Potsdam Declaration's demands for surrender, the order for the A-bombs was given. The Allies banked on the terrible destruction leading to a loss of national morale and eventual capitulation.

The world's first weaponized nuclear bomb, "Little Boy," was dropped on Hiroshima, an industrial city and logistical center for military operations. The explosion instantly killed some 70,000 residents, with an equal number succumbing to horrific burns and radiation poisoning within a year. The Japanese government considered surrender on condition that their own lives be saved, but failed to make any decision, hoping that the Americans had only a single bomb.

Nagasaki, a shipbuilding and arms-producing port on the northwest coast of Kyushu, was the target of the second A-bomb, "Fat Man." Falling in the Urakami Valley among arms factories and the largest church in Asia, the bomb's blast was muted by hilly terrain, limiting the death toll to approximately 75,000 over the next year. This bomb, along with Russia's invasion of Manchuria, forced the Japanese to surrender. Today, the Hiroshima and Nagasaki peace memorials remain powerfully emotive sites.

of the Korean War in 1953, Japan signed the U.S. Security Treaty, letting American bases remain on its soil. In 1955, Yoshida lost the vote to the new Liberal Democratic Party, which remained in power almost continuously until 2009.

Modern Japan (1989–present): When Japan joined the United Nations in 1956, the economy was growing at twice the predicted rate. Thanks to soaring industry, exports, and good living standards, the country had recovered by 1958.

With the renunciation of war now written into the constitution, Japan is technically forbidden a military. However, its SDF (self-defense force) still receives $41 billion in funding, about one percent of the GDP: By budget it has the eighth-largest military in the world. Widespread rioting erupted in 1960 with the renewal of the U.S. Security Treaty, as the presence of American military bases in Japan, along with SDF's hamstrung status, continued to chafe the small sector of xenophobic ultranationalists.

> With the renunciation of war now written into the constitution, Japan is technically forbidden a military.

The Tokyo Olympic Games made 1964 a landmark year for Japan. In the same year, the country launched the *Shinkansen*—then the fastest train service in the world. Come 1970 and the International Exposition in Osaka, Japan had a formidable world-class economy based on a widening spectrum of quality industrial products.

Weathering oil shocks in both 1973 and 1979, Japan's spectacular growth prevailed but drew international flak in the 1980s for huge trade surpluses; fraught with tariff barriers, its markets were virtually closed to the outside world. In 1972 the Lockheed bribery scandal forced the resignation of Prime Minister Tanaka Kakuei and exposed endemic corruption in the ruling Liberal Democratic Party.

The death of the Showa emperor in 1989 marked the end of an era for Japan. With the accession of his son Akihito in 1990, the Heisei era finds the country facing an uncertain future. The miracle ended with the collapse of the Bubble Economy in 1991; the resulting recession has since subsided, but not the social malaise.

The generation gap between baby boomers and today's young adults remains a social worry. The former grew up in a rapidly growing Japan and retired before the bubble burst; today's youth struggle to find work, let alone the lifetime employment of their parents, and with Japan's considerable affluence, heavy overtime for little increase in standard of living holds less appeal. Crime statistics remain enviably low, but juvenile offenses and the incidence of social reclusion have soared. Many Japanese blame the erosion of traditional values on materialism, and a modern-day moral and spiritual vacuum. Natural disasters, such as the Great East Japan Earthquake of 2011 (see sidebar p. 161) have added to the sense of uncertainty toward the future; if the scrambled political response to the disaster is any indication, the nation does not have much by way of leadership to guide it.

Still, a cautious optimism surrounds the upcoming 2020 Tokyo Olympics. Many hope that the games will give the country a boost as it did last time, a chance to put a new foot forward on the international stage. Construction is booming, and English schools are filled to capacity in anticipation: With the arrival of the Olympic flame, the world may yet see a bold new era of Japan's colorful history. ■

The 2020 Tokyo Olympics

Japan has hosted the Olympics three times: in Tokyo in 1964, Sapporo in 1972, and Nagano in 1998. The first time was seen by many as Japan's big move onto the international stage, its grand party after a difficult postwar recovery and decades of aggression in Asia. Hopes are high that the second Tokyo Olympics will be as successful.

Tokyo's New National Stadium in Shinjuku will host the city's second summer Olympics in 2020.

Current Prime Minister Abe Shinzo is banking heavily on the Olympic and Paralympic Games, with the hope that they give a 20 percent boost to 2015 GDP figures and increase the number of tourists annually from 10 million in 2013 to 20 million by 2020. Economists are divided on whether the games can provide lasting economic benefit, and critics argue that the money would be better spent on rebuilding tsunami-hit areas, but there's no doubt that a successful event would be a huge boost to national morale.

Japan's present circumstances are a lot different from those of six decades ago. The economy has limped since the mid-90s, the populace has aged rapidly, and the country is still recovering from the Great East Japan Earthquake of 2011. While a sporting event can only hope to take on the first of those challenges, optimism is running high, and Japan is keen to show the world its most hospitable side.

The Tokyo Olympics will feature five new sports: baseball/softball, karate, skateboarding, sport climbing, and surfing.

The events will be held in two main areas in the city: the Heritage and Tokyo Bay zones. The former will include famous venues from the 1964 event such as the Budokan (p. 69) and Yoyogi National Gymnasium, south of Meiji-jingu (pp. 83, 86), as well as a new Olympic Stadium in Jingu-gaien, the outer gardens of Meiji-jingu, accessible by Kokuri-tsukyogijo or Shinanomachi stations. The more spacious Tokyo Bay area will host another 12 venues, and soccer games will be played in nearby cities, such as Yokohama.

The main consideration in attending the games is where to book a room. Although services such as Airbnb will absorb some of the influx, this will not nearly meet demand as Tokyo homes are tiny and a spare room is a rare luxury. The usual last-resort places—capsule hotels, love hotels, Internet cafés—will certainly be full, so you'll need to make a reservation somewhere. If you are willing to take what will be very crowded trains into the metropolis, commuter towns such as Saitama, Kawasaki, and Chiba offer cheaper accommodations.

The Arts

Symmetry plays no part in Japanese aesthetics. A millennium ago, Japanese temple complexes abandoned the regular plan of the Chinese model. Ceramic tea bowls are often irregularly shaped, and composition in prints and paintings is often off-center, with as much white space as subject matter. In speech, prose, poetry, and visual arts, the implicit is often preferred to the explicit.

During the 13th century, Zen Buddhism (see p. 27) inspired radically new forms and concepts, influencing painting, calligraphy, and poetry. Tea drinking, ritualized in China by Ch'an (Zen) monks seeking no more than a means of staying awake

Kakizome (the first writing of the year) at Tokyo's New Year's Calligraphy Contest

during meditation, was transformed into a deeply aesthetic and philosophical ceremony in Japan. As developed by, among others, the great tea master Sen-no-Rikyu (1522–1591), *chado* or *chanoyu*—the Way of Tea—spurned ostentation and ushered in a new sense of aesthetics.

The tearoom is small, spotless, and plain. It contains a *kakemono* (hanging scroll) and a flower arrangement in the *tokonoma* (alcove); often simple or rough in appearance, the tea bowls at first belie their master craftsmanship. The kakemono can be a work of calligraphy (often a poem) or an ink painting; like the flower arrangement, it should reflect the mood and hues of the season. The tearoom is a space for the appreciation of different art forms in harmony.

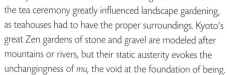

The tearoom is a space for the appreciation of different art forms in harmony.

In requiring works created specially for it, chanoyu engendered other forms, notably *ikebana*—the art of flower arrangement. Zen and the tea ceremony greatly influenced landscape gardening, as teahouses had to have the proper surroundings. Kyoto's great Zen gardens of stone and gravel are modeled after mountains or rivers, but their static austerity evokes the unchangingness of *mu,* the void at the foundation of being.

Chanoyu and its correlative arts always reflect *wabi* (quiet taste) and *sabi* (rustic simplicity). These are the criteria for *shibui* (sober refinement), the paramount principle of Japanese taste, whereby less is more. Although not always so refined, aesthetics still preoccupy the Japanese, from the painstaking wrapping of gifts and the elaborate presentation of food to clusters of artificial flowers in toilets.

Traditional Architecture

Japanese architecture is based on wood. The often brightly painted, symmetrical, and purely Chinese designs of the great Buddhist temples of Horyu-ji (see pp. 240–243), near Nara, gradually gave way to the subdued dark wood of the Japanese style. Shinto shrines also took cues from Chinese architecture, although some of the oldest and most sacred, like those at Ise and Izumo, predate Chinese influence and replicate the prehistoric originals.

The raised structure of Ise Jingu is modeled after an ancient granary. Older shrines such as this have thatched roofs, with rafters alternating like crossed fingers placed against the ridge-pole. Others, like the shrine at Izumo, imitate ancient headmen's houses. At the gabled end of Shinto shrines, including many of those in the Chinese style, are the distinctive ornamental *chigi*—large crossed beams protruding from the roof like horns.

Beginning in the 16th century, the heads of the supporting pillars and crossbeams were sometimes carved, often with embellishments in gilded metalwork. Most shrines and all temples stand on foundations of stone and display sweeping tiled roofs with eaves sloping elegantly upward.

Many temple complexes have a five-story pagoda, a feature that reflects the Chinese geomantic principle of the elements: earth, water, sky, wind, and fire. Most castles, regardless of the number of floors inside, also show five roof levels on the exterior. As with most Japanese wooden architecture, these intricate buildings have been constructed with mortise-and-tenon joints that lock beam and post together without nails.

The traditional Japanese house is raised on low stilts, sometimes above a foundation. The single-story model is said to emulate the aristocratic dwelling of the 12th century, but between the 17th and mid-19th centuries two and sometimes three stories became common. The walls consist of a bamboo framework set between exposed support pillars and coated with daub. They are then plastered and often whitewashed on the outside, while inside they are either plastered or coated with a smooth daub made from paper pulp. Such traditional houses are light, airy, and designed to open onto the outside world, rather than to seal it off as in the West. As a result of being uninsulated and open to the elements, traditional homes are often very cold in the winter.

Roofs vary according to place and time. They can be steep and narrow to shed snow or wide and sweeping to provide shade. Thatch was ubiquitous until the 16th century, even on samurai dwellings, but is used today only on a few old farmhouses and some historic buildings. Cedar-shingled roofs appeared later; they can still be seen on some Shinto shrines. Clay tiles, first used in towns during the 17th and 18th centuries, became widespread. The roofs of modest homes now commonly display many cheaper alternatives, including metal, corrugated iron, and plastic.

Many temple complexes have a five-story pagoda, a feature that reflects the Chinese geomantic principle of the elements: earth, water, sky, wind, and fire.

The cost of building a traditional house is prohibitive today, calling upon vanishing skills and increasingly scarce wood. Many modern homes are prefabricated, incorporating concrete slabs and plastics—materials also used to build houses in the traditional style.

Originally reserved for official buildings, Western architecture first appeared during the late 19th century. It was typically massive, of red brick and Victorian in style, and was greatly influenced by British architect Josiah Conder (1852–1920); Tokyo Station was built by one of his pupils in 1914.

Multistory apartment buildings of reinforced concrete, built according to utilitarian rather than aesthetic criteria, are dominant in cities. However the profile of modern architecture was heightened during the 1960s with many remarkable buildings, notably Tange Kenzo's structures for the 1964 Olympic Games. Highly regarded internationally, architects such as Tange and Ando Tadao often incorporate traditional concepts into modern buildings to striking effect.

Literature

The *Kojiki (Record of Ancient Matters)* and the *Nihon Shoki (Chronicles of Japan),* eighth-century history books that meld creation myths and fact, held sway over Shinto belief and national thinking for more than a millennium. The eighth-century

Matsumoto-jo, in Nagano Prefecture, with its traditional five-story design

Man'yoshu (Collection for Ten Thousand Generations) is a compilation of 4,500 poems by emperors and aristocrats as well as ordinary people. Many are in the brief, evocative *tanka* style—a forerunner of the better known *haiku* (see below) and a poetry form still in fashion.

The great advances in literature during the Heian period (see pp. 34, 36–37) were mainly due to female writers of *nikki* (diaries) and *monogatari* (tales)—the world's oldest true novels. Most prominent were those written by the courtiers Sei and Murasaki Shikibu, who created literary milestones around the year 1000. Sei Shonagon's candid *Makura Soshi (The Pillow Book)* is a compilation of vivid (and often unabashedly bitchy) observations of life at court. Murasaki's 54-chapter *Genji Monogatari (The Tale of Genji)*, tracing the rise and fall of a philandering prince, is one of the classics of world literature.

After the 13th century, literature was eclipsed for almost 400 years by war—though war itself was the source of inspiration for the great classic *Heike Monogatari (The Tales of Heike)*, an epic prose poem recounting the wars between the Taira and Minamoto clans. Often recited or sung, Heike-style epics were adapted for the theater; the melancholy and richly evocative Noh plays of Zeami Motokiyo (1363–1444) are outstanding for their poetic sensitivity.

During the Edo period (see pp. 39–41), plays were written interchangeably for the Bunraku puppet theater and Kabuki drama, notably by Chikamatsu Monzaemon (1653–1725), often regarded as a Japanese equivalent of William Shakespeare. Monzaemon's plays were mainly historical, but the most popular were contemporary tragedies about doomed lovers running afoul of the rules of caste and society. Social and dramatic realism came to color both the theater and novels—the latter revived as a genre after 600 years. Many novels, most notably those by Ihara Saikaku (1642–1692), were satires recounting the adventures of profligates and prostitutes in the Floating World (see pp. 80–81).

The Japanese Sankai Juku *butoh* company performs in countries around the world.

In poetry, the 17-syllable haiku was brought to perfection by Matsuo Basho (1644–1694; see sidebar p. 158). A low-ranking samurai who gave up the sword for the pen, the wandering Basho produced haiku anthologies based on his journeys—masterpieces that are still widely revered today.

The Meiji period (see pp. 41–43) brought Western realism to the Japanese novel. Among the first modern novelists were Mori Ogai (1862–1922) and Natsume Soseki (1867–1916). The novels of Nagai Kafu (1879–1959) cast a wistful glance at the vanishing Floating World in the 1900s. Women writers emerged for the first time since the Heian period, among them the tragically short-lived novelist Higuchi Ichiyo (1872–1896) and the poet and scholar Yosano Akiko (1878–1942).

The postwar period was something of a renaissance highlighted by the best work of established writers such as Nobel laureate Yasunari Kawabata (*Snow Country,* 1948) and Tanizaki Junichiro (1886–1965), whose masterpiece, *The Makioka Sisters,* was banned by the militarists. A wealth of emerging talent included Yukio Mishima, Abe Kobo, Endo Shusaku, and Oe Kenzaburo, winner of the Nobel Prize for Literature in 1994. Murakami Ryu's *Almost Transparent Blue* reflects youthful nihilism during the 1970s. Among the most popular current authors are the surrealist Haruki Murakami *(The Wind-Up Bird Chronicle, Norwegian Wood)* and the lightweight Banana Yoshimoto *(Kitchen),* deplored by traditionalists as an indicator of the growing superficiality of Japanese taste.

Theater & Dance

The sacred masked dance of *kagura,* taking the form of pantomime and featuring musical and vocal accompaniment, goes back to ancient times. Still performed during Shinto festivals, it is the source of inspiration for other forms of dance and drama. *Bugaku,* which survives in imperial ceremonies, and *gagaku* are of Chinese origin. They were forms of music and dance performed at the court in Heian times. More popular types of entertainment were *dengaku* (field music, originating in peasant dances) and *sarugaku* (monkey music), both based on kagura. During the 14th century, sarugaku was refined into Noh, which means "skill." Under the patronage of shogun Ashikaga Yoshimitsu, the art was perfected by Kan'ami Kiyotsugu (1333–1384) and his son Zeami Motokiyo (see p. 51), who turned Noh

EXPERIENCE: A Visit to a Japanese Theater

There are few sights as unmistakably Japanese as the lurid makeup and bright red wig of a Kabuki actor. An Edo-period theater form, all-male Kabuki *(kabuki-bito .jp/eng)* is pure medieval bombast and sensationalism. The name comes from the old verb *kabuku*: to act eccentrically. Odd voice modulation, strange dramatic poses, and bursts of movement all characterize the form, making it surprisingly accessible, even without an audio guide. The plots, too, tend to be fairly straightforward: Spoiler alert!—there's a lot of failed romance and tragic death.

Takarazuka Revue *(kageki.hankyu .co.jp)* is the flip side of Kabuki, in several ways. The drama troupe based in Kansai's Takarazuka city is exclusively female and does mostly Western-themed musicals. And unlike Kabuki, where few would go so far as to say that the *onnagata* (see p. 54) were pretty, the revue's players have a consistent doe-eyed look that extends rather oddly to the male characters (think guerrilla bombers in eye shadow and impeccably clean Spanish

fashions in an adaptation of Hemingway's *For Whom the Bell Tolls,* which ran in 2011). Takarazuka, though more earnest in its style, is just as bizarre as Kabuki and a lot of fun. The productions are well orchestrated and the singing is top class.

Places to See Kabuki
Kabukiza Theatre, Tokyo *(4-12-15 Ginza, Chuo-ku).* Rebuilt in 2013, this is the only place where you can see Kabuki every day.
Minamiza Theatre, Kyoto *(198 Nakano-cho, Yamato-oji-nishiiru, Shijo-dori, Higashi-yama-ku).* This theater runs plays on an irregular basis except in December, when the top national actors perform.

Places to See Takarazuka Revue
Takarazuka Grand Theater, Takarazuka *(1-1-57 Sakaemachi, Takarazuka-shi).* The headquarters of Takarazuka offers performances daily.
Tokyo Takarazuka Theater *(1-1-3 Yurakucho, Chiyoda-ku).* Troupes rotate between here and the headquarters.

EXPERIENCE: Karaoke—Japanese Style

No trip to Japan is complete without an evening of *karaoke* (pronounced "car-ah-okay"), Japan's infamous contribution to popular music culture. Hold your groans: This isn't the crummy system dominated by a chorus of drunks in the bar back home. Such bar-style karaoke culture has largely been replaced with "karaoke boxes"—private, somewhat soundproof rooms. The latest sound systems have a large catalog of Western hits and can embellish even the worst warbling, but half the fun of karaoke is hamming it up for the delight of close friends.

On arrival, tell the front desk how many people your party has and how long you intend to stay. All-you-can-drink plans are popular, usually guaranteeing a memorable (or perhaps mercifully less remembered) evening. Choose a song from the catalog and enter the number on the remote control; alternately, spell the band or song name on the touch-screen controller. The staff can help, too. Before choosing a song, try to remember a few of the lines, making sure you actually know the melody. When in doubt, go with Queen's "Bohemian Rhapsody," a perennial expat favorite. When your specified time is nearly up, the staff will call the box and ask if you'd like to extend: Say *mo ichijikan* for one more hour!
Shidax Kabukicho (*1-5-2 Kabuki-cho, Shinju-ku, Tokyo, tel 03/3204-8833*). Just east of the entrance to Kabuki-cho.
Super Jankara Kawaramachi (*296 Narayacho, Kawaramachi Takoyakushi-agaru, Nakagyo-ku, Kyoto, tel 075/212-5858*). One of Kyoto's largest, with cosplay costumes for rent.

into a great classical theater form. Noh has a repertoire of five categories: Using poetic language and an exquisitely costumed cast of three, it enacts tales of gods, ghostly warriors, elegant nobles, mad women, and demons. Noh performances are traditionally accompanied by a *kyogen* (comic interlude), a derivative of sarugaku.

Noh became the preserve of the samurai elite; during the Edo period, commoners were forbidden to see it. Early in the 17th century, however, a woman named Okuni presented a new kind of dance drama for the people of Kyoto. Called Kabuki, it soon enchanted Edo and the rest of the country. It was often a front for prostitution, and the shogunate attempted to kill it to placate standard prostitutes, whose turf had been invaded. They banned actresses from the stage, but Kabuki rebounded with an all-male cast; the female roles were played by *onnagata* (woman-forms). Flamboyant and fast moving in contrast to Noh, Kabuki featured gaudy costumes, spectacular sets, and special effects. The scripts used contemporary language and embraced modern themes.

The same applies in miniature to the popular contemporary Bunraku puppet theater; the works of many playwrights, including the great Chikamatsu (see p. 51), are staged in both forms. One-third life-size, each stringless marionette is manipulated by as many as three handlers on stage (their presence is soon forgotten). Bunraku remains one of the world's most refined forms of puppetry.

Until Western-style alternatives, such as the all-female Takarazuka Revue, gradually came to eclipse it after the mid-19th century, Kabuki remained synonymous with popular theater in Japan. It retains a wide following and, like Noh, is a revered facet of Japan's national cultural heritage.

Apart from an enduring profile in festivals and drama, dance never evolved much as an independent form until the 19th century. During the 18th century, geisha and dancing girls in the entertainment quarters borrowed heavily from Kabuki, and it is in this form that *nihon buyo*—traditional Japanese dance—survives today.

Plays have been written and performed in the Western tradition in Japan for more than a century. Ballet and modern dance have surpassed nihon buyo and command a wide following. *Angura* (underground) dance and theater made waves in the late 1960s, notably with *butoh* (the dance of darkness), cofounded by Hijikata Tatsumi (1928–1986) and Ohno Kazuo (1906–2010). Arising from the darkness of Japan's postwar devastation, butoh is a rebellious, individual, and visceral form whose spiritual roots lie in Kabuki and Noh. Widely influential outside Japan, it lacks the domestic following of other more codified and restrained styles. Much the same applies to Japan's avant-garde theater; led by Kara Juro and Terayama Shuji during the 1970s, the movement has seen the emergence of several troupes that are admired overseas. From the dance innovations of Teshigawara Saburo to the stylish theatrical productions of Ninagawa Yukio, Japanese dance and theater come increasingly under the global spotlight.

Music

The grand and sedate *gagaku* (court music) orchestra, using instruments from T'ang-dynasty China, has remained in use for imperial, Shinto, and Buddhist ceremonies for more than a thousand years. Its main instruments are the *biwa* (a large teardrop-shaped lute), *koto* (a 13-stringed zither), side-blown flutes, and percussion, including the *tsuzumi* shoulder drum and the huge, vertically played *da-daiko* drum.

Shomyo, chanting of Buddhist ritual, exerted a strong influence on singing styles in Japan; itinerant monks often gathered alms by singing epic poems to a biwa accompaniment. The epic poem singing style gave rise to *naga-uta* (long songs), influential on the Noh theater in the 15th century, which in turn engendered the *joruri* singing adopted in the 17th century by the Kabuki theater. Joruri was also practiced by geisha in the Floating World as well as by blind minstrels, who had a monopoly on singing epic poems until 1871.

During the Edo period, the *shamisen* gradually replaced the biwa. The shamisen, introduced from China via Okinawa, is a three-stringed lute with a long, thin neck and a small, round sound box covered in snakeskin (in Okinawa), animal skin (on mainland Japan), or plastic (on a budget). Adopted in the Kabuki theater, the shamisen soon became the instrument of choice for geisha, blind minstrels, and folk music. The Edo period also saw the appearance of the *shakuhachi*, a bamboo flute about 18 inches (45 cm) long. Its unique tone gives the player much scope for expression.

The classic singing technique, plaintive and heavily stylized, is an acquired taste for many modern Japanese used to Western harmony. Composed using the pentatonic scale, traditional Japanese music is not always easy listening to the unaccustomed ear—but it is worth the effort.

> **Shomyo, chanting of Buddhist ritual, exerted a strong influence on singing styles in Japan; itinerant monks often gathered alms by singing epic poems to a biwa accompaniment.**

Western music accompanied the Portuguese in the 16th century but was soon forgotten with the closure of the country. Returning in the form of military bands during the 1860s (most samurai clans wanted one), Western music had a colossal and lasting impact. Japanese symphony orchestras, such as the Saito Kinnen and Tokyo Symphony, are among the world's finest, and the country has produced many outstanding Western-style musicians, among them conductor Ozawa Seiji and pianist Uchida Mitsuko. During the 1960s, composers such as Takemitsu Toru combined gagaku with contemporary Western music to explore new horizons of sound.

> **The influence of karaoke on J-Pop is immense, as difficult songs have little chance of being included in the machines.**

Enka, crooning love ballads from the early 20th century, have largely fallen out of popularity, but the outside world still remembers the megahit "Sukiyaki" by Sakamoto Kyu. Representative of the struggle to gain popularity abroad, the song was renamed after a Japanese beef stew because "Ue o Muite, Arukou" ("I will walk looking up . . . so that my tears won't fall," the song says) was too hard for Westerners to remember. The average J-Pop song, however, is a saccharine, forgettable tune sung by a large group of pretty people chosen for their faces and dance moves, such as the supergroup AKB48. The influence of karaoke on J-Pop is immense, as difficult songs have little chance of being included in the machines. Alas, many creative musicians chafe under the current hit-of-the-week culture.

Visual Arts

Painting: In early Japan, painting was Chinese in form and exclusively Buddhist in content. Among the earliest examples are the murals in the main hall of Horyu-ji near Nara, executed in the seventh century. During the Heian period (794–1185), painting took a more Japanese turn, with landscapes and scenes from court life decorating screens and sliding doors; portraiture and illustrated scrolls also became popular.

In the Kamakura period (1185–1333), art of this kind came to be called *yamato-e* (Japanese painting) as distinct from *kara-e* ("outside" paintings in the Chinese tradition). The yamato-e tradition favored fine detail and vivid colors. Focusing on black-and-white, kara-e was characterized by *sumi-e* (ink paintings); the school progressed with the spread of Zen Buddhism and reached its zenith in the 15th century with Sesshu (1420–1506), a monk whose works depicted real (as opposed to the hitherto imaginary) landscapes.

From the late 16th century, wealthy warlords lavished patronage on the rival Kano school, which combined elements of kara-e and yamato-e to embellish the interiors of houses and castles with magnificent works. Motonobu (1476–1559) and Eitoku (1543–1590) were Kano's finest artists. Thanks to the growing patronage of wealthy merchant princes, the established schools flourished alongside growing demand for purely decorative art. This was met notably by the Rimpa school, of which Ogata Korin (1658–1716), famed for his composition of irises on a golden screen door, was a major exponent.

Hishikawa Moronobu (d. 1694), a prominent painter in the Kano style, was the first master—though not the inventor—of *ukiyo-e*, woodblock prints depicting the Floating World. The works of ukiyo-e masters such as Kitagawa Utamaro (1753–1806), Katsushika Hokusai (1760–1849), and Ando Hiroshige (1797–1858) caused the Japonism sensation in Europe during the 19th century and strongly influenced the Impressionists.

Sculpture: Archaeological excavations have unearthed Jomon-period statuettes and the Kofun era's more sophisticated *haniwa* clay figures (see p. 32). The latter, representing humans, animals, and buildings, were put in the grave mounds of chieftains, paralleling the Chinese practice.

Bronze figures of the Buddha were first introduced from Korea during the sixth century. Although Buddhism continued to dictate the same formal conventions as the original Sino-Korean prototypes, the Japanese were soon making their own. Styles changed with the introduction of new sects and materials: Wood allowed fitting many fine pieces together to create the multiarmed Kannon statues; sculpted lacquer statues achieved new levels of expression and were light enough to carry by hand when fires broke out.

In the secular world, wooden sculpted portraits became quite common to commemorate both noted priests and secular dignitaries. Sculpture thrived in miniature, too. Swords and armor often displayed fine decorative metalwork; many *netsuke,* the wood or ivory toggles used for attaching small medicine cases *(inro)* to kimono sashes, were tiny sculptures of consummate skill. As demand for these declined in the 19th century, former metalworkers and netsuke carvers turned to statuettes and figurines.

Modern Art: The resounding impact of Western art during the Meiji period prompted many Japanese artists to study in Paris, among them the influential

Yashuda Kan's "Shape of Mind" sculpture gives passersby pause for thought in midtown Tokyo.

Kuroda Seiki (1866–1924), founder of the first Western-style art school in Japan. Traditionalists' opposition led to the official division of *nihon-ga* (Japanese painting) and *yo-ga* (Western painting), with the latter deprived of government sponsorship. Nevertheless, all significant Western art movements have produced major Japanese representatives from the 1900s to the present day. Although they incorporate Western styles, nihon-ga painters continue to thrive.

Film: Born with the flickering images of a Kabuki actor in 1896, Japanese cinema took off during the 1910s with hundreds of one-reelers borrowing themes and actors from Kabuki theater.

Directors perfecting their craft during the 1920s absorbed Russian (Eisenstein), American (D. W. Griffith), and German (Expressionist) film technique. Among them were Mizoguchi Kenji (1898–1956) and Ozu Yasujiro (1903–1963), whose films progressed from rickety, silent one-reelers to masterpieces of world cinema.

In 1951 Kurosawa Akira's period drama *Rashomon* won the grand prize (the Golden Lion) at the Venice Film Festival. Mizoguchi's *The Life of Oharu* won the festival's international award in 1952, and his exquisite medieval ghost story *Ugetsu* won the Silver Lion the next year. At its zenith, epitomized by Ozu's *Tokyo Story* (1953), a poignant portrait of a rural family overwhelmed by social change, Japanese cinema earned global accolades and had far-reaching influence.

Meanwhile, to counter the onslaught of television, major Japanese film companies increasingly churned out formula flicks. Despite a vogue in the 1960s for the Japanese Nouvelle Vague cinema epitomized by Oshima Nagisa (*In the Realm of the Senses,* 1976; *Merry Christmas Mr. Lawrence,* 1983), film audiences declined tenfold between 1958 and 1998. Fighting off bankruptcy during the 1970s, the venerable Nikkatsu Company, founded in 1912, launched soft-core *roman poruno* (porno romance), a genre in which many prominent directors and actors cut their teeth until hard-core video killed it overnight. Some directors sought financing abroad, including Kurosawa (both in Russia and the U.S.) and Oshima (in France); others, like Imamura Shohei (*Ballad of Narayama,* 1983), sought independent financing at home.

The 1980s saw the emergence of successful independent directors, especially the late Itami

Old Japan meets new in a manga girl in kimono.

EXPERIENCE: Try Your Hand at Manga

You know Pokémon from *Princess Mononoke*, *Evangelion* from *ecchi*, and *Great Teacher Onizuka* from *One Piece*. You've practiced drawing doe eyes until your arm ached, and now it's time to take your art one step further and study manga and anime style in Japan.

Serious students should check out the programs at **Kyoto Seika University** (*kyoto-seika.ac.jp/eng/edu/manga*), a pioneer in manga studies, drawing style, and animation technique. **Nihon Kogakuin College** (*ncie.neec.ac.jp/en/creators/anime*) is another industry leader. A one-year minimum full-time Japanese course or JLPT Level 2 would be necessary to survive these programs.

If you'd just like to try your hand at the style, check out the **Kyoto International Manga Museum** (*kyotomm.jp*), which runs drawing workshops for beginners and practiced artists.

Juzo (*Tampopo, Taxing Woman*). The trend continues, despite small audience figures and the fact that two-thirds of films seen in Japan are foreign. Best known for hard-boiled cop movies, Kitano Takeshi has won many international awards for such films as *Hanabi* (1997) and *Zatoichi* (2004). Younger talent (e.g., Kawase Naomi, Koreeda Hirokazu) scores highly on the international agenda; Japan's quality cinema audience may be small but is reliable enough to make indie film directors flourish, if not rich. Major company formula films include anime movies, *yakuza* gangster movies, comedies, and period dramas—though the only ones to break into the Western market have been animated films, particularly from Studio Ghibli (*My Neighbor Totoro, Spirited Away*).

Manga & Anime: Successor to the throne of popular art is manga (comic books) and its TV counterpart, anime (Japanese-style animation). Perhaps second only to food for its soft power, anime is an international craze, with its adult themes, high-quality art, and diverse stories. Watching anime and reading manga are favorite pastimes for all but the oldest generation, as the subject matter ranges from giant robots to quirky high-school romance to the trials of your average long-suffering salaryman. The most famous names to have arrived in North America are *Astro Boy, Dragonball, Sailor Moon*, and *Pokémon*, but you'll score points with the locals if you know of present hit anime such as *One Piece, Yowamushi Pedal, One Punch Man,* or *Haikyuu!!*

Martial Arts

Although baseball and soccer are more popular, Japan's martial arts are treated with reverence and studied diligently. They originally arrived from China along with Buddhism: The core concepts had already been developed by monks as they honed techniques to defend themselves against bandits on their travels.

The oldest Japanese fighting arts are *kenjutsu* (based on the samurai art of swordsmanship), *jujutsu* (unarmed combat of medieval origin), and *kyujutsu* (ancient archery formalized during the Kamakura period). The suffix *-jutsu* means "skill"—especially skills useful to samurai warriors; it was replaced by *-do* (the Way) during the Meiji era. Although martial arts always involved spiritual as well as physical discipline, the emphasis

A craftsman hones his tools for weaving in the Nishijin textiles area in Kyoto.

shifted to the former during the 19th century. *Kendo,* the Way of the Sword, was introduced into the curriculum during the 19th century and is still widely practiced in schools and universities by both girls and boys. The same applies to a lesser degree to *kyudo* (archery), which adopts Zen's emphasis on mindfulness and concentration. Wearing padded armor and helmets to protect the face, kendo practitioners duel with swords of split bamboo; winning is determined according to five principles and the quality of strikes against eight strategic points on the opponent's body armor.

Martial arts are taught by masters in schools known as *dojo.* Most use the *dan* ranking system, whereby proficiency is measured from first to sixth dan, designated with colored belts worn on tunics; black generally denotes the highest level.

Judo, a synthesis of jujutsu, spiritual training, and other old fighting arts, involves grappling and body throws. It was introduced in the 1900s and became a national sport in the 1930s, but like all martial arts it was banned as a feudal remnant by the Occupation authorities. Reinstated in 1950, judo had already found experts around the world before its inclusion in the Tokyo Olympic Games in 1964, when to the disappointment of the Japanese the gold medal went to a Dutchman.

Karate ("empty hand"), a close relative of kung fu, was originally of Chinese origin. Adopted and developed in Okinawa due to a royal ban on weapons 500 years ago, the style did not reach mainland Japan until the 1900s. Akin to other martial arts in its demands for dedication and spiritual concentration, karate calls upon a variety of blows with the hands, fists, and feet, setting it apart from "soft" martial arts that redirect an attacker's energy, rather than confronting it directly.

Aikido, founded by Ueshiba Morihei during the 1920s and based on ancient arts of self-defense, is the most spiritually oriented of the martial arts. The emphasis is entirely on defense; throws are achieved by deftly using the opponent's momentum against him. Borrowing movement from classical Japanese dance, aikido also involves Zen-style meditation to enhance the flow of *ki*, the life force, through the practitioner's body.

Crafts

The rapid pace of modernization in Japan led inevitably to the loss of countless aspects of its former culture, but the survival of certain traditional crafts is one of the country's marvels. Efforts have been made to preserve them, not least through a system designating older practitioners of traditional arts and crafts as Intangible Cultural Properties or Living National Treasures. The fact that arts and crafts are hereditary businesses has helped to perpetuate them, as has the survival of the traditional ceremonies and pastimes in which they are used. Works by officially treasured craftspeople are rare and revered; even those by lesser masters can be dauntingly expensive. Fortunately a vast range of marvelous handicrafts are still affordable, though unlikely to be really cheap if made in Japan.

Ceramics: Japanese pottery goes back to the ancient Jomon culture, but remained rough and practical until techniques from China and Korea became established in the sixth century. Japanese potters continued to make Korean-style ware through the 18th century. Glazed ceramics arrived with the introduction of three-color glazes during the 7th century, but it was not until the 14th century that renewed contacts with China prompted the refinements and sophistication for which Japanese ceramics are renowned.

The tea ceremony ushered in stylistic innovations epitomized by the deceptively rough-hewn quality of ware such as Karatsu, Hagi, and Raku. As Hideyoshi's army retreated from its failed invasion of Korea in 1592, it enslaved many Korean potters. By the early 17th century, they were producing porcelain in Arita in Kyushu, especially the blue-and-white ware (and later polychrome, too) commonly called Imari. Along with polychrome Satsuma ware, Imari is still seen as most representative of Japanese ceramics today. Mass production caused a decline in traditional ceramics in the late 19th century, but there are still a hundred noted kilns and many master potters active in Japan, especially in Kyushu.

Paper: The surfaces and mats used in brush-and-ink painting and calligraphy are traditionally made from *washi*–paper handmade from wood pulp, especially mulberry bark. Although manufacture dwindled with the introduction of Western paper, washi is still in demand for such

Land of Ninja

Ninja, those mysterious masters of stealth and espionage, are hugely popular in film, Japanese comics, and animation, but are hard to spot in modern Japan. If you are traveling with children who like throwing stars and smoke bombs, check out the **Iga-ryu Ninja Museum** (*1117 Uenomarunouchi, Iga, Mie Prefecture, tel 0595/23-031, iganinja.jp*). Iga was a traditional ninja stronghold, and several old houses still have hidden trapdoors. In Tokyo, try **Ninja Akasaka** (*1F Akasaka Tokyu Plaza, 2-14-3 Nagata-Cho, Chiyodu-Ku, tel 03/5157-3936, ninjaakasaka.com*). This pricey, ninja-themed eatery scores points for its backflipping waiters.

uses as calligraphy, origami (paper folding), fans, decorations, paper dolls, and traditional stationery. In different thicknesses, plain, dyed, printed and decorated, and sometimes incorporating flecks of gold leaf and colored fragments, washi is sold in stationery and specialty stores.

Lacquerware: Common throughout East Asia, lacquer has long been associated primarily with Japan; in 18th-century England, red or black lacquering for furniture was known simply as Japanning. In Japan, *nuri* (lacquer) and *urushi-mono* (lacquered things) have rarely gone out of fashion since their height from the late 17th to the 19th centuries. *Tansu* (chests), boxes for various uses, tea caddies, combs and hair ornaments, wooden bowls, saké cups, and ceremonial *bento-bako* (packed meal boxes) are still produced by modern craftsmen, notably in Ishikawa, the Kiso Valley, and Okinawa. Authentic urushi-mono use a painstaking process involving three coats of lacquer, and their production commands high prices; plastic imitations, especially tableware, abound today. Often featuring inclusions of gold leaf and mother-of-pearl, beautifully painted designs are enhanced with a deep, glossy finish. Black, red, and occasionally green were once the more common colors, along with rarer *maki-e* (lacquerware with silver and gold leaf), but some of today's craftsmen create striking designs in a wider array of subtle (and not so subtle) hues.

Wood & Bamboo: The traditional Japanese home has little furniture, low tables and chests *(tansu)* being the notable exception. Popular overseas, antique tansu command increasingly high prices but remain a good buy in Japan. Although made with considerable skill and still expensive, modern equivalents are often machine finished and tend to have painted gloss where there should be a patina.

Many handcrafted objects are made of wood, notably lacquerware. Trays and bowls, turned on a lathe and hand finished, are often sold polished rather than lacquered.

Bamboo is popular for tea-related utensils and flower holders. It is either sectioned and shaped into a vase or cut into thin strips and woven into a variety of attractive shapes, for displaying on a surface or for hanging. Disposable chopsticks are the most common wooden tool in daily use: 24 billion pairs a year are thrown out. ∎

Girls' Day Doll Displays

The favorite toys of Japanese children have traditionally been dolls. *Hina-matsuri* (March 3) is Girls' Day, celebrated in homes with a display of dolls *(ningyo)* representing members of an old imperial court. Not toys but family heirlooms, such dolls are often beautifully dressed and crafted; fine examples, antique or modern, can be dauntingly expensive. (Boys' Festival on May 5 finds an equivalent in miniature suits of armor and samurai warrior dolls.)

Evolving partly from the *haniwa* figurines of the Kofun period (see p. 32), dolls have long been used as ritual charms in Japan and figure prominently among the country's folk arts. The most primitive are the cylindrical wooden *kokeshi*, but more refined types are still produced, notably in Kyoto, Hakata, and Saga Prefectures.

Perhaps it's no wonder that Japan remains crazy about cute little plastic figures and highly detailed models of interplanetary fighting robots.

The world's most populous metropolis, Japan's economic epicenter, and frontline of fashion, technology, and culture

Tokyo

Tokyo is a city of sensory overload: Come prepared to be richly stimulated!

Tokyo

In 1603, Edo—the precursor to Tokyo—was a fishing hamlet clustered around a crumbling fort. This became the military capital, replacing Kyoto. By the 18th century, it was the world's largest city; today, Greater Tokyo has more than 35 million inhabitants.

Viewed from the Roppongi Hills Mori Tower, the vast scale of the largest city on Earth is evident.

Established by shogun Tokugawa Ieyasu, Japan's great conquering unifier, Edo was originally constructed around a colossal castle (on the current site of the Imperial Palace), with the ruling samurai living within the walls; artisans, merchants, and the populace lived in the *shitamachi* (Low City), which extended eastward to the banks of the Sumida-gawa. Frequent fires necessitated the rebuilding of the wooden city.

Despite the setbacks of conflagrations, Edo was marked by social stability and economic growth. The problem of rebellious, warring *daimyo* was resolved by the alternate residence system, wherein each province's lord had to live in Edo in symbolic attendance on the shogun every other year, maintaining a financially exhausting second home. Their families remained in Edo when they went home, essentially hostages against foment, and all marriages were sanctioned by the shogun, preventing alliances of great clans. The presence of so many wealthy daimyo fuelled the growing merchant class, and Edo became a great city of art, craft, and pleasure.

Of Edo's many fires, the Great Meireki Fire of 1657 (aka Furisode-no-kaji—the long-sleeve fire) was the worst. Legend attributes the cause to a long-sleeve kimono—worn by a girl who died of unrequited love. The kimono was given to a temple, whose priests then sold it to another girl, who also died—a pattern repeated three times. The priests finally threw the kimono into a brazier, but a gust of wind sent it skyward to ignite the temple and a blaze that killed more than 100,000 people.

During the period of Sakoku—the national closure (1637–1868) during which no foreigner could enter nor any Japanese person leave the country on penalty of death—Edo became the cradle of Japanese

urban culture. After 1868 it served as the new home of the imperial family, which left Kyoto after a thousand years of history, and the nucleus for Western influences and modernization. Renamed Tokyo (Eastern Capital), the sprawling metropolis was a city of firsts, boasting Japan's first railroads, brick buildings, factories, gas, electricity lines, trams, and telephones.

INSIDER TIP:

To get around Tokyo, get the hassle-free prepaid train pass Pasmo or the Suica. These allow you to zip through on trains, subways, and buses.

—SHIGEO OTSUKA
Editor in chief,
National Geographic Japan

NEED TO KNOW

Reaching Tokyo

Tokyo is served by two airports, Haneda and Narita. Haneda is south of the city center, just half an hour from Tokyo Station by rail. It was formerly limited to domestic flights, but has a new international terminal and receives long-haul flights. Narita International Airport remains Japan's busiest terminal for flights abroad. It can be reached from Tokyo Station via the Narita Express (53 min.) or by shuttle bus in just over an hour, depending on traffic.

Coming from other parts of Japan, you can reach Tokyo by the Shinkansen "bullet trains" from Kyoto and Osaka (2.5 hours), Nagano (1.5 hours), and Sendai (1.5 hours) and even farther afield, though at nearly 5 hours to Hakodate on Hokkaido or Fukuoka on Kyushu, a quick flight may be worthwhile without the JR Pass (see Travelwise p. 354).

Getting Around

The 158 rail and metro lines, 2,210 stations, and 40 million other daily passengers make Tokyo's transit system the busiest and most extensive in the world. To get from A to B, access Google Maps, as streets are rarely named and the district-block-building address system is hard for even the Japanese to use. A data-only SIM card with b-mobile is recommended (see Travelwise p. 356).

In Tokyo, the JR Pass is limited to the Yamanote and Chuo lines. Whether you get the JR Pass or not, buy a Suica smart card ($) and charge it with about $10/day in urban areas. This card can be used everywhere in Tokyo and in most other cities. Just tap it at the gate and the fare will be calculated automatically. The balance can be refunded when you leave.

For more information on Excursions from Tokyo, see pp. 103–124.

Very little of Edo remains, and most of older Tokyo was destroyed by the Great Kanto Earthquake in 1923 and the incendiary pounding of World War II. Postwar reconstruction changed the old city beyond recognition. As visitors approach the urban-industrial sprawl en route from Narita Airport to downtown Tokyo, first impressions are grim. Yet for all the lack of urban planning and the concrete, "Western-style" architecture—designed for earthquake resistance or budgetary restraint rather than aesthetics—Tokyo can still surprise with moments of unexpected beauty: the contrast of a shrine surrounded by skyscrapers; the delicate arrangement of a *kaiseki* dish; the low light on a museum's National Treasure; or the fluorescent blaze enticing diners to endless epicurean delights. Modern-day Tokyo is a sensory kaleidoscope.

Behind busy central thoroughfares, quieter residential districts have their own temple, shrine, market, and main street. As echoes of the past resound in neighborhoods such as Ueno and Asakusa, the future looms in the skyscraper clusters near Tokyo Bay. One thing is certain: Tokyo never rests. Repeat visitors find change happens fast, as the core of Japanese society struggles to stay ahead of a rising Asia, chasing the tail of the future. Ultimately it is that energy that brings visitors back to this electrifying and fascinating metropolis. ■

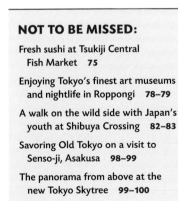

NOT TO BE MISSED:

Fresh sushi at Tsukiji Central Fish Market 75

Enjoying Tokyo's finest art museums and nightlife in Roppongi 78–79

A walk on the wild side with Japan's youth at Shibuya Crossing 82–83

Savoring Old Tokyo on a visit to Senso-ji, Asakusa 98–99

The panorama from above at the new Tokyo Skytree 99–100

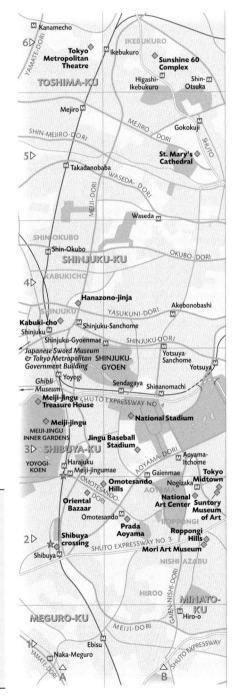

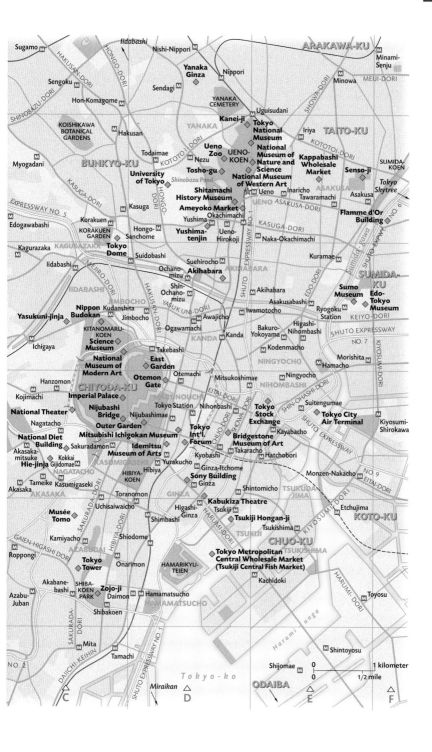

Sugamo
Nishi-Nippori
ARAKAWA-KU
Minami-Senju
Minowa
MEIJI-DORI
Iidabashi
HAKUSAN-DORI
HONGO-DORI
Nippori
Yanaka Ginza
Sengoku
Sendagi
YANAKA CEMETERY
SHOWA-DORI
Uguisudani
Iriya
TAITO-KU
Hon-Komagome
Kanei-ji
YANAKA
KOTOTOI-DORI
SHINOBAZU-DORI
KOISHIKAWA BOTANICAL GARDENS
Hakusan
Tokyo National Museum
National Museum of Nature and Science
Kappabashi Wholesale Market
Senso-ji
SUMIDA-KOEN
Myogadani
Todaimae
Ueno Zoo
UENO-KOEN
Nezu
Tosho-gu
National Museum of Western Art
Tokyo Skytree
BUNKYO-KU
University of Tokyo
Shinobazu Pond
Shitamachi History Museum
Ueno
Inaricho
ASAKUSA
Asakusa
KASUGA-DORI
Ameyoko Market
Okachimachi
UENO ASAKUSA-DORI
Tawaramachi
EXPRESSWAY NO. 5
Edogawabashi
Kasuga
Yushima
Flamme d'Or Building
Korakuen
KORAKUEN GARDEN
Hongo-Sanchome
Yushima-tenjin
Ueno-Hirokoji
Naka-Okachimachi
Sumida-gawa
SHUTO EXPWY
Kagurazaka
KAGURAZAKA
Tokyo Dome
Suidobashi
KASUGA-DORI
Kuramae
SUMIDA-KU
Iidabashi
IIDABASHI
MEJIRO-DORI
Ochanomizu
Akihabara
AKIHABARA
Edo-Tokyo Museum
Ichigaya
Shin-Ochanomizu
Akihabara
SHUTO EXPRESSWAY
Sumo Museum
Yasukuni-jinja
Nippon Budokan
Kudanshita
YASUKUNI-DORI
Jimbocho
Awajicho
Iwamotocho
Asakusabashi
Ryogoku Station
KEIYO-DORI
NO. 6
KITANOMARU-KOEN
Science Museum
Ogawamachi
Bakuro-Yokoyama
Higashi-Nihombashi
SHUTO EXPRESSWAY NO. 7
National Museum of Modern Art
Takebashi
KANDA
Kanda
Kodenmacho
Morishita
KIYOSUMI-DORI
Hanzomon
East Garden
Otemachi
NINGYOCHO
Hamacho
Kojimachi
CHIYODA-KU
Otemon Gate
Mitsukoshimae
Ningyocho
NIHOMBASHI
Imperial Palace
MARUNOUCHI
Suitengumae
EITAI-DORI
Shin-Ohashi-Dori
National Theater
Nijubashi Bridge
Nijubashimae
Tokyo Station
Nihonbashi
Tokyo Stock Exchange
Tokyo City Air Terminal
Kiyosumi-Shirokawa
Nagatacho
Outer Garden
Mitsubishi Ichigokan Museum
Tokyo Int'l. Forum
Kayabacho
SHUTO EXPRESSWAY
National Diet Building
Sakuradamon
Idemitsu Museum of Arts
Bridgestone Museum of Art
Takaracho
Monzen-Nakacho
NO. 9
Akasaka-mitsuke
Kokkai
Gijidomae
KASUMIGASEKI
Yurakucho
Kyobashi
Hatchobori
EITAI-DORI
Hie-jinja
Tameike
Kasumigaseki
HIBIYA-KOEN
Hibiya
Ginza-Itchome
KOTO-KU
NAGATACHO
Sony Building
Ginza
Shintomicho
TSUKUDA-JIMA
Akasaka
Toranomon
Uchisaiwaicho
GINZA
Etchujima
AKASAKA
Musée Tomo
SAKURADA-DORI
Higashi-Ginza
Kabukiza Theatre
Tsukiji
Tsukishima
Kamiyacho
Shimbashi
Tsukiji Hongan-ji
Tsukishima
GAIEN-HIGASHI-DORI
HIBIYA-DORI
Shiodome
TSUKIJI
KIYOSUMI-DORI
Roppongi
Tokyo Tower
Onarimon
HAMARIKYU-TEIEN
Tokyo Metropolitan Central Wholesale Market (Tsukiji Central Fish Market)
CHUO-KU
TSUKISHIMA
Akabane-bashi
SHIBA-KOEN PARK
Zojo-ji
Daimon
Kachidoki
HARUMI-DORI
Toyosu
Azabu-Juban
Shibakoen
HAMAMATSUCHO
Hamamatsucho
Harumi unga
Mita
DAIICHI-KEIHIN
Tamachi
Shintoyosu
NO. 2
SHUTO EXPRESSWAY NO. 1
Tokyo-ko
Miraikan
Shijomae
Shijomae
0   1 kilometer
0   1/2 mile
ODAIBA

C   D   E   F

Marunouchi: Old Edo Castle

The heart of Tokyo centers on the green space where Edo Castle used to be and the current Imperial Palace now stands. What was once home to loyal samurai families' great estates within the castle's outer moat now plays host to immensely wealthy corporations, the palace gardens, fine museums, and some early Western-style buildings such as the newly renovated Tokyo Station.

Cherry blossoms festoon the Chidoriga-fuchi moat around the Imperial Palace.

Tokyo

Visitor Information

✉ Tokyo Station, west exit

🕐 7:30 a.m.–8:30 p.m.

gotokyo.org

Imperial Palace

🅰 67 C3

✉ 1–1 Chiyoda, Chiyoda-ku

☎ 03/5223-8071

🕐 Palace tours at 1:30 p.m., by reservation. Garden: 9 a.m.–5 p.m., 4 p.m. in winter

Ⓜ Otemachi

The site of the **Imperial Palace** (Kokyo) has seen several important structures. Originally home to the 1457 fort of Edo's founder, feudal lord Ota Dokan, the location was chosen by shogun Tokugawa Ieyasu for his new castle and capital in the 1590s. In 1888, a palace was added here for Emperor Meiji, but it was destroyed in the fire-bombing of 1945. The stone walls and surrounding moats are part of the original Edo-jo complex, as is the restored Ote-mon gate, which stands beyond the Nijubashi access bridge and

before the East Garden, the actual site of Edo-jo. Elegantly landscaped with ponds and pines, the garden contains the ruins of Edo-jo and the 100 Guard Office, built in 1863—the last remaining original structure.

The **East Garden** (Higashi-gyoen) and the ruins of **Edo-jo** are open year-round, but the Imperial Palace itself, rebuilt in 1968, is open only by reserved tour. The lack of activity in what was once the heart of the nation leaves some Japanese visitors feeling depressed, but come April, the cherry trees along the moats burst

INSIDER TIP:

There is no better way to explore Tokyo than with a city walk. The JNTO's website (www.jnto.go.jp) has great walking itineraries.

—ROB GOSS
National Geographic contributor

into bloom and young lovers shyly sit under their boughs in a decidedly hopeful atmosphere.

The park on the north side of the Imperial Palace grounds, **Kitanomaru-koen,** is notable for museums and the **Nippon Budokan** (*2-3 Kitanomaru-koen, tel 03/3216-5100*), a martial arts stadium now largely used for rock concerts and the upcoming Olympic Games. The **Science Museum** (Kagaku Gijutsukan; *2-1 Kitanomaru-koen, tel 050/5541-8600, www.jsf.or.jp*), less than a quarter of a mile (300 m) southeast, doesn't have the reputation of the national equivalent in Ueno (see p. 93), but hands-on exhibits make it a hit with schoolchildren.

The **National Museum of Modern Art** (Kokuritsu Kindai Bijutsukan) is to the right of the park entrance. This is one of Japan's finest modern art museums, with a collection focusing on contemporary artists and tracing the major developments in Japanese art since the Meiji era. The **Crafts Gallery** (Kogeikan), housed in the adjacent old Imperial Guard Headquarters of 1911, presents exhibits including ceramics, basketware, dolls, lacquerware, and metalwork.

East of the palace is the **Marunouchi business district.** Of many early modern brick buildings that once existed here, only Tokyo Station, renovated in 2012 for its centennial, and the Bank of Japan's old building stick out among the glassy towers. One new-old addition is the **Mitsubishi Ichigokan Museum,** a 2010 replica of Mitsubishi's banking headquarters, originally constructed in 1894 as the first Western building in Marunouchi. The attractive brick building now houses four annual art exhibits. Kitty-corner from this is the ultramodern Tokyo International Forum's "Glass Building," an ethereal ship sailing among stodgy skyscrapers. ∎

Kitanomaru-koen
 67 C4
✉ Just south of Kudanshita, a short walk from north exit of Imperial Palace East Garden
🚇 Kudanshita

National Museum of Modern Art
 67 C4
✉ 3-1 Kitanomaru-koen, Chiyoda-ku
☎ 03/5777-8600
🕐 10 a.m.–5 p.m. (Fri. 10 a.m.– 8 p.m.), closed Mon.
💲 $
🚇 Takebashi
www.momat.go.jp

Mitsubishi Ichigokan Museum
 67 D3
✉ 2-6-2 Marunouchi, Chiyoda-ku
☎ 03/5405-8686
🕐 10 a.m.–6 p.m., closed Mon.
💲 $$$
🚇 Tokyo Station
mimt.jp

Karoshi: Japan's Modern Killer

Karoshi or "death from overwork" is an apt description for Japanese business culture. Karoshi can be heart failure or stroke occurring in young staff with no history of illness, but the definition has been broadened by court verdicts to include work stress–related suicide, which claims 2,000 lives yearly. Government estimates put one in five workers—those logging more than 60 hours a week—at risk. In 2015 a new recruit at advertising giant Dentsu committed suicide after months of overwork, prompting the president to resign and the nation to once again question its self-sacrificing, collectivist, *"Ganbatte!"* (Do your best!) work culture.

Modern Architecture

Japan's architectural transformation from wood to reinforced concrete began in the late 19th century but really took off—and upward—with mass reconstruction during the postwar period. Much of Japan's architecture looks inspired by city-of-the-future features in sci-fi comic books of the 1950s, while the monster *danchi*—state apartment buildings—parallel Soviet architectural brutalism.

Mode Gakuen Cocoon Tower

Due to little urban planning, Japan's urban environments are a fascinating heterogeneous mix. Rickety wooden houses often stand wedged between structures of reinforced concrete or austere temples; even Las Vegas could envy the palatial Chinese rococo architecture of the *onsen* (hot spring) resort, the neon-splashed *pachinko* (pinball) parlor, or the outrageous kitsch of the love hotel.

The soaring economy resulted in the *kenchiku bumu* (architecture boom), which saw many fine heritage buildings torn down through the 1980s. Most towns can boast a share of noteworthy modern buildings; Japanese contemporary architecture frequently incorporates traditional aesthetic concepts to great effect.

Foreign Architects in Tokyo

The list of works by major architects in the capital reads like an international hall of fame, with Le Corbusier and Frank Lloyd Wright alongside homegrown architectural stars such as Tange Kenzo and Ando Tadao. A notable landmark is New York architect Rafael Viñoly's vast Tokyo International Forum Building in Yurakucho, completed in 1996—a kind of indoor city famous for its colossal glass atrium crossed by walkways. British architect Norman Foster's Century Tower was built in 1991 near Ochanomizu; U.S. architect Peter Eisenman was responsible for the Koizumi Lighting Theater, and, out in Koiwa, a suburb of Tokyo, the strange Nunotani (NC) Building looks as if it's about to fall apart. French architect Jean Nouvel designed the pointed oval of the Dentsu Building (2002), which towers over Hamarikyu-teien.

Responsible for a few of Tokyo's most surreal constructions, some foreign architects are more famous as such in Japan; at home they are designers. Britain's Nigel Coates made the Wall Building in Hiroo—with a Roman facade embellished with scrap metal. In Asakusa, Frenchman Philippe Starck's quirky Flamme d'Or Building (1989) houses the Asahi Super Dry Beer Hall. Devised by premier developer Minoru Mori, the 29-acre (11.6 ha) Roppongi Hills complex (2003) in Azabu is a showcase for both domestic and international architects as well as for innovative urban green spaces.

Japanese Modernism

The 1980s saw the rise of several important Japanese architects, notably Isozaki Arata (Shukosha Building, Fukuoka, 1974–1975; Tokyo Globe Theater, 1988) and Osaka's extraordinary self-taught Ando Tadao (Children's Museum, Himeji, 1989; Chichu Art Museum, Naoshima, 2004). The most universally famous is Tange Kenzo, noted first for his remarkable stadium buildings for the 1964 Tokyo Olympics and the striking hyperbolic planes forming a massive cross in the structure of St. Mary's Cathedral (1964). Completed in 1991, Tange's colossal granite-and-glass Tokyo Metropolitan Government Building, a monumental blend of modernism and cathedral Gothic, is one of the most visited new buildings in Japan. It soars above western Shinjuku, where skyscrapers first emerged after the Olympics. A great area for vertical architecture, Shinjuku is bleak at ground level; most people find the architecturally less remarkable eastern side of the district more colorful and congenial.

Not that all modern buildings in Tokyo are cold. With its sci-fi shapes, the extraordinary Tokyo Metropolitan Gymnasium is a 1990s answer to Tange's Olympic architecture of the 1960s. Imaginative, eclectic, and effective, Takahiko Yanagisawa's 1995 Museum of Contemporary Art, in Kiba-koen, was designed as an update on the old counterpart in Ueno. Herzog and de Meuron's Prada Store on Omotesando is a charming tower of convex diamond-shape glass panes, and Tange Associates' Mode Gakuen Cocoon Tower (2008) uses a curved steel lattice wrapped around a glass oval to symbolize the nurturing character of this education-based skyscraper situated in Shinjuku.

EXPERIENCE: A Night in a Capsule Hotel

Temples and soaring skyscrapers aside, the architecture that leaves the most lasting impression on travelers may be the capsule hotel. Built for salarymen who work past the time of the last train home, capsule hotels have rows upon rows of slightly claustrophobic "rooms," typically 3 feet by 3 feet by 6 feet (.9 m x .9 m x 1.8 m), offering enough space for the average Japanese man to sit up and stretch out. Each capsule has a reading light, a mini TV, and a curtain for privacy, but luggage has to be stored in lockers. You can soak in the large communal baths, then hit the town and stagger back like a proper salaryman. You can check in at any time, which is an advantage over the strict, early curfews of many hostels. Most capsule hotels are for men only, but the growing female workforce has led some to open women-only floors, guarded by a front desk. The following are capsule hotels worth experiencing:

Green Plaza Shinjuku Capsule Hotel *(1-29-2 Kabukicho, Shinjuku, Tokyo, tel 03/3207-4923, hgpshinjuku.jp)*. Tokyo's first capsule hotel, this massive 630-room beehive has a communal bath. The policy is men-only (and no tattoos), but a women's spa on the ninth floor has an open sleeping area.

Nine Hours *(588 Teianmaeno-cho, Teramachi-dori Shijo-sagaru, Shimogyo-ku, Kyoto, tel 075/353-7337, ninehours.co.jp)*. This stylish new capsule hotel, with separate men's and women's sections, has an all-white theme reminiscent of a spaceship and is close to Kyoto's entertainment district.

Shinjuku Kuyakushomae Capsule Hotel *(Toyo Bldg. 3F, 1-2-5 Kabuki-cho, Shinjuku-ku, Tokyo, tel 03/3232-1110, capsuleinn.com /shinjuku)*. This capsule hotel caters to the Kabukicho late-night scene. The public bath is men-only, but there's a women's floor available too.

Ginza

During the 19th century, Ginza became the showcase for Western-style development, with cafés and restaurants appearing between Western boutiques and department stores. Today, Ginza rivals New York's Fifth Avenue, with the pantheon of global haute couture represented by glittering shrines to fashion. Among the Western brand shops are several traditional Japanese department stores full of eye-poppingly expensive items—great to explore, even if the prices put you off.

Global-brand shops are found along Chuo-dori in Ginza.

The district's best shopping opportunities are concentrated around Ginza Station running north up Chuo-dori, a large street that becomes a pedestrian mall on weekends. However, lesser brands and edgier upstarts spill over into the side streets, which are well worth exploring if you have time for some leisurely browsing.

The Japanese shopper's obsession with brands can be bewildering: In essence, the huge popularity of designer labels is due to the widely held beliefs that only the best will do, that if you pay more you will automatically get better quality, and that appearances are reality.

Young, rich housewives occupy the most stylish

component of Ginza's clientele, but the real money is with the immaculately dressed grandmothers. This generation grew wealthy before the Bubble Economy collapsed. Their era of lifetime jobs and pension plans left them with money to spend, unlike the significantly poorer generations of the last 20 years.

Nowhere is this more apparent than in the prestigious Japanese department stores **Wako** and **Mitsukoshi** at Ginza Station. These are two of the oldest and best places to be seen shopping for exquisite traditional goods and classy styles.

Ginza Entertainment

The winking neon of small bars in Ginza backstreets may be enticing, but many of the exclusive hostess clubs are among the most expensive watering holes in the world. Not all of Ginza's wining and dining options are so expensive though; you'll find less costly options toward Hibiya and Yurakucho, where the adventurous can seek out the little beer-and-yakitori joints that operate under the railroad tracks.

The area is a nucleus of art galleries, with dozens between Ginza 1- to 4-chome and Kyobashi, and from Ginza 5- to 8-chome. The accent is on the contemporary—mainly Japanese but including some Western artists. The **Idemitsu Museum of Arts** (Idemitsu Bijutsukan), covering 26,900 square feet (2,500 sq m), houses Tokyo's finest private collection of Japanese art and ceramics. The collection

has pottery fragments from archaeological excavations all over Asia. Chinese ceramics include Song-dynasty and T'ang-dynasty three-color ware, as well as fine antique Japanese pottery styles such as Seto, Oribe, Kutani, Karatsu, and Kakiemon. This eclectic museum also features Zen calligraphy and ink painting, most notably by the 17th-century monk Sengai.

INSIDER TIP:

If electronic gadgets and widgets are your thing, take at least an hour or two to peruse the latest prototypes in the Sony Showroom in Ginza.

—KENNY LING
National Geographic contributor

The **Sony Showroom** in the funky new Ginza Place building (*5-8-1 Ginza, Chuo-ku, tel 03/3573-5307, 11 a.m.–7 p.m.*) has all the electronics titan's latest and greatest gadgets and makes for a pleasant diversion from sightseeing.

Another good option if you want a break from walking outdoors is the **Bridgestone Museum of Art** (Burijisuton Bijutsukan), an excellent private museum. Owned by Japan's foremost tire manufacturer, it specializes in major French Impressionists but also contains works by Modigliani and Picasso and some important old masters, including Rembrandt. The museum also

Idemitsu Museum of Arts
- 67 D3
- ✉ 9F Teigeki Bldg., 3-1-1 Marunouchi, Chiyoda-ku
- ☎ 03/3213-9402
- ⏰ 10 a.m.–5 p.m. (Fri. 10 a.m.–7 p.m.); closed Mon.
- 💲 $$
- 🚇 Hibiya or Yurakucho

www.idemitsu.com /museum/honkan

Bridgestone Museum of Art (under renovation until 2019)
- 67 D3
- ✉ 1-10-1 Kyobashi, Chuo-ku
- ☎ 03/3563-0241
- ⏰ 10 a.m.–6 p.m. (Fri. 10 a.m.–8 p.m.); closed Mon.
- 💲 $$$
- 🚇 Kyobashi

bridgestone -museum.gr.jp

Kabukiza Theatre

🅰 67 D3

✉ Ginza 4-12-15, Chuo-ku

☎ 03/3545-6800

💲 $$–$$$$$

🚇 Higashi-Ginza or Ginza

kabuki-za.co.jp

focuses on *yo-ga* (Japanese art in the Western tradition) and includes works by the Paris-based artist Tsuguharu (or Léonard) Foujita (1886–1968).

Five minutes' walk along Harumi-dori from Ginza Station is the recently rebuilt **Kabukiza Theatre** one of Japan's prime spots for watching this memorably bizarre form of 17th-century drama. Even without an audio guide, it is still possible for non-Japanese speakers to follow the twists and turns through multiple loves, murders, and betrayals. Don't worry if you lose the plot: The manner of acting is a fascinating study for lovers of drama. Nothing is left to improvisation, and every move, glance, and pose has been long established by a master as the proper way to portray that story.

INSIDER TIP:

Although convenient for a night out, capsule hotels can be noisy due to all-hours check-in. Buy earplugs at a pharmacy and take the upper bunk so that late arrivals don't wake you.

—PERRIN LINDELAUF
National Geographic writer

All Kabuki plays are set to traditional music and the archetypal *pon!* of a small drum that punctuates particularly dramatic sentences; keep a look out for the especially entertaining heroes wearing vibrant red and white *kumadori* makeup. ∎

Making Conversation in Japan

So you've found some locals who speak some English and you'd love to pick their brains about Japan—that's great, but tread carefully.

Japanese humility and sense of privacy mean that you'll be pulling teeth to get them to speak about themselves. And even if they do, they'll dismiss their own lives as of little interest. Similarly, the Japanese are wary of giving offense and will only reluctantly offer an opinion on politics, religion, or sex—many young people get around the issue by never having an opinion at all!

The only real taboos are the imperial family and its mythical origins, but discussion of the actions of the Japanese military during World War II and the aftermath of the atomic bombs are likely to make people uncomfortable. Criticism of whaling and whale meat, although rarely eaten or even seen, can arouse an angry defense of Japanese cuisine.

Instead, give your new friends a chance to talk about their interests. Travel, food, hobbies, sports, and popular culture are perennial topics. Asking for advice about what to see or do in their hometown is another great conversation starter. Japanese society is insular, so meeting a foreigner is often a treat and a chance to ask about other countries. Bear in mind that the strain of speaking in English and worries over making grammar mistakes tend to make the Japanese shy, slow speakers. A couple of beers later, however, you'll find them more loquacious. If all else fails, the national topic is the weather. Remember *"atsui!"* (it's hot), and *"samui!"* (it's cold) and you're set.

Tokyo Bay

Amid the concrete sprawl of metropolitan Tokyo, it is easy to forget that it is a port town. Odaiba, largest of the bay's artificial islands, has several family-friendly museums and amusement parks. The north side of the bay features Tsukiji, the massive wholesale market that supplies the metropolis with seafood and ensures that millions of fresh delicacies reach the tables of Tokyo every day. It's not to be missed.

A mile (1.6 km) southeast of the palace lies the **Tsukiji Central Fish Market** *(5-2-1 Tsukiji, Chuo-ku, tel 03/3541-2640, tsukiji-market.or.jp, closed Sun., holidays, and 2nd & 4th Wed., subway: Tsukiji)*, where most of Tokyo's fresh fish is received and sold. The market opens to the general public at 9 a.m.: It's hectic and children are not allowed in this busy workplace, but it is a fascinating display of sea creatures needed to feed Tokyo daily. Pick up some fresh sushi in the adjacent warren of little eateries for an unusual breakfast. Note that Tsukiji may move to new facilities at nearby Toyosu in time for the 2020 Olympics, but an ongoing battle over the site's benzene contamination may yet block the move.

On your way to the Tsukiji market, you will probably pass a curious Buddhist temple. **Tsukiji Hongan-ji** *(3-15-1 Tsukuji, Chuo-ku, tel 03/3541-1131, outside Tsukiji subway station)* was built in 1935 to replace a 17th-century original destroyed in the 1923 earthquake. It was designed to evoke the classical Indian temple style by the celebrated architect Ito Chuta.

South of Ginza and a ten-minute stroll from the fish market, is **Hamarikyu-teien.** Turned into

Tuna arrives at the Tsukiji Central Fish Market.

a landscaped pleasure garden in 1709 from reclaimed land owned by the shoguns, the garden fell into disuse following damage in one of the city's great fires. It passed to the Imperial Household

Hamarikyu-teien

- 67 D2
- 1-1 Hamarikyu-teien, Chuo-ku
- 03/3541-0200
- 9 a.m.–5 p.m.
- $
- Shiodome

tokyo-park.or.jp

Miraikan

- 67 D1
- 2-3-6 Aomi, Koto-ku
- 03/3570-9151
- 10 a.m.–5 p.m., closed Tues.
- $$
- Fune-no-kagakukan

**www.miraikan.jst
.go.jp**

**BOAT TRIP TO
ASAKUSA:** Take a
45-min. boat ride to
Asakusa, leaving from
Shimbashi Station ($$).

Agency in 1869 and became the Detached Palace Garden. Graced with a lavish Western-style pavilion, it was used for entertaining foreign dignitaries.

Today the pavilion is gone, replaced by attractive teahouses. Although Hamarikyu's horizons are walled off by high-rise buildings, it remains a fine landscape garden and a haven of green. Hamarikyu is a stop on the boat trip on the Sumida-gawa between Hinode pier (near Hamamatsucho) and Asakusa. Boats pass every half hour.

If you find downtown too frenetic, escape like a Tokyoite to Odaiba. The island, literally named "Fortifications," was built as a cannon emplacement to discourage hostile powers from barging into the bay for some gunboat diplomacy, like Commodore Perry did with his infamous "black ships" (see p. 41). Nowadays the cannons have given way to spacious, interactive museums, malls and amusement parks. The **Miraikan**

(National Museum of Emerging Science and Innovation) is both kid friendly and cutting edge: The exhibits on some of the latest technology are interactive and there's English signage. Fans of Kenzo Tange's architecture should see the **Fuji Television Building,** notable for its oddly suspended sphere. The **Oedo Onsen Monogatari** hot-spring complex *(2-3-6 Aomi, Koto-ku, tel 03/5500-1126, ooedoonsen.jp, 11 a.m.–9 a.m., $$$$, Yurikamome line: Telecom Center)* was built to resemble an Edo-period town, and video game maker Sega's **Joypolis** *(1-6-1 Daiba, Minato-ku, tel 03/5500-1801, tokyo-joypolis.com, 10 a.m.–10 p.m., $$$$, Rinkai line: Tokyo Teleport)* has an arcade amusement park. Last, Odaiba holds **Tokyo Big Sight,** the convention center that hosts **Comiket,** the massive biannual manga convention. Anime fans should also visit DiverCity Tokyo Plaza to see the "life-size" 59-foot-tall (18 m) Gundam robot. ■

Hamarikyu-teien offers Tokyoites a refuge from concrete and glass.

A Geek's Pilgrimage in Japan

Forget the temples and sushi for a while: Some tourists in Japan go straight for the geekery, seeking out the latest in high-tech gadgets, the newest video games, the most obscure anime, and everything ninja they can get their hands on.

So, how *otaku* (geeky) are you? Here's a list of must-dos on the geek's pilgrimage of Japan.

- Go directly to otaku mecca, the Tokyo district of **Akihabara,** and load up on limited-edition plastic models and Japan-only video games. Visit a *dojinshi* (small press comic) shop, then catch a performance by an **AKB48** troupe (see p. 97).
- Visit one of Akihabara's famous **maid cafés** for the ultimate experience in kitschy *"kawaii!"* ("cute!" see sidebar p. 97).
- Attend the August or December **Comiket** *(comiket.co.jp),* when half a million manga fans descend upon the Tokyo Big Sight convention center to buy dojinshi, meet anime or video game celebrities, or join the 15,000 others who show up in cosplay for this manga mega-event *(comiket.co.jp).*
- Admire thousand-year-old swords at the **Japanese Sword Museum** in Tokyo (see p. 89), or watch smiths hammer out new *katana* at the **Bizen Osafune Sword Museum** in Okayama-ken (see pp. 275–276).
- Practice your *shuriken* throwing skills at the **Iga-ryu Ninja Museum** in Iga, Mie Prefecture (see sidebar p. 61), explore the secrets of **Ninja Temple** in Kanazawa, and try your best ninja sneak on the intentionally squeaky floors in Nijo Castle.
- Forget hotels! A real geek sleeps only in **Internet cafés,** where a $20 overnight stay gets you a booth with a sofa, a computer or a TV and video game console, a huge manga library, and unlimited soft drinks! There are even showers.
- In Tokyo, visit the **Ghibli Museum** (see pp. 101–102), home of Miyazaki Hayao's beloved films *(My Neighbor Totoro, Spirited Away, Princess Mononoke, Ponyo).*
- While in Kansai, be sure to pay homage to

A maid café waitress in Akihabara waves to prospective customers.

the Godfather of Anime and creator of Astro Boy at the **Tezuka Osamu Manga Museum** (see p. 252).
- If you dare, sit through the famous Power Rangers show at Kyoto's **Toei Kyoto Studio Park** (see p. 218).
- Don't miss the mesmerizing **Kyoto International Manga Museum** (see p. 203) for a rare look at the medium's early history.
- Spend several sessions in a *purikura* (print club), fancy photo booths complete with skin-whitening, eye-enlarging, glitter-spraying auto-photoshop. Barely recognizable shots of your mug through the lens of idealized Japanese beauty are hilarious souvenirs.
- Cruise **Sennichimae Doguya-suji** (see p. 247), Osaka's kitchen tool street, for all manner of restaurant kitsch and strange cooking paraphernalia. You'll find all the culinary equipment you need to cook up a perfect *takoyaki* when you get back home.
- Bring your 'Mons to battle at **Pokémon Centers** in most of Japan's big cities, too.

Roppongi

A couple of miles (3 km) southwest of the Imperial Palace, Roppongi developed, along with nearby Azabu and Hiroo, as a residential area for expatriates when foreign embassies multiplied there in the 1950s. Renowned then as now for its foreign restaurants and nightclubs, it became a favorite with the Japanese for Western-style entertainment. The Art Triangle Roppongi, completed in 2007, brings together three excellent museums showcasing fine modern art.

Roppongi's National Art Center, Tokyo

Roppongi (Six Trees) rivaled Shinjuku for its proliferation of discos in the late 1970s and became one of Tokyo's most fashionable districts during the 1980s. Although still cosmopolitan and sophisticated, in recent years it has exploded as an entertainment district as raucous as any. In the process it has become more tacky, and visitors should be on their guard against aggressive foreign touts and spiked drinks, an otherwise rare danger in Japan. Still, it remains one of the best and most attractive and accessible options for a night on the dance floor in Tokyo.

Tokyo Tower

During the development frenzy of the 1950s, Tokyo had to have its Eiffel Tower. Devised for radio/TV transmission, the 1,092-foot (333 m) Tokyo Tower was erected in 1958 on land that had belonged to Shiba-koen. Then cherished, it is now widely seen as an ugly red-and-white blight on the capital's cityscape. However, improved lighting has turned it into a surprisingly attractive feature of the nocturnal skyline. A decent Tokyo panorama is visible from the top observation platform, but for views of a higher elevation the new Tokyo Skytree (see pp. 99–100) is a much better bet.

Zojo-ji was moved to what is now Shiba-koen in 1598, where it was the centerpiece of a vast temple city. Razed and rebuilt more than once, the temple has had a tumultuous history. After being torched during the Meiji Restoration, it was burned by a vagrant in 1909 before being destroyed during World War II. The *sanmon* (two-storied) gate, built in 1605, is a miraculous and magnificent survivor. One of the very few buildings of such antiquity in Tokyo, it is designated an Important

INSIDER TIP:

Follow the overhead expressway down to Nishi Azabu Crossing, where the backstreets on the left abound with quieter bars and restaurants.

—KENNY LING
National Geographic contributor

Cultural Property. The main hall, built in 1974, contains several treasures, including the huge old temple bell.

Another famous old survivor in the area is the Nitenmon gate, which now stands on land belonging to the Tokyo Prince Hotel (*3-3-1 Shiba-koen, Minato-ku, tel 03/3432-1111*); other parts of the compound, including the old Tokugawa burial ground, now find themselves within the confines of a private golf club.

The **Roppongi Hills** complex, completed in 2003, has titanic residential/office towers set in among pleasant green spaces, which are a rarity in many other parts of Tokyo. This futuristic urban planning concept offers Tokyoites an impressive array of options for culture, entertainment, shopping, and dining.

Art Triangle Roppongi

In addition to its great night views, the rooftop **Mori Art Museum** showcases an impressive range of contemporary international art and is the southern tip of the **Art Triangle Roppongi,** a trio of museums. Its other points are the relocated **Suntory Museum of Art** (*3F Tokyo Midtown Gardens, 9-7-4 Akasaka, tel 03/3479-8600, suntory.co.jp/sma, 10 a.m.–6 p.m., until 8 p.m. Fri. and Sat., closed Tues., $$$*), which has an outstanding collection of lacquerware, painting, and ceramics in the new Tokyo Midtown complex, and the excellent **National Art Center, Tokyo** (*7-22-2 Roppongi, tel 03/5777-8600, www.nact.jp, 10 a.m.–5:30 p.m., 7:30 p.m. on Fri., closed Tues., $$$*), which has no permanent collection but focuses on exhibitions.

At the north end of the district of Roppongi, the **Musée Tomo** makes for a fine contrast with the Art Triangle museums. Here you'll find an intimate, carefully chosen collection of modern Japanese ceramics. For lovers of the tea ceremony (see p. 227), the Musée Tomo is well worth a leisurely visit. ∎

Tokyo Tower

- 🅰 67 C2
- ✉ 4-2-8 Shiba-koen, Minato-ku
- ☎ 03/3433-5111
- 🕐 9 a.m.–11 p.m.
- 💲 $$
- 🚇 Kamiyacho

tokyotower.co.jp

Zojo-ji

- 🅰 67 C2
- ✉ 4-7-35 Shiba-koen, Minato-ku
- ☎ 03/3432-1431
- 🕐 9 a.m.–5 p.m.
- 🚇 Daimon, Shibakoen, or Onarimon

www.zojoji.or.jp

Mori Art Museum
- ✉ 53 Roppongi Hills Mori Tower, 6-10-1 Roppongi
- ☎ 03/5777-8600
- 🕐 10 a.m.–10 p.m., closed Tues.
- 💲 $$$
- 🚇 Roppongi

mori.art.museum

Musée Tomo
- 🅰 67 C2
- ✉ 4-1-35 Toranomon, Minato-ku
- ☎ 03/5733-5131
- 🕐 11 a.m.–6 p.m., closed Mon.
- 💲 $$$
- 🚇 Kamiyacho

musee-tomo.or.jp

The Water Trade—What Goes On in Japan After Dark

The origin of the term *mizu shobai* ("water trade") is endlessly debated. The more prosaic interpretation is that the "water" is simply the alcohol upon which the trade floats; the more poetic is that the business reflects the impermanence of life itself. The ancestor of today's mizu shobai was the *ukiyo*—the Floating World, a name ascribed to the pleasure quarters in major towns during the 17th century.

Drinking and dining under the tracks at Yurakucho, Tokyo

The focus on prostitution in the ukiyo was greater than in the mizu shobai, but, like today's amusement districts, the old pleasure quarters boasted a whole gamut of other entertainments—especially of a bibulous kind. The quarters declined during the 19th century with the rise of more general amusement districts elsewhere; the word "ukiyo" simply died with them.

The reliance on alcohol in Japanese culture hasn't gone anywhere, though; indeed, the incredible profusion of bars, pubs, and cabarets has deeper roots than the desire for a good time. A major feature of Japanese culture is *tatemae* and *honne*: "public pleasantries" and "one's personal opinion," respectively. Daytime business discussions are full of polite agreements, but once the excuse of feigned or real drunkenness is in place, the Japanese feel able to speak their minds. Much of the real day's business goes on after dark, and corporate budgets for entertaining expenses have grown as Japan has prospered.

Postwar Shinjuku

During the postwar period, Tokyo's big emerging amusement district was Shinjuku. Although prostitution flourished there, Shinjuku really took off when racketeers erected rows of ramshackle drinking dives in the rubble east of the train station in 1946. Bars, already popular as "cafés" during the 1920s, were all the rage in Japan during the 1950s. The traditional *nomiya* (drinking shop), with its red paper lantern outside, now had a serious rival. The tone was ostensibly American. Sporting Western fashions, the girls enticing customers to drink were hostesses, and the owners of the establishment were *mama-san* and/or *masutaa* (master). These characters, the mainstays of the mizu shobai, signaled the demise of the teahouses and the geisha of prewar times, as their establishments increased in numbers, standing, and price.

Hostess Bars

Hostess bars are fewer since the recession, especially in Ginza, but remain for the most part exorbitantly expensive. A small minority traffics in prostitution, but not the better clubs. Hostess bars are often luxuriously appointed, but the experience generally holds little appeal for Westerners. Pretty girls in designer dresses cajole and flatter the tired salaryman's ego, pouring drinks, lighting cigarettes, and singing karaoke with him. There may be flirtatious banter, but nothing more. Hostesses are very good at arousing a customer's desire, so that he keeps coming back—mostly in vain.

Things are seldom what their English name implies. A hostess bar is usually called a "club" (*kurabu*), which it may be, and sometimes "supper club," which it is not. Be wary of piano bars, for some keep hostesses. If one sits at your table, you will be charged accordingly.

Another postwar bar legacy is the misnamed *sunakku* (snack), the hostess bar's poorer relative. Most popular in the countryside, sunakku are generally variants of the ubiquitous karaoke bar. The majority are harmless, but beware, some are downright sleazy; generally sunakku are best avoided unless you are taken by friends. In fact, this is the general rule for smaller bars in the mizu shobai. If a bar is inconspicuously hidden

Dance Clubs

Dance clubs in Japan are fairly accessible, though cover charges can be high. Despite the belief that "Japanese don't dance," clubs ranging from multifloor complexes to private salsa studios are a way of life for some young people. Salsa in particular has made a big splash. Introduced by immigrant Japanese Peruvians on their return to the homeland, salsa can be studied and practiced, rather than improvised, and was a perfect fit for the Japanese mentality, though the unsmiling concentration of some such dance partners can be a bit disconcerting at first.

behind a thick door, the chances are that patrons have been introduced; wandering in unaccompanied feels a bit like intruding in a private living room—in a sense, it is. Home is not the place for socializing in Japan; the bar, presided over by a mama-san who knows all her customers by name, makes a handy substitute.

Until as recently as 15 years ago, frequenting mizu shobai was strictly the preserve of the Japanese male. However, "host clubs" for women are becoming popular in areas like Shinjuku's Kabuki-cho, although most foreign women find the plain-faced, peacocked hosts to be merely the latest laughable oddities of the age-old water trade.

Shibuya

Brash and hip, Shibuya is one of Tokyo's most lively wards. Fashion is king here, whether in the cheap, fad-of-the-minute shops near Shibuya Station, strutting past designer-brand stores on Omotesando-dori, or in full cosplay glory around Harajuku Station. Also home to Yoyogi-koen and Meiji-jingu, one of Japan's largest shrines, Shibuya offers an oasis of welcoming greenery in the big city.

Shimenawa, braided straw ropes, ward off evil spirits at Meiji-jingu shrine.

TEMPLES & SHRINES: All temples in Japan are Buddhist and all shrines are Shinto. Temples and shrines are usually part of a complex; the area covered by a complex can be extensive.

Shibuya originally grew up around a major railroad terminal. Shibuya Station developed rapidly after the 1923 earthquake, when many people moved to the area from devastated Asakusa, and it is the commuter gateway between the capital and Yokohama. Nowadays the station is staggeringly busy, and Shibuya Crossing, the intersection in front of the station, plays host to a flash mob of scurrying pedestrians every time traffic stops.

From the end of the 1970s, Shibuya's Seibu and Parco department stores were harbingers

of high fashion. When nearby Harajuku became the city's prime teenage hangout, Shibuya took the overflow, especially on narrow Center Gai Street opposite the station. The trendy bars, cafés, and boutiques spread out from here over a decade and cemented Shibuya's status as the ultimate fashion mecca for students.

Among the department stores are **Tokyu Hands,** devoted to crafty DIY projects, and **Bunkamura** (culture village), a multimedia exhibition space with an international flavor, both owned by Seibu's rival department store company, Tokyu. Tokyu's brand-new **Hikarie** shopping center, east of the station, caters to a more mature scene.

Following busy, boutique-lined Aoyama-dori northeast, you arrive at the tail end of **Omotesando-dori,** a leafy boulevard with a high concentration of designer fashion shops. Notable are the Prada store, with its bulbous glass frontage, and the long **Omotesando Hills,** designed by architect Tadao Ando. **Cat Street,** a left turn two blocks before Meiji-dori, is funkier than conservative Omotesando.

Avant-garde Tokyo

Haute couture gives way to avant-garde youth fashion as Omotesando ends in Harajuku, where teens flock to Takeshita-dori, a narrow alley with several edgy boutiques. Harajuku Station faces **Yoyogi-koen,** a park built on the former site of U.S. Occupation staff buildings, and the whole area retains an aura of foreignness that originally drew Western designer brands. Even more alien are the

cosplayers who show up here on Sundays to flaunt their costumes, whether they be neo-Gothic, Lolita-esque, or something else.

Meiji-jingu

Just west of Harajuku Station is the entrance to Tokyo's greatest shrine, **Meiji-jingu,** dedicated to the spirits of Emperor Meiji and his wife Empress Shoken, rulers during the passage from feudal to modern Japan. Construction began in 1915, a year after the death of Empress Shoken, and was completed in 1920.

The shrine was destroyed during World War II, but rebuilt in 1958. It stands in a broad courtyard with characteristically sweeping architecture of unadorned cypress wood beneath a roof of copper tiles. The fine cloister adjoins the main hall and is hung with bronze lanterns. The main approach behind Harajuku, a shaded avenue of majestic camphor trees, features at the entrance a towering *torii* gateway made of gigantic cypress trees from Taiwan. ■

Yoyogi-koen
- 66 A3

Meiji-jingu
- 66 A3
- 1-1 Kamizono-cho, Yoyogi, Shibuya-ku
- 03/3379-5511
- Dawn to dusk; Treasure House 9 a.m.–4 p.m.
- $: Inner gardens; $: Treasure House
- Meiji-jingumae or Harajuku

meijijingu.or.jp

MEIJI-JINGU PERFORMANCES: Noh and *kagura* (see p. 53) performances are held in the shrine courtyard on Emperor Meiji's birthday (Nov. 3). Meiji-jingu is Tokyo's most popular shrine for observances over the New Year holiday, when its visitors number around a million.

Tokyo's Face Mask Phenomenon

Don't worry; you didn't miss a pandemic announcement—it's just hay fever season again. The surgical mask has long been a Japanese institution: Due to monoculture Japanese cedar plantations created around the capital in the postwar years, huge clouds of pollen inundate the Greater Tokyo area, forcing

many to wear masks. Their second function is for cold season. In crowded trains, it's easy to catch someone's cold, so the masks are worn not to prevent catching cold, but to avoid giving one and inconveniencing others. It takes just one sneeze in a packed train for the necessity of these masks to become clear.

Two Walks Through Shibuya

Sights tend to be scattered in Shibuya, but as a rule of thumb, the southwestern part is mainly concerned with shopping and entertainment and the northwestern sector, though it too has plenty of shops, focuses on the Meiji-jingu and surrounding parkland.

Shoppers on Takeshita-dori, a youthful Omotesando offshoot

Walk 1: Shibuya

Start at the Hachiko exit of Shibuya station, named after the statue of a faithful dog. Wade through the incredible crowd of pedestrians to cross the **Shibuya Scramble ❶**, an intersection that floods with people each red light. After crossing, turn left at the world's busiest Starbucks into the **Center Gai ❷** pedestrian shopping street, a youth culture mecca full of cheap clothing stores. When the street hits a T-intersection, turn right and right again to walk down the street parallel to Center Gai. The businesses here are mainly international brands and reasonable *izakaya*. One block past the cylindrical police box, turn left up **Spain-zaka ❸** (Spain Slope),

NOT TO BE MISSED:

• Shibuya Crossing • Dogen-zaka's Love Hotels • Meiji-jingu
• Nezu Museum

a narrow alley full of little boutiques, a few Spanish and French restaurants, and a vaguely Mediterranean style. At the top of the alley, turn right and walk past the Uniqlo and Gap stores to the broad boulevard headed back to the station. You'll pass **Muji,** a popular "no name" store with a minimalist aesthetic, then **Kinokuniya,** a large bookshop, and finally the **Disney Store** in the incongruously grotesque Humax Pavilion Building.

When you pass the first **Seibu** department store, turn left and walk under the train tracks. **Nonbei Yokocho** ❹ (Drunkard's Alley) is a fascinating watering hole that has been fostering its namesake since the 1950s. Many of the 36 tiny old bars have just four or five seats. Back out in front of Shibuya Station, walk a block east to the **Hikarie** ❺ department store. It has a fine view of the district from the 11th floor and the d47 travel store, bringing together the best-designed items from all across Japan.

To end your tour, walk past the station and up **Dogen-zaka** ❻ or "Love Hotel Hill." To see the lurid architecture, spot shy couples, or take a break yourself, turn right at the red gate of **Hyakkendana** ❼ (100 Shops), which was

once the entrance to a hip area and now is a mix of clubs, love hotels, and old restaurants redolent with the nostalgic atmosphere of an earlier, less electric Japan.

Walk 1

🗺 See area map pp. 66–67

▶ Hachiko Square

🕐 2 hours

↔ 2.5 miles (4 km)

▶ Hyakkendana

Walk 2

🗺 See area map pp. 66–67

▶ Harajuku Station

🕐 2 hours

↔ 1.7 miles (2.8 km)

▶ Aoyama Cemetery

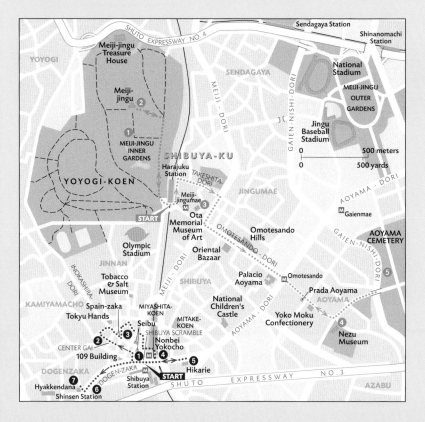

Walk 2: Aoyama-Harajuku

Start at Harajuku Station. Enter the path on your left (signposted in English) leading into Yoyogi-koen (Yoyogi Park) and Meiji-jingu (see p. 83). Just inside the park, keep your eyes peeled for young cosplayers in fantastic styles and their aging rockabilly counterparts, Asian Elvises with receding hairlines

INSIDER TIP:

In Shibuya, check out the small alley called Nonbei Yokocho (Drunkard's Alley) near the train station by the rail tracks. It's lined with tiny bars and food joints, each about the size of a minivan.

—DAISUKE UTAGAWA
National Geographic Traveler
contributing editor

and outrageously large pompadours. After 220 yards (200 m), you will come to the entrance to the **Meiji-jingu Inner Gardens** ❶ (Meiji-jingu-gyoen). The beautiful 150-acre (60 ha) park is noted for its lily pond in summer and its 126,000 trees, contributed from all over Japan when the garden was created in 1920. Much cherished by the Emperor Meiji and Empress Shoken, the iris garden is particularly lovely in June, when displays of hundreds of varieties bloom along a broad serpentine bed. Continue along the same path to one of Japan's most important shrines, **Meiji-jingu** ❷. While here, check out the Meiji-jingu Treasure House (Homotsuden), which displays a collection of state costumes and miscellaneous items belonging to Emperor Meiji, including the imperial carriage *(follow signs from the shrine's Harajuku entrance, closed 3rd Fri. each month)*. After your visit, retrace your steps to Harajuku Station. Turn left and after 160 yards (150 m) you'll find, on your right, narrow Takeshita-dori—a shopping alley usually packed with teenagers. At the end of the alley is the intersection with Meiji-dori. Turn right and walk down the avenue toward the next intersection. The cream-colored building with the cylindrical facade on your right is Laforet Harajuku, with boutiques inside.

Just behind the Laforet building is the *ukiyo-e*-themed **Ota Memorial Museum of Art** ❸ (Ota Kinen Bijutsukan; *1-10-10 Jingu-mae, tel 03/5777-8600, ukiyoe-ota-muse.jp, 10:30 a.m.–5:30 p.m., closed Mon. & last three days of each month, $$*). The Ota collection of 12,000 *ukiyo-e* prints is probably the largest privately owned collection in Japan. The museum is laid out in Japanese style, with a small rock garden and a tearoom downstairs.

Make your way down Meiji-dori again to the intersection and turn left onto Omotesando-dori. For a quick detour, turn right at the Bulgari shop to explore Cat Street for 20-something fashions with prices back on planet Earth. Farther along Omotesando-dori is the popular Prada store, eye-catching with its frontage built entirely of convex glass rhombi. Next, cross over the intersection with Aoyama-dori and walk some 550 yards (500 m) to the **Nezu Museum** ❹ (Nezu Bijutsukan; *6-5-1 Minami Aoyama, tel 03/3400-2536, www.nezu-muse.or.jp, 10 a.m.–5 p.m., closed Mon., $$$*). Located in a quiet residential district, this notable museum stands in a delightful Japanese garden replete with ponds and teahouses (still used for tea ceremonies). Despite its small size, the museum boasts one of the country's finest collections of Japanese (as well as Chinese and Korean) classical and Buddhist art, including the famed 17th-century screen painting of irises by Ogata Korin. Turn left and walk five minutes to the peaceful **Aoyama Cemetery** ❺, Tokyo's most fashionable place to be buried and a popular spot for *hanami* (see p. 94).

Shinjuku

Shinjuku means "new inn," taking its name from the taverns that grew up around this 17th-century post town on the highway outside Edo. The town rapidly grew and was known for its large unlicensed red-light district. Respectability came with the building of Shinjuku Station in 1885, now the busiest train terminal on Earth. After the 1923 earthquake, Shinjuku became a major hub of reborn Tokyo and today is its liveliest nightlife district.

Kabuki-cho offers a kaleidoscope of nocturnal temptations.

Following the Tokyo Olympics in 1964, Shinjuku took off—mostly upward—as the "new heart of Tokyo." Starting with the Keio Plaza Hotel, completed in 1972, the western side of Shinjuku developed a forest of skyscrapers. Tange Kenzo's new Tokyo Metropolitan Government Building became the colossal centerpiece in 1991. Combining plush hotels, official buildings, shopping areas, a lovely park, and a raucous amusement district, the marvelous eclecticism of Shinjuku is archetypically Japanese.

East Shinjuku

Make sure you leave plenty of time if you catch a train at Shinjuku Station: Getting lost in the crowded station labyrinth is something that happens even to locals. Exits from the subway lines lead into a gigantic underground shopping mall, and the surges of people in every direction at rush hour merely add to the confusion above ground.

Anywhere else, **Kabuki-cho** in East Shinjuku would be Sin City, but the Japanese do not believe in sin. As in other amusement districts, all the facets of pleasure

Kabuki-cho

🗺 66 A4

Hanazono-jinja

- 66 A4
- 5-17-3 Shinjuku, Shinjuku-ku
- 03/3200-3093
- Shinjuku Sanchome

exist here cheek by jowl: eating, drinking, movies, game arcades, and sex. Out of some 3,000 entertainment outlets, the 300 devoted to sleaze are signaled by tuxedoed touts in doorways or skimpily clad girls enticing customers inside. The streets, a blaze of electric signs and shining neon, are lined with speakers blaring come-ons and deafening music. The range of fantasies, perversities, and plain old prostitution to be experienced behind closed doors is likely as intense. The prevalence of the "water trade" (see pp. 80–81) is said to be a result of the stress of Japanese society, an ambivalence toward paid sex, and the world's lowest rates of sexual activity, thus the most convoluted kinks.

With many great restaurants and thousands of bars, Kabuki-cho attracts about 500,000 visitors every night; at the evening's end, pub-crawling salarymen—and increasingly, their female counterparts—totter through the streets, propping each other up. Tokyo's main gay neighborhood, Ni-chome, is east of Shinjuku Sanchome station, with hundreds of little bars crammed together.

For a sense of what Kabuki-cho looked like in harder times, wander through **Omoide Yoko-cho** (Memory Lane), a warren of narrow alleys full of little *izakaya*, just north of Shinjuku Station. The humorous nickname "Shomben Yokocho" (Piss Alley) came from the lack of toilets and general aroma of the area in bygone days; it's grungy, smoky, and full of character, but not that malodorous anymore. Some bars are for regulars only, so try to make eye contact with the staff and get a big *"irrashai!"* (welcome!) before rubbing elbows with the locals.

Heading west, **Hanazono-jinja** provides a pleasant retreat from the sheer lunacy of Kabuki-cho. Dedicated to Inari, the deity of

EXPERIENCE: Feel the Shinjuku Squeeze

A quintessentially uncomfortable Tokyo experience is rush hour in Shinjuku train station. The largest rail hub in the capital, Shinjuku is also the world's busiest, registered in *Guinness Book of World Records* for the 3.64 million passengers that pass through it daily. During the morning rush (8 a.m.–9 a.m.), the crowds are so intense that dozens of station attendants line the platform to jam limbs through the doors, and instances of the windows shattering from the pressure of bodies are not unheard of.

Is this fun? No, but standing on the platform to watch Shinjuku's clockwork chaos is a must for train lovers. The Yamanote and Chuo lines are arguably the craziest. To experience one of the most crowded places on Earth, buy the cheapest ticket from the vending machine and then ride the press of commuters down to a platform, taking photos of the sea of black-haired, business-suited salarymen grimly facing the daily trial. When you leave, show the ticket to the gate attendant and tell her you made a mistake. She'll let you through and refund you. Should you have to ride during rush hour, buy a face mask to prevent catching a cold, put some loud music in your headphones, and let the crowd hold you up, rather than trying to hold on to anything.

gain and grain, the shrine was moved to its present site during the 17th century. The rather unprepossessing shrine comes into its own during Tori-no-Ichi—the chicken festival—on November 3.

Bargain hunters should head for Map Camera (mapcamera .com) in Shinjuku. Its two floors of Canon and Nikon equipment offer used cameras and equipment at very good prices.

—KEN SHIMIZU
National Geographic photographer

Shinjuku National Garden
(11 Naito-cho, Shinjuku-ku, tel 03/3350-0151, 9 a.m.–4 p.m., closed Mon., $) belonged to the regional governor of Naito during the Edo period, then to the imperial family, before becoming a public park after World War II. Lying to the southeast of Shinjuku, this is not only one of the city's largest parks at 150 acres (60 ha) but also one of the most beautifully landscaped, with sections devoted to both Japanese- and Western-style gardens. Its 1,300 cherry trees make it a highly popular location for blossom viewing in April.

West Shinjuku

Leaving Shinjuku Station by the west exit places you in a popular warren of cut-price camera stores. Awe-inspiring as the tall buildings are, they are utterly devoid of anything so prosaic as human warmth. That said, Tange's impressive 797-foot (243 m) **Tokyo Metropolitan Government Building,** completed in 1991 and inspired by European cathedrals, boasts one of Tokyo's best views, with Mount Fuji often visible from its twin observatories.

However, for panoramic views at night, it is hard to beat the one from the nearby Keio Plaza Hotel's Sky Lounge Aurora.

Tokyo Metropolitan Government Building

🅰 66 A3
✉ 2-8-1 Nishi-Shinjuku, Shinjuku-ku
☎ Observatories: 03/5320-7890
🕐 North Tower 9:30 a.m.–10:30 p.m., closed 2nd & 4th Mon.; South Tower 9:30 a.m.–5 p.m., closed 1st & 3rd Tues.
🚉 Tochomae

gotokyo.org/en /tourists/info/ observatory.html

A staggering 3.64 million passengers squeeze on and off the trains at Shinjuku Station every day.

Medieval history buffs shouldn't miss an opportunity to visit the **Japanese Sword Museum** (Touken Hakubutsu-kan). Three National Treasure *tachi* swords from the Kamakura period (1185–1333) are on display, each as keen as it was 800 years ago, as well as many *katana* (long swords) and *wakiza-shi* (short swords). ∎

Japanese Sword Museum

🅰 66 A3
✉ 4-25-10 Yoyogi, Shibuya-ku
☎ 03/3379-1386
🕐 10 a.m.–4 p.m., closed Mon.
💲 $$
🚉 Odakyu line: Sangubashi

touken.or.jp

Northwest Tokyo: Iidabashi to Ikebukuro

Northwest Tokyo is often seen as a poor cousin to the glitter and culture of more fashionable districts, but it has its own distinct character and memorable sights. Between Ikebukuro, Tokyo's second busiest commuter portal, and the Imperial Palace lie the controversial Yasukuni-jinja, a small geisha district, and the Tokyo Dome megaplex, home to the Yomiuri Giants, the oldest and most popular baseball team nationwide.

Tokyo Dome, the capital's storied sports arena

Yasukuni-jinja
- 🅰 67 C4
- ✉ 3-1-1 Kudan-kita, Chiyoda-ku
- ☎ 03/3261-8326
- 🕐 6 a.m.–6 p.m.; Yushukan 9 a.m.–4:30 p.m.
- 💲 Yushukan: $$
- 🚇 Kudanshita

www.yasukuni.or.jp

Right outside the Imperial Palace is **Yasukuni-jinja,** a shrine devoted to those who died for the Emperor; its name ironically means "Peaceful Country Shrine." Yasukuni was originally built after the Meiji Restoration in 1869 to honor soldiers who had perished fighting for the restoration of the emperor, but it soon grew to enshrine the spirits of all the 2.5 million Japanese who are estimated to have died serving the nation throughout its history.

A major sore point with China and Korea, Yasukuni also enshrines Class-A war criminals such as general and prime minister Tojo Hideki; the sharp contrast between Hiroshima's respect for the horror of war and Yasukuni's glorification of organized murder can irritate otherwise disinterested visitors.

The adjacent **Yushukan** museum contains various traditional military hardware, which again fails to communicate regret for Japanese militarism of the early 20th century. If you can ignore these things, the shrine is attractive, quiet, and popular for its cherry blossoms.

The neighborhood of **Kagurazaka** once had pride of place just outside the north walls of Edo-jo, a spot for the powerful to dine and enjoy geisha entertainment in exclusive establishments. The geisha have all but disappeared, but the cobbled, narrow backstreets are still full of attractive *ryotei* (high-class restaurants). Kagurazaka remains one of Tokyo's most charming semiresidential districts and is a pleasure to walk around at night.

Baseball in Tokyo

Forget sumo: Baseball is king in Japan, and the **Tokyo Dome** is a great place to catch a professional game. The major differences between American and Japanese baseball are the use of a smaller, harder-wound ball and the tactical ploy of smaller plays to get on base, rather than big swings in the hope of hitting home runs.

The Yomiuri Giants (*www.giants .jp*) are the nation's most popular team, and their fans are serious about their organized cheers. (See sidebar p. 246 for more about the Japanese fanaticism for baseball.)

The Tokyo Dome complex also contains the **LaQua** hot-spring resort, which draws its water from 5,580 feet (1,700 m) underground (proving the old adage that if you dig deep enough in Japan, you'll hit hot water). After soaking, take a nap in one of the anterooms; there's an overnight charge if you'd like to stay.

Ikebukuro is designated as one of Tokyo's major subcenters, gateway to the sprawl north of the metropolis. The station is dominated by the usual department stores jousting for dominance—Seibu, Tobu, and Marui—but beyond the station the shopping scene is a shade younger than Shibuya (see pp. 82–83), catering to teens with limited budgets. There's more mall in the

INSIDER TIP:

Baseball fans won't want to miss Japan's Hall of Fame: It's inside the Tokyo Dome, home to the Yomiuri Giants.

—LARRY PORGES
National Geographic Books author

Sunshine 60 Complex east of the station, but Otome-dori, along the northwest side of the complex, is a mini version of Akihabara's (see pp. 96–97) *otaku* culture, with shops devoted to anime and cosplay. More mainstream, the **Tokyo Metropolitan Theatre** holds a variety of events, including performances by the Tokyo Metropolitan Orchestra. ∎

Iidabashi

🅰 66 B6

Tokyo Dome

🅰 66 C5

✉ 3-1, Koraku, Bunkyo

🚇 Suidobashi, Korakuen

www.tokyo-dome .co.jp

Ikebukuro

🅰 66 B6

Sunshine 60 Complex

🅰 66 B6

✉ 3-1 Higashi-Ikebukuro

☎ 03/3989-3331

🕐 10 a.m.–10 p.m.

🚇 Ikebukuro

Tokyo Metropolitan Theatre

🅰 66 A6

✉ 1-8-1 Nishi-Ikebukuro

☎ 03/5391-2111

🚇 Ikebukuro

geigeki.jp

Ueno

Just north of Central Tokyo, Ueno Hill (now Ueno-koen) is dotted with shrines and temples erected by the Tokugawa shoguns. Famous for its cherry trees, it was favored by aristocrats for *hanami*—cherry blossom viewing. The site of the only major battle resisting the Meiji Restoration, the hill was a stronghold for some 2,000 Tokugawa loyalists routed by Japan's first modern army in 1867. The fleeing survivors torched the buildings of the Tokugawas' Kanei-ji.

Prayerful students leave their requests at Yushima-tenjin.

Ameyoko Market

🅰 67 D5

🚇 Subway & Train: Ueno

The hill area became the city's first public park in 1873 and was used for popular national exhibitions; the art gallery built for the second exhibition in 1892 was the predecessor of the Tokyo National Museum.

Ueno Park contains outstanding museums, Tosho-gu shrine, temples, Ueno Zoo, and Shinobazu Pond, which is particularly delightful in summer, and the whole area explodes in cherry blossoms and drunken gaiety each spring.

With the expansion of railways, Ueno Station increased in importance after the start of the 20th century as the gateway to northern Japan. Following the devastation of World War II, the station area found many thousands of homeless Tokyoites sheltering under the elevated tracks. Since the 1950s, the area has attracted a large number of poor farmers from Northern Honshu (Tohoku); they would leave their snowbound fields in winter to seek employment in Tokyo—often in vain. Since the 2011 Great East Japan Earthquake devastated Tohoku, more have poured in.

Many visitors to Ueno are northern day-trippers; the area accordingly is filled with department stores and shopping options to suit all budgets. The district includes a rather seedy if spirited entertainment area, but tucked away in the streets just below the park are some vintage restaurants and shops that make Ueno one of Tokyo's most fascinating areas. Less than 20 minutes from Ginza on the Hibiya or Ginza subway lines, Ueno could hardly present a greater contrast to that district's glitz.

Visiting Ueno

Today's colorful **Ameyoko Market,** alongside Ueno Station, is a legacy of the black market that thrived in the postwar period. The name is short for Ameya-yokocho (Candy Store Alley), so called after the candy stalls that were often fronts for other goods—especially those made in the United States.

This is Tokyo's liveliest market and the last with something of the flavor of an Asian bazaar. Stalls sell jeans of every known brand and configuration, aloha shirts, leather jackets, bags, and sneakers next door to dried squid and bonito flakes, groceries, and fresh fish. The prices of famous-brand clothing are the same as elsewhere, but bargains and discounts abound on everything else. Halfway down the alley is Tokudai-ji, a little Buddhist temple located above a collection of sundry stores.

Yushima-tenjin, also called Yushima Tenman-gu, was originally

INSIDER TIP:

To experience Ameyoko Market in Ueno at its liveliest, go in the early evening, when many of the vendors offer end-of-the-day discounts.

—ROB GOSS
National Geographic contributor

built in the 14th century and restored during the 19th. The shrine is dedicated to Sugawara-no-Michizane (845–903), a Heian-period statesman and scholar later deified as the patron of learning. Yushima-tenjin is particularly revered by students praying for success in exams, as well as for its garden of plum trees, which attract large crowds when they blossom between mid-February and mid-March.

To the northwest of Ueno-koen, **Yanaka,** maintained as a temple town during the Tokugawa era, still has more than 80 temples, most managing funeral rites in nearby Yanaka Cemetery. There are so many temples that the streets are scented with incense. A survivor of both the 1923 earthquake and wartime air raids, this is the last sad bastion of Taisho-era Tokyo. Yanaka is close to the University of Tokyo (Japan's most prestigious seat of learning) and the University of Fine Arts and has been favored by academics, artists, and intellectuals since Meiji times.

Ueno-koen

From Ueno Station, take the west gate entrance, where you will find an information desk. Walk north to the **National Museum of Nature and Science** (Kokuritsu Kagaku Hakubutsukan). Presenting many aspects of science and natural history, the museum is a firm favorite with schoolchildren and sometimes holds large-scale special exhibitions.

About three minutes' walk south of the science museum, the **National Museum of Western Art** (Kokuritsu Seiyo Bijutsukan), opened in 1959, was designed by Le Corbusier. The museum's collection includes European old master paintings such as El Greco's "Crucifixion," Rodin sculptures ("The Thinker" and "The Burghers of Calais"), French Impressionists, and works by modern artists such as Max Ernst and Jackson Pollock.

Yushima-tenjin
🅰 67 D5
✉ 3-30-1 Yushima, Bunkyo-ku
☎ 03/3836-0753
🕐 6 a.m.–8 p.m.
🚇 Yushima
www.yushimatenjin.or.jp

Yanaka
🅰 67 D5

Ueno-koen
🅰 67 D5
✉ Ueno-koen, Taito-ku
🚇 Ueno

National Museum of Nature and Science
🅰 67 E5
✉ 7-20 Ueno-koen, Taito-ku
☎ 03/3822-0111
🕐 9 a.m.–5 p.m., 8 p.m. on Fri., closed Mon.
💲 $$
🚇 Ueno
www.kahaku.go.jp

National Museum of Western Art
🅰 67 D5
✉ 7-7 Ueno-koen, Taito-ku
☎ 03/3828-5131
🕐 9:30 a.m.–5:30 p.m., 8 p.m. on Fri., closed Mon.
💲 $
🚇 Ueno
nmwa.go.jp

EXPERIENCE: Celebrate Hanami

Hanami, Japan's cherry blossom viewing parties, are a national institution, and a great opportunity to make new friends, whether in quiet contemplation of beauty and its transitory nature or in raucous drinking parties.

Strollers enjoy hanami at Ueno Park.

Hanami has a long history in Japan, originating in parties held by the imperial court and then spreading to the samurai class. The *sakura* (cherry) is held above all other flowers because its petals fall immaculate, a symbol of beautiful youth cut short that has been celebrated by everyone from poets to samurai warriors as they prepared to die.

Worldly transience, however, need not get in your way of experiencing a great Japanese party. You'll find most hanami in parks, where blue tarps are laid down and people stake out the best places for hours prior to the start of the festivities.

Once everyone gathers, huge quantities of alcohol and food are produced, often bought at nearby stalls or from local convenience stores. Not everyone gets drunk, of course, some preferring just to take photos and enjoy the falling petals, but a boozy, boisterous time is typical.

The variety of cherries is boggling. The most beloved, Somei Yoshino, has a pale pink, five-petaled flower that suits Japanese sensibilities with its simple lines and subdued color. This variety blooms early, typically in the first week of April, and is the flower that the weather report's "sakura forecast"

refers to. Other varieties, such as Shiro-yama-zakura (white mountain cherries) and Yaezakura (a general term for flowers with more than five petals), bloom later in April. With the flower front moving northward starting in March, there's usually a good chance for you to witness the wonder of the blossoms somewhere in Japan in March or April.

Great Hanami Spots:

Ueno Park, Tokyo (see p. 92): Boisterous crowds relish the blossoms in Tokyo's most famous spot.

Shinjuku National Garden, Tokyo (see p. 89): The small entrance fee and no-alcohol policy keep away the rowdiest revelers, making this park and its 1,500 trees a good choice for families.

Shirakawa Canal, Gion, Kyoto (see p. 211): Cherry blossoms and weeping willows over the cobbled streets and canal of this traditional geisha district are an iconic Japanese sight.

Yoshino, Nara Prefecture (see p. 244): One of the most ancient hanami sites; the trees carpet the mountainside, blooming in stages over a month.

At the south end of the park is the **Shitamachi History Museum** (Shitamachi Fuzoku Shiryokan), a two-story museum founded in 1980. Upstairs are exhibits and artifacts that afford fascinating glimpses into the lives of the *edokko*—the proud but often very poor inhabitants of the "Low City" of Edo and Tokyo. Downstairs, the reconstructed shops, workshops, and homes of the Edo and Meiji periods, brought to life with wax figures, provide a nostalgic picture of a different way of life that has long since vanished.

Ueno Zoo (Ueno Dobutsuen), which opened in 1882, is particularly popular for its pandas. The grounds contain a pagoda and teahouse of Edo-period vintage, as well as a section of Shinobazu Pond devoted to cormorants. The animals are well cared for, but if the sight of animals in cages distresses you, bypass this place.

Regrettably eclipsed these days by Ueno Zoo and the monorail connecting its two halves is **Toshogu** *(9-88 Ueno-koen, Taito-ku, tel 03/3822-3455, 9 a.m.–dusk, $)*. This opulent shrine, noted for its rich Chinese-style carvings and Kano-school (late 16th-century) paintings in the prayer hall, is an Important Cultural Property. Among Tokyo's oldest shrines, it remains as it was when completed in 1651. To the south of the shrine approach is its famous peony garden *(mid-April to mid-May)* containing a range of some 200 varieties. ◼

Shitamachi History Museum

🅰 67 D5
✉ 2-1 Ueno-koen, Taito-ku
☎ 03/3823-7451
🕐 9:30 a.m.– 4:30 p.m., closed Mon.
💲 $
Ⓜ Ueno

www.taitocity.net /zaidan/shitamachi

Ueno Zoo

🅰 67 D5
✉ 9-83 Ueno-koen, Taito-ku
☎ 03/3828-5171
🕐 9:30 a.m.–5 p.m., closed Mon.
💲 $$
Ⓜ Ueno

www.tokyo-zoo.net

Tokyo National Museum: The Capital's Top Attraction

In the north part of Ueno Park, Japan's largest museum, Tokyo National Museum (Tokyo Kokuritsu Hakubutsukan; *13-9 Ueno-koen, Taito-ku, tel 03/3822-1111, www.tnm.jp, 9:30 a.m.–5 p.m., open till 8 p.m. Fri. Mar.–Dec., open until 6 p.m. weekends April–Sept., closed Mon., $$, subway & JR trains: Ueno),* houses the world's best collection of Japanese art. It comprises 86,456 works of art, plus nearly 2,000 on permanent loan; the Japanese collection includes 84 National Treasures and 521 Important Cultural Properties. It is impossible to display everything simultaneously, so exhibits are shown on a rotating basis.

The 25 rooms of the **Main Building** (Honkan, built in 1937) are devoted to Japanese art. The first floor is divided into art forms, with Buddhist sculpture, lacquerware, swords, and ceramics on the right, modern painting and sculpture on the left, and the art of Japan's indigenous peoples in the back. The second floor is arranged thematically into exhibits as diverse as the refined tools of the tea ceremony and the fearsome and flamboyant costumes of the ruling samurai class. The exhibits can be seen in a leisurely two hours, and the objects represent the best of Japanese culture.

Right of the main hall, the nine-room 1968 **Gallery of East Asian Art and Antiquities** (Toyokan) exhibits Chinese and Central Asian Buddhist statuary, Chinese and Korean ceramics, lacquerware, paintings, and a handful of Egyptian relics. The 1909 **Hyokeikan Gallery,** right of the main hall, and the 1999 **Heiseikan** are used for temporary exhibits. The **Gallery of Horyu-ji Treasures** (Horyu-ji Homotsukan) hosts a collection of 318 treasures from the great seventh-century Horyu-ji near Nara, donated to the imperial family in 1878. The displays include sculptures, furniture, ironwork, painted scrolls, masks, and textiles.

Akihabara

Every *otaku* (see p. 77) heads to Akihabara (Electric Town), to the northeast of Central Tokyo, the center for anime, video games, cosplay, and electronics. Born as a black market for radio parts after World War II, Akihabara grew into a center for virtual realities; computers, video games, and robotics all thrive here, as does Japan's industry of hypercuteness.

Colorful cosplayers abound within Japanese youth subculture.

Akihabara
🗺 67 D4
🚇 Subway & Train: Akihabara

Akihabara Radio Center
✉ 1-14-2 Sotokanda, Chiyoda-ku
☎ 03/3251-0614
🕐 10 a.m.–7 p.m.

Yellow Submarine
✉ 1-15-16 Sotokanda, Chiyoda-ku (just south of the Radio Center)
☎ 03/5298-3123
🕐 10 a.m.–8 p.m.

Akihabara's humble beginnings can be traced to the **Akihabara Radio Center,** a scruffy warren of tiny shops just west of Akihabara subway station, under the Sobu line's tracks. It would take a true electronics nut to be able to name all the bits and bobs available in tiny booths, from industrial-grade switches and transformers to antique vacuum tubes. Also notable are the tiny glass lockers of one cubic foot that can be rented to display and sell a couple of items, sort of a physical eBay (we've come full circle!).

Esoteric components aside, Akihabara is full of big-name electronics shops, and while they offer goods duty-free and with international voltage (see Travelwise p. 356), they are the same as in any major city. The one exception is **Sofmap,** which deals in barely used equipment, but you'll have to check the voltage. The real reason to visit "Akiba" is for its specialty shops. First, head to the UDX Building's **Tokyo Animation Center,** just northwest of the station. The center occasionally puts on a special event, but its small shop has a great map of Akihabara. Several branches of **Yellow Submarine** sell all manner of collectibles, particularly anime or video game characters, as well as ready-to-wear cosplay. **Toranoana** specializes in *dojinshi* small-press comics, with big-name manga on the lower floors, dojinshi in the middle, and three floors of adults-only, mind-bendingly creative perversity. Do you dare to go to the top floor?

Akihabara's Alternative Realities

Video game fans should check out any of the several arcades, as well as "antique" games and systems for sale at **Super Potato** (Suupaa Poteto). Bask in the good old days of the Nintendo Entertainment System (Famicom), Sega Genesis (Mega Drive), original PlayStation, and their ilk and pick up weird, Japan-only games (you'll need a Japanese console to run them).

Akiba is also great for people-watching. Look for random people in cosplay walking down the main Chuo-dori or young women in a caricature of a French maid's outfit, luring shy young men to maid cafés (see sidebar below). The **Akihabara Don Quixote** building has both the maid café **@home** and a theater dedicated to the cultural pandemic of **AKB48,** a 64-member all-girl bubblegum-pop-idol group. One of the largest grossing acts in the world, AKB is designed to foster fandom among young men and teenage girls with daily shows, "handshake tickets" in CD cases, blogs, TV shows, and a dreamer-friendly "no boyfriends" policy. Photos of the girls are everywhere; if you've chosen a favorite, you're already on a slip-pery slope down into the abyss of true otaku. ∎

Toranoana

✉ 4-3-1 Sotokanda, Chiyoda-ku

☎ 0800/1004-315

🕒 10 a.m.–10 p.m.

AKB48

✉ 4-3-3 Sotokanda, Chiyoda-ku

☎ 03/5298-6848

🕒 Shows at 6:30 p.m. Special tickets available to foreign visitors; to avoid the lottery system, reserve a month in advance.

💲 $$$$

www.akb48.co.jp

EXPERIENCE: Akihabara's Maid Cafés

The maid café, an Akihabara institution, is the perfect place to go to observe Japan's obsession with excessive cutesi-ness and its *otaku* (geek) culture in the wild. The "maids" you'll meet are young women in cartoonish versions of French maid uniforms who'll greet you with deep bows and cries of "Welcome back, Master! Right this way, Princess!" They'll bat their superextended eyelashes at you, pretend to trip over their own shoes, giggle nervously, and flatter you endlessly. The whole performance comes off as silly, not sexy. The customers you'll observe are typically the shy, video game–playing and manga-reading young men who frequent Akihabara's niche-market hobby shops.

The maid café offers young men a safe place to interact with the opposite sex in a controlled environment, the market for which reveals how badly socialization is suffering in the age of the text message.

Maid cafés also draw curious young couples, awkward middle-aged men, and the sort of office lady who makes the pil-grimage to Tokyo Disneyland—the capital of *kawaii!* (cute!)—at least once a year.

As far as the cafés themselves go, the food tends to be overpriced and subpar, but the dishes come with a campy song and dance, which is fine if you like being under the spotlight. A coffee and a laugh at a maid café such as **@home** *(Don Quijote Akihabara 5F, 4-3-3 Sotokanda Chiyoda-ku, tel 03/3254-7878, 11:30 a.m.–10 p.m., cafe-athome.com)* sets in stark contrast the many men who throw down considerably more money for hostesses to flatter them and fill their drinks.

Asakusa

The very heart of the old city, Asakusa remains Tokyo's most colorful and traditional district. Combining old-fashioned Japanese refinement with the brash and lively aspects of a working-class neighborhood, this northeast area along the Sumida-gawa has a great atmosphere. The addition of the brand-new Tokyo Skytree, the world's tallest tower, makes Asakusa a must-see.

Tokyo Skytree offers views as far as Mount Fuji on a clear day.

The sights here are mainly in the area around **Senso-ji,** one of the few Buddhist temples in Japan to constitute such a strong focus for a neighborhood—a privilege normally reserved for Shinto shrines. Senso-ji is approached from Kaminarimon, the Thunder Gate, renowned for its colossal central red paper lantern and the fierce guardian deities on either side. Beyond it is the Nakamise, an avenue of souvenir and specialty stores.

Senso-ji (also called Kannon-sama) has been standing on the same spot for more than a millennium; legend has it that the temple was built by three fishermen in the seventh century. After finding a statuette of Kannon, goddess of mercy, in their nets, each dreamed that the deity told him to build the temple. It was restructured several times from the 9th century, and took its final form early in the 17th. This version survived the earthquake in 1923, but vanished completely during World War II. The gigantic concrete replacement, built in 1958 with a sweeping roof of 70,000 clay tiles, is sufficiently imposing to do justice to the original; the same applies to the five-story pagoda to the west of the temple. Paintings on the ceiling of the main

INSIDER TIP:

An interesting way to get to Asakusa is via the canals of Tokyo, by catching the ferry from Hamarikyu.

—DAISUKE UTAGAWA
National Geographic Traveler
contributing editor

hall are originals saved from the bombing. In the temple courtyard stands a huge bronze cauldron of burning incense; it is considered auspicious to spread its smoke over your head.

On the banks of the Sumida-gawa, **Sumida-koen** has long been a favorite place for cherry blossom viewing despite its unattractive concrete embankment. *Yakatabune* pleasure boats are hired for private parties, especially for the Sumida fireworks display. A cheaper option is to take the Sumida-gawa cruise from Azuma-bashi Bridge to Hamarikyu-teien (see pp. 75–76). The trip is not especially scenic, but offers a welcome sit-down after sightseeing. The Azumabashi skyline is dominated by three very different buildings: Asahi Breweries' big frothy pint of a headquarters and Flamme d'Or Beer Hall—dubbed the "gold turd building" by locals—and the new Tokyo Skytree, rising above them.

The **Tokyo Skytree** is at the top of Tokyo's new attractions and, at 2,080 feet (634 m), the tallest tower in the world. You'll need to see a chiropractor for all the neck-craning involved in a visit. The subway station was built directly under the tower, so

Senso-ji
- 67 E5
- 2-3-1 Asakusa, Taito-ku
- 03/3842-0181
- 6 a.m.–5 p.m.
- Asakusa

senso-ji.jp

Tokyo Skytree
- 67 F5
- 1-1-2 Oshiage, Sumida-ku
- 0570/55-0634
- 8 a.m.–10 p.m.
- $$$$ to Tempo Deck, additional $$$ to Tembo Galleria
- Oshiage or 15-min. walk from Asakusa

tokyo-skytree.jp

Sumo Wrestling in the Flesh

If one of Japan's six 15-day sumo tournaments is on when you visit Tokyo's Sumo Stadium (see p. 100), attend a day of matches, as tickets are reasonable and fun is assured. At first glance it seems to be overweight men in diapers slapping each other, but up close these massive athletes impress with the explosive power of their legs and their surprising agility. Each match begins with both wrestlers tossing salt into the circular earthen ring to purify it. They then squat facing each other and lean forward onto their knuckles to signal that they are ready. Once they both touch down at the same time (this can take a couple minutes of psychological warfare), they launch at each other, using slaps, pushes, and throws to either knock the other down or push him out of the ring. Matches usually end within seconds, often with dramatic reversals or throws that land several hundred pounds of wrestler on a rich person in the front row.

Matches start in the early afternoon with young, low-ranking wrestlers and end in early evening with the top-ranked matches. Unlike many other sports, it is possible to walk around the stadium and see the wrestlers warming up, if just to mentally compare physiques.

By far the best part of sumo is when the reigning *yokozuna* (top-ranked wrestler) is defeated in an upset in the day's final match. The stadium explodes in hoots and cheers, and everyone throws their seat cushions at the ring in a shower of spinning blue squares.

Edo-Tokyo Museum

 67 E4

✉ 1-4-1 Yokoami, Sumida-ku

☎ 03/3626-9974

🕐 9:30 a.m.–5:30 p.m., 7:30 p.m. on Sat., closed Mon.

$ $$

🚇 Ryogoku

edo-tokyo-museum .or.jp

it is difficult to appreciate the scale upon arrival. Rather, walk east from Asakusa Station and enjoy the view from a distance. Unlike the Tokyo Metropolitan Government Building or the Mori Tower, Skytree looks over Tokyo from the outside, granting a rare sense of the whole city and views of Mount Fuji in clear weather. Even on a smoggy day, the glass floors make for a thrilling vertiginous experience.

As you walk around Asakusa, you may find yourself coveting the plastic food displays you see in restaurant windows. One stop south from Asakusa *(subway: Tawaramachi)* is **Kappabashi wholesale market** (Kappabashi Dogugai). Here you can buy gastronomic emblems like a forkful of spaghetti suspended above a plate, or plastic sushi.

Across the Sumida-gawa from Asakusabashi Station is an astounding building, seemingly from the realm of science fiction, that houses the **Edo-Tokyo Museum** (Edo-Tokyo Hakubutsukan). With a fascinating array of exhibits evoking Tokyo's past, this is the city's prime

history museum. It lies east of the main national **Sumo Stadium** (Kokugikan). While you are in the area, visit the **Sumo Museum** (Sumo Hakubutsukan; *sumo.or.jp*) near the stadium entrance to learn more about this ancient sport. ■

Echoes of Edo

Edo lingers on in countless place-names. **Marunou-chi** (meaning "inside the walls") was where the samurai elite lived. **Ginza** (Seat of Silver) gets its name from a long-gone coinage mint. **Akasaka** (Red Hill) was once used for growing plants yielding a red dye. Edo continues too in certain district characteristics: **Nihonbashi** was the haunt of high finance in samurai days, and still is; and the site of the **Yoshiwara** licensed quarter, banned in 1957, is now the realm of "soap-land" massage parlors.

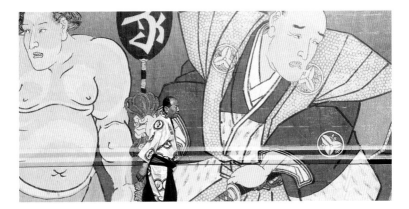

Man meets myth outside Tokyo's Sumo Stadium.

More Places to Visit in Central Tokyo

Akasaka

Going southeast from the Imperial Palace, close to Kasumigaseki district and the Diet Building in Nagatacho, Akasaka is devoted to both business and upscale entertainment. **Hie-jinja** (*hiejinja.net/en*) also called Sanno-sama, was the favorite shrine of the Tokugawa shoguns and the focal point of the grandest festival in Edo. Accessible via a steep path straddled by rows of small red *torii* (shrine gateways), this is a very pleasant haven. In mid-August, Hie-jinja stages Takigi Noh (outdoor Noh theater) performances of some of the most representative plays in the repertoire—an unmissable experience.

Akasaka, though primarily the domain of paper-pushing bureaucrats, has recently been the site of massive demonstrations against the government handling of the Great East Japan Earthquake and any further use of nuclear power. This is all the more fascinating as the Japanese tend to be averse to public displays of emotion or mischiefmaking. A festive atmosphere has dominated recent activism—and such protests are worth checking out if something big is happening during your visit.

🗺 67 C3 🚇 Akasaka-mitsuke; Kokkai Gijidomae for Hie-jinja

Jimbocho

The focus for antiquarian booksellers since the 1880s, this is Tokyo's main center for books new and used. Its stores yield used books in many languages, as well as woodblock prints and delightful Edo-period illustrated paper books. It also is home to Shueisha, the manga publisher known for *Weekly Jump* manga magazine. The bookstores extend from Jimbocho subway station, going left toward Kanda along Yasukuni-dori.

🗺 67 D4 🚇 Jimbocho

Ningyocho

Farther south, near the Tokyo City Air Terminal, is Ningyocho, one of Tokyo's oldest neighborhoods. Site of the original Yoshiwara pleasure quarter built in 1617, it remained a major theater district until Asakusa took over in the 1870s. Ningyocho (Doll Town) was named for the many workshops making and repairing puppets for the Bunraku theater. Leveled by the 1923 earthquake but unscarred by wartime bombing, the neighborhood has many buildings dating from the 1920s. The traditional shops selling *wagashi* candy, green tea, and *sembei* crackers are among Tokyo's most venerable.

🗺 67 E4 🚇 Ningyocho

More Places to Visit in Tokyo's Outlying Districts

Ghibli Museum

A 20-minute train ride west of Shinjuku is this must-see museum, home to characters of Japan's most beloved animation company, Studio Ghibli (pronounced *ji-bu-ri*). Set in a forested park, the Ghibli Museum uses simple interactive exhibits to explain the process of hand-drawn animation that is used for all of Ghibli's films. A small theater also screens nine original shorts not shown anywhere else with simple, delightful stories that do not require any Japanese language ability. The Cat-Bus from Totoro is also present and big enough for all passengers to live the dream. *ghibli-museum.jp* 🗺 66 A3 ✉ 1-1-83 Saiennai, Shimorenjaku, Mitaka-shi 🚇 Train: 15-min. walk from Mitaka Station 🕐 10 a.m.–6 p.m.; closed Tues. Four entrance times daily: limited tickets by advance purchase only, either from foreign

The leafy green gardens of the Ghibli Museum

travel agencies or through Lawson convenience store Loppi kiosks in Japan. See website for details. $ $$

Kawagoe

A castle town important to the shogunate because of its proximity to Edo, it is now home to 300,000 people living an hour from Tokyo on the northwestern commuter belt. After a fire in 1893, local merchants used clay to build *dozozukuri*—structures combining home and business—which still stand, some as museums. The local Kita-in temple includes a pagoda and dates from the 17th century. 105 B3 Hon-Kawagoe (60 min. from Shinjuku on Seibu Shinjuku line)

Ogasawara-shoto

Official administration places the Ogasawara archipelago in Tokyo, but it's actually some 620 miles (1,000 km) southeast in the Pacific. Most of the 2,000-odd inhabitants live on **Chichi-Jima** (Father Island), with the rest on **Haha-Jima** (Mother Island). Now off-limits to visitors, **Iwo-Jima** was the site of one of the fiercest battles of World War II. The climate is subtropical and there are several plants, a species of wood pigeon, and a kind of snail that are endemic to the archipelago, which is why it was designated a World Natural Heritage site. Local operators run scuba diving, whale-watching (see sidebar

p. 307), and dolphin-swim tours in the pristine waters, and there are a few fine beaches too. There are also good hiking trails, but you'll need a licensed guide to enter the nature reserves. Haha-jima, the remotest inhabited point in Japan, has excellent stargazing. Sixty inns cater to vacationers; be sure to book ahead as camping is not permitted. *www.ogasawara mura.com* See map on inside front cover Journey time 24 hours, one ferry weekly (*ogasawarakaiun.co.jp*)

Takao-san

Tokyo's western urban sprawl fades into the hills and forests around 1,970-foot (600 m) Takao-san, a perfect day trip—but crowded on weekends. Hiking trails to and from the summit are signposted; there is a cable car. Near the summit is Yakuo-in temple, famous for its Hiwatari festival *(second Sun. in Mar.),* when devotees walk unharmed on beds of hot coals. In the valley are the delightful **Ukai Tori-Yama** *(3426 Minami Asakawa-machi, Hachioji-shi, tel 042/661-0739, 11:30 a.m.–10 p.m., closed Tues.)* and **Chikutei** *(2850 Minami Asakawa-machi, Hachioji-shi, tel 042/661-8419, 11:30 a.m.–9:30 p.m.)* restaurants, featuring authentic traditional buildings in garden settings. 107 B2 Takaosan-guchi (Keio line or Chuo line from Shinjuku, changing for the Keio-Takao line at Takao); journey time 55 minutes

Iconic Fuji-san soaring above the Kanto plain, beckoning hikers, with Yokohama, Kamakura, and historic Nikko all within reach

Excursions From Tokyo

Choshukaku house in the Sankei-en Garden, built in 1623 during the Edo period

Excursions From Tokyo

Tokyo makes an excellent base for a number of excursions into the surrounding areas. The most popular day trips are to Yokohama, Kamakura, and Fuji-Hakone and farther afield to Nikko. Yokohama is the closest to Tokyo, but a trip to Nikko will introduce you to some of the region's best known historic sights.

The sacred Shinkyō Bridge over the Daiya River

Yokohama is Japan's second largest city, but it forms a contiguous mass of urban landscape with Tokyo, so second place is usually given to Osaka. Despite being fused to the capital and just 30 minutes away by train in the modern day, Yokohama has long had a distinct character arising from its status as Japan's most important 19th-century maritime gateway to the outside world. The nation's largest Chinatown can be found here, and the port was once the main base for occupation forces after World War II.

Kamakura was also set up by a group of soldiers, but in this case it was the Minamoto clan establishing the Kamakura shogunate, which ruled Japan from 1180 to 1333. As the capital of early medieval Japan, Kamakura is profuse with temples and pretty gardens. Despite being part of Tokyo's commuter belt (55 minutes from Tokyo Station), it feels like a world apart, which may explain why so many writers, such as early modern stars Yasunari Kawabata and Natsume Soseki, have been attracted to it.

Nikko is essentially a grand mausoleum, built to honor the founder of the later Tokugawa shogunate, Tokugawa Ieyasu. The period of the Tokugawa reign, called the Edo

NOT TO BE MISSED:

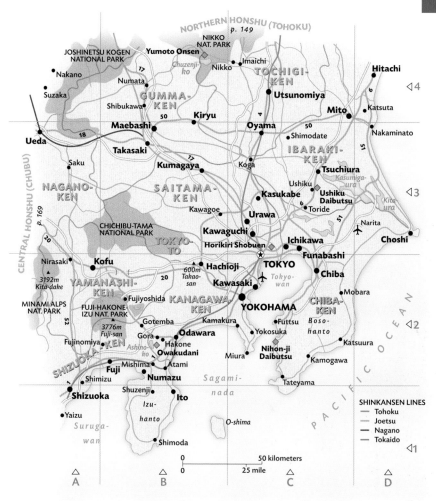

period, held for 265 years, and Nikko is a fine representation of the wealth, power, and ostentation that its rulers enjoyed. It can be reached from Tokyo by train for JR Rail Pass holders with a transfer at Utsunomiya, but it is faster (1 hr. 50 min.) to take the private Tobu Nikko line from Asakusa.

The spiritual and cultural importance of Mount Fuji cannot be overstated. Its image symbolizes Japan itself, and it has long been a place of pilgrimage, purification, and fearful prayer against devastating eruption. When you've conquered the mountain, the area has excellent hot springs, too. The Chuo and

Area of map detail

Fujikyuko lines connect Tokyo with Kawaguchi-ko (2.5 hr.) beneath Fuji, and Odawara (35 min.) is the closest JR station to Hakone's resorts. ■

Yokohama

It seems just a continuation of Tokyo's gigantic urban sprawl, but Yokohama is Japan's second largest city and its largest port. Yokohama has a fascinating history as one of the first ports opened to foreigners in 1858, an atmosphere retained by the colorful Chinatown and a large (albeit somewhat contentious) U.S. Navy base in nearby Yokosuka.

Yokohama's Chinatown is a food lover's delight.

Yokohama

⚐ 107 C2

Visitor Information

✉ Yokohama Station

☎ 045/441-7300

🕑 9 a.m.–7 p.m.

🚉 Yokohama

Silk Museum

✉ 1 Yamashita-cho, Naka-ku

☎ 045/641-0841

🕑 9:30 a.m.–5 p.m., closed Mon.

💲 $

🚉 Minato Mirai line: Nihon Odori

silkcenter-kbkk.jp /museum

The central Kannai district has been transformed with imaginative and architecturally striking developments. This applies especially to the Minato Mirai 21 development to the west, dominated by the **Landmark Tower,** at 971 feet (296 m) one of the tallest buildings in Japan. On clear days, the view from the 69th floor to Mount Fuji is breathtaking.

While you are there, take in the **Yokohama Port Museum** (2-1-1 Minato Mirai, Nishi-ku, tel 045/221-0280, nippon-maru.or.jp, $$), which offers exhibits about Japanese and world shipping, as well as the Nippon Maru, a beautiful tall ship built in 1930. The port was the point of departure for Japan's once colossal silk trade, detailed in the **Silk Museum** (Shiruku Hakubutsu-kan), whose fascinating exhibits focus on silk processing, textiles, and trade.

On the promontory to the south is the **Sankei-en Garden** (58-1 Honmoku San-no-tani, Naka-ku, tel 045/621-0634, 9 a.m.–5 p.m., $). Laid out in 1906, it incorporates a 15th-century pagoda and other buildings moved from various places throughout Japan.

For many, however, the city of Yokohama's star attraction lies in Japan's largest **Chinatown** and its wealth of restaurants, sundry goods stores, and pharmacies. ■

Kamakura

Overlooking Sagami Bay, Kamakura, founded in 1180, was perfect as both a samurai stronghold and a temple city; it was the capital of Japan until 1333. Now a plush residential town on Tokyo's outer commuter belt, hilly Kamakura retains a collection of Zen temples, ancient shrines, and samurai-era relics to justify its reputation as one of the must-sees in Japan.

Kamakura's sights (65 temples and 19 shrines) are far too many to be visited in a single day. They are largely distributed on a loop around Kamakura Station, with most of the major ones to the north. Five of the most important Zen temples of the Rinzai sect, collectively known as the **Kamakura Gozan,** still stand, but only **Engaku-ji** and **Kencho-ji**—the most popular— retain period buildings. Both of these are closer to Kita-Kamakura, the train station to the north. The famous Great Buddha, however, sits farther southwest and is reached more comfortably by bus or local train from Kamakura Station.

One way to cover the area is to arrive at Kita-Kamakura and zigzag through the temples. Or begin with a round-trip to the Great Buddha in the south and return to Kamakura Station. From there, go northeast along Wakamiya-oji, the wide main boulevard, to the National Treasure Museum and Tsurugaoka Hachiman-gu, then continue northwest to Kita-Kamakura Station. There are recommended hiking routes on a bilingual map posted outside Kamakura Station. Copies are available from the visitor center. If the crowds become too much, visit some of the smaller, quieter

temples and shrines, particularly east of Tsurugaoka Hachiman-gu.

Kamakura's colossal **Great Buddha** (Daibutsu) sits in the precincts of **Kotoku-in Temple** and is one of the two largest premodern bronze Buddhas in Japan (the other is in Todai-ji in Nara; see pp. 237–239). Cast in 1252 and 37 feet (11 m) high, this seated Buddha was once housed in a vast wooden hall that was swept away by a tidal wave in 1495. With its serene countenance enhanced by the elegant flow of drapery, this is an intriguing work

Kamakura

107 C2

Visitor Information

✉ Outside Kamakura Station

☎ 0467/22-3350

🕐 9 a.m.–5 p.m.

Kotoku-in Temple

✉ 4-2-28 Hase

☎ 0467/22-0703

💲 $

🚆 Enoshima line: Hase

kotoku-in.jp

The Daibutsu (Great Buddha) at Kotoku-in Temple

Hase-dera

✉ 3-11-2 Hase

☎ 0467/22-6300

🕐 8 a.m.–5 p.m.

💲 $

🚃 Enoshima line: Hase

hasedera.jp

National Treasure Museum

✉ 2-1-1 Yukinoshita

☎ 0467/22-0753

🕐 9 a.m.– 4:30 p.m., closed Mon.

💲 $

🚃 Yokosuka line: Kamakura

Tsurugaoka Hachiman-gu

✉ 2-1-31 Yukinoshita

☎ 0467/22-0315

🕐 8:30 a.m.–6 p.m.

💲 $ (museum)

🚃 Yokosuka line: Kamakura

tsurugaoka -hachimangu.jp

Engaku-ji

✉ 409 Yamanouchi

☎ 0467/22-0478

🕐 8 a.m.–4:30 p.m., public meditation held 1:20 p.m. on Sat., 9 a.m. on 2nd & 4th Sun.

💲 $

🚃 Yokosuka line: Kita-Kamakura

of art. The statue is hollow—a ladder inside gives access to shoulder level.

Less than a quarter of a mile (400 m) south is **Hase-dera** with a breathtaking view over Sagami Bay. Founded in the eighth century, this temple was rebuilt by shogun Ashikaga Yoshimasa (who also built Kyoto's Ginkaku-ji) in 1459. The temple stands beyond a beautiful garden in the precinct. Close to the steps to the buildings, as well as to the west of the compound, are serried ranks of hundreds of statues of Jizo, typically festooned with bibs and children's toys. The patron deity of travelers and children, Jizo is venerated especially by women as the guardian of the souls lost in terminated pregnancies. The main Amida Hall and Kannon Hall are open to the public (unlike in most temples). They contain fine Buddha figures, but Kannon Hall is renowned for its great Juichimen (11-faced) statue of Kannon, deity of compassion. Carved in 721 from a giant camphor log, the splendidly gilded figure stands some 30 feet (9 m) high.

Presenting a wealth of exhibits revealing facets of Kamakura's rich history, the **National Treasure Museum** (Kokuhokan) is noted for its collection of temple treasures and fine Buddhist artworks.

Tsurugaoka Hachiman-gu is a shrine dedicated to Hachiman, Shinto deity of war. The original 11th-century shrine burned down in 1191, but was rebuilt on nearby Tsurugaoka—the Hill of Cranes. Fire struck again six centuries later; most of the current structures date from 1828. The

shrine is cherished for its view and the beauty of its fine vermilion buildings—but most of all for its historical associations. The shrine's Mai-den (dance stage) is revered as a replica of the one on which Shizuka, beloved of the ill-fated hero Minamoto Yoshitsune (1159–1189), performed centuries ago. A festival remembers Shizuka and her struggles to reunite with her lover each September (14–16) with dances and demonstrations of *yabusame* (horseback archery). Yoshitsune's fratricidal half brother and founder of the Kamakura shogunate, Yoritomo, is buried just to the east, on the site of his former palace.

Temples

Engaku-ji is the first temple by distance, about 110 yards (100 m) southeast of Kita-Kamakura Station. It was founded in 1282 to commemorate those who fell during the Mongol Wars. Most of the buildings finally succumbed to the earthquake of 1923. Current structures are mainly concrete reproductions, but the beautifully carved two-story

Sanmon Gate of 1780 survives, as does the great bell, cast in 1301. Closed to the public, the oldest extant building is Shariden Hall, which contains a reliquary said to hold one of the Buddha's teeth. The compound has two small gardens: Obai-in, a mausoleum for the 13th-century Hojo family rulers, and Butsunichi-an, where green tea is served.

About 280 yards (250 m) southwest of Engaku-ji and across the train tracks, **Toke-ji** is set in a leafy valley. A former nunnery, this temple is also known as Enkiri-dera (Divorce Temple, or "fate-cutting temple"). In the 1600s, divorce—exclusively a male privilege—came to be recognized as the only refuge for battered wives.

A year spent here made a woman's divorce official. The temple's directives inspired Japan's first divorce law in 1873. The complex embraces **Matsugaoka Treasure House,** a museum with items relating to the temple's history.

Kencho-ji, about half a mile (600 m) southwest of Kita-Kamakura, stands among majestic cedars. The most important of Kamakura's five main Zen temples, it was founded by a Chinese Zen master in 1253. It is now headquarters to the Kencho-ji branch of Rinzai. The current buildings date from the mid-17th century; cast in 1255, the great bronze bell near the Sanmon Gate is a National Treasure. Behind the main Ryuoden (Dragon King Hall) is a fine garden laid out by Zen master Muso Kokushi. ■

Toke-ji

- ✉ 1367 Yamanouchi
- ☎ 0467/22-1663
- 🕐 8:30 a.m.–5 p.m.
- 💲 $
- 🚇 Yokosuka line: Kita-Kamakura

tokeiji.com

Kencho-ji

- ✉ 8 Yamanouchi
- ☎ 0467/22-0981
- 🕐 8:30 a.m.–4:30 p.m.
- 💲 $
- 🚇 Yokosuka line: Kamakura

hasedera.jp

Seeking Out the Big Buddhas

Don't get too impressed: The **Kamakura Buddha** and his 52-foot (16 m) older brother at Todai-ji in Nara aren't the biggest boys on the block. There are more than a dozen bigger Buddhas scattered across Japan, peering down over small towns and quiet rice fields, totally off the tourist radar.

The biggest, the **Ushiku Daibutsu** (2083 Kunocho, Ushiku-shi, tel 029/889-2931, 9:30 a.m.–4:30 p.m., Joban line to Ushiku, bus to Ushiku Daibutsu-Mae, $$) in Ibaraki Prefecture, stands a staggering 328 feet (100 m) tall, two and a half times taller than the Statue of Liberty.

The second biggest, the **Dai-Kannon** in Kaga city, Ishikawa Prefecture (Hokuriku line to Kagaonsen), is a gold 240-foot (73 m) monstrosity holding a baby in its arms the size of the Nara Daibutsu. It is now closed due to finances, but the crumbling grounds can be explored.

Nihon-ji Daibutsu is Japan's largest premodern Buddha, built out of a stone cliff in 1783. At 98 feet (30 m), it sits twice the height of Nara's Daibutsu. (184-4 Motona, Kyonanmachi, Awa-gun, Chiba Prefecture, tel 0470/55-1103, Uchibo line to Hamakanaya, 8 a.m.–5 p.m., $$).

Nearly all of these big Buddhas are of modern construction, built in the 20th century. Some were genuine postwar peace memorials, but others seem to be the efforts of wealthy people to buy credit for the afterlife. The rash of Buddha-building ended in 1994, after the Bubble Economy and its wild expenditures screeched to a halt. Now many towns see these edifices to excess as embarrassing eyesores–but it's not an easy task in Japan to tear down a well-intentioned Buddha.

Buddhism

Of the 300 million Buddhists worldwide today, about a third are Japanese. That the function of Buddhism in modern Japan is mainly funereal may seem grim, but death is only the gateway to rebirth; the midsummer Buddhist O-Bon festival of the dead involves much merrymaking. At other times, thousands of Japanese join in prayers, ceremonies, and retreats from the stress of day-to-day living at peaceful Buddhist temples.

Buddhist priests offer a meal to the spirit of the saintly monk Kukai.

Buddhism has shaped Japan. As in Europe at the end of the Dark Ages, monks held the keys to knowledge. Initially Korean and Chinese, they taught numeracy and literacy, built temples, roads, and cities, and laid the foundations of culture, government, and law.

The Philosophy

Buddhism is based upon the discourses of the philosopher Siddhartha Gautama (circa 563–483 B.C.), born in what is now southern Nepal. Posthumously known as the Buddha (Enlightened One), his verbal teachings were later written down by his disciples. According to Buddhism, existence is full of *dukkha:* transience and dissatisfaction. The source of dukkha is desire in the mind—to live, to get,

to have, to avoid pain—and thus the only escape from endless suffering is to master the mind and cease clinging to things, to people, to a sense of self, even to life. The practice of Buddhism is meditation—sitting quietly to watch and understand the mind. Buddhism grew out of the Hindu belief that all beings would be reincarnated endlessly based on their karma or meritorious deeds each life. The goal of Buddhism is to break this cycle of unhappy lives perpetuated by spiritual desire with one final, peaceful life and to be reborn no more. Thus *nirvana* is not the achievement of godlike wisdom, but a snuffing out of the suffering that agitates humans.

There are two main Buddhist doctrines: the original Theravada, practiced today mainly in Sri

Lanka and Southeast Asia, and the later Mahayana, or Great Vehicle, which, after spreading to Tibet and China, was adopted in Mongolia, Korea, and Japan. The former focuses on achieving nirvana within this lifetime and is considered a more personal, inward-looking Buddhism, whereas Mahayana argues for a social Buddhism: Instead of becoming Buddhas, we should become bodhisattvas, enlightened beings who stay on Earth to help others become enlightened before joining the Buddha in "heaven."

Buddhism in Japan

Mahayana Buddhism, brought by Korean emissaries in either 538 or 552, was decreed the state religion in Japan by Prince Shotoku in 593. The religion progressed substantially during the mid-eighth century under Emperor Shomu, who established temples and monasteries throughout his realm. When monks in Nara started politicking, the emperor sent the monks Saicho and Kukai to China to bring back rival forms of Buddhism to break Nara's power. Saicho founded the vigorous, ascetic Tendai sect on top of Mount Hiei, which stood in sharp contrast to pampered city monks below. Tendai was adopted as the state sect and Nara's power waned. Kukai (774–835) returned to Japan to found the Shingon sect, which advocated an esoteric Buddhism in which wisdom could not be transmitted through texts but only in secret teachings and fiery rituals. Shingon's influence had overtaken that of Tendai by the end of the Heian era, as idle nobles adored its dramatic flair for ritual. Today it counts some 12 million followers.

The Jodo and Jodo Shinshu schools were created by Honen (1133–1212) and his disciple Shinran (1173–1262), respectively. These worship the Amida (Pure Land) Buddha and believe that salvation resides in repeatedly chanting *Namu Amida Butsu* ("Glory to Amida Buddha"). Achieving Enlightenment through meditation seemed like an impossible task for laypeople, who flocked to this simple teaching.

Both sects have a membership of millions; the Shinshu branch has the largest following of all Japanese sects. The priest Nichiren (1222–1282) based the sect he founded (Nichiren-shu) upon the Lotus Sutra, arguing that all other texts were spiritually damning. Although his aggressive zeal earned him the displeasure of the shogun and a four-year exile to Sado-ga-shima (see pp. 195–196), his Nichiren-shu school has a huge following today in part because he popularized Buddhism by throwing out certain rules (monks can marry, eat meat, and drink alcohol). Its many subsects include the modern Soka Gakkai. With millions of devotees worldwide, it exerts considerable influence on Japanese politics through Komeito—the "clean government party."

(see pp. 195–196)

INSIDER TIP:

Visitors of any faith will benefit from the deep breathing and mind emptying of Buddhist meditation. And exhale . . .

—JUSTIN KAVANAGH
National Geographic Travel Books editor

Zen (*Ch'an* in Chinese, from the Sanskrit *dhyana*, or meditation), founded in China by the Indian monk Boddhidarma in the sixth century, was introduced in Japan by the Japanese monks Eisai (1141–1215) and Dogen (1200–1253), respectively the founders of the Rinzai and Soto sects. Setting aside sutras, Zen is imparted verbally from master to disciple and holds that Enlightenment is attainable in this life only through sitting meditation (*zazen*). Focusing on self-discipline, frugality, and hard work, Zen also bestowed spiritual concepts upon the martial arts, making it appealing to the samurai. It brought innovations to calligraphy, poetry, and painting, introduced the tea ceremony, and virtually reinvented flower arrangement as an art in itself. Zen's influence is still much in evidence in Japan today.

Nikko

Even a quick stay in Tokyo should include Nikko, the best historical day trip from the metropolis. The small town sits on the edge of a beautiful national park and has preserved some astonishingly ostentatious shrines to the founders of the Tokugawa shogunate, retaining a sense of the medieval government's power, money, and aesthetic tastes.

Shouyo-en (garden) at Rinno-ji

Nikko

🅼 107 C4

Visitor Information

✉ Tobu Nikko Station, 4-3 Matsubara-cho

☎ 0288/53-4511

🕐 8:30 a.m.–5 p.m.

Sitting at the edge of Nikko's historical sights in the western half of the city, the elegantly curved vermilion **Shinkyō Bridge** (Sacred Bridge) spans the Daiya-gawa. Two *torii* (gateways) mark the ends of the bridge, which was formerly used only for ceremonial purposes. Built in 1636, it commemorates an old legend about the eighth-century priest Shodo Shonin, said to have crossed the river on this spot on the backs of two gigantic serpents. The bridge was reconstructed in 1907, shortly after being washed away in a flood.

Rinno-ji, the first sight within the Sannai historical district, is on the right along the main Omotesando-dori to **Tosho-gu,**

the shrine which is less than a quarter of a mile (400 m) farther north. Founded by Shodo during the eighth century and maintained by the Buddhist Tendai sect, the temple is renowned for its Sanbutsudo (Hall of the Three Buddhas), erected in 1648. The three large gilded and lacquered statues inside represent the thousand-armed Kannon on the left, the Amida-Nyorai Buddha in the center, and the unusual Bato (horse-headed) Kannon on the right. Featuring a horse's head jutting from the forehead, this incarnation of the deity of compassion is devoted to animal welfare. The nearby Gohotendo, containing other statues, is notable for the Sorinto, a large bronze pillar inscribed with 10,000 sutras (Buddhist texts) and bearing 24 bells. Exhibiting various items connected with the temple's history, the Treasure Hall (Homutsuden) has a beautiful garden behind it.

When the great shogun Tokugawa Ieyasu died in 1616, Nikko was selected as the site for his mausoleum. At Ieyasu's request, this was a modest affair, but in 1634 Ieyasu's grandson, Iemitsu, began building the Tosho-gu shrine on a scale commensurate with his grandfather's stature. Some 15,000 craftsmen, among them the finest carpenters, carvers, and painters in the land, worked on the project, the cost of which today would translate into hundreds of millions of dollars. Incorporating some 2.5 million sheets of gold leaf, the shrine's lavish buildings

remain paradigms of the ornate style of the late 16th-century Momoyama period. They have both admirers and detractors: The Tosho-gu structures are a far cry from the simple elegance of classic Japanese taste, reflecting the rococo excess of Ming-dynasty China and the parvenu taste of military dictators. Still, if they tend to be massive and overdecorated as a whole, charm and subtleties lie in a wealth of detail, particularly in the hundreds of intricate polychrome carvings, many based on designs supplied by major exponents of the Kano school of painting. Several of the buildings are designated Important Cultural Properties and National Treasures.

INSIDER TIP:

There's no English signage or pamphlet offered in Tosho-gu, so the ¥500 audio guide is worth getting.

—PERRIN LINDELAUF
National Geographic Books author

As you proceed through a giant stone torii gateway along Omotesando-dori leading to the shrine, on your left is a five-story pagoda built in 1818 to replace a 1650 original destroyed by fire. Flanked by two fierce protective kings and featuring ornate carvings, the great vermilion Omotemon is the true gate to Tosho-gu. Beyond this are the Sanjinko, three storehouses

Rinno-ji
✉ 2300 Sannai
☎ 0288/54-0531
🕐 8 a.m.–5 p.m
💲 $

Tosho-gu
✉ 2301 Sannai
☎ 0288/54-0560
🕐 8 a.m.–4:30 p.m.
💲 $$$ (shrine),
$$ (art museum),
$$ (treasure house)

containing sacred trappings for the shrine's great festivals (Warrior Processions, May 18 and October 18). The last of these structures displays fanciful carvings of elephants. The unpainted Shinkyusha (sacred stable), containing a single effigy of a white horse, bears a delightful bas-relief sequence of monkeys, including a famous "Hear No Evil, Speak No Evil, See No Evil" trio. Monkey spirits were once believed to protect horses.

Next is a granite water cistern; Shinto worshippers pause here to wash hands and rinse mouths before proceeding into the sacred precinct.

Proceeding past the next torii gateway and up more stairs, you will find a drum tower on the left and belfry to the right, behind which lies the Yakushi-do *(extra fee for access),* a Buddhist structure featuring a huge ink drawing on the ceiling of the Naki-ryu (roaring dragon). The 17th-century original was lost with the building in a fire in 1961. The current reproduction offers the same novelty: As visitors clap their hands, the reverberations are believed to resemble the sound of a dragon's roar.

Back along the main path and up more steps is the amazing 36-foot (11 m) **Yomeimon** (Gate of Sunlight). The ornamentation seen thus far reaches a florid climax here: The structure is alive with 400 gilt polychrome carvings of Kano-school design depicting giraffes, lions, dragons,

The Sennin Gyoretsu festival at Tosho-gu

birds, flowers, and phoenixes, along with Chinese children, sages, and immortals. One of the columns has been deliberately carved upside down to appease evil spirits; it was believed that, without this imperfection, the lavish artistic overkill might otherwise have aroused their ire.

Through the gate to the left is the **Mikoshigura**—a building housing *mikoshi,* sacred palanquins carried in festivals. Straight ahead are the gorgeously decorated Haiden (Oratory) and Honden (Main Hall).

To the right of the Yomeimon is a corridor leading toward the Sakashita-mon gate. Just before the gate you'll see another small portal, whose lintel features a much-cherished carving of a sleeping cat—the "Nemuri-neko"—by 17th-century sculptor Jingoro. Beyond the gates, a long stone stairway through a cedar grove leads to Ieyasu's tomb, whose austere design comes as something of a relief. Outside the shrine are the **Tosho-gu Treasure House** and the **Tosho-gu Museum of Art,** both of which exhibit items pertaining to the Tokugawa shoguns, including armor, swords, and paintings.

Futarasan-jinja & Taiyuin

There are three Futarasan shrines, dedicated to the deities of Mount Nantai (formerly Futara-san), in the Nikko area. The Okumiya (Inner Shrine), near the peak of the mountain itself, is the most sacred, and the Chugushi (Middle Shrine) stands by the lake of Chuzenji-ko; the third, beside the Daiya-gawa, was called Honsha (Head Shrine). Founded by the priest Shodo in the eighth century, these shrines originally had Buddhist connotations, but were given exclusive

Shinto status in 1868. To reach the riverside **Futarasan-jinja,** from Omotesando-dori turn left along the Ue-Shinmichi path at the crossing before the Omotemon Gate. The buildings date back to 1619. The ornate lacquered *karamon* (Chinese

Futarasan-jinja

- ✉ 2307 Sannai
- ☎ 0288/54-0535
- 🕐 8 a.m.–5 p.m., 9 a.m.–4 p.m. in winter
- 💲 $$$ (multiple entry ticket), $ (garden)

Shrine & Temple Merchandise

During festivals, many large Shinto shrine and Buddhist temple compounds look like markets. Stalls sell delicacies such as *tako-yaki* (barbecued octopus dumplings) and fried noodles, as well as toffee apples, candy, cheap toys, and souvenirs. The main buildings trade briskly in religious trinkets, notably key ring–size *mamori* (talismans) against misfortune, as well as *omikuji* (fortune papers). For around ¥100, you pull a numbered stick out of an oblong box and are given the paper with the corresponding number. Rolled up, the paper is tied to a tree (the right one is the one festooned with fortune papers) to enhance good fortune and, hopefully, avert any bad luck headed your way.

Nikko National Park

⛰ 105 B4

Chuzenji-ko

⛰ 105 B4

🚌 Bus from JR Nikko Station to Chuzenji Onsen (approx. 50 min.)

Yumoto Onsen

🚌 Bus from JR Nikko Station (approx. 80 min.)

Edo Wonderland

✉ 470-2, Karakura, Nikko, Tochigi Prefecture

☎ 0288/77-1777

🕐 9 a.m.–5 p.m., closed Wed. except hols.; closed Dec. 8–21

💲 $$$$

🚌 Tobu Kinugawa line: Kinugawa Onsen, then 15-min. bus

edowonderland.net

gate) stands before the main hall; both the hall and oratory are designated Important Cultural Properties. The shrine stands amid magnificent cedar trees; from here, you can take an invigorating stroll toward the Nantai-san foothills.

West of Futarasan is **Taiyuin** (also called Taiyuin-byo), the mausoleum (1653) of the builder of Tosho-gu, shogun Tokugawa Iemitsu. To find it, as you go north toward Tosho-gu along Omotesando-dori, turn left onto the Shita-Shinmichi path just before the stone torii gateway. The precinct embraces several Important Cultural Properties. Taiyuin is beautifully ornamented but less bombastic than Tosho-gu.

More subdued than the shrines, the **Tamozawa Imperial Villa** (*$$*), a ten-minute walk from the Shinkyō Bridge, is Japan's only extant villa from its early modern Meiji period. The massive 106-room wooden building mixes styles from the Edo, Meiji, and Taisho periods and served as a retreat for Emperor Hirohito (Showa) and the current emperor, Akihito, during World War II.

Outlying Nikko

If you have an extra day or more to spare, the 540-square-mile (1,400 sq km) area of **Nikko National Park** offers several scenic wonders and some outstanding hiking trails. With its dramatic mountain backdrop, **Chuzenji-ko** (Chuzenji Lake) can be admired on foot or by taking a cruise or

renting a rowboat. You'll enjoy fine views of the lake from Chanokidaira, where the viewing platform is accessible by cable car from Chuzenji Onsen.

Nearby is the spectacular 318-foot (97 m) **Kegon-no-Taki Waterfall,** renowned for its spectacular display of rainbows in the spray on sunny days. **Yumoto Onsen** resort enjoys a reputation for its hot-spring experience; you can reach it by bus or on foot from Chuzenji-ko. Its *onsen* hotels are perfect for relaxing after an afternoon of exhilarating mountain hiking from Ryuzu Waterfall to the north of Chuzenji-ko.

Southeast, on the Kinugawa line from Nikko, Kinugawa Onsen is a gaudier, more conventional onsen resort than Yumoto, but for those traveling with children, it is close to **Edo Wonderland,** a theme park with reconstructed period buildings and samurai-oriented attractions. Adults might find this tacky, but kids often love it. ∎

Mount Fuji, Hakone & Izu

The image of Japan's premier natural wonder is everywhere—on postcards, calendars, travel brochures, and old woodblock prints. Split between Yamanashi and Shizuoka Prefectures, Fuji-san is the centerpiece of Fuji-Hakone-Izu National Park. Whether you are set on climbing Japan's most famous peak, luxuriating in an *onsen* or taking the perfect photo from the surrounding lakes, you'll find this region is guaranteed to delight.

Hakone is renowned for its views of Fuji-san, particularly as mirrored in the waters of beautiful Ashino-ko. With the region's many onsen resorts, its fuming volcanic valleys, the scenic Fuji Five Lakes area, and the presence of Fuji-san itself, this is not surprisingly one of the most cherished areas for recreation and relaxation in Japan. Hakone makes a perfect day trip from Tokyo, but with so much to see and some outstanding hotels (especially the landmark Fujiya, one of Japan's first Western-style hotels; see Travelwise p. 367), treating yourself to an overnight stay will make this a more rewarding experience.

One constant proviso is the weather: If it is cloudy or wet, Fuji-san often totally vanishes. Also, you should be aware that the sacred mountain gets very crowded on weekends.

Hakone

A loop of the Hakone region starts at Hakone-Yumoto, a popular onsen town. There you transfer to the Hakone Gozan line to Gora. Gora is the beginning of a funicular tram/cable car relay over the mountains along Hakone's big lake, Ashino-ko. On the way there, you'll pass a worthwhile detour, **Hakone Open-Air Museum** (Chokoku-no-Mori Bijutsukan;

Mount Fuji, Japan's sacred mountain

1121 Ni-no-Taira, Hakone-cho, tel 0460/82-1161, hakone-oam.or.jp, 9 a.m.–4:30 p.m., $$$$, Hakone Tozan line to Chokoku-no-mori), a highly regarded repository of 19th-century and contemporary

Climbers enjoy the view through the swirl of sulphurous steam in Owakudani.

Hakone
⬛ 107 B2

Visitor Information

✉ Hakone Yumoto

☎ 0460/85-8911

🕑 9 a.m.–5:45 p.m.

🚄 Shinkansen: Odawara (1 hr. from Tokyo)

Pola Museum of Art

✉ 1285 Kozukayama, Sengokuhara

☎ 0460/84-2111

🕑 9 a.m.–5 p.m.

💲 $$$$

🚌 13-min. shuttle from Gora Station

polamuseum.or.jp

Japanese and Western sculpture; there is a pavilion devoted entirely to Picasso, and a collection of 26 sculptures by Henry Moore is displayed outdoors.

Another excellent museum, the **Pola Museum of Art,** is a quick shuttle away from Gora should the weather turn foul. A large private collection, the museum displays works from 19th-century French Impressionists and the first wave of Japanese artists to study Western styles around the same time period.

From Gora, take the funicular tram for a ten-minute trip to the summit of Soun-zan. You can alight at any of the four stops on the way. Koen Kami is the stop for the **Hakone Museum of Art** (Hakone Bijutsukan; *1-min. walk from the station,*

tel 0460/82-2623, 9:30 a.m.–4 p.m., closed Thurs., $$), noted for its Chinese and Japanese ceramics.

From Soun-zan, hop on the cable car to Togendai. Within ten minutes, the car passes over a valley of jagged rocks, craters, and bubbling mud, where steam jets from the crevices and fumaroles belch sulfurous vapors. This is **Owakudani** (Great Boiling Valley). Weather permitting, there is a fine view of Fuji-san to the northwest. You can take a closer look at the inferno from the Owakudani Exploration Path circumventing it. Before setting out, be sure to check ahead with the tourist information staff regarding conditions, since area trails are sometimes closed due to the toxic gases emitted by the mountain. The building alongside the cable car station houses a panoramic restaurant.

Board the cable car again to make the spectacularly scenic descent toward **Ashino-ko.** On a fine day, Fuji-san will be perfectly mirrored in the calm surface of the lake. You can get a closer look by taking a ferry from Togendai, where the cable car terminates, to Hakone-machi or Moto-Hakone. The trip takes about 40 minutes; tickets should be purchased from the cable car terminal before boarding. If you are on a day trip with a train to catch back to Tokyo, you can get the bus back to Odawara from Hakone-machi (outside the pier building) or Moto-Hakone (from Hakone Barrier) every 10 or 20 minutes.

Hakone Attractions

The two stops, about half a mile (1 km) apart, have sights worth visiting nearby. Almost 220 yards (200 m) to the north of Hakone-machi is **Hakone Barrier Station** (Hakone Sekisho-ato). The original structure vanished long ago, but the replacement on the same spot reproduces the checkpoint set up for intercepting travelers along the old Tokaido Road between Kyoto and Edo, a system designed for social stability that made travel possible only with the government's permission. From here, the Suginamiki, a splendid avenue of cryptomeria trees planted more than 350 years ago, parallels the main road for about three-quarters of a mile (1.2 km) to Moto-Hakone.

Hakone Gongen-jinja stands among dense woods in the foothills of Mount Koma. Marked by a huge red *torii* gateway emerging photogenically from the lake north of the Moto-Hakone bus stop, it is one of central Japan's largest shrines, founded some 1,200 years ago. Minamoto Yoritomo hid here in 1180 after a defeat during his ultimately successful campaign against the Taira clan. The shrine features a soaring cedar grove along the approach

INSIDER TIP:

In Owakudani try the *kuro-tamago*, eggs cooked in the hissing volcanic vents. Although black-shelled and sulfurous, the eggs supposedly add seven years to your life (2.5 eggs maximum!).

—PERRIN LINDELAUF
National Geographic writer

and a treasure hall with important historical relics.

If you have plenty of time, there is a popular hiking route along a preserved section of the old Tokaido Road from Moto-Hakone to Hakone-Yumoto. Very little of this essential link between Tokyo and Kyoto has been preserved, though you'll be following its general path on the Tokaido Shinkansen or Meishin Expressway. Hiroshige's series of woodcut prints "The 53 Stations *(continued on p. 123)*

Fuji-san: Sacred Mountain

The world's most beautiful volcano, its image immediately recognizable, Fuji-san is the highest mountain in Japan at 12,388 feet (3,776 m).

The sacred volcano has long been revered by followers of Japan's native Shinto religion.

The name Fuji-san is believed to mean either "second to none" in Japanese or "god of fire" in the indigenous Ainu language.

As Japan's highest point, Fuji was formed as a result of three tectonic plates—the Okhotsk, Amurian, and Philippine Sea plates—intersecting beneath it and causing a tremendous amount of magma to push to the surface over the millennia.

Although the sacred volcano is currently top dog in Japan, it is a relative upstart. Starting as a welling of magma at the foot of two older volcanoes, Old Fuji formed its cone over the course of several dramatic explosions between 11,000 and 80,000 years ago, burying its neighbors. Eight thousand to 11,000 years ago another huge lava flow piled up on Old Fuji and formed the current cone.

Fuji-san has erupted ten times since the eighth century, last blowing its top in 1707. The spectacular two-week eruption terrified the citizens of Edo 75 miles (120 km) away, turning skies dark during the daytime and coating the city with ash. The volcano has been quiet for 300 years, but the tremors of the Great East Japan Earthquake put immense pressure on a magma chamber approximately 9 miles (15 km) below the surface, causing volcanologists to warn of the possibility of another eruption of Mount Fuji.

The Sun Goddess Amaterasu

Whether raining down fire or not, Fuji-san is the almighty among mountains worshipped in ascetic Shinto-Buddhism (see sidebar pp. 248–249) and has been revered as sacred since prehistoric times. For the religious, climbing Fuji-san is the chance to commune with Amaterasu, sun goddess and ancestor of Japan's imperial line. Although many hikers now take the shortcut up to the Fifth Station and hike overnight, pilgrims traditionally began at Fuji-Yoshida's Fuji Sengen-jinja, a shrine devoted to the mountain goddess, then hiked several extra hours through the day and stayed in a lodge near the peak overnight before rising early to watch dawn break and shout *"Banzai!"* ("Hurrah!") at the appearance of Amaterasu.

Although forbidden to women until 1868—supposedly for reasons of "spiritual purity"—the volcano is now ascended annually by more than 250,000 people of both sexes and all ages during the July–August climbing season. As many as one-third of the climbers come from overseas, hoping to see a stunning sunrise with views of Tokyo and across the Japan Alps.

Indeed, views of and from Fuji have long been considered the most beautiful in the country. In the late Edo period, famous woodblock printers Hokusai and Hiroshige both made series of prints entitled "Thirty-six Views of Mount Fuji"; Hokusai then doubled down with "One Hundred Views of Mount Fuji." When the woodblock *ukiyo-e* style first hit Europe, it created a sensation, and the particular emphasis on Fuji-san by these artists founded the mountain's global status as a place of beauty and significance.

Despite all this, the mountain has traditionally been less charming up close. A veritable dump for decades, Fuji was littered with the cast-off rubbish of hikers, and the trail stunk of poorly built, badly overloaded toilets. As a result, the first attempt to register Fuji-san as a World Heritage site was rejected. Since then, volunteer efforts have removed tons of trash from Japan's most sacred mountain and better facilities have been built, making the climb a crowded but much more pleasant experience.

INSIDER TIP:

Altitude sickness is possible on Fuji-san, if you ascend too quickly. Go slow, drink a lot of water, and sleep a little in one of the huts near the top to acclimatize.

—KEN NOGUCHI
Alpinist and environmentalist

Volcanoes & Earthquakes

The most active Japanese volcanoes are those in Kyushu (notably Aso, Unzen, and Sakurajima). However, the presence of hot springs, geysers, pools of boiling mud, and emanations of sulfurous fumes in the land around the foothills of many others, including Fuji-san, belies their dormancy. Volcanic activity and the movement of tectonic plates deep underground make Japan particularly earthquake-prone.

Japan experiences as many as 2,000 earthquakes annually, usually too small to be recorded except on sensitive seismographic equipment. Registering over 7.0 magnitude, temblors such as the Great Kanto Earthquake of 1923, the Kobe quake of 1995, and the Great East Japan Earthquake of 2011 have all caused devastating damage and loss of life. The Kanto plain is considered especially vulnerable. For centuries, major earthquakes have hit the Tokyo-Yokohama region roughly once every 70 years, so the next one is widely regarded as overdue.

Strong earthquakes offshore often trigger tsunami—colossal seismic waves that can have calamitous effects when they come crashing inland onto Japan's vulnerable archipelago. Much of Kamakura was destroyed by a tsunami in 1495, and 2011 saw the devastation of Tohoku's coast in a 45-foot (15 m) tidal wave.

(See also Earthquakes on p. 359 of Travelwise.)

EXPERIENCE: Climbing Fuji-san

The Japanese have an oft-repeated saying: "A wise man climbs Fuji-san once, but only a fool climbs it twice." This is taken as an article of faith by a people for whom Fuji is the most sacred of mountains, and many beginner hikers set out to climb the great volcano and watch sunrise from the top during the brief summer climbing season.

Mount Fuji's climbing season runs from July 1 to August 31.

Fuji-san (Mount Fuji) doesn't require any special training or gear—there are chains where the going is a little rocky—but you shouldn't take Fuji lightly just because your bus is full of energetic old-timers.

Despite the short summer climbing season, Fuji-san sees the most injuries per year of any mountain in Japan, and a large number of those are tourists completely unprepared for sudden rain or temperatures below freezing in mid-summer. Call visitor information to get the latest forecast. Climbing out of season is possible but ill-advised: Except for the first two weeks of September, the huts will be closed and conditions can quickly become dangerous.

Making the Trek

Be sure to pack a rain suit, good hiking shoes, a warm top, a hat, sunscreen, ¥100 coins for the toilets, and extra batteries for your headlamp if you plan on doing the overnight climb. Food and drink is pricey, so bring your own, especially water, as the risk of altitude sickness is higher if you become dehydrated.

The traditional **Yoshida Trail** starts at the town of Fuji-Yoshida, but most take the bus from Kawaguchi-ko up to the Fifth Station, cutting out five hours of climbing. From the parking lot to the peak takes about six hours, so if you aim to climb overnight and watch dawn, the bus arriving at 10 p.m. is the latest feasible start.

The trail follows switchbacks past the five remaining stations to the summit, with 16 rest huts along the way. The snake of glowing lights moves as slow as the slowest hiker, and bottlenecks are common, so fast hikers should consider the **Subashiri Trail** on the east slope, which gets only 11 percent of Fuji's traffic. Resting for a few hours in a hut to regain energy and acclimatize is recommended, but book ahead, as they get very crowded (www.city.fujiyoshida.yamanashi.jp/div/english/html/climb.html). After shouting "Banzai!" ("Hurrah!") at sunrise, enjoy the views of the clouds far below and the glittering lakes, then descend by the **Gotemba-guchi** track and enjoy racing through the soft volcanic sand. After climbing Fuji-san, you really will feel like you are walking on air. For tour information: fujimountainguides.com.

of the Tokaido" gives a sense of the beauty and difficulty of making this journey, glimpses of which still remain among the ancient cedars. Paved as far as the Amazake-Jaya teahouse, the walk takes three and a half hours and passes the temples of Saun-ji, Shogen-ji, and Soun-ji.

As the area's most popular onsen resort, Hakone-Yumoto is predictably garish, but it's a good choice for the onsen experience. Moreover, a long soak in hot water might be just the ticket after a good hike. If you are here on Culture Day, November 3, don't miss the Hakone Daimyo Gyoretsu, a procession of 170 people dressed as samurai and princesses in their palanquins, which departs Soun-ji at around 10 a.m. The best part is the crier at the head of the procession who bellows the traditional warning call, *"Shitaaaaaa Niiiiiii!"* ("On your knees! On your knees! The lord approaches!") A commoner who didn't heed this would likely see his head fly; luckily, festivalgoers can skip the genuflection without risk of decapitation.

Fuji Five Lakes

With its outstanding scenery, including densely forested mountains and idyllic views of Fuji-san, the nearby Fuji Five Lakes (Fuji-go-ko) area has not gone unnoticed; the banks of the larger lakes, **Yamanaka-ko** and **Kawaguchi-ko,** have been substantially developed, particularly the latter. The best sight lines in Kawaguchi-ko are achieved by climbing the ropeway up Tenjo-san, a 3,622-foot (1,104 m) peak next to the lake.

This affords fine views of Fuji-san and the lake below, but if the weather is foul, check out the **Fuji World Heritage Center,** which has exhibits on its geology.

The areas around the lakes of Sai-ko, Shoji-ko, and Motosu-ko are pristine. In sinister contrast to the happy holidaymakers, the **Sea of Trees** (Aokigahara Jutai) near Shoji-ko is the most likely place for suicide in Japan—so much so that signs urging people not to give up hope are posted in the area. Up to a hundred bodies are found in this forest every year, and the area is reputed to be haunted by the souls of these unhappy people. ■

Literary Izu

Shuzenji (see map p. 105 B1) is an *onsen* and temple town in the center of the Izu Peninsula. Shuzenji first gained a romantic reputation as a place of political exile, execution, and intrigue: The murder of shogun Minamoto Yoriie, son of Yoritomo (see p. 37), was one of several incidents to give the village a tragic air. Attracted by its history, early modern writers such as Yasunari Kawabata and Natsume Soseki came to take the waters and write. Soseki spent a long convalescence here with a life-threatening gastric ulcer. After many days without food, his first swallow of food inspired the haiku: "Through my guts / spring trickles / the taste of porridge."

Fuji-san
🗺 107 B2

Visitor Information
📋 Fuji Yoshida, outside the station
☎ 0555/22-7000; English info line: 0555/24-1236
🕐 9:30 a.m.–6 p.m.
� Fujikyuko line: Kawaguchiko or highway bus from Shinjuku; buses depart 6:45 a.m.–4:45 p.m. daily in July & Aug. Reservation a month in advance recommended.

Fuji World Heritage Center
✉ 6663-1 Funatsu, Fujikawaguchiko-machi, Minami-tsuru-gun
🚌 Tour Retro Bus from Kawaguchiko Station to Kawahara Visitor-Mae stop (5 min., free)
☎ 0555/72-0259
🕐 8:30 a.m.–7 p.m. July–Aug.; closes at 5 p.m. in off-season
💲 $ (new building)

Izu-hanto

◭ 105 B1–B2

MOA Museum of Art

✉ 26-2 Momoyama Atami, Shizuoka

☎ 0557/84-2511

🕓 9:30 a.m.– 4:30 p.m., closed Thurs.

💲 $$$

🚃 Tokaido line: Atami

moaart.or.jp

Izu-hanto

The southern end of Fuji-Hakone-Izu National Park flanks the Izu Peninsula, famous for its hot-spring resorts and coastal scenery. Close to Tokyo, this is Japan's most popular resort area and is often over-crowded. Where the famous scenic assets have been under-mined by indiscriminate hotel development, resorts such as Atami have become tawdry and overpriced. That said, Atami possesses the **MOA Museum of Art** (MOA Bijutsukan); its famous collection of Japanese and Chinese art includes several National Treasures.

The area, which includes the Izu Seven Isles offshore, has a reputation for great seafood. The less ostentatious hot-spring *ryokan* (traditional inns) around Shimoda, where

Commodore Perry landed his black ships in 1853 (see p. 41), or inland at Shuzenji offer a peaceful off-peak getaway. But unless you are in Japan for some time, Izu-hanto, unlike Fuji-Hakone, should not be a high priority. ■

Japanese holidaymakers enjoy the ocean at Shirahama Beach on Izu-hanto.

Japan's second largest island and final frontier—a pristine wilderness of breathtaking lakes, mountains, and volcanoes

Hokkaido

Hokkaido squirrel, a native subspecies of red squirrel

Hokkaido

The Japanese have long regarded Hokkaido, their second largest island, as a wilderness. In feudal times, it was seen as a wasteland, called Ezo, inhabited only by the indigenous Ainu peoples (see sidebar p. 132). Today it attracts lovers of the outdoors. With the Japan Sea to the west, the Pacific Ocean to the southeast, and the Sea of Okhotsk to the northeast, Hokkaido Prefecture represents 22 percent of the national landmass with just 5 percent of the population.

Although lonely outposts in southern Hokkaido existed during the feudal era, exploitation of the island began only in 1859, when Hakodate was opened as one of Japan's first five treaty ports. Major development started after the Meiji Restoration in 1868, but demographic and economic growth really took off after World War II, when millions of Japanese who had colonized Manchuria after its occupation in 1931 were repatriated. Most settled in the south of Hokkaido, particularly in the capital, Sapporo.

Hokkaido's wilderness, still roamed by brown bears, offers thrilling landscapes of forests, mountains, and lakes—the latter often in the calderas of extinct or dormant volcanoes. Many volcanoes are active, and the island's abundant hot springs supply some of Japan's favorite *onsen* resorts. Best known is Noboribetsu Onsen, 72 miles (116 km) south of Sapporo, which lies within Shikotsu-Toya National Park.

NOT TO BE MISSED:

The rugged terrain also makes for great hiking, with long, isolated trails across the Daisetsuzan massif on the center of the island and up the Shiretoko Peninsula, Japan's most remote piece of the great outdoors.

Soya-misaki

6

Hamatombetsu

Horonobe

Esashi

Embetsu

Otoineppu

Omu

Okoppe

Mombetsu

Sea of Okhotsk

Shiretoko-misaki

SHIRETOKO NAT. PARK
1254m ▲ Shiretoko-dake

5

Shumarinai-ko

Nayoro

Yubetsu

Utoro

1661m ▲ Rausu-dake

Rausu

RUSSIA

Shibetsu

Engaru

Abashiri

39

Kitami

Bihoro

Kawayu Onsen

Shibetsu

4

Asahikawa

2290m ◇
Sounkyo Gorge

Asahi-dake

Kussharo-ko

Mashu-ko

Naka-Shibetsu

Nemuro

Fukagawa

39

DAISETSUZAN NATIONAL PARK

AKAN NAT. PARK

Akan-ko

▲ 1371m
O-akan-dake

Takikawa

Ashibetsu

2077m ▲
Tokachi-dake

Onneto-ko

▲ 1499m
Me-akan-dake

Akan Kohan

Bibai

Furano

Ashoro

KUSHIRO-SHITSUGEN NATIONAL PARK

44

Mikasa

Kami Shihoro

Akkeshi

3

Iwamizawa

Yubari

Shimizu

Kushiro

F

Eniwa

Hidaka

Obihiro

38

Atsunai

E

Chitose

Tomakomai

Mombetsu

Taiki

Hiroo

PACIFIC OCEAN

Urakawa

Erimo

2

Erimo-misaki

SHINKANSEN LINES
— Hokkaido

0   50 kilometers
0   25 miles

C

D

Area of map detail

Tokyo

The island's climate is Siberian, with long, cold winters and short, cool summers. Two of Japan's finest ski resorts, Furano and Niseko (see sidebar p. 130), offer winter sports. Many Japanese travel to Sapporo to see the elaborate ice sculptures in Odori Park during February's Snow Festival.

Although Hokkaido has coal, iron ore, electronics, and car industries, it mainly thrives on forestry products and agriculture. Here you'll see Japan's only wheat fields, much fruit growing, and dairy farming; Hokkaido supplies 75 percent of Japan's milk products (and the ice cream is superb!). With rich fishing grounds offshore and plentiful rivers, the island is the country's premier supplier of trout, salmon, crab, scallops, and other seafood. ■

Sapporo & Beyond

The fifth largest city in Japan, Sapporo is dynamic and modern. It is also the gateway to Japan's only true wildernesses. Laid out with the help of American urban planners in 1871, Sapporo is best known for its fresh food, world-famous beer, and lively snow festival. Friendly and cosmopolitan, Sapporo is certainly worth an overnight stop, at the very least as the main transport hub to other parts of the island.

Crossed east to west by **Odori-koen,** a park that cuts a swath of lawns, trees, monuments, and fountains through the center of the city, Sapporo is surprisingly

The Sapporo Snow Festival melts hearts young and old.

green. The park is also the center of the action for the annual **Yuki Matsuri** (Snow Festival; *Feb. 1–12, snowfes.com*). Huge snow and ice sculptures line the park, and a snowman-building area is set aside for kids. Odori is crowned at its eastern end by the 482-foot (147 m) **TV Tower,** offering great night views from its 295-foot (90 m) observation deck (*9 a.m.–10 p.m., $$*). The legacy of the American urban planners is a city that is easy to get around: Sapporo is a city where the streets have no names. Unlike elsewhere in Japan, addresses follow a numbered grid system: The Sapporo railroad station, for instance, is at North 5, West 3.

Sapporo's sights are mainly concentrated in the city center. Among them, about 550 yards (500 m) southwest of the station, are the **Botanical Gardens** (Hokudai Shokubutsu-en), a lovely oasis of green established in 1886. In addition to thousands of varieties of (mainly alpine) plants and trees, both local and imported, the gardens include the **Ainu Museum** (Hoppo Minzoku Shiryoshitsu), displaying historical Ainu crafts and artifacts. Also on the grounds is a museum devoted to local wild-life—alas, of the stuffed variety.

Other buildings surviving from early days are the 1888 **Old Hokkaido Government Building** *(no admission);* when Hokkaido was just beginning to attract mainland settlers, the building was called the Colonization Commission. Built of red brick in the 19th-century neo-Baroque style popular in Meiji-period Japan, it is attractive in its setting of lawns and greenery but less likely to impress visitors used to similar buildings in the West.

Architectural pride is reserved for the **Clock Tower** (Tokei Dai), the symbol of Sapporo and the single most photographed sight in the city. Built of wood in 1878 for Sapporo Agricultural College, it resembles a charming old New England schoolhouse and stands incongruously dwarfed between adjacent towers of concrete, some 440 yards (400 m) south of Sapporo Station.

Sapporo is known as an indoor city; if the crowds appear to thin in winter, you can be sure they're down in the huge underground shopping mall in Susukino or the 0.75-mile (1 km) Tanuki-koji shopping arcade, with shops that have operated there for a hundred years. These areas lie to the south of Odori. The latest addition is the futuristic **Sapporo Factory** *(tel 011/207-5000, 10 a.m.–8 p.m.),* just south of Sapporo Station, a shopping and leisure complex featuring trees, streams, an old redbrick brewery, and other buildings, all within an atrium spanned by the largest glass roof in Japan.

The **Sapporo Beer Museum** *(Biiru Hakubutsukan; N7 E9, Higashi-ku, tel 011/748-1876, www.sapporo-bier-garten.jp, 11 a.m.–7:30 p.m., closed Mon., $, shuttles from Sapporo Station North Gate),* located east of the station, is owned by Hokkaido's most famous brand name and focuses on its 1891 brewery, which has free tours and samples of the brews. The adjacent **beer garden** is a vast restaurant and one of the most popular spots in town.

The local specialty, *jingisukan* (Genghis Khan), is lamb grilled on a convex skillet, named because Mongolian warriors were thought to grill lamb on their round helmets, though this

Sapporo

⚠ 126 B3

Visitor Information

✉ Sapporo Tourist Information Center, Sapporo Station

☎ 011/213-5088

🕐 8:30 a.m.–8 p.m.

sta.or.jp

Botanical Gardens

✉ N3 W8, Chuo-ku

☎ 011/221-0066

🕐 9 a.m.–4 p.m., gardens closed Mon.

💲 $, greenhouse: $

NEED TO KNOW
Reaching Hokkaido
Due to the great distance from Japan's other main centers, flying to Sapporo's New Chitose Airport remains the most popular means of reaching Hokkaido. ANA and Japan's other airlines run several flights due to Hokkaido's popularity as a vacation destination.

Although the Shinkansen now extends as far north as Hakodate, the train is only recommended with the JR Pass, as the trip from Tokyo to Sapporo takes about 8 hours and otherwise costs about as much as a flight.

Getting Around
Train service covers all but the most remote corners of Hokkaido, but service is less common and slower than on Honshu. Buses cover more remote locations, such as national park trailheads, but car rental is popular in this far-flung region.

Historical Village of Hokkaido

✉ 50-1 Konopporo, Atsubetsu-cho, Atsubetsu-ku

☎ 011/898-2692

🕐 9 a.m.–5 p.m., closed Mon. Oct.–April; reserve guides one week in advance

💲 $$

🚌 JR bus from JR Shin Sapporo

kaitaku.or.jp

Otaru

🗺 126 B3

Visitor Information

www.city.otaru.lg.jp

Otaru Museum

✉ 1-3-6 Temiya, Otaru-shi

☎ 0134/33-2523

🕐 9:30 a.m.–5 p.m., closed Tues.; guides available by reservation

💲 $

🚌 20-min. walk from Otaru Station

isn't likely true. The modern, high-tech **Hokkaido Brewery** *(542-1 Toiso Eniwa-shi, 011/748-1876)* is outside town and conducts tours, if you can't get enough beer culture.

The Susukino amusement quarter to the south of the town center counts some 6,000 bars, restaurants, and places of entertainment—from swanky crab restaurants to cabarets in the red-light category. Located due south of Sapporo Station, Susukino's **Ramen Alley** (Ramen Yokocho) is the main rival to Fukuoka's *yatai* (see p. 315) for the best ramen noodles in Japan. This narrow alley of a dozen or so tiny noodle eateries is so popular that you will probably have to wait in line. The noodles with crab are worth the wait, but skip the bowl with the big slab of butter and corn on top.

If you wonder about the Hokkaido of the past, you can visit the **Historical Village of Hokkaido** (Hokkaido Kaitaku-no-mura), just

beyond the eastern boundary of the city. This impressive open-air museum combines some 60 buildings dismantled in Sapporo and other parts of Hokkaido and reerected here. They include Sapporo's old main train station, homes, stores, and businesses, as well as structures from farming and fishing villages. Transport around the 133-acre (54 ha) site is by sleigh in winter and horse-drawn trolley the rest of the year.

Otaru

On the coast west of Sapporo is Otaru, once one of the most vital commercial and fishing ports on Hokkaido and still a ferry terminal. Just 40 minutes from Sapporo by train, this attractive town is now virtually a suburb of its neighbor. You'll find several Western-style buildings dating back to Otaru's Meiji-era heyday, among them the restored Offices of the Nippon Yusen Co., built in 1906 by Satate Shijiro, a pupil of British architect Josiah Conder.

Otaru's most interesting buildings are concentrated east of the city around the port; almost all are **warehouses** dating from the 1890s that have been restored and converted into shopping areas, cafés, and microbreweries. One of these, constructed in the Chinese style in 1893, is the **Otaru Museum** (Otaru-shi Hakubutsukan), displaying facets of local history. Endlessly described as "romantic" in tourist brochures, the 0.8-mile (1.3 km) **Otaru Canal Walk** takes you on a pleasant urban stroll. ∎

EXPERIENCE: Niseko Skiing

About three hours west of Sapporo by bus is Niseko, Japan's best ski resort. Thanks to frosty winds from Siberia, Niseko's four resorts on Mount Annupuri (4,291 feet/1,308 m) have some of the finest, deepest powder in the world—hardly news to Australians, who flock here for the best skiing in Asia. The view of conical Yotei-zan is thrilling, and Niseko offers great après-ski hot springs. The region is also known for rafting and hiking. For information, see *nisekotourism.com* and *niseko.ne.jp*

Shikotsu-Toya National Park

Close to Sapporo, this park of nearly 230 square miles (600 sq km) combines Hokkaido's most beautiful scenery with an abundance of hot springs. The park gets its name from Toya-ko to the southwest and Shikotsu-ko in the east. These lakes are the highlights of the areas that constitute the park's main sections. A third area, north of Toya-ko, centers on the conical Yotei-san, often called Ezo-no-Fuji for its resemblance to its more famous counterpart on Honshu.

Oyunuma Pond, a thermal lake in Noboribetsu

The northernmost ice-free lake on Hokkaido, scenic **Shikotsu-ko** is ringed by volcanic mountains; a paradise for walkers, climbers, and nature lovers in summer, it remains popular year-round with fishermen. Despite being only about an hour from Sapporo, the 30-square-mile (77 sq km) caldera lake is remarkably unspoiled. The gateway is **Shikotsu Kohan,** a village lying in the woods on the lake's eastern shore. Even the *onsen* have remained rustic, with the emphasis on *rotenburo* (outdoor baths). A long soak is the perfect way to finish a good day's hike around the local peaks.

Among the best of many hiking options, **Monbetsu-dake**

Shikotsu-Toya National Park

🗻 126 B3

Visitor Information

✉ 142 Toyako-cho Onsen-machi

☎ 0142/75-2446

🕐 9 a.m.–6 p.m.

🚌 Toyako Onsen bus terminal

laketoya.com

The Ainu

The Ainu were the original inhabitants of Honshu. Light skinned and often wavy haired, they are unrelated to the Japanese; anthropologists believe they are descendants of Caucasians from prehistoric Siberia.

The Korean forebears of the Japanese drove the Ainu in Honshu northward. By the ninth century, the Ainu had been forced into Ezo (today's Hokkaido), then considered by the Japanese to be an icy wasteland. This viewpoint changed in the Meiji period, when rapid growth spurred many Japanese to immigrate to the open lands of Hokkaido to make a new life for themselves, once again bringing them into conflict with the Ainu. Oppression and slavery in medieval Japan gradually morphed into efforts at assimilation: Ainu culture and language were forbidden, and under heavy discrimination the Ainu were forced to adopt the Japanese way of life.

Today the Ainu are thought to number about 24,000. Intermarriage between the Ainu and the Japanese has been so long practiced that recent surveys show only about 200 people left with all four grandparents of pure Ainu descent.

Their culture, which embraces carving and woodcraft, vividly patterned textiles, and epic songs, has no close relatives. The bear features heavily in traditional life: Hunted for its meat and fur, the bear was the most sacred of the spirits, and important ceremonies were held to send this helpful god back to the Eastern Heaven.

The future of Ainu culture is unclear. Tourism has boosted the stature of the Ainu, and the Ainu Museum in Poroto Kotan (see p. 133) has fine exhibits, but the daily dances are a sign of a preserved, rather than vibrant, tradition. A 1997 court ruling recognized their rights, but whether this unique people will make a comeback after centuries of repression is yet to be seen.

Noboribetsu Onsen

126 B3

Visitor Information

60 Noboribetsu Onsen-cho

0143/84-3311

9 a.m.–6 p.m.

Muroran line: Horobetsu

noboribetsu-spa.jp

(2,841 feet/866 m) is closest to the village and easiest to summit (less than two hours). **Eniwa-dake** (4,331 feet/1,320 m) is the hardest: A round-trip hike takes five to six hours and should be abandoned if it rains, as conditions can quickly turn hazardous.

Tarumae-zan (3,415 feet/1,041 m) to the south is the most popular walk—and the most volcanic. It takes about half an hour to reach the summit from Station 7, itself accessible in three hours from Shikotsu Kohan on foot. The alternative is to take a taxi, as there is no bus. Transport around the Shikotsu lake area is at best highly sporadic, so a car comes in handy, though most hotels and youth hostels rent bicycles on a daily basis.

Toya-ko, the smaller of the park's two lakes, has an island right in the center, with an animal population that includes Ezo deer (Hokkaido was formerly called Ezo). The more popular of the two lakes, with an abundance of hot springs all around the shore, Toya-ko draws onsen enthusiasts throughout the year.

Just to the south is the highly active **Usu-zan,** which shouldn't be missed by anyone interested in volcanoes. The latest eruption in spring 2000 caused widespread evacuations of the area.

Check with the local authorities if you plan to visit this area.

Usu-zan is the parent of the volcano known as **Showa Shin-zan** (New Mountain), which first appeared in a farmer's field at the foot of Usu-zan in 1943; it is now nearly 1,320 feet (400 m) high, and growing. Unless informed otherwise, you can safely take a cable car up to an impressive view of the infernal landscape inside Usu-zan's crater rim and beyond the lake to Yotei-san in the distance.

spanning a desolate, evil-smelling landscape belching sulfurous fumes and steam from fissures in discolored rocks, not to mention the poisonous-looking, violently bubbling Oyunuma Pond.

Farther northeast is the coastal town of **Shiraoi,** noted for the reconstructed Ainu village at **Poroto Kotan.** Although the town features performances for tourists, it was set up by the Ainu themselves and boasts a particularly good **Ainu Museum.** ■

**Poroto Kotan
Ainu Museum**

✉ 2-3-4
Wakakusa-cho,
Shiraoi-cho

☎ 0144/82-3914

🕐 8:45 a.m.–5 p.m.

$ $$

🚉 Muroran line:
Shiraoi

ainu-museum.or.jp

INSIDER TIP:

About an hour's drive outside Sapporo, you can luxuriate at Maruoka Hot Springs (marukoma.co.jp) on the shore of Shikotsu-ko. The place is rustic, remote, and simply heavenly.

—DAISUKE UTAGAWA
National Geographic Traveler
contributing editor

Near the park's southern coast is **Noboribetsu Onsen,** which boasts the greatest volume of hot spa water in Japan—11,023 tons (10,000 tonnes) a day—and nine different kinds of spring water to cure whatever ails you.

Monster hotels aside, Noboribetsu does have the advantage of awe-inspiring **Hell Valley** (Jigokudani), with viewing platforms and wooden walkways

A woman sews traditional cloth at Poroto Kotan Ainu Museum.

Hakodate & Beyond

Hakodate, on the Oshima-Hanto Peninsula in the far southwest of Hokkaido, has recently been linked to the mainland by Shinkansen, and it is also one of the most rewarding cities to visit in the prefecture. No other city has quite so many reminders of Meiji- and Taisho-period Japan.

The night view over Hakodate, viewed from Mount Hakodate

Hakodate

🅰 126 B2

Visitor Information

✉ 12-13 Wakamatsu-cho

☎ 0138/23-5440

🕐 9 a.m.–7 p.m.

🚆 JR trains from Aomori (2 hr.) or from Sapporo (3 hr. 30 min.)

hakobura.jp

Though Hakodate is a popular gateway to Hokkaido, many Japanese visitors confine their trips to the Hakodate area alone, which evokes Japan's early exchanges with the West and encapsulates much of the frontier history of the island.

In 1864 the shogunate built **Goryokaku** (Five Corner Fort) to defend this important outpost from foreign aggression. Ironically, it was besieged by Japanese soldiers during the Hakodate War of 1869, when the shogun's troops made a futile last stand against the imperial forces during the Meiji Restoration. The citadel itself, an early attempt at a Western-style fortification, has disappeared, but the curious star shape of the walls is still much in evidence on a hilltop east of the city as the highlight of popular park **Goryokaku-koen.** The moat serves as a boating pond, and the whole star shape becomes a vast floral centerpiece during the cherry blossom season. Adjacent **Goryokaku Tower,** though reminiscent of an air-traffic control tower, is

INSIDER TIP:

For the ultimate view of Hakodate, take the cable car up Hakodate-yama as the sun sets. The twilight vistas from the top are truly stunning.

—DAISUKE UTAGAWA
National Geographic Traveler
contributing editor

worth ascending to appreciate the shape of the citadel.

The city lies on a narrow spit of land, with the sea to the north and south. Beside the town is 1,100-foot (335 m) **Hakodate-yama,** accessible either on foot or by cable car. The view from the top is spectacular. **Motomachi,** the western side of town, occupies part of the slope; it is renowned for buildings from the city's late 19th- and early 20th-century heyday. Most of these structures are open as museums (see pp. 136–137). Old buildings also pepper the area near the waterfront: Warehouses have been preserved and transformed into attractive shopping areas, exhibition spaces, and café-restaurants brewing their own beer. Streetcars are still the city's main form of public transportation; one dating from 1913 is still in service for tourists.

Painted signs and mountains of bright orange king crabs and hairy crabs characterize Hakodate's colorful morning market (*asa ichi*), just south of the railroad station. It comprises some 400 stalls selling fish, seafood, fruit,

and other local produce, both wholesale and retail. Open for breakfast, the local noodle restaurants are famed for their seafood soup dishes. The market opens at 4 a.m. with the sale of fresh catches and closes in the early afternoon, though some stalls remain open for tourists. Some of the wooden buildings in the picturesque alleyways out back look as if they have been around as long as Hakodate itself.

On the eastern side of the city is Yunokawa Onsen spa area; just over half an hour to the north is scenic Onuma Quasi-National Park (see p. 138). Beautiful **Cape Esan-misaki,** about 37 miles (60 km) east of the city, is cherished for two volcanic peaks carpeted with azaleas and alpine plants in late spring and summer. ■

Goryokaku Tower

✉ 43-9 Goryokaku-cho

☎ 0138/51-4785

🕐 8 a.m.–7 p.m. April 21–Oct. 20; 9 a.m.–6 p.m. Oct. 21–April 20

💲 $$

🚋 Streetcar: Goryokaku-koen Mae, then 7-min. walk

goryokaku-tower .co.jp

Hakodate: Gateway to the West

Hakodate city was an unlikely place for a sudden dose of foreign culture, but when Commodore Perry's gunboat diplomacy shattered Japan's seclusion policy (see p. 41), it was agreed in 1854 that two ports be opened for refueling and provisioning American steamboats going to and from China. The naval gateways were Hakodate and Shimoda, near Tokyo. A consul, Townsend Harris, was permitted to live in Shimoda; he convinced Japan to open trade ports lest they be forced open as the British had done in China. Similar treaties with other nations were soon signed, and traders and missionaries swarmed into Hakodate, creating a bewildering mix of foreign cultures. Today the old consulates, residences, and churches are among the city's top sights (see pp. 136–137).

A Walk in Hakodate

Hakodate is a small city. If you have seen the park of Goryokaku-koen and the morning market, you can take this walk around Motomachi and the waterfront area after lunch.

The Russian Orthodox Church in Hakodate

Take the streetcar or bus to **Hakodate Dokku-mae** or take a taxi to the **Foreigners' Cemetery ❶** (Gaikokujin Bochi). If you're coming from the streetcar/bus stop, head southwest up Uomi-zaka, take the right fork, and stay on the same road. The cemetery is on the right, overlooking the bay. A poignant reminder of Hakodate's cosmopolitan history, it contains the graves of Americans (including two of Commodore Perry's sailors, who died on the trip in 1854), British, Chinese, and Russians. From the cemetery, double-back to the first main road, turn right at the school, and turn right again two blocks later, heading uphill to the **Old Russian Consulate ❷**

NOT TO BE MISSED:

Foreigners' Cemetery • Old British Consulate • Old Branch Office of the Hokkaido Government • Russian Orthodox Church

(Kyu Roshia Ryoji-kan), built in 1908 to replace the original of 1858. The redbrick exterior is not imposing, but the interior conveys the atmosphere of the tsarist era.

Next, walk downhill and take the fifth street on the right, at the Bentencho 3 traffic signal, then walk four blocks to reach the brick **Chinese Memorial Hall.** Rebuilt after a fire in 1907, it looks as if it belongs in old Shanghai—which, in a sense, it does. Completed in 1912, it was constructed by builders, carpenters, and sculptors specially brought over from Shanghai, but is no longer open to the public. Head downhill, then turn right at the tram tracks. One block later, you will find yourself before the green Soma Company building, a neoclassical wooden office building of the early Taisho period (1912–1926) that still functions as such. Across the street is the **Hakodate City Museum of Northern Peoples ❸** (tel 0138/22-4128, 9 a.m.–7 p.m., $), which has a good collection of Ainu and Siberian artifacts. The broad avenue going uphill in front of the building leads to the main sights of **Motomachi.** As you walk up, the white building with the blue-trimmed arched windows on your left is the **Old British Consulate ❹** (Kyu Igirisu Ryoji-kan; tel 0138/27-8159, 9 a.m.–7 p.m., $). In service from 1859 to 1934 and now a popular setting for weddings, the consulate contains a museum and a cozy tearoom (with a wax Buckingham Palace guard) construed in Japan as "English-style."

At the top of the avenue is the park of **Motomachi-koen,** dominated by an imposing gray wooden building with an elegant Grecian portico: the **Old Branch Office of the Hokkaido Government ⑤** (Kyu-Hokkaido-cho Hakodate-shicho chosha; *tel 0138/27-3333, 9 a.m.–7 p.m., $*). Built in 1909, it contains a museum of early photography, including what is allegedly the first snapshot ever taken in Japan: Commodore Perry during his trip to Hakodate in 1854. Just behind here is the **Old Public Hall.** This delightful building was built of wood in the colonial style by a Japanese architect in 1910 and has been repainted in grayish mauve with yellow trim around the windows and friezes.

From the top of Motomachi-koen, take the cobbled lane on the left. About 380 yards (350 m) farther on your left, you'll see the candy-box charm of the **Russian Orthodox Church ⑥** (Hakodate Harisutosu-sei Kyokai; *tel 0138/23-7387, 10 a.m.–5 p.m., $*), built in 1916. Almost alongside, on the other side of

---

📷 See area map pp. 126–127
▶ Foreigners' Cemetery
🕓 4 hours
↔ 3.5 miles (5.6 km)
▶ Waterfront

---

the lane, is the 1924 Gothic-style **Roman Catholic Church** (Katorikku Motomachi Kyokai). On the same street lies the **Episcopal Church** (Sei Yohane Kyokai), built by missionaries in 1874 and rebuilt with futurist renovations in 1979. Just east of it is the **Hakodate-yama Cable Car Station** (*tel 0138/23-3105, 10 a.m.– 10 p.m.*), which takes you to the summit for a spectacular view over the city and harbor.

Coming down again after enjoying the vista of the town and port, walk northeast for about 15 minutes toward the **waterfront.** As you reach the road running parallel to the seafront, you'll see to your right a large redbrick building with high rounded arches—the **Hakodate Meiji Hall ⑦** (Hakodate Meijikan; *tel 0138/ 27-7070, 9:30 a.m.–6 p.m.*). A post office until 1955, it has since been converted into a glass studio and shopping precinct. Around back are a number of 19th-century storage buildings, the **Kanemori warehouses,** now converted into stores, exhibition and event spaces, and café-restaurants, including **Bay Hakodate** and **Hakodate History Plaza.** Farther north along the waterfront you'll find the **Hakodate Beer** microbrewery-restaurant, a good place for refreshment after your 3.5-mile (5.6 km) walk. The walk ends at Hakodate Station, but dinner on the waterfront is a perfect way to wind up your tour of the town.

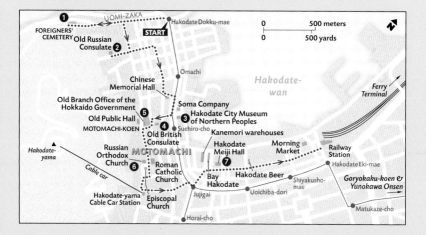

Onuma Quasi-National Park & the South

Located toward the east of the Oshima Peninsula in western Hokkaido, Onuma Quasi-National Park is just north of Hakodate. At the center is 3,717-foot-high (1,133 m) Komaga-take, an active volcano famed for the beauty of its craggy peaks and gentle slopes, which in summer are carpeted with spectacular displays of alpine flowers.

Lake Onuma, with the sharp peak of Mount Komaga-take in the background

Onuma Quasi-National Park

🗻 126 B2

Visitor Information

✉ Beside JR Onuma Koen Station

☎ 0138/67-2170

🕐 8:30 a.m.– 5:30 p.m.

🚉 JR Hakodate line from Hakodate (50 min.) or Super Hokuto Express (20 min.)

Walkers and climbers are rewarded with views south of the mountain over the twin lakes **Onuma,** which gives the park its name, and **Konuma.** Both are outstanding beauty spots. Onuma, whose waters reflect Komaga-take, is dotted with scores of tree-covered islets famed for their spectacular displays of autumnal color. **Lake Konuma** is no less scenic; Ezo deer roam its perimeter, and the lake's three islands are the winter habitat of wild swans.

Renting a bicycle from the train station is the best way to see both of the lakes at your own pace; alternately, climbing Komaga-take will take about two and half hours round-trip, including the demanding bike ride up to the Sixth Station parking lot.

Southwest of the park, near the point of the peninsula joined to Honshu by the Seikan Tunnel, lies **Matsumae.** This is virtually the only place on Hokkaido that retains vestiges of its feudal past. Its castle is a reproduction of the original built in 1854 and destroyed after the feudal era ended in 1868, though the main gate is original. ■

Daisetsuzan National Park & Central Hokkaido

Right in the heart of Hokkaido, Daisetsuzan National Park covers some 890 square miles (2,300 sq km), making it Japan's largest national park. Its backbone is a mountain range known as the "roof of Hokkaido," culminating in 7,513-foot-high (2,290 m) Asahi-dake. The park and its mountains are famed for a massive caldera, rugged, snow-dotted volcanic terrain, and spectacular waterfalls, in addition to the hot springs sprinkled about the foothills.

One excellent area for hiking is the 15-mile (24 km) **Sounkyo Gorge,** with its rich tapestry of color in the fall and lovely waterfalls, some of which cascade 500 feet (150 m) down a sheer drop, in particular over the Obako and Kobako cliffs.

From the massive, steaming caldera of Asahi-dake, it is possible to make a five-day traverse of the range over rolling volcanoes, snowfields, and windswept wastes all the way to **Tokachi-dake.** This passage takes you over several spectacular Ainu-named peaks such as Tomuraushi and Oputateshike. There is a scarcity of huts, which keeps the majority of hikers away and makes this one of the best hikes for nature lovers in all of Japan (note the boil water advisory in the sidebar below).

Below Tokachi-dake lies the town of **Furano**—an area important for its winter sports, scenery, and agriculture. With its excellent snow conditions, Furano often hosts international ski events.

A major producer of grapes, potatoes, beans, asparagus, and other vegetables, the area around the Tokaichi foothills has become popular among Japanese tourists for its vast fields of lavender. These are truly beautiful in full bloom, but a word to the wise: Stay away from the lavender ice cream—some flavors belong in bath soap only. ■

Asahi-dake
🗻 127 C4
Visitor Information
☎ 0166/97-2153
🚌 Bus from JR Asahikawa
www.daisetsuzan.or.jp

Sounkyo Gorge
🗻 127 C4
Visitor Information
☎ 0165/85-3350
🚌 Bus from JR Asahikawa
sounkyo.net

Furano
🗻 127 C4
Visitor Information
✉ JR Furano Station
🚌 Nemuro line: Furano
furanotourism.com

Dangerous Creatures

There is little wildlife to witness in the mountains of Japan, but brown bears do still roam here. If you happen on a bear when you're not hiking in a group, make plenty of noise and back away slowly. Likewise, much ado is made over the *habu,* a poisonous viper, but its bite is rarely fatal; mind your footing and be noisy if you have to bushwhack on Kyushu or the Okinawan Islands. Leeches are a more common pest encountered in some of the damper ranges, but they can be discouraged by rubbing salt into your socks or wearing gaiters. The eggs of *Echinococcus,* a parasitic tapeworm spread by foxes, contaminate some water sources in Hokkaido, but are easy to avoid: Infection can be fatal, but simply boiling water is sufficient to stay safe. Most deadly of all is the *suzume-bachi,* or giant Asian hornet, whose sting kills several dozen people a year. If you hear a mini-helicopter buzz near you, stay cool and don't swat—they usually sting in self-defense.

Rishiri-Rebun-Sarobetsu National Park & the Far North

Up in the far northwest of Japan, this national park comprises the beautiful and hiker-friendly islands of Rishiri and Rebun; on the mainland opposite is the Sarobetsu Plain, a strip of coastal swampland some 21 miles (34 km) long.

The peak of volcanic Rishiri-zan

Rishiri-Rebun-Sarobetsu National Park

🗺 126 B6

Visitor Information

✉ Inside Oshidomari ferry terminal

☎ 0163/82-2201 (Oshidomari ferry)

🕐 8 a.m.–5 p.m.

🚆 Soya line: Wakkanai, then ferry, 105 min., to Rishiri-to or 2 hr. to Rebun-to

Located just to the north of the Sarobetsu Plain, the remote coastal town of **Wakkanai** has a reputation for bleakness. Many Japanese come here just to view the disputed island of Sakhalin (presently in Russian possession) to the north, then continue on to nearby **Soya-misaki**—the cape that is the northernmost point in Japan—just to say that they've been there. As far as the average traveler is concerned, Wakkanai is primarily a jumping-off point for the two

breathtaking islands a short distance from the western coast.

The rounded island of **Rishiri-to** is crowned by a conical volcano often compared to Fuji-san, the magnificent 5,646-foot (1,721 m) **Rishiri-zan.** This is the island's main draw; there are several trails to the summit, including one for serious climbers. None of the routes is especially easy. To ascend and descend Rishiri-zan takes about ten hours, but there are less strenuous walks through lower, greener hills dotted with alpine

Hokkaido's Bears

Hokkaido is home to the Ussuri brown bear (*Ursus arctos lasiotus*). Bears are shy of humans, but can be very dangerous if frightened or hungry. In bear country, travel in a group, and carry a bell to warn bears of your approach. If you spy a cub, don't approach it—the mother is usually close by. Bears have always been sacred to the Ainu—an honor lost on the animals, who were often sacrificed and eaten.

flowers, notably to the scenic **Hime-numa Pond.** The visitor information center at the island ferry terminal in Oshidomari has maps and guides describing the various trails in English, although the staff does not speak English. If you're planning to climb, bring proper clothing, as it can be bitterly cold, with plenty of ice and snow even in high summer. You will also need to carry water, as there is none on the mountain.

If you are not of the mountaineering persuasion, the visitor center rents out bicycles. The single road around the island links various picturesque fishing hamlets with the ports of **Oshidomari** in the north and **Kutsugata** in the west, where there are the largest number of places to stay.

Rebun-to, a narrow, wedge-shape isle some 9 miles (15 km) long, is smaller than Rishiri but more interesting—at the very least for the sheer variety of its scenery.

Famous for carpets of hundreds of varieties of alpine flowers in summer, its rolling hills culminate in 1,607-foot (490 m) **Rebun-dake.** The most popular hiking routes on Rebun run along the west coast, taking in cliffs, remote fishing hamlets, and a striking array of wooded and marine scenery. Details of the trails are available at the hotels and youth hostels on the island, many of which organize hiking parties.

There are two main ports, Kafuka in the south and smaller Funodomari in the north; both offer a range of accommodations, as do the villages of Motochi in the southwest and Shiretoko on the southern tip. Bicycle rental is available from most hotels and

INSIDER TIP:

Take a ferry from Wakkanai port to the island of Rebun-to. From spring to summer, this abounds with alpine flowers, including the indigenous Rebun Atsumori So.

—SHIGEO OTSUKA
Editor in chief
National Geographic Japan

minshuku (guesthouses), and all communities are linked by a bus service. Rebun and Rishiri are at their best from June to September.

Back on the mainland lies the **Sarobetsu Genya Plain,** the remaining area of the park, famous for its summer flowers, especially irises, lilies, and rhododendrons. ∎

Rebun-to
126 B6
Visitor Information
Inside Kafuka ferry terminal
8 a.m.–5 p.m.
www.rebun-island.jp

Going Wild in Hokkaido

Situated at the northernmost extreme of Japan's long string of islands, Hokkaido is a magnet for those who love hiking, birding, skiing, or just being out in nature. In summer, you'll see brown bears, who long ago crossed the frozen ocean from Russia, or spot cunning foxes hunting in carpets of alpine wildflowers. In winter, walk on ice floes, witness white-tailed sea eagles or the mating rituals of red-crested cranes, and, as night descends on this wintry wonderland, enjoy a long, hot soak in an *onsen* as the snow falls.

Hiking through the virgin forests of the Shiretoko Peninsula is a scenically rewarding experience, whatever the season.

Hiking

Hokkaido is a heaven for hikers. Walkers can enjoy blooming tapestries of alpine flowers on Rishiri Island (see pp. 140–141), embark on a five-day trek in Daisetsuzan National Park (see p. 139), or take a three-day hike (60 km) through the Kiritappu wetlands *(contact Kiritappu Ecotours Navi, email: porch1986@almond.ocn.ne.jp)*. The Kiritappu Wetland National Trust also runs boardwalk, boot trekking, flower, mountain-bike, or cross-country skiing ecotours *(tel 153/62-4600, kiritappu.or.jp)*. These are also great ways to spot the area's rare birds (see sidebar p. 143) such as the Eurasian oystercatcher *(Haematopus ostralegus)* and the Chinese egret *(Egretta eulophotes)*.

Water Adventures

Although the main attractions of the region are undoubtedly the volcanically heated waters of its many onsen towns and resorts, the seas of Hokkaido also lure more aquatically adventurous souls. Ice floe walking tours (in buoyant dry suits) are offered for those who want to experience the frozen Sea of Okhotsk firsthand *(Shinra ecotours, tel 0152/22-5522, shinra .or.jp, $$$$; or Shiretoko Shari Tourist Association, tel 0152/22-2125, shiretoko.asia, $$$$)*. Qualified divers can rent wet suits and regulators and discover the frigid underworld beneath the drift ice *(tel 0152/24-2888, email info@iruka-hotel .com, iruka-hotel.com, $$$$$)*.

A great way to see more of the northern seabirds is to take a boat trip out onto any of Hokkaido's three seas. Trawlers can be chartered from the port of Ochiishi *(Ochiishi Nature Cruise c/o Ken's Inn, tel 090/5988-7838, minsyuku-takano.com, or tel 0153/27 2772,*

Hokkaido: land of volcanic mountains, hot springs, and restful, restorative *onsen* resorts

EXPERIENCE: Watch Birds of Japan's North

Apart from the red-crowned crane (*Grus japonensis*; see sidebar p. 147), the Steller's sea eagle (*Haliaeetus pelagicus*; photo below) is the star avian attraction in these parts. The sea eagle is a National Monument of Japan, but for the native Ainu, the Blakiston's Fish Owl is the central creature in their animist belief system and considered the guardian of the village. The woods of Shiretoko Peninsula are pocked from the beakwork of white-backed woodpeckers, and in summer you may spot the Japanese Green Pheasant (Japan's national bird), the Bohemian waxwing, the Eurasian Nuthatch, or the Long-tailed Rosefinch. The Sea of Okhotsk brims with cormorants, and Hokkaido's lakes are graced with balletic processions of whooper swans. Guided tours are available from **Marumi Cruises** (*tel 0153/88-1313, shiretoko-rausu.com*) and **Abashiri Nature Cruise** (*tel 0152/44-5849, abakanko.jp/naturecruise*).

www.ochiishi-cruising.com) to view the natural habitats of Cape Nosappu and the bird-colonized islands of Yururi and Moyururi.

Winter Sports

Hokkaido is one of Asia's great ski destinations, offering long winter seasons when powdery snow lies thick on the pistes, particularly in Niseko (see sidebar p. 130). The Sheraton Hokkaido Kiroro Resort offers package holidays with airport transfers (*tel 011/788-4080, sheraton.com /hokkaidokiroro*), and Daisetsuzan (see p. 139) is dotted with ski areas, such as the Furano Ski Resort (*tel 0167/22-1111, princehotels.co.jp/ski /furano*), host of ten FIS Alpine Ski World Cups.

Those of a gentler disposition might enjoy snowshoe hikes through the Shiretoko's virgin forests: Head to Shiretoko National Park Nature Center and take one of the many trails—the Furepe waterfall trail is especially scenic in winter (*tel 0152/24-2114, center.shiretoko .or.jp, or tel 0152/22-2125, shiretoko.asia*).

Whale-watching

The seas around Shiretoko's World Heritage site are home to pods of orca whales in spring and sperm whales in summer, and many whale-watching tours are offered locally (*tel 0153/87-3360, rausu-shiretoko.com*).

The Northeast: Abashiri & Shiretoko National Park

Shiretoko, literally "world's end," is Japan's most remote locale, a narrow peninsula of true wilderness offering visitors the country's largest remaining population of wildlife, a hot spring waterfall, and rugged hiking in every season.

A family of Sika deer in Shiretoko National Park

Abashiri

🗺 127 D4

Visitor Information

✉ 4-5-1 Minami Sanjohigashi (N of Katsuradai Station)

☎ 0152/44-5849

🕐 9 a.m.–6 p.m.

🚆 Seihoku line: Abashiri, from Sapporo (5.5 hr.)

abakanko.jp

Say "Abashiri" to most Japanese of the baby-boomer generation, and they fondly think back to a prison rather than to the town. It's all due to an early 1970s gangster-movie series that featured tattooed antiheroes in a snowbound maximum-security lockup. Built on **Tento-zan** near the city in 1890, the prison has been moved to new premises, and the old one has been turned into **Abashiri Prison Museum** (Hakubutsukan Abashiri Kangoku; *1-1 Yobito, Abashiri-shi, tel 0152/ 45-2411, kangoku.jp, 8:30 a.m.– 5 p.m., $$$*). Now populated with

wax figures, Japan's Alcatraz is a grim if fascinating reminder of the harsh, chilly conditions endured by prisoners in prewar Japan. Also on Tento-zan is the interesting **Hokkaido Museum of Northern Peoples** (Hoppo Minzoku Hakubutsukan); it provides insights into the Ainu, Siberians, Inuit, and North American First Nations—and the connections among them. Abashiri is also home to the **Okhotsk Ryuhyo Museum** (Okhotsk Ryuhyo-kan; *244-3 Tento-zan, Abashiri-shi, tel 0152/43-5951, 8:30 a.m.–*

6 p.m., $$). With its subzero temperatures and great blocks of ice, it shows summer visitors what they missed of the pack ice in winter. Hardier visitors can try Mombetsu, 56 miles (90 km) northwest of Abashiri, to see the ice floes on the Sea of Okhotsk in midwinter; come February, the sea is frozen to the horizon, and sightseeing excursions are provided aboard an icebreaker.

Above all, Abashiri is the gateway to **Shiretoko National Park,** Japan's only true wilderness, which was granted UNESCO World Heritage site status in 2005. Shiretoko includes peaks and dense forests and occupies the last 30 miles

INSIDER TIP:

Avoid hiking after sunset, when bears are most active on Hokkaido. If you meet one, don't shout or turn your back. Move slowly backward and don't run.

—KENNY LING
National Geographic contributor

(50 km) of a rugged peninsula extending some 45 miles (70 km) into the Sea of Okhotsk. A road runs along the coast to the town of **Utoro** in the west and connects with the small town of **Rausu** in the east. Beyond it, there are no more roads: Fox, deer, and bear roam the last 25 miles (40 km) of the peninsula. The area can be

explored on foot or by sightseeing boat from Utoro (a three- to four-hour trip around the cape).

Some 6 miles (10 km) northeast of Utoro is one of the park's highlights, the **Shiretoko Five Lakes** (Shiretoko-go-ko), where wooden walkways encircle bodies of water in pristine forest crisscrossed by hiking paths. Another 6 miles (10 km) farther on is **Kamuiwakka-no-taki,** a thermal river, the hot waters of which cascade down waterfalls and form natural *onsen* bathing pools. Bring swimwear and shoes with soles for gripping slippery rock; otherwise you will fall prey to vendors waiting to rent out straw sandals at very inflated prices.

Of the many walks within Shiretoko park, the most popular is the ascent of **Rausu-dake** (5,450 feet/1,661 m), the highest peak in the volcanic range at the park's center. Allow up to five hours for the climb. From the peak, you can walk north to **Io-zan** (5,125 feet/1,562 m), the volcano that heats the water at Kamuiwakka-no-taki; the trek to the peak and back takes around eight hours.

Many serious hikers swear by the Shiretoko Iwaobetsu Youth Hostel (*youthhostel.or.jp),* some 3 miles (5 km) north of Utoro, which organizes hiking expeditions. If you're planning to explore the remote tip of the peninsula, traveling in a group is recommended. Bear attacks are rare in Japan, but with 600 or so living on a narrow peninsula, the likelihood of spotting one is high. Hang your food at night and make lots of noise. ∎

Hokkaido Museum of Northern Peoples

✉ 309-1 Azashiomi

☎ 0152/45-3888

🕐 9:30 a.m.– 4:30 p.m. Oct.– June; 9 a.m.– 5 p.m. July–Sept.; closed Mon.

💲 $$

🚌 Bus from JR Abashiri Station to Hoppo Minzoku-Hakubutsukan-Mae stop

hoppohm.org

Shiretoko National Park

🗺 127 E5

Visitor Information

✉ JR Shiretoko-Shari Station

☎ 0152/23-2424

🕐 8:30 a.m.– 5:30 p.m.

🚌 Senmo line: Shari, then bus to Utoro Onsen (50 min.) or Iwaobetsu (40–50 min.)

center.shiretoko.or.jp

Shiretoko Nature Office

Visitor Information

✉ JR Shiretoko-Shari Station

☎ 0152/22-5041

sno.co.jp

Rausu

Visitor Information

☎ 0153/89-2036

kamuiwakka.jp

The East: Akan & Kushiro-Shitsugen National Parks

Southwest of Shiretoko Peninsula, toward the center of the eastern wing of the island of Hokkaido, lies Akan National Park, an idyllic preserve of dense virgin forest, clear lakes, and volcanic mountains. The town of Kushiro (see sidebar p. 147) to the south is the most convenient access point for the parks.

A bevy of swans adorns Akan-ko.

Often regarded as the eastern equivalent of Shikotsu-Toya (see pp. 131–133) and likewise endowed with hot springs, Akan is less accessible and therefore less crowded. The park encompasses three main lakes: Akan in the southwest, Mashu to the east, and Kussharo just north of center. Dotted with small islands and surrounded by forests, **Akan-ko,** with its alpine scenery, is famous for the curious plant balls called *marimo (Aegagropila sauteri)* that form in its water. A species of pondweed growing in a perfectly spherical shape, the marimo can grow up to the size of a soccer ball, but it takes centuries. The **Akan Kohan Eco Museum Center** *(tel 0154/67-4100, 9 a.m.–5 p.m.)* contains displays that explain these strange "special national treasures."

Akan-ko offers a multitude of hot springs, especially in the resort of **Akan Kohan** on the southern shore. It doesn't have much to offer other than a sad Ainu "village" tourist trap, but it's a convenient base for climbing 4,498-foot (1,371 m) **O-Akan-dake.** With its trailhead some 3 miles (5 km) northeast of Akan Kohan, it can be ascended and descended in about six hours. However, the

---

EXPERIENCE: *Tancho*-Watching in the Wetlands

The *tancho* or red-crowned crane *(Grus japonensis)*, a graceful white bird with a spot of red on its head, was for centuries a symbol of longevity until the development of modern Japan almost drove it to extinction. Believed extinct in the early 20th century, a dozen birds were found in the Kushiro Wetlands in 1924 and protected by the government. Following a "Special Natural Monument" designation in 1967, an artificial breeding program was instituted and the tancho population began to rebound, resulting in the 1,200 semi-tame birds now fed in the wetlands.

The **Akan International Crane Center** (*tel 0154/66-4011, 9 a.m.–5 p.m., $, Akan bus from Kushiro Station to Tanchonosato stop*) and the **Onnenai Boardwalk** (*tel 0154/65-2323, Akan bus from*

Kushiro Station to Onnenai Visitor Center) are the most convenient spots to see the cranes, but the best way to experience the wildlife up close is by canoeing deep into the marshy recesses of the wetlands. The **Toro Nature Center** on Toro-ko has English-speaking guides and a broad variety of tours (*dotoinfo.com /naturecenter*), from short explanatory walks to half-day canoe trips down the Kushiro-gawa.

---

most interesting local hike is up **Me-Akan-dake** (4,918 feet/ 1,499 m), which is not only the highest mountain in the park but also one of the most active volcanoes in Japan. Me-Akan has erupted 15 times since 1800, most recently in 1988. There are a number of ways to reach the summit; the most common is via a trailhead at lovely **Onneto-ko,** a lake nestled in the depths of a thick forest. The lake is accessible from Akan Kohan by bus. If you climb Me-Akan, take warm, waterproof clothing, as the weather is notoriously unpredictable. Once you reach the unearthly landscape near the summit, with its discolored ponds and steaming vents, you might find the air a little too sulfurous for comfort.

Mashu-ko is a caldera lake surrounded by sheer cliffs. More

than just an intense shade of blue on a clear day—a rarity, as Mashu is notorious for fog—the exceptionally pure lake water happens to have one of the world's highest transparency ratings, with visibility to a depth of 115 feet (35 m). A good base in the area is the wooded resort of **Kawayu Onsen** to the west of the lake, which is much more pleasant and unspoiled than Akan Kohan. Just south of Kawayu Onsen, another great volcanic hiking opportunity looms in the form of **Io-zan** (Sulfur Mountain). At only 1,680 feet (512 m), it's a less arduous trek than Me-Akan, taking less than an hour. In geothermal terms, however, Io-zan pulls out all the stops: Its fascinating, extraterrestriallooking landscape is alive with bubbling pools and vents belching sulfurous steam.

Akan National Park
🗺 127 D4–E4

Visitor Information
✉ 2-6-20 Akanko Onsen, Akan-cho Kushino-shi (in front of Akan Hotel)
☎ 0154/67-2254
🕐 9 a.m.–6 p.m.
🚌 Akan bus from JR Kushiro Station to Akan Kohan

lake-akan.com

Kawayu Onsen
🗺 127 E4

Visitor Information
✉ 2-3-40 Kawayu Onsen
☎ 0154/83-2670
🕐 9 a.m.–5 p.m.
🚌 Senmo line: Kawayu Onsen, then 10-min. bus to town center

Kushiro-Shitsugen National Park

 127 E3–E4

Visitor Information

✉ Information counter inside JR Kushiro Station

☎ 0154/22-8294

🕐 9 a.m.–5:30 p.m.

🚌 Akan bus from JR Kushiro Station (40 min.)

Kushiro

 127 E3

Visitor Information

www.kushiro
-kankou.or.jp

Kawayu is approximately midway between Mashu-ko and **Kussharo.** The largest lake on Hokkaido, Kussharo-ko has a 35-mile (57 km) circumference. At **Sunayu Onsen** on a beach on its eastern shore, the heat of the underground water rises to warm the sand. If you take a dip in summer, be careful: The lake is renowned for its Nessie relative, the monster Kusshie.

South of Akan National Park is the newer **Kushiro-Shitsugen National Park.** The main attraction here is **Kushiro Wetlands** (Kushiro Marshland Observatory, 6-11 Hokuto, Kushiro-shi, tel 0154/56-2424, 8:30 a.m.–5:30 p.m., $), Japan's largest wetland (75 square miles/200 sq km) and a major bird sanctuary.

The wetlands are a seasonal home to the endangered tancho (Japanese red-crowned crane; see sidebar p. 147); the park acts as their winter habitat. Up to 60 inches (152 cm) tall, these graceful cranes are famous for complex mating dances. Both national parks are reached from the city of **Kushiro,** the industrial hub of eastern Hokkaido. ∎

INSIDER TIP:

Watch carefully for the strange mating dances of the tancho. You won't feel so bad about your own personal dramas once you've seen their bizarre courtship.

—PERRIN LINDELAUF
National Geographic writer

Eco-paparrazzi: Red-crowned cranes or tancho are the stars at Kushiro-Shitsugen National Park.

Tohoku's isolated *onsen* and historic towns, where winters are cold, but the locals are warm

Northern Honshu (Tohoku)

Lantern detail at the Nebuta Festival

Northern Honshu (Tohoku)

Tohoku means "northeast," but when the haiku poet Basho (1655–1694) made his famous journey to the eponymous region at the top of Honshu in 1689, it was just the "deep north." Mountainous, wild, and often bitterly cold in winter, Tohoku was extremely remote in those days. Some of it still remains so.

Like much of the side of Honshu on the Sea of Japan, western Tohoku is known as *yuki guni* (snow country). Tohoku was the last dwelling place of the Ainu people on Honshu before they were driven to Hokkaido about a thousand years ago; until recently, much of it was underdeveloped and desperately poor.

Fast-forward to the present: Two decades of Shinkansen expansion have made Tohoku's major centers accessible, yet the region retains the mystique of the deep north due to a sparse population and limited public transportation.

Those who make the trip will be rewarded with quiet, rustic *onsen*, great hiking, and a handful of historical spots. Northernmost Aomori Prefecture is home to the Shirakami Beech Forest, a World Heritage site, and eerie

Area of map detail

Tokyo

Osore-zan, a sulfurous wasteland believed to be a netherland between here and the hereafter. On the Sea of Japan, Akita Prefecture's claims to fame are the samurai town of Kakunodate, the crater lake Tazawa-ko, and milky-watered Nyuto Onsen. Neighboring Yamagata Prefecture is known for the Dewa Sanzan, a trio of sacred mountains, and skiing in Zao Onsen.

The Pacific side of Tohoku was hit hard by the tsunami that followed the Great East Japan Earthquake of 2011, yet other areas escaped relatively unharmed. Matsushima, with its pine-covered islets, has one of Japan's best views; the islands acted as a breakwater and spared the town. The once magnificent inland city of Hiraizumi retains excellent old temples from its heyday 900 years ago.

The Pacific coastline, however, remains devastated, and the nuclear accident cleanup at the Fukushima reactors is ongoing (see p. 161). Although the danger has now passed, the sight of foreigners coming to visit is still a huge moral boost to the people of this stricken region. ■

NOT TO BE MISSED:

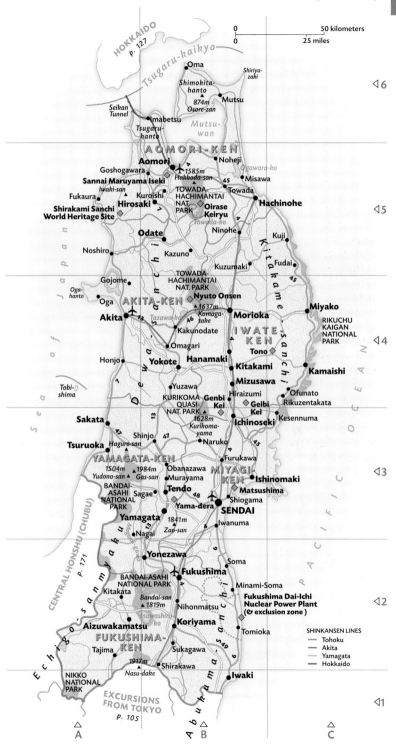

HOKKAIDO
p. 127

Tsugaru-kaikyo

Oma

Shiriya-zaki

Shimokita-hanto

874m
Osore-zan

Mutsu

Seikan Tunnel

Imabetsu

Tsugaru-hanto

Mutsu-wan

AOMORI-KEN

Aomori

Goshogawara

Noheji

Misawa

Ogawara-ko

1585m
Hakkoda-san

Towada

Sannai Maruyama Iseki

Iwaki-san

Fukaura

Kuroishi

TOWADA-HACHIMANTAI NAT. PARK

Hachinohe

Hirosaki

Oirase Keiryu

Shirakami Sanchi World Heritage Site

Towada-ko

Ninohe

Kuji

Odate

Kazuno

Noshiro

Kuzumaki

Fudai

Gojome

TOWADA-HACHIMANTAI NAT. PARK

Oga-hanto

Oga

AKITA-KEN

Nyuto Onsen

Morioka

Miyako

1637m
Komaga-take

RIKUCHU KAIGAN NATIONAL PARK

Akita

Tazawa-ko

IWATE-KEN

Kakunodate

Omagari

Tono

Honjo

Yokote

Hanamaki

Kitakami

Kamaishi

Tobi-shima

Yuzawa

Mizusawa

Hiraizumi

Ofunato

KURIKOMA QUASI-NAT. PARK

Genbi Kei

Geibi Kei

Rikuzentakata

Sakata

1628m
Kurikoma-yama

Ichinoseki

Kesennuma

Tsuruoka

Shinjo

Naruko

Haguro-san

YAMAGATA-KEN

Furukawa

1504m
Yudono-san

1984m
Gas-san

Obanazawa

Murayama

MIYAGI-KEN

Ishinomaki

BANDAI-ASAHI NATIONAL PARK

Sagae

Tendo

Matsushima

Shiogama

Yama-dera

SENDAI

Yamagata

1841m
Zao-san

Iwanuma

Nagai

Yonezawa

Soma

Fukushima

Minami-Soma

BANDAI-ASAHI NATIONAL PARK

Kitakata

Bandai-san
1819m

Nihonmatsu

Fukushima Dai-Ichi Nuclear Power Plant
(& exclusion zone)

Inawashiro-ko

Koriyama

Aizuwakamatsu

Tomioka

FUKUSHIMA-KEN

Tajima

Sukagawa

1917m
Nasu-dake

Shirakawa

Iwaki

NIKKO NATIONAL PARK

EXCURSIONS FROM TOKYO
p. 105

CENTRAL HONSHU (CHUBU)
p. 171

Sea of Japan

Dewa-sanmyaku

Kitakami-sanchi

Ou-sanmyaku

Echigo-sanmyaku

Abukuma-sanchi

PACIFIC OCEAN

0 50 kilometers
0 25 miles

SHINKANSEN LINES
— Tohoku
— Akita
— Yamagata
— Hokkaido

6

5

4

3

2

1

A   B   C

Aomori-ken

Prior to the colonization of Hokkaido in the 19th century, Aomori was the world's end for insular Japan. It's harsh, Siberian winters and great distance from civilization meant that the prefecture was largely spared the overdevelopment that has been the norm in much of Honshu. While it lacks the rich history of other regions, ancient archaeological sites prove that people have lived here since Neolithic times.

Pinwheels entertain the spirits of dead children at Osore-zan, halfway between heaven and hell.

Sannai Maruyama Iseki

🅰 151 B5

✉ 305 Oaza Sannai, Aza-Maruyama, Aomori-shi

☎ 017/766-8282

🕐 9 a.m.–6 p.m.

🚍 Bus from Aomori Station

sannaimaruyama.pref .aomori.jp

Featuring reconstructed Jomon-period (see p. 32) dwellings and open to the public, the most famous sites are in Korekawa, near the town of Hachinohe on the east coast, and especially at **Sannai Maruyama Iseki,** the impressive site of a village 5,000 years old just south of Aomori city. Until the 1970s, Aomori was regarded as a cultural backwater; today it is revered by the Japanese as a nostalgic repository of customs, festivals, and folklore.

Aomori is famous for horses, although much less so than in premodern times; always an agricultural region, it now prospers as a leading national provider of rice, vegetables, and fruit and is a major producer of processed foods. With coastlines on both the Pacific and the Japan Sea, Aomori is renowned for its fish and seafood.

The capital, **Aomori,** lies in the north of the prefecture between Tsugaru-hanto and Shimokita-hanto. Blitzed during World War II, the city is now entirely modern. Nevertheless, this is another of those cities that prove indispensable to travelers exploring a region—in this case, especially those who are going on to Hokkaido.

If you do stop over, take a look at the **Munakata Shiko Memorial Museum of Art** (Munakata Shiko Kinenkan), devoted to the eponymous modern woodblock print master, a native son. Despite Aomori's plentiful hotels and *ryokan,* be warned: The city's accommodations are often fully reserved during holiday periods, especially for Nebuta Matsuri in early August (see sidebar p. 154).

Aomori-ken is divided into three peninsular districts: Shimokita in the northeast, Nambu to the southeast, and Tsugaru in the west.

South of Aomori lies **Towada-ko,** one of Japan's prettiest lakes.

The outlet river, the Oirase-Keiryu, cuts through a forest of beech, painted maple, Mongolian oak, and horse chestnut; although a road closely follows the river, the 9 miles (14 km) of trail along the rapids and falls are pleasant.

Tsugaru-hanto is most famous for the **Shirakami Range,** designated a World Heritage site for its virgin beech forest. Beech once carpeted Japan, but it was considered useless except as firewood: This rare concentration survives due to its remoteness. The complex, multilevel ecosystem is a delight compared with the cedar monoculture that replaced it across the country.

Iwaki-san *(5,330 feet/ 1,625 m, chairlift 9 a.m.–4 p.m., $$, bus from Hirosaki bus terminal)* is Tohoku's Mount Fuji and has excellent views over the Shirakami Range and to the sea. The summit of the volcano is a moderate four-hour hike from the base or an hour round-trip from the top of the chairlift. While not particularly tall, Iwaki towers above its surroundings

Aomori City

🅰 151 B5

Visitor Information

✉ By Aomori Station central exit & 2F Shin-Aomori Station

☎ 017/723-4670 or 017/752-6311

🕐 8:30 a.m.–7 p.m.

🚄 Tohoku Shinkansen from Tokyo (3.5 hr.)

✈ Tokyo (Haneda) to Aomori airport (1 hr. 20 min.)

en-aomori.com

Munakata Shiko Memorial Museum of Art

✉ 2-1-2 Matsubara

☎ 017/777-4567

🕐 9 a.m.–5 p.m., closed Mon.

💲 $

🚌 Bus from Aomori Station (15 min.)

munakatashiko -museum.jp

NEED TO KNOW

Reaching Tohoku

The Tohoku region is primarily served by the JR East Tohoku Shinkansen, which extends from Tokyo through the major cities of Fukushima (1.5 hr.), Sendai (1.5 hr.), Morioka (2 hr.) and Aomori (3 hr.), then on to Hokkaido. "Mini-Shinkansen" branch lines serve Yamagata and Akita Prefectures on the west coast.

The region's airport are largely domestic, with a few connections in East Asia. A flight from west Japan makes sense if you are short on time and don't have a JR Pass.

Getting Around

Tohoku's cities are compact and transit is easy to understand, limited to the JR line, a private subway, and a few bus routes. For more remote locales in the countryside, you'll need to take a bus.

Hirosaki

 151 B5

Visitor Information

✉ 1F JR Hirosaki Station

☎ 0172/26-3600

🕐 8:45 a.m.–6 p.m.

🚃 JR Ou line: Hirosaki

hirosaki-kanko.or.jp

Hirosaki-jo

✉ Hirosaki-koen

☎ 0172/33-8733

🕐 9 a.m.–5 p.m., closed Nov. 24–Mar. 31

💲 $

Osore-zan Bodai-ji

✉ 3-2 Usoriyama, Tanabu, Mutsu-shi

☎ 0175/22-3825

🕐 6 a.m.–6 p.m., closed Nov.–April

💲 $

🚃 Bus from Shimokita Station, Mutsu City (45 min.)

and offers some spectacular 360-degree views.

Iwaki-san looks down on **Hirosaki,** Japan's greatest producer of apples and one of Tohoku's few historical towns. Hirosaki prospered during the Edo period, but nowadays its fame is limited to fruit and 5,000 cherry trees planted about its little castle, **Hirosaki-jo.** The keep, rebuilt smaller after a fire in 1810, fails to impress if you've seen bigger or older ones, but it combines with the **Historical House Preservation Area,** where several 19th-century missionaries lived in Western-style homes, and **Zenrin-gai,** the Zen temple district, for a traditional character little seen in the north. The Hirosaki Cherry Blossom Festival *(April 23–May 5)* is the best time to go, but the town fills up quick, so book ahead.

Shimokita-hanto is known for the weird, strangely twisted

Nebuta Matsuri

In early August, festival-lovers from all over Japan come to Nebuta Matsuri, when thousands of revelers dance in a parade (whose origins are forgotten) featuring colossal illuminated floats. One theory is that the festival commemorates a legendary, ninth-century warrior named Sakanoue-no-Tamuramaro, who led imperial forces to the far north to conquer local tribes. Tamuramaro's successful strategy consisted of placing huge lanterns around the hills at night; when the hapless tribesmen came out to investigate the lanterns, they were captured. The *nebuta,* which represent the lanterns, are gigantic illuminated paper structures colorfully painted with mythical figures.

INSIDER TIP:

The rice paddy art of Inakadate village is a must-see in the Hirosaki area. Every year, villagers create images using rice paddies as their canvas. Behind the village hall, a giant image can be seen in summer and early fall.

—HIROMI ISHII
Senior staff editor
National Geographic Japan

cliff formations along the rocky **Hotoke-ga-ura** coast on its western side, and spooky **Osore-zan** (Mount Dread), a gray volcanic waste believed to be closely connected to the Buddhist conception of both heaven and hell.

Visitors make small piles of stones to the memory of the dead or plant a brightly colored pinwheel among the hissing vents for the spirits of dead children to play with while waiting for their parents to join them in the afterlife. Large crows feast upon the offerings, and their calls add to an already eerie atmosphere.

The nearby lake and surrounding mountains represent Buddhist heaven in a geographic cosmology also seen at Tateyama (see p. 189). In **Osore-zan Bodai-ji,** the main temple adjacent to the wastes, the living line up patiently for hours to speak to an *itako,* a blind female medium, who can facilitate contact with relatives in the afterlife. ∎

Akita-ken

Akita lies along the Japan Sea south of Aomori, hemmed in by mountains to the north, east, and south and 70 percent forested. Skiing, hiking, and *onsen* draw many to the mountains, and the crater lake Tazawa-ko, deepest in Japan, is a favorite summer spot. Kakunodate retains one of the best extant samurai districts, and Nyuto Onsen offers a rare mixed bathing experience.

Winters are cold and snow-bound on Akita's higher ground, but the plain on the milder seaward side is subject to the high rainfall common to much of the west coast of Japan. There can be seasonal extremes of temperature; situated halfway down on the coastal side, the prefectural capital of Akita city records temperatures dropping to 14°F (−10°C) in winter and soaring to 93°F (34°C) in summer. Particularly lush, the agricultural lowlands take in productive rice-growing districts, some yielding the highest quality crop in the country.

Archaeological finds have shown that the region was inhabited at least 20,000 years ago, probably by tribes related to the Ainu (see sidebar p. 132). The army of the Yamato court took Akita in 658 and drove the Ainu ever farther north; Akita City grew out of a permanent garrison established in the eighth century. In 1602, the year before he founded the national government that would last for centuries, shogun Tokugawa Ieyasu appointed the Satake clan as the first lords of Akita. The Satake later moved to Kakunodate, and until the fall of the shogunate in 1867, rule of the province was shared by families who collectively constituted the Akita clan.

The Nishimonai Bon Odori, an annual dance to honor deceased ancestors

The city of **Akita** is an excellent base for touring the region. Except for the ruins of the foundations and a recent reconstruction of a lookout tower—both in **Senshu-koen**—nothing remains

Akita
◪ 151 A4
Visitor Information
☎ 018/832-7941
🕐 9 a.m.–5 p.m.
www.city.akita.akita.jp

Masakichi Hirano Museum of Fine Art

- ✉ 1-4-2 Nakadori, Akita-shi
- ☎ 018/833-5809
- 🕐 10 a.m.–6 p.m.
- 💲 $
- 🚶 10-min. walk from Akita Station

Tazawa-ko

- 🗺 151 B4

Visitor Information

- ✉ JR Tazawako Station
- ☎ 0187/43-2111
- 🕐 8:30 a.m.– 5:30 p.m.
- 🚉 Akita Shinkansen: Tazawako (3 hr. from Tokyo)

Nyuto Onsen

- 🗺 151 B4

Visitor Information

- 🚌 Bus from Tazawako Station (40 min.)

nyuto-onsenkyo.com

of Satake-jo or the old town. But in August the city comes into its own with the colorful **Akita Kanto Festival** (August 3–6, www .kantou.gr.jp), when crowds arrive for the spectacle. The parade features some 200 men using their foreheads, hips, shoulders, and palms to balance clusters of lighted paper lanterns atop tall, thick bamboo poles. The poles, each bearing 20 lanterns, weigh about 110 pounds (50 kg) apiece. The **Masakichi Hirano Museum of Fine Art,** meanwhile, features "Events of Akita," said to be the world's largest painting.

At 1,394 feet (425 m), **Tazawa-ko** is the deepest lake in Japan. It is renowned for the views of the surrounding peaks, notably Komaga-take, and their reflections in the intense blue of its crystal clear water. The Tazawa-ko area has several nearby ski resorts but lures visitors year-round. A favorite with Japanese vacationers, the lake can be chockablock with swimmers, rented rowboats, and pleasure boats in high summer; choose off-peak periods to make the most of its great scenery. You can tour its 12-mile (20 km) circumference by bus, but the most pleasant way is to rent a bicycle from one of the outlets on either side of the Tazawa-kohan bus terminal. The area has plenty of accommodations in all categories, including campgrounds.

If you like walking, buses from Tazawa-kohan take 50 minutes to reach Komagatake-Hachigome. From there, it is just over an hour's walk to the summit of

INSIDER TIP:

The Japanese expression regarding mixed-bath etiquette is "don't show off and don't stare." Strutting about brazenly is as bad as being goggle-eyed. Be cool!

—PERRIN LINDELAUF
National Geographic writer

Komaga-take (5,369 feet/ 1,637 m), the starting point for several hiking trails through fine alpine scenery. If you have the stamina, one option is to make a day's trek north over Eboshi-dake and then down to the group of remote baths at **Nyuto Onsen.**

From Akita, Eboshi-dake is actually called Nyuto-san—Mount Nipple—because its peak appears suggestively pointed. The cluster of onsen dubbed "Nipple Hot Springs" are famous for their milky waters and rustic charm, with the oldest of the resorts, **Tsurunoyu** (*50 Kokuyurin Senda tsuizawa Tazawa Aza, Senboku-shi, Akita-ken, tel 0187/46-2139, 7 a.m.–10 p.m., tsurunoyu.com*), going back 350 years. If the region's name isn't sufficiently suggestive, Tsurunoyu is one of the few onsen in Japan with mixed bathing. There are segregated indoor baths and one *rotenburo* (outdoor bath) for women only, but the main rotenburo is the full monty, nothing but a hand towel and the opaque water for modesty. The social aspect of families and couples chatting together is relaxing, but even the savvy traveler may experience a certain terror when a large group of chatty, opposite-sex old-timers piles into the bath.

Around 15 minutes west of Tazawa-ko is **Kakunodate,** the prefecture's most famous town. Between late April and early May, thousands go there to see the fantastic tunnels of blossoming cherry trees planted along a one-mile (1.5 km) stretch of the **Hinokinai-gawa.** But the trees, river. All that remains of the castle is the hill upon which it stood; the original town center, which lay to the north of it, has vanished. The new town, still divided into a northern samurai quarter and a southern quarter for merchants, contains a substantial number of old wooden houses. The most impressive are concentrated in the **Buke-yashiki,** the unmissable old samurai quarter.

The houses stand behind wooden walls and stately gateways on a long avenue flanked

Kakunodate
 151 B4

Visitor Information

✉ Kakunodate Station

☎ 0187/54-2700

🕐 9 a.m.–6 p.m., to 5:30 p.m. in winter

🚄 Akita Shinkansen: Kakunodate (3 hr. 20 min. from Tokyo)

kakunodate-kanko.jp

The author and a friend enjoy the milky waters of Nyuto Onsen.

planted as recently as 1934, are a recent complement to some substantial historical attractions. Founded as a castle town in 1620 by Akita clan lord Ashina Yoshi-katsu, Kakunodate succumbed to fires over the years. However, it was flooding that determined its relocation farther south along the by weeping cherries, many of them planted 300 years ago. Although most of the houses are privately owned, six of them—Kawarada, Aoyagi, Odano, Iwahashi, Ishiguro, and Matsu-moto—are open to the public. The houses date from the twilight of the samurai in the early to

Aoyagi Samurai Manor Museum

✉ 3 Omotemachi Shimocho, Kakunodatemachi, Senboku-shi

☎ 0187/54-3257

🕐 9 a.m.–5 p.m.

💲 $

samuraiworld.com

Ishiguro Samurai House

✉ 1 Omotemachi Shimocho, Kakunodatemachi, Senboku-shi

☎ 0187/55-1496

🕐 8:30 a.m.–5 p.m.

💲 $

Kaba Craft Denshokan Museum

✉ 10-1 Omotemachi Shimocho, Kakunodatemachi, Senboku-shi

☎ 0187/54-1700

🕐 9 a.m.–5 p.m.

💲 $

mid-19th century. These buildings are mainly modest rather than grand and feature charming gardens; some display collections of heirlooms and memorabilia ranging from samurai relics to Western appliances.

The **Aoyagi Samurai Manor Museum** is the most touristy, as the owners have developed five of the buildings in their compound into little exhibits on samurai life. The quality here varies widely: The armory has an impressive collection of swords, rifles, and armor, but the folk craft museum is one of many such exhibits across Japan, and the Haikara-kan, devoted to 19th-century imported Western culture, is unlikely to impress foreign visitors.

The **Ishiguro Samurai House,** on the other hand, is still the residence of the Ishiguro family, once important retainers for the local feudal lords. The house is broader and more aristocratic, with multiple gates for visitors of varying importance and two huge earthen-walled

storehouses in the back, now used for exhibits of the family's heirlooms. The smiling ladies at the souvenir stands are real-life samurai descendants, too.

With cherry blossom viewing a prime attraction, it is perhaps not surprising that the wood and bark of the cherry are the materials of choice for Kakunodate's attractive local handicrafts. The place to trace the historical development and to see the finest examples of *kabazaiku* (cherry bark craft) is **Kaba Craft Denshokan Museum.** Working in one of the museum rooms, an in-house artisan is always happy to demonstrate his craft.

The museum is otherwise devoted to antiques, including armor, clothing, lacquerware, and old and new examples of Kakunodate's recently revived Shiraiwa pottery. This is distinguished by its earthen hues, with subtle, semi-transparent overglazes in lighter colors. There is a sales area offering quality local crafts at prices comparing favorably with the town's specialty stores. ■

Matsuo Basho (1644–1694)

Japanese poetry packs rich imagery and emotional power into few words. As the Zen influence gained ground from the 14th century on, the concept of "less is more" pervaded. Epitomizing this is haiku—an evocative, often elegiac verse form in which the 31 syllables of classical *tanka* poetry (the main poetic form from the 9th to 13th centuries) were slashed to 17. Of all haiku exponents, none is so revered as Basho. Born a samurai, Basho

turned to poetry when his lord died, distinguishing himself with the new haiku form. He habitually roamed the country for months on end, interspersing his travel diaries with haiku masterpieces. *The Narrow Road to the Far North*, recording a journey through Tohoku in 1689, is considered his greatest work. Frail and prematurely aged, Basho died on the road, succumbing to food poisoning at an inn on his way to Kyushu.

Sendai & Matsushima

Tohoku's largest city, Sendai, is the capital of Miyagi-ken and a popular base for visiting Matsu-shima Bay, which, along with Miyajima (see pp. 286–288) and Amanohashidate (Kyoto Prefec-ture), is one of the "three great views" of Japan. Since the Great East Japan Earthquake of 2011, Sendai has become a major center for reconstruction and refugees from the coast.

Sendai

The warlord Date Masamune built **Aoba-jo** in 1602. The castle was ruined long ago, but its foundations still lie in the city park *(1 Kawauchi, Aoba-ku, 022/227-7077, 9 a.m.–5 p.m., museum $$)*. Other vestiges of the Date legacy were obliter-ated with most of Sendai dur-ing World War II. Along with the usual covered shopping arcades and a lively street mar-ket, Sendai has attractive tree-lined boulevards and is home to Kokubuncho, Tohoku's larg-est nightlife district.

Two buildings that miracu-lously survived the war are the Date family mausoleum, the 16th-century **Memorial Hall** (Zuihoden; *23-2 Otamayashita, Aoba-ku, tel 022/262-6250, zuihoden.com, 9 a.m.–4:50 p.m., $$)*, and the ornate **Osaki Hachiman-gu** *(4-6-1 Hachiman, Aoba-ku, tel 022/234-3606, oosaki-hachiman.or.jp/pop)*, built in 1607. The surrounding hills boast hiking trails and hot springs, as well as beautiful scen-ery in the gorges of Futakuchi and Raira-kyo and especially near the town of **Naruko,** renowned for its curative spas. Near Sendai, too, is the 180-foot (55 m) **Akiu Otaki,** among Japan's most spectacular waterfalls.

Southeastern Sendai, including the airport, was completely inun-dated during the 2011 tsunami, and parts of the town of Natori were wiped off the map. To get a sense of the damage, take the airport train to the penultimate station, Mitazono, and walk north-east through the barren fields until you hit the concrete foundations of what were once coastal homes.

Sendai

📍 151 B3

Visitor Information

✉ Sendai Station

☎ 022/222-4069

🕐 8:30 a.m.–7 p.m.

🚄 Tohoku Shinkansen: Sendai

The drama of the Matsushima landscape

Matsushima

🅰 151 B3

Visitor Information

✉ 5-min. walk from Matsushima-kaigan Station

☎ 022/354-2263

🕐 9:30 a.m.– 4:30 p.m.

matsushima-kanko .com

Matsushima Bay Cruise

☎ 022/365-3611

💲 $$$

🕐 10 a.m.–3 p.m., 50-min. cruises hourly

Kanran-tei

✉ 56 Chonai, Aza, Matsushima

☎ 022/353-3355

🕐 8:30 a.m.–5 p.m., until 4:30 p.m. in winter

💲 $

Zuigan-ji

✉ 91 Chonai, Aza, Matsushima (7-min. walk from Matsushima-kaigan Station)

☎ 022/354-2023

🕐 8 a.m.–5 p.m., until 3:30 p.m. in winter

💲 $$

Entsu-in

✉ 67 Machiuchi, Aza, Matsushima

☎ 022/354-3206

🕐 8:30 a.m.–5 p.m.

💲 $

Matsushima

Basho, the traveler-poet (see sidebar p. 158), was said to be so struck by the beauty of **Matsushima Bay** that he penned the immortal lines: "Matsushima ya! / Ah-ah Matsushima ya! / Matsushima ya!" Although the haiku may be a joke attributed to him, the bay is still breathtaking.

The panorama inspired the very place-name: *Matsushima* means "pine island." With some 200 pine-covered islets sprinkled about a sweeping bay, the view is lovely. Although it can be crowded, the promenade makes for a pleasant stroll, and a long red footbridge ($) links the coast to Fukuura-jima, one of the larger islands, which has been partially tamed into a pleasant park. Regular cruise boats head out into the bay, passing among the stony islands and their stubborn, storm-bent pines. The town owes both its livelihood and its existence to these islands: Forming a natural breakwater, they held back the tsunami when other towns with massive, man-made breakwaters were completely overwhelmed.

Temples & Treasures

Standing on an islet connected to the promenade by a short bridge is **Godai-do.** This curious little temple was built in the ninth century and rebuilt in 1600 by Date Masamune. The interior is opened only three times a century, but you can view the fine carvings of zodiac animals at the top of the pillars. Flanked by pines, Godai-do complements the view over the sea.

West of Godai-do is **Kanran-tei,** the "water-viewing" pavilion. Once a teahouse at the castle of warlord Toyotomi Hideyoshi in Kyoto, it was presented to Date Masamune and moved here, to a cliff-top site, in the late 16th century. Used as a moon-viewing pavilion by generations of Date lords, it contains a small museum exhibiting Date memorabilia.

The beauty of **Zuigan-ji** is a fitting counterpart to the panorama on the bay, near which it lies. Founded in 828 by the Tendai sect, Zuigan-ji became a Zen temple during the 13th century. It declined during the Era of Civil War (1467–1603) but was restored in 1604 by Date Masamune. The Hondo is most notable for carved doors and bright, gold-leaf paintings on sliding screen doors. The paintings are reproductions, but the originals are on display in the adjacent **Seiryuden Treasure Museum,** along with Buddhist art and statues of the Date family and notable monks.

Outside the temple, rows of **hermitages** have been carved into a solid wall of rock. Many contain images of the Buddha, hewn from the stone. It is said that acolytes had to carve their way in and spend time meditating inside—an arduous path to Enlightenment!

The temple precinct of **Entsu-in,** just next door to Zuigan-ji, contains the mausoleum of Date Masamune's grandson Mitsumune, set in a quiet glade of cedars. It has a lovely garden, mostly devoted to a flower not usually found in Japanese gardens—the rose. ■

The Great East Japan Earthquake & Tsunami of 2011

At 2:46 p.m., March 11, 2011, the Great East Japan Earthquake, a 9.0-magnitude megathrust, struck the eastern coastline of Tohoku. The earthquake was the fourth most powerful in a century of records, creating a tsunami up to 45 feet (15 m) high that washed fishing villages out of isolated coves, poured deep inland over flat farmland, and triggered a nuclear meltdown.

As survivors watched the tsunami from high ground, the most enduring problem had already begun: The backup cooling system for Tokyo Electric's (TEPCO) Fukushima nuclear reactors, placed close to the shore to save money, was knocked offline, resulting in a meltdown of their fuel rods. Initially denying that there was any danger, the government and TEPCO failed to quickly evacuate much of the surrounding area, even as a plume of radioactive cesium was contaminating it. The radiation panic that ensued crippled the economy, spawned a food scare, and drove away tourists, although most of the country registered only a minuscule increase in background radiation.

While the government floundered and the utility cited a tsunami "outside imagination" to evade criminal negligence, the Japanese themselves were picking up the pieces. Massive volunteer efforts ran overloaded shelters, and the survivors displayed a patient, orderly perseverance that amazed the world. Five years after the disaster, 100,000 of Tohoku's evacuees remain in temporary housing. The debris of their former lives has been sorted into piles waiting for disposal, and the reactors, though heavily damaged, have been stabilized. Although radiation in the worst areas has fallen significantly, many refugees are suspicious of government assurances that the present levels are safe. Refugee life has also taken its toll: 1,607 died from initially-sustained injuries, but an equal number have died from stress-related problems, including suicide.

The 45-foot (13.7 m) high tsunami inundated coastal towns and drowned thousands.

Silver Lining

The massive power restrictions in 2011 during the nationwide reactor safety checks gave Japan a strong impetus to go green. Energy-conservation is popular, and the private use of solar power is growing. The people have rallied against the future use of nuclear power, so politicians have begun to talk of 20 percent renewable energy to reduce nuclear dependency.

Both government and independent watchdogs are closely monitoring radiation levels in the air and food of hardest-hit Fukushima Prefecture. Although the situation has improved, Tohoku is still struggling. Many of the young have left permanently, and the economy has limped. More than anything, Tohoku's people need moral support. Only an upswing in visitors to the region will provide the reassurance that they have not been forgotten.

Iwate-ken

Long known as the "deep east" for its remoteness, Iwate is second only to Hokkaido in size and low population density. Its main historic claim to fame is the old town of Hiraizumi, where the hero Minamoto Yoshitsune met his death. Today Hiraizumi is just a small town, but some of the relics from its glorious past are among the most impressive in Japan.

Boating in Geibi-kei Gorge

Morioka, Iwate's prefectural capital, is publicized as a "castle town" (the castle was destroyed during the 1870s) and even as "Little Kyoto." But short of a pleasant riverbank, green spaces, and the occasional district with a few mid-19th- to early 20th-century vestiges, the city's sole attraction is the *wanko soba* "experience" (see sidebar p. 164). It is a congenial place nevertheless, and as a station on the Tohoku Shinkansen from Tokyo, it makes a handy stop-over for visiting the prefecture. Taking in all the sights would require an overnight stay, but visiting Chuson-ji and Motsu-ji takes about four hours.

Iwate-ken has plenty of unspoiled space with plenty of fine scenery, especially in the national parks. There is **Rikuchu Kaigan National Park** to the east, with its stark seascapes of rocky coves and 650-foot (200 m) cliffs, and **Towada Hachimantai National Park** *(bus from Morioka Station to Hachimantai Chojo, 2 hr.)* to the west. In addition to being another nucleus of hot springs, Hachimantai is renowned for its scenery, as well as for the option of skiing until June, notably cross-country through forests. To the south is **Kurikoma Quasi-National Park,** where the alpine scenery is truly spectacular when aflame with colors in the autumn. Kurikoma lies near Ichinoseki, the transfer point for the town of Hiraizumi.

West of coastal Kamaishi is the quiet town of **Tono,** famed as Japan's superstition capital due to folklorist Yanagita Kunio's *The Legends of Tono* (1912). Based on interviews with a Tono man who had memorized a hundred local folktales, the still-popular book features creatures such as *kappa* water imps and shape-shifting foxes. Tono's L-shaped *magariya* thatched farmhouses derived their unique shape from having stables directly attached to the homes to protect horses, a major product of the region, through the frigid winters: Folk village **Tono Furusato Mura** features several of them. Tono is also a good choice for countryside bicycling or hiking amid its outlying rice paddies and hills.

Visiting Hiraizumi

The main avenues of modern **Hiraizumi,** unusually broad for a small rural town, faintly echo the layout of an ancient Sino-Japanese city. Hiraizumi has a strangely melancholy atmosphere; you become eerily aware of a lost city beneath your feet—underlined by such discoveries as the foundations of a 12th-century settlement when a private house was redeveloped in 1998.

Once consisting of no more than a remote garrison and two temples, Hiraizumi grew into a city of 100,000 people—the jewel of the northeast—when Fujiwara

Kiyohira turned it into a regional capital in the early 12th century. Mining gold, producing silk, and breeding horses, Hiraizumi rivaled even Kyoto in opulence for more than a century. The northeastern Fujiwara dynasty held the city until, greedy for gold and horses, Minamoto Yoritomo's troops invaded in 1189.

INSIDER TIP:

If visiting Tono in early August, be sure to join in the lighthearted fun of the Manuke-bushi Festival, a comical costumed dance on the streets of the town.

—JUSTIN KAVANAGH
National Geographic Travel Books editor

Hiraizumi declined rapidly and suffered a number of fires over the centuries, becoming no more than a backwater with an illustrious past.

Hiraizumi's finest attraction is the splendid hilltop precinct of **Chuson-ji.** Founded in 850, Chuson-ji was greatly enlarged by Fujiwara Kiyohira, who built 40 halls during the 1120s. Including monks' quarters, the precinct counted 300 structures, but nearly all were destroyed during a fire in 1337. Current buildings date mostly from the late Edo period, including a fine **Noh stage** built in 1853. All that remains of the original temple is the **Sutra Hall** (Kyozo) and the breathtaking

Morioka
 151 B4

Visitor Information

✉ JR Morioka Station

☎ 019/625-2090

🕐 9 a.m.–5:30 p.m.

🚃 Tohoku Shinkansen: Morioka (2.5 hr. from Tokyo).

Tono
151 C4

Visitor Information

✉ Outside JR Tono Station

☎ 0198/62-1333

🕐 8 a.m.–7 p.m.

🚃 JR Kamaishi line: Tono

tonojikan.jp

Tono Furusato Mura

✉ 5-89-1 Kamitsukimoshi, Tsukimoshi-cho, Tono-shi

☎ 0198/64-2300

🕐 9 a.m.–4 p.m.

💲 $$

🚃 Bus from Tono Station (25 min.)

Hiraizumi
151 B4

Visitor Information

✉ Outside Hiraizumi Station

☎ 0191/46-2110

🕐 8:30 a.m.–5 p.m.

🚃 JR Tohoku Honsen line: Hiraizumi

hiraizumi.or.jp

EXPERIENCE: The *Wanko Soba* Eating Contest

Morioka's culinary claim to fame is *wanko soba*: buckwheat noodles in little cups. History tells us that a local lord seemed to enjoy his noodles more when cut up and served by the mouthful, although he likely never imagined that wanko soba would morph into the intense eating competition it is today.

Having paid ($$$), you are informed by your waitress that (a) a normal soba serving is equivalent to 15 cups, (b) the average for a man is 50, and (c) the day's record is probably somewhere between 140 and 165.

You lift your bowl up to the waitress standing by, and she dumps another cup's worth into your bowl. You then sprinkle it with various little toppings or wolf it down and ask for another. The waitresses, mostly sadistic elderly ladies, eagerly push the noodles upon those willing to compete, with admonishments such as "go go go!" "You can do it!" and "You're a man, you can't be full yet!"

Depending on the restaurant, you may have to slam the lid down on top of the bowl to prevent your waitress from giving you more noodles. The noodles themselves range from typical to fairly tasty, but the main point is the lively atmosphere of several tables engaged in noodle death matches and the prospect of facing off against a friend.

To test your will and your stomach in the wanko soba eating contest, visit **Azumaya** (1-8-3 Naka-No-Hashi-Dori, Morioka-shi, tel 019/622-2252, wankosoba -azumaya.co.jp).

Chuson-ji

- ✉ 202 Koromoseki, Hiraizumi-cho
- ☎ 0191/46-2211
- 🕐 8:30 a.m.–5 p.m.
- 💲 $$
- 🚶 20-min. walk from Hiraizumi Station

Motsu-ji

- ✉ 58 Osawa, Hiraizumi-cho
- ☎ 0191/46-2331
- 🕐 8:30 a.m.–4:30 p.m.
- 💲 $$
- 🚶 7-min. walk from Hiraizumi Station

motsuji.or.jp

Golden Hall (Konjiki-do), commissioned in 1124. Housed within a large protective concrete building, this tiny hall is one of the greatest National Treasures. Intricately carved, inlaid with mother-of-pearl, lacquered, and gilded, it enshrines altars graced with outstanding golden Buddhist carvings. Beneath them lie the mummified bodies of Fujiwara Kiyohira and three of his descendants. Much like Kyoto's Kinkaku-ji (see p. 216), the Konjiki-do was restored to its original blazing golden brightness in the 1960s. Still, many people find the sheen gaudy and prefer the haunting beauty of the weathered patina that the original structure had gained over 800 years. Painted in gold on indigo paper, some of the 5,300 illustrated sutras formerly in the Kyozo are now in the nearby **Treasure Hall** (Sankozo). Also containing several sculptures designated as National Treasures, the Sankozo holds such a wealth of temple relics and Heian-period artifacts that a new annex was built to accommodate them in 1999.

Elevation & Poetry

Chuson-ji precinct stands atop a hill with splendid views over the surrounding plain. The approach is through a magnificent grove of tall cedars, but the slope is pretty steep. You can stop at the tiny Edo-period shrine dedicated to Yoshitsune on the way up and refresh yourself in an old thatched farmhouse charmingly converted into a café.

Motsu-ji, founded in the mid-9th century, was the largest temple in northern Japan during the 12th century. Declining along with the rest of Hiraizumi, its several pagodas, 40 halls, and 500 monastic dwellings all burned down in several fires. Built in 1989, the present **main hall** is an uninspiring emulation of the Heian-period style; the precinct's only really old building is the 17th-century **Jogyo-do** hall. Archaeologists uncovered the foundation stones of several original buildings in the late 1960s, and later excavation revealed the rocks constituting the artificial watercourses and pond of a lost **garden.** Now beautifully restored, it is the only complete extant example of a Heian-period Jodo (Pure Land) sect garden, landscaped in emulation of Buddhist paradise. The precinct also includes an iris garden containing 300 varieties; visitors come from all over Japan to see the flowers between mid-June and mid-July. On the fourth Sunday in May, the Gokusui-no-en (Floating Poetry Festival) finds contestants in Heian-period garb floating cups of saké down the garden's stream. The objective is to compose a poem before your cup reaches the end—a garden-party game now 900 years old.

East of Hiraizumi is scenic farmland and the **Geibi-kei,** a deep river gorge with 330-foot-high (100 m) cliffs on either side, especially scenic in the fall when the trees burst into a blaze of color on all sides. While the boatmen's patter mainly consists of corny "dad-jokes," the traditional songs they render in the perfect acoustics of the narrow gorge make a boat ride here a hauntingly beautiful experience. ■

Geibi-kei Boat Trip

☎ 0191/47-2341
🕐 8:30 a.m.–4:30 p.m., 90-min. cruises, 10 times daily
💲 $$$
🚶 5-min. walk from Geibi-kei Station

The plates pile up as the competition intensifies in the *wanko soba* eating contest.

Yamagata-ken

Yamagata-ken embraces the southwestern boundary of Tohoku. It is a prime agricultural region—in the 30 percent of it that is not mountain and forest. Yamagata's climate varies as much as its topography; ski resorts remain open on Gas-san in high summer, when temperatures on the plain can reach record highs for Japan. Out of the four million annual tourists here, most come to ski resorts, leaving much of the prefecture refreshingly unspoiled.

A tiny subtemple perches cliffside at Yama-dera.

Yamagata City
🅰 151 B3
Visitor Information
✉ JR Yamagata Station
☎ 023/647-2266
🕐 9 a.m.–5:30 p.m.
🚄 JR Yamagata Shinkansen from Tokyo to Yamagata Station (2 hr. 50 min.)

data.yamagata kanko.com/english

A boon for both farming and tourism, the Mogami-gawa and its tributaries flow from the southwest to the northwest. Near the town of Sakata, tour boats ply the spectacular **Mogami Gorge—**the appeal lying as much in the folk-singing skills of the boatmen as in the scenic beauty of the steep cliffs flanking the river. Yamagata thrives in winter, with ski hills on nearly all its mountains and

at least one *onsen* (hot spring) in every village. Well known for both, **Zao-san** in the southeast also attracts walkers and nature lovers year-round with its fine alpine scenery. Undamaged in World War II, Yamagata's towns suffered from Japan's ubiquitous postwar architectural brutalism; though convenient as bases for regional exploration, they retain precious few sights.

The prefectural capital city,

Yamagata, is a convenient base, especially for winter sports on Zao-san and for visiting **Yama-dera** (also called Risshaku-ji), the Mountain Temple, one of Tohoku's most celebrated historical and religious sites. Yama-dera dates from 860, when Ennin, its founding priest, is said to have chipped away at the rocks to build the **Main Hall** (Konponchu-do). Although the structure was rebuilt in 1356, the Buddhist figure enshrined here dates to the ninth century; the flame before it has burned for more than a thousand years. The temple comprises some 40 buildings perched on peaks and cliffsides; a trek for the hardy, the route from the bottom of the path to the temple winds up 1,100 stone steps through the woods, past spectacular views of the valley below, to the uppermost **Inner Sanctum** (Oku-no-in). The poet Basho (see sidebar p. 158) wrote a haiku about Yama-dera during his Tohoku journey of 1689:

> The quiet—
> shrilling into the rocks
> the cicada's cry

The northwestern town of **Sakata,** on the Mogami-gawa estuary, was the main trade link with Kyoto in feudal times; sadly, it lost many historical buildings in a 1976 fire. It still has one old samurai house, the **Former Honma Family Residence** (Honma-ke Kyu-hontei), which harks back to the ruling Honma clan, and Sankyo Soko, a district preserving 12 warehouses built in 1893. Sakata is the ferry port for **Tobi-shima,** a tiny island off the west coast popular both as a bird

sanctuary and as a resort for fishing and diving.

Just south of Sakata, the city of **Tsuruoka** was the feudal domain of the Sakai family, but the only reminders today are the castle moats and the interesting open-air **Chido Museum** (Chido Hakubutsukan). Several buildings of the Sakai family in the vicinity were taken down and reerected here in a park.

INSIDER TIP:

For a spiritual uplift, wander into the retreat site on Mount Haguro in Yamagata and take the 2,446 stone steps— the oldest in Japan— up to the five-story pagoda on the peak.

—KENNY LING
National Geographic contributor

Tsuruoka is convenient as a gateway to the **Three Dewa Mountains** (Dewa Sanzan), a trio of peaks ranking among the most sacred in Japan. Along with Fuji-san and On-take in Nagano Prefecture, the Dewa Sanzan are the holiest of all the objects of worship of Shinto mountain cults. Because the Dewa trio— Haguro-san (1,358 feet/414 m), Gas-san (6,494 feet/1,980 m), and Yudono-san (4,933 feet/ 1,504 m)—respectively symbolize birth, death, and rebirth, they are supposed to be visited in that order. Of the thousands going on

Yama-dera
- 151 B3
- ☎ 023/695-2816
- ⏰ 8 a.m.–4 p.m.
- $ $
- 🚆 JR Senzan line: Yama-dera

Sakata
- 151 A3

Visitor Information
- ☎ 0234/24-2233
- ⏰ 9 a.m.–6 p.m.

sakata-kankou.com

Former Honma Family Residence
- ✉ 12-13 Niban-cho, Sakata
- ☎ 0234/22-3562
- ⏰ 9:30 a.m.– 4:30 p.m.; closes at 4 p.m. Nov.–Feb.
- $ $$
- 🚌 Bus from Sakata Station (6 min.)

Tobi-shima
- 151 A4

Tsuruoka
- 151 A3

Visitor Information
- ✉ 1F Tsuruoka Station
- ☎ 0235/25-7678
- ⏰ 9:30 a.m.– 5:30 p.m.

Chido Museum
- ✉ 10-18 Kachushin-machi, Tsuruoka-shi
- ☎ 0235/22-1199
- ⏰ 9:30 a.m.– 4:30 p.m.
- $ $$

EXPERIENCE: Yamabushi—Mountain Monkhood

The Dewa Sanzan are an important train-ing ground for *yamabushi*—the "monks who lie in the mountains" —followers of Shugendo, a religion embracing both Shinto and Buddhism that attempts to gain spiritual power from the mountain gods through extreme asceticism, such as immersion in ice-cold water in winter or being suspended by one's heels over sheer cliff edges. Most yamabushi practice in their free time but the **Ideha Culture Museum** (*Toge, Haguro, tel 0235/62–4727, 9 a.m.–4:30 p.m., $, only Japanese spoken*) runs a three-day yama-bushi course at the beginning of Septem-ber for beginners, which includes meditation in the mountains, vigorous running along mountain trails, learning to blow a conch horn, and light fasting. Call in May or June to reserve.

Dewa Sanzan

- 🗺 151 A3
- 🚌 Bus: Tsuruoka Station to Haguro (50 min.)

Dewa pilgrimages, a few belong to the *yamabushi* sects (see sidebar above) that have wandered and worshipped these mountains for centuries. Although athletic hik-ers may claim otherwise, visiting all three requires an overnight stopover. There are several *shukubo* (shrine or temple lodgings, see p. 257) in the Toge district at the foot of Haguro-san.

Haguro-san—the lowest and easiest to climb—is the most visited of the holy trio. Dedicated to the three deities, the **Sanshin**

Gosaiden Shrine stands at the summit, along with a museum of temple memorabilia. If you are unfit, you should probably stay at the bottom, but the good news is that the way up includes a waterfall and a fine 14th-century pagoda; the bad news is that from the latter, there are still 2,446 stone steps to climb to the summit! You can also take a bus to the top and walk down. **Gas-san** has a shrine at the top, but getting there can be quite a trial due to its long-lasting snowpack. Accordingly the mountain is best known for skiing. Snowfalls of up to 26 feet (8 m) close even the ski slopes until mid-April; they remain open until the end of July. Ideal for hiking in late summer, Gas-san is justifiably famous for its spectacular scenery.

The last of the trio, **Yudono-san,** is also the holiest. The walk from the road to the shrine at the top takes only 15 minutes. The object of worship is a rock stained bright brick red by the iron in the spring welling up around it. So sacred is it that visitors are asked to remove footwear and refrain from taking photographs. ■

A priest prepares for the New Year's Eve Festival (Matsuri) at Dewa-sanzan jinja.

The city of Nagoya, Japan's fourth largest, and gateway to Chubu, plus time-capsule mountain villages and towns rich with traditional crafts

Central Honshu (Chubu)

Miko (shrine maidens) perform at Otaue-sai harvest festival at Atsuta-jingu.

Central Honshu (Chubu)

Chubu, which means "central section," is the middle part of the island of Honshu—the very center of Japan. Its nine prefectures have a wealth of different topographical, climatic, and cultural features. Chubu is divided into two main regions: Tokai on the Pacific side and Hokuriku on the Sea of Japan.

The great Tokaido Road between Edo and Kyoto in feudal times got its name from Tokai—the eastern sea. Today's Tokai region has more transportation arteries between Tokyo and southwestern Japan than ever before, including the Centrair airport on Ise Bay. Heavily industrialized and densely populated along the coast, the area has few major tourist sites, so foreign travelers stopping here en route to the district of Kansai are comparatively few. For those on their way to Hokuriku and the Japan Alps, the Nagoya region is a convenient gateway. Although it is one of the most industrialized areas of all, it still has some worthwhile scenic and historical sights, from Nagoya's history as the homeland of the

Tokugawa clan and the impressive Nagoya-jo, to its deep connection with automotive giant Toyota, based in a city of the same name also in Aichi Prefecture.

Hokuriku, the snowy region facing the Sea of Japan, has a great deal to recommend it. From Nagoya, you can move up toward Nagano via the ancient Nakasendo mountain highway through the Kiso Valley, or through Gifu to Kanazawa in the west, or north to Takayama. Nagano is synonymous with the best of Japanese alpinism and the North Alps, also known as the Hida Range, offer one of the best multiday hikes in Asia. The range, which separates Gifu, Nagano, and Toyama Prefectures, can be hiked from peak to peak with views all the way to Mount Fuji.

Historical and cultural destinations of major importance, Kanazawa and Takayama are also less touristic than towns in Kansai, offering the charms of "little Kyoto" without the same press of visitors. Both towns have well-preserved Edo-period districts, the former the domain of samurai and geisha, the latter of wealthy lumber merchants.

Northern Nagano and Niigata receive an extraordinary dump of snow, transforming quiet mountain villages into wintry hot spring havens and attracting skiers from Japan and abroad. Hence the area has long been called *yukiguni*, or "Snow Country." Off the coast of Niigata-ken is lovely Sado-ga-shima; once reserved for political exiles, it is now a scenic lure for those fleeing the crowds and pressure of urban Japan. In summer the island reverberates with the sound of huge *taiko* drums during the Kodo drumming festival held by the internationally renowned Sado troupe. ∎

NOT TO BE MISSED:

Area of map detail

Tokyo

🏔 151 A3

SHINKANSEN LINES
— Tohoku
— Joetsu
— Hokuriku
— Tokaido

0 ——————— 50 kilometers
0 ——————— 25 mile

Sado-ga-shima

934m
▲ Donden-yama
Ryotsu

Murakami ◁6

Aikawa • Sawata
Mano

Shibata
Niigata ⊕ BANDAI-ASAHI NATIONAL PARK

Ogi

Niitsu
Shirone

NIIGATA-KEN ◁5

Sea of Japan

Sanjo
Tochio

Kashiwazaki

Nagaoka

Ojiya

Wajima   Suzu
Noto-hanto

Nanao
Hakui

Toyama-wan

Himi
Shimminato

Joetsu

Itoigawa

Arai
2454m
Myoho-san

Iiyama
Nakano
Suzaka

Tokamachi

Yuzawa Onsen

JOSHINETSU KOGEN NAT. PARK

◁4

Echigo-sanmyaku

NORTHERN HONSHU (TOHOKU)   P. 149

Uozu   CHUBU SANGAKU NATIONAL PARK
Nagano

Takaoka   8
Toyama
Tonami

Tateyama
Omachi
Kurobe Dam

EXCURSIONS FROM TOKYO   P. 103

Kanazawa

ISHIKAWA-KEN   **TOYAMA-KEN**

Komatsu
HAKUSAN NATIONAL PARK

Kaga

Shirakawa-go

3180m
Yariga-take

3190m
Hotaka-dake

Ueda
18

Saku

Matsumoto

NAGANO-KEN

Eihei-ji
2702m
Haku-san

Takayama

Katsuyama
Ono

Fukui
Sabae
Echizen

Shirakawa-go

Hida Minzoku Mura

Kamikochi
Shiojiri
Okaya
Suwa
Chino

North Alps

Narai
Kisoji
Kiso
Fukushima

CHICHIBU-TAMA NATIONAL PARK

Wakasa-wan

Tsuruga

FUKUI-KEN

GIFU-KEN

Mino

3063m
Ontake-san

Tsumago
Agematsu

3192m
Kita-dake

Nirasaki
Kofu   ◁3

YAMANASHI-KEN

Fujiyoshida
FUJI-HAKONE-IZU NAT. PARK

Obama

Minokamo

Nakatsugawa
Iida

MINAMI-ALPS NAT. PARK

South Alps

3120m
Akaishi-dake

3776m
Fuji-san

Gotemba

KANSAI   P. 229

Gifu

Inuyama   Ena

Seto

Fujinomiya

Ogaki
Ichinomiya

NAGOYA

Toyota

Shitara

Tenryu-gawa

SHIZUOKA-KEN

Mishima
Atami

Fuji
• Shimizu
Numazu

Ito

Kariya
Centrair ⊕ **Okazaki**
Handa
Gamagori

AICHI-KEN

Fujieda

Shizuoka
Yaizu

Izu-hanto

O-shima ◁2

Kakegawa
Toyohashi
Kosai
Hamamatsu

Suruga-wan

Shimoda

Ise-wan

△B

△C

Nii-shima

IZU SHICHITO

Kozu-shima

Miyake-jima ◁1

△D

Mikura-jima
△E

Aichi-ken

Although important agriculturally, Aichi-ken is better known for its industrial output: electronics, chemicals, ceramics, textiles, and 40 percent of the nation's cars. Because of this and the drab highway scenery on the flatlands, most travelers skip Aichi. For those with time, however, it has its rewards. The regional capital, Nagoya, is a transportation hub with many good hotels, making it a convenient base for exploring the Tokai region and the southern Japan Alps.

Cars of many makes and vintage are displayed at the Toyota car museum.

Nagoya

⬛ 171 B2

Visitor Information

✉ Nagoya Station
☎ 052/541-4301
🕐 9 a.m.–7 p.m.
🚄 Shinkansen from Tokyo (1 hr. 45 min.) or Osaka (1 hr.)

nagoya-info.jp

Coastal Aichi-ken is dotted with beach resorts and hot springs, but there is little of cultural or historical interest. Also, the resorts and spas are scattered; to make the most of them, you will need plenty of time or a car. North of the coast, Aichi-ken shares mountains with Nagano-ken (see pp. 186–187) and Gifu-ken; if you have your own transportation, you can cover miles of beautiful countryside laced with rivers. The jewel in Aichi's crown is the historic hill town of Inuyama (see pp. 174–175), with the oldest original castle in Japan.

   Nagoya is Japan's fourth largest city. Inhabited since prehistoric times, it rose to prominence in

the 16th century as Japan's three greatest military leaders completed the unification of the country. While Oda Nobunaga and Toyotomi Hideyoshi were from Nagoya, Tokugawa Ieyasu, founder of the military dynasty that ruled Japan until 1867, was born in Okazaki, 38 miles (60 km) southeast. Nagoya was virtually obliterated during World War II, and the vestiges associated with its great warrior sons were lost.

Nagoya Castle

Nagoya-jo, built in 1612 by Tokugawa Ieyasu for his son Yoshinao, was famous for the *shachi-hoko*–golden dolphins topping the keep's gables. The pride of the city, it was destroyed in 1945 and rebuilt in 1959. Stone and plaster were eschewed for cheap concrete, but it's difficult to tell from the well-restored exterior. The **National Treasure Honmaru Palace,** which once sat within the keep's walls, suffered the same fate in the war, but by 2009 reconstruction had begun, this time with all traditional methods and materials. The first stage opened in 2013, complete with re-created Kano-school screen paintings; a viewing platform overlooks the continuing construction process.

Established in the third century, **Atsuta-jingu** houses the ancient Kusanagi Sword—which, along with the mirror in Ise-Jingu (see p. 258) and the jewel in the Imperial Palace in Tokyo, comprises the nation's imperial regalia. None of these is on display; rather, the appeal of Atsuta-jingu is in its thick camphor forest and mysterious shrines, occluded by fences to keep the curious at a safe distance. The small **treasure hall** displays relics related to the shrine,

including an astoundingly massive 86-inch (2.2 m) great sword.

From Nagoya Station, take the subway to Ozone, where a short walk south leads to the **Tokugawa Art Museum** (Tokugawa Bijutsukan). The 10,000 items of the Tokugawa family treasury include calligraphy, paintings, ceramics, armor, and swords. The model teahouse and Noh stage capture the grandeur of the age and put the associated treasures in their appropriate setting. The star attraction is the celebrated 12th-century Genji Scroll, the oldest surviving set of text and illustrations of Lady Murasaki's great tenth-century novel, *The Tale of Genji*. Because of its extreme fragility, the original is exhibited only once a year; what you normally see is a reproduction.

Aichi's grand tradition of craftsmanship is displayed at the **Toyota Commemorative Museum of Industry and Technology** *(4-1-35 Noritake Shinmachi, tel 052/551-6115, www.tcmit.org, 9:30 a.m.–4:30 p.m., closed Mon., $),* which relates the company's growth from an upstart weaving

Nagoya-jo

- ✉ 1-1 Honmaru, Naka-ku
- ☎ 052/231-1700
- 🕐 9 a.m.–4 p.m.
- 💲 $$
- 🚇 Meijo line: Shiyakusho

**www.nagoyajo.city
.nagoya.jp**

Atsuta-jingu
- ✉ 1-1-1 Jingu, Atsuta-ku
- ☎ 052/671-4151
- 🕐 Treasure hall 9 a.m.–4:10 p.m.
- 💲 $ (treasure hall)
- 🚇 Meitetsu line: Jingu-mae

atsutajingu.or.jp

Tokugawa Art Museum

- ✉ 1017 Tokugawa-cho, Higashi-ku
- ☎ 052/935-6262
- 🕐 10 a.m.– 4:30 p.m., closed Mon.
- 💲 $$$
- 🚇 JR Chuo or Meijo lines: Ozone

**tokugawa-art-
museum.jp**

(see p. 258)

NEED TO KNOW

Reaching Chubu
South Chubu and Nagoya are served by the Chubu Centrair International Airport, a busy terminal with regular flights to the rest of Asia. ANA also provides domestic service to distant domestic locales, such as Fukuoka, Naha, Sapporo, and Ishigaki.

Nagoya is also just 100 minutes from Tokyo by Shinkansen. A recent extension to the Hokuriku Shinkansen line means

that there is now rapid transit available from Tokyo to Nagano (1.5 hours) and Kanazawa (3 hours).

Getting Around
Outside the cities, this mountainous area is well-served by JR lines and bus routes. To reach Fukui and Takayama, you'll need to take regular express trains. For buses to ski areas and trailheads, check with the station's tourist info counter.

The Pull of *Pachinko*

Ablaze with colored neon, *pachinko* (from *pachin*—slap—and *ko*, a ball) took off during the 1950s. In this vertical pinball game, hundreds of ball bearings clatter along the pins and traps on the machine's gaudy face as customers spend hours trying to aim them toward valuable targets.

Tales of little old ladies eking out an existence to play the game permeate pachinko culture. There is even a profession of "pin straighteners," whose job consists of straightening the pins on the machine face to remedy bending from ostensible overuse. Prizes include cookies and cigarettes, usually exchanged for cash through a backstreet pigeonhole (but don't tell anyone—gambling is technically illegal in the country). Amazingly, the profits from pachinko top the entire service industry in Japan.

Noritake Garden

- ✉ 1-36 Noritake-Shinmachi, 3-Chome, Nishi-ku
- ☎ 052/561-7290
- 🕐 10 a.m.–5 p.m.
- 💲 $$
- 🚌 Meguru sightseeing bus: Noritake Garden

www.noritake.co.jp/mori

Inuyama

- 🗺 171 B3

Visitor Information

- ✉ Inuyama Station
- ☎ 0568/61-6000
- 🕐 9 a.m.–5 p.m.
- 🚌 Meitetsu Inuyama line: Inuyama. (*Note: Inuyama-Yuen Station is more convenient for the sights.*)

ml.inuyama.gr.jp

Inuyama-jo

- ✉ 65-2 Kitakoken
- ☎ 0568/61-1711
- 🕐 9 a.m.–4:30 p.m.
- 💲 $$
- 🚌 Meitetsu Inuyama line: Inuyama-Yuen, then 15-min. walk

machinery maker to global auto titan. Exhibits start with Toyota's cotton processes and the earliest hand-molded car prototypes and end at live demonstrations of the major steps in a modern assembly line. English-speaking guides are available to visitors on Sundays.

Nearby, **Noritake Garden** commemorates Japan's best known china company. Set about an original brick factory, the garden includes a museum, gallery, and craft center where visitors can paint and fire their own dishes. Train buffs will love the **SCMaglev and Railway Park** (*3-2-2 Kinjofuto, Minato-ku, museum.jr-central.co.jp, 10 a.m.–5 p.m., closed Tues., $$$, Aonami line: Kinjofuto*), which houses old trains and decommissioned Shinkansen models. The park also details the Maglev system set to roll out in 2027. At 361 miles an hour (581 kph), the Maglev will cut the Tokyo-Nagoya commute from 100 minutes on the 186-mile-an-hour (300 kph) Shinkansen to just 40 minutes.

About one mile (1.5 km) east of the station, the focal **Sakae** district comprises restaurants, bars, shopping centers, and an underground mall. **Osu,** to the south, is a more animated downtown neighborhood with a colorful arcade leading to the popular **Osu Kannon Temple,** which holds a good flea market on weekends.

On the south bank of the Kiso-gawa on the boundary between Aichi-ken and Gifu-ken, the pleasant town of **Inuyama** and its surroundings are a favorite Nagoyite weekend excursion. Along with fine scenery and a historic castle, it has some unusual sights, including the Meiji Village architectural museum and Japan Monkey Park.

Set on a cliff overlooking Kiso-gawa, the small four-story **Inuyama-jo** is one of Japan's finest castles. In fact, built in 1537, it is the oldest still in its original state. It is also the only one that is privately owned, having remained the property of the Naruse family since 1618. The castle's survival is miraculous: When it was seized from its owners in 1871, the buildings surrounding the keep were destroyed. Damaged in an earthquake in 1891, the castle was returned to the Naruse family in 1895 on the condition that they restore it—and they did. The viewing platform on the top offers a wonderful panorama over the river and valley. A three-minute walk east of the castle, on the grounds of the Meitetsu Inuyama Hotel, is the inviting garden of **Uraku-en.** In the garden is the **Jo-an,** a celebrated 17th-century teahouse, moved here from Kyoto.

Fertility Shrines

Tagata-jinja, a short distance south of Inuyama, across from Tagata-jinja-mae Station, is one of Japan's 40 or so remaining phallic shrines. Tagata is renowned for its rousing Bumper Harvest Festival (Tagata Honen Sai, March 15). The huge wooden phallus leading the parade is enshrined in the main hall, and many more in an array of improbable sizes are displayed in the adjacent building. Exhibiting rocks and stones suggesting male and female genitalia, parts of the precinct are also festooned with small *ema*—votive plaques left by

those entreating the gods to find them partners or grant offspring. Stronger on content than form, the shrine buildings are utilitarian.

Tagata's female counterpart is the more demure **Oagata-jinja.** Set in wooded hills and attractively constructed, it provides insights into feminine Shinto practices: Girls leave their dolls here to be burned as a rite of passage to womanhood. Some women crawl through the miniature *torii* gateway in the open-sided pavilion to increase their fertility.

Inuyama's most curious attraction is the open-air village museum of **Meiji-mura,** where lucky buildings go when they die. More than 60 early Western-style structures have been moved here: Highlights include the facade and lobby of Frank Lloyd Wright's Tokyo Imperial Hotel, Kyoto's St. John's Church, and the old Sapporo telephone exchange. You can ride around the village on antique streetcars and a steam railroad. ■

Tagata-jinja
- ✉ 152 Tagata-cho, Komaki-shi
- ☎ 0568/76-2906
- 🚇 Komaki line: Tagata-jinja-mae

Oagata-jinja
- ✉ 15-min. walk east of Gakuden Station
- ☎ 0568/67-1017
- 🕐 9:30 a.m.–5 p.m.
- 🚇 Komaki line: Gakuden

Meiji-mura
- ✉ 1 Uchiyama, Inuyama-shi
- ☎ 0568/67-0314
- 🕐 9:30 a.m.–5 p.m., 9 a.m.–9 p.m. in summer
- 💲 $$$$
- 🚇 Bus from Inuyama Station (20 min.)

meijimura.com

Japan's first *pachinko* parlor opened in Nagoya in 1948; such arcades are now everywhere in Japan.

Kanazawa & Hokuriku

To the Japanese, the name Hokuriku evokes the high mountains, the deep winter that Yasunari Kawabata elegized in his Nobel Prize–winning *Snow Country,* and old towns that still retain their Edo-period character. The region loosely comprises the prefectures of Ishikawa, Toyama, Nagano, Niigata, and northern Gifu, centered around the North and Central Japan Alps, the narrow plains along the Sea of Japan, and the vibrant city of Kanazawa.

Shirakawa-go's farmhouses are preserved amid rice paddies.

Coming north from Nagoya, you arrive at Gifu's Takayama (see pp. 182–184), a charming old town set at the gateway to the deeper mountains with a well-preserved merchant district. From Takayama, buses run to the village of Shirakawa-go, famous for its thatched-roof houses, or east to Kamikochi (see p. 189), arguably the most beautiful mountain valley in Japan. The Japan Alps, running south from Toyama-ken and into Gifu and

Nagano (see pp. 186–187) are home to superb skiing, hiking, and mountain scenery, with the cities of Toyama, Nagano, and Matsumoto (see p. 188) as excellent bases for exploration.

Along the Sea of Japan, Ishikawa-ken is noted for its long history of fine craftwork and Kanazawa's well-preserved samurai and geisha quarters. The prefectural capital is also home to Kenroku-en, one of Japan's three best gardens. Skipping east along the largely industrial coast of Toyama-ken you arrive in **Niigata-ken,** notable for great ski hills and *onsen* a short Shinkansen ride from Tokyo and for the island of **Sado-ga-shima,** headquarters of Kodo, the world-famous *taiko* drumming group (see sidebar p. 196).

Kanazawa History

Kanazawa was the capital of the old fiefdom of Kaga, which came to be governed by the Buddhist Jodo Shinshu sect as an autonomous republic in 1488. Conquered by warlord Oda Nobunaga in 1583, it thrived as a prominent center for arts and crafts, including ceramics (see sidebar below), textiles, gold leaf, and paperware, as well as traditional *Kaga ryori* cuisine and *wagashi* (Japanese confectionery). These all still continue today. Noh theater also flourished in Kanazawa, and the Ishikawa Prefectural Noh Theater is now one of Japan's most important centers for Noh.

Having survived World War II unscathed, Kanazawa abounds in historical sights. Several are in or near **Kenroku-en.** Designated one of the three great gardens of Japan, Kenroku-en is named after the *kenroku* (six combinations) considered ideal for gardens: spaciousness, serenity, venerability, scenic views, subtle design, and coolness provided by watercourses. Originally the stroll garden of Kanazawa-jo, it was enlarged and completed in 1819 and opened to the public in 1871. There are some 12,000 trees of 150 species within this masterpiece of landscaping, which encompasses artificial hills, ponds, and waterways flanked by irises

INSIDER TIP:

At Chirihama Nagisa Driveway, 65 miles (40 km) north of Kanazawa, you can drive directly on the sandy shore for five miles (8 km).

—HIROMI ISHII
Senior staff editor
National Geographic Japan

Kanazawa

◭ 171 B4

Visitor Information

✉ Kanazawa Station

☎ 076/232-3933

🕐 8:30 a.m.–8 p.m.

🚆 JR Joetsu Shinkansen from Tokyo to Nagaoka, then change for limited express (4.5–5 hr.)

kanazawa-tourism .com

Kenroku-en

✉ 1 Kenrokumachi

☎ 076/234-3800

🕐 8:30 a.m.–8 p.m.

💲 $

🚌 The tourist loop bus runs from Kanazawa Station to Kenroku-en-shita (or the Seisonkaku-mai stop for Seisonkaku-mae).

www.pref.ishikawa .jp/siro-niwa /kenrokuen/e

Kanazawa Ceramics

A center for ceramics since feudal times, Kanazawa is known for both Ohi tea-ceremony pottery and Kutani ware, with its multiple colors and bold designs. Craft shops selling pottery dot the town, and antique ware is displayed in museums such as the **Ishikawa Prefecture Museum of Traditional Products and Crafts** (1-1 Kenroku-machi, Kanazawa, tel 076/262-2020, ishikawa-densankan.jp, 9 a.m.–5 p.m., closed Thurs., $) and the

Ishikawa Prefecture Museum of Art (2-1 Dewa-machi, Kanazawa, tel 076/231-7580, ishibi.pref.ishikawa.jp, 9:30 a.m.–6 p.m., $), both near Kenroku-en. In the southwest of town, the **Kutani Pottery Kosen Kiln** (5-3-3 Nomachi, Kanazawa, tel 076/241-0902, 9 a.m.–4:30 p.m.) welcomes visitors. You can arrange to visit workshops through the Visitor Information Center. North of Kenroku-en, the **Ishikawa Local Products Shop** sells local crafts.

21st-Century Museum of Contemporary Art

- ✉ 1-2-1 Hirosaka
- ☎ 076/220-2800
- ⏱ 10 a.m.–6 p.m., closed Mon.
- 💲 $, $$ for special exhibits
- 🚌 Loop bus: Hirosaka stop

kanazawa21.jp

D. T. Suzuki Museum

- ✉ 3-4-20 Honda-machi
- ☎ 076/221-8011
- ⏱ 9:30 a.m.– 5 p.m., closed Mon.
- 💲 $

kanazawa-museum .jp/daisetz

The 21st-Century Museum of Contemporary Art

Nomura House

- ✉ 1-3-32 Naga-machi
- ☎ 076/221-3553
- ⏱ 8:30 a.m.– 5:30 p.m.
- 💲 $$

in season. Yet Kenroku-en's scale, impressive as it is, precludes the intimacy of a true garden— it is more accurately described as a park and can get very crowded between 11 a.m. and 3 p.m.

Just to the north outside Kenroku-en is the impressive **Ishikawamon Gate,** the last sur-viving structure of Kanazawa-jo, which burned down in 1881. At the southern end of the garden the **Seisonkaku Villa,** built in 1863, is noted for the delicacy of its interiors. The grounds include an elegant teahouse and a garden with gnarled pines and streams meandering beneath the veranda.

South of the garden lies a cluster of museums, the foremost of which is the popular **21st-Century Museum of Contem-porary Art,** opened in 2004

to much acclaim for its regular exhibits of the best of Japanese artists and international stars. Typi-cal of much postmodern art, the exhibits swing widely between the sublime and the self-aggrandizing.

The open layout and public exhibit areas make it good for wandering and for energetic kids.

Students of Zen (see sidebar p. 179) shouldn't miss the recently opened **D. T. Suzuki Museum,** a 10-minute walk to the south of the garden. Daisetz Suzuki is the best known proponent of Zen in the West. His English translations influenced a whole generation of American thinkers, among them the Beats, such as Kerouac, Gins-berg, and Snyder. The museum has a peaceful meditation room set in the middle of a mirror-still pool.

Just north of Kanazawa-jo Park is **Omicho Market,** a boisterous cluster of shops selling seafood straight from the Sea of Japan and a collection of sushi restaurants to serve it up as fresh as possible. Similar to the massive Tsukiji Central Fish Market in Tokyo (see p. 75), Omicho is lively, but it's less intense and more accessible.

Samurai & Geisha Areas

About half a mile west of the garden, the old earthen walls that flank the lanes of the Nagamachi samurai quarter make the area picturesque. However, most of the buildings are private, and few are original structures. In the 1910s the remains of **Nomura House** (Nomura-ke) were restored by a shipping magnate who added part of a samurai house he owned in his hometown. Although not quite authentic, the building is highly evocative. Best viewed from the veranda or from upstairs while sipping green tea, the exquisite little garden of rocks and watercourses is a masterpiece of miniature landscaping. Nearby stands the **Nagamachi Yuzen-kan,** a silk-dyeing center that was once a teahouse. Here you can watch *kaga yuzen* artisans intricately hand-painting silk textiles (children are not admitted). The **Kanazawa Shinise Memorial Hall** (Kanazawa-shi Shinise Kinenkan), once a wooden pharmacy in the town center, has been dismantled and reerected here as a museum exhibiting local crafts and showing shop interiors of the late 1800s.

Three old geisha districts remain in Kanazawa. Kazue-machi along Asano-gawa is charming, as is the Nishi-Chaya-gai quarter in the southwest. The finest is **Higashi-Chaya-gai** to the northeast. The streetlights and buildings here remain unchanged since the 19th century, although the geisha who once frequented these districts are now reduced to a mere 50 or so. The 190-year-old **Kaikaro** is a teahouse, its decor an inspired blend of the traditional and the contemporary, featuring an inner garden of shards of glass. A few doors away is **Shima** *(1-13-21 Higashiyama, tel 076/252-5675),* a delightful old geisha house with original fixtures and furnishings, now a museum.

On the slopes of tranquil **Teramachi,** the temple district in the south of town, are some 70 temples and shrines. None are considered major, but several are interesting, among them Gannen-ji, visited by the 17th-century poet Basho; Akan-ji (also called Neko-dera–Cat Temple–a

former feline cemetery); and Daien-ji, which has a fine Zen garden. West of Teramachi is the famous **Myoryu-ji,** also known as the Ninja Temple. The first impression is that the temple is nothing special, but appearances are deceptive—intentionally so. Built in the 1640s, the temple complex presents an ingenious labyrinth of 21 secret chambers, hidden stairways, and trapdoors designed as escape routes; despite its nickname, Myoryu-ji was a government outpost built to protect local lords in case of attack. Tours of the temple's secrets are held every 30 minutes, by reservation only. ■

Zen Riddles

Zen is famous for the use of *koan,* riddles designed to point at the nature of reality without explaining, so students can make the realization on their own through long meditation. The pop-culture example is "What is the sound of one hand clapping?" But there are many other koan to pique one's interest: "If you meet the Buddha, slay him: Even a great teacher can become the object of desire and prevent one's own Enlightenment." "Sickness and medicine correspond to each other. The whole world is medicine. What am I?" "The world is such a wide world, why do you answer a bell and don ceremonial robes?"

Nagamachi Yuzen-kan

- ✉ 2-6-16 Nagamachi
- ☎ 076/264-2811
- 🕐 9 a.m.–4:30 p.m.
- 💲 $
- 🚌 Loop bus: Korinbo stop

kagayuzen-club.co.jp

Kanazawa Shinise Memorial Hall

- ✉ 2-2-45 Nagamachi
- ☎ 076/220-2524
- 🕐 9:30 a.m.–5 p.m.
- 💲 $
- 🚌 Loop bus: Korinbo stop

Myoryu-ji

- ✉ 1-2-12 Nomachi
- ☎ 076/241-0888
- 🕐 9 a.m.–4:30 p.m., until 4 p.m. in winter
- 💲 $$; reservations required for 40-min. tour; no English spoken
- 🚌 Loop bus: Hirokoji stop

myouryuji.or.jp

Japanese Gardens

Gardening, according to a recent government poll, is the fifth most popular hobby in Japan; there are 38 million keen gardeners in this densely populated country with little space. Lack of a backyard is no deterrent: The sills and facades of small suburban homes are festooned with pots, while bonsai cultivators tend dwarf trees high on the balconies of urban apartment buildings.

Autumn in the Japanese garden at the Adachi Museum of Art, Shimane Prefecture

The average garden is small; neither crammed with variegated blooms nor geometrically arranged in lawns and beds, its function is contemplative. Rather than transforming nature, it strives to imitate it and shuns symmetry. The garden path uses stones of irregular shape instead of aligned bricks or flagstones; paths may consist of stepping-stones, even over dry land. Fine rocks are considered as important as plants and command high prices. The most important criteria are color and shape. Rocks may be chosen to suggest, for instance, mountains, boats, or animals, especially turtles.

Early Gardens

Gardening came to Japan in the sixth century with Chinese culture and Buddhism. Long lost in China, a few early prototypes survive in Japan, where the Japanese used them to develop gardening concepts of their own. Gardens are described in the tenth-century *Tale of Genji* and had become common by then among the clergy and aristocracy—the biggest being stroll gardens laid out around large ponds. A garden abandoned during the 12th century was recently unearthed during archaeological excavations at Motsu-ji in Hiraizumi, Tohoku (see pp. 164–165), and has now been restored; it included an artificial lake, man-made rock formations, and an artificial watercourse. Typically landscaped to represent the Buddhist universe, the ponds and rocks were arranged to evoke oceans and islands.

The garden in Kyoto's Daikaku-ji retains the 215,000-square-foot (20,000 sq m) pond called Osawa-no-Ike, originally designed by the ninth-century emperor Saga. It also once had a dry waterfall, perhaps pioneering the common use of smaller stones that, often striated, are placed in rows to subtly mimic the flow of bodies of water.

Gardening manuals appeared during the 13th century but became more common in the 15th, when gardening trends diversified and spread through the influences of Zen Buddhism and the tea ceremony. Zen introduced a minimalist approach to temple gardens, sometimes landscaping them with expanses of raked sand and rocks alone (as in Ryoan-ji in Kyoto). Exalting naturalism, tea masters favored lush, wooded glades floored with moss and stepping-stones to harmonize with the teahouse, as well as the sight and sound of flowing water.

Gardening for All

During the Edo period (1603–1868), commoners took up gardening; most current concepts emerged from practices and manuals popular at the time. There are three main styles: *tsukiyama* (artificial mountain or landscape garden), *karesansui* (dry landscape in which watercourses are suggested by using stones), and *chaniwa* (a garden surrounding a teahouse). Gardens may combine them, but strict conventions dictate the positioning of the different kinds of appropriate stone lanterns *(toro),* bamboo fences, and bridges of wood or stone. Sometimes incorporating all three styles in miniature, *tsuboniwa*—small gardens in domestic courtyards—can be real gems showcasing gardening as a master craft. Gardens require planning: How will the shadows of the rocks fall? How striking will the elements look from different angles? Consider the climate: With rocks shining against the intense greens of damp moss and foliage, some gardens look best in the rain.

Although the Japanese appreciate thousands of varieties of flower, some are reserved for *ikebana* arrangements, while others—potted plants such as chrysanthemums—are used exclusively for seasonal displays. The traditional garden excludes all but a few indigenous species: iris, lotus, and flowering shrubs such as camellia, azalea, hydrangea, and tree peony—an early arrival from China in the sixth century. Large gardens are often wooded, with trees such as cherry and plum, and even tiny ones like display pines, maples, and bamboo. Trees and shrubs may be cut, trimmed, twisted, and dwarfed into any shape—but for a Japanese garden, forget about roses and lawns.

Bonsai, horticulture's small wonder

EXPERIENCE:
Grow Your Own Bonsai

If you fall in love with Japanese gardens, consider taking up bonsai. The art of growing trees in miniature through careful pruning allows even the apartment-dwelling Japanese to have small gardens. Start with *The Complete Book of Bonsai* by Harry Tomlinson: This has excellent photographs to both inspire and instruct, as well as information on shaping North American or European plants, in addition to the Japanese mainstays. Diehard enthusiasts should look into **Bonsai Network Japan** *(j-bonsai.com)* in Shizuoka, which runs one-day tours and three-month semiprivate classes in English.

Takayama

Delightful Takayama, on the western slopes of the Japan Alps in Gifu-ken, was the capital of the old province of Hida. The name Takayama, meaning "high mountain," conveys the remoteness of what was once a vital town. Its carpenters reputedly played a large part in the building of ancient Kyoto and Nara. As its reputation for woodcrafts spread, Takayama continued to prosper. It has declined in the modern era, but its very remoteness has helped preserve it.

A hidden craftsman manipulates *karakuri* dolls (windup mechanical puppets) in the Karakuri Museum.

Takayama

🅜 171 B3

Visitor Information

✉ Outside station

☎ 0577/32-5328

🕐 8:30 a.m.–7 p.m.

🚆 Hida line: Hida Express from Nagoya to Takayama (2 hr. 30 min.)

www.hida.jp/english

travel.kankou-gifu.jp

Today the town retains sufficient historical sights to justify the hackneyed designation "Little Kyoto"—mainly for its Teramachi temple district. Yet Takayama is nothing like Kyoto; no realm of samurai, priests, and literati, it grew up as a town of farmers, artisans, and merchants. Its charm lies in the remarkably well-preserved streets of merchant houses and venerable saké breweries concentrated in the Sanmachi Suji district, which also contains shops, taverns, and inns of similar vintage. Takayama's role as the hub of a rich folk culture is evidenced in its museums.

Although Takayama is small, it takes a good day to see the sights on the east side of the Miya-gawa alone; a stopover is highly recommended. Be sure to try *sansai* (mountain vegetables), Hida beef, which is known to rival that of Kobe, and the acclaimed local saké during your stay.

Hida Kokubun-ji, northeast of the train station on the west riverbank, was founded by Nara's pious emperor Shomu in 746. The temple has been burned down and rebuilt since, so all that remains of the original is a ginkgo tree thought to be 1,200 years old; next to it stands a three-story **pagoda** from 1821.

Despite the temple's long history, the 16th-century main hall fails to impress—continue on to the **Sanmachi Suji** district after a quick look. This traditional neighborhood consists of old merchant houses that flourished in the Edo period when it enjoyed close business ties with the Tokugawa shogunate via Takayama Jinya. The buildings are notable for their low, almost hunched aspect despite the otherwise expensive cypress furnishings and construction: Afraid of disrespecting their samurai overlords, the merchants built their homes lower than the gate of the government office across the river.

Kusakabe Folk Museum (Kusakabe Mingeikan) is located on the eastern bank of Miya-gawa. The building, built in 1879 as a merchant's home and warehouse, is a fine example of Takayama carpentry. Now a museum, it displays all the fixtures it contained when open for business during the 19th century. Next door, the interior of **Yoshijima House** (Yoshijima-ke; 1-51 Ojin-machi, tel 0577/32-0038, $) is not to be missed. A masterpiece of traditional Japanese domestic architecture, its soaring framework of huge crossbeams and posts stretches high up under the roof.

Takayama Museums

Also in the Sanmachi district are two noteworthy museums: the new **Takayama Museum of History and Art** and the **Fujii Folk Museum,** a private collection. The former was built into six old storehouses and displays all the accoutrements of the wealthy merchant class. The Fujii Folk Museum is filled with old-fashioned rural tools and pieces of metalwork.

Twice yearly (April 14–15 and October 9–10), the Takayama Festival draws thousands with its colorful procession of complex puppet-machine floats, each displaying ingenious sleight of hand accomplished with simple rods and strings. If you miss the festivals, stop by the new **Karakuri Museum** (a museum of mechanical puppetry), a five-minute walk east of the Sanmachi district, where demonstrations of this traditional art form are given every 30 minutes. The **Festival Floats**

Exhibition Hall next door holds four of the eleven floats from the festival and also puts on regular performances for the public.

Across the river from the southern end of the Sanmachi Suji district lies **Takayama Jinya** (Historical Government House), the sole remaining Edo-period government office in Japan. Originally built for the Kanemori rulers in 1615, the building was the seat of government through the Tokugawa shogunate and the return to imperial rule. The oldest

Takayama's Morning Markets

If you're an early riser, you'll find plenty of local color in Takayama's morning markets (asa-ichi), which trade daily in the produce and flowers grown by local farmers, as well as in handicrafts. Both markets are open from 7 a.m. to noon, one at Jinya-mae near Takayama Jinya and the other on the eastern bank of the Miya-gawa, across from Kajibashi bridge.

section is the 400-year-old granary. The largest in Japan, it pays tribute to the heavy taxes of rice levied on the area's poor mountain people and the frequent revolts that resulted. The heavily used government officials' rooms were rebuilt in the 19th century; a collection of smaller servants' rooms, kitchens, and scribes' rooms were reconstructed in 1996.

Kusakabe Folk Museum
- ✉ 1-52 Ojin-machi
- ☎ 0577/32-0072
- 🕐 9 a.m.–4:30 p.m.
- 💲 $
- www.hida.jp/english

Takayama Museum of History and Art
- ✉ 75 Kamiichino-machi
- ☎ 0577/32-1205
- 🕐 9 a.m.–7 p.m.
- www.hida.jp/english

Fujii Folk Museum
- ✉ 69 Kamisanno-machi
- ☎ 0577/35-3778
- 🕐 9 a.m.–5 p.m., closed Wed.
- 💲 $$
- www.hida.jp/english

Karakuri Museum
- ✉ 53-1 Sakura-machi
- ☎ 0577/32-0881
- 🕐 9 a.m.–4:25 p.m.
- 💲 $$
- www.hida.jp/english

Takayama Jinya
- ✉ 1-5 Hachiken-machi
- ☎ 0577/32-0643
- 🕐 8:45 a.m.–5 p.m.
- 💲 $
- www.hida.jp/english

Shirakawa-go

🗺 171 B3–B4

✉ Ogimachi Visitor Center

☎ 05769/6-1013

🚌 Bus from Takayama (1 hr. 40 min.)

shirakawa-go.org

Hida-no-Sato

✉ 1-590 Kamiokamoto-machi

☎ 0577/34-4711

🕐 8:30 a.m.–5 p.m.

💲 $$

🚌 Bus from number 1 gate at station to Hida-no-Sato (fast bus takes 10 min., slow bus 30 min.); then 20-min. walk SW of station

www.hida.jp/english

While much of the building seems empty, the interrogation room stands out. Its uniquely Japanese torture device involves sitting Japanese-style on one's calves on top of a piece of sharply corrugated wood with heavy stones in one's lap.

Also on the eastern side of town is **Shiroyama-koen,** a park renowned for its alpine views and spring displays of cherry blossoms; look for the feudal castle ruins.

Shoren-ji (under renovation) in the northwestern part of the park originally stood in Shirakawa-go (below), 20 miles (32 km) northwest of Takayama. The temple was rebuilt here in 1960, when the lake formed by a new dam drowned its site. The 1504 **Main Hall** is much admired as an example of Muromachi (1338–1573) temple architecture. There is a pleasant landscape garden adjacent.

If you follow the paths through Shiroyama-koen, you will come to **Teramachi,** the temple district. The Higashiyama Walking Route (2 miles/3.5 km) is well signposted in English throughout and passes 13 temples and five shrines.

Shirakawa-go

The charming village of **Ogimachi** in the nearby World Heritage site Shirakawa-go has 114 traditional thatched-roof farmhouses in a living village. Several are open as museums, including the four-story Wada House and the Kanda House, which lacks exhibits but feels more like a home. The village is best visited in the winter for the iconic view of chalets buried in the snow

and because the cold keeps many tourists away. If you stay overnight in a farmhouse, you'll have Ogimachi to yourself. Alternately, check out **Ainokura,** a tiny village an hour away with 15 gassho-zukuri farmhouses (see below) and a fraction of the tourists.

INSIDER TIP:

The old town center of Sanmachi Suji holds an antiques market on the seventh of each month from May through October. Good pieces aren't cheap, but the prices still beat Kyoto or Tokyo.

—KENNY LING
National Geographic contributor

If you don't have time to explore Shirakawa-go, stop by **Hida-no-Sato,** an open-air folk museum that consists of old thatched farmhouses rescued from valleys flooded by hydroelectric projects or that could no longer be maintained. The "village" is artificial, but has good English explanation of the gassho-zukuri architectural style, with steep roofs in the shape of hands pressed together in prayer to shed snow, as well as the system of smoke-blackened beams held together only with straw ropes, which enable the houses to flex under heavy winter loads. There is also a good explanation of the process of raising silkworms and regular folk song performances. ■

Eihei-ji

Sleepy Fukui Prefecture's star attraction is Eihei-ji, one of two head temples of Soto Zen Buddhism. Soto is considered the "soft school" of Zen, different from the Kyoto-based Rinzai Zen. Soto monks face the wall instead of each other while meditating for better concentration. Soto also places primary importance on *zazen* (sitting meditation), whereas Rinzai makes more use of *koan*—nonsensical riddles that are designed to point to the true nature of being.

Soto Zen monks face the wall to reduce distraction during meditation.

The temple complex, along with Koya-san (see pp. 254–257), is one of the few places where the visitor can witness living Buddhism in action in Japan. Built up a steep hillside, the temple buildings are set in a deep valley full of old trees, and the place has a well-worn, lived-in feel.

The complex was originally founded in 1244 by the popular monk Dogen, who was dissatisfied with the political struggles of the Tendai sect on Mount Hiei and felt that Rinzai placed too much emphasis on the mental gymnastics of koan riddles. He called for a return to the seated meditation of Sakyamuni, the historical Buddha.

The great Sanmon Gate is the oldest structure in the complex, rebuilt in 1749, and while the others—including the Buddha Hall, the Priests' Hall, and the Dharma Hall—have all been rebuilt, the sheen of polish that 200 resident monks put on everything gives the unadorned, burnished wood a timeless look. Architecture aside, the real interest is in quietly observing the black-robed monks as they go about their chores. Rising at 3:30 a.m., they spend hours every day in seated meditation, reading sutras, gardening, cleaning, cooking, and welcoming guests. You can stay at Eihei-ji for one to three nights and train with the monks in residence, but you must already be affiliated with Soto Zen. ∎

Eihei-ji

🅰 171 B3

✉ 5-15, Shihi, Eiheiji-cho, Yoshidagun, Fukui

☎ 0776/63-3640

💲 $

🚌 Bus from Fukui Station (30 min.)

global.sotozen-net .or.jp/eng/temples /jp/eiheiji.html

Nagano-ken

Japan is a land of many mountains—but to the Japanese, Nagano-ken is *the* alpine prefecture. Western-style mountaineering was first introduced here more than a century ago; in 1998, Nagano city was host to the Winter Olympic Games. Apart from winter sports, visitors can enjoy hiking in summer and autumn, especially around Kamikochi.

Zenko-ji offers meditative grounds high in the mountains of Central Honshu.

Nagano

🗺 171 C4

Visitor Information

✉ 2F JR Nagano Station

☎ 026/226-5626

🕐 9 a.m.–7 p.m

🚆 JR Shinkansen from Tokyo to Nagano (1 hr. 40 min.)

go-nagano.net

After coming under the spotlight in 1998, Nagano reverted to the quiet lifestyle of a prefectural capital. A small modern city, it has few sights, but it is friendly and cosmopolitan, and it makes a comfortable base for trips into the surrounding mountains. The town's one truly outstanding temple is **Zenko-ji.** So important is the temple to the town that

Chuo-dori, the main street, runs northward up to it in a dead straight line, a distance of one mile (1.5 km) from Nagano Station. Founded around 660, Zenko-ji's all-embracing tradition of worship reflects the dawn of Buddhism in Japan, but it belongs to no specific sect and is revered by all. Zenko-ji has admitted women both as worshippers and priests for centuries, even when most sacred precincts were male preserves. Of paramount importance to pilgrims, it receives up to eight million visitors annually. Those numbers swell every six or seven years for the Gokaicho ceremony honoring the Ikko Sanzon Amida Nyorai statue. Too sacred for mortal eyes, the statue traditionally remains hidden. The next Gokaicho will take place in either 2021 or 2022.

Main Hall & Gates

The temple's destruction in 1700 prompted a reorientation of the compound; built in 1707, the colossal **Main Hall** (Hondo) stands on a site northeast of its original counterpart. The **Nio-mon,** first of the two huge gates along the approach, was rebuilt in 1918. The imposing facade of the Main Hall does justice to the magnificence of the lofty interior. Incense wafts high up into the gilded shadows of an ornate coffered ceiling hung with gigantic gold lamps; the atmosphere is awe-inspiring.

One of the main attractions—a ticket to heaven—is to touch the **key of paradise** (an icon set in wood) beneath the main altar. Claustrophobes, be warned: To touch the key, you need to grope along the wall through a long, narrow tunnel in pitch darkness. If you fail to touch the key, take heart: The relief at seeing a glimmer of light at the end is symbolically equated with Enlightenment.

Scribes are on hand to commemorate pilgrims' visits

with a temple seal; for a small fee, they will stamp your notebook (visitors can collect stamps from temples and shrines throughout Japan) and embellish it with votive calligraphy.

Nagano is a convenient base for hiking and skiing, particularly the Myoko range to the north. There is excellent year-round hiking up the west side of **Myoko-san** through wetlands

INSIDER TIP:

There are countless skiers' gems to be found in Nagano-ken. Personal favorites are Zao (Yamagata) and Tenjindaira (Gunma). Come mid-January to mid-February for the deepest powder.

—ANDREW LEA
Founder, snowjapan.com

full of flowers and ski runs ending at hot-spring resorts on the east. A more challenging hike is the four-day traverse south from **Shirouma-dake,** the "white horse peak" that looms over the Hakuba ski area. The ridgeline trail is vertiginous and requires chains in many places.

Of the seven ski resorts, Myoko Suginohara stands out for its 5.2-mile (8.5 km) run, the longest in the nation, and Akakura remains popular for families with easy runs and an *onsen* at the base. ■

Zenko-ji

- ✉ 491 Motoyoshi-cho
- ☎ 026/234-3591
- 🕐 Dawn to 5:30 p.m.
- 💲 $: Inner Sanctum & walk in the dark *(okaidan meguri),* main hall free
- 🚌 Bus: Daimon stop from Nagano Station

Myoko-san

- 🗺 171 C4
- ✉ By Myoko Kogen Station
- ☎ 0255/86-3911
- 🕐 10 a.m.–5 p.m, closed Wed.
- 🚌 Access via Myoko Kogen Station (40 min. from Nagano)

Matsumoto

Matsumoto, in the central highlands, is the southwestern equivalent of Nagano (see pp. 186–187) and is similarly used as a base for mountain excursions and activities. The city center is bland, but it retains some venerable backstreets. The Metoba-gawa flows through Matsumoto east to west, and the townscapes along the banks are an engaging jumble of old and new.

The Utsukushigahara Open Air Museum: Alfresco art for outdoor types

Matsumoto

⚑ 171 C4

Visitor Information

✉ IF JR Matsumoto Station

☎ 0263/32-2814

🕐 9 a.m.–5:45 p.m.

🚃 JR Shinonoi line from Nagano (50 min.) or JR Chuo Honsen line's "Azusa" limited express from Shinjuku Station, Tokyo (2 hr. 40 min.)

www.matsumoto -tca.or.jp

Utsukushigahara Open Air Museum

✉ 2085-70 Takeshi kamihoniri, Ueda-shi

☎ 0268/86-2331

🕐 9 a.m.–5 p.m., closed Nov.–April

💲 $$

Ruled by the Ogasawara clan in the 14th and 15th centuries and taken over by the Ishikawa in the 16th, Matsumoto was a castle town. **Matsumoto-jo** *(4-1 Marunouchi, tel 0263/32-2902, 8:30 a.m.–4:30 p.m., $$)* is one of Japan's finest castles. Only a hint of white accentuates the black wooden walls and dark-tiled roofs of this National Treasure, nicknamed Karasu-jo (Crow Castle). The name, possibly derived from its shape, is more probably due to the contrast with the White Heron Castle of Himeji (see pp. 253). First constructed in 1504, the castle reached its final form in the 1590s. A spectacular alpine panorama unfolds from the platform on the five-story **main keep.** The interior—actually six floors (most Japanese castles have five stories outside and six inside)—displays an arsenal of

guns, swords, and armor. **Nihon Minzoku Shiryokan Museum,** attached to the castle, showcases many exhibits, including the Honda Clock Collection. The **Japan Ukiyo-e Museum** (Nihon Ukiyo-e Hakubutsukan; *2206-1 Shimadachi, Koshiba, tel 0263/ 47-4440, 10 a.m.–4:30 p.m., closed Mon., $$$)* has the country's largest collection of *ukiyo-e,* or woodblock prints.

Matsumoto is noted for scenic spots less than 30 minutes away by bus, notably the 6,500-foot (2,000 m) **Utsukushigahara Plateau** (Utsukushigahara-kogen), famed for mountain views, carpets of alpine flowers, and the **Utsukushigahara Open Air Museum,** where some 400 works lay scattered across an alpine meadow. Matsumoto also provides easy access to the Kamikochi Valley. ∎

Kamikochi & the North Alps

The Kamikochi Valley, cutting through the Japan Alps west of Matsumoto, is a narrow glen in Chubu Sangaku National Park. The valley lies at 5,000 feet (1,525 m) above sea level between Yake-dake to the southwest, Kasumizawa-dake to the east, and the Hotaka range to the north. Averaging 10,000 feet (3,050 m), these peaks are among Japan's highest.

A favorite hiking ground since the introduction of alpinism to Japan in the 19th century, **Kamikochi** is a gateway for several excellent hikes, especially in October when the foliage sets the slopes ablaze in reds and yellows. Day-trip trails follow the

INSIDER TIP:

The earliest easy hiking in the North Alps is in mid-July: Before that you'll need crampons or risk being caught in the severe storms of the rainy season.

—PERRIN LINDELAUF
National Geographic writer

Azusa-gawa up to Yoko Lodge with stunning views of 10,466-foot (3,190 m) **Oku-Hotaka-dake,** Japan's third highest peak, and popular weekend loop tracks go up to **Yari-ga-take,** the sharp "Spear Peak" or through the colorful Kara-sawa Valley and up to Oku-Hotaka.

Once on the ridgeline, even longer hikes extend farther north, including a weeklong trek that ends in Toyama-ken at

Tateyama, a popular pilgrimage spot, and **Tsurugi-dake** (Sword Peak; 9,839 feet/2,999 m), known as Japan's scariest nontechnical climb, with a knife-edge ridgeline leading into a short vertical cliff ascent assisted by chains.

The abundance of staffed lodges along this route obviate the need for camping gear, but in the high seasons (August and October) be aware that the lodges can't turn anyone away, so you may end up spooning with strangers. Whether you haul your gear up the slopes or get friendly with other hikers, the peaks are worth it. ∎

Kamikochi

🅰 171 C4

Visitor Information

✉ Kamikochi bus terminal

☎ 0263/95-2405

🕐 7 a.m.–4:30 p.m.

🚉 Matsumoto Dentetsu line from Matsumoto Station to Shin-Shimashima (30 min.), then 1 hr. 5 min. by bus to Kamikochi (bus service runs from mid-April–mid-Nov. only)

kamikochi.or.jp

Hotaka-dake overlooks Kappa Bridge in Kamikochi.

EXPERIENCE: Japan—A Hiker's Paradise

With its icon of snowcapped Fuji-san, Japan thinks of itself as a hiker's country. But it wasn't always so. A hundred years ago, the mountains were fearsome places, the realm of the gods, where only ascetic priests dared climb to learn their secrets. It wasn't until a pair of mountaineering Englishmen, William Gowland and Walter Weston, began scaling peaks and spreading the word about Japan's great landscape that locals started to lace up their boots.

Fast-forward a hundred years: Hiking is hugely popular, with well-marked trails, staffed lodges, and buses running directly from major centers to busy trailheads. The islands' long north–south orientation and tumultuous tectonic history make for a broad variety of landforms and ecosystems—from the snowy, hissing volcanoes of the Daisetsuzan Range to the temperate ridgeline hikes of the Japan Alps and the semi-tropical jungle of Yakushima island in Kagoshima.

The mountains have long been a spiritual testing ground, a place of purification, and home of the gods. Temples hide in deep valleys, weathered shrines dot the peaks, and hearing the blast of an ascetic priest's conch horn reverberating through the mountains is magical, a call to Japan's ancient past.

More than anything, it is the Japanese themselves that make the mountains so pleasant. Shared interest in hiking and shared suffering on steep sections make it easy for outsiders to be accepted. You'll be taken care of, given snacks and drinks, and your safe arrival will be asked after in the evenings. Although the signage is almost exclusively in Japanese, there will always be someone on the trail to give directions and make shy conversation. Indeed, the cardinal rule for hiking in crowded Japan is that if you're alone, you're in the wrong place.

INSIDER TIP:

Before leaving your lodge, check the mountain forecast (*tenki yo-hoh*), as the closest village data will likely be different.

—PERRIN LINDELAUF
National Geographic author

The **Kamikochi Valley Loop** (see p. 189) is a moderate, well-maintained course that takes in Hotaka-dake, the third tallest peak in Japan at 10,466 feet (3,190 m). The best time to hike this three-day loop is October, when the hills begin to blaze red. The hut below Mount Hotaka's peak offers wonderful views.

The **Tsurugi-dake Circuit** (*alpen-route.com*) in the North Alps offers a holy mountain and Japan's scariest peak. This circuit has a fascinating cultural side, as the geography is seen to represent Buddhist cosmology: Rolling Tateyama is easygoing, lofty, and with its mountaintop temple, represents the heaven of Enlightenment. Below, the valley's volcanic "hells" spit boiling mud and hiss sulfuric gases. Nearby Tsurugi-dake (Sword Peak) doesn't look all that sharp until you scramble over its razor ridges and cling to chains on its sheer walls.

Climbing **Mount Fuji** at dawn is on every hiker's must-do list. A once-in-a-lifetime hike, Fuji-san (see p. 122) is convenient to Tokyo: Buses run to the Kawaguchi-ko-guchi Fifth-Stage trailhead from Shinjuku Station. Time your walk so you can sleep in a hut near the top, then walk the remaining stage to watch dawn from the summit.

The **Daisetsuzan** traverse offers the hiker five adventurous days of rolling, snow-patched volcanoes. Daisetsuzan or "Great Snow Mountain" (see p. 139) rises out of the center of Hokkaido, a patchwork of new and old volcanoes. Huts dot half the traverse, but the need to camp and to cook every meal keeps a large number of casual hikers away.

The Kiso Region

Modern Japan has paved over most of its medieval highways, but not in the Kiso region, where the Nakasendo—the mountain highway between Tokyo and Kyoto—and its post towns still exist. Eleven towns lie along the highway in this narrow, cedar-lined valley, preserving the lifestyle of the footsore traveling merchant, the princess in her palanquin, and the samurai on horseback, rushing to the capital.

Tsumago retains a timeless atmosphere.

Kisoji (the Kiso route, aka the Nakasendo) was never as popular as the lowland Tokaido Road, which saw three-quarters of all the traffic between Kansai and Tokyo. The latter has been covered up by the Tokaido train lines and the Meishin expressway in modern Japan, but Kisoji, thanks to its remoteness and narrow valley location, was partly bypassed when mountain highways and train lines were constructed. The region's towns of Narai, Tsumago, and Magome suffered decline as foot travel became a thing of the past, but their fortunes turned in the 1960s, when the traditional architecture of these towns was reevaluated by a modernizing Japan.

Narai, once dubbed "Narai of the 1,000 Houses," was the most important post town on the Nakasendo. There are fewer than 1,000 today, but venerable houses still flank the 0.75-mile (1.2 km) main street, which looks much as it did 200 years ago, down to the old wells for slaking travelers' thirsts. Just behind it lie charming rustic shrines and temples. Some houses are now museums and craft shops; others, such as the saké brewery, an old lacquerware workshop, and the famous Echigoya Inn, maintain their ancestral function. You can visit a large

Kisoji
🅰 171 C3
🚆 JR Chuo Honsen line: Matsumoto–Nagoya
kisoji.com

Narai
🅰 171 C3
Visitor Information
✉ Inside JR Shiojiri Station
☎ 0263/54-2001
🕐 9 a.m.–6 p.m.

Kiso Fukushima

171 C3

Visitor Information

- Beside JR Kiso Fukushima Station
- 0264/22-4000
- 9 a.m.–6 p.m.
- JR Chuo Honsen line from Matsumoto (40 min.)

Agematsu

171 C3

Visitor Information

- In front of Agematsu Station
- 0264/52-4820
- 9 a.m.–5 p.m.

Tsumago

171 C3

Visitor Information

- 2159-2 Azuma
- 0264/57-3123
- 8:30 a.m.–5 p.m.
- Bus from JR Nagiso Station

Magome

Visitor Information

- Opposite Toson Kinenkan
- 0573/69-2336
- 8:30 a.m.–5 p.m.
- Bus from JR Nakatsugawa Station (30 min.)

lacquerware store and museum in **Hirasawa,** about half a mile (1 km) north. About the same distance north of this is **Niekawa,** which maintains a replica of its old *sekisho* (barrier station), where the identities of travelers were checked.

To the south, **Kiso Fukushima** is Kisoji's largest town. Part of it was badly damaged by fire in 1947 and subsequently rebuilt. The old section on the hill, overlooking the Kiso-gawa, was largely spared and retains an antiquarian charm. As at Niekawa, there is a handsome replica of the old barrier station. West of the village is Mount Ontake, one of Japan's most sacred mountains. Tragically, it erupted in 2014, killing 57 hikers, and its peak remains off-limits.

The next major station you reach is riverside **Agematsu,** which offers a breathtaking view over the Kiso-gawa gorges. Known as a center for woodcraft, the town's workshops are open to the public, and the scent of cedar is heavenly.

The jewel in Kisoji's crown is **Tsumago,** 15 miles (25 km) southwest of Agematsu. This village marks the start of the best preserved section of the old Nakasendo, which leaves the river and highway behind for the ancient road, 6 miles (9.5 km) of pleasant walking south to Magome. Tsumago has been officially protected since 1968; the town's buildings have been beautifully restored, with communication lines buried underground and TV aerials hidden. Highlights include a palatial wooden official

residence (now the local museum) and a post office, both dating from the 1860s. Tsumago's only drawback is that it feels like a museum, particularly as the often daunting crowds of visitors vastly outnumber the residents. Best appreciated in the evening and early morning, Tsumago is a delightful place to stay. The 18th-century house on the main street, famous for the tree growing right against its facade and featured on local postcards, is still a *ryokan* (inn). If you intend to do the walk, inquire at the Visitor Information Center about luggage forwarding to Magome, the southern terminus, as both villages are best experienced with a restful overnight stay.

Heading south from Tsumago, you pass through the hamlets of Otsumago, Kudaritani, and O-daki, taking in the pretty farmland and a pair of waterfalls. Depending on the season, you will see mountains reflected in the flooded rice fields, lush shades of green, or vivid autumn hues. After the Magome-toge (Magome Pass) a modern road restarts, and there is bus service if you'd like to skip the last 2 miles (3 km) to **Magome.** Touristy but with picturesque mountain views, the town marks the southern end of the historical Kisoji. Rebuilt after several fires and now primarily famous for local writer Shimazaki Toson (1872–1943), an early proponent of Western styles for Japanese themes, the village has traded some of its historical patina for fresh blood and new businesses serving walkers. ∎

Futuristic Convenience in Japan

Part of the enduring image of Japan is that of the sci-fi metropolis, crawling with robots and high-tech conveniences. Yet in past decades, other countries have developed high-speed trains, Apple has eclipsed Sony in electronics, and vending machines have become more sophisticated worldwide. Despite the rest of the planet catching up, Japan is largely perceived as a world leader in technological progress thanks to three cultural touchstones: *omotenashi* (hospitality), *benri* (convenience), and *kaizen* (improvement).

Omotenashi literally means "without surface" and describes the whole-hearted, rather than superficial devotion to one's guests that is core to the Japanese sense of hospitality. This way of thinking is ancient, and it can be seen in everything from the cool towel offered in a restaurant on a hot summer day to how a tea master sprinkles water in the street to tamp down dust before your arrival. Good service is of absolute importance in Japan, and today's businesses strive to outdo each other in little gestures.

The essential term *benri* is the clearest example of this. If whole-hearted devotion maxes out at smiles and anticipating needs, convenience, or having something immediately at hand when required, is where much of Japan's current focus lies. Convenience stores, found everywhere, make a mockery of the junk-food dispensaries in North America, selling everything from fresh vegetables to smartphone battery packs, booze, and business shirts. Vending machines are even more ubiquitous and carry a broad range of products.

It isn't enough to merely be convenient. The concept of *kaizen* has trickled into Western business vernacular, and it refers to continual small step improvement rather than radical change within an organization or workflow. While this sometimes results in *chindogu* or "unuseless gadgets" that cause more trouble than they are worth, here are some of the latest improvements in service and convenience you will find:

The ANA Boeing 787 Dreamliner offers unprecedented passenger comfort.

- the new full-flat beds in business class on All Nippon Airways' 787 Dreamliners
- Ferris wheel–style stacked parking garages
- braille on the top of beer cans
- washlet toilets that dry and deodorize
- the call-server buttons in busy restaurants
- the detachable end of a toothpick to rest the used toothpick on
- rice ball packaging that keeps seaweed dry and separated until you pull a tab to open it
- bank machines that can receive a loose handful of change or dispense coins
- photocopy machines and ATMs in all convenience stores
- karaoke machines that let you change the key of the music to better suit your range and prevent crimes against music
- easy-ordering vending machines in restaurants—great for non-Japanese speakers
- Internet cafés where you can stay the night and take a shower

Yuzawa Onsen

A mere 77 minutes by Shinkansen from Tokyo, Yuzawa Onsen in Niigata Prefecture is ideal for a day of skiing. Siberian winds pick up moisture on the Sea of Japan and dump 460 inches (11.7 m) of annual snowfall on this region nicknamed Yukiguni or "Snow Country." Sixteen ski resorts are located around this *onsen* town, which is also known for excellent saké.

Yuzawa Onsen

⊠ 171 D4

Visitor Information

✉ Inside JR Echigo-Yuzawa Station

☎ 025/785-5505

🕐 8:30 a.m.–6 p.m.

🚄 JR Joetsu Shinkansen to Echigo-Yuzawa Station (77 min. from Tokyo)

e-yuzawa.gr.jp

Snow Country Museum

✉ 354-1 Oaza-Yuzawa, Yuzawa-machi

☎ 025/784-3965

🕐 9 a.m.–4:30 p.m., closed Wed.

💲 $

Skiing is a relatively new pastime in Japan, the oldest ski hill being established in nearby Myoko in 1937. The main draw for remote mountains has been their hot springs: for warmth, health, and pleasure. Many prestigious onsen such as Yuzawa trained local women to entertain as geisha. Unlike their wealthy city counterparts, whose activities were strictly limited to the arts, mountain geisha ranged from entertainers to love interests to post-bath prostitutes, and their lot was often an unhappy one.

Novelist Yasunari Kawabata, Japan's first Nobel laureate in the arts, wrote his prize-winning novel *Yukiguni* while staying in Yuzawa Onsen; the tale beautifully recounts a doomed romance between a local geisha and a Tokyo man. **Takahan,** the same 800-year-old *ryokan* he stayed in while writing, is still in business and is one of several excellent onsen ryokan (see Travelwise p. 372), its bath open to nonguests, too *($$$)*. The geisha are now long gone, but the **Snow Country Museum** preserves traces of old mountain life: straw raincoats, displays on raising silkworms, and photos of the geisha.

In Kawabata's novel, the geisha were already on the decline and skiing had just been introduced; it's hard to say whether the writer would recognize modern Yuzawa and its huge resorts. **GALA Yuzawa Ski Resort** *(tel 025/785-6543, galaresort.jp, closed May 8–Dec. 16, day passes $$$$$)* is convenient for day trips, its own Shinkansen station connecting directly to a gondola to take skiers up to the resort on Takatsukura-yama (3,875 feet/1,181 m).

Those with more time should hop on a shuttle bus from Echigo-Yuzawa Station to one of the more remote, less busy resorts. At the station, check out the **Pon-shukan** *(tel 025/784-3758),* a rice and saké shop. For ¥500 you can get five tokens that allow you to sample from 117 different kinds of saké from Niigata breweries. ∎

Snowboarders at GALA Yuzawa Ski Resort, Yuzawa Onsen

Sado-ga-shima

Few islands have as varied a history as Sado-ga-shima: First used as an ocean-bound prison, it then enjoyed a gold rush and recently saw the establishment of Kodo, a *taiko* drumming group that sets the island to a powerful beat each summer at its Earth Celebration festival.

A demon dances to the drums of Sado's *ondeko* music.

Sado differs from other remote islands because of the regular injections of dissident culture it received over the centuries. Emperor Juntoku was sent here for fostering a rebellion in 1221 against the Kamakura shogunate, and although he died 22 years later without being pardoned, he brought with him the culture of the aristocracy. In a similar fashion, firebrand monk Nichiren was banished here for criticizing the government and calling all other monks heretics: He brought with him an impassioned, populist Buddhism

that made many converts and established many temples on the island before his eventual pardon. Among several artists and writers, Noh master playwright Zeami was sent here as an old man on the angry impulse of a shogun, and partly thanks to him Sado-ga-shima has a rich history of Noh plays, unusual for a largely rural area.

The discovery of gold in 1601 changed Sado's fortunes, but it still remained a place of exile, as convicts were sent here for hard labor. At one point, the most productive gold mine in

Sado-ga-shima

⬛ 171 C5–C6

Visitor Information

✉ Near ferry terminal at Ryotsu

☎ 0259/23-3300

🕐 8:30 a.m.– 5:30 p.m.

🛳 Ferry from Niigata to Ryotsu, (2 hr. 20 min.); jetfoil from Niigata (1 hr.)

visitsado.com
mijintl.com

Kodo Drummers

Accompanying dancing and parades, traditional Japanese festival combos incorporate flutes with a gamut of percussion instruments, including giant upright *taiko*, hand drums, and wooden clappers—all orchestrated with dexterous precision. Among them, Sado's *ondeko* drumming is paramount; founded in 1981, its Kodo

troupe stands at the pinnacle of the art. Kodo drummers train long and hard, living according to a monastic regime near Ogi in the south. The Kodo organization created Sado's international Earth Celebration *(third week of August, kodo.or.jp)*, a weeklong festival of music and dance where the island resounds to the beat.

Sado Kinzan

- ✉ 1305 Shimoaikawa
- ☎ 0259/74-2389
- 🕐 8 a.m.–5:30 p.m., 8:30 a.m.–5 p.m. in winter
- 💲 $$
- 🚌 Bus from Ryotsu port

Ogi

- ▲ 171 C5

Visitor Information

- ✉ 1935-26 Ogimachi, W of the post office
- ☎ 0259/86-3200
- 🕐 8:30 a.m.– 5:30 p.m.
- 🚌 Bus from Sawata (65 min.)
- ⛴ Ferry from Naoetsu, Honshu (2 hr. 40 min.)

Sadokoku Ogi Folk Culture Museum

- ✉ 270-2 Shukunegi, Ogi-machi
- ☎ 0259/86-2604
- 🕐 8:30 a.m.–5 p.m., closed Mon. Dec.–Jan.
- 💲 $

the world, the **Sado Kinzan,** outside the sleepy village of **Aikawa,** saw a huge gold rush and a population of 100,000, more than the whole island's current population. After falling production in the 19th century and the mine's final closure in the 1990s, a museum to its history was established, with fine descriptions of medieval mining techniques, such as the old bamboo water pump systems.

With the collapse of mining, tourism has risen to fill the void as urbanites seek out some self-imposed exile away from the bustle of busy lives. Of the two ports, **Ryotsu** is more convenient, but if you are coming for the Earth Celebration, **Ogi** is the center of the action. The island is divided into three main districts: the rugged north; the developed, rice-producing center; and the cultural south. Nowadays Sado is most famous for the Kodo drumming troupe, but if you miss the Earth Celebration (see sidebar above), Ondeko Demon Dances, out of which Kodo developed, are held throughout the year.

Ryotsu is a developed port, but **Sado Nogaku-no-sato,**

a museum dedicated to the island's Noh culture, is well worth a look. Across the island is **Mano,** the former island capital and erstwhile prison home to exiled emperor Juntoku. From the town, a popular walking trail passes through rice fields and by temples to **Mano Go-ryo,** Juntoku's tomb.

In the south, the village of Ogi is a quiet port, once responsible for shipping out Sado's gold. The **Sadokoku Ogi Folk Culture Museum** has a replica of the boats used to transport this heavy, precious cargo. Outside the lively three days of Kodo's Earth Celebration, the main form of tourist entertainment is paddling around the bay in tub-shaped *taraibune* boats, traditionally used to collect seaweed or shellfish from the coastline. Rent a bike and head west along the coast, noting the giant 59-foot (18 m) Jizo statue poking out of the hillside on the way to the village of **Shukunegi,** a national historic site with an attractive collection of old homes, clustered together in the narrow bay. ∎

Geisha slipping down narrow alleyways, the still of a Zen garden, and the spiritual heartland of traditional Japanese culture

Kyoto

A garden lantern in the surrounds of Shoji-ji Temple

Kyoto

Japan's capital from 794 to 1868, Kyoto remains the finest repository of the nation's history, the best glimpse of an enduring "Old Japan." Long a center of political power struggles and religious foment, the city has two palaces, two castles, and some 1,600 Buddhist temples and 400 Shinto shrines, including 15 UNESCO World Heritage sites.

There are still some traditional neighborhoods, too, but the departure of the emperor for Tokyo in 1868 left Kyoto with an identity crisis that continues to this day: "Keep up" with other modern, ugly Japanese cities or preserve the city's traditional beauty and risk irrelevance?

Indeed, visitors expecting an incense-scented Shangri-la are shocked by the architectural mishmash of Kyoto Station and its slapdash concrete environs. Don't worry: Despite poor first impressions, Kyoto remains an attractive city once you seek out its gems. It lies in a U-shaped valley, with major sights such as the Imperial Palace and Nijo Castle in the center and the majority of temples, shrines, and traditional districts against the wooded hills, where they escaped Kyoto's frequent fires. North of Kyoto Station is the Kawaramachi shopping district and downtown; east, across the Kamo-gawa, lies Gion, the most famous of the city's five geisha districts. Beyond Gion is Higashiyama, a low mountain range full of ancient temples, including Kiyomizu-dera, Nanzen-ji, and Ginkaku-ji. Likewise, west, in the Arashiyama mountains, another large concentration of excellent temples is found, along with the Okochi Villa and Kyoto's celebrated Bamboo Grove.

In planning a trip to Kyoto, remember that it's easy to overdose on traditional architecture and multiarmed Buddhas. A little background reading helps appreciate differences, but the ideal Kyoto day has a healthy mix of elements such as gardens, religious iconography, geisha-spotting, fine art, a Shinto festival, or sublime *kaiseki*, Kyoto's haute cuisine. The ancient capital is also the place to try traditional culture such as flower arrangement, Zen meditation, or the tea ceremony. Stop by Kyoto Station's tourist information center to grab a map and see what's on, as there is often a little festival underway at a shrine or temple somewhere.

Perhaps the best aspect of this large city with a long history and so many hidden gems is that visitors are able to discover their own Kyoto. Beyond the pages of this chapter lie hundreds more intriguing temples and ancient shrines, storied sweetshops, and hidden gardens. Even long-term residents remark in surprise at the endless discoveries to be made. While Kyoto struggles against the tide of modernity, that magic of old Japan still lingers for those willing to look for it. ∎

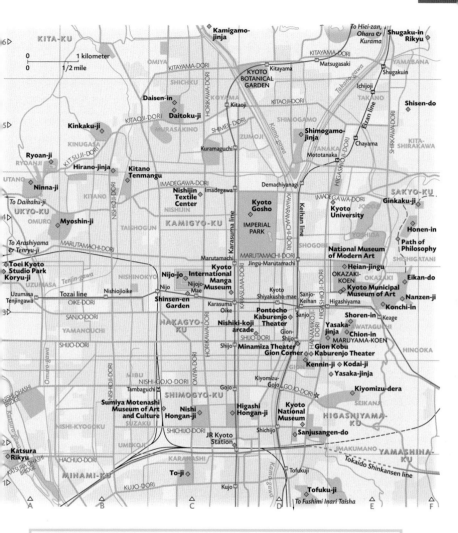

NEED TO KNOW

Reaching Kyoto

Kyoto is served by Kansai's two airports, Itami and Kansai International (KIX). Itami, also known as Osaka International, ironically only deals with domestic flights. Just 50 minutes by Limousine Bus, it's closer to Kyoto and a great option for a quick flight with ANA from Tokyo. KIX handles the region's international flights. The HARUKA Express airport train runs directly to Kyoto in just 75 minutes, and you can use the JR Pass on it. Kyoto is also served by the Tokaido Shinkansen, just over two hours from Tokyo.

Getting Around

In addition to several intercity railway lines, Kyoto is bisected by two subway lines and has extensive bus service. Cycling is also great to see Higashiyama.

Central Kyoto

Central Kyoto has largely been taken over by the typical Japanese urban landscape, but a few major sights, their proximity to the city center denoting their importance, lie within walking distance of Kyoto Station or the Karasuma subway line, which runs north-south through the middle of the city.

A "praying for peace" float at the Gion Matsuri festival

Kyoto

Visitor Information

✉ 2F Kyoto Station (next to Isetan dept. store)

🕐 8:30 a.m.–7 p.m.

☎ 075/343-0548

kyoto.travel

www.pref.kyoto.jp /visitkyoto/en

Take a quick trip up Kyoto Tower across from the train station to get your bearings before heading out. If pressed for time, catch a bus from in front of the station direct to Higashiyama in eastern Kyoto (see pp. 204–211), which has the best one-day concentration of sights.

Kyoto was founded, among other reasons, as an attempt to escape the rising political power of the large temples in Nara, so when it was laid out in classical Chinese grid style, space was allotted for only two temples, **To-ji** (East Temple) and Sai-ji (West Temple), built in 796. They sat on either side of the south gate, the Rashomon, popularized by Kurosawa's film of the same name. Sai-ji was lost to fire and never rebuilt, but To-ji was rebuilt repeatedly due to the influence of prominent monk Kukai (see sidebar p. 294), who was given charge of the temple in 823. He turned it into a huge seminary, four times its present size. The **Kondo** (Main Hall; 1606) is a National Treasure, as are some of the eighth- and ninth-century works of religious art in the **Kodo** (Lecture Hall; 1491), which contains 21 renowned statues of Buddhas and Buddhist guardians. More stunning iconography is in the **Treasure House** (Homotsukan), which is open only in the spring and fall. The grounds contain extensive gardens and the stunning pagoda built by Tokugawa Iemitsu in 1644: At 187 feet (57 m), it's the largest in Japan. Every month on the 21st, a large flea market is held here.

Buddhist influence was once again out of hand with the rise of populist Pure Land Buddhism (Jodo Shinshu sect; see sidebar below), but warlord Toyotomi Hideyoshi attempted to exert some control by granting the sect land for **Nishi Hongan-ji.** The temple, just northwest of Kyoto Station, is one of two headquarters for the sect. It has exquisitely ornate halls: The gold-leaf-encrusted **Founder's Hall** (Goei-do) dates to 1636 and has a statue of the founder, Shinran, while the **Amida-do** has excellent Kano-school paintings. The best parts of the temple are the beautifully painted **Daisho-in** hall and **Hiunkaku** pavilion, which were once part of Hideyoshi's castle, but you can see them only in October.

Jodo Shinshu Sect

Founded by the priest Shinran (1173–1224) in 1224, the Jodo Shinshu (Pure Land New Faith) sect of Buddhism rejects the need for vegetarianism, asceticism, and celibacy for the priesthood. Instead, it teaches that Enlightenment may be achieved simply by repeatedly chanting a mantra exalting the Amida Buddha: "Nama Amida Butsu." Seen as a political threat, the sect was persecuted. But so great was its following that Toyotomi Hideyoshi realized that his campaign to unite Japan would fail without it; he built Nishi Hongan-ji in Kyoto in 1591. Jodo Shinshu now counts 12 million followers worldwide.

Higashi Hongan-ji, the other headquarters of the sect, was founded when Hideyoshi's successor, shogun Tokugawa Ieyasu, fostered a feud between the heirs to Nishi Hongan-ji, splintering the sect and reducing its power. Reduced power isn't really what comes to mind looking at the temple's **Goei-do,** a building whose size is rivaled only by Todai-ji in Nara (see pp. 237–239). Rebuilt after a fire in 1895, the temple lies north of Kyoto Station.

A fragment of the old Floating World endures at the **Sumiya Motenashi Museum of Art and Culture,** just west of Nishi-Hongan-ji. This last remaining *ageya* or grand banquet hall of the old Shimabara entertainment district once held huge parties with large numbers of geisha. The 17th-century building has some 20 rooms that mix the open space of samurai style with the refinement of smaller teahouses.

The old heart of the city is **Kyoto Gosho,** the Imperial Palace. The original palace was built by Emperor Kammu in 794 and stood northwest of the present site for more than 500 years. The current palace was a noble's villa the imperial family often visited, and it became the de facto palace in 1331 when the original location was abandoned after a series of disastrous fires. The spacious pine-covered grounds and large walled palace were home to the throne for the next 500 years until they were abandoned by Emperor Meiji in his move to Tokyo in 1889. Truth be told, the large enthronement building and

To-ji

- 🗺 199 C1
- ✉ 1 Kujo-cho, Minami-ku
- 🕐 8:30 a.m.– 5:30 p.m., closes 4:30 p.m. Sept.– Mar.
- ☎ 075/691-3325
- 💲 $
- 🚇 Kintetsu line: Toji; or 15-min. walk from Kyoto Station

Nishi Hongan-ji

- 🗺 199 C2
- ✉ Hanayacho Sagaru, Horikawa-dori, Shimogyo-ku
- 🕐 5:30 a.m.– 6 p.m.
- ☎ 075/371-5181
- 🚌 City Bus 9

Sumiya Motenashi Museum of Art and Culture

- 🗺 199 C2
- ✉ 32 Nishi-Shinyashiki Ageya-cho, Shimogyo-ku
- ☎ 075/351-0024
- 🕐 10 a.m.–4 p.m., closed Mon.
- 💲 $$
- 🚇 JR Sanin line: Tambaguchi

Kyoto Gosho

- 🗺 199 D4
- ✉ Kyoto Gyoen-nai, Kamigyo-ku
- ☎ 075/211-1215
- 💲 English-language tours (50 min.) at 10 a.m. & 2 p.m. Mon.–Fri.; reservations required. See also sidebar p. 202.
- 🚇 Karasuma line: Imadegawa

Nijo-jo

🗺 199 C3

✉ Nijojo-cho, Horikawa Nishi-iru, Nijo-dori, Nakagyo-ku

☎ 075/841-0096

🕐 8:45 a.m.–5 p.m.

💲 $$ (including garden)

🚇 Tozai line: Nijojo-mae; JR Sanin line: Nijo; City Bus 9, 12, 50, or 101: Nijojo-mae

private quarters feel a little sad: Politically irrelevant while the shogunate held power, they sat empty afterward. It's easy to understand why Kyotoites wept when the emperor left. Still, the surrounding park provides open, quiet space, and the long walls of the palace are quite photogenic.

West of the palace lies **Nijo-jo**, a castle built in 1603 for shogun Tokugawa Ieyasu's visits to Kyoto. More of a gilded palace with a moat, the castle is a showy display of wealth intended to humble the cash-strapped imperial court and prove that the military was truly in power. A few relics of the military remain: The anti-ninja "nightingale" floors squeak loudly, a hawk-themed room was dedicated to storing arms, and small chambers next to the shogun's seat once concealed lurking bodyguards.

Many of the sliding doors are blinding gold-leaf reproductions, standing in for the Kano-school originals, which are displayed in the adjacent museum. The bright new reproductions alongside original screens give a sense of how intimidating the reception chambers once were. In contrast,

the residential rooms are painted in a subdued black ink.

The center of Kyoto nowadays is the shopping district around Kawaramachi and Shijo streets. Their intersection is dominated by the large department stores Takashimaya and Marui: Shops spread out north and west from there. A block west of Kawaramachi are three shopping arcades: Shinkyogoku, Teramachi, and Nishiki-koji. **Shinkyogoku** is full of cheap youth fashions and lurid souvenir shops for out-of-town students on field trips. You may not find anything to buy, but the street is prime people-watching

INSIDER TIP:

The bus network in Kyoto is easy to use and covers most of the major sights. Buy a ¥500 day pass and English-language bus map from the ticket office at Kyoto Station.

—ROB GOSS
National Geographic contributor

Permission to Visit

Permission from the Imperial Household Agency is required before you visit the palaces and imperial villas in Kyoto. Non-Japanese visitors are generally able to visit the same day if they apply before 9:40 a.m. at the Imperial Household Agency in Kyoto. You can save yourself time and uncertainty by gaining advance permission on the Imperial Household

Agency website (*sankan.kunaicho.go.jp*). Visitors under 18 must be accompanied by an adult. Only one Japanese person is allowed to accompany each foreigner, thus passports for foreign residents are required to confirm your nationality. Permission must similarly be obtained from the Imperial Household Agency for the Katsura and Shugaku-in villas.

territory. **Teramachi** or "Temple Town" took its name when Hideyoshi forced many temples to move here so that Buddhism could be better controlled. The arcade is lined with stylish shops as well as a collection of good craft stores; north of Oike-dori, Teramachi has excellent antiques stores, too. Perpendicular to Teramachi is the **Nishiki Market.** Once called the Kitchen of Kyoto, this narrow arcade is now primarily devoted to local specialties, particularly the expensive, refined ingredients for *kaiseki*. With piles of mysterious pickles, rows of razor-sharp knives, Japanese sweets for tea ceremonies, and hundred-dollar matsutake mushrooms, the shops here are nothing short of fascinating. There are lots of samples on offer, but be considerate of the "no photos" signs, where posted.

Pickled vegetables at the Nishiki Market

Kyoto's main nightlife district is just east of Kawaramachi, focused on the cherry-lined Kiyamachi street and the narrow alley of Pontocho. Kiyamachi, despite its attractive little canal draped with cherry trees, is a fairly standard collection of bars, reasonably priced *izakaya* pubs, and hostess cabarets, somewhat quieter than a similar-size city because Osaka sucks some of the wind out of Kyoto's nightlife. Running parallel, Pontocho is one of Kyoto's five geisha districts, and because it is narrow, it is one of the best places to spot a *geiko* or *maiko* walking to an appointment. The restaurants are more expensive than Kiyamachi, but more accessible than those of nearby Gion (see pp. 210–211), another

geisha district, and dining along the Kamo-gawa in the summer is one of Kyoto's great pleasures. Geisha and maiko dances are put on at the **Pontocho Kaburenjo Theater** May 1–24.

Fans of anime culture should pop into the **Kyoto International Manga Museum,** a large reading library with exhibits on the history and evolution of manga—Japanese comics—its big names and prominent themes. Translated volumes are also available, and the Astroturf lawn here is great for energetic kids. Would-be illustrators should also check out their workshop programs, where kids can color manga pages and serious students of the style can get advice from a manga artist. ■

Pontocho Kaburenjo Theater

- ⚠ 199 D3
- ✉ Pontocho, Sanjo-sagaru, Nakagyo-ku
- ☎ 075/221-2025
- 💲 $$$$
- 🚆 Keihan line: Sanjo

Kyoto International Manga Museum

- ⚠ 199 C3
- ✉ Karasuma-Oike, Nakagyo-ku
- ☎ 075/254-7414
- 🕐 10 a.m.–6 p.m., closed Wed.
- 💲 $$
- 🚆 Tozai line: Karasuma-Oike

kyotomm.jp

East Kyoto: Higashiyama

Kyoto's Higashiyama (East Mountain) district is its most beautiful, with diverse temples, attractive traditional architecture, and the largest geisha district in Japan. Kiyomizu-dera, the most popular temple in Kyoto, should be at the top of everyone's list. From there, an easy half day can be spent exploring quieter temples, important shrines, or narrow cobbled lanes between Gion's teahouses.

Daina-no-gi Festival at Heian-jingu

Kiyomizu-dera

🗺 199 E2

✉ 1-294 Kiyomizu, Higashiyama-ku

☎ 075/551-1234

🕐 6 a.m.–6 p.m.

💲 $

🚌 City Bus 100 or 206: Kiyomizu-michi or Gojo-zaka; Keihan line: Kiyomizu-gojo, then 20-min. walk

kiyomizudera.or.jp

Kiyomizu-dera, sitting up against the forested hills of Higashiyama, is an ideal starting spot for the neighborhood. The temple predates Kyoto's creation: First established in 778 around a pure spring from which it took its name, Kiyomizu is dedicated to the Eleven-Headed Kannon, the bodhisattva who hears all prayers. The temple's current buildings date from the 17th century, but the **Hondo** (Main Hall) is a National Treasure and architectural feat belying its age. Sitting on a steep hillside, the Hondo has a large stage extending out from the central altar chamber, supported by 40-foot (12 m) wooden pillars. The view of Kyoto from the stage is superb, particularly when the temple's *sakura* are in bloom, but the height inspired a superstition that jumping and surviving would grant a wish. Even today, bold action in Japan is called "leaping from the stage at Kiyomizu." Below the stage is the **Otowa Waterfall,** a trickle of spring water that visitors drink for its purifying properties. Before you leave, walk to the east entrance of the hillside **Otani Cemetery** for the view over thousands of tombs. For a sense of scale, remember that many enshrine the bones of whole family branches over many generations.

The lanes below the temple are chockablock with souvenir shops. Most of it is cheap junk—except the umbrellas with handles like sword hilts, which no would-be ninja should face a rain shower without. The area is also known for its own style of pottery, *Kiyomizu-yaki,* characterized by a rich blue or green glaze. Turning north and downhill, you clear the kitsch and enter a fine neighborhood of

EXPERIENCE: *Zazen*

Zen differs from other sects of Buddhism in that it attempts to get back to the original experience of the historical Buddha. Zen followers set aside sutras, ceremonies, and ascetic rituals to focus on simple sitting meditation—*zazen*—from which the sect takes its name. A famous Zen *koan* (riddle) states: "If you meet the Buddha, slay him," meaning that even a great teacher can become an object of desire and prevent one's Enlightenment.

Sitting meditation, the observation of the mind, and contemplation of koan make up much of Zen practice. Several temples across Japan open their meditation halls for public sittings alongside practicing monks. This is a great opportunity to experience "zen," so poorly understood in the West, for one's self.

Start by sitting cross-legged, either with both ankles resting on your thighs or with the left tucked under if the "full lotus" position is too difficult. Sit up straight and concentrate on slow regular breathing. The key is not trying *not* to think, but rather to restrain the mind from chasing after each thought that pops up. Rather, observe the thoughts that arise, and let them go. If you find concentration difficult, ask for the *kyo-saku* or "encouragement stick." Bow to a passing monk, and he'll administer four quick smacks to your back with a long paddle. The sting helps focus and fights off sleepiness; but don't worry, it sounds much more painful than it is.

Tofuku-ji, Kyoto Experience zazen in a delightful 14th-century meditation hall (*Sundays, 6:30 a.m.–7:30 a.m.*).

Nazen-ji, Kyoto (*April–Nov.: 6–7 a.m. 2nd & 4th Sun. each month; Dec.–Mar.: 6:30–7:30 a.m.; closed Aug.*)

Shunko-in, Myoshin-ji, Kyoto Meditation sessions in English (*Most days at 9:30 a.m., $$$$, see shunkoin.com*)

Engakuji, Kamakura (*Sat. at 1:20 p.m.; 2nd & 4th Sun. at 9 a.m., includes 1-hr. lecture*)

---

traditional homes. Kyoto used to look like this everywhere, which makes these remaining patches of traditional architecture all the more precious.

The next stop is **Kodai-ji,** a Zen temple built in 1605 to the memory of Toyotomi Hideyoshi with his widow's prayers and Tokugawa Ieyasu's money, perhaps because the founder of the Tokugawa shogunate felt guilty for taking the country away from the dead man's young heir. The temple suits Hideyoshi's sense of style: Not exactly exuding Zen simplicity, it features a gate from his castle in Fushimi, the elaborate **Founder's Hall** (Kaisando) decorated with masterwork paintings from the Kano and Tosa schools, and a mortuary chapel covered in lacquer and gold inlay.

Continuing north past the rickshaw drivers (*$$$$$*), the cobbled lane reaches **Maruyama-koen,** Kyoto's best-loved park for *hanami* (see p. 94), when its paths are crammed full of stalls hawking snacks, booze, and toys. In mid-March the park is the centerpiece for **Hanatouro** (*hanatouro.jp*), a weeklong illumination of the Higashiyama district.

Just outside the park is **Chion-in,** the head temple for the Jodo sect and thus one of the most important in the nation. Religious

Kodai-ji

199 E2

526 Shimogawara-cho, Kodaiji, Higashiyama-ku

075/561-9966

9 a.m.–5 p.m.

$$

City Bus 206: Higashiyama-Yasui

kodaiji.com

Chion-in

- 🅰 199 E3
- ✉ 400 Rinka-cho, Higashiyama-ku
- ☎ 075/531-2111
- 🕐 6 a.m.–4:30 p.m., gardens 9 a.m.– 4 p.m.
- 💲 $
- 🚌 City Bus 206: Chionin-mae

chion-in.or.jp

Heian-jingu

- 🅰 199 E4
- ✉ 97 Nishi Tenno-cho, Okazaki, Sakyo-ku
- ☎ 075/761-0221
- 🕐 6 a.m.–6 p.m. Mar.–Sept.; closes at 5 p.m. Oct.–Feb.
- 💲 $$
- 🚌 City Bus 4, 5, or 6: Kyoto Kaikan Bijutsukan

heianjingu.or.jp

National Museum of Modern Art

- 🅰 199 E3
- ✉ Okazaki Enshoji-cho, Sakyo-ku
- ☎ 075/761-4111
- 🕐 9:30 a.m.–5 p.m., closed Mon.
- 💲 $
- 🚇 Tozai line: Higashiyama

www.momak.go.jp

Kyoto Municipal Museum of Art

- 🅰 199 E3
- ✉ Okazaki Park, Sakyo-ku
- ☎ 075/771-4107
- 🕐 9 a.m.–5 p.m., closed Mon.
- 🚇 Tozai line: Higashiyama

reformer Honen founded this temple in 1175; much like his student Shinran, who founded the Jodo Shinshu sect (see sidebar p. 201), he proposed faith and prayer, rather than individual meritorious behavior, to be the only way the average person could achieve Enlightenment. Critics argued that this "make a donation and say *Namu Amida Butsu*" model degraded the religion, but there's no denying that Honen's philosophy has had mass appeal. The temple has Japan's largest gate, standing 79 feet (24 m) tall, and the largest bell, weighing 81.5 tons (74 tonnes) and requiring 17 monks to ring. The **Hondo** (Main Hall) is under renovation until 2019, but the grounds are open.

Next door is **Shoren-in** (*69-1 Sanjobo-cho, Awataguchi, Higashiyama-ku, tel 075/561-2345, shorenin.com, 9 a.m.–5 p.m., $*), a temple surrounded by ancient camphor trees. Technically a part of the Tendai sect of Mount Hiei (see p. 113), it was built in the 12th century for members of the imperial family who were practicing monks; the beautifully painted sliding screens give Shoren-in the air of an imperial villa, and the gardens are among the city's best.

From Shoren-in, walk down to Sanjo-dori, where a massive red *torii* gate looms in the distance, announcing the entrance to **Heian-jingu.** As its bright red paint and green tile suggest, this is one of Kyoto's relatively new shrines, built in 1895 to commemorate the 1,100th anniversary of the city's founding and to deify Emperor Kammu, its founder.

The shrine is actually a two-thirds scale-reproduction of the original Heian-period (794–1185) imperial palace, and although they are jarring, the loud colors are historically accurate. The somber, unpainted wood of many contemporaneous temples is actually a failure to repaint their gaudy original murals. Behind the ornate buildings lies a large garden containing cherries, maples, azaleas, and lily ponds, making it worth a visit year-round. Heian-jingu is also the starting point for Jidai Matsuri, held October 22. This "Festival of the Ages"

INSIDER TIP:

In Kyoto, visit the Kanga-an *(kangaan .jp)* to the north of the Imperial Palace for a great vegetarian meal prepared by monks.

—TAKUYA NISHIMATSU
Kyoto City Tourism office manager

was begun to cheer up Kyotoites recently bereft of the emperor's presence and consists of a parade of people in the various lavish fashions of Kyoto's history.

The area around the shrine—Okazaki—is notable for a cluster of museums. The **National Museum of Modern Art** primarily exhibits work of 20th-century artists from Kansai, and the **Kyoto Municipal Museum of Art** holds a mix of local and global exhibitions. The **Fureaikan** (*Okazaki Seisoji-cho, Sakyo-ku, tel 075/762-2670, miyakomesse.jp/fureaika, 9 a.m.– 5 p.m., Tozai line: Higashiyama*),

Women in kimonos take in Nanzen-ji's gardens.

beneath the Miyako Messe conference hall, displays Kyoto traditional crafts, from textiles to ceramics to Buddhist altars.

East of Okazaki, **Nanzen-ji** is one of Japan's most important Zen temples. The temple complex started out as an Imperial villa: One of Emperor Kameyama's mountain retreats was haunted and only the meditation of a Zen monk was able to calm the spirit. Impressed, Kameyama granted the monk part of the estate in 1291 and supported the temple's construction. By 1334 Nanzen-ji was so large and powerful, thanks to the support of the throne and the shogunate, that it was declared the head temple of the city.

Despite being sacked and burned by the warrior-monks of Mount Hiei, Nanzen-ji was repeatedly rebuilt in a style that struggles to mix Zen simplicity with the ostentatious tastes of the Momoyama-period rulers. The **Sanmon** gate is pure Zen: Standing alone, not demarcating any obvious border, it alludes to a famous collection of *koan* entitled "The Gateless Gate" or "The Gate to Emptiness," a metaphor for Buddhism itself. The **Seiryo-den,** a National Treasure building from Emperor Go-Yozei's own palace, is all baroque excess. Tigers and phoenixes parade across its Kano-school gold-leaf screens, making *(continued on p. 210)*

Nanzen-ji

🗺 199 E3

✉ 86 Fukuchi-cho, Sakyo-ku

☎ 075/771-0365

🕐 8:40 a.m.– 5 p.m. Mar.– Nov.; closes at 4:30 p.m. Dec.– Feb.

💲 $$

🚇 Tozai line: Keage; City Bus 5: Nanzen-ji or Eikando-michi

Higashiyama Walk

This walk takes in several of Kyoto's best known sights; allow yourself extra time if you plan to visit any of the places on the way. It will probably take a full day to follow the route and stop off for sightseeing and refreshments.

Zen refinement and Toyotomi Hideyoshi's opulent tastes mix at Kodai-ji.

From Gojo-zaka bus stop, walk up Gojo-zaka slope, veering right for 550 yards (500 m) up to **Kiyomizu-dera ❶**, Kyoto's most famous landmark (see pp. 204). The temple buildings were erected in 1633; perched on pillars on top of a cliff, the main hall is designated a National Treasure. Having admired the view from up here—particularly beautiful in the cherry blossom season—wander down the narrow lane called **Kiyomizu-zaka.** The number of craft and souvenir stores selling everything from kitsch to beautiful Kiyomizu-yaki ceramics is

NOT TO BE MISSED:

Kiyomizu-dera • Ninen & Sannen-zaka • Kodai-ji • Yasaka-jinja

overwhelming; 19th-century Western visitors did not dub the street "Teapot Alley" for nothing.

At the bottom of the lane, turn to your right down the staircases called **Sannen-zaka** and **Ninen-zaka**. This will bring you

INSIDER TIP:

Be sure not to miss Kiyomizu-dera and the narrow lanes around Ninen and Sannen-zaka: This area's teahouses, inns, and shops feel like the quintessence of Japan.

—KENNY LING
National Geographic contributor

into Kyoto's prettiest little lanes, full of teahouses, traditional inns, and classy restaurants. To your left is the five-story, 128-foot-high (39 m) **Yasaka-jinja Pagoda ❷**, built by shogun Ashikaga Yoshinori in 1440. Follow the street on your right—passing Ryozen Kannon Temple, notable for a colossal statue of the Buddhist deity Kannon, 80 feet (24 m) high—to **Kodai-ji ❸** (see p. 205), which dates from 1606. The grounds include an elegant garden, and the screens inside the buildings are decorated with fine art.

Proceed north 650 yards (600 m), then cross through **Maruyama-koen,** notable as Kyoto's most popular place for *hanami* (see p. 94), centered on its ancient weeping cherry tree. Chion-in's massive hall is under construction, but its gate is astounding and its bell is Japan's largest. From here, walk 220 yards (200 m) north past Chion-in's huge gate to **Shoren-in ❹** (see p. 206), noted for its excellent 17th-century paintings inside and for its landscape garden, one of Kyoto's most famous. Retrace your steps as you leave, walking 550 yards (500 m) down to **Yasaka-jinja ❺**, the shrine favored by residents of Gion and known locally as Gion-san (see p. 211). From here you can go on to explore Gion (see pp. 210–211) or call it a day at the Gion bus stop, opposite the *torii* gateway in front of the main entrance to Yasaka.

▲	See area map pp. 198–199
➤	Gojo-zaka bus stop
⏱	3–4 hours
↔	1 mile (1.5 km)
➤	Gion bus stop

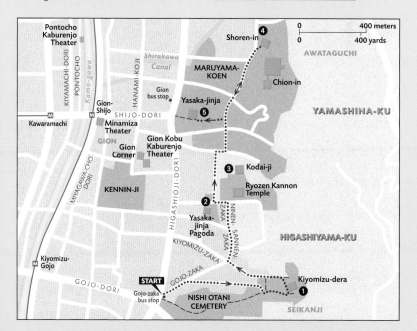

Eikan-do

199 E3
48 Eikando-cho, Sakyo-ku
075/761-0007
9 a.m.–4 p.m.
$$
Tozai line: Keage; City Bus 5: Nanzen-ji or Eikando-michi

eikando.or.jp

for quite a contrast with the austere landscape gardens.

Some of the old temple-town atmosphere remains. Several subtemples in the precinct are open to visitors. **Konchi-in** has a garden built by Kobori Enshu, the master gardener—and vegetarian restaurants line the road leading to the main gate. **Eikan-do** sits just next door to Nanzen-ji and is famous for its maples and unusual statue of Amida. Legend has it that the monk Eikan was pacing around the altar in prayer, when the statue climbed down and started walking with him. Shocked, Eikan stopped, so the Amida looked over his shoulder, saying, "Eikan, you're slow!" This Mikaeri-Amida (Looking-back Amida), frozen in that position, symbolizes his patience even for those who are slow to come to him.

Gion

Gion, Kyoto's biggest traditional entertainment district, stretches out between Maruyama-koen in Higashiyama and the Kamogawa in the west, north, and south of Shijo-dori. Although much of the original sprawling pleasure quarter has been replaced by stacks of bars and cabarets in garish concrete buildings, the core of old geisha teahouses and exclusive restaurants around Hanami-koji remains the best preserved in the nation. Gion is wonderful to explore, especially beautiful after dark, when the soft lantern-light casts shadows over the narrow cobbled streets and the latticework of old buildings. You may even spot one of the remaining 300 *geiko* or *maiko* (apprentice geisha) as she steps from a taxi

A chef works along Shirakawa Canal, one of Kyoto's best spots for *hanami* and fine dining.

into a restaurant or walks down one of the narrow alleys, avoiding the tourist cameras. South of Shijo, **Hanami-koji** preserves numerous fine old buildings, but be aware that the old "*ichigen-san, okotowari*" (no introduction, no service) system still exists, so many places won't serve you unless a previous customer will vouch for you. Walk three blocks north of Shijo along Hanami-koji and turn left on Shinbashi-dori, where another cluster of beautiful old buildings follows the Shirakawa Canal, lined with cherry and willow trees.

Although the teahouses are largely inaccessible, the local geiko and maiko put on dances at the **Gion Kobu Kaburenjo Theater** on Hanami-koji every April and at the **Gion Kaikan Theater** near the entrance to Yasaka-jinja every November. **Gion Corner,** a small theater next to Gion Kobu, has daily performances of traditional arts, including maiko dances. The entertainment scene isn't all about geisha, though: On the corner of Shijo and the Kamo-gawa, the **Minamiza,** the most celebrated old theater in Japan, holds regular Kabuki performances. The biggest show is in December; Kyoto Station's tourist information center has the complete listings.

Gion is also home to two key religious centers: Yasaka-jinja and Kennin-ji. **Yasaka-jinja** sits at the end of Shijo-dori, announced by a large Buddhist-style gate built when Shinto and Buddhism were closely entwined. The patron shrine of Gion, Yasaka has long been Kyoto's most popular place

INSIDER TIP:

When sizing a kimono, sleeves should cover the wrists, and the hem should hide the ankles. Kimonos are worn left over right: The opposite is unlucky, as it is for the dead.

—INOUE NAOYA
Kimono shop owner

for *hatsumode,* the first shrine visit of the new year, and thousands of kimono-clad celebrants line up here every January 1. The shrine is also the center for Gion Matsuri, a grand parade of tall wooden floats held in July that dates back 1,100 years. Sitting just south of Hanami-koji is **Kennin-ji,** Kyoto's oldest Zen temple. Eisai, the monk who introduced Zen and tea to Japan in the late 12th century, built this temple despite the opposition of rival sects; one can only wonder at the concentration it took to meditate on the doorstep of a pleasure quarter. The large *karesansui* (dry landscape) garden around the **Abbot's quarters** (Hojo) and the 575-foot (175 m) ceiling painting of a pair of dragons in the **Lecture Hall** (Hatto) are notable.

If Hanami-koji is too crowded, check out the little visited Miya-gawa-cho, one of Kyoto's smaller geisha districts. Turn west from the north gate of Kennin-ji and turn south (left) one block before the Kamo-gawa. This charming street is often deserted and is just as photogenic as central Gion. ■

Gion Corner

◮ 199 D3

✉ Gion Hanamikoji-dori

☎ 075/561-1119

🕐 Performances daily 6 p.m. & 7 p.m. mid-Mar.–Nov.; Fri.–Sun. only Dec.–mid Mar.

💲 $$$$

kyoto-gioncorner .com/global/en.html

Kennin-ji

◮ 199 D3

✉ 584 Komatsu-cho, Higashiyama-ku

☎ 075/561-6363

🕐 10 a.m.–5 p.m. Mar.–Oct.; 10 a.m.–4:30 p.m. Nov.–Feb.

💲 $

🚃 Keihan line: Gion-shijo

kenninji.jp

Geisha

Most Japanese have seen true geisha only on television or in festival parades. Genuine geisha entertain the political and industrial elite in exclusive traditional *ryotei* restaurants, and *cha-ya* (teahouses)—both antiquarian establishments boasting inner gardens. Numbering about 100,000 before World War II, the geisha declined with the rise of the bar hostess after the war; they now number less than 1,000.

A young *maiko* in Gion

The geisha have their origins in the pleasure quarters—the Floating World—of 300 years ago. More than mere bordellos, the great Green Houses of the 17th-century pleasure quarters offered banquets enhanced by courtesans adept at singing and dancing. Itinerant entertainers and musicians often accompanied them, the most skilled being dubbed *otoko geisha* (male arts people). By the 1700s, the best female entertainers became known as *geiko* (arts girls). To call them by any other name in Kyoto would

ruffle their fine plumage, but elsewhere the generic "geisha" stuck.

The geisha, her face whitened and her mouth reduced to little petals of brilliant red, became a living work of art, an icon of womanhood. Spirited, garrulous, talented, and sexy, she had all the dazzle that Confucian strictures forbade in a virtuous wife. Geisha are also table entertainers, sought for their wit and powers of conversation. Even in advanced years, geisha continue to be revered as exponents of traditional performing arts.

At first, many geisha doubled as prostitutes. Infuriated by the rivalry, the courtesans successfully petitioned the government to pass a law forbidding geisha to sleep with customers in the pleasure quarters. As a result, the profession went upscale.

Modern-day Geisha

Today's geisha earns a lot of money. She has to, in order to pay for an apprenticeship that leaves her indebted to her *okiya* (geisha house) and for her wardrobe, which includes a collection colored according to each season. She shuns wearing the same kimono in front of the same customers twice. Modern lifestyles have influenced the geisha: Formerly dependent on finding a *danna*—a wealthy patron/lover—to support her career, modern geisha are no longer under such economic pressure. Similarly, the practice of auctioning off a geisha's virginity is now illegal and extinct.

Previously, girls trained as geisha from childhood; nowadays they start in their late teens or even after graduating from university. Hundreds of girls still aspire to become geisha, but only three out of ten weather the harsh training as

INSIDER TIP:

The best place to spot geisha in Gion is the intersection of Hanami-koji and Shijo streets. Go in the early evening, but keep a respectful distance.

—CHRIS ROWTHORN
Writer, insidekyoto.com

maiko (apprentices) at the okiya, where they are strictly schooled in singing, dancing, playing the shamisen (Japanese three-stringed lute), and deportment. The harshest mistress is apparently the uncomfortable wooden neck-prop used to keep their complex hairstyles from becoming ruined while they sleep.

You might see geisha in Kyoto's Gion (see pp. 210–211), where the maiko—gaudy little dolls with whitened faces—bustle along, pigeon-toed on high sandals, while the geisha glide past in their silken finery with regal nonchalance. The traditional geisha districts of Gion, Pontocho, and Kamishichiken are small enough that it is possible to spot one of Kyoto's 300 remaining geisha. Don't bother looking in Tokyo: The metropolis of 35 million souls has only 60 practicing geisha. Geisha are not as old-fashioned as they seem. Their conversational skills are utterly contemporary, and they pride themselves on being able to talk to anyone about anything. If geisha disappear, it will not be because they are out of tune with the times, but a matter of simple economics. Catering to a dwindling elite, they have priced themselves out of the market.

Geisha and maiko prepare to perform the *Miyako Odori* (Cherry Dance) in Kyoto.

West Kyoto

Away from the city center, residential western Kyoto has several large temple complexes—Buddhist villages in themselves—that developed in what were once the city's outskirts. Less convenient than eastern Kyoto, big-name temples, an important shrine, and a center for weaving make a bus trip worthwhile.

The Nishijin textiles area is a cloth-lover's wonderland.

Nishijin Textile Center

🅜 199 C4

✉ Horikawa-Imadegawa Minami-iru, Kamigyo-ku

☎ 075/451-9231

🕐 10 a.m.–6 p.m.

🚇 Karasuma line: Imadegawa

nishijin.or.jp

Nishijin, Kyoto's most famous textiles district, lies several blocks west of the palace. Originally established to produce kimonos and obi for the court, this weaving district grew increasingly wealthy in the prosperous Edo period—7,000 looms once operated in the area. Although the weavers have adopted modern power looms to stay competitive, the finest obi are still woven by hand, the fingernails used to pluck the thin silk strands. At the **Nishijin Textile Center,** you can watch weavers at work, try your hand at the loom, and see regular kimono fashion shows.

Farther west along Imadegawa-dori, **Kitano Tenman-gu** is one of Kyoto's most important shrines, dedicated to the scholar Sugawara-no-Michizane. Slandered and exiled in 903 to Kyushu, he died longing for the capital. When a series of disastrous lightning strikes devastated central Japan, including the properties of his accusers, Kitano Tenman-gu was built to appease his spirit. The grounds are the site of the Tenjin-san flea market on the 25th of each month and are beautiful in March when the plum trees bloom. Likewise, adjacent **Hirano-jinja,** rarely visited by foreigners, is a great spot for *hanami*, with 500 cherry trees.

Buses bound for Kita-oji Terminal go past the vast temple complex of **Daitoku-ji.** A walled city of 24 subtemples on 27 acres (11 ha), Daitoku-ji is a world apart from the busy street outside and preserves the cloistered atmosphere of a monastery. Established in 1324 and burned down in the Onin War (1467–1477), Daitoku-ji's existence is owed to one of the

INSIDER TIP:

Get into the local scene at Kitano Ten-mangu and haggle for goods at the monthly flea market (25th) offering everything from antique kimonos to bonsai trees.

—GREG KOCH

Tour Guide, handsonkyoto.com

most fascinating monks in Japanese history, Ikkyu Sojun (1394–1481). An eccentric iconoclast, Ikkyu left the rich, power-grubbing Zen temples of Kyoto for severe training and poverty in Shiga. Once he achieved Enlightenment, he began to eat meat, get drunk, and brazenly go to brothels in his monk's robes. Much like a self-contradictory *koan*, his behavior was a calculated challenge to calcified dogma and the hypocrisy of "mouth Zen," which turned a blind eye to pederasty between

monks and their disciples. In his old age, he badgered wealthy merchants into funding the temple's reconstruction. Ikkyu was never comfortable in an abbot's robe and preferred the company of his lover, a blind woman 40 years his junior, subject of dozens of racy poems that would have made Shakespeare blush.

The tea master Sen-no-Rikyu was also deeply involved with Daitoku-ji. Having renovated the **Sanmon** gate, he put a statue of himself among its Buddhist images, but when the *daimyo* Toyotomi Hideyoshi discovered he'd been walking beneath Rikyu, he ordered the tea master to commit suicide. Among the several subtemples only a handful are open: **Daisen-in** stands out for its excellent sand garden, and **Koto-in** is notable for its maples and bamboo.

Kitano Tenman-gu

🅰 199 B4
✉ Bakuro-cho, Kamigyo-ku
☎ 075/461-0005
🕐 5 a.m.–6 p.m.
🚌 City Bus 50 or 101 from Kyoto Station, 201 from Demachiyanagi Station

kitanotenmangu
.or.jp

Daitoku-ji

🅰 199 C5
✉ Daitokuji-cho, Murasakino, Kita-ku
☎ 075/491-0019
🕐 Subtemples: 9 a.m.–4 p.m.
🚌 City Bus 205 or 206: Daitokuji-mae

zen.rinnou.net

Japanese Textiles

The beauty of Japanese textiles is legendary; the prices of even used silk kimonos and brocade obi (kimono sashes) have escalated sharply in recent years. Using hand-cut stencils and rice paste applied to the fabric, *yuzen* is a skillful dyeing technique that produces patterns of great complexity, especially in Kyoto and Kanazawa. Okinawa, too, produces beautiful textiles; the hand-painted colorful *bingata* designs, often representing stylized flowers and birds, are the most famous. Rustic *aizome* cotton textiles, mainly dyed with natural indigo, are often exquisitely printed or tie-dyed. Used for garments, bags, and hats commonly sold in gift shops, sophisticated variants of aizome find new applications among fashion designers.

The stone garden at Ryoan-ji defies easy interpretation.

Kinkaku-ji

- 199 B5
- 1 Kinkakuji-cho, Kita-ku
- 075/461-0013
- 9 a.m.–5 p.m.
- $
- City Bus 205: Kinkakuji-michi

About 1.5 miles (2 km) west of Daitoku-ji is **Kinkaku-ji,** also known as the Golden Pavilion. A small, three-story villa covered in gold lacquer without, and gold leaf within, the pavilion was built by shogun Ashikaga Yoshimitsu (1358–1408), an aesthete whose reign was largely marked by failure. Abdicating his powers to his nine-year-old son, he focused on building something worthy of the heavenly paradise of the Buddhas. The retirement villa is semantically ambiguous: As a symbol of extreme wealth and power it would be more easily understood, but as a Zen temple, which it became after Yoshimitsu's death, its worldly opulence jars the senses. Burned down in 1950 by a monk (whose madness is fictionalized in Mishima's *The Temple of the Golden Pavilion*), the current reconstruction feels fake

INSIDER TIP:

Listen to the stones, appreciate the simple palette of plants, and feel the emptiness within the design to increase awareness and learn to see in new ways.

—MARK HOVANE
Kyoto Garden Experience

to some, though regularly rebuilt shrines rarely face the same criticism. Whatever your reaction, it can't be denied that the pavilion, surrounded by a pond and set against a forested hillside, is a striking edifice in its own right.

Ryoan-ji (1473), just southwest, has what is probably the most famous Zen garden in all of Japan. The site attracts tourist busloads to match. The garden, a walled rectangle about the size of a tennis court, runs along the veranda of the temple's main building and consists of 15 large rocks in a sea of raked white gravel. Only 14 of the stones are visible from any point on the veranda; it is said that it is a Zen exercise to see the last invisible stone. The meaning of the garden is unclear, perhaps by design. The utter simplicity of stones, moss, and white space refuses easy mental categorization, forcing the mind to slow and wrestle with an intentional absence of meaning. Sadly, the garden tends to be packed, making quiet reflection impossible. Try to visit on weekdays just before closing, especially in rainy weather. The surrounding stroll gardens are excellent and largely ignored if the stone garden is too crowded.

Continuing southwest along the forested edge of the city you'll reach World Heritage site **Ninna-ji.** The temple started as a palace for retired emperors and still preserves one palace building, the **Goten,** notable for its gardens. By 888 it was converted to a temple of the Shingon sect, but its abbots were all imperial princes and the **Kondo** and **Miedo** halls were brought from the old Imperial Palace, preserving an imperial atmosphere. The five-story pagoda is particularly attractive as the backdrop of the temple's dwarf cherries, which bloom late each spring.

Myoshin-ji is a walled temple complex like Daitoku-ji, 15 minutes' walk southeast of Ninna-ji.

A total of 46 temples line the ancient cobbled roads, each walled away in small cells of private quiet. Of the few that are open to the public, **Taizo-in** has a wonderful garden and does short *zazen* classes, as does **Shunko-in** (see sidebar p. 205), which also preserves some relics of the Christians who once owned the temple and hid the objects of their forbidden faith within seemingly innocuous Buddhist iconography. Myoshin-ji is excellent for wandering about: You'll have nearly every subtemple to yourself, and the gardens of even the lesser known temples make for a peaceful moment of reflection. ■

Hikikomori & NEET

Two categories of Japanese youth are making a dramatic break with the ethos of their hardworking parents: the *hikikomori* and the NEET. The former are teens who lock themselves in their rooms, unable to cope with the world. The causes range from Japan's rigid social hierarchies and intense pressure on youths to permissive mothers and absent, overworked fathers. The related NEET (Not in Employment, Education, or Training) lives at home on his parents' pension and does little other than lounge about and meet friends. The collapse of lifetime employment and insane overtime are blamed for this trend.

Ryoan-ji
- 199 A5
- 13 Goryono-shitamachi, Ryoan-ji, Ukyo-ku
- 075/463-2216
- 9 a.m.–5:30 p.m. Mar.–Nov.; 8:30 a.m.–5 p.m. Dec.–Feb.
- $
- City Bus 59 from Sanjo-Keihan-mae to Ryoanji-mae or 50 from Kyoto Station to Ritsumeikan Daigaku-mae

www.ryoanji.jp

Ninna-ji
- 199 A4
- 33 Ouchi, Omuro, Ukyo-ku
- 075/461-1155
- 9 a.m.–5 p.m.; closes 4:30 p.m. Dec.–Feb.
- $
- City Bus 10 or 26: Omura-Ninnaji-mae; JR Sanin line: Hanazono, then 20-min. walk

ninnaji.or.jp

Myoshin-ji
- 199 A4
- Miyoshinji-cho, Hanazono, Ukyo-ku
- 075/461-5226
- 9 a.m.–4:40 p.m.; closes 3:40 p.m. Nov–Feb.; closed for lunch
- $
- JR Sanin line: Hanazono; City Bus 60, 91, or 93: Myoshinji-mae

myoshinji.or.jp

Arashiyama

Although eastern Kyoto preserves more of the worldly aspects of the former city, the peaceful west is felt to reflect Kyoto's aesthetic and spiritual heart. Even the emperors and aristocrats in ancient times liked to get away from the urban bustle, and when they did, their favorite escape lay in Arashiyama (Storm Mountain).

Koryu-ji
- 199 A3
- 32 Hachioka-cho, Uzumasa, Ukyo-ku
- 075/861-1461
- 9 a.m.–5 p.m. Mar.–Nov.; closes at 4:30 p.m. Dec.–Feb.
- $$
- City Bus 71, 72, or 73: Uzumasa-Koryuji-mae; JR Sagano line: Uzumasa

Today this hilly western edge of the city is both a popular area for strolling and a choice site for luxurious suburban homes.

On the way to Arashiyama, stop by **Koryu-ji,** Kyoto's oldest temple. Prince Shotoku, Buddhism's strongest early supporter, ordered the construction of this temple in 603 to house a statue of the Miroku Nyorai, the Buddha of the Future. Still the centerpiece of the temple, it seems insignificant among larger statues in the

Treasure Hall (Reihokan), but a closer look reveals why it was chosen as the first National Treasure of Japan. This Asuka-period (552–645) image, likely carved from red cedar in Korea, bears an expression reminiscent of the Mona Lisa. Eyes closed, a slight smile across his lips, he seems to be savoring this exquisite present moment; the emotion conveyed across the centuries is sublime. Of the other structures, the Taishi-den (1720) contains a statue of Shotoku believed to be a self-portrait; the Keigu-in (or Hakkakudo, Eight-Sided Hall), another National Treasure, dates from 1251 and enshrines another image of the prince.

The Uzumasa neighborhood where Koryu-ji is located was once home to Japan's early film studios, but all that now remains is **Toei Kyoto Studio Park** (Eiga Mura), a theme park and film set for period dramas. It's cheesy, but the samurai versus ninja shows that seem to spontaneously erupt as you walk about the sets can be fun. The Anime Museum describes Toei's animation projects, from *Dragon Ball* and *Sailor Moon* to recent hit *One Piece*; less glamorously, Toei is also guilty of creating the Power Rangers and their various spin-offs.

Arashiyama is to natural beauty what Higashiyama is to well-preserved architecture. The

Bamboo Grove on the way to Okochi Sanso in Arashiyama

INSIDER TIP:

Parents traveling with bored kids will find relief at Toei Kyoto Studio Park, where the Power Rangers put on live-action martial arts shows.

—PERRIN LINDELAUF
National Geographic writer

trees on the slopes of Arashiyama burst ablaze with color every spring and fall, drawing incredible crowds. A five-minute walk from JR Saga-Arashiyama Station, the main street running north–south through Arashiyama is full of good restaurants and faces **Tenryu-ji,** the most famous temple within the district.

Emperor Go-Daigo's death in 1339 brought to end a tumultuous era: He wrested power from the Kamakura shogunate only to be so inept that his own general, Ashikaga Takauji, seized control and installed a puppet emperor while Go-Daigo launched armies from Yoshino, near Nara (see pp. 234–243). When a monk dreamed of Go-Daigo's angry spirit in the form of a dragon rising from a river near the emperor's old villa, the famous monk Muso Kokushi urged Takauji to build a temple and appease his enemy's ghost. Thus the Temple of the Heavenly Dragon was founded as Kyoto's first large Zen seminary, with Muso laying out the gardens, which are the real attraction here. Focused on a pond with the mountains as backdrop, they are

particularly beautiful when the maples redden in November.

Exiting through the back gate of Tenryu-ji brings you to Kyoto's beloved **Bamboo Grove,** where a narrow lane winds through a dense old grove bathed in green light. The lane splits at the base of **Okochi Sanso** (*9 a.m.–5 p.m., $$*), the private villa of samurai movie star Okochi Denjiro. Its entrance fee effectively rebuffs the hordes in the bamboo forest from this little-known garden in Kyoto. Narrow paths wind up the side of Mount Ogura, where the wealthy actor and follower of Zen labored 30 years to build an extraordinary sprawling garden with views of Kyoto, Arashiyama, and the Hozu-gawa gorge. When the *sakura* are in bloom, the surrounding mountains seem to float atop them.

Turning right at the villa, you'll cross the tracks of the Romantic Train (*$$*), an open-air tram that runs along the Hozu-gawa gorge to the other side of the mountains. A good half-day loop from here starts with one of the hourly trains from Torokko Arashiyama (or Saga-Arashiyama Station). From there it's 20 minutes to Kameoka where a waiting shuttle bus connects with the Hozu-gawa Boat Ride (*9 a.m.–3:30 p.m., $$$$$*). This two-hour trip passes through the same gorge, bringing you back to the Togetsukyo Bridge, and is pleasant amid November's maples. The last train to do this course leaves at 3:10 p.m.; reserve a boat ticket from the train station.

Farther north of Okochi Sanso, the crowds thin out and you'll largely have the scattered temples

**Toei Kyoto
Studio Park**

◪ 199 A3

✉ 10 Higashi-hachioka-cho, Uzumasa, Ukyo-ku

☎ 075/864-7716

🕐 9 a.m.–5 p.m.

💲 $$$$ (adult), $$$ (child)

🚃 JR Sagano line: Hanazono or Uzumasa; City Bus 71, 72, or 73: Uzumasa-Koryuji-mae;

toei-eigamura.com

Tenryu-ji

◪ 199 A4

✉ 68 Susukinobaba-cho, Tenryuji, Saga, Ukyo-ku

☎ 075/881-1235

🕐 8:30 a.m.–5:30 p.m. April–Oct.; closes at 5 p.m. Nov.–Mar.

💲 $

🚃 JR Sagano line: Saga-Arashiyama

tenryuji.com

Daikaku-ji

☎ 4 Osawa-cho, Saga, Ukyo-ku

☎ 075/871-0071

🕐 9 a.m.–4:30 p.m.

💲 $

🚌 City Bus 28: Daikaku-ji; Kyoto Bus 61 from Sanjo-Keihan-mae or 71 from Kyoto Station

daikakuji.or.jp

Kozan-ji

☎ 8 Umegahata-Toganoo-cho, Ukyo-ku

☎ 075/861-4204

🕐 8:30 a.m.–4 p.m.

💲 $

🚌 City Bus 8: Takao (from Shijo-Karasuma Station)

Jingo-ji

☎ Takaocho Umegahata, Ukyo-ku

☎ 075/861-1769

🕐 9 a.m.–4 p.m.

💲 $

🚌 City Bus 8: Takao (from Shijo-Karasuma station)

to yourself. Both **Jojakko-ji** and **Nison-in** are notable for their maples, whereas **Takiguchi-dera** and **Gio-ji** are famous for stories of heartbreak. At the former, a rejected woman whose love had become a monk wrote her feelings in blood on a stone, then committed suicide; at the latter, a 21-year-old dancer named Gio rejected the world and became a nun when Japan's most powerful clan leader, Taira-no-Kiyomori, ditched her for another woman. Her usurper then broke it off with Kiyomori and joined the temple, too—one can only assume he had that effect on women. More somberly, thousands of stone Buddhas cover the grounds of **Adashino Nembutsu-ji,** commemorating the unknown dead who were thrown into pauper's graves here for centuries. The endless rows of tombs and worn, nearly featureless statues can be pretty spooky.

Farther north into the mountains is **Takao,** a village notable for its vibrant maples, steep mountain slopes, and a trio of excellent temples. Foremost among them is World Heritage site **Kozan-ji.** Not only is the temple home to Japan's first tea plantation, but its humorous National Treasure, "The Scrolls of Frolicking Animals and Humans," is considered the nation's first example of the manga style. Downriver, **Saimyo-ji** is a charming little temple over a red-painted bridge, but it is **Jingo-ji,** high on the ridge over the valley, that gets the most visitors in Takao. Founded in 781, the temple was taken over by famed monk Kukai (see sidebar p. 294) in 809. He resided here as

INSIDER TIP:

INSIDER TIP:

Saiho-ji is a gardening buff's delight, worth the entry fee for its quiet and its historic influence on gardening design.

—LARRY PORGES
National Geographic Books editor

abbot for 14 years, preparing to spread the estoteric Buddhism he learned in China across the country. The temple is stunning amid the maple trees, and tourists enjoy tossing little clay discs down into the valley to dispose of bad karma.

Northeast of central Arashiyama lies **Daikaku-ji,** a palace built for Emperor Saga's retirement, later converted to a temple. Like Ninna-ji (see p. 217), this temple's close connection to the throne meant that its abbots were always imperial princes. Although it was founded in the Heian period, the magnificent buildings here date to the 16th century. Outstanding paintings by major exponents of the Kano school—Motonobu, Eikoku, Sanraku, and Tanyu—are displayed here, as well as works by Ogata Korin of the 18th-century Rimpa school. The large boating pond adjacent to the temple, Osawa-no-ike, was also built by Emperor Saga and is striking for the spaciousness of its view when most Kyoto gardens make the most of enclosed spaces. Like much of Arashiyama, the pond is stunning in April and November.

Though somewhat distant from the rest of the sights,

Katsura Rikyu: A perfect blend of plant, stone, and water

southern Arashiyama has two of the best gardens in Kyoto. Generally considered to be a model combination of classical Japanese architecture and landscaping, **Katsura Rikyu** (Katsura Imperial Villa) was built by the imperial prince Toshihito in 1615 because *The Tale of Genji,* his favorite book, referred to moon-viewing parties along the Katsura-gawa (aka Hozu-gawa). The villa itself is closed, but its setting is a triumph of landscape design. Set about a pond, the garden is laid out in a series of visual surprises, its appearance vastly different from each viewpoint the winding paths lead to. The finest details have been carefully planned: Pine branches are pruned into fluffy balls of needles, moss grows along the edges of old bridges, and the precise placement of a spreading pine prevents arriving guests from seeing the whole garden at once. Even a rice field seen through the trees outside the villa was purchased to prevent its development, a rare bit of urban planning foresight for Japan.

Saiho-ji, a Nara-period temple restored in 1339, is considered to have the finest garden of Muso Kokushi (1275–1351), its lush profusion of moss set around a pond giving the temple the nickname Koke-dera (Moss Temple). More than 120 varieties of moss carpet the garden floor. The fragility of this moss led the temple's administration to severely limit the number of visitors: Application must be made by postcard a week in advance, visitors have to sit through an hour of Zen lecture or sutra copying before their tour, and the admission fee, at ¥3,000, is one of the most expensive in the country. ∎

Katsura Rikyu
- 199 A1
- Misono, Katsura, Nishikyo-ku
- Tour reservations required, see sidebar p. 202
- Hankyu Kyoto line: Katsura, then 20-min. walk; City Bus 33 from Kyoto Station to Katsura Rikyu-mae

Saiho-ji
- 225 A1
- 56 Jingatani-cho, Matsuo, Nishikyo-ku
- $$$$$. Tour only. Apply for tours at least 1 week prior by self-addressed, stamped postcard.
- City Bus 63 or 73: Kokedera

Southeast Kyoto & Fushimi

Southeastern Kyoto's sights are spread out but among the best that the city has to offer: Fushimi Inari, shrine of thousands of *torii* gates; the Kyoto National Museum, second only to the Tokyo National Museum; and Sanjusangen-do, which holds an army of ancient Buddhas.

The *torii* tunnel leading through Fushimi Inari Taisha

Kyoto National Museum
- ⓜ 199 D2
- ✉ 527 Chayamachi, Higashiyama-ku
- ☎ 075/541-1151
- 🕒 9:30 a.m.–5 p.m., closed Mon.
- 💲 $
- 🚉 Keihan line: Shichijo

www.kyohaku.go.jp

Sanjusangen-do
- ⓜ 199 D2
- ✉ 657 Mawari-cho, Sanjusangen-do, Higashiyama-ku
- ☎ 075/561-0467
- 🕒 8 a.m.–4:30 p.m.
- 💲 $$
- 🚉 Keihan line: Shichijo

To explore this area, either walk 20 minutes from Kyoto Station to Shichijo Station on the Keihan line, which has several local stops, or take the JR Nara line from Kyoto Station to sights farther south. Walking or the bus are the best way to get to the **Kyoto National Museum.** Originally built to house art belonging to the imperial family, the museum grew to some 12,000 pieces, particularly the fragile treasures that local temples and family couldn't preserve themselves. The Collections Hall has excellent exhibits on Japanese art, from Buddhist iconography to painting, ceramics, textiles, and metalwork, such as masterwork swords.

Across the street, you'll find **Sanjusangen-do,** the longest wooden building in the world, named after the 33 galleries between its pillars. Inside the temple, Kannon statues stand in rows ten deep, each of the thousand human-size images festooned with arms (for saving worlds) and heads (for hearing the prayers of the faithful). A total of 124 of them date from the temple's founding in 1164; the rest are copies carved after a fire in 1249. Tradition dictates that you try to find one that looks like someone you know. In the middle sits a giant Kannon, carved by master sculptor Tankei.

This and the wind and thunder guardians are National Treasures.

A quick train hop south brings you to **Tofuku-ji,** one of the five main Zen temples of Kyoto. Founded in 1236, this Rinzai-sect temple has several impressive buildings dating to the 14th century, among them the attractive Meditation Hall (Zendo), the lavatory and bath (Tosu and Yokushitsu), and the two-story, 72-foot-tall (22 m) Sanmon gate, a National Treasure. Tofuku-ji's grounds are more extensively gardened than other Zen temples. A bridge stretches across a small ravine full of maple trees, creating the impression of being engulfed in fire come November (that is, if you aren't engulfed by people— the crowds are legendary). A variety of dry landscape gardens use gravel raked in different patterns or moss grown around square stones to impressive effect.

Fushimi Inari Taisha lies about half a mile (1 km) south of Tofuku-ji. There are about 40,000 Shinto shrines dedicated to the deity Inari around the country, and this one, said to have been founded in the early eighth century, is the most important of all. The shrine covers the slopes of Inari-yama, the trails between lesser shrines to other deities lined with countless bright red torii gates. This torii tunnel is the product of donations made to the shrine. If you turn back, you'll see that the reverse side has the names of famous firms and the date of their donation. Inari is the god of rice and, by extension, wealth, so many

businesspeople come here to pray for success or to buy a charm of a fox, the messenger of Inari.

About 3 miles (5 km) southeast of Fushimi Inari Taisha is **Daigo-ji.** Approached via an avenue of cherry trees, this vast temple compound covers much of Daigo-yama. Founded during the mid-ninth century and belonging to the Shingon sect, Daigo-ji is favored by followers of Shugendo, a stringent form of Buddhist asceticism. Comprising more than 70 buildings and subtemples, the precinct is divided into Shimo (Lower) Daigo and Kami (Upper) Daigo, with a steep path some 2 miles (3 km) long dividing them. Visiting both constitutes a pleasant hike taking up a whole afternoon. The structures of Kami Daigo, former Buddhist seminaries, were built between the 12th and 16th centuries. Most of the Shimo Daigo buildings were destroyed during the 15th-century Onin Wars; they were extensively restored and rebuilt in the 16th century by order of Toyotomi Hideyoshi, who was known to hold *hanami* here. The notable exception is the five-story **pagoda,** erected in 951. It is not only the oldest building in Kyoto but the oldest of its kind in Japan. Rebuilt by Hideyoshi, the ornate **Sanpo-in** subtemple is noted for its Kano-school paintings as well as an outstanding landscape garden. Nearby is the **Hoju-in trea-sure hall** *(open April 1–May 25 & Oct. 1–Nov. 25).* It is renowned for its fabulous collection of scrolls, paintings, sculptures, and miniature shrines. ■

Tofuku-ji
- 199 D1
- ✉ 15-778 Honmachi, Higashiyama-ku
- ☎ 075/561-0087
- 🕘 9:30 a.m.– 4:30 p.m.
- 💲 $
- 🚉 JR Nara or Keihan line: Tofukuji

Fushimi Inari Taisha
- 225 B1
- ✉ 68 Yabunouchi-cho, Fukakusa, Fushimi-ku
- ☎ 075/641-7331
- 🕘 Dawn to dusk
- 🚉 JR Nara line: Inari; Keihan line: Fushimi-Inari

Daigo-ji
- 225 C1
- ✉ 22 Ogicho Daigo-Higashi, Fushimi-ku
- ☎ 075/571-0002
- 🕘 9 a.m.–4:30 p.m.
- 💲 $$
- 🚉 Tozai line: Daigo

daigoji.or.jp

North Kyoto

The northern reaches of Kyoto begin to mix with the surrounding countryside, and rice fields form the backdrop for famous temples and shrines. In the northeast the wildly popular Path of Philosophy is a prime spot for a stroll beneath the *sakura* come spring, and the villages north of the city preserve the traditional rustic style that is little seen in Kyoto city.

The Aoi Matsuri festival at the Shimogamo-jinja

Shimogamo-jinja

✉ 59 Shimogamo Izumigawa-cho, Sakyo-ku

☎ 075/781-0010

🕐 Dawn to dusk

🚃 Keihan line: Demachiyanagi

www.shimogamo-jinja .or.jp

The Kamo-gawa meets the Takano-gawa at one of Kyoto's oldest, most sacred spots, **Shimogamo-jinja.** This ancient shrine predates the founding of Kyoto; the Hata clan, living in the region before the arrival of Emperor Kammu, considered this forested delta home to Kamotaketsunomi-no-Mikoto, the local guardian deity, a belief taken up by Shinto priests arriving with the emperor. The shrine structures were built along with the new capital and Shimogamo-jinja rose to great prominence during the Heian period. The primeval forest surrounding the shrine buildings gives us an idea of what the ancient Kyoto valley looked like, and the Aoi Matsuri, Japan's oldest and most beloved religious procession, is held here each May. Starting on the 3rd with displays of horseback archery, the festival culminates with a grand parade from the palace to the shrine on the 15th, including dances from the festival's inception in 545.

Shimogamo's sister shrine, **Kamigamo-jinja,** is also a World Heritage site. Farther up the river, it enshrines the thunder god that quickens the earth, Wakeikazuchi, and has been important to agriculture since its inception in 678. It is notable for twin cones of sand in the shrine precinct, said to be points of ancient purity where the gods descend.

From **Nanzen-ji** (see p. 207), the **Path of Philosophy** (Tetsugaku-no-Michi) winds along a canal on the edge of Higashiyama and past several minor temples. The walking route earned its name from the consti- tutional that philosopher Nishida Kitaro took here each day. The cherry trees that line the canal have become so famous that you aren't likely to do much philoso- phizing here in April, but you can go early to beat the crowds. The route ends at **Ginkaku-ji,** the Silver Pavilion built by Ashikaga Yoshimasa, grandson of the cre- ator of Kinkaku-ji. The Silver Pavil- ion was intended to be an escape from a shattered country that his weakening shogunate could no longer hold together. The main building is surprisingly not coated in silver—Yoshimasa moved in as

soon as it was built and he never got around to silvering it. He did finish the garden, however, an attractive combination of walking- garden and dry landscape that harkens back to the comparatively peaceful Heian period. Sadly, the statue of Yoshimasa that Kyotoites used to pay to clobber was taken down in 1877. Ginkaku-ji is quite small and fills quickly, so try to go early or late and on a weekday.

If you take the little road left of Ginkaku-ji's gate, you'll hit the trailhead to climb **Daimonji- yama,** the prominent mountain with the Chinese character for "great" cut into its bald face. This is a great little 90-minute round- trip hike with the best views over the city. The character, like the others scattered across the moun- tains of the city, is lit on fire each August 16 for the Gozan Okuribi festival, which guides ancestral spirits back to their resting places.

In the far northeast of Kyoto, in the western foothills of Hiei-zan, is **Shugaku-in Rikyu** (Shugaku-in

Kamigamo-jinja

- ✉ 339 Kamigamo Motoyama, Kita-ku
- ☎ 075/781-0011
- 🕐 8 a.m.–4:50 p.m.
- 🚌 City Bus 9 from Kyoto Station to Kamigamo Misonobashi (also passes by Shimogamo- jinja)

kamigamojinja.jp

Ginkaku-ji

- 🗺 199 E4
- ✉ 2 Ginkakuji-cho, Sakyo-ku
- ☎ 075/771-5725
- 🕐 8:30 a.m.–5 p.m.
- 💲 $
- 🚌 City Bus 100 from Kyoto Station to Ginkakuji-mae

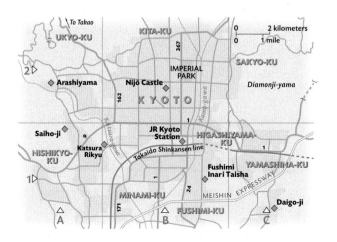

Shugaku-in Rikyu

- 199 F6
- Yabuzoe, Shugaku-in, Sakyo-ku
- Tour reservations required, see sidebar p. 202
- City Bus 5 from Kyoto Station to Shugakuin Rikyu-michi (about 1 hr.), then 15-min. walk

Shisen-do

- 199 E5
- 27 Monguchi-cho, Ichijoji, Sakyo-ku
- 075/781-2954
- 9 a.m.–5 p.m.
- $
- Eizan line: Ichijoji, then 10-min. walk; City Bus 5 from Kyoto Station to Ichijoji-Sagarimatsu-cho, then 5-min. walk

kyoto-shisendo.com

Sanzen-in

- 540 Raigoin-cho, Ohara, Sakyo-ku
- 075/744-2531
- 8:30 a.m.–5 p.m.
- $$
- Kyoto Bus 17 from Kyoto Station

Jakko-in

- 676 Kusao-cho, Ohara, Sakyo-ku
- 075/744-3341
- 9 a.m.–5 p.m.
- $$
- Kyoto Bus 17 from Kyoto Station

Imperial Villa), built by the Tokugawa shogunate for former emperor Gomizuno-o in the early 17th century. The grounds are divided into three large gardens with *chaya* (teahouses) in each. Like its southwestern counterpart, the Katsura Rikyu (see p. 221), this palace is a fine example of landscape architecture, with buildings beautifully complementing their surrounding ponds, pathways, and trees. The uppermost Kamino-Chaya garden contains the **Rin'un-tei teahouse,** which has a fine view over the city.

Shisen-do (a poet's hermitage) is a ten-minute walk south of Shugaku-in Rikyu. Ishikawa Jozan, a samurai turned poet and scholar of Chinese classics, had this peaceful retreat built in 1641.

The neighborhood is also known for a famous battle of Miyamoto Musashi, the greatest swordsman in Japanese history and author of *The Book of Five Rings.* Having challenged and maimed or killed the heads of the Yoshioka sword school, Musashi was challenged again, but this time a huge posse was out to kill him. Using a highly unorthodox two-sword style, he ambushed the gang of swordsmen, killing the remaining heir to the school, decimating the rest, and escaping unharmed. A descendant of the pine tree where they fought still stands on the road to Shisen-do.

Unspoiled rural areas lie to the north of Kyoto. The valleys of Kurama and Kibune are favored mountain getaways for Kyotoites; **Kibune** is known for its scenic riverside *ryokan* (inns).

INSIDER TIP:

Every aspect of the tea ceremony is prepared to please the senses, to help us slow down and savor life. Don't worry about the rules; just enjoy the harmony of the elements.

—YUKO KARIYAZAKI
Director, HUG International Exchange Association

Surrounded by wooded hills at the foot of Hiei-zan, **Ohara** is a small town renowned for its scenery—especially for its autumnal landscapes and maple trees. The 16th-century temple **Sanzen-in** has an exceptionally beautiful garden, 10th-century main hall, and 16th-century buildings. Nearby **Shoren-in,** set in an extensive precinct, is noted as a training center for *shomyo* sutra chanting. Between the two is the garden temple of **Jikko-in,** reached by a steep flight of stone steps, where one can contemplate the delights of the setting while sipping green tea. The famed **Jakko-in** nunnery lies northwest of Ohara. When the Minamoto clan finally defeated the Taira in 1185, the survivors tried to drown themselves in the sea. Among them were Lady Kenreimon-in and her son, seven-year-old Emperor Antoku. To her chagrin, Kenreimon-in was saved. She became a nun, spending the rest of her life here in melancholy contemplation. ∎

EXPERIENCE: The Japanese Tea Ceremony

A tea ceremony is a great way to sample a broad array of Japanese arts. Originally developed as an exercise in presence of mind by Zen monks, the tea ceremony was then taken up by samurai warriors seeking to focus their minds before battle. It was perfected by Japan's greatest tea master, Sen-no-Rikyu, who elevated it to the highest form of art while maintaining focus upon *wabi-sabi*, a current of quiet simplicity and rustic beauty that runs through the Japanese aesthetic.

Every part of the tea ceremony is in harmony with the season or occasion, from the color of participants' kimonos to the meaning of the calligraphy on the hanging scroll, the choice of flowers decorating the alcove, the tea bowls used, and the sweet served before the tea.

Tea ceremonies are typically held in small teahouses set in gardens or in tearooms within larger homes. Guests sit around the hearth in the center of the floor where the host prepares the hot water and begins to whisk the powdered green tea into a thick, frothy drink. As a guest, you should try to kneel Japanese fashion, on your calves, with your back straight. If this proves impossible, crossing your legs is acceptable. Make sure to eat the sweet given to you before you drink your tea, as this prepares the palate for the bitter tea. When a bowl of tea is placed before you, bow with the host, lowering your head toward your hands, placed on the tatami mats before her. Then, pick up the bowl with both hands, placing it on the left palm, and rotate it 180 degrees, clockwise, in three short turns, so that the "good side" of the bowl,

Freshly whisked powdered green tea *(matcha)*

which has been placed facing you, will face the other guests. Raise the bowl and drink silently in three or four sips, finishing with a small slurp so that the host knows you are finished. Lower the bowl and rotate it counterclockwise so that the good side once again faces you and place it on the tatami. When the host takes your bowl back, bow as you did before.

After drinking, it is polite to inquire about the pieces of art used in the ceremony, or to comment on the beauty of the setting by way of reflecting on a shared experience.

Best places for attending a tea ceremony:

HUG International Exchange Association (e-hug.jp, $$) holds twice yearly, accessible tea ceremonies at the Kyoto Imperial Palace Park and organizes tea ceremonies with guests dressed in kimonos.

Joukeian *(joukeian.gotohp.jp, $$$$$).* This small teahouse near Tofuku-ji offers peak tea ceremony experiences in English, from candlelit night courses to the full four-hour *chaji* tea ceremonies.

The Women's Association of Kyoto *(wakjapan.com, $$$$$).* This course incorporates all the traditional cultural aspects of the tea ceremony, including a lesson on preparing the powdered green tea, while wearing kimonos, of course.

Uji

Uji city, about 9 miles (15 km) southeast of Kyoto was one of the first places in Japan to boast a tea plantation and still enjoys a national reputation for the premium quality of its green tea. It is also known for cormorant fishing in the Uji-gawa, which can be viewed by boat from mid-June through August. Above all, Uji is famous for the beautiful temple of Byodo-in.

Byodo-in, one of Japan's most celebrated temples

Uji

Visitor Information

- Outside Byodo-in
- 0774/23-3334
- 9 a.m.–5 p.m.

kyoto-uji-kankou.or.jp

Byodo-in

- 116 Uji Renge, Uji-shi
- 0774/21-2861
- 9 a.m.–5 p.m.
- $$
- JR Nara line or Keihan Uji line: Uji, then 10-min. walk

byodoin.or.jp

Built as a villa by Fujiwara-no-Michinaga (966–1024), the most powerful man behind the throne in Heian times, **Byodo-in** was converted into a temple in 1052. The other palatial buildings were all lost to fire in 1336, but the **Phoenix Hall** (Hoo-do), built in 1053, still stands. It is fortunate that this is one of the remaining buildings of the period, as it represents the apogee of Heian architecture. Mirrored in the pond around it, the hall evokes a phoenix *(ho-o)* alighting; the buildings flanking the central body represent extended wings.

Inside, beneath an ornate, intricately carved canopy inlaid with mother-of-pearl, is a beautiful statue of Amida (Amithaba), Buddha of Mercy. The surrounding walls are adorned with 52 charming delicate statuettes of Buddhist deities. Other walls are decorated with period murals, but the paintings on the doors are reproductions. The originals can be seen in the **Treasure Hall** (Homutsukan), as can the original statues of the male and female phoenixes on the roof and the old temple bell.

Along the temple approach are several tea merchants' shops that offer a chance to taste the subtleties of different grades of green tea. Don't pass on the delectable *matcha*-flavor *kakigori* (shaved ice): The local version, called Uji Kintoki, comes with little rice cakes and sweetened *azuki* beans. ■

Ancient pilgrimage routes, raucous cries of *"Irrashai!"* (Welcome!) in Osaka and Kobe's restaurants, and Japan's earliest history

Kansai

Deer at the Nara-koen

Kansai

The Kansai region is Japan's heartland, home to much history, tradition, and culture. Here scattered clans first consolidated into the Yamato kingdom and Buddhism first took root. Other than Kyoto (see pp. 197–227), the region is notable for the cities of Nara, Osaka, and Kobe and a rich religious heritage in the countryside of Wakayama.

The Imperial capital before Kyoto, ancient Nara is second only to its successor in historical wealth, with temples dating back to the earliest existence of Japanese Buddhism. Religious history is deep in Kansai: South of Nara, the mountain temple complex of Koya-san offers one of the few opportunities to experience Esoteric Buddhism firsthand, and the Kii Peninsula, rugged with lush mountains, is home to Japan's oldest Shinto shrine, Ise-jingu. The area is also crisscrossed with the Kumano Pilgrimage trail, which once linked Kyoto with sacred shrines and healing hot springs throughout the region. Trekkers can look forward to a six-day walk from the trailhead near Tanabe city to Nachi Taisha, an important shrine at Japan's tallest waterfall.

Not to be overshadowed by history, Osaka and Kobe, two very modern cities, are worth a visit for their own distinct characters. Mercantile, friendly Osaka is crazy for food, but not the delicate treats of pompous Kyoto or the overpriced dishes of Tokyo; here, you eat till you burst. Osaka's has the best nightlife in all of western Japan, concentrated around the Umeda and Namba districts, and prices are quite reasonable compared to other big cities.

Cosmopolitan Kobe, once one of the few ports permitted to accept foreign ships, has risen from the ashes of the devastating 1995 Great Hanshin Earthquake and is now notable as one of the loveliest cities in Japan. Its district of old Western homes, the small Chinatown, and that delectable but pricey Kobe beef are all worth checking out. Hot spring lovers should make a detour to the countryside north of Kobe. The Arima and Kinosaki hot-spring resorts have more than a thousand years of relaxing history, and the inns are accustomed to welcoming foreign guests.

West of Kobe in Himeji city lies the greatest original castle, Himeji-jo. After five years of restoration that finished in 2015, this "White Crane Castle" positive gleams. Medieval history fans should not miss this excellent example of traditional architecture.

Shiga Prefecture has its own original castle, Hikone-jo, east of Lake Biwa, and the mountaintop temple complex that looms over Kyoto from Mount Hiei, Enryaku-ji. Long a poor cousin to Kyoto, Shiga now sports the excellent Miho Museum, which, given the time, is worth a special trip for its Bond-villain-base architecture and superlative private collection.

If you pass through Kansai during cherry blossom season, make the special trip to Yoshino, where mountain cherries carpet the

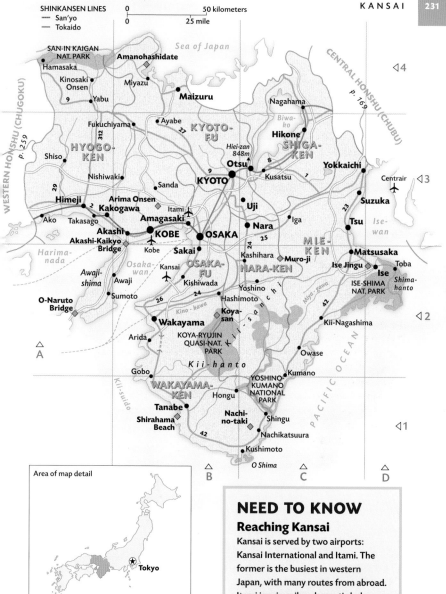

SHINKANSEN LINES
— San'yo
— Tokaido

0   50 kilometers
0   25 mile

Sea of Japan

SAN-IN KAIGAN NAT. PARK
Hamasaka
Kinosaki Onsen
Amanohashidate
Miyazu
Yabu
Maizuru
Nagahama
WESTERN HONSHU (CHUGOKU) p. 259
CENTRAL HONSHU (CHUBU) p. 169
Fukuchiyama
Ayabe
KYOTO-FU
Biwa-ko
Hikone
SHIGA-KEN
Shiso
HYOGO-KEN
312
Hiei-zan 848m
Otsu
Yokkaichi
Nishiwaki
Sanda
Kusatsu
Centrair
KYOTO
Himeji
Arima Onsen
Kakogawa
Itami
Uji
Suzuka
Ako
Takasago
Akashi
Amagasaki
Nara
Iga
Tsu
Ise-wan
Harima-nada
KOBE
OSAKA
Kobe
Sakai
Kashihara
Muro-ji
MIE-KEN
Matsusaka
Akashi-Kaikyo Bridge
Osaka-wan
Kansai
OSAKA-FU
NARA-KEN
Ise Jingu
Ise
Toba
Awaji-shima
Awaji
Kishiwada
Yoshino
ISE-SHIMA NAT. PARK
Shima-hanto
O-Naruto Bridge
Sumoto
Hashimoto
Kii-Nagashima
Wakayama
Koya-san
KOYA-RYUJIN QUASI-NAT. PARK
Arida
Owase
Gobo
Kumano
WAKAYAMA-KEN
YOSHINO KUMANO NATIONAL PARK
Hongu
Tanabe
Shirahama Beach
Nachi-no-taki
Shingu
Nachikatsuura
Kushimoto
O Shima

Area of map detail

Tokyo

hills and the bloom gradually rolls upslope over a three-week period, much longer than usual. Likewise, travelers in the area in mid-August should try to catch a game of the high school baseball championship at Koshien Stadium, near Kobe—it makes March Madness look sedate in comparison. ∎

NEED TO KNOW
Reaching Kansai
Kansai is served by two airports: Kansai International and Itami. The former is the busiest in western Japan, with many routes from abroad. Itami is primarily a domestic hub, popular with business travelers.

Getting Around
Efficient service from multiple rail and subway lines leads to almost all tourist destinations in the region, although the highway bus is a slower, cheaper option for some of the more distant corners.

Mount Hiei

Hiei-zan, about 5 miles (8 km) northeast of Kyoto city center, holds a special place in the city's history. In the ninth century, the priest Saicho founded the Tendai sect, a rigorous, ascetic form of Buddhism endorsed by the state to combat the influence of the powerful Nara temples. According to ancient Chinese geomancy (divination based on geographical directions), the northeast is the unluckiest direction, so Hiei-zan was considered the ideal place for Saicho to build a temple complex to protect the city from evil influences.

Hiei-zan
🗺 231 C3

Enryaku-ji
✉ 4220 Sakamoto-honmachi, Otsu-shi, Shiga-ken
☎ 0775/78-0001
🕐 8:30 a.m.–4:30 p.m.; closes early in winter
💲 $$
🚌 Kyoto Bus: Buses from Kyoto Station or Sanjo Station bound for Hiei-zan, such as the Hiei-zan Driveway Bus (1 hr.)

hieizan.or.jp

Enryaku-ji, Saicho's focal temple, spread across the mountain into a temple city of more than 3,000 buildings. During Saicho's lifetime, even emperors studied Buddhism at Enryaku-ji. Seeking the legal immunity of the clergy, many bandits and thieves fled to the mountain and became warrior-monks to defend Hiei-zan's real monks from . . . bandits and thieves. By the 11th century, these warrior-monks were raiding rival temples, slaughtering their clergy, and even bullying the emperors, going so far as to set fire to the city on numerous occasions. Remaining politically and militarily powerful for centuries, the monks were eventually deemed a threat by the great warlord Oda Nobunaga, whose army killed some 3,000 monks and burned Enryaku-ji in 1581. Partially restored by Toyotomi Hideyoshi, the monastery never regained its former size or power.

INSIDER TIP:

A scenic route to Hiei-zan: Take the Keihan or Eizan line to Yase-Hieizan-guchi Station; the nearby cable car takes you to the top of Hiei. From there, you're just a 30-minute walk from Enryaku-ji.

—KENNY LING
National Geographic contributor

Among the notable buildings of the temple are the central Konpon-Chu-do and Daiko-do (Great Lecture Hall) in the Toto (eastern precinct) and the Shaka-do (Shak-yamuni Hall) and Sorinto pagoda in the Saito (western precinct). With its temples set in a forest of soaring cedars, the quieter western side seems the more deeply steeped in peace, piety, and the mystic ambience of Buddhism. ■

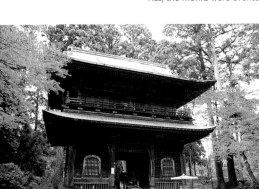

Enryaku-ji is resplendent as the leaves start to turn.

Shiga-ken

Lake Biwa (Biwa-ko), in Shiga-ken east of Kyoto, is named for an ancient Japanese lute whose shape it resembles. At 260 square miles (674 sq km), it is Japan's largest and best known lake. The scenery is no longer quite as picturesque as it was when celebrated in 19th-century woodblock prints, but several places are worth exploring.

Biwa-ko dominates the center of rural Shiga Prefecture, just east of Kyoto. Shiga has a handful of great sights, and its friendly residents welcome foreign visitors.

Busy **Otsu,** the prefectural capital, is a good base for seeing **Ishiyama-dera** and the **Miho Museum** *(tel 0748/82-3411, 10 a.m.–5 p.m., closed Mon., $$$, Ishiyamadera Station, then Teisan bus–50 min.),* both tucked into the mountains between Shiga and Kyoto. The former, an eighth-century Shingon-sect temple set among large boulders and maple trees, is most famous as the place where Murasaki Shikibu began the world's first novel, *The Tale of Genji.* In the art scene, the Miho Museum was founded by wealthy textiles heiress Koyama Mihoko in 1997 in the forested hills southeast of Ishiyama-dera. The museum itself sits like a subterranean lair hidden mostly beneath a ridgeline, but extensive skylights illuminate what is perhaps Japan's best collection of Western and Middle Eastern antiquities.

East of the mountains, you'll find **Shigaraki** *(Tourist Center, tel 0748/82-2345, 9 a.m.–5 p.m.),* one of the six old pottery regions of medieval Japan. The style—rough-hewn, simple, and rustic—came to be celebrated by masters of the tea ceremony for its very lack of refinement. In the modern day, Shigaraki is a major producer of *tanuki* (raccoon dog) statues. These mischievous characters from folklore stand outside many restaurants in Japan, bringing luck to their proprietors should they behave like one, with a toothy smile, a big hat (preparation against bad luck), promissory notes (a symbol of trust), and big testicles—"money bags" in Japanese slang—the mark of generosity.

On the other side of Biwa-ko, **Hikone** is notable for its well-preserved 17th-century castle, one of only four National Treasure castles. Not as tall as Matsue-jo or Himeji-jo, **Hikone-jo** makes up for it by perching on a steep hill with commanding views over the surrounding town. ■

Shiga-ken
- 231 C3

Visitor Information

en.biwako-visitors.jp

Ishiyama-dera
- ✉ 1-1-1 Ishiyama-dera, Otsu-shi
- ☎ 077/537-0013
- 🕐 8 a.m.–4 p.m.
- 💲 $
- 🚊 Keihan Ishiyama-sakamoto line: Ishiyamadera

Hikone-jo
- ✉ 1-1 Konki-cho
- ☎ 0749/22-2742
- 🕐 8:30 a.m.–5 p.m.
- 💲 $$

The underground walkway of the Miho Museum

Nara & Environs

Nara is a small city; its unhurried ambience seems designed to avoid disturbing the long sleep of its illustrious ancestors. While Kyoto's grandeur emerges from a comparatively recent past, Nara and its environs contain buildings of such antiquity that their very survival is quite astonishing. Japanese civilization first appeared in the Nara Basin; ancient burial mounds of the Kofun period (see p. 32) are on view within the modern city confines.

Bronze lanterns hang outside Kasuga Taisha.

Nara
🅜 231 C3

Visitor Information
✉ 23-4 Kamisanjo-cho
☎ 0742/22-3900
🕐 9 a.m.–9 p.m.

narashikanko.or.jp

In 710, Empress Gemmei founded the city of Heijo, then intended as a permanent capital. About 1 mile (2 km) west of modern Nara, the city was modeled on China's mighty T'ang-dynasty city of Chang'an, the cosmopolitan hub of the Silk Road and the most sophisticated metropolis of the ancient world.

Profoundly affected by Chang'an, Nara was Japan's window on the world. Its temple treasures include ancient Chinese, Korean, Indian, and even Persian artworks, and experts still wrangle over the influences displayed by its art and architecture.

Though Nara gave its name to an era of great progress, it never realized the permanence to which it originally aspired. Emperor Kammu built Heian-kyo (Kyoto) in 794, after which Nara slumbered, despite remaining an important center for Buddhism. Natural disasters, fires, and redevelopment obliterated much of ancient Nara over the centuries, but some of its seventh- and eighth-century temples still stand.

Occupying the northeastern quarter of the city are the 1,235 acres (500 ha) of **Nara-koen,** a park roamed by approximately 1,500 tame deer. Japan's largest city park, it embraces some of Nara's greatest treasures, including the world's largest bronze sculpture (see pp. 237–238).

The rest of the city is unremarkable; there are picturesque older neighborhoods in Naramachi to the southwest, but preservation outside religious contexts is not much of a priority. Though Nara is a small city, the volume of tourists that pass through is nothing short of phenomenal. The major sights can be covered on a day trip from Kyoto.

INSIDER TIP:

Nara has a good but somewhat limited range of accommodations. If you plan to stay overnight, book ahead (see Travelwise pp. 374–376).

—BARBARA NOE
National Geographic
Travel Books author

One of the main temples of the Hosso sect of esoteric Buddhism, **Kofuku-ji** was founded in 669 by the wife of Fujiwara Kamatari, an ancestor of the family that ruled Kyoto during the Heian period. Moved to its present location when Nara became the capital in 710, this temple complex comprised 175 buildings at the zenith of the Heian period. As regional conflict increased after the 1150s with the decline of the Fujiwara dynasty, Kofuku-ji raised an army of warrior-monks to support the Minamoto clan's forces, which were defending the ruling Fujiwara from the Taira clan. The warrior-monks were defeated in 1180 by a Taira army, which set the temple buildings ablaze. After defeating the Taira, shogun Minamoto Yoritomo set about restoring Kofuku-ji.

A disastrous fire destroyed most of those buildings in 1717, but the **Northern Octagonal Hall** (Hokuen-do) and **three-story pagoda** survive intact from the Kamakura period. The **five-story pagoda** and **Eastern Golden Hall** (Tokon-do) date from the early 15th century. Reflected in nearby **Sarusawa Pond** (Sarusawa-no-ike), the pagoda is one of Nara's most photographed sights. Various halls of Kofuku-ji contain a number of outstanding early Buddhist sculptures, as does its **Treasure Hall** (Kokuhokan) museum, which is most notable for the exquisitely expressive Ashura guardian, a masterpiece of the dry-lacquer construction technique produced in 734.

The **Nara National Museum** (Kokuritsu Hakubutsukan) is 550 yards (500 m) east of Kofuku-ji. Built in 1895, the **West Gallery** contains an impressive collection of Buddhist art, including paintings, calligraphy, sculptures, and decorative arts

Kofuku-ji
- ✉ 48 Noborioji-cho
- ☎ 0742/22-7755
- 🕐 9 a.m.–5 p.m.
- 💲 $$
- 🚉 Kintetsu Nara line: Kintetsu Nara

www.kohfukuji.com

Nara National Museum
- ✉ 50 Noborioji-cho
- ☎ 0742/22-7771
- 🕐 9:30 a.m.–5 p.m., closed Mon.; open until 7 p.m. Fri. April–Oct.
- 💲 $$
- 🚉 Kintetsu Nara line: Kintetsu Nara

www.narahaku.go.jp

Kasuga Taisha

✉ 160 Kasugano-cho

☎ 0742/22-7788

🕐 6 a.m.–6 p.m.

🚌 Bus: Kasuga Taisha-Omotesando stop, then a 650-yd. (600 m) walk east

kasugataisha.or.jp

from the seventh century through the Kamakura and Edo periods. In 1973 the **East Gallery** was added, and is devoted to archaeological artifacts unearthed in the Nara region. Museum exhibits change on a regular basis; some items in the West Gallery are so precious and fragile that they are exhibited only once a year (see the museum's website for schedules; expect massive crowds). The same applies to the treasures formerly kept in the Shoso-in Hall of Todai-ji. These include items of Chinese, Indian, and Persian origin or influence, reflecting Nara's ancient connections to the Silk Road.

Kasuga Taisha, founded by the Fujiwara clan as a family shrine in 768, is on the southeastern edge of Nara-koen, less than a mile (1.5 km) east of the National Museum. It comprises four main **Honden** halls—three dedicated to divine warriors and one to the deified ancestors of the Fujiwara line. Epitomizing the Chinese temple style in vogue between the seventh and tenth centuries, Kasuga is an architectural paradigm: Other shrines around Japan with pillars of vermilion wood and sweeping Chinese roofs are often described as being in the Kasuga style. Like most major Shinto shrines, the main buildings have been ritually demolished and identically rebuilt. With the exception of the old **Oratory** (Haiden) and the **Function Hall** (Naoraiden), the rest of Kasuga was last reerected—for the 56th time—in 1893. The shrine approach, 875 yards (800 m) long, is bordered by some 2,000 **stone lanterns**

Nara Deer

Deer reached Japan before even the Japanese, having crossed continental land bridges during the Ice Age. Divine messengers, according to Shinto belief, they have roamed Nara for centuries. Over generations, the herd in Nara-koen, numbering some 1,500, has perfected the doe-eyed look that guarantees maximum handouts. Stalls trade briskly in deer feed; *shika sembei* (deer crackers) are allegedly often munched by foreigners who mistake them for local delicacies.

Deer are greedy. They have been accused of overturning trash cans—and even small people. Males can be mildly dangerous during mating season. Feed them carefully: They are cute, but not completely tame.

donated by devotees since the 11th century. A thousand more, made of bronze, hang elegantly from the eaves of the buildings closer to the main precinct. Twice a year, during the Setsubun Festival in early February and the Bon festival in August, the lighted lanterns present an enchanting spectacle enhancing the hallowed atmosphere of the shrine.

A modern building next to the parking lot near the shrine's main entrance, the **Treasure House** (Homutsuden) displays a collection of historical shrine objects, including Noh masks and the trappings of Shinto ritual, ceremonies, and festivals. To the left of the shrine approach, the **Man'yo Botanical Garden** (Kasuga Taisha Shin-en) boasts all 300 plant species mentioned in the *Man'yoshu,* a celebrated eighth-century anthology of many thousands of poems.

Beyond the road flanking Nara Park to the south is **Shin Yakushi-ji.** The temple was founded in 747 by Komyo, consort of Emperor Shomu, as a means of praying for the emperor's recovery from an eye infection. The only surviving original structure is the **Main Hall** (formerly the dining hall), renowned for the sculptures (all National Treasures) it contains. The main object of worship is the effigy of the seated **Yakushi Nyorai,** the Healing Buddha, flanked by an 11-faced Kannon (Buddhist god of mercy) and the Juni-Shinsho (12 divine generals). These tall, exquisitely wrought clay statues of generals in full armor actually number 11: One went AWOL centuries ago. Other notable treasures in the compound are the gilt-bronze **Ko-Yakushi** Buddha and a rare Heian-period painting of Nirvana.

Todai-ji, on the northwestern edge of Nara-koen, about 1 mile (2 km) northeast of Nara Station, is most famous for the mighty bronze Buddha, the Daibutsu. Emperor Shomu (701–758) built the temple (completed in 752) to accommodate a colossal bronze statue of the Dainichi Buddha (Vairocana) that he had commissioned. Having previously renounced the world and retired

The huge Buddha at Todai-ji

as a monk, Shomu emerged from seclusion to conduct the grand dedication ceremony for the statue in 752, with foreign monks attending from India and China. These visiting holy men brought the lavish gifts still preserved in the Nara National Museum (see pp. 235–236). Like Kofuku-ji, Todai-ji was torched during the conflicts ending the Heian period in 1185.

Todai-ji

✉ 406-1 Zoshi-cho

☎ 0742/22-5511

🕐 7:30 a.m.–5 p.m.; closes at 5:30 p.m. April–Sept.

💲 $$

todaiji.or.jp

Shin Yakushi-ji

✉ 1352 Takabatake-cho

☎ 0742/22-3736

🕐 9 a.m.–5 p.m.

💲 $$

🚌 Bus: Wariishi

The finely sculpted octagonal **bronze lantern** in front of the main hall is an eighth-century original. The massive **Great South Gate** (Nandaimon) before the entrance also dates from the eighth century, although it was substantially restored in the 12th century after collapsing during a typhoon. The fierce guardian deities standing in niches on either side—splendid wooden carvings 26 feet (8 m) tall—are attributed to Kamakura-period sculptor Unkei and his school.

Due to fires and natural disasters, most of the precinct's buildings are 16th- and 17th-century reproductions, notably the **Hall of the Great Buddha** (Daibutsuden), rebuilt for the last time in 1708. It measures 187 feet (57 m) wide by 164 feet (50 m) deep and 157 feet (48 m) high. Although smaller than its predecessor, the hall is still one of the world's largest wooden structures—it had to be to house the **Daibutsu**, the biggest bronze statue in the world. The massive size is key to a certain irony: As the Buddha of ultimate emptiness and void, the statue suggests

that even the greatest things are fleeting and impermanent.

Indeed, during the 1,200-year history of the Daibutsu, it has been damaged by multiple fires and lost its head twice during earthquakes. It was last restored in 1692. The seated colossus, weighing 550 tons (500 tonnes) and incorporating 290 pounds (103 kg) of gold, soars 53 feet (16 m) above its pedestal. Its sheer scale tends to undermine the artistry intended by its Korean designer, but the statue still induces awe.

The main effigy is surrounded by statues of Kannon and two heavenly guardians, dating to the 17th and 18th centuries. A huge pillar to the right of the Daibutsu is thought to open the path of Enlightenment to those able to crawl through the hole the size of the Daibutsu's nostril in the base—a privilege reserved for the small and the slim (see sidebar below).

The **Nigatsu-do Hall** (Second Month Hall), rebuilt in 1669, contains statues of Kannon that only the elite clergy have ever seen. It is celebrated for its view

EXPERIENCE: The Nostril of Enlightenment

If Todai-ji's whopper Buddha (the Daibutsu) seems intimidating, fear not! There are shortcuts, even to the lofty state of Enlightenment that is *nirvana*.

Scurry beneath its inscrutable gaze to one of the large supporting columns of the hall on the right. In its base is a small hole, the same size as one of the statue's nostrils, and it is believed that if you can just squirm through—clambering into the

mind of the Buddha, as it were, there'll be no need for all that meditation and Enlightenment will come as easily as a sneeze.

A crawl through the nostril may be an easy feat for kids, but for the rest of us less supple souls, we must heed the wisdom passed down through the ages: "Those who would crawl into the Buddha-mind go arms first."

over the city from the veranda, as well as for the Omizu-tori (Water-Drawing) Festival (March 1–14), whose torchlight processions attract thousands.

The **Sangatsu-do Hall** (Third Month Hall) has stood since the eighth century and is Todai-ji's oldest structure. The period sculptures it contains are National Treasures, as are other artworks and buildings in the precinct; they include a tall statue of Kannon attributed to Roben and 14 other major effigies. The two halls are some 330 yards (300 m) east of the Daibutsuden. Other treasures, including those placed there by Emperor Shomu himself, were once kept in the **Shoso-in,** north of the precinct. This long rectangular building on stilts still stands, but the treasures were moved to the Nara National Museum (see pp. 235–236) in 1963.

Beyond Nara

About 3 miles (5 km) west of Nara is **Toshodai-ji,** headquarters of the Ritsu school of Buddhism. The temple was built in 759 by the Chinese priest Ganjin (Jian zhen) at the invitation of Emperor Shomu. Opposition from Chinese bureaucrats, five shipwrecks, and bouts of illness that finally left him blind delayed Ganjin's arrival for ten years. Entirely Chinese in design, Toshodai-ji's main buildings survive as paradigms of Nara-period architecture. Statues inside the **Main Hall (Kondo),** among them the focal Dainichi Buddhas carved by Chinese sculptors, are National Treasures.

Nara Crafts

Nara craftsmen and women still fashion *Kogakumen* dance-drama masks and rough-finished wooden *itto-bori* dolls. Both were used in ancient religious ceremonies. Buddhism brought with it many arts from China, especially calligraphy and ink painting. To this day, Nara remains the center for turning out brushes and *sumi* ink tablets. Made of deer, horse, rabbit, squirrel, or badger hair, brushes come in a range of sizes for different functions. Sumi or *yoboku,* made from the soot of bulrushes, is combined with glue from deer horn to form a cake said to improve with age. Depending on the desired intensity of the ink, other ingredients may include *beni* (crimson safflower dye), powdered oyster shell, and even musk; some formulas are secrets handed down for generations.

Originally the assembly hall of the Nara court, the **Lecture Hall** (Kodo) was moved here when the temple was built. Although it retains revealing details about Nara-period palace architecture (not least, front pillars that curve slightly to alter their perspective), its overall form has been lost through repairs and alterations over the centuries.

The **Founder's Hall** (Miei-do) contains a famous sculpted portrait of Ganjin; more fine works of Buddhist art are exhibited in the **Shin-Hozo Treasure House,** open twice annually *(late Mar.–late May & mid-Sept.–early Nov.).*

Yakushi-ji, less than half a mile (800 m) south of Toshodai-ji, was founded in the seventh century. Once one of the Seven Great Temples of Nara, it is the

Toshodai-ji
- ✉ 13-46 Gojo-cho
- ☎ 0742/33-7900
- 🕐 8:30 a.m.–5 p.m.
- 💲 $$
- 🚃 Kintetsu Kashihara line: Nishinokyo, then 10-min. walk

www.toshodaiji.jp

Yakushi-ji
- ✉ 457 Nishinokyo-machi
- ☎ 0742/33-6001
- 🕐 8:30 a.m.–5 p.m.
- 💲 $$$
- 🚃 Kintetsu Kashihara line: Nishinokyo, then 5-min. walk

Horyu-ji

✉ 1-1 Horyuji
Sannai, Ikaruga-
cho, Ikoma-gun
☎ 0745/75-2555
🕐 8 a.m.–5 p.m.
💲 $$$
🚆 JR Kansai line:
Horyuji

www.horyuji.or.jp

headquarters of the Hosso sect. Yakushi-ji's grand buildings are long gone, but the Toto pagoda, 108 feet (33 m) high and dating from 730, is prized for its elegance and for the unique architectural feat of making its three stories appear as six. The Main Hall (Kondo), rebuilt in 1976, houses a National Treasure—the bronze Yakushi Triad depicting the Yakushi Nyorai Buddha (associated with healing) and attendant bodhisattvas. These once-golden statues, cast in the 720s, have been smoked a glossy black by fires over the centuries. Another National Treasure is the seventh-century statue of Sho-Kannon in the Eastern Hall (Toin-do), built behind the pagoda in 1285.

Paramount among all Japan's great temples and revered for its pride of place in Japanese Buddhist culture, **Horyu-ji**

(see diagram pp. 242–243) was founded in 607 by Prince Shotoku, architect of the first national constitution (see sidebar opposite) and first strong supporter of Buddhism. The temple complex is said to have been rebuilt after a fire in 670, although some historians doubt the fire ever occurred. Either way, four of the buildings, remaining as they have been for more than 1,300 years, are the oldest standing wooden structures on Earth.

With several buildings from the Heian and Kamakura eras, as well as additions from the 15th to 19th centuries, the complex includes a hall opened in 1998 to house the Kudara Kannon, a masterpiece of wood sculpture and the temple's most famous statue. Horyu-ji, a UNESCO World Heritage site, holds more than 2,300 items considered of historical

Horyu-ji, founded in 607 by Prince Shotoku, has the oldest standing wooden structures on the planet.

importance—190 of them are Important Cultural Assets or National Treasures. The temple is divided into the larger **Western Precinct** (Sai-in), lying beyond the 15th-century **Great South Gate** (Nandaimon), and the smaller **Eastern Precinct** (To-in), which embraces Chugu-ji, a subtemple.

The seventh-century **Main Hall** (Kondo) houses some of the era's most important bronze and wooden sculptures, visible only through wooden lattices. The hall is also dark, making it hard to see the murals depicting paradise. Badly damaged in a fire in 1949, these have been beautifully restored. To the left of the Kondo stands the magnificent seventh-century **Five-story Pagoda** (Goju-no-To), the oldest in Japan; 110 feet (33 m) high, it contains an elaborate clay sculpture on the first floor, with figures illustrating various Buddhist myths. North of the main compound at the point where the cloisters meet, the **Great Lecture Hall** (Daikodo) and the statues within date from the tenth century; the original was struck by lightning.

Also replacing a damaged predecessor, the 13th-century **West Round Hall** (Saiendo) stands on a hill and contains an eighth-century Yakushi Nyorai image—the oldest dry-lacquer statue in Japan. The

INSIDER TIP:

Some people try to read about Zen in books, but that's no good. You have to feel it in your legs and back to understand.

—REV. YAMATO
Daisen-in, Daitoku-ji

two long halls on either side of the central compound were once monks' quarters; built during the Kamakura period, the one on the east side is the **Hall of Prince Shotoku's Soul** (Shoryoin) and contains a statue of the prince wrought in the Heian period.

Prince Shotoku Taishi (574–622)

When Empress Suiko acceded to the throne in 593 in Asuka, Japan's first capital, power was assumed by Shotoku, the prince regent. One of Japanese history's most remarkable figures, Shotoku spurred great cultural and architectural advances through the ties he forged with China. Based on Chinese concepts, the Seventeen Articles he devised amounted to Japan's earliest constitution. Government was centralized for the first time, and all the people became imperial subjects—making their incomes taxable by local rulers only with the emperor's approval. A great scholar and devout Buddhist, Shotoku sponsored the building of temples in the Asuka area, including Horyu-ji near Nara. Posthumously deified, the prince has since become shrouded in legends about an immaculate birth and a life abounding with multiple miracles. In a more secular vein, the saint's portrait once adorned Japan's 10,000-yen note.

Horyu-ji

Five-story Pagoda (Goju-no-To)

Sutra Repository (Kyozo)

Main Hal (Kondo)

Central Gate (Chumon)

Important Cultural Properties

National Treasures

Great Lecture Hall
(Daikodo)

Bell House
(Shoro)

Hall of Prince
Shotoku's Soul
(Shoryoin)

Passing through the ancient East Main Gate (Todaimon) brings you to the Eastern Precinct, with its octagonal seventh-century **Hall of Dreams** (Yumedono) pavilion. Dominating the statues it contains is a wooden portrait of the deified Prince Shotoku; his gilded likeness is remarkably preserved. Just east of this is **Chugu-in,** a nunnery housing Japan's oldest embroidered picture—and the exquisite seventh-century **Miroku Bosatsu,** a Buddha statue of exceptional grace and serenity.

Though many of Horyu-ji's treasures are now in Tokyo's National Museum (see sidebar p. 95), about a thousand remain in the **Gallery of Temple Treasures** (Daihozoden) just east of the main precinct. Among them is the Dream-Changing Kannon sculpture, sought out for changing nightmares into auspicious dreams. A small, exquisitely decorated lacquered shrine, the Tamamushi Tabernacle belonged to Empress Suiko. The intricate metalwork on its surface once held thousands of iridescent wings of the *tamamushi* beetle. ∎

Key to Site Plan

1 Great South Gate
(Nandaimon)
2 Central Gate
(Chumon)
3 Main Hall (Kondo)
4 Five-story Pagoda
(Goju-no-To)
5 Great Lecture Hall
(Daikodo)
6 Sutra Repository
(Kyozo)

7 Bell House (Shoro)
8 Inner Sanctuary
(Kami-no-Mido)
9 West Round Hall
(Saiendo)
10 Hall of Prince Shotoku's
Soul (Shoryoin)
11 Gallery of Temple
Treasures (Daihozoden)
12 Kudara Kannon Hall
(Kudara Kannon-do)

13 East Main Gate
(Todaimon)
14 Hall of Dreams
(Yumedono)
15 Reliquary Hall
(Shariden)
16 Hall of Buddhist
Teachings (Denpodo)
17 Bell House (Toin Shoro)

Nara-ken

Too often, visitors are so taken with Nara the city that they forget about Nara the prefecture. There is much here that is worthwhile. Refreshingly rural and mountainous, the countryside boasts beautiful temples and is said to harbor the legendary heartland of the cherry tree. Indeed, the hills around Yoshino village are cloaked in the palest pink blossoms each spring.

Hase-dera sits in secluded woodlands.

Yoshino

🗺 231 C2

Visitor Information

✉ 2430 Yoshino-yama

🕐 9 a.m.–4 p.m.

☎ 0746/32-1007

🚉 Kintetsu Yoshino line: Yoshino

yoshinoyama-sakura .jp

one never barred female visitors. The buildings are noted examples of seventh-century architecture; several are National Treasures, as are the statues within. The five-story **pagoda** is among the most photographed buildings in Japan.

Amid forests of tree peonies and cherry trees, **Hase-dera** (Temple of Flowers; *731 Hase, Sakurai-shi, $, tel 0744/47-7001*) is a popular temple in late spring despite its remote location. Founded in 686 and enlarged by Emperor Shomu, who built the main hall, Hase-dera was once a cherished preserve of Nara-period aristocracy. Containing a celebrated 26-foot (8 m) statue of Kannon, god of mercy, the **Main Hall** (Hondo) is reached by a covered flight of stone steps.

Legend has it that cherry trees originated in the town of **Yoshino,** where they were planted in the seventh century by En-no-Gyoja, a priest said to have placed a curse on anyone who dared to cut them down. The warlord Toyotomi Hideyoshi nearly invoked the curse when his 5,000-person *hanami* was rained out for three days. Hideyo-shi was so angry that he threatened to scorch the mountainside if the local followers of En-no-Gyoja didn't do something about the weather. The ascetics prayed fervently, and sunny skies spared Yoshino the next day. ∎

According to tradition, **Muro-ji** (*78 Muro, tel 0745/93-2003, 8:30 a.m.–5 p.m., $$, Kintetsu Osaka line: Muroguchiono*), beautifully situated in a peaceful wooded valley, was founded in 681 (the exact date is not known). Rebuilt in 824 by the priest Kukai (see sidebar p. 294), the temple is known as the "women's Koya"; unlike the temple Kukai founded on Koya-san (see pp. 254–257), this

Osaka

Gregarious, direct, and occasionally brash, Osakans are known as Japan's sharpest businesspeople, the best jokers, and serious foodies. Despite being totally rebuilt after the war, the city has a handful of excellent sights, great nightlife, and excellent transportation to the rest of Kansai.

Officially, Osaka is Japan's third city. Because Tokyo and Yokohama are close enough to constitute a single megalopolis, however, most people consider Osaka to be the second. Its location on a sweeping bay prompted its use as a port during the reign of Emperor Nintoku, so Osaka has been a primary trading center since the fourth century. While samurai fortunes fell from the late 17th century on, merchants grew ever more wealthy and powerful, especially in Osaka. As the city established its position as the national hub of trade and industry, it saw the foundation of many of Japan's biggest brand names, among them the electronics giants Panasonic, Sanyo, and Sharp and video game maker Capcom.

Under the patronage of merchant princes, Osaka flourished as a center for the dramatic arts, particularly when many Kabuki actors moved here after the devastation of Edo in the great fire of 1657. Osaka was renowned for its Bunraku (see p. 54), and today it remains the national center for this unique form of puppetry.

A prime target during World War II, the city was flattened, and all of Osaka's historic assets vanished. The castle **Osaka-jo**

Tsutenkaku tower overlooks Osaka's Shin-Sekai district.

Osaka

231 B3

Visitor Information

✉ JR Osaka Station, Central Concourse, north side

🕐 8 a.m.–8 p.m.

☎ 06/6345-2189

Museum of Oriental Ceramics

✉ 1-1-26 Nakanoshima, Kita-ku

☎ 06/6223-0055

🕐 9:30 a.m.–5 p.m., closed Mon.

💲 $$$

🚇 Midosuji line: Yodoyabashi

www.moco.or.jp

survived, but it was already a concrete copy (built in 1931) of its predecessor. But don't let modern Osaka put you off: This city of 2.6 million boisterous sybarites has Japan's best nightlife—and its widest spectrum of fine food.

With a JR loop line running around the perimeter and a subway network crisscrossing the city, Osaka is easy to get around. **Kita-ku** (northern sector) encompasses Osaka Station, surrounded by a vast warren of every imaginable kind of restaurant above- and belowground. This is the main business district. Its focus is **Umeda,** an area notable for its labyrinthine shopping mall and soaring modern architecture, such as the sleek **Umeda Sky Building,** a 40-story,

twin-towered titan erected in 1993 with a great observation deck *(10 a.m.–10 p.m., $$).*

Umeda is a major cluster of corporate headquarters on Nakanoshima, home to the **Museum of Orient Ceramics,** which contains a world-class selection of Persian, Chinese, Korean, and Japanese ceramics. The history of the gradual shift in styles as ceramics technology was imported to Japan is fascinating.

Also in Nakanoshima, you'll find the **National Museum of Art Osaka.** The museum puts on a variety of Western and Japanese exhibits—these can be hit or miss, so check the website to see what's on.

Dominating the city skyline east of center, the current version

Koshien: Baseball Fever

Japan gives the U.S. a run for its money in the baseball-crazy department as the nation grinds to a halt every spring and summer for two national high-school baseball championships at **Koshien Stadium** *(1-8-2 Koshiencho, Nishinomiya, tel 0180/997-750, Hanshin line: Koshien),* between Osaka and Kobe. The media focus on these teenagers is intense, and the populace loves their struggles, triumphs, and moments of heartbreak, such as when the defeated scoop up handfuls of "sacred" infield dirt and vow to return.

As the tournaments are packed with games, the tickets are reasonably priced and easy to get. Half the fun is watching the madness of the crowd, as the Japanese are most comfortable when acting in an organized group. Buses full of supporters from distant towns paint sections of the stadium in their own colors.

There are songs and dances devised by each region to cheer on their boys, and the partisan sections often stand through entire games, chanting to the directions of militant cheer conductors and their energetic brass bands. Foreigners are often made into honorary lucky charms, dragged into the dances and fed beers and snacks—another example of sport in Japan lowering cultural barriers, similar to hiking (see p. 190).

The tournament typically runs from August 8 to 21, with four matches a day for the first ten days, all viewable on a single ticket. The seating is divided into sections: behind home plate, the first- and third-base "Alps" partisan cheering sections, and the outfield. Behind home plate is under the awning and slightly more expensive for the shade *($$$$),* but the Alps *($$$)* are a riot.

of **Osaka-jo** is an impressive concrete reproduction of the old castle set on its massive original walls and girded by the city's largest park, popular in the spring for its cherry blossoms.

Minami-ku (South Ward), a veritable city of covered arcades, is Osaka's most energetic and colorful district. In its northern part, **Shinsaibashi** (shinsaibashi.or.jp), you'll find the youthful fashion followers' hangout of **Amerika-mura** (America Village), which offers the anthropologically minded visitor to Japan a prime people-watching opportunity.

The lively **Shinsaibashi-suji** arcade runs down to the **Namba** area and its main entertainment district, **Dotombori** (dotonbori .or.jp). A rainbow array of signs and a cacophony of sound advertise the area's theaters, bars, and pachinko parlors (see sidebar p. 174)—as well as more risqué entertainments. Also boasting Osaka's largest mass of restaurants catering to all budgets, Dotombori is not surprisingly the city's most popular hangout.

Restaurants cluster along the neon-lit Dotombori-gawa and around the main artery of Namba Station. Choosing one is half the fun, as restaurant staff scurry after pedestrians with their menus and chefs bellow "Irrashai!" (Welcome!) from their kitchens to welcome customers. On the other end of the scale, dozens of Japan's top-rated, astronomically priced restaurants are here, too. If you are concerned about walking into a place that is beyond your budget, look for

INSIDER TIP:

Beware high-priced restaurants in Namba hiding behind innocuously marked entrances. Ask to see the menu at the door (menu-o misete kudasai).

—PERRIN LINDELAUF
National Geographic author

the plastic food representations outside (the universal mark of cheap-to-reasonable).

East of Namba is **Nippon-bashi,** also known as **Den Den Town** (nipponbashi.toraru.com). "Den" comes from denki—electricity—as this is one of the biggest shopping districts for electronics in Japan. Although Den Den Town has lost pride of place to the newer, massive Yodobashi Camera in Umeda, it has become a major center for otaku culture, western Japan's version of Akihabara (see pp. 96–97), complete with maid cafés, shops filled with collectible robot figurines, and people roaming about in various states of cosplay.

Running north–south between Namba and Nipponbashi is **Sennichimae Doguya-suji,** an arcade market devoted to cooking equipment, plastic display food, and anything else you might need to reproduce something you ate here or open a Japanese restaurant. Prices are reasonable here, but it's a great (continued on p. 250)

National Museum of Art Osaka

✉ 4-2-55 Nakanoshima, Kita-ku

☎ 06/6447-4680

🕐 10 a.m.–5 p.m.; 10 a.m.–7 p.m. Fri.; closed Mon.

💲 $, $$$ for special exhibitions

🚇 Yotsubashi line: Higobashi

www.nmao.go.jp

Osaka-jo

✉ 1-1 Osaka-jo, Chuo-ku

☎ 06/6941-3044

🕐 9 a.m.–5 p.m.

💲 $ keep, grounds free

🚇 Osaka Loop line: Osakajokoen

osakacastle.net

Tsutenkaku

✉ 1-18-6 Ebisuhigashi, Naniwa-ku

☎ 06/6641-9555

🕐 9 a.m.–8:30 p.m.

💲 $$

🚇 Sakaisuji line: Ebisucho

tsutenkaku.co.jp

Shinto

Being Shintoist is virtually synonymous with being Japanese. Almost everyone is involved in Shinto rituals at some time: Newborn children are presented at the shrine, and many marriage ceremonies are Shinto.

The Way of the Gods

Meaning "the Way of the Gods," Shinto originated among the tribes of prehistory. It is rooted in an animist folk religion, worshipping *kami*—the gods believed to inhabit all things under, and including, the sun. Whether inaugurating building sites or factories, or at the shrine itself, Shinto ceremonies suggest extreme antiquity. Waving leafy branches toward cardinal points to ward off evil spirits, the priest is assisted by *miko* (shrine maidens) whose slow, simple motions evoke ancient, solemn rituals passed down over millennia.

Ancient Chinese influences gradually turned Shinto into an ancestor cult; it was believed that everyone, especially emperors, would become kami (spirit gods) after death. Different communities share the basic religion, but believe in variants; tiny hamlets boast a shrine for a protective god, and even homes contain a miniature *kamidana* (god shelf) to enshrine kami. Early Buddhist proselytizers claimed that major kami were merely incarnations of their Buddhas; the overlap resulted in confusing syncretic temple-shrines. With worshippers moved by awe, reverence, and superstition rather than faith or piety, Shinto is devoid of doctrine or ethics. Its priesthood is a hereditary post serving the community by maintaining the shrine.

The Shrine

A Shinto shrine is recognizable by the *torii* (gateway) at its entrance. Shrines are often decorated in white and red, the respective ritual colors of male and female. Being formless, the ancient gods go undepicted, but paired stone *komainu* (lion dogs) often stand at the entrance to guard the shrine against evil. Some shrines contain statues of animals considered divine messengers—especially the fox, the familiar (servant) of Inari, deity of the hearth and harvest. Horses are often featured in shrines: Originally presented to shrines to invoke the kami, horses were later replaced by more convenient *ema* (horse pictures), a wooden plaque with a horse painted onto it, on which one writes a wish to the gods. Nowadays, despite the horsey name, ema may have a variety of animals on them, especially those from the Chinese zodiac.

State Shinto

The name Shinto came into use only when the vague, heterogeneous beliefs were formalized and separated from Buddhism in 1872 as the nationalistic state religion based on emperor worship. State Shinto exalted the *Kojiki (Record of Ancient Matters)* and *Nihon Shoki (Chronicles of Japan).* Completed in the early eighth century, both books begin with the Shinto creation myths and chronicle the reigns of emperors from 697 B.C. to A.D. 660, the first 14 being mythical. Seen as politically expedient, the books reinforced an emperor's rule by establishing his divinity. Japan, its population, and the gods were all progeny of the female Izanami and the male Izanagi, parents of the sun goddess Amaterasu, who was the ancestor of Emperor Jimmu—the first of an unbroken imperial line and the source of Japanese superiority in the eyes of ultranationalists, even though State Shinto was repudiated after the war.

Beliefs & Rituals

Many Shinto cults focus on volcanoes and mountains, and a few on phallic variants of human fertility. Primarily Shinto is a farmer's religion, bound to crop cycles; the emperor's duties still include the ceremonial

A *miko* (shrine maiden) bears a branch of the sakaki evergreen tree, used for purification in Shinto ceremonies.

planting and harvesting of rice on palace grounds. From convivial New Year bonfires in remote country shrines to spectacular annual *matsuri* (festivals) attended by hundreds of thousands, Shinto binds communities. Matsuri feature processions of ornate *mikoshi* (portable shrines). Some 70 million people visit shrines at New Year to pray for the guardianship of the gods, whose assistance is invoked for a safe journey, success in exams or business, the birth of a healthy child, or protection against illness. Shinto shuns impurity and the pollution of blood, death, and dirt. When entering a shrine, use the cisterns by the shrine entrance to wash your hands and rinse your mouth. Pour the water into your hand to drink. Ring the gong to alert the kami to your presence, throw a coin—five yen is luckiest—into the offering box. Bow twice with hands together, pray, then clap twice, bow again, and back away from the shrine. If few believe intrinsically today, everyone plays it safe. It was always so: Moved to tears before the altar at Ise-jingu, the 13th-century priest Saigyo said, "I know not at all if anything deigns to be there."

Spa World

✉ 3-4-24 Ebisuhigashi, Naniwa-ku

☎ 06/6631-0001

🕐 10 a.m.– 8:45 a.m. the next day

💲 $$$ (daytime), $$$$ (24 hr.)

🚇 Osaka Loop line: Shin-Imamiya

spaworld.co.jp

Kaiyukan (Osaka Aquarium)

✉ 1-1-10, Kaigan-dori, Minato-ku

☎ 06/6576-5501

🕐 10 a.m.–8 p.m.

💲 $$$$

🚇 Chuo line: Osakako

kaiyukan.com

spot for window-shopping, too.

Just south of Den Den Town is **Shin-Sekai,** Osaka's most colorful neighborhood. Literally dubbed "New World" when it was a hip district at the turn of the 20th century, Shin-Sekai is now either nostalgic or crusty, depending on your generosity. The narrow pedestrian streets are full of discount clothing stores, smoky dens where old men play endless games of mah-jongg, and cheap restaurants selling *kushi-katsu* (fried food on skewers) or fugu (see sidebar p. 21). The tower at the center, 338-foot-tall (103 m) **Tsutenkaku,** is a beloved Osaka landmark and it enshrines Billiken, an odd "god" adopted from an American doll, whose feet grant luck when rubbed. Despite being rough around the edges and despite what some worried elders may tell you, Tsutenkaku isn't dangerous. It's a great area to explore

with a camera or to grab a bite to eat—and enjoy enticements to "come to our place, it's the third best in Shin-Sekai!"

Rounding out the list of strange experiences is nearby **Spa World,** a kind of super *onsen* that has an unbelievable collection of Asian and European bath styles, from Balinese architecture to Roman baths and Finnish saunas. On the subject of water, Osaka's aquarium, the **Kaiyukan,** is one of the world's largest. The star attraction is a whale shark in the giant central tank, but there are exhibits on the fauna from all around the Pacific Ring of Fire. If that isn't enough to tame unruly children, consider **Universal Studios Japan** *(usj.co.jp),* which has a strong anime theme mixed into the classic attractions: The Water World show, for instance, has been converted to a *One Piece* anime-themed pirate battle. ∎

Osaka Aquarium, also known as Kaiyukan

Kobe & Hyogo Prefecture

The city of Kobe sits on the southern slope of Mount Rokko, on the west side of Osaka Bay. A trading post from ancient times, Kobe rose to prominence when the city opened its doors to foreign traders as one of Japan's first treaty ports. In so doing, it acquired a substantial foreign population and a degree of cosmopolitanism—both of which it retains today.

The night view of Kobe Port Tower and Kobe Maritime Museum

A large city sandwiched between Mount Rokko and the sea, Kobe is one of Japan's most livable urban centers, not something lost on the first foreign traders to be allowed into Japan in the early Meiji period. Sitting high on the mountain slopes, the Kitano district features several of the early Western-style homes and religious buildings. The upscale neighborhood is on the whole quite charming, with a variety of cafés and boutiques. South of Sannomiya Station, Kobe's central hub, is **Nankin-machi,** western Japan's only Chinatown. The street is packed with good restaurants; Kobe enjoys a high caliber of foreign food thanks to its long contact with the outside world. Farther downhill is the port, watched over by the bright red **Kobe Port Tower.** The tower withstood the 1995 Great Hanshin Earthquake that devastated Kobe's traditional wooden homes and left 6,000 dead. Also along the port is the **Great Hanshin-Awaji Earthquake Memorial** (*www.dri.ne.jp*), which researches disaster mitigation techniques and preserves scenes of Kobe's devastation.

Takarazuka, a bedroom town between Kobe and Osaka,

Kobe

 231 B3

Visitor Information

✉ Inside JR Sannomiya Station; another booth on 2nd floor of JR Shin-Kobe Station

☎ 078/322-0220 or 078/241-9550

🕐 9 a.m.–7 p.m.

feel-kobe.jp

Tezuka Osamu Manga Museum

✉ 7-65 Mukogawa-cho, Takarazuka

☎ 0797/81-2970

🕐 Open daily 9:30 a.m.– 5 p.m., closed Wed. Sept.–June

💲 $$

🚇 Hankyu Takarazuka line: Takarazuka

tezukaosamu.net

Arima Onsen

✉ 7-65 Mukogawa-cho, Takarazuka

☎ 078/904-0708

🕐 9 a.m.–7 p.m.

arima-onsen.com

would be indistinguishable from other such towns if not for a pair of unusual attractions. The **Tezuka Osamu Manga Museum** describes the life of Tezuka Osamu, Japan's Walt Disney and the godfather of anime, who grew up in Takarazuka. Falling in love with its nature, he learned his drawing skills by illustrating local insects. His respect for life led him to become a doctor, but after qualifying he went back to drawing manga (comics) and anime: His creations include the robot Astro Boy, vigilante doctor Black Jack, and Kimba the White Lion, although his complete body of work runs to 150,000 pages. His final words are said to be, "I'm begging you, let me work!" The museum houses exhibits on his life and work, as well as a good library of translated comics, an animation center, and a theater screening his anime. Takarazuka is also known for the Revue (see sidebar p. 53), which was founded by Hankyu Railway's owner, Kobayashi Ichizo, to increase tourist traffic to the station. Increase it has: Takarazuka's all-female troupe has developed a cult following.

Farther afield in Hyogo-ken are two fine *onsen*, Arima and Kinosaki. **Arima Onsen** is right in Kobe's backyard, directly behind Mount Rokko. The baths here have been popular for 1,400 years, since early emperors began to take the waters for their health. There are two kinds of spring water running here: the "gold bath," a rusty brown-gold alkaline water featuring a very high iron and salt content, said to be good for the skin, and the "silver bath," a mix of carbonic acid and radon. Each kind has a public bath available for day-trippers, and most of the *ryokan* in town allow nonguests to use their baths for a fee.

Kinosaki Onsen *(tel 0796/32-4141, kinosaki-spa.gr.jp)* is opposite Kobe, on the Japan Sea coast. Unlike other onsen towns, Kinosaki is notable for the *soto-yu* (outside bath) system: Guests don *yukata* (light kimonos) and walk from bath to bath throughout the village, rather than using only the baths in their ryokans. There are seven in total, ranging from the super-onsen Sato-no-yu next to the station—with a variety of baths and saunas, including a "penguin sauna" (actually a walk-in refrigerator) to Gosho-no-yu, built to resemble a traditional palace. ■

Kobe Beef

Kobe beef, the world's most famous, most expensive meat, sits at the pinnacle of the *wagyu* (Japanese beef) tables, its tender muscle and delicate fat marbling a cut above anything else. You may think you've tried it back home, but like "champagne," the term "Kobe beef" is used indiscriminately to sell lesser products. Only 3,000 head of the Tajima breed are designated Kobe beef a year: The meat must have that melt-on-the-tongue high fat content and excellent texture to be certified. To meet these specifications, the cows are given only the best feed and are massaged to keep them happy, but the beer drinking is just a legend. The cheapest five-ounce sirloin will run you $60, and steaks over $200 are not uncommon, but you can eat Kobe beef for less at lunchtime, when the portions are smaller. (See Travelwise pp. 374–375 for a Kobe beef restaurant recommendation.)

Himeji

H [...] dium-size city 34 miles (55 km) west of Kobe, was almost obliterated by bombs d [...] d War II, so it is quite miraculous that its magnificent castle still stands. Also known a [...] -jo (White Heron Castle) for its whitened woodwork and plaster walls, Himeji-jo i [...] ed Japan's most beautiful stronghold. Restored in 2015, the keep gleams whiter t [...] in centuries.

Built by local warlords on the site of a 14th-century fortress in 1581, **Himeji-jo** was restored and upgraded during the 1600s by Ikeda Terumasa, son-in-law of shogun Tokugawa Ieyasu. Its ownership passed through various noble samurai families until the Meiji Restoration in 1868. Standing on massive unmortared walls and comprising scores of *yagura* (arrow storehouses), watchtowers, and other buildings around its magnificent main *donjon,* the castle stands today as it was finished in 1618. Complete with slits in the walls for firing arrows and guns—and chutes for pouring boiling oil on invaders—this formidable fortification remains remarkably preserved, as it was never attacked. Of three moats, the outer one is now buried; it once separated the castle from the town.

Between the castle buildings stretch beautifully landscaped areas with lawns and flowering trees—exemplifying the samurai way of melding an unyielding defensive structure with refined living spaces. The main donjon displays the traditional five-story roof structure while it conceals six stories—and a cellar beneath. Echoing the balance between martial might and aesthetic sensibilities, the architectural delicacy of Himeji-jo belies its strategic impregnability. ◾

Himeji
 231 A3
Visitor Information
✉ Inside JR Himeji Station
☎ 079/287-0003
🕐 9 a.m.–7 p.m.
himeji-kanko.jp

Himeji-jo
✉ 68 Hon-machi
☎ 0792/85-1146
🕐 9 a.m.–4 p.m. (last admission), 5 p.m. in summer
💲 $$
 Sanyo Shinkansen or Sanyo Main line: Himeji, then 15-min. walk north

The gleaming white walls and roof of the recently restored Himeji Castle

Wakayama-ken

Wakayama Prefecture, despite being on the doorstep of Osaka's Kansai International Airport, is worlds apart. Once you leave Wakayama city, you enter the Kumano region, one of the earliest cradles of Japanese spirituality. Pilgrimage routes lace the mountains of the Kii-hanto, a broad peninsula containing some of Japan's most ancient shrines. Buddhism has an important home here, too, at the mountain monastery of Koya-san.

Pilgrims walk through Okunoin cemetery on the Buddhist mountain of Koya-san.

Koya-san

231 B2

Visitor Information

✉ By Senjuinbashi-mae bus stop

☎ 0736/56-2616

$ $$$ (joint ticket)

🕐 8:30 a.m.–7 p.m.

🚉 Nankai Koya line: Gokurakubashi, then cable car to Koya-san; Nankai Rinkan bus to Senjuinbashi-mae

eng.shukubo.net

In the peninsula's northwest, hilly Koya Ryujin Quasi-National Park is the site of **Koya-san,** Japan's best known Buddhist mountain retreat. At about 3,300 feet (1,005 m), Koya-san culminates in a plateau covering 5 square miles (12 sq km). It was here that Kukai (774–835), founder of the Shingon sect of Buddhism, first established a seminary in 816. The exclusive preserve of monks, the Koya-san temple city was forbidden to women until 1873. Frequent fires have left no buildings older than the 12th century; several, in fact, were reconstructed early in the 20th century, but unlike many older temples,

even the new ones have a lived-in, well-used atmosphere thanks to the large monastic community that still practices here. **Kongobu-ji,** erected by the warlord Toyotomi Hideyoshi in 1592 and containing fine Kano school screen doors, became the focal temple—and is still the headquarters—of the Shingon sect.

Koya-san is divided into two main areas: the **Danjo Garan,** just southwest of Kongobu-ji, and the **Okuno-in** to the east. In the Danjo Garan complex is the **Treasure House** (Reihokan), with thousands of wonderful exhibits, many of them registered National

Treasures. T...sive cemetery...00 graves ar...ments have ac... or more than 1...nese histor... afterlife pole-positi... Buddha of the Futur... tsu) arrives here s... he **Mausoleum of Tokugawa Ieyasu** is one such placeholder; his main tomb is in Nikko (see pp. 112–116).

In the deepest part of the cemetery is the **Mausoleum of Kukai,** surrounded by ancient cedars. "Mausoleum" is perhaps a misnomer: He is believed to be in eternal meditation, awaiting the Miroku Butsu. In any case, it is the best place to see regular ceremonies conducted by the monks of Koya-san. Just south is the **lantern hall.** Among its 11,000 luminaries, two

have been burning continuously since the tenth century.

The secular part of Koya-san, with all the attributes of an ordinary small town, has no hotels. The majority of the million-odd visitors it receives annually are pilgrims; 51 of the 117 temples in the vicinity provide lodgings known as *shukubo* (see p. 257). Like many places, Koya-san is much quieter once the day-trippers leave, but **Okuno-in** is positively magical in the evening, when the stone lanterns along the winding forest path are lit with flickering candles.

The spiritual roots of the Kii Peninsula go far beyond the upstart 1,300-year-old Japanese Buddhism, extending along a network of ancient pilgrimage trails called the **Kumano Kodo** (see sidebar below). These crisscross the rainy,

Kongobu-ji

✉ 132 Koyasan, Koya-cho, Ito-gun

☎ 0736/56-2011

$ $

🕐 8:30 a.m.–5 p.m.

koyasan.or.jp

Kumano/Tanabe

🗺 231 C2 & 231 B1

Visitor Information

✉ Outside Kii-Tanabe Station

☎ 0739/34-5599

🚆 Kuroshio Express train to Kii-Tanabe Station (2 hr. from Shin-Osaka Station)

tb-kumano.jp

EXPERIENCE: Walk the Kumano Kodo Pilgrimage Trail

Several old pilgrimage routes run through the Kumano region, but the most popular is the Nakahechi route, which starts at the coast in Tanabe and heads inland to Hongu Taisha, the same route traveled by emperors of old on their pilgrimages from Kyoto. The full walk is 35 miles (56 km), but the shorter route below allows for time at the shrines and a bath at Yunomine Onsen.

Grab a map from the tourist office at **Kii-Tanabe Station** tourist office in the morning and catch a Ryujin bus to the **Hosshinmon-oji** stop deep in the mountains. *Oji* are subsidiary shrines of the Kumano deities, serving as waymarkers, places for prayer, and resting spots. Hosshinmon-oji symbolizes the gate to Enlightenment and the entrance to the

grounds of **Kumano Hongu Taisha** (see p. 256), Kumano's most sacred shrine. Following the trail, the next shrine you'll reach is **Fushiogami-oji,** a viewpoint that first reveals the former site of Hongu Taisha in the valley below. Destroyed in a huge flood in 1889, the current shrine is farther inland, but Japan's largest *torii* marks its original riverside spot. From here, descend to Kumano Hongu Taisha's sacred halls, then follow the river through the gate and old shrine precincts.

Leaving the river, take the Dainichi-goe trailhead to **Yunomine Onsen,** a great place to stay. Yunomine has 1,800 years of history and was long believed to cure many diseases; it was also used for purification prior to visiting Hongu Taisha, where visitors are spiritually reborn.

Kumano Hongu Taisha

- ✉ 100-1 Hongu, Hongu-cho, Tanabe-shi
- ☎ 0735/42-0735
- 💲 $
- 🕐 8:30 a.m.–5 p.m.
- 🚌 Ryujin bus from Kii-Tanabe Station to Hongu Taisha-mae stop (2 hr.)

hongutaisha.jp

Kumano Nachi Taisha

- ✉ 1 Nachi-san, Nachi-Katsuura-cho, Higashi-Muro-gun
- ☎ 0735/55-0321
- 🕐 6 a.m.–5 p.m.
- 🚌 Nachisan bus from Katsura Station to Nachisan stop

Kumano Hayatama Taisha

- ✉ 1 Shingu, Shingu-shi
- ☎ 0735/22-2533
- 🕐 Dawn to dusk
- 🚌 15-min. walk from Shingu Station

Ryujin Onsen

- 🚌 Ryujin bus from Kii-Tanabe Station

mountainous World Heritage region, connecting Kansai's cities to shrines of legendary power and hot springs of miraculous healing. The origins of Shinto are lost to history (see pp. 248–249), but the shrines of nearby Ise (see p. 258), and the three in Kumano—Hongu, Hayatama, and Nachi—were once considered as essential to one's spiritual well-being as Mecca. By the early tenth century Japan's emperors were making grand processions over well-built stone trails, in an effort to purify themselves before death.

Ironically, much of the Kumano Kodo isn't "pure" Shinto: Mixed together since Buddhism's introduction, Shinto-Buddhist syncretism (i.e., my *kami* is your Buddha) was widespread until politicians forcibly separated them in order to sprinkle some Divine Right of Kings over their newly restored Emperor Meiji, the center of Shinto belief (see p. 41). The region is one of the few that has retained syncretic shrine/temples and double-naming of the local deities; it is considered highly sacred to the mountain-priests of *Shugendo* asceticism.

To experience Kumano, it's best to walk a section of the ancient pilgrimage trail, linking the purification of the hot springs with the satisfaction of arriving at a major shrine on foot. Of the three grand shrines, **Kumano Hongu Taisha** is the most important, the confluence of all four Kumano pilgrimage routes. **Kumano Nachi Taisha** originated in worship of the 436-foot (133 m) **Nachi Falls** (Nachi-no-Otaki). **Kumano Hayatama Taisha,** while lacking some of the solemn atmosphere of Hongu, is worth visiting to complete the circuit.

Kumano has three *onsen* towns, each distinct and memorable. **Kawayu Onsen's** hot water bubbles up from the bottom of a passing river, so as you dig a hole in the stony bank, it gradually becomes a bathtub. In the winter a "thousand-person bath" is built in the riverbank.

Yunomine Onsen (*Ryujin bus from Kii-Tanabe Station, 1 hr. 45 min.*) is one of the oldest, but **Ryujin Onsen** is perhaps the finest. Set in a narrow valley over a river, the *ryokan* **Kamigoten** was once the villa of the local *daimyo*—and you can stay in his gold-leaf encrusted bedroom for less than you'd think (see p. 376). ∎

Persimmon Sushi to Go

Nara and Wakayama's culinary claim to fame is *kakinoha-zushi*: mackerel sushi wrapped with persimmon leaves. Nara sits inland, far from fishing ports, so what fish the locals traditionally ate was either small river *ayu* (sweetfish) or ocean fish preserved for transport. Kakinoha-zushi is a form of *oshi-zushi* (pressed sushi), where fresh mackerel or salmon is salted and then treated with vinegar to prevent spoiling. The next day the fish is pressed into a bed of rice, sliced, and wrapped in persimmon leaves. A weight is then put on top to press the sushi together overnight. The persimmon leaves and the extra sugar in the rice both inhibit the growth of bacteria, making this local dish ideal for the deep mountains of Nara and Wakayama.

EXPER␣␣␣␣␣␣␣ *hukubo* Stay

For all the t␣␣␣␣␣␣␣ ␣at goes on in Japan, you'd be hard-pressed to see an actual monk during "to␣␣␣␣␣␣␣ ␣ed, many temples have become little more than sightseeing spots or inherit␣␣␣␣␣␣␣ ␣ where the project of Enlightenment has been all but replaced by memoria␣␣␣␣␣␣␣ parishioners.

An e␣␣␣
M␣␣␣
mo␣␣␣␣␣␣␣␣␣␣␣␣␣␣of
th␣␣␣␣␣␣␣␣␣␣␣␣␣␣d
␣␣␣␣␣␣␣␣␣␣␣␣␣␣␣␣␣
Esoteric Buddhism for nearly 1,200 years. Koya-san was founded in 816 by Kukai (see sidebar p. 294), a great religious reformer. The 117 temples sprawling across the highland valley bustle with monks and the faithful, as Koya-san is one of the few places where one can stay at a *shukubo* or temple-inn.

Bibbed Jizo bodhisattvas watch over travelers and children.

The 53 shukubo lodge serious pilgrims and curious tourists alike, offering simple Japanese-style rooms and traditional monk cooking, called *shojin-ryori* (ascetic cuisine), which forbids the consumption of animals and any exciting vegetables, such as onions and garlic. So while the simple vegetable tempura, tofu, vegetable hot pot, and miso soup won't wow the senses, they are all part of the experience.

The best aspect of a shukubo stay is participating in the ceremonies held each day. Depending on the temple, visitors may join sitting meditation, copy a sutra, help tidy the temple grounds, or watch the morning ceremony. Guests typically rise at dawn to join the morning chant of sutras. As

the monks chant, guests are asked to offer incense and meditate silently.

Afterward, many temples conduct an exciting *goma* or fire ritual. To the chant of sutras and the beat of a drum, the monks prepare a small hearth in an intimate hall dedicated to this ceremony. The deity Fudo Myo'o, one of the Mantra Kings, destroyer of delusion, glares down at the ceremony from his lofty pedestal.

A monk blesses the table, the opening of the hearth, and the hearth itself, representing the purity of body, speech, and mind, respectively. He then lights a fire that leaps almost to the ceiling and adds oil, incense, grains, water, and rice. The consumption of

these elements symbolizes the conversion of delusion to wisdom. As the chanting climaxes, the monk stokes the fire with a fan, drawing huge tongues of flame. Suddenly the fire dies, spent of its fuel and symbolic import, and guests are permitted to approach the fearsome statue of Fudo Myo'o, who drives out delusion, cutting ignorance with his sword of wisdom and binding up one's personal demons with his rope. As for his glare? That means, "Aren't you a Buddhist yet? Convert!"

Koyasan Shukubo Temple Lodging Association (*eng.shukubo.net*) has listings and reservation instructions. **Eko-in** (*ekoin .jp*) holds a popular goma each morning.

Ise

Jutting east into the sea, the Shima Peninsula is covered by the Grand Shrine at Ise, Ise-jingu, the most sacred in all Shinto for nearly 2,000 years and endpoint for one of the most important pilgrimage routes in the region. Such is Ise-jingu's primacy that it is correctly known only as Jingu, The Shrine. The Kintetsu Yamada line makes Ise a convenient day trip from Osaka.

Weaving by hand in Ise-jingu

Ise

🅰 231 D2

Visitor Information

✉ Kintetsu Ujiyamada Station, 2-1-43 Iwabuchi

☎ 0596/23-9655

🕐 9 a.m.–5:30 p.m.

🚆 JR from Nagoya to Ise-shi (2 hr.) or Kintetsu Yamada line from Osaka or Kyoto (2 hr.)

Ise-jingu

✉ Ujitachi-cho

☎ 0596/24-1111

🕐 Dawn to dusk

🚆 10-min. walk from Ise-shi or Ujiyamada Stations to Geku

isejingu.or.jp

Of Japan's thousands of Shinto shrines, **Ise-jingu** is paramount. The precinct comprises 125 subsidiary shrines consecrated to a host of deities, all set amid wooded hills and streams. The chief structures are the **Outer Shrine** (Geku), dedicated to Toyouke-Omikami (goddess of harvests, homes, and food), and the **Inner Shrine** (Naiku), dedicated to the sun goddess Amaterasu-Omikami (mythical ancestor of the emperor and the Japanese race). The two buildings stand 4 miles (6 km) apart, but they are connected by a bus that runs every 15 minutes. Made of fresh *hinoki* (cypress) wood from the Kiso mountains (see pp. 191–192), the main shrine buildings are ritually dismantled and identically reconstructed every 20 years; the process took place for the 62nd time in 2013.

The shrine buildings—simple, unadorned, and thatched—are akin to ancient granaries; the design features distinctive ornamental *chigi* (crossed beams protruding from the gabled ends of the roofs). The main, or inner, halls of both shrines, accessible only to high priests and the emperor, lie behind a series of enclosures fenced in various traditional styles. Unfortunately the structures can only be seen by peeking over fences.

The Sacred Bronze Mirror

The outside of the Geku is reached via three *torii* gateways and along a curving avenue of towering cryptomeria trees. After crossing the bridge over the Isuzu-gawa, the approach to the Naiku is similar; enhanced by the worship of countless millions over 2,000 years, the atmosphere is awe-inspiring. The inner sanctum of the main hall of the Naiku contains one of Japan's great imperial treasures: the sacred bronze mirror said to have been given to the first emperor by Amaterasu. Covered by layers of cloth placed over it since the third century, the mirror has not been glimpsed by anyone—priests or emperors—since the day it was cast. ∎

Divided into San-in—the northern area along the Sea of Japan—and San-yo, the southern coastal region and gateway to the charming islands of the Inland Sea

Western Honshu (Chugoku)

Ceremony at Itsukushima-jinja Shinto shrine

Western Honshu (Chugoku)

Chugoku is the western part of Honshu, between the island of Kyushu to the west and Hyogo-ken to the east. Coined in the distant past when only the area between Kyushu and Kanto came under any governmental administration, Chugoku literally means the "middle country."

The south coast is called San-yo, literally the "sunny side of the mountains," whereas the north coast along the Sea of Japan is known as San-in, "in the shadow of the mountains" or, less flatteringly, the "backside of Japan." The remoter San-in region, which covers Shimane and Tottori Prefectures (the latter with miles of sand dunes) as well as northern Yamaguchi, boasts a unique combination of rural farmland, rugged coasts, and historical towns—an increasingly popular alternative for those seeking the pleasures of an older, quieter Japan.

Following the paths of the great trunk roads of feudal times, the main highways and Shinkansen railroad lines from Tokyo to the island of Kyushu run through San-yo. This region includes the gateways to Shikoku and the islands of the Inland Sea, reached both by ferry and by bridge; it also takes in the prefectures of Okayama in the east and Yamaguchi (the southern part) to the west, with Hiroshima in between. Compared to San-in, the region is more developed, wealthier, and with more big-name sights, but it lacks the quiet beauty of the more rural north coast. ■

NOT TO BE MISSED:

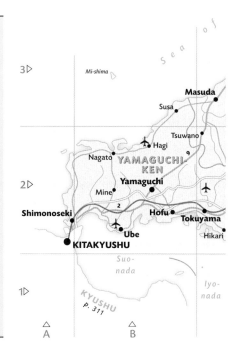

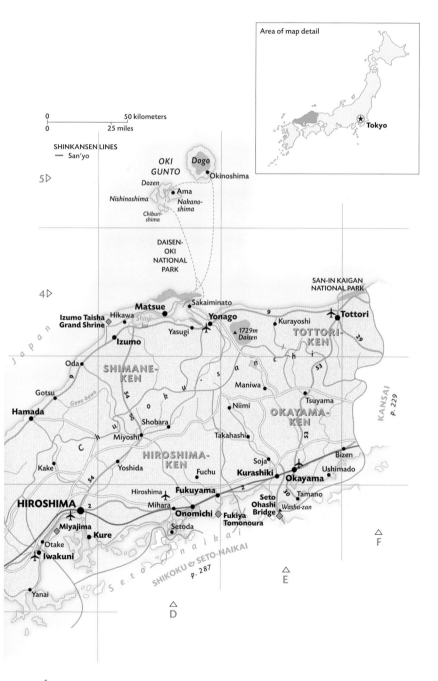

Area of map detail

★ **Tokyo**

0 ___ 50 kilometers
0 ___ 25 miles

SHINKANSEN LINES
— San'yo

**OKI
GUNTO**

Dogo

• Okinoshima

Dozen

• Ama

Nishinoshima   • *Nakanoshima*

*Chiburi-
shima*

**DAISEN-
OKI
NATIONAL
PARK**

5▷

4▷

**SAN-IN KAIGAN
NATIONAL PARK**

• Sakaiminato

Matsue   *Shinji-
ko*   **Yonago**   ✈ **Tottori**

Hikawa   • Kurayoshi   9

**Izumo Taisha
Grand Shrine** ◇   Yasugi ✈   ▲ 1729m
Daisen   **TOTTORI-
KEN**   29

Izumo •

Oda •   • Maniwa   53

Gotsu •   **SHIMANE-
KEN**   • Niimi   • Tsuyama

Hamada •   Shobara •   54   **OKAYAMA-
KEN**   53   **KANSAI**
p. 229

Miyoshi •   Takahashi •

**HIROSHIMA-
KEN**   Soja •   Bizen •

Kake •   Yoshida •   • Ushimado

54   Fuchu •   **Kurashiki** •   ✈

Hiroshima ✈   **Fukuyama**   **Okayama** •

HIROSHIMA 2   Mihara •   2   30   • Tamano

Miyajima ◇ ✈   **Onomichi** • ◇ **Fukiya**   **Seto
Ohashi
Bridge** ◇   *Washu-zan*

• Otake   **Kure** •   Setoda •   **Tomonoura**

✈ **Iwakuni**

Seto・naikai

• Yanai   **SHIKOKU & SETO-NAIKAI**
p. 287

Japan

Gono-kawa

F△

E△

D△

C△

San-in

Despite being one of the most attractive regions in the country, the San-in coast of northern Chugoku is often omitted from travelers' itineraries. The oversight is probably due to its location on the shores of the Sea of Japan, so notorious for snowy winters and abundant rainfall that potential visitors seem to forget it has a summer. Consequently, the San-in coast remains comparatively rural—and little spoiled by development.

Candles light the way for ancestral spirits at a ceremony in Hagi.

The region has justifiably earned an off-the-beaten-path reputation. The main San-in railroad meanders along a coast largely devoted to fishing and farming, where life is more leisurely than in most of Japan. But San-in has more than excellent seascapes and mountain scenery to recommend it. The old coastal town of Hagi preserves picturesque reminders of its feudal past, as does inland Tsuwano. Matsue, adopted home of 19th-century Greek writer Lafcadio Hearn (see sidebar p. 267), retains a fine castle. Nearby Izumo is famed for Izumo Taisha, the second most sacred Shinto shrine in the country after Ise. Shimane-ken embraces the Oki-shoto Islands, with towering sea cliffs and a rich local history. And with a modicum of common sense, San-in is a great place to hitchhike, with stunning coastal views and friendly locals who rarely have the chance to meet and talk to foreigners.

Hagi

Hagi, with its beautifully pre-served samurai quarter, evoca-tive castle ruins, pottery kilns, beaches, and attractive seascapes, is often regarded as the gem of the San-in coast. While Japan remained sealed to the outside world, Hagi produced the Choshu clansmen most instrumental in overthrowing the old samurai regime and bringing about the Meiji Restoration of 1868.

Hagi has long had a reputation for pottery, particularly tea cer-emony vessels. The ware typically displays a deceptively rough-hewn quality. About a hundred kilns are open in the vicinity.

The main sights congregate in the west, on the delta of the Hashimoto-gawa. The town is small enough to negotiate on foot, but there is a lot to see. Arm yourself with the excellent English-language booklet from the visitor information center, then head out exploring.

On the eastern confines is the 1691 **Toko-ji.** Built as a Mori

INSIDER TIP:

The best way to get around Hagi is by bicycle. Rent one at Higashi-Hagi Station or from one of several hotels.

—ROB GOSS
National Geographic contributor

memorial temple, this is the graveyard of the first and odd-numbered generations of the Mori clan; it mirrors **Daisho-in** (*4132 Tsubaki, tel 0838/22-2124, 8 a.m.–4:30 p.m., $*), in the south-west, which commemorates the even-numbered Mori. Behind the Toko-ji you'll find an avenue that is flanked by stone lanterns.

Matsue

Situated on the eastern shore of Shinji-ko and just inland from the coast, Matsue is a charming mix of traditional districts, mod-ern city, and ubiquitous water.

(continued on p. 266)

Hagi
- 🅰 260 B2

Visitor Information
- ✉ JR Higashi-Hagi Station
- ☎ 0838/25-3145
- 🕐 9 a.m.–5:45 p.m.
- 🚄 JR San-in line from Matsue (3.5 hr.)

hagishi.com

Toko-ji
- ✉ 1647 Chinto
- ☎ 0838/26-1052
- 🕐 8:30 a.m.–5 p.m.
- 💲 $
- 🚌 Maaru Bus: Tokoji-mae (from Higashi-Hagi)

Matsue
- 🅰 261 D4

Visitor Information
- ✉ North of JR Matsue Station
- ☎ 0852/21-4034
- 🕐 9 a.m.–6 p.m.

www.kankou
-matsue.jp

NEED TO KNOW

Reaching Western Honshu

Access to the cities of the Pacific-facing Sanyo region couldn't be easier: Just hop on the Shinkansen. From Osaka, the San-yo Shinkansen links Okayama (45 min.) and Hiroshima (80 min.), and local transfers connect the smaller cities of Onomichi and Kurashiki.

On the San-in side of Chugoku there is no Shinkansen service. Although there are JR express trains, these are no faster than highway buses and cost more,

unless you have a JR Pass. If coming from Tokyo, check flights with ANA to the domestic airports on the north coast: You could save a lot of time.

Getting Around

The small cities of Chugoku are linked by JR West rail service and otherwise largely rely on bus service at the municipal level. Kurashiki, Onomichi, Hagi, and Tsuwano are compact, lending themselves well to walking.

A Hike Through Hagi

If you stroll at a leisurely pace, it takes most of a day to cover all the sights mentioned in this walk. If you omit Teramachi or rent a bicycle, the time can be cut to three hours.

Hagi's homes preserve the atmosphere of samurai days.

The best starting point for an exploration of Hagi is the **Hagi Uragami Museum** (Kenritsu-Hagi Bijutsukan; *586-1 Hiyako, tel 0838/24-2400, www.hum.pref.yamaguchi .lg.jp, 9 a.m.–5 p.m., closed Mon., $*), which lies just outside the traditional Horiuchi and Jokamachi districts. The museum displays a local entrepreneur's exquisite collection of *ukiyo-e* prints and Asian pottery, including local Hagi ware.

After visiting the museum, head west toward Horiuchi, the inner moat district, around the ruins of Hagi-jo. On the way, you will come to the old **Kuchiba Residence** ❶ (Kuchiba-ke Jutaku). Although the house is closed to the public, the gate in front of it, the largest in Hagi, is listed as an Important Cultural Property. A few minutes northwest is the **Mori Clan Tenant House** ❷ (Kyu-Asa Mori-ke Hagiyashiki Nagaya; *Horiuchi Shizuki-koen, tel 0838/25-2304, 8 a.m.–6:30 p.m.*

NOT TO BE MISSED:

Horiuchi Shizuki-koen • Ruins of Hagi-jo • Hananoe Teahouse • Kumaya Museum

April–Oct., 8:30 a.m.–4:30 p.m. Nov.–Feb., 8:30 a.m.–6 p.m. Mar., $ with Hagi-jo ruins), the largest of the samurai houses open to the public. Containing rather dusty memorabilia, it gives an impression of austerity. Like most samurai in 1868, the Mori, who were instrumental in bringing down the shogunate, were anything but rich.

From here, walk about 220 yards (200 m) north to reach **Horiuchi Shizuki-koen** ❸ (Horiuchi Shizuki-koen-nai; *tel 0838/25-1826, 8 a.m.–6:30 p.m. April–Oct., 8:30 a.m.–4:30 p.m. Nov.–Feb., 8:30 a.m.–6 p.m. Mar., $ with Mori*

House), a spacious park extending down to the beach, and the **ruins of Hagi-jo** ④. The castle ruins are a lovely place to wander, at the very least for the views over the sea. More than just moats, ramparts, and scattered foundation stones, these ruins include sections of collapsing outer walls and wooded areas where roof tiles litter the undergrowth. Just northwest of the ruins is the **Hananoe Teahouse** ⑤ (Hananoe Chatei), where you can sip green tea in a charming traditional garden. Check out the Hagi-jo kiln on the way out of the castle's main gate.

It's a pleasant walk east around the promontory toward **Kikuga-hama Beach.** Just south of it, along the ocher-colored mud walls of the Horiuchi district, is the Mori Outer Gate and, to its east, the old **Sufu Residence** featuring beautiful latticed windows. The **Masuda Residence,** 220 yards (200 m) eastward along the same street, is not open to the public, but you can still admire it.

Backtrack half a block and head south to the **Hagi Museum** (tel 0838/25-6447, 9 a.m.– 5 p.m., $), which has an in-depth explanation of the city's role in the Meiji Restoration and English-speaking guides, though it will mainly appeal to history buffs. Crossing the old moat

you will enter Jokamachi. Walk north to **Kikuya Residence** ⑥ (Kikuya-ke Jutaku; 1-1 Gofuku-machi, tel 0838/25-8282, 8:30 a.m.–5:30 p.m., $$). Representative of a wealthy Edo-period merchant's home, it was built in the mid-17th century and retains many original fixtures and furnishings. A museum in a converted *kura* (storehouse) features samurai memorabilia and antique dolls.

From here walk to the **Kumaya Museum** ⑦ (Kumaya Bijutsukan; 47 Imauo-no-Tana-machi, tel 0838/25-5535, 9 a.m.–4 p.m., closed irregularly, $$), an impressive collection of Hagi memorabilia, including pottery, scrolls, and painted screens, exhibited in a converted 18th-century kura. You are now in the **Teramachi** district, home to about 20 temples. Although of relatively minor interest, some are charming enough to make this a rewarding ramble if time permits. Stretching east from the north of Shizuki-koen, Kikuga-hama Beach is scenic and pristine; cap your walk in summer with a swim.

- 🗺 See area map pp. 260–261
- ▶ Hagi Uragami Museum
- 🕓 3 hours to full day
- ↔ 2.3 miles (3.6 km)
- ▶ Teramachi district

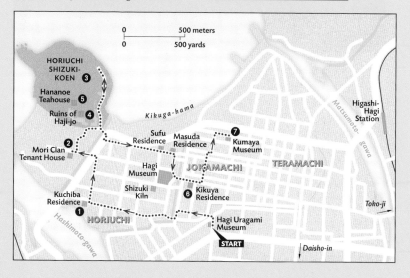

Matsue-jo

- ✉ 1-5 Tono-machi
- ☎ 0852/21-4030
- 🕐 8:30 a.m.–6:30 p.m. April–Sept.; closes 5 p.m. Oct.–Mar.
- 💲 $$, foreigners $
- 🚌 Bus: Matsue Station to Kencho-mae stop

The neighborhood of the castle can been seen in half a day, but it's worth considering Matsue as a base for exploring the region's more distant sights, such as the Oki Archipelago, Izumo Taisha, and the Adachi Museum.

Matsue-jo, completed in 1611, was built by the lords of the Horio clan. The five-story main keep, which conceals a sixth floor inside, underwent renovations opposite) described it as brooding over the city and "fantastically grim." It no longer dominates the skyline as it once did, but this is a fine castle and certainly dark and grim-looking—if only because of the black wood on the facade. Inside is a fine collection of armor and samurai memorabilia.

From the castle grounds, it is a delightful walk north down

Matsue-jo towers among the red leaves of fall in Matsue city.

Buke-yashiki

- ✉ 305 Shiomi-nawate Kitahori-cho
- ☎ 0852/22-2243
- 🕐 8:30 a.m.–6:30 p.m. April–Sept.; closes 5 p.m. Oct.–Mar.
- 💲 $
- 🚌 Bus: Koizumi-Yakumo-Kinenkan-mae

www.city.matsue
.shimane.jp/kankou
/jp/e/buke.htm

some 30 years later. Matsue-jo changed hands through several feudal families until it was taken from the Matsudaira family during the Meiji Restoration. Spared the destruction wrought on most feudal edifices, the keep and several buildings from the 17th century remain intact, distinguishing Matsue-jo as the only original castle standing in western Japan. Lafcadio Hearn (see sidebar a wooded hill to reach the old district of **Shiomi-nawate,** a row of samurai residences beneath the castle along the north side of the moat. Among them are the Meimei-an teahouse and garden, and the **Buke-yashiki,** a samurai residence.

Along the way, stop at the **Jozan Inari-jinja,** an enchanting shrine devoted to the god of rice and wealth. Hundreds of small,

INSIDER TIP:

Invoke the master of the Japanese ghost story by visiting Lafcadio Hearn's favorite shrine, Jozan Inari-jinja. This spooky shrine is devoted to the fox deity.

—KENNY LING
National Geographic contributor

moss-covered, crumbling stone fox effigies litter the precinct. Hearn would stop in here on his way to teach at Matsue Junior High School.

The **Lafcadio Hearn Residence** (Koizumi Yakumo Kyukyo) is in Shiomi-nawate. You will be handed a pamphlet at the entrance with a passage about the garden that Hearn so loved. He described it in *Glimpses of Unfamiliar Japan,* which he wrote here in 1891. It was here too that Hearn penned his famous compilation of ghost stories, *Kwaidan*. The garden is threadbare, ready now for restoration rather than reverent preservation. Although you are left wondering if it ever had a kitchen or a bathroom, the rest of this small, charming house is intact. By all accounts, the Hearn/Koizumis were happy here, even though they occupied the house a mere seven months. More poignant still is the adjacent **Lafcadio Hearn Memorial Museum** (Koizumi Yakumo Kinenkan). One exhibit is Hearn's desk, specially made with disproportionately long legs—his only eye was so shortsighted that he had to work inches from the paper. Here, too, are his Japanese pipes, the suitcases he carried to Japan from America, and the phrases painted on sheets of newspaper with which he taught his children English.

Matsue was part of the region of Izumo, which is regarded as a cradle of Japanese civilization. Six miles (10 km) south of the city is **Fudoki-no-Oka,** where archaeologists have unearthed objects dated from the first century A.D. The **Yakumotatsu Fudoki-no-Oka Museum** displays jewels, swords, and pottery from the

Lafcadio Hearn Residence

 315 Kitahori-cho

☎ 0852/23-0714

🕐 8:30 a.m.–6:30 p.m. April–Sept.; closes 5 p.m. Oct.–Mar.

💲 $

Lafcadio Hearn Memorial Museum

 322 Okudani-machi

☎ 0852/21-2147

🕐 8:30 a.m.–6:30 p.m. April–Sept.; closes 5 p.m. Oct.–Mar.

💲 $

🚌 Lake line bus from JR Matsue Station to Koizumi Yakumo Kinenkan-mae

Yakumotatsu Fudoki-no-Oka Museum

 456 Obacho

☎ 0852/23-2485

🕐 9 a.m.–5 p.m., closed Tues.

💲 $

🚌 Ichibata Bus: Matsue to Fudoki-no-Oka-mae

Lafcadio Hearn (1850–1904)

Lafcadio Hearn, the son of a Greek mother and an Irish father, left Greece at age six after his parents divorced. After a lonely childhood with an aunt in England, he emigrated to the U.S. at 19, where he became a successful journalist. Posted to Japan in 1890 as a correspondent for *Harper's,* he married Koizumi Setsu, a woman of samurai descent, and became a Japanese citizen, adopting the name Koizumi Yakumo. His compelling period pieces express an enchantment with his adopted land. He later wrote the more penetrating *Japan: An Attempt at Interpretation,* but is best remembered for his masterful retellings of Japanese ghost stories and folktales. The frail, partially sighted Hearn died age 54 and was buried in Tokyo's Zoshigaya cemetery. Few foreigners are more beloved in Japan, where Koizumi Yakumo is revered as only a true Japanese writer could be.

Adachi Museum of Art

✉ 320 Furukawa-cho, Yasugi-shi

☎ 0854/28-7111

🕐 9 a.m.–5 p.m. Oct.–Mar.; closes 5.30 p.m. April–Sept.

💲 $$$$, half price for foreigners

🚉 JR Sanin line: Yasugi, then shuttle bus

www.adachi -museum.or.jp

Izumo Taisha Grand Shrine

⛰ 261 D4

☎ 0853/53-3100

🕐 6 a.m.–8 p.m.

🚉 JR Sanin line: Izumoshi, then bus to Seimon-mae

many grave tumuli in the area. In the vicinity are two very old Shinto shrines: **Kamosu-jinja**, with its 17th-century buildings, and **Yaegaki-jinja**, whose treasure house exhibits a rare tenth-century fragment of a shrine mural.

The **Adachi Museum of Art**, 40 minutes east of Matsue, is a must-see garden and museum. The huge garden, ranked number one in Japan for 13 years running, is comprised of six different garden styles, from a moss garden to a dry landscape to an emphasis on bright Japanese maples. If you can tear yourself away from the gardens, the fine collection of modern Japanese paintings inside focuses on Yokoyama Taikan (1868–1958), who was famous for introducing Western techniques into the Japanese style,

INSIDER TIP:

At Izumo Taisha, listen for traditional Japanese music that signifies the sacred dances of the Oracle with 240 mats.

—KENNY LING
National Geographic contributor

resulting in softer lines and more chromatic gradation.

Izumo Taisha

About four miles (6.5 km) northwest of Izumo city is the oldest of all Shinto shrines, **Izumo Taisha Grand Shrine** (see sidebar below). Izumo figures prominently as the backdrop for Shinto creation myths laid down in the *Kojiki* and *Nihon*

Izumo: Conference Hall of the Gods

The convolutions of Japanese mythology could give the Greek gods a run for their money, so it is no surprise that Izumo's ancient shrine originates in a spat between sun goddess Amaterasu and a lesser deity, Okuninushi. Japan's oldest historical documents tell that Okuninushi had built himself a mighty nation, but Amaterasu coveted it. When he refused to hand it over, she resorted to increasingly forceful methods of persuasion. When he finally gave in to the more powerful goddess, she rewarded him with the grand shrine of Izumo and the important spiritual portfolio of Things Unseen (*en-musubi*). Okuninushi's alternate name, En-Musubi—literally "fate-tying"—refers to all the connections that humans form between each other.

Such is the primacy of fate in our lives that each year all of the gods of Japan's various shrines leave home and congregate here in the tenth month of the lunar calendar, traditionally called *kan-na-zuki* or "the month without gods" in Japan.

The gods spend the month discussing the fates of us petty mortals, so this month is especially important for marriage-hopefuls, who go to Izumo Taisha to pay court to the assembled gods. While marriage has supposedly climbed higher on En-Musubi's meeting agendas over the centuries, superstition says that one should never go to the shrine with a betrothed or romantic partner—En-Musubi will be angry that he wasn't consulted first and doom the union. You've been warned!

The giant *shimenawa*, Shinto braided straw ropes to ward off evil spirits, at Izumo Taisha

Shoki—chronicles compiled in the seventh century. The origin of Ise-jingu (see p. 258) is thought to go back 1,700 years; Izumo Taisha predates even that. According to legend, the shrine was originally built for the god Okuninushi when he assumed control of the fates of mankind.

Rebuilt at intervals—though not on the regular 20-year intervals of Ise—the main shrine buildings at Izumo Taisha are quite recent, dating mainly from 1874. The precinct, surrounded by hills, is pleasantly wooded. It incorporates two long rectangular halls called *juku-sha,* which are provided to accommodate all eight million Shinto gods believed to visit annually in October. Shinto gods take a vacation at that time; the deities pack their bags and head for Izumo, where the month of October is called *Kami-ari-Zuki* (the month when the gods are there). The precinct has a **treasure house** containing historical and religious artifacts connected to the shrine.

Many worshippers come to Izumo Taisha to pray for success in marriage, this being one of the god Okuninushi's spheres of interest (along with medicine, fishing, and silkworm culture). Izumo Taisha Grand Shrine can be comfortably visited on a day trip from Matsue.

Tottori

The least populous prefecture in Japan, Tottori is much the opposite of the prefectures to the south. Unlike the industrialized, milder Pacific coast, Tottori is rugged, hot, and wild, home to San-in Coast National Park, dramatic sand dunes, and Mount Daisen, a volcano rising nearly straight from the sea.

(continued on p. 272)

Tottori

🔼 261 E4

Visitor Information

✉ Outside station

☎ 0857/22-3318

🕐 8:30 a.m.–5 p.m.

🚆 Access: Limited Express Super Hakuto from Osaka (2.5 hr.)

torican.jp

Tsuwano Walk

A beautiful little castle town hidden in the mountains, Tsuwano makes for a great compact walk with a mix of historical buildings, forest trails, and great views.

Carp swim in the streets of Tsuwano.

As you exit Tsuwano Station, the visitor information office is to your right. Pick up a map and take a peek in the connected **Shisei Kuwabara Photograph Museum** *(tel 0856/72-1771, $)*, devoted to a local-born photojournalist known for his work on the Minamata Disease environmental disaster.

Across the street, another native son's work is on display: The **Mitsumasa Anno Art Museum ❶** *(tel 0856/72-4155, 9 a.m.–5 p.m., $$)* has a large collection of the painter's whimsical, international award–winning work.

NOT TO BE MISSED:

Maria Seido • Kakuozan Yomei-ji • Taikodani Inari-jinja • Ruins of Tsuwano-jo • Mori Ogai Memorial Museum

From the visitor information office, turn right and follow the tracks south, then cross them at the first opportunity, doubling back until you are behind the station. From here, take the road straight into the mountains to **Maria Seido ❷**. This charming wooden Catholic church, was built in 1951 to commemorate the 153 "hidden" Christians who were imprisoned here. The forcible opening of Japan by U.S. Commodore Perry (see p. 41) emboldened Japanese Christians who had kept the faith for 240 years in Nagasaki to reveal themselves. The government imprisoned 3,394 of them and tortured the most stubborn faithful in Tsuwano. 37 died during their "reeducation" between 1868 and 1872.

From the churchyard, turn left into the Jujika-no-Michi (Road of the Cross), a tree-lined path dotted with scenes from Christ's final days. Turn left into the road as you reach it, then turn right into the grounds of a small but stately temple, **Kakuozan Yomei-ji ❸** *(Ro-107 Ushiroda, tel 0856/72-0137, 8:30 a.m.– 5 p.m., $)*. Built in 1420 as a contemplative retreat, it boasts fine painted interior screen doors and an attractive garden. Exit through the main gate. When the temple path meets the road, turn right, cross the tracks again, then follow the road about half a mile (700 m) and turn sharp right into a secondary road with a large *torii* gate over it. Enter the grounds of Yasaka-jinja, a shrine on your right.

From here, make the winding trek up a concrete stairway through a tunnel formed by well over a thousand bright red torii gateways. At the top is **Taikodani Inari-jinja** ❹ *(tel 0856/72-0219, 9 a.m.–4 p.m.)*; established in 1773, it is one of the most important shrines devoted to Inari, the deity of commerce. From the south side of the shrine, a path leads to the chairlift for the **ruins of Tsuwano-jo** ❺ *($)*; following a beautifully scenic four-minute ride, this conveyance stops at a point about ten minutes' walk from the castle ruins, which in turn command a breathtaking view over the town and toward Mount Aono across the valley. Take the chairlift down again and walk downhill. The road ends at a high school, where you turn right. Take the first left and then the footbridge over the river. Go straight one block and on your right you should see the **Mori Ogai Memorial Museum** ❻ *(Mori Ogai Kyutaku; 283 E, Machida, tel 0856/72-3210, 9 a.m.–5 p.m., closed Mon., $$ museum, $ residence grounds)*. Mori was a fascinating man: A military doctor who traveled throughout Europe, he became a pioneer of realism in Japanese literature.

With extra time, walk 15 minutes south to **Nagomi-no-Sato** ❼, *(E 256 Washihara, tel 0856/72-4122, 10 a.m.–9 p.m., closed Thurs., $$)*, a hot spring, and take a dip to wash away the sweat you've worked up so far. From the museum, head north on Tonomachi-dori, Tsuwano's main drag. The street is flanked by houses from the feudal period; their white plaster walls are characteristically patterned with panels of dark gray cross-hatching. Channels of clear water containing thousands of carp run along Tonomachi-dori—a sight particularly lovely when the irises are in full bloom in June.

Some of the houses here are open as museums, notably the **Musée de Morijuku** ❽ *(Morijuku Bijutsukan; 542 Morimura, tel 0856/72-3200, 9 a.m.–5 p.m., closed Mon. $)*, which was once a wealthy farmer's house. Endowed with a fine garden, it now exhibits the works of local contemporary artists.

Just over the bridge is the Catholic church, a delightful building dating from 1931. From here the avenue narrows to become Tsuwano's main street, where you will find local saké breweries (ask for a sample!) and shops selling *washi* paper and *genji-maki*—a cake featuring a layer of sponge around a filling of sweet bean jam.

Finally, stroll through the **Japan Heritage Center** ❾ *(Ro-253 Ushiroda, tel 0856/72-1901, 9 a.m.–5 p.m., closed Mon.)*; it harbors an extensive collection of woodblock prints depicting Tsuwano over its history.

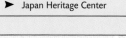

⚠	See area map pp. 260–261
►	Tsuwano Railway Station
⊕	4 hours
⬌	4 miles (6.5 km)
►	Japan Heritage Center

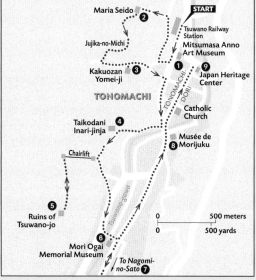

Tottori Sakyu

- 🚌 Bus stop no. 0 to Sakyu Kaikan (30 min.)

Sand Museum

- ☎ 0857/20-2231
- 🕐 9 a.m.–6 p.m.
- 💲 $$

sand-museum.jp

Uradome Kaigan Island Boat Tours

- ✉ 2182 Otani, Iwami-cho, Iwami-gun
- ☎ 0857/73-1212
- 🕐 9 a.m.–4 p.m. Mar.–Nov. (40-min. tours)
- 💲 $$$
- 🚌 Bus from Tottori Station to Shimameguri Yuransen Noriba-Mae stop (40 min.)

Oki Archipelago

- ☎ 0851/22-1122 (Oki Kisen ferry line)
- ⛴ Ferries and high-speed boats twice daily to Oki Kisen. Inquire at Matsue Visitor Information.

www.oki-kisen.co.jp

Provincial **Tottori** city is a warm, largish town, famous for the nearby **Tottori Sakyu** (Sand Dunes). A result of strong northwestern winds, sand carried down in the Sendai-gawa, and the violent churn of the sea, these impressively large dunes just out of the coastline, at times up to 165 feet (50 m). The view is particularly impressive at sunset, as the light crosses the wind-etched slopes on an oblique angle. On the edge of the dunes, **Sakyu Geopark** explains the geology at work, and locals offer rides on homesick-looking camels. Also nearby is the **Sand Museum,** which houses large sand sculptures made by internationally renowned artists. The subjects rotate yearly: In 2016 they were based on the Rio Olympics.

The dunes form part of the **Uradome Kaigan,** a sandy, windswept coastline incorporated into San-in Kaigan National Park, stretching from northern Kyoto Prefecture to Tottori city. Forty-minute boat tours of the craggy sea cliffs run out of Iwami; the Uradome white sand beach around the cape is one of the most popular on the Sea of Japan.

West of Tottori city lies Daisen, an old volcano close to the sea with great views of the coast. Not particularly large at 5,672 feet (1,729 m), Daisen still impresses with its vertical prominence, towering over surrounding farmland. Daisen is part of Daisen-Oki National Park, which encompasses the **Oki Archipelago** (Oki Shoto) offshore from Shimane Prefecture. Once used to exile rebellious emperors, Oki is well off the beaten path. The most attractive island is Nishinoshima. Its 843-foot (257 m) sea cliffs are Japan's highest, and their grassy tops are populated by grazing horses reputed to have been washed there when Kublai Khan's armies were scattered in a storm in 1281. You'll have a hard time believing you are still in Japan. ∎

The Future of Nuclear Power

After the 1973 oil crisis, the Japanese government saw nuclear power as a clean, cheap alternative to imported fossil fuels, despite the recent memory of the A-bombs of World War II. The 2011 meltdown in three cores of the Fukushima No. 1 Nuclear Power Plant and irradiation of the surrounding prefectures dispelled this illusion.

All 50 reactors were subsequently shut down for inspection, and their return has been accompanied by bitter protest by many Japanese, who fear a similar accident may one day poison their fields or sicken their children. Given suspicion toward these idled reactors, a shift to renewable energy is likely despite big-business interests and a lack of government initiative.

Whatever the future holds, Japan's energy status quo has been shattered irrevocably.

San-yo

The San-yo coast lies on the Seto-naikai (Inland Sea); it enjoys mild winters and summers that are less humid than in most of Japan, giving it a reputation as the Far Eastern equivalent of the Mediterranean, complete with olive trees. As the main trade route between Tokyo and Kyushu runs through San-yo, the area has seen much more development than the north. At the same time, the San-in can't compare to the sights of wealthy cities on the sunny side of Japan.

The great floating gate (O-Torii) on Miyajima Island, near Itsukushima-jinja

Japanese vacationers flock to resorts on islands just offshore, but beaches are not really the region's major attractions. Okayama-ken, comparatively little spoiled inland, has some beautiful scenery, while its capital, Okayama, is distinguished by one of Japan's greatest gardens, Koraku-en. The nearby town of Kurashiki has a delightful old quarter along a canal and is a significant center for the arts.

The highly industrialized region of Hiroshima-ken is most visited for Hiroshima city, forever associated with the atomic bombing in 1945. But the millions of visitors to Hiroshima's commemorative Peace Memorial Park and museum often bypass the prefecture's other sights.

Just offshore and traditionally hailed as one of Japan's most scenic spots is the island of Miyajima, with the seaside shrine of Itsukushima-jinja, famed for its huge red *torii* emerging from the sea. The picturesque port town of Tomo-no-Ura and, above all, the temple town of Onomichi are also worth a look.

Ferry ports in Hiroshima-ken and Okayama-ken serve the

Swordsmiths at the Bizen Osafune Sword Museum. Below: A razor-sharp *katana*

Okayama-ken

⚠ 261 E3

Visitor Information

okayama-japan.jp

Takahashi

⚠ 261 E3

Visitor Information

✉ Beside JR
Bitchu-Takahashi
Station

☎ 0866/22-8666

🕐 9 a.m.–5 p.m.

🚃 JR Hakubi line
from Okayama
to Bitchu-
Takahashi
(30 min.)

islands of the Seto-naikai and
Shikoku, though Shikoku is
more convenient via the gigantic
bridges of Naruto-Ohashi
(from Hyogo-ken via Awaji-shima
island) and Seto-Ohashi, south
of Okayama, as well as the
Shimanami-Kaido
bridge system
south of Onomichi.

Okayama-ken

Okayama-ken can be
divided into the regions
of northern and southern
Bicchu to the west, Mima-
saka to the northeast, and
Bizen in the southeast; Bizen
includes Okayama city. Though
the coastal areas are somewhat
urban-industrial, the prefecture is rich in scenery, history,
and art—and there is more to
Okayama-ken than the castle
gardens of Okayama.

During the past two decades,
local authorities have been
concentrating increasingly on
tourism and thus undertaking
conservation and restoration
programs. In northern Bicchu,
near **Takahashi** city, you can
see the fine 17th-century castle
Bicchu Matsuyama-jo (*1 Uchi-
sange, Takahashi-shi, tel 0866/22-
1487, 9 a.m.–5:30 p.m. April–Sept.,
closes at 4:30 p.m. Oct.–Mar., $,
bus from JR Bitchu-Takahashi Station),* preserved samurai houses
in **Ishibiya Furusato village,**
and **Raikyu-ji** (*18 Raikyuji-cho,
Takahashi-si, tel 0866/22-3516,
9 a.m.– 5 p.m., $),* noted for its
landscape garden with raked
sand offsetting stones and
azalea bushes shaped to look
like waves.

In northern Bicchu's hills is the
village of **Fukiya,** which preserves
merchant houses from the Edo

INSIDER TIP:

Bridge buffs should
check out the Seto
Ohashi Memorial
Bridge Museum,
(tel 0877/45-2344);
it displays models of
many famous bridges
throughout the world.

—LARRY PORGES
National Geographic Books editor

period, when the local economy
thrived on copper mining.

Although its castle is now
gone, **Tsuyama** city in Mima-
saka has interesting vestiges of
feudal days: a samurai quarter,
the Shuraku-en garden, and
the mid-19th-century Tsuyama
Archive, one of Japan's first centers of Western learning. Nearby,
there is also **Tanjo-ji,** an Important Cultural Property erected at
the birthplace of Honen, founder
of the Jodo sect of Buddhism.
Tsuyama is known for its *onsen,*
but there are several more in
Maniwa, where the pastoral
scenery, complete with grazing
cows, could almost be mistaken
for Switzerland. In the nearby
Soja region is the eighth-century
Hofuku-ji, which is noted for a
lovely pagoda standing in bold
vermilion against a background
of green hills.

Southern Bicchu is best known
for **Kurashiki** (see pp. 277–279),
but it also has some pleasant
resorts offshore, notably on the
islands of Mukuchi, Shiraishi,
and Manabe. The area includes

Tamashima and its temple
Kibi-ji, renowned for its unusual
Chinese garden. Looking out
over the islands of the Inland Sea,
the panorama from the top of
Washu-zan was legendary—until
the completion of the colossal
7.5-mile-long (12.3 km) **Seto
Ohashi,** the bridge connecting
Honshu to Shikoku, in 1988. If its
six sections now dwarf the islands
they span, the bridge is an amazing feat of engineering and a sight
in its own right.

Encompassing Okayama city,
the southeastern region of **Bizen**
is famous for its pottery (see
sidebar p. 276). An abundance of
iron not only affected the color
of the pottery, but also made
Bizen a center for swordmaking
(see sidebar, below). The **Bizen
Osafune Sword Museum** is

Fukiya
Visitor Information

☎ 0866/29-2222
🕓 9 a.m.–4:30 p.m.

Tanjo-ji
✉ 808 Satogata,
Kumenan-cho,
Kume-gun
☎ 0867/28-2102
🕓 9 a.m.–4:30 p.m.
💲 $

Bizen
🅰 261 F3
Visitor Information

🚉 JR Imbe Station
☎ 0869/64-1100
🕓 9 a.m.–6 p.m.
🚉 JR Ako line
from Okayama
to Imbe Station
(40 min.)

Katana

The Japanese sword, commonly referred
to as *katana*, holds a special place in the
country's culture. Each blade is at once
an artifact of a medieval arms race, in
which the sharpest and strongest swords
were instrumental to victory, and also
the symbol of the proud samurai warrior
class, whose strong spirit the Japanese
still look to in peaceful days.

It is the artistry of katana, however,
that elevates them far above mere
weapons. Holding the blade toward the
light, look down the blade and note
the pattern in the folded steel, the
smooth or jagged line down its length
called the *hamon,* which marks where the
edge was tempered. Note the groove,
cut for lightness and strength and the
name chiseled into the blade. You won't
be likely to view these fine works as mere
weapons again.

EXPERIENCE: Make Your Own Bizen Pottery

One of the "big six" ceramic centers from medieval times, Bizen gained a reputation for unglazed stoneware prized for both appearance and durability.

The popularity of Bizen ware grew during the 15th century, when its rough-hewn quality was prized by tea masters. The high iron content of the clay gives Bizen its typically deep red to dark brown color; it is often used to make roof tiles. Varied firing techniques alter the color and produce a variety of subtle effects. The streets around Imbe Station abound with workshops such as **Kibido** (bizenyaki kibido.com), which offers free tours of its kiln. The **Friends of Bizen-yaki Ceramics Society** (touyuukai.jp) inside Inbe Station runs workshops on weekends and can help you make a reservation elsewhere during the week. Next to the station, the **Bizenyaki Museum** (9 a.m.–5 p.m., $) describes the history of the style.

Bizen Osafune Sword Museum

- ✉ 966 Osafune, Osafune-cho, Setouchi-shi
- ☎ 0869/66-7767
- 🕐 9 a.m.–5 p.m., closed Mon.; smithy demos on 2nd Sun. monthly
- 💲 $
- 🚕 Taxi from JR Osafune Station

Okayama

- ▲ 261 E3

Visitor Information

- ✉ JR Okayama Station B1
- ☎ 086/222-2912
- 🕐 9 a.m.–8 p.m.
- 🚄 San-yo Shinkansen from Tokyo (3 hr. 15 min.)

okayama-japan.jp

the best place to learn about the craft of these exquisite blades, from their forging to the artistry that goes into their fittings. Once a month, swordsmiths fire up the forge to demonstrate how the steel of a *katana* is folded for strength and the complex tempering method required for that recognizable curve. There may also be demonstrations on polishing and sharpening. On the Bizen coast is **Ushimado,** a resort prized for its olive groves, marine views, and Mediterranean climate.

Okayama is best known for **Koraku-en** (1-5 Koraku-en, Kita-ku, tel 086/272-1148, okayama -korakuen.jp, 7:30 a.m.–6 p.m. Mar. 20–Sept., 8 a.m.–5 p.m. Oct.–Mar. 19, $), one of Japan's three greatest stroll gardens, a distinction shared with Kenroku-en in Kanazawa (see pp. 177–178) and Kairaku-en in Mito. Koraku-en was commissioned by feudal lord Ikeda Tsunamasa in 1686 and completed in 1700. This master-piece of landscaping, with ponds, watercourses, and hilly artificial islands, was carefully devised to use the castle as borrowed scen-ery. Here teahouses and elegant pavilions stand on lawns against backdrops of maple, cherry, and apricot trees. Streams are crossed by various bridges and enhanced in June with displays of irises.

Other remnants of Okaya-ma's past were flattened with most of the city during World War II, including **Okayama-jo** (2-3-1 Marunouchi, Kita-ku, tel 086/225-2096, 9 a.m.–5 p.m., 9 p.m. in Aug., $$ with Koraku-en, $ castle only), which once stood at the heart of the city. The castle was initially built in 1573. Painted black, it was dubbed U-jo—Crow Castle—in contrast to the famous White Heron Castle at Himeji. The current version was built in 1966, and though only the moon-viewing turret remains from the original, the reproduc-tion of the main *donjon* is realistic enough to provide a magnificent background to Koraku-en. Inside the stronghold is a museum of samurai armor, weapons, and lacquerware.

Okayama has several other fine museums, all located in a "cultural zone" near Koraku-en. In a striking building by architect Okada Shinichi, the **Okayama Prefectural Museum of Art** (Okayama-kenritsu Bijutsukan) displays works by some of the region's greatest artists, including the ink painter Sesshu (1420–1506), the painter/writer/master swordsman Miyamoto Musashi (d. 1645), and the woodblock print master Utagawa Kuniyoshi (1797–1861).

The **Orient Museum** (Oriento Bijutsukan) contains Asian antiquities and is one of the finest museums of its kind in Japan. The **Hayashibara Museum of Art** (Hayashibara Bijutsukan) is devoted to the priceless objects and memorabilia belonging to the Ikeda clan, which ruled Okayama until 1868; its exhibits include furniture, swords, and Noh costumes, several designated National Treasures. The **Yumeji Art Museum** (Yumeji Bijutsukan; *2-1-32 Hama, Naka-ku, tel 086/271-1000, yumeji-art-museum.com, 9 a.m.– 5 p.m. closed Mon., $$*) shows many works by Yumeji Takehisa, a painter beloved in Japan; the quintessence of the early Taisho era (1912–1926), this native son of Okayama depicted willowy beauties in a style akin to European Expressionism.

Traveling 9 miles (15 km) west, you can reach **Kurashiki** by train from Okayama in roughly 15 minutes. The modern part of town near the station is unremarkable, but follow the signs for Kurashiki Bikan Chiku to discover one of Japan's most charming townscapes. Mirrored in a still canal crossed by humpbacked

Okayama Prefectural Museum of Art

✉ 8-48 Tenjin-cho, Kita-ku
☎ 086/225-4800
🕐 9 a.m.–5 p.m., closed Mon.
💲 $

pref.okayama.jp /seikatsu/kenbi

Orient Museum

✉ 9-31 Tenjin-cho, Kita-ku
☎ 086/232-3636
🕐 9 a.m.–5 p.m., closed Mon.
💲 $$

www.orientmuseum.jp

Hayashibara Museum of Art

✉ 2-7-15 Marunouchi
☎ 086/223-1733
🕐 10 a.m.–5 p.m., closed Mon.
💲 $$

Boat tours take visitors through the Kurashiki Bikan historical quarter.

Kurashiki

261 E3

Visitor Information

✉ Beside
  JR Kurashiki
  Station

☎ 086/424-1220

🕐 9 a.m.–7 p.m.

🚉 San-yo line
  from Okayama
  Station (15 min.)

kurashiki-tabi.jp

stone bridges and bordered by willow trees, sedate and carefully maintained old wooden merchant houses stand alongside the town's quintessential warehouses. Kurashiki means "a spread of warehouses." The town found a new use for the warehouses beginning in 1889, when an important cotton textile mill was located in Kurashiki.

The warehouse buildings are typically whitewashed, with

Masks at the Japan Rural Toy Museum in Kurashiki

attractive black-and-white tiled features on the facades. Several have been turned into museums, reflecting Kurashiki's important role as a center for arts and culture—its assurance of preservation during the modern era.

This happy state of affairs is thanks largely to the Ohara family, owners of the Kurashiki Spinning Corporation, which thrived before World War II. A great lover of Western art, Ohara Magosaburo amassed a collection—acquired by connoisseur Kojima Torajiro on his behalf—that warranted the creation of the **Ohara Museum of Art** (Ohara Bijutsukan).

Graced with a Grecian facade, this outstanding museum opened in 1930; substantially enlarged since then, it is now one of the finest museums in Japan. Don't let the paradox of traveling to Japan to find a museum devoted to Western art deter you from seeing a collection that would be equally impressive in Europe. Indeed, some of the works by Western-style Japanese artists may lead you to conclude they deserve a much wider international reputation. Western art is displayed in the two-story **Main Gallery** (Honkan), featuring a substantial array of works by artists ranging from El Greco to Jasper Johns, with Gauguin, Monet, and Munch in between. The **Annex** (Bunkan) exhibits 19th-century and contemporary Japanese works in the Western tradition. Featuring rooms devoted to British ceramicist

Bernard Leach and modern print master Munakata Shiko, the **Craft Gallery** (Kogeikan) also displays works by notable Japanese craftsmen of the modern era. The **Asiatic Gallery** (Toyokan) displays Kojima's remarkable collection of ancient Oriental art, including Chinese Sung- and T'ang-dynasty polychrome figurines.

INSIDER TIP:

Become a child again at the Japan Rural Toy Museum: You'll find dolls, masks, a world record–breaking spinning top, and kites to make your spirit fly.

—ROB GOSS
National Geographic contributor

Other notable museums include the **Kurashiki Museum of Folkcraft** (Kurashiki Mingeikan), with some 800 household items from Japan and around the world attractively laid out in a row of storehouses, and the **Japan Rural Toy Museum** (Nihon Kyodogangukan), with a collection of around 40,000 folk toys and dolls, including many from other countries. Some of them are downright spooky—half the fun is discovering the creepiest doll in the bunch, though that wasn't likely the museum's intended purpose. The **Kurashiki Archaeological Museum** (Kurashiki Kokokan) displays mainly artifacts discovered in Okayama.

The far-reaching Ohara cultural legacy has prevented the indiscriminate redevelopment that has blighted all too many places in Japan; indeed, the city view from Achi-jinja on the hill just north of the Bikan district reveals the contrast between black tile roofs and hodgepodge reinforced concrete. As Kurashiki proves, conservation pays, which is good news for all of Japan's beautiful old places. Although tiny in area, Kurashiki's Bikan district has such a wealth of things to see that it takes up the best part of a day. You could treat yourself to a pleasant overnight stay, especially in one of the historical *ryokan*. The Oharas' old textile factory still stands, cleverly converted into **Ivy Square**, an attractive complex of exhibition spaces, craft workshops, restaurants, cafés, stores, and a hotel.

Onomichi

Onomichi is about midway between the cities of Okayama and Hiroshima, on a hill that offers a beautiful view over the islands of the Inland Sea. Established as a port during the 13th century, it prospered from trade with Ming China during the 14th century. Until the end of the Edo period, it remained important as a center for shipping agents and for ferries to Shikoku.

Today the town around the foot of the hill is largely industrial, but from higher ground the view over the Onomichi Channel, where ships cross in both directions, has all the charm of an *(continued on p. 282)*

(continued on p. 282)

Ohara Museum of Art
- ✉ 1-1-15 Chuo
- ☎ 086/422-0005
- 🕐 9 a.m.–5 p.m., closed Mon.
- 💲 $$$

ohara.or.jp

Kurashiki Museum of Folkcraft
- ✉ 1-4-11 Chuo
- ☎ 086/422-1637
- 🕐 9 a.m.–5 p.m. Mar.–Nov.; 9 a.m.–4:15 p.m. Dec.–Feb.; closed Mon.
- 💲 $$

Japan Rural Toy Museum
- ✉ 1-4-16 Chuo
- ☎ 086/422-8058
- 🕐 9:30 a.m.–5 p.m.
- 💲 $

japan-toy-museum.org

Kurashiki Archaeological Museum
- ✉ 1-3-13 Chuo
- ☎ 086/422-1542
- 🕐 9 a.m.–5 p.m., closed Mon. & Tues.
- 💲 $

Onomichi
- 263 D2

Visitor Information
- ✉ JR Onomichi Station, South Gate
- ☎ 0848/20-0005
- 🕐 9 a.m.–6 p.m.
- 🚅 Shinkansen from Okayama or Hiroshima to Shin-Onomichi Station

ononavi.com

Obake—Ghosts & Demons

If you travel in Japan in midsummer, you will find TV and theaters airing an annual crop of horror movies, Kabuki programs featuring ghost plays, and haunted rides drawing crowds in amusement parks. Children will be glued to the comical animated adventures of Ge-Ge-Ge-no-Kitaro, the little boy who battles ghosts and demons. The Japanese say the perfect antidote to the sultry heat is a nice cool shiver of fear, but the traditions surrounding summertime spirits go back some 1,500 years.

Osore-zan: **Offerings to the dead on Mount Dread**

Comprising several species of goblin and demon, as well as the spirits of humans, animals, and even trees or umbrellas, Japan's army of demons is unmatched in the real world. These things are called *bakemono—obake* for short—meaning monsters or changelings. In the West, ghost stories are mainly for wintertime; in Japan obake walk abroad mainly during O-Bon, a Buddhist festival for the dead starting mid-July—a highlight of the summer holidays. Like the Christian All Saints festival, O-Bon is a time for remembrance. Families visit the graves of relatives

and pray for them before home altars. During O-Bon, the spirits of the dead return for a monthlong visit. The celebrations (dancing, feasting, fireworks) are to welcome them home, but some of the evil dead are said to jump aboard the bandwagon.

Many kinds of bakemono are unrelated to O-Bon. The Setsubun Festival (Feb. 3 or 4) is for driving out *oni*—horned ogres with an appetite for human flesh. The little clay figurines of froglike imps seen in gift shops represent *kappa*. Said to inhabit lonely streams and rivers, the cute-looking kappa were nonetheless feared for sucking out the entrails of those venturing into the water—an appetite long emphasized to deter children from dangerous water play.

The winged *tengu*, inhabiting alpine forests, is a demon sometimes depicted with a stubby beak but more usually with a fierce scarlet face and an outsize nose. Originating in ancient masked drama, tengu masks often adorn the walls of Japanese bars and restaurants. The kindness of the tengu depends mainly upon the moral character of the beholder. Popular myth has it that the great 12th-century military hero Minamoto Yoshitsune was taught the art of swordsmanship as a child by a wise old tengu he encountered in a forest.

INSIDER TIP:

Many trees in Japan are believed to be inhabited by spirits, called *kodama*, **and cutting down such trees is said to bring great misfortune.** *Shimenawa*, **braided ricestraw ropes, are often used to ward off evil spirits.**

—JUSTIN KAVANAGH
National Geographic Travel Books editor

Animal spirits, especially foxes, figure prominently in Japanese folk beliefs. Myths about foxes are of Chinese origin, but they were adapted by the Shinto belief system. Represented as a statue around shrines dedicated to Inari, god of grain and gain, the fox is believed to be the deity's messenger. Not always benign, its ability to assume human form inspired many a ghostly tale; in former times, the insane were often presumed to be possessed by fox spirits. A mammal unique to Japan, the *tanuki* or raccoon dog is similarly believed to be able to change its shape.

The appearance of *kitsune-bi* (fox fire), incandescent marsh gas or will-o'-the-wisp in the countryside, is said to augur hauntings by *yurei*—ghosts. As in the West, the ghosts are thought to be transparent, but they drift away into nothing below the waist. Yurei, earthbound spirits regarded as having unfinished business (usually revenge for the wrongdoings that took their lives), were greatly feared.

Tales of ghosts and demons formed the main themes of Noh plays; the tales were celebrated in storybooks and woodblock prints by, among others, Katsushika Hokusai (1760–1849). Some are well known, as recounted by the 18th-century author Ueda Akinari, but maybe the greatest writer of the genre was Lafcadio Hearn (1850–1904), still revered in Japan by his adoptive name of Koizumi Yakumo (see sidebar p. 267). Many Japanese ghost stories are as chilling as any in the West—eat your tell-tale heart out, Edgar Allan Poe!

A Tengu mask at Sennin Gyoretsu Festival, Tosho-gu

Senko-ji

✉ 15-1 Higashi Tsuchido-cho

☎ 0848/23-2310

🕐 9 a.m–5 p.m.

elaborate scale model. Above all, Onomichi is a temple town and a location much favored by Japanese writers and intellectuals since the early 20th century. On the strength of a 1981 hit movie by director Obayashi Nobuhiko that was set in Onomichi, the town acquired further acclaim.

Onomichi's temples and other sights can easily be covered in a walking tour, starting in **Senkoji-koen.** The path is steep, so it is

famous writers exalting the view, which is probably at its best from outside the temple itself. From here, walk about 440 yards (400 m) eastward downhill to **Fukuzen-ji,** built in 1573 and noted for its carved gates. It is quite a climb north from here to **Saikoku-ji,** but well worth the effort. Founded in the ninth century, this Buddhist temple is immediately identifiable by the gigantic *waraji* (straw sandals) at

The Seto Ohashi bridge

best to take the cable car near Nagaeguchi bus stop up to the hilltop in Senkoji-koen, which is famed for its cherry trees and azaleas.

On the **Bungaku-no-Komichi** (Path of Literature) down through the park to **Senko-ji,** commemorative stones standing in the pines are carved with the words of

the Nio-mon gate. From here a further trek of a hundred steps takes you up to the main hall and three-story pagoda. As you walk back down, take a look at the antiquarian charm of the small **Josen-ji.** Next, walk five minutes east to **Saigo-ji;** built in 1543, the main hall and gate are fine examples of late Muromachi-period (1341–1555) architecture.

Onomichi is also a gateway to the **Shimanami Kaido,** a series of bridges linking Honshu with Shikoku through six islands in the Seto-naikai (Inland Sea; see pp. 308–310). The route makes a pleasant island-hopping bicycle journey (Onomichi to Imabari on Shikoku takes about eight hours). Anime fans should make a side trip to the nearby coastal village of **Tomonoura** (access by bus via JR Fukuyama Station, an hour from Onomichi): Full of charming old buildings crowded around a beautiful bay, it is Japan's best preserved Edo-period port and was also the inspiration for Miyazaki Hayao's movie Ponyo.

Hiroshima

"Hiroshima" is a synonym for the horror of war. It attracts campaigners for peace and nuclear disarmament from Japan and the rest of the world. Yet Hiroshima is also the prefectural capital of an important industrialized coastal region, a thriving new city whose optimistic inhabitants seldom mention the bomb.

The **Hiroshima Peace Memorial Park** (Heiwa Kinen-koen) and **Hiroshima Peace Memorial Museum** provide current and future generations with warnings from the past. The shell of a building known as the **A-Bomb Dome** (Genbaku Domu) illustrates history textbooks all over the world. Hiroshima's Industry Promotion Hall until the morning of August 6, 1945, it is now a World Heritage site, preserved much as it was after the explosion. The hypocenter—the

point above which the bomb detonated—was about 110 yards (100 m) southeast of this hall.

Monuments commemorating the tragedy, in which 140,000 citizens were killed instantly or fatally irradiated in the world's first use of an atomic weapon, stand approximately in the park's center. The **Children's Peace Monument** (Genbaku-no-Ko-no-Zo) is festooned with garlands of thousands of colored paper cranes, a traditional "get well" symbol still made by schoolchildren all over Japan for the

INSIDER TIP:

To island-hop across the Shimanami Kaido bridges by bicycle, go to the Onomichi Port Rent-a-Cycle Terminal (tel 0848/22-5332, 7 a.m.– 6 p.m., $$) outside JR Onomichi Station.

—KENNY LING
National Geographic contributor

benefit of ailing survivors. At the center is the **Cenotaph** (Genbaku Shibotsusha Ireihi). It stands in front of the rectangular Peace Pond, where the **Flame of Peace** (Heiwa-no-To) burns: It will not be extinguished until the last nuclear weapon is destroyed.

The **Hiroshima National Peace Memorial Hall for the Atomic Bomb Victims** houses photographs of those killed and testimonies of the survivors.

Hiroshima

🅰 261 C2

Visitor Information

✉ JR Hiroshima Station, South Gate

☎ 082/261-1877

🕐 9 a.m.–5:30 p.m

✉ 1F Rest House, Peace Memorial Park

☎ 082/247-6738

🕐 8:30 a.m.–6 p.m

🚄 Shinkansen from Tokyo (4 hr.) or Kyoto (1 hr. 45 min.)

hiroshima-navi.or.jp

Hiroshima Peace Memorial Museum

✉ 1-2 Nakajima-cho, Naka-ku

☎ 082/241-4004

🕐 8:30 a.m.– 6 p.m.; closes at 5 p.m. Dec.–Feb.

💲 $

🚋 Tram: Genbaku-Domu-mae

www.pcf.city .hiroshima.jp

Hiroshima-jo

✉ 21-1 Moto-machi, Naka-ku

☎ 082/221-7512

🕐 9 a.m.–6 p.m.; closes at 5 p.m. Dec.–Feb.

💲 $

🚌 Maipu Loop Bus Orange Route: Hiroshimajo stop

Shukkei-en

✉ 2-11 Kaminobori-machi, Naka-ku

☎ 082/221-3620

🕐 9 a.m.–6 p.m.

💲 $

South of the cenotaph, the **Peace Memorial Museum** (Heiwa Kinen Shiryokan) completes the picture. Exhibits include detailed before-and-after scale models, disturbing photographs, burned and tattered school uniforms, a twisted tricycle, and melted bottles, tiles, and metal appliances.

Reminders of the prewar city are few. **Hiroshima-jo,** a concrete copy of the 16th-century castle obliterated by the bomb, contains a museum on Hiroshima's medieval past. The garden of **Shukkei-en,** laid out in 1620, had to be completely restored. This "shrunk scenery garden" was built for the enjoyment of the tea ceremony,

The Flame of Peace in Hiroshima Peace Memorial Park

with an emphasis on making the space feel larger than it actually is through a variety of symbolic geographic features. **Fudo-in** (*3-4-9 Ushita Shin-machi, tel 082/221-6923*), a temple built on the Ota-gawa in the mid-14th century, miraculously escaped damage; the main hall is a

National Treasure. Crossed by broad rivers, Hiroshima is a pleasant small city; distinctly hedonistic, it has a lively shopping arcade on Hon-dori street and the two raucous entertainment districts of Nagarekawa and Yagenbori, chock-full of bars and restaurants. The local dish is the Hiroshima version of *okonomiyaki:* Unlike Kansai's pancake-batter, cabbage and topping mix, the dish consists of fried noodles, cabbage strips, and an egg to hold it together.

Miyajima

Miyajima is one of Japan's three traditionally designated great scenic spots—the others are Amanohashidate and Matsushima, near Sendai (see p. 160). Literally "Shrine Island," Miyajima has been home to sacred Itsukushima-jinja for 1,500 years. Seeming to float above the water, the shrine's huge red *torii* gateway is as much a symbol of Japan as Mount Fuji.

Just half an hour by train from Hiroshima (about an hour by tram or ferry), Miyajima (also known as Itsukushima) can be visited comfortably in an afternoon. Yet there is so much to see that a whole day is recommended. An overnight stop is not cheap, but you'll have the place to yourself.

Miyajima has scenic attractions year-round, from springtime cherry blossoms to autumn displays of maples in **Momijidani Park** (Momijidani-koen), and from beaches and seascapes to the wooded heights of Mount Misen. The perimeter of the island is almost 19 miles (30 km), making a bicycle the perfect way to get around. You can rent one next to the pier as you arrive; a battery-assisted model is a good idea, as some of Miyajima's hills are quite steep. Tame deer roam the island at will, especially in the vicinity of the shrine and Momijidani-koen.

All the sights are concentrated on the north side of the island and up on Mount Misen. Extending along the coast between the ferry terminal and Itsukushima-jinja, Miyajima's little town is charming—if somewhat overwhelmed by souvenir stores.

Itsukushima-jinja, dedicated to three sea goddesses who were daughters of the Shinto god Susano-o, is said to have been founded during the reign of Empress Suiko in 593. It reached its definitive form in 1168 under the patronage of Taira-no-Kiyomori (1118–1181), the great leader of the Heike (or Taira) clan and penultimate Heian-era ruler. The shrine, flanked by elegant covered corridors, is noted for its sweeping thatched roofs and the intense orange color of its delicate woodwork. Built on pillars right over the sea and appearing to float on the water at high tide, it is a truly outstanding example of Heian-period shrine architecture. Rows of bronze lanterns hang from the eaves; when these are lit on festive occasions along with the many stone lanterns on the shrine's coastal approach, the effect is magical. The famous **torii** is 175 yards (160 m) out from the shrine landing and stands 53 feet (16 m) high; made of camphor

wood, it was rebuilt in 1875 for the eighth time. The shrine precinct includes a nationally revered 16th-century Noh stage, used in sacred Jin-Noh performances (April 16–18). Just southwest of the shrine, the modern **treasure house** contains some 4,000 objects, 130 of which are

INSIDER TIP:

On Miyajima, buy yourself a *shakushi*, a wooden rice scoop invented here by an Edo-period Buddhist priest and now adapted nationwide for dishing up rice.

—PERRIN LINDELAUF
National Geographic writer

Important Cultural Properties or National Treasures; these include fans, swords, armor, masks, and a famous set of painted sutra scrolls that once belonged to the Heike clan.

South of Itsukushima-jinja, a short climb brings you to the enchanting **Tahoto pagoda,** built in 1523. From here, the view over Itsukushima-jinja and the bay is spectacular. On the way you should visit **Daigan-ji,** responsible for the upkeep of Itsukushima-jinja until Shinto-Buddhist syncretism was outlawed in 1868. Miyajima's most important temple is **Daisho-in,** higher up to the southwest, which once oversaw the shrine's administration.

Miyajima
🗺 261 C2
Visitor Information
✉ Inside ferry building
☎ 082/944-2011
🕐 9 a.m.–6 p.m.
🚉 JR Sanyo line: Miyajima-guchi; tram to Hiroden Miyajima-guchi (70 min.)
⛴ Ferry from Peace Memorial Park to Miyajima (45 min.)
visit-miyajima-japan.com/en

Itsukushima-jinja
✉ 1-1 Miyajima-cho
☎ 0829/44-2020
🕐 6:30 a.m.–6 p.m. Mar.–mid-Oct.; closes at 5:30 p.m. mid-Oct.–Nov., Jan.–Feb.; closes at 5 p.m. Dec.
💲 $

Daigan-ji
✉ 3 Miyajima-cho
☎ 0829/44-0179
🕐 8:30 a.m.–5 p.m.

Daisho-in
✉ 210 Miyajima-cho
☎ 0829/44-0111
🕐 8 a.m.–5 p.m.

The summit of **Mount Misen,** accessible via a cable railway or a 90-minute walk, is well worth visiting. Apart from a breathtaking panorama over the Inland Sea from the summit, this 1,740-foot (530 m) mountain features **Monkey Park** (Misen Yaen-koen). A sighting of the monkeys is not guaranteed—they often retire to the forest—but be aware that the animals can be fractious, and always keep a safe distance. Near the summit are a number of small temples, including one said to have been frequented by the priest Kukai (774–835), founder of the Shingon sect of Buddhism.

Up a hill north of Itsukushima-jinja is evidence of the ancient melding of Shinto and Buddhism: The main hall of the **Toyokuni-jinja, Senjokaku,** is famous for its library of Buddhist sutras. Senjokaku means "Hall of a Thousand Mats," though its floor size is equivalent to just 857 tatami mats (approximately 14,300 square feet/1,330 sq m). This impressive open-sided building, reputedly made from the wood of a single camphor tree, was commissioned by Toyotomi Hideyoshi in 1587 to honor the war dead. The original intention was to paint it red to match the magnificent early 15th-century, five-story pagoda next to it, but Hideyoshi died the following year and the building was never completed. The hall contains thousands of *shakushi*—wooden rice scoops—left as votive offerings to the gods. Originating with soldiers about to leave for the front during the Sino-Japanese War of 1894, the custom emerged from a superstitious play on words: *Meshi-toru* means "to take rice," but a homonymous verb means "to conquer." ∎

INSIDER TIP:

Beware—the primates of Mount Misen Monkey Park have been known to attack. Avoid eye contact and never try to feed them.

—ROB GOSS
National Geographic contributor

The Kibiji Cycling Path

Just outside the western confines of Okayama is Kibiji, a plain combining scenic beauty with historic temples and shrines. In recent years, it has earned plaudits for a marvelous cycling path that takes in its main sights. From Okayama Station, four stops on the Kibi line brings you to Kibitsu, where you can rent a bicycle. Start with **Kibitsu-jinja,** renowned for its architecture and long covered walkway. Pedal to **Tsukuriyama burial mound** (a fifth-century tumulus), then on to **Bicchu Kokubun-ji,** with its beautiful five-story pagoda rising above the rice fields. Near here is **Soja,** birthplace of the monk Sesshu (1420–1506), the great painter and calligrapher. The 12.5 miles (20 km) of the trip to Soja will have taken you past several more temples, shrines, and burial mounds. Another 2.5 miles (4 km) north of Soja Station is **Hofuku-ji,** where Sesshu studied as a child. After seeing it, cycle back to Soja to drop off your bike.

Thousands of islets dotting the Seto-naikai (Inland Sea), the channel between Honshu and Shikoku, smallest of Japan's four main islands

Shikoku & the Seto-naikai

Water lily pond

Shikoku & the Seto-naikai

The smallest of Japan's main islands, Shikoku lies south across the Seto-naikai from Honshu. Shikoku means "four countries," referring to the feudal provinces of Sanuki, Awa, Iyo, and Tosa, now respectively the four prefectures of Kagawa (in the northeast of the island), Tokushima (south of Kagawa), Ehime (along the Inland Sea and westward), and Kochi (facing the Pacific).

Old Japan lives on in Shikoku. Long isolated, Shikoku was a realm of Buddhism pilgrimages and quiet fishing villages, the last mountainous refuge for the Taira clan, driven out of Kyoto by the rival Minamoto clan 800 years ago. Three huge bridges, the Great Seto Bridge, Shimanami Sea Route, and the Akashi Strait Bridge, the first built in 1978 and latter two in 1998, have gradually transformed Shikoku and its surrounding islands and enabled the industrialization of the northern coast, yet most of the region remains quiet and rural. Indeed, the same high mountains and deep, lush valleys that permitted the Taira to lose their pursuers remain much as they were, impenetrable to the best efforts of Japan's concrete industry.

The prefectural capitals—Tokushima, Kochi, Matsuyama, and Takamatsu—are not immune to slapdash modern architecture, but retain

NOT TO BE MISSED:

a laid-back pace long gone from Honshu's bustling cities. Fine castles survive in Kochi and Matsuyama, and the latter also has Japan's oldest known hot spring, Dogo Onsen. In the summer, Tokushima and Kochi hold vibrant traditional dance festivals that draw thousands of tourists, eager to watch or join in the fun.

The deep countryside is most inviting. An 88-temple pilgrimage wends through

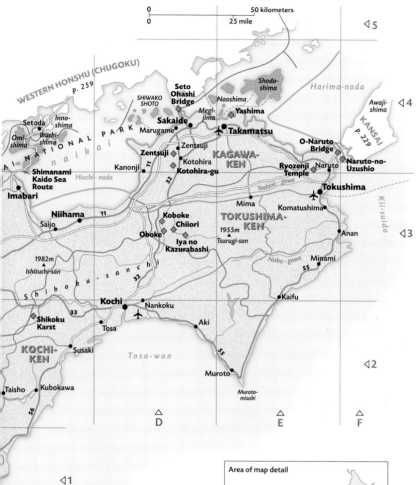

mountainous valleys and up to hilltop temples where the hypermodern Japanese portray a different side of themselves, walking from temple to temple to shed worldly passions. The industrial north coast gives way to orange groves and farmers apt to load you up with an armful of produce as you pass. The emerald green Yoshino River, deep in Tokushima Prefecture, offers great white-water rafting

(Class 3–4). Often overlooked—literally, as one passes overhead on the Great Seto Bridge—the islands of the Seto-naikai or Inland Sea are transforming from fishing hamlets and former pirate isles to an art-lover's mecca. ■

Shikoku

With a mountainous topography and peaks reaching nearly 6,500 feet (2,000 m) in the east and center, Shikoku's landscapes are lush and scenic. Farming villages stand against hilly backdrops, fishing villages cling to rugged coastlines, and deserted beaches line the south coast. Shikoku is endlessly described as "off the beaten path." Despite modern bridges linking the north coast to Honshu, Shikoku retains a pace of life all its own.

Chefs prepare *sanuki udon* by hand in Tsurumaru.

Shikoku also has religious resonance. Sanuki Province was the birthplace in 774 of Kukai (known posthumously as Kobo Daishi), the founder of the Shingon sect of Buddhism (see sidebar p. 294). Eighty-eight temples make up the most important pilgrimage route in Japan, a total of about 870 miles (1,400 km).

The *henro*—pilgrims in Shikoku— believe that walking your way around all these temples is the way to rid yourself of the 88 worldly passions, thereby bringing you closer to salvation.

For less pious folks with tight schedules, covering just the main sights and delights of Shikoku is feasible in about four days.

INSIDER TIP:

There's a huge variety of *sanuki udon* dishes, but if it's your first time, try a basic soup and focus on the noodles' taste and delightful texture.

—PERRIN LINDELAUF
National Geographic writer

Takamatsu

The bridges between Shikoku and the mainland have undermined Takamatsu's status as the island's most important port, but the capital of Kagawa-ken is still the nucleus for ferries serving islands on the Seto-naikai. One of the longest bridges in the world, the colossal **Seto Ohashi** (Seto Great Bridge) linking Kagawa-ken to Honshu has itself become a tourist site (see p. 275), but the prefecture is best known for its more traditional aspects.

Takamatsu was originally the castle town that headed the feudal realm of Sanuki; **Takamatsu-jo,** built in 1588, was later held by the Matsudaira clan until the 1868 Meiji Restoration. Sections of moats, ramparts, and turrets are all that now remain, but **Tamamo-koen,** containing the ancient castle ruins, is a very pleasant park.

Takamatsu was badly damaged during air raids in World War II, and its surviving sights are precious few; among them, **Ritsurin-koen,** one of Japan's most beautiful gardens, is paramount. Laid out south of the city in the 17th century, this gorgeous stroll garden was once attached to a villa built by the Matsudaira lords and destroyed after the Meiji Restoration. Ritsurin-koen took more than a century to complete and is often compared to Koraku-en in Okayama (see p. 276), one of Japan's three great gardens. Skillfully incorporating the pine-clad slopes of Shiun-zan to the west, this masterpiece of landscaping is graced with ponds, curved bridges spanning meandering watercourses, artificial islands, and elegant teahouses. Any Japanese, however, will tell

Takamatsu
🅰 289 E4
Visitor Information
✉ JR Takamatsu Station
☎ 087/826-0170
🕐 9 a.m.–8 p.m.
🚃 JR Seto-Ohashi line from Okayama (1 hr.)

Tamamo-koen
✉ 2-1 Tamamo-cho
☎ 087/851-1521
🕐 8:30 a.m.–5 p.m.
💲 $
🚃 JR Kotoku line: Takamatsu

Ritsurin-koen
✉ 1-20-16 Ritsurin-cho
☎ 087/833-7411
🕐 7 a.m.–5 p.m.
💲 $
🚃 Kotoden line: Ritsurinkoen

NEED TO KNOW
Reaching Shikoku

Shikoku is linked to Honshu by three bridges, the Akashi Strait and O-Naruto bridges in the east, the Seto Bridge in the north, and the Shimanami Kaido Sea Route in the west. The only rail connection is via Okayama and the Seto Bridge to Takamatsu. With time and a JR Pass, most of Shikoku is easy to access, but domestic airlines have regular flights to Shikoku, saving considerable time to Kochi or Matsuyama. The highway bus can also be a faster and cheaper option if you want to travel over the west or east bridges.

Getting Around

JR Shikoku connects most parts of the island, but you'll need a bus to reach some of the remote mountains. Takamatsu, Kochi, and Matsuyama are all served by simple tram lines.

Shikoku Mura

- ✉ 91 Yashima
  Naka-machi
- ☎ 087/843-3111
- 🕐 8:30 a.m.–5 p.m.
- 💲 $$
- 🚉 JR Kotoku line:
  Yashima, then
  15-min. walk

Isamu Noguchi Garden Museum

- ✉ 3519 Mure,
  Mure-cho
- ☎ 087/870-1500
- 🕐 Tours on Tues.,
  Thurs., Sat. 10 a.m.,
  1 p.m., & 3 p.m. by
  reservation
- 💲 $$$$
- 🚉 Kotoden Shiyo line:
  Yakuri, then 20-min.
  walk

isamunoguchi.or.jp

you Takamatsu is most famous for *sanuki udon,* a firmer variant of the popular, thick wheat noodles. The best places bang out noodles in an open kitchen.

To the east of Takamatsu lies **Yashima,** a plateau with fine views of the Inland Sea and famous as a battleground of the 12th-century Gempei War. Nearby, **Shikoku Mura,** an open-air museum displaying several beautiful old farmhouses from the island, replicates the famous Iya vine bridges (see pp. 295–296) and has a Kabuki stage that sometimes hosts performances. Between the Yashima plateau and rocky Mount Goken lies the **Isamu Noguchi Garden Museum,** the former home and atelier of the internationally renowned modernist sculptor and

INSIDER TIP:

The Isamu Noguchi Garden Museum is an intriguing mix of East and West. To take a guided tour, you'll need to make a written reservation.

—LARRY PORGES
National Geographic Books editor

landscape designer. Half-Japanese Noguchi mixed western abstract modernism with Japanese subtlety in a host of media, from basalt to balsawood. The inspiring garden contains an eclectic range of 150 sculptures, including the smooth basalt "Energy Void" and "Sun at Midnight" and borrows

Pilgrims climb the 785 stone steps of Kotohira-gu, shrine of the god travelers.

EXPERIENCE: Become a Henro

Many ancient pilgrimage routes crisscross the Japanese landscape (e.g., the Kumano Kodo; see sidebar p. 255), but the most popular of modern times is the 88-temple loop of Shikoku Island (*tourismshikoku.org/henro*). According to legend, the circuit was founded by the monk Kukai (known posthumously as Kobo Daishi, the Great Saint), founder of the esoteric Shingon sect of Japanese Buddhism. Pilgrims dressed all in white walk from temple to temple around the island, pursuing *nirvana* and shedding the 88 worldly passions in an 870-mile (1,400 km) journey that takes more than two months on modern roads and well-kept trails, although most pilgrims go by bus or car these days.

Walking a section of the pilgrimage route is a great way to meet Japanese people, from fellow pilgrims and monks to the farmers whose lands you'll cross.

If you don't have a month to devote to a successful reincarnation, there are several sections that cover popular temples spread over a short distance. **Ryozen-ji** (*126 Ryozenji, Oasacho Bando, Naruto, tel 088/689-1111, 7 a.m.–5 p.m.*), north of Tokushima, is Temple 1 and a good place to acquire the white robes, straw hat, staff, and temple logbook of a pilgrim. From there, the first ten temples are scattered over 25 miles (40 km) of the Yoshino-gawa, making for a fine two-day mini pilgrimage.

For day trips, **Matsuyama city** has eight temples and **Dogo Onsen** offering hot-spring balm for aching legs. **Zentsu-ji**, the birthplace of Kukai, is another good day trip. While there, hedge your spiritual bets and say a prayer at nearby **Kotohira-gu**, home to the Shinto god of travelers.

from the scenery of the adjacent mountains for a peaceful, contemplative atmosphere.

Kotohira

Southwest of Takamatsu is the region of Kotohira, wherein lies Kotohira-gu, one of Japan's most sacred Shinto shrines. Just 4 miles (6 km) north of Kotohira-gu is Zentsu-ji, the birthplace of the Buddhist saint Kukai, founder of the Shingon sect (see sidebar p. 294). Devotees believe that Shikoku's 88-temple pilgrims' route was devised by Kukai himself.

Kotohira-gu, better known as Kompira-san, is the most important of Shikoku's Shinto shrines. Located on the forested slope of Zozu-san, a 1,640-foot (500 m) hill, the shrine is dedicated to Omono-Nushi, god of seafarers and travelers. Particularly awe-inspiring to many of its visitors is the prospect of an hour's climb up 785 stone steps through the woods to get there. The ascent is not as dire as it sounds (except during a heat wave), because the shrine's buildings are well positioned for splitting the journey into easy stages. Climbing to Kompira-san is well worth the effort, both for the spectacular view of the Sanuki Plain and for the National Treasure shrine itself.

After passing through the imposing two-story **Main Gate** (O-mon) and along an approach lined with stone lanterns, you reach the **Treasure Hall** (Homotsukan), with ceramics, Noh theater masks,

Kotohira

- 289 D4

Visitor Information

- Main street bet. JR Kotohira and Kotoden Kotohira Stations
- 0877/75-3500
- 10 a.m.–6 p.m.

Kotohira-gu

- 291 D4
- 892-1 Kotohira-cho
- 0877/75-2121
- 6 a.m.–5:30 p.m.
- $$ Treasure Hall, $$ Shoin
- JR Dosan line: Kotohira, then 15-min. walk

Zentsu-ji

- 289 D4
- 3-3-1 Zentsuji-cho, Zentsuji-shi
- 0877/62-0111
- 6 a.m.–5 p.m.
- $
- JR Dosan line: Zentsuji, then 20-min. walk

zentsuji.com

Naruto Whirlpools

- Viewable from Uzu-no-Michi walkway under the Naruto Bridge
- 9 a.m.–6 p.m.
- $$. Boats every 30 min. from Naruto Pier ($$$$)
- JR Naruto line: Naruto, then Rosen Bus to Naruto-koen

painted scrolls, and armor among the exhibits. The National Treasure **Shoin** reception hall on the next level, which dates from 1659, contains screen doors decorated by 18th-century landscape painter Maruyama Okyo (1733–1795), the greatest of a school of naturalistic painters influenced by Western art.

A more arduous walk farther up the hill leads you on to the **Asahi-no-Yashiro** (Shrine of the Rising Sun), dating from the 1830s and famed for its ornate carvings. The next stage leads to the **Honden,** the main hall, built on stilts on a steep incline in a fashion similar to Kiyomizu-dera temple in Kyoto (see p. 204).

On the same level is the **Ema-do,** a hall filled with votive offerings in maritime themes, including model ships. Another half hour up lies the inner shrine (Okusha), with goblin statues and a fabulous view.

Near the steps leading to the

Kukai

Kukai (774–835) had a very productive life. In addition to founding a new sect, he engineered dams; wrote more than 50 volumes on philosophy, literature, and religion; composed Chinese poetry; and brought a new style of calligraphy to Japan. He established the Shikoku Island pilgrimage route (see sidebar p. 293) and achieved Enlightenment in a cave on Cape Muroto. According to folktales, he slew dragons and threw his *vajra* (a ceremonial mace) from China and found it again on Mount Koya; some argue he created the Japanese syllabaries of *hiragana* and *katakana*. If you doubt it, just go and ask him: He's still alive in his tomb on Mount Koya, so they say.

entrance to the shrine compound at the bottom of the hill is the **Kanamaru-za Kabuki Theater** (*1241 Kotohira-cho, tel 0877/73-3846, 9 a.m.–5 p.m., $*), Japan's oldest Kabuki theater. Built in 1835 and restored in 2003, the theater still puts on performances each April (*$$$$$, tickets sell out in Feb.*). In other months, guides reveal its features, including trapdoors, the revolving stage, and sliding doors to control the natural lighting.

Zentsu-ji, 4 miles (6 km) to the north of Kotohira-gu, is one of the most important temples of the Shingon sect and one of the most famous in Japan. Number 75 on the pilgrim route, it is said to have been founded by Kukai in 813 on the spot where he was born, though none of the original buildings still survive. With magnificent old camphor trees that Kukai loved as a child, the precinct has a grand five-story **pagoda** and a **Treasure Hall** containing exhibits brought back from China by Kukai himself.

Tokushima-ken

On the east of Shikoku, Tokushima-ken is both the start and terminus of the 88-temple pilgrimage around Shikoku. The prefecture arguably has the island's best natural sights: the emerald green Yoshino-gawa with Class 3–4 rapids, lush Tsurugi-san, and the Naruto Whirlpools. In August, four days of mad dancing take over Tokushima city for the best party in Japan.

Shikoku's natural sights start

right at its doorstep: During high or low tide (one each in daylight), the normally placid Inland Sea beneath the O-Naruto Bridge swirls into the 65-foot-wide (20 m) **Naruto Whirlpools** as tidal currents race between the Naruto Peninsula and Awaji-shima, seeking to balance with the Sea of Japan. The best whirlpools can be seen around a full moon, when the tides are strongest, either by tourist boat or from the **Uzu-no-Michi Promenade,** beneath the bridge.

Flowing into Tokushima city is the deep green Yoshino-gawa, pouring forth from narrow, limestone valleys all set about with dense semitropical forest. Dammed at its source in Kochi-ken, the river has reliable Class 3–4 rapids in Koboke and Oboke Gorges, suitable for adventurous beginners. The typhoon season in September is a good time to hit these world-class rapids. Tsurugi-san (6,414 feet/1,955 m), high above the gorges, is the second tallest mountain on Shikoku and has a moderate trail to its summit.

East of Oboke Gorge lies the **Iya Valley,** where local activists are struggling to preserve traditions of old, rural Japan. Alex Kerr, author of *Lost Japan* and *Dogs and Demons*—books that lament Japan's reckless modernization—bought a 300-year-old farmhouse here in 1972. Dubbed **Chiiori,** the thatched-roof house is the center of the Chiiori Trust, which restores old homes to be used as guesthouses and works to revitalize Japan's rural economy with tourism and organic agriculture. Guests participate in restoring old buildings, farming, or planting trees in the area.

Between Chiiori and the Oboke Rapids is the vertiginous **Iya-no-Kazura Bashi** (Vine Bridge;

Oboke & Koboke Rapids

- ✉ 221-1 Ikadagi Otoyo-cho, Nagaoka-gun, Kochi-ken
- ☎ 0877/75-0500
- 🕐 Full-day & half-day tours
- 💲 $$$$$
- 🚆 JR Dosan line: Tosa-Iwahara (2 hr. 20 min. from Tokushima)

happyraft.com

Chiiori

- ✉ 209 Tsurui Higashi-iya, Miyoshi city
- ☎ 0883/88-5290
- 🕐 Day visits 12:30 p.m.– 2 p.m.
- 💲 $, stays: $$$
- 🚆 Kodo bus from Oboke Station to Wada, then 80-min. walk

chiiori.org

The Kazura Bashi (Vine Bridge) in the Iya Valley

Tokushima

289 E3

Visitor Information

In front of Tokushima Station

☎ 088/622-8556

🕐 9 a.m.–7 p.m.

🚆 Express train from Takamatsu (1 hr. 15 min.)

Awa Odori Kaikan

✉ 2-20 Shinmachibashi

☎ 088/611-1611

🕐 9 a.m.–9 p.m.

💲 $, dances $$

🚆 JR Kotoku line: Tokushima

dawn to dusk, $$), one of the few remaining traditional bridges in Japan. The powerful Taira clan, defeated in the 12th-century Genpei War, fled to Shikoku and often severed such vine bridges over deep gorges to cut off the pursuing Minamoto clan. No chance of that in modern, safety-obsessed Japan: The vines are replaced every three years and reinforced with steel cables.

The prefectural capital, **Toku-shima,** was severely damaged in World War II air raids and is probably a nicer place to live than to visit. But what it lacks in tourist sights it makes up for with its rich heritage of arts and crafts. Work-shops and exhibits are devoted to *washi* papermaking, *aizome* indigo dyeing (notably for the local *shi-jira* textiles), and *otani yaki*—local

pottery. Plain and unadorned earthenware, otani pottery is devoted mainly to kitchenware and utilitarian items—including huge jars for fermenting soybeans to make miso paste. Some jars are more then 6 feet (1.8 m) tall, and potters work in pairs to turn them.

Open to the public at various locations around the town, some of the workshops offer hands-on opportunities to try out the crafts yourself. Find out what is on offer at the **Tokushima International Strategies Center** (*6th floor of JR Tokushima Building, tel 088/656-3303, topia.ne.jp, 10 a.m.–6 p.m.*).

Tokushima is also renowned for Awa Ningyo Joruri, a form of puppet theater originating in the 17th century. It is similar to the Bunraku of Osaka, but with larger, heavier puppets; the

---

Shikoku's Summer Dance Festivals

Despite protestations to the contrary, the Japanese do dance. Numerous dance fes-tivals are held across the country, particu-larly during August around the O-Bon holiday, and these wild, citywide parties often last for days. Adding to the excite-ment, spectators are regularly dragged from the crowd into the dancing parade; the appearance of being forced obviates any embarrassment about joining in, allowing otherwise shy visitors to throw themselves into the moves with as much abandon as the locals.

Of all the festivals, **Awa Odori Mat-suri** *(Aug. 12–15)* is the most famous. Inspired by a raucous party 400 years ago, the dance is easy enough to do at a casual stagger—a good thing, consider-ing the amount of alcohol flowing over the four-day festival. More than 200

teams of dancers in period dress wend through Tokushima between 6:30 p.m. and 10:30 p.m. or give performances on stages scattered throughout town. If you can't make it to Tokushima, Tokyo's Toshima ward puts on a smaller Awa Dance at the end of August.

Also on Shikoku, Kochi city (see p. 306) holds the **Yosakoi Odori Matsuri** *(Aug. 9–12).* Yosakoi, literally "Come Tonight," Dance Festival, started out as a traditional O-Bon dance with wooden hand-clappers punctuating the moves of the dancers, but since World War II the troupes have incorporated styles such as samba and hip-hop. The resulting variety doesn't preclude participation though; the tourism office can introduce you to a traditional troupe that can supply a cos-tume and quickly teach you the moves.

The streets come alive at Shikoku's dance festivals, such as at Awa Oduri in Tokushima.

performances are surprisingly expressive. The best performances are given at the **Inugai Noson-butai** in spring or fall; amateur groups can be seen twice daily at the **Awa Jurobe Yashiki** *(184 Motoura Miyajima; tel 088/ 655-2202; 9:30–5 p.m., shows at 11 a.m. & 2 p.m., $)*, which also has displays explaining the use and history of the traditional puppets.

Above all, Tokushima is famous for the frenzied **Awa Odori Matsuri** (see sidebar opposite), a popular and boisterous festival. A throng of tens of thousands, most in traditional costumes from all over Japan, winds its way through the town, dancing to the hypnotic carnival music of flute and drums.

If you miss the festival, stop by the **Awa Odori Kaikan,** a hall that puts on several dance performances daily and explains the history of the festival. Spectators

are usually pulled into the dance, as at the festival. "We are fools to be dancing and you are a fool to be watching," goes the chant, "so why not join in and dance?" Why not, indeed?

Matsuyama

Matsuyama is the capital of Ehime-ken, which stretches along the northern part of Shikoku to the west coast. Presenting the traveler with a perfect balance between the rustic and the historic, this highly scenic prefecture is quintessential Shikoku. Ishizuchi-san in the south offers fine alpine panoramas.

The city of Matsuyama is mainly modern and nondescript, except for the handful of noteworthy sights that survived World War II. Its principal attraction is the well-preserved **Matsuyama-jo.** Built on a hill above the city by

Matsuyama
 288 C3
Visitor information
✉ JR Matsuyama Station
☎ 089/931-3914
🕐 8:30 a.m.– 8:30 p.m.
🚃 JR Yosan line from Takamatsu (2.5 hr.)
iyokannet.jp

Matsuyama-jo
✉ 1 Marunouchi
☎ 089/921-4873
🕐 9 a.m.–5 p.m.; park: 6 a.m.– 9 p.m.
💲 $
🚃 Iyo Tetsudo Tram line: Okaido

Matsuyama Municipal Shiki Kinen Museum
- ✉ 1-30 Dogo-koen
- ☎ 089/931-5566
- 🕐 9:30 a.m.–5:30 p.m., closed Tues.
- 💲 $, English audio guide available
- 🚃 Iyo Tetsudo Tram line: Dogo Onsen (20 min. from JR Matsuyama Station)

Shiki-do
- ✉ 16-3 Suehiro-cho
- ☎ 089/945-0400
- 🕐 8:30 a.m.–4:40 p.m.
- 💲 $

Iyo Textile Museum
- ✉ 1200 Kumano-dai
- ☎ 089/922-0405
- 🕐 8 a.m.–4 p.m.
- 💲 $

feudal lord Kato Yoshiaki between 1602 and 1627, the castle was taken over by Gamo Tadachika when Kato was posted to Northern Honshu.

The castle fell into the hands of the Matsudaira family in 1635 and was presented to the city by a descendant in 1923. Damaged by lightning in the 18th century, the main donjon was rebuilt in 1854; several turrets were damaged in arson attacks during the 1930s, and other buildings succumbed to bombing in World War II. However, the castle compound is intact overall. The harness tower,

especially when the cherry trees blossom in April.

Matsuyama is where Natsume Soseki (1867–1916), the most celebrated of all early modern Japanese novelists (his portrait once graced the 1,000-yen note), taught English as a young man and found inspiration for his novel *Botchan.* Soseki's boardinghouse has been restored as the **Gudabutsu-an,** now used for tea ceremonies and haiku poetry sessions. As the birthplace of the influential master poet Masaoka Shiki (1867–1902)—a close friend of Soseki's—Matsuyama is

Straw pilgrim sandals at Ishite-ji

which contained military equipment and was rebuilt in 1968, is the only building to have been restored with concrete; all the others have been painstakingly put back exactly as they were, using wood and original carpentry techniques. Exhibits inside the castle include paintings, armor, and swords (none labeled in English). The castle grounds, reachable by cable car, are pleasant for strolling,

regarded nationally as a center for haiku. **Matsuyama Municipal Shiki Kinen Museum** was built to commemorate the poet, along with Matsuyama's literary past. Just southeast of Matsuyama Station is a copy of Shiki's house— the **Shiki-do,** which stands on the precinct of Shoshu-ji.

Eight of the 88 temples on the pilgrims' circuit—all worth visiting for their architecture and

EXPERIENCE: Staying in *Ryokan*

Ryokan, Japanese traditional inns, are a full cultural package that will push you out of your comfort zone, without breaking the bank. On entering the building, you'll don slippers, and the staff will usher you to a traditional Japanese room. The floors are covered with cool tatami (woven straw) mats, sliding paper doors fill the rooms in soft light, and a private garden typically sits just outside the window.

You will be served tea, and given a *yukata* (light kimono) to wear to the bath. After changing, you pad down to the hot-spring bath, often built with a view of a garden, the sea, or the mountains, where you strip naked and soak with the other guests of your gender (see p. 322). Private "family baths" are sometimes available, too. After bathing, you'll return to a feast laid out in your room, with multiple little dishes of refined delicacies. The ryokan staff scurry to and fro, kneeling to refill beer glasses and rice bowls and bringing out endless little courses, from fresh sashimi and hot pots cooked over paraffin stoves to odd local pickles. Breakfast is also quite large, but with a focus on Japanese staples such as fish, rice, and miso soup. The staff will lay out your futon mattress after dinner, complete with the crunchy but so cool buckwheat-husk-filled pillow to carry you off to sleep.

For ryokan stays, see Travelwise: Tokyo (pp. 363–367), Nikko (pp. 367–368), Hokkaido (pp. 368–369), Sapporo (p. 369), Akan National Park and Akita-ken (pp. 368, 370–371), Takayama (p. 372), Kyoto (pp. 372–374), Nara (p. 375), and Hagi (p. 376).

---

setting—are in Matsuyama, but the most revered is **Ishite-ji,** No. 51, in Dogo Onsen.

In the northwestern confines of the city is the **Iyo Textile Museum** (Mingei Iyo Kasuri Kaikan), devoted to *Iyo Kasuri,* an intricate local weaving process that uses cloth dyed with natural indigo. Matsuyama is also well endowed with stores selling Ehime crafts, notably objects of woven bamboo and ceramics—especially the bold yet simple blue-on-white *tobe-yaki* ware, made today much as it was 300 years ago.

Dogo Onsen

About 2.5 miles (4 km) northeast of Matsuyama is one of Japan's oldest spas. Mentioned in seventh-century historical records, Dogo Onsen is said to date back to the age of the gods. Legend has it that the curative properties of Dogo's water were first noted when a white heron miraculously mended a broken leg by dipping it into the hot jet spouting from a rock; the notion of bathing for sheer pleasure came later.

Whatever the myth, the Dogo area was the administrative and cultural capital of Iyo—now Ehime—until the end of the 16th century. Along with a number of temples and shrines and a delightful streetcar station dating to the 1900s, the area is dotted with resort hotels. These inevitably include monumental kitsch palaces, but the oldest and most famous of the baths is the **Dogo Onsen Main Building**

Dogo Onsen

 288 C3

Visitor Information

✉ In front of Dogo Onsen Station

☎ 089/921-3708

🕐 8:30 a.m.–5 p.m.

🚃 Iyo Tetsudo Tram line: Dogo Onsen

Dogo Onsen Main Building

✉ 5-6 Dogo Yunomachi

☎ 089/921-5141

🕐 6 a.m.–11 p.m.

💲 $ bath only, $$ bath with tea and sweets, $$$ private bath with tea and sweets

 Iyo Tetsudo Tram line: Dogo Onsen

Isaniwa-jinja
- ✉ 173 Sakuradani-cho
- ☎ 089/947-7447
- 🕐 Dawn to dusk
- 🚋 Iyo Tetsudo Tram line: Dogo Onsen

Ishite-ji
- ✉ 2-9-21 Ishite
- ☎ 089/977-0870
- 🕐 8 a.m.–5 p.m.
- 💲 $ Treasure Hall
- 🚌 Iyo Tetsudo Bus: Ishiteji-mae

(Honkan), an elaborate wooden structure built in Japanese castle style in 1894 and the basis for the fantastical bathhouse of Miyazaki Hayao's blockbuster anime *Spirited Away*. Upstairs is the **Yushinden,** a special bath reserved for the Meiji imperial family, and a room said to have been used regularly by writer Natsume Soseki when the building was new. After luxuriating in the Kami-no-Yu (Water of the Gods) bathroom, you are served tea in a large tatami hall—an enticing experience with a certain fin-de-siècle appeal.

Just southeast of the Honkan is the imposing **Isaniwa-jinja.** Built in 1667 with a central tower in the Chinese style and adorned with intricate carvings, it is one of only three shrines in Japan to show the distinctive architecture devoted to Hachiman, a war god.

Another landmark of Dogo,

Ishite-ji means "stone hand temple" (a local lord is said to have been born with his hand clutching a stone). Founded by Emperor Shomu in 728, this temple is No. 51 on the pilgrim route and is said to have been rebuilt by Kukai himself (see sidebar p. 294)—though if Kukai had really built all the temples ascribed to him, he must have been an architect rather than a priest. The oldest and most noteworthy buildings date from the early 14th century: the beautiful **entrance gate** flanked by statues of fierce Deva kings, the **Main Hall,** and an especially fine **three-story pagoda.** All three are designated Important Cultural Properties. The **Treasure Hall** contains some 300 exhibits pertaining to the history of the temple and the pilgrimage.

Over and above the cultural

Dogo Onsen's main bath, built circa 1894

Near the entrance to the temple of Ishite-ji, you'll find a shop selling proper pilgrim garb: white robe, conical hat, staff, and straw sandals.

—PERRIN LINDELAUF
National Geographic writer

and historical, Ishite-ji's main attractions reside in the weird and wonderful. With pond-side statuary on a par with garden gnomes, and a spooky "mantra cave" in which you grope through a dark tunnel toward a cavern illuminated with 1970s-style psychedelic lamps and cosmic mandalas, much of the precinct is like a Buddhist amusement park. Up the hillside are dozens more Buddhist shrines and monuments, notably serried ranks of statuettes of Jizo, the guardian deity of children, travelers, and the unborn. For those who want to look the part of the Japanese pilgrim, note the 1950s-vintage mannequins modeling the gear outside the shop near the entrance.

Uchiko

It would be a shame to visit Matsuyama without traveling a mere 30 miles (50 km) southwest to the lovely rural town of Uchiko. Until the end of the 1920s, Uchiko's main industry was the manufacture of candle wax extracted from the berries of local sumac trees; its output met about one-third of national demand for everything from candles to crayons. Concentrated in the district of **Yokaichi-Gokoku,** the former workshops and merchant houses still stand.

Few Japanese towns can boast quite so many preserved and restored buildings as Uchiko. Painted white and cream and trimmed with black-and-white plaster work, Yokaichi-Gokoku's fine buildings are now part of a preservation area. Yokaichi-Gokoku is a single street about 650 yards (600 m) long; along the way, several buildings have been designated as Important Cultural Properties. Some of the restored buildings are still private houses, such as the **Hon Haga Residence** (Hon-Haga-tei), built by the family that launched the Uchiko wax business in 1886; you can admire the house and its garden only from the street. However, the Haga family's 19th-century waxmaking factory and attached private residence in the north of Yokaichi district, once the area's largest waxmaking concern, is now Uchiko's star attraction, magnificently restored as the enthralling **Japanese Wax Museum and Kami Haga Residence** (Mokuro Shiryokan-Kami-Haga-tei; see sidebar p. 303). The museum is next to the **Machiya Shiryo-kan,** a town house dating from the 1790s and restored as a period museum in 1987.

Unfortunately, the government subsidizes restoration only in designated areas, so some equally remarkable houses outside the Yokaichi district are in a sorry state of repair. However,

---

Uchiko

  288 B2

Visitor Information

✉ Beside JR Uchiko Station

☎ 0893/43-1450

🕐 9:30 a.m.–5 p.m.

🚃 JR Yosan line from Matsuyama (25 min.) or Uwajima (50 min.)

iyokannet.jp

Japanese Wax Museum and Kami Haga Residence

✉ 2696 Uchiko

☎ 0893/44-2771

🕐 9 a.m.–5 p.m.

💲 $

🚃 JR Yosan line: Uchiko

Omori Warosoku-ya, in Yokaichi-Gokoku, the last candlemaker's shop

Uwajima

🗺 288 B2

Visitor Information

✉ Across from JR
Uwajima Station

☎ 0895/23-5530

🕐 9 a.m.–6 p.m.

🚆 JR Yosan
line from
Matsuyama
(1 hr. 20 min. by
limited express)

uwajima-tourism.org

the **Uchiko-za Theater,** a Kabuki theater built in 1916 just south of the Yokaichi area, was splendidly restored in 1985. Also preserved is a former pharmacy converted into the **Museum of Commercial and Domestic Life** (Akinai to Kurashi Hakubutsukan; *1938 Uchiko, tel 0893/44-5220, 9 a.m. –4:30 p.m., $*), which uses wax mannequins to show what business was like there in the early 1920s. Exhibits in the rear building reflect the history of Uchiko arts and crafts.

Much of Uchiko's pretty countryside is devoted to farming (rice, shiitake mushrooms, persimmons, grapes) and to forestry. The continuing exodus to large cities, as in most rural areas, is causing economic decline. One recent countermeasure has been the introduction of "Sightseeing Farms," where you can pick your own pears,

INSIDER TIP:

Our sightseeing farms are mostly vineyards: You can pick and eat your fill for a fee. Come to the tourism office and we'll find you a farm in season.

—MIZUGUCHI YUMIKO
Uchiko town tourism bureau staff

peaches, grapes, or apples.

Though often struggling, traditional industries—including candles and paper products such as lamps and umbrellas—survive in the area, too.

Uwajima

The more pleasant for seeming underpopulated, Uwajima's wide boulevards and modern buildings merely enhance the lazy pace of this small port city on Shikoku's west coast. If you are taking the ferry from Uwajima to Kyushu, the city merits a peek for two noteworthy sights: its castle and Taga-jinja, a Shinto shrine with an irresistibly bizarre sex museum.

Uwajima-jo *(1 Marunouchi, tel 0895/22-2832, 9 a.m.–4 p.m., $)* was originally built in 1595, then taken over in 1616 by Masahide, son of Date Masamune, lord of Sendai. The castle remained in the Date family until the Meiji Restoration of 1868. Reduced from the original five stories, the three-story main keep—one of only 12 surviving feudal castles nationwide—is virtually all there is. The keep has been rebuilt several times and was restored in 1962. It is quite a trek up the hill to get there; some say that is why no one took the trouble to destroy it—the fate of most other feudal castles during the Meiji era. Just as likely, it was simply not important enough. Hardly larger than a sizable mansion—but elegantly proportioned in white and perfectly charming—the castle stands in a beautiful park with a fine view over the city.

Taga-jinja is one of the 40-odd Shinto shrines still devoted to fertility deities. It stands in a small garden with miniature ponds and dry water pieces (stones arranged to suggest bodies of water) decked out with stone effigies of phallic gods. Already very small, the main hall is further dwarfed by the monster wooden phallus parked alongside it. To the back of it is a small building crammed with curious votive offerings, such as lengths of women's hair and broken dolls, but what really dominates the whole is the large concrete **sex museum.** Though mainly Japanese, exhibits also hail from India, Tibet, Latin America, and elsewhere; here are three floors of erotic and pornographic prints, paintings, bronze figurines, ceramics, curios, magazine clippings, and photographs.

However tempted you are, don't even think of laughing at anything in front of the high priest who mans the ticket booth. Having amassed this exhaustive and highly eccentric collection

Taga-jinja

- 1340 Fujie
- ☎ 0895/22-3444
- 8 a.m.–5 p.m.
- $$ sex museum, shrine free
- JR Yosan line: Uwajima

Wax Wonders

Be sure to visit the magnificently restored Japanese Wax Museum and Kami Haga Residence (Mokuro Shiryokan-Kami-Haga-tei; see p. 301), the Haga family's 19th-century waxmaking factory and attached private residence in the north of Yokaichi-Gokoku. Here you can see all the domestic furnishings and professional tools arranged in a fascinating display.

To see how candles are made in the 21st century, visit the workshop called **Omori Warosoku-ya** (tel 0893/43-0385, closed Tues. & Fri.) on Yokaichi-Gokoku, where candlemaking has been a family business for generations.

Togyu-jo

✉ 496-2 Aza-Ippomatsu, Warei-cho

☎ 0895/25-3511

🕐 Noon–2 p.m., Jan 2, 1st Sun. of April, July 24, Aug. 14, 4th Sun. of Oct.

💲 $$$$$, $$$$ with reservation

www.tougyu.com

himself, he takes a dim view of those who fail to take it seriously. "Even the emperor has sex," he sternly admonishes.

Uwajima's other claim to fame is *togyu*—sumo for bulls. The animals, which weigh almost a ton each, lock horns; the winner is the one that drives the other out of the ring. The practice is said to have emerged from the late 17th century, when the crew of a foundering Dutch ship presented their rescuers with a pair of bulls. At **Togyu-jo**, togyu is staged only five times annually.

Kochi-ken

Quiet, laid-back, and semitropical Kochi Prefecture may as well be on another planet from the bustle of Tokyo. One of the least populous prefectures in Japan, Kochi is heavily forested, mountainous, and interlaced with the most natural rivers in the nation. Once a place of political exile, the prefecture's fresh food, including its spring and fall bonito catches, and its surprisingly unspoiled environment draw more and more visitors each year.

Though its mild climate and fertile land (yielding two rice crops annually) have made it a choice place of habitation since prehistoric times, Kochi was sufficiently remote for mainland governments to exile renegades there during the medieval period. Kochi remained extremely poor until the last quarter of the 20th century. Before the Meiji period (1868–1912), it consisted of two fiefdoms, Hata and Tosa; the latter became increasingly dominant during the feudal era. Governing from Kochi-jo, the castle that still stands in the town that is now the prefectural capital (see p. 306), the Tosa lords ultimately emerged as some of the main opponents of the tottering Tokugawa shogunate in the 1860s. Among the dissenting Kochi samurai was Sakamoto Ryoma, one of the greatest architects and heroes of the Meiji Restoration, which he instigated by uniting the Satsuma and Choshu clans (from modern-day Kagoshima and Yamaguchi Prefectures, respectively). Statues commemorate Ryoma in front of Kochi Station and at

Nakahama Manjiro or John Manjiro (1827–1898)

One of Japan's most extraordinary heroes, Nakahama Manjiro was born in a poor hamlet near Ashizuri-misaki. Shipwrecked at 14 on an uninhabited island far off the coast of Honshu in 1841, he and his fellows were rescued months later by a U.S. whaling ship. For the next four years, Manjiro traveled the world with the crew. The captain recognized the boy's potential and took Manjiro back to Massachusetts, where he studied English, mathematics, and navigation as John Manjiro. He returned to Japan in 1851 and worked as an interpreter during the negotiations between Commodore Matthew Perry and the shogunate in Edo. These talks played a key role in opening up the country. Manjiro pioneered the teaching of English at what later became the University of Tokyo and traveled abroad as one of Japan's first diplomats after the Meiji Restoration of 1868.

Kochi is famous for *tataki-katsuo*—seared bonito—served with raw garlic.

Katsura-hama, a famous moon-viewing beach south of Kochi city, but you are likely to see his face on everything from buses to cookies to men's room doors in Kochi. Assassinated in 1867 at only 31, he never saw the restoration occur a year later.

Such political foment long past, Kochi now draws stressed-out urbanites in seek of a bit of green and blue. Outdoor pursuits run the gamut here, but surfing, whale-watching (see sidebar p. 307), and kayaking are Kochi's best offerings. In the west, the unpolluted **Shimanto-gawa,** the only river in Japan without large-scale dams, is the nation's cleanest. The crystal clear waters rush down from lush, densely forested mountains, evidence of the heavy rainfall the region receives each year. If canoeing isn't your thing, an open-air trolley runs along the river from Kubokawa Station to Ekawasaki Station before heading to Uwajima (see pp. 302–304) each summer. Farther west, near the border with Ehime-ken, is the popular and scenic **Shikoku Karst,** featuring alpine pasture-lands with curiously formed out-croppings of limestone.

The Pacific coast of Shikoku used to be much given to whaling, but with the decline of many species and the international ban on hunting the leviathans, whale-watching tours have given whalers a viable alternative. Finally the coast narrows down to scenic **Cape Ashizuri** (Ashizuri-misaki), noted as a popular whale-watching spot and as the birthplace of one of

Kochi

289 D2

Visitor Information

JR Kochi Station

088/823-4016

8:50 a.m.–
5:15 p.m.

JR Dosan line
from Takamatsu
(2 hr.)

visitkochijapan.com

Kochi-jo

Marunouchi
1-2-1

088/824-5701

9 a.m.–4:30 p.m.

$

Streetcar:
Kochijo-Mae

**kochipark.jp
/kochijyo**

Japan's most remarkable heroes, Nakahama Manjiro or John Manjiro (see sidebar p. 304).

The center of **Kochi,** some 6 miles (10 km) from the coast and flanked on three sides by the Kuma, Kagami, and Kokubu Rivers, contains a fine feudal castle, and is otherwise known for its huge platters of seared bonito, everything Sakamoto Ryoma, and its friendly, hard-drinking locals. Kochi is compact and easy to get around by streetcar.

It was the castle **Kochi-jo,** on a strategic hilltop originally called Kochi-yama, that gave the prefecture its name. Initiated by the Tosa lord Yamauchi Kazutoyo in 1601, construction lasted a decade. The main keep suffered serious damage in a fire in 1727 and was rebuilt some 20 years

later on a smaller scale; with its lovely garden setting, the castle complex became a charming aristocratic residence rather than the belligerent tower that its nickname, "Hawk Castle," evokes.

In addition to samurai memorabilia, the **museum** inside the castle displays a Roman alphabet written by Nakahama Manjiro.

For a little contrast to the stately keep on the hill, stop by the **Former Yamauchi Residence** (1-3-35 Takajomachi, tel 088/832-7277, 7 a.m.–5 p.m.), a row house used as a barracks for the Yamauchi family's guards, now an Important Cultural Property preserving the humble lodgings of a poor samurai. Reflecting Kochi's rural face, a picturesque market held on Sundays runs from the main gate of the castle for half a mile

The seas around Katsurahama offer excellent whale-watching opportunities.

EXPERIENCE: Whale-Watching in Japan

Whaling remains one of the least popular aspects of Japanese culture abroad. Mentioning Japan's so-called research ships, used to hunt hundreds of whales yearly, will almost guarantee discomfort or an argument. In reality, almost no one eats whale meat anymore: The most vociferous supporters of the industry are sensitive nationalists and the old-timers who had to chew up the tasteless rubber in their wartime school lunches.

More good news is that formerly depleted whaling grounds have become whale-watching areas as the local industry collapsed and the whales gradually returned. Elsewhere whalers have turned to tourism as the market for their controversial haul becomes smaller.

In Shikoku's Kochi Prefecture, former whaling cooperatives put on tours around Cape Ashizuri, where whales and dolphins gather year-round for the fish congregating near the outlet of the clean Shimanto-gawa. Daily tours run for 3–4 hours from several ports in **Tosa Shimizu** city (shimizu-kankou.com).

In Okinawa, **Zamami-jima's local whale-watching association** (www.vill .zamami.okinawa.jp/whale/english.html) runs two 2-hour boat tours daily in the winter during humpback mating season.

The remote **Ogasawara Islands** (see p. 102), 620 miles (1,000 km) off the coast of Tokyo, also have humpback and sperm whale-watching tours, as well as dolphin swimming experiences. You'll find several companies running trips (ogasawaramura.com). Most tours cost approximately $60 per person and all require reservations.

(1 km) along Otesuji-dori— a tradition since the Edo period. Try out exotic varieties of citrus fruit, powdered turmeric to ease a burgeoning hangover, or ginger tonic drinks, among other local produce. Just down the street is **Hirome Ichiba**, a raucous food court of eateries popular day and night with locals and visitors. It's a good place to sample *tataki-katsuo* (seared bonito). Find a table first, then place an order at a stall.

You could also visit **Katsura-hama**, on Urado Bay about 7.5 miles (12 km) south of Kochi city, a beach popular over centuries for moon-viewing (swimming is not allowed) and one of Sakamoto Ryoma's favorite spots. Indeed, a large bronze statue of Sakamoto continues to glower out across the Pacific from the beachhead, and the **Sakamoto Ryoma Memorial Museum** pays tribute to Japan's recently voted "most popular historical figure." The lack of English signage disappoints, but the museum website provides an excellent introduction to Ryoma-mania. Surfers will prefer beaches east of Kochi.

Across the Kokubu-gawa lies Mount Goda, site of temple 31, **Chikurin-ji,** noted for its five-story pagoda and 1,200 years of history, and the **Makino Botanical Gardens.** Dedicated to Tomitaro Makino, Japan's most accomplished botanist, the expansive garden includes Kochi flora, plants discovered by Makino, a greenhouse of South American rarities, and a museum to the botanist's work. ∎

Sakamoto Ryoma Memorial Museum

✉ 830 Urado-Shiroyama
☎ 088/841-0001
🕐 9 a.m.–5 p.m.
💲 $
🚌 My-Yu Bus: Kinenkan-mae stop

ryoma-kinenkan .jp/en/

Chikurin-ji

✉ 3577 Godai-san
☎ 088/882-3085
🕐 8:30 a.m.–5 p.m.
💲 $ (treasure house & garden)
🚌 My-Yu Bus: Chikurinji stop

The Seto-naikai

Few views outside the Aegean equal those on the Seto-naikai—the Inland Sea. At sunset, the myriad islands fade back into the horizon or seem to detach themselves against the coastline of Honshu or Shikoku to the south.

The view from the top of Akashi Strait (Akashi Kaikyo) Bridge

Oyamazumi-jinja

- ✉ 3327 Miyaura
- ☎ 0897/82-0032
- 🕐 8:30 a.m.–5 p.m.
- 💲 $$ (treasure house)

Once the realm of pirates and isolated fishing hamlets, the Seto-naikai has struggled to retain a local economy and a sense of identity after the construction of the Great Seto and Akashi Strait Bridges during Japan's economic boom, which, rather than isolating the locals, made their islands accessible and susceptible to the lure of big mainland cities. Recent years have seen some success against the tide of depopulation and economic stagnation. History buffs flock to Omi-shima's **Oyamazumi-jinja,** a militant shrine with the best collection of medieval armor and blades in Japan. The Benesse Corporation's extensive art collection has single-handedly revived Nao-shima with its world-class museums. Likewise, the 43 miles (70 km) of the Shimanami Sea Route, a highway stringing together nine small islands, is a popular rent-a-cycle trip and makes formerly remote island gems a pleasant bike ride out of Onomichi.

Coming from Kobe, buses cross the Akashi Kaikyo Bridge to Awaji Island, the largest of the group, and pass over the Naruto Whirlpools (see p. 295) to Tokushima Prefecture. Alternatively, the Great Seto Bridge connects Okayama (see p. 276) and western Kagawa Prefecture, stopping at three of the islands on the way. The westernmost link is the Seto-uchi Shimanami Kaido (Sea Route), connecting Onomichi and Matsuyama (see pp. 297–299). Regular ferry services to the islands also run from Takamatsu and Matsuyama, as well as most ports on the mainland.

The Islands

Awaji-shima is sadly best known as the epicenter for the Great Hanshin Earthquake, which leveled many of Awaji's homes and great swaths of Kobe. Striking on January 17, 1995, at 5:46 a.m., the 7.2-magnitude quake caught many in bed, unable to shelter, killing more than 5,200 and leaving 300,000 homeless (compare to the Tohoku Earthquake's 9.0 magnitude—see p. 161). This pleasant but innocuous island is close enough to Kobe to function as a suburban park, its most famous sight being the Naruto Whirlpools, between it and Shikoku.

Ikuchi-shima, Omi-shima, and Inno-shima are all main stopping points on Seto-naikai tour-boat routes from the San-yo coast, although the Shimanami Kaido bridge system means they can also be visited by car, bus, or bicycle.

The focus of **Ikuchi-shima** is **Setoda,** a pleasant little town embracing all the island's main sights. You get spectacular panoramas over the Inland Sea from **Kojo-ji,** built on the hilltop in 1403 and graced with a fine three-story pagoda. But the majority of the 500,000 tourists flocking to Ikuchi-shima annually are drawn down Setoda's main street to **Kosan-ji** (tel 0845/27-0800, 9 a.m.– 5 p.m., $$$). Erected in 1936, Kosan-ji is one of Japan's greatest

INSIDER TIP:

Big-city galleries tend to look down on photography as art, so Naoshima's Art House Project often hosts exhibitions by ambitious young photographers showing edgy new work.

—MITSUHIRO MATSUDA
Art House Project photographer

contributions to world kitsch. Brainchild of a wealthy arms dealer turned monk, the grounds contain much gaudier reproductions of famous Japanese religious buildings, including Nikko's Tosho-gu and Kyoto's Kinkaku-ji. Curious visitors can learn about the island's past at the **Setoda History & Folklore Museum** (tel 0845/26-6204), located on

Awaji-shima
▲ 289 F4
Visitor Information
✉ 1F Awaji Service Area
☎ 0799/72-0168
🕐 8 a.m.–5 p.m.
🚌 Express bus from JR Sannomiya Station (Kobe) to Awaji Interchange bus stop (30 min.)
hyogo-tourism.jp /english/area/awaji .html

Ikuchi-shima
▲ 289 C4
Visitor Information
✉ 200-5 Setoda-cho, Sawa
☎ 0845/27-0051
🕐 9 a.m.–5 p.m.

Omi-shima

📍 289 C4

Visitor Information

✉ 3260 Miyaura at the Shimanami-no-eki Mishima waystation

☎ 0897/82-0002

🕐 8:30 a.m.–5 p.m.

Inno-shima

📍 289 C4

Visitor Information

✉ 2F, ferry terminal at Habu

☎ 0845/26-6111

🕐 8:30 a.m.–5 p.m.

Naoshima

📍 289 E4

Visitor Information

✉ Inside ferry terminal at Miyanoura

☎ 087/892-2299

🕐 9 a.m.–6 p.m.

naoshima.net

the seaward end of the main street.

The pleasant and hilly island of **Omi-shima** was the favored abode of pirates in medieval times. Its **Oyamazumi-jinja** is as old as any Shinto shrine in Japan and is dedicated to a powerful god of protection who has drawn warriors over the centuries seeking aid or leaving weapons behind as tokens of gratitude. The Treasure Hall contains a superlative collection of swords and armor.

Inno-shima now depends upon farming, especially flowers and fruit, but this island was once a pirate stronghold, notably for the Murakami clan. Up on a hill is **Konren-ji,** which was the family temple and graveyard; next to it is their castle, known as **Innoshima Suigun-jo Pirate's Castle.** Heavily restored, the three remaining buildings are now a museum. A walk up **Shirataki-yama,** the hill

dominating the island, will take you along a path flanked by more than 500 stone effigies of the Buddha and reward you with a superb view over the sea.

Shodo-shima (visitor information inside Tonosho ferry terminal, tel 0879/62-2009, www.town.shodo shima.lg.jp, 8:30 a.m.–5 p.m.), or "little bean island," is famous for its soybeans and olives. Visitors appreciate the island's quiet atmosphere and scenic gorges, **Kanka-kei** and **Choshi-kei,** the former accessed by cable car, the latter accompanied by monkeys.

From the port of Marugame, to the west of Takamatsu on Shikoku, you can visit the **Shiwaku-Shoto** group, comprising about a dozen islands. The most notable is **Hon-jima** where you'll find a street of attractive late Edo-period houses faced with white plaster ornamented with black and white tiles. ∎

Naoshima: The Island of Art

Easily reached by ferry, from Okayama or Takamatsu, unique Naoshima is an art lover's delight. The alluring underground **Chichu Art Museum** (3449-1 Naoshima-cho, tel 087/892-3755, benesse -artsite.jp, 10 a.m.– 6 p.m., closed Mon., $$$$) was designed by master of concrete Ando Tadao, the architect responsible for all three museums on Naoshima. It features Claude Monet works lit by filtered sunshine and James Turell's "light as art" installations. Equally impressive is **Ando's Benesse House Museum** (Gotanji Naoshima-cho, tel 087/892-2030, 8 a.m.–8 p.m., $$), with a collection that includes works

by Pollock, Hockney, and Warhol. Added in 2010, the **Lee Ufan Museum** (1390 Naoshima-cho, tel 087/892-3754, 10 a.m.–6 p.m., closed Mon., $$) displays the Korean-born artist's often dramatically simple paintings and sculpture in another stark Ando bunker.

The best way to get around Naoshima is by minibus, which stops at Honmura. Here artists have turned traditional buildings into studios under the name of the **Art House Project.** Temporary exhibits run mainly in the summer, and the permanent installations include one by Turell that plays off our ability to gradually see in the dark.

Volcanic Kyushu, closest island to the Asian mainland, for centuries a gateway to China, Korea, and the rest of the world

Kyushu

Guardian lion at a Confucian shrine, Nagasaki

Kyushu

The Japanese are fond of comparing Kyushu, with its mild climate, vivid blue-green seas, and citrus trees, to the Mediterranean. The character of the residents is also described as Mediterranean, with traditional Japanese reserve taking a backseat to more demonstrative temperaments.

Kyushu means "nine regions," which is what it embraced in ancient times. Today it comprises seven prefectures: Fukuoka, Oita, Kumamoto, Nagasaki, and Saga in the north, and Kagoshima and Miyazaki in the south. The southernmost of Japan's main islands and the third largest, it is linked to Western Honshu by road and rail via an undersea tunnel. The island is heavily industrialized—especially the north—and wealthy: In 2003, its gross domestic product of $430 billion equaled one percent of the world total, with most of that from Fukuoka-ken.

Vibrant and hedonistic Fukuoka, the prefectural capital, is the logical starting point for exploring Kyushu. This cosmopolitan city is enlivened by travelers arriving from the Asian mainland by ferry. Fukuoka's fusion- and street-food culture reflects a cultural gregariousness and a taste for the exotic.

Area of map detail

Tokyo

NOT TO BE MISSED:

The party atmosphere of Fukuoka's street-stall restaurants **314–316**

Praying for scholastic success at Dazaifu's Tenman-gu **317**

A riverboat tour of Yanagawa **319**

Soaking in the colorful hot springs of Beppu **320–321**

Kumamoto-jo, one of Japan's finest castles **323–324**

Nagasaki's history, before and after the atomic bomb **325–332**

The pottery towns of Saga-ken Prefecture **334–335**

Northern Kyushu is just 125 miles (200 km) from Korea, making Nagasaki closer to Shanghai than to Tokyo. Kyushu was Japan's cradle of civilization, and its history reflects its worldliness. Archaeological sites in Saga-ken reveal the first evidence of rice farming, introduced to Japan from Korea. The global reputation of ceramics from Karatsu and Imari was built upon the skills of Korean craftsmen in the 16th and 17th centuries. The first Europeans to come to Japan were Portuguese sailors shipwrecked off the southern Kyushu coast in 1543. They introduced the Japanese to firearms and tobacco. Vestiges of bygone relations with Europe, both mercantile and religious, survive in Nagasaki city, notwithstanding the horrific destruction wrought by the atomic bomb in 1945.

Kyushu shows more volcanic activity than the rest of Japan and has many hot springs. Aso-san boasts the largest caldera on Earth and is the most visited of Kyushu's volcanoes. There are several volcanoes in Miyazaki-ken, known for its *onsen* and beach resorts. Sakurajima, the Japanese equivalent of Vesuvius, smolders just over the bay from Kagoshima, earning the city the designation "the Naples of Japan." ■

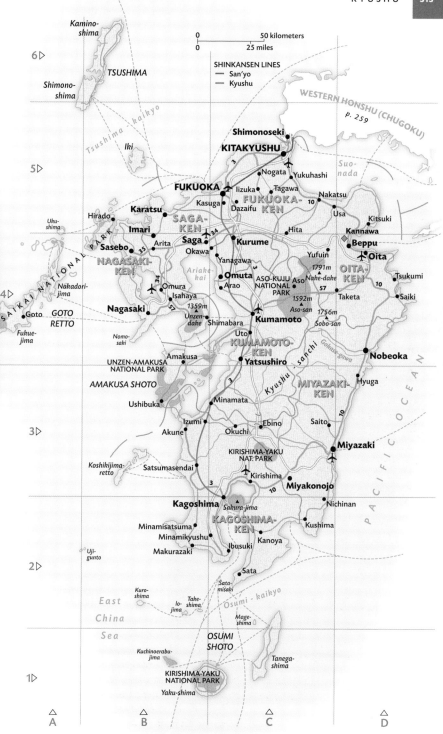

Kamino-
shima

TSUSHIMA

Shimono-
shima

SHINKANSEN LINES
— San'yo
— Kyushu

50 kilometers
25 miles

WESTERN HONSHU (CHUGOKU)
p. 259

Tsushima -kaikyo

Iki

Suo-
nada

Shimonoseki
KITAKYUSHU

• Nogata • Yukuhashi

FUKUOKA ✈ Iizuka Tagawa
Kasuga Dazaifu **FUKUOKA-**
KEN Nakatsu
10 Usa • Kitsuki

Uku-
shima

Hirado • **Karatsu**
Imari **SAGA-**
KEN Hita **Kannawa**
Beppu

PARK

Sasebo Arita 35 **Saga** ✈ 34 **Kurume** Yufuin **Oita**
Okawa Yanagawa 1791m **OITA-**
Nakadori- *Ariake-* *Nake-dake* **KEN** Tsukumi
jima *kai* **Omuta** **ASO-KUJU** Aso 57 Taketa 10
NAGASAKI- Omura **NATIONAL** 1592m • Saiki
KEN Isahaya Arao **PARK** *Aso-san* 1756m
Nagasaki 57 1359m Shimabara **Kumamoto** *Sobo-san*
Goto • Unzen- Uto *Gokase-gawa*
GOTO *dake* **KUMAMOTO-** **Nobeoka**
Fukue- **RETTO** *Nomo-* **KEN**
jima *saki* **Yatsushiro** Hyuga *PACIFIC*
UNZEN-AMAKUSA Amakusa • **MIYAZAKI-**
NATIONAL PARK *Kyushu -sanchi* **KEN**

SAIKAI NATIONAL

AMAKUSA SHOTO Minamata
Ushibuka • Izumi Ebino Saito
Koshikijima- Akune Okuchi **Miyazaki**
retto Satsumasendai **KIRISHIMA-YAKU**
NAT. PARK 10 **Miyakonojo**
3 Kirishima
Kagoshima Nichinan
Minamisatsuma *Sakura-jima* **KAGOSHIMA-**
Minamikyushu **KEN** Kushima
Makurazaki Ibusuki Kanoya
Uji-
gunto Sata

East Kuro- Take-
China shima *Io-* shima Sata-
jima *misaki* *Osumi -kaikyo* Mage-
Sea shima

OSUMI
SHOTO
Kuchinoerabu-
jima
KIRISHIMA-YAKU
NATIONAL PARK Tanega-
shima
Yaku-shima

OCEAN

A   B   C   D

6

5

4

3

2

1

Fukuoka

Fukuoka is fast becoming the international hub of Kyushu. Lying on a broad bay, Fukuoka is divided into two: the northeastern sector, Hakata, which embraces the port; and Fukuoka itself, which lies on the western bank of the Naka-gawa. Kyushu's capital is mercantile, energetic, and hedonistic. What Fukuoka lacks in historical sights is made up for with delicious specialties (pork bone ramen and spicy cod roe), boisterous nightlife, and striking architecture.

Canal City Hakata adds color to Fukuoka's cityscape.

After building their castle at the outset of the Edo period, the ruling Kuroda clan gave the name Fukuoka to the samurai quarter newly dominating the plebeian and merchant harbor-town of Hakata. It was under this name that the two sections of town were administratively reunited in 1886, but local inhabitants—overwhelmingly descended from commoners rather than samurai—preferred to call it Hakata. They still do, and true native citizens like to be called Hakatakko; the city's main station is JR Hakata.

From ancient times, the port of Hakata had been the gateway for exchanges with China and Korea, though contacts with the mainland were not always peaceful. Hakata twice played a decisive role in fending off Mongol emperor Kublai Khan's attempts to invade Japan. Massive and technologically superior Mongol forces attacked in 1274 and 1281; after the first attack a 12-mile (20 km) anti-Mongol wall was built along the coast. Each invasion was spoiled by typhoons, which the hastily-built Mongol ships could not survive. This fortuitous intervention has been venerated ever since as *kamikaze*—the wind of the gods, a name adopted by Japan's suicide pilots in World War II. Parts of the wall still stand at Iki-no-Matsubara, Nishijin, and Imazu.

Fukuoka's is distinguished by its excellent cuisine and its development as a modern, international travel hub. Hakata Station, the gateway to Kyushu for most travelers, underwent massive development to coincide with the launch of the new Shinkansen line across Kyushu in March 2011: Its sparkling white interior and department store megaplex have shifted the city's shopping core to the east. The shopping district of Tenjin has broad green boulevards lined with designer stores and one of Japan's most pleasant underground shopping malls beneath Watanabe-dori, designed in a cobblestone pseudo-European motif.

A night on the town is the best way to see Fukuoka shine. The city is famous for the best ramen soup in Japan, *tonkotsu* ramen, which is made from long-boiled pork bones. The stock is rich and thick, and the number of eateries boasting original recipes is staggering. Fukuoka is also renowned for *mentaiko* (spiced cod roe) and *motsunabe* (intestines hot pot). If you think you've handled Japanese cuisine well so far, here's your chance to take it up a level or two. Mentaiko is an acquired taste: Spicy and rich, it is best eaten on rice and in small amounts. Motsunabe is much more delicious than it sounds. Beef or pork intestines, soft and fatty, are cooked with a heap of vegetables in miso stock and are one of the best kinds of offal to eat in Japan (among the alternatives are grilled cow lungs!).

The main entertainment district is **Nakasu,** an island in the middle of the Naka-gawa, said to rival even Tokyo's Kabuki-cho for hedonistic excess. All along the river are *yatai* (portable restaurant stalls), set up each evening and dishing up inexpensive food in a friendly, steamy atmosphere. Yatai also set up in Tenjin, along Showa-dori. If you want to rub elbows with locals and have a real Japanese experience, this is it.

Fukuoka's historical sights center on the shrine of

Fukuoka

  313 C5

Visitor Information

✉ JR Hakata Station
☎ 092/431-3003
🕐 8 a.m.–9 p.m.
🚄 Shinkansen from Tokyo (5 hr.)

yokanavi.com/en

Kushida-jinja

✉ 1-41 Kami-Kawabata-machi, Hakata-ku
☎ 092/291-2951
🕐 9 a.m.–10 p.m.
🚄 Kuko line: Gion or Nakasu-Kawabata

NEED TO KNOW

Reaching Kyushu

Shinkansen lines connect Kyushu with Honshu, 5 hours from Tokyo to Fukuoka. The "bullet train" runs down the west side, from Fukuoka to Kumamoto (37 min.) and Kagoshima (100 min.), but those without the JR Pass should consider the two-hour flight from Tokyo to Fukuoka, Nagasaki, or Kumamoto (ana.co.jp), as it is often cheaper than the train.

Getting Around

The Kyushu Shinkansen fails to extend across much of the island, so you'll need to take JR Kyushu express trains to reach Nagasaki, Beppu, Miyazaki, and areas of interest in central Kyushu, such as Mount Aso. In order to reach Yakushima or the Goto Islands it is necessary to take a ferry from Nagasaki or Kagoshima, respectively.

Kyushu at the Crossroads of Art & Culture

The long association with mainland Asian has influenced Kyushu more than the rest of Japan, nowhere more so than in the art world. Two major museums, the **Kyushu National Museum** in Dazaifu (p. 318) and the **Fukuoka Asian Art Museum** (see below), capture Kyushu's role at the crossroads of cultural exchange. The former sets itself apart by considering Japanese art within the context of styles developed in Korea and China and along the Silk Road. Unlike similar museums,

it has replica exhibits of the artifacts that crossed Asia and came to influence Japan, which visitors can freely handle or try to make themselves. The Fukuoka Asian Art Museum approaches art from the other end, attempting to represent modern Asian styles that have grown and evolved out of traditions relatively untouched by Western art influence. It steers clear of highbrow notions of art, including examples of folk craft and popular art that have largely been ignored until now.

Hakata Machiya Folk History Museum

- ✉ 6-10 Reisen-machi, Hakata-ku
- ☎ 092/281-7761
- 🕐 10 a.m.–6 p.m.
- 💲 $
- 🚉 Kuko line: Gion or Nakasu-Kawabata

hakatamachiya.com

Fukuoka Asian Art Museum

- ✉ 7-8F, Riverain Center Bldg. 3-1 Shimokawabata-machi
- ☎ 092/263-1100
- 🕐 10 a.m.–8 p.m., closed Wed.
- 💲 $
- 🚉 Kuko line: Nakasu-Kawabata

faam.city.fukuoka.lg.jp

Shofuku-ji

- ✉ 6-1 Gokusho-machi, Hakata-ku
- ☎ 092/291-0775
- 🕐 8 a.m.–5 p.m.
- 🚉 Kuko line: Gion

Kushida-jinja and its exciting summer festival, Hakata Gion Yamakasa *(July 10–15).* Giant 33-foot-tall (10 m) floats covered in battling papier-mâché warriors are run through the city as thousands of men in loincloths chant *"Yoisa!"* A float is kept on display at the shrine, and the **Hakata Machiya Folk History Museum,** just to the east, has a good video on the festival, as well as displays on Fukuoka's old city life.

From the west side of the shrine, walk north through the Kawabata shopping arcade to see another float on display and check out the arcade's strange mix of Buddhist altar shops, fashionable boutiques, and shoe shops from the last millennium.

The arcade ends at Riverain, a modern shopping and arts complex and a fitting symbol for modern Fukuoka. In addition to designer-brand shops, it houses the **Fukuoka Asian Art Museum,** which exhibits notable works from all over Asia. Next door, traditions are carried on at the **Hakata-za,** a popular kabuki theater *($$$$$).*

The best museum in town is the **Fukuoka City Museum** (Fukuoka-shi Hakubutsukan; *3-1-1 Momochihama, Sawara-ku, tel 092/845-5011, museum.city.fukuoka.jp, 9:30 a.m.–5:30 p.m., closed Mon., $, subway: Nishijin).* It details the city's history and relationship with mainland Asia. While you are there, pop by nearby Fukuoka Tower for a great view over the city, especially at night.

World War II destroyed most of Fukuoka's historical sights, but it is worth checking out **Shofuku-ji, Tocho-ji** (*2-4 Gokusho-machi, Hakata-ku, tel 092/291-4459, subway: Gion),* and **Hakozaki-gu** (*1-22-1 Hakozaki, Higashi-ku, 092/641-7431, 9 a.m.–4:30 p.m., $, subway: Hakozaki-Miya-mae).* The temples were founded for the Rinzai Zen and Shingon sects of Buddhism, respectively, when their founders returned from China, though the former is mostly closed and the latter is modern, albeit with a gigantic 33-foot-tall (10 m) wooden Buddha. Hakozaki-gu, founded in 923, is a shrine dedicated to the god of war. ∎

Dazaifu

Almost a suburb of Fukuoka and just 40 minutes away by train, Dazaifu was Kyushu's seat of government from its establishment in A.D. 664 until it began to decline at the end of the 12th century. It was also important as a center for trade with China.

The raked stone gardens of Komyozen-ji

The area's greatest draw is **Dazaifu Tenman-gu,** dedicated to Sugawara-no-Michizane, a wrongfully exiled tenth-century scholar who was posthumously deified as Tenjin, the Shinto god of literature and learning, when a series of calamities in the capital raised suspicion that Michizane's vengeful spirit was on the loose. It's hard to say whether deification has appeased him: Despite more than 12,000 Tenjin shrines and endless hopeful prayers from students before their university entrance exams, the test results seem to suggest he is a fickle god. Students flock here to pay their respects. The shrine was founded

in the tenth century, but the current **Main Hall,** featuring ornate carving beneath its thatched roof, was built in 1591. The precinct encompasses plum and camphor trees, as well as irises; along the approach is a watercourse spanned by a celebrated hump-backed bridge. To the right of the Main Hall is an apricot tree that, according to legend, uprooted itself from Michizane's Kyoto garden and followed him to Dazaifu. It is said to have stood on this spot for a thousand years.

Look for craftsmen painting ceramic Hakata dolls in the shops near the shrine. A Fukuoka specialty, the dolls represent

Dazaifu

 313 C5

Visitor Information

✉ Dazaifu Station

☎ 092/925-1880

🕐 9 a.m.–5 p.m.

🚉 Nishitetsu line: Dazaifu, change at Futsukaichi (25 min.)

Dazaifu Tenman-gu

✉ 4-7-1 Saifu

☎ 092/922-8225

🕐 6:30 a.m.–7 p.m.

 $ (treasure house)

Komyozen-ji

- ✉ 2-16-1 Saifu
- ☎ 092/922-4053
- 🕐 9 a.m.–4:30 p.m.
- 💲 $

Kyushu National Museum

- ✉ 4-7-2 Ishizaka
- ☎ 092/918-2807
- 🕐 9:30 a.m.– 5 p.m., closed Mon.
- 💲 $ (permanent collection), $$$ (special exhibition)

kyuhaku.com

Dazaifu Exhibition Hall

- ✉ 4-6-1 Kanzeon-ji
- ☎ 092/922-7811
- 🕐 9 a.m.–4:30 p.m., closed Mon.
- 🚌 Bus from Dazaifu Station to Dazaifu Seicho-ato stop

Kaidan-in

- ✉ 5-7-10 Kanzeon-ji
- ☎ 092/922-4559
- 🕐 9 a.m.–4 p.m.
- 💲 $
- 🚌 Bus from Dazaifu Station to Kanzeonji stop

Kanzeon-ji

- ✉ 5-6-1 Kanzeon-ji
- ☎ 092/922-1811
- 🕐 9 a.m.–5 p.m.
- 💲 $
- 🚌 Bus from Dazaifu Station to Kanzeonji stop

traditional dancing girls; while the craftsmanship is exquisite, they tend to be aesthetically insipid.

The overwhelming majority of the hordes visiting the Tenman-gu never give a passing thought to **Komyozen-ji,** a Zen temple not five minutes' walk to the south. It was founded during the 13th century, though the current buildings date from the Edo period. Refined and simple, they feature expanses of tatami matting surrounded by verandas of polished wood—all intended simply for sitting and contemplating the lovely garden. A masterpiece of landscaping, it features white gravel "seas" beautifully raked around rocks resembling islands, and green "land" pieces consisting of mosses and trees. Try moving from one vantage point to another; the garden has been designed so that the view is perfect from any angle.

Opened in 2005, the **Kyushu National Museum** is a strikingly modern, expansive facility that looks at local history through the lens of interaction and cultural exchange with Korea, China, and beyond via the Silk Road. Dazaifu may seem an odd place for Japan's fourth national museum (after Tokyo, Kyoto, and Nara), but its position as an early center of trade and civilization offers strong justification. The museum shows how Japanese culture has related to, evolved from, and been influenced by those of other nations.

As for Dazaifu's early history, only traces can still be seen. The ancient government office, the **Tofuro,** was a vermilion wooden

structure with a tiled roof; all that remains are the massive foundation stones, embedded in an expanse of grassland. The same applies to vestiges of earthen walls and embankments to the west and north toward **Ono-jo,** a fortress built on a hill to defend Dazaifu.

Just south of the Tofuro, you can find out more about the ancient city at **Dazaifu Exhibition Hall.** At the foot of Shioji hill is **Chikuzen Kokubun-ji** *(4-13-1 Kokubu).* Only foundation stones remain from the huge temple precinct built by Emperor Shomu in 741, but the present temple contains a fine eighth-century Buddha statue.

Another historical site is the **Kaidan-in,** an ordination hall that was one of only three in Japan during the eighth century. ∎

A Treasure Hall of Buddhas

Next to the Kaidan-in, to the east, is **Kanzeon-ji,** once rivaling even Chikuzen Kokubun-ji in size. Although the old structures vanished long ago, the temple's current buildings date from the 17th century. The bell (*bonsho*), cast around 745, is from the original temple and is reputedly Japan's oldest. Do not miss the Treasure Hall, which contains an outstanding collection of Buddhist statues from the 8th to 12th centuries.

Yanagawa

The picturesque little town of Yanagawa lies some 25 miles (40 km) south of Fukuoka. Like most former castle towns, Yanagawa lost its castle following the Meiji Restoration; it was burned to the ground in 1873. The three moats remained, however, forming a canal network that criss-crosses Yanagawa and is now used to ferry tourists to the town's various historical spots.

Punting is a relaxing way to take in Yanagawa.

Yanagawa

🅰 313 C4

Visitor Information

✉ Yanagawa Station

☎ Information
& river trips:
0944/74-0891

🕐 9 a.m.–5 p.m.

🚆 Nishitetsu-
Omuta line from
Fukuoka Station
(45 min. by
limited express)

yanagawa-net.com

**Ohana Villa,
Shoto-en Garden
& Seiyokan**

✉ 1 Shin Hoka-
machi

☎ 0944/73-2189

🕐 9 a.m.–6 p.m.

💲 $

ohana.co.jp

**Kitahara Hakushu
Memorial Hall**

✉ 55-1 Okinohata

☎ 0944/73-8940

🕐 9 a.m.–5 p.m.

💲 $

**Former Residence
of the Toshima
Family**

✉ 49-3 Onidomachi

☎ 0944/73-9587

🕐 9 a.m.–5 p.m.,
closed Tues.

💲 $

The main focus is the **Ohana Villa,** built in 1697, but the only true survivor of the era is the villa's **Shoto-en Garden,** laid out with a pond encompassing dwarf pines and rocks to emulate Matsushima Bay in Tohoku (see p. 160). Next to it is the **Seiyokan,** a Western-style mansion built by Yanagawa's feudal lords in the 1880s. The two buildings contain museums: In the Tachibana house are displays of Meiji-period memorabilia and utensils, while the Ohana Villa has a beautiful collection of Edo-period artifacts that includes Noh costumes, armor, and miniature painted books.

The north side of the town embraces a number of quaint temples, restaurants, and shops. The picturesque streets by the canal have several old traditional houses, notably the birthplace of the celebrated poet Kitahara Hakushu (1885–1942), now open as the **Kitahara Hakushu Memorial Hall,** and the **Former Residence of the Toshima Family** (Kyu Toshima-ke Jutaku), a thatched samurai home built in the tea-ceremony-house style dated to the early 19th century. ∎

Beppu

The town of Beppu sits in an area overflowing with volcanic hot springs and is *the* place for hot-water hedonism in a nation nuts about the art of the bath. From the flashy new resort to the nostalgic old *ryokan* and the super spa to the sand bath, Beppu has it all.

Red clay glows and steams from Beppu's subterranean fires.

The Promised Land for lovers of the long, leisurely soak, Beppu reigns supreme over all *onsen* resorts in Japan. Yet this distinction hardly qualifies it as a paragon of refinement—quite the contrary. Matched only in the realm of science fiction, Beppu is gaudy, outlandish, and fascinating. In this contender for the title of the world's most geothermal city, natural hot water cooks food and heats houses in winter. Onsen tourists roam the streets in cotton *yukata* (light kimonos) emblazoned with their hotel's crest, even in the town center.

Of the eight onsen areas, the most important are **Beppu Onsen** in the center of town, **Kankaiji** on the hill to the west, and **Kannawa** to the northeast. The **Ekimae Koto Onsen** bathhouse in central Beppu, which is open 24 hours a day, goes back to the 1930s, but the most venerable is the **Takegawara** *(16-23 Moto-machi, tel 0977/23-1585),* an imposing wooden building dating from 1879 where—apart from the usual mineral-rich hot water—the main attraction is the *suna-yu* (sand bath). Steam filtering up from the boiling water underground heats the sand, which is shoveled over you. Lying buried up to your neck, you sweat away your cares—and quite possibly, if you stay long enough, your skin, too. Suna-yu is also available at **Shoningahama** beach on the eastern side of the seafront and is a treat not to be missed by any visitor to Beppu.

If you're after sheer luxury and the latest in onsen technology, hilly **Kankaiji Onsen** is for you. The views over Beppu Bay are

INSIDER TIP:

Hot-spring baths (*onsen*) are one of Japan's great pleasures, but also a place where travelers can easily annoy locals. To avoid any glares, wash and rinse thoroughly before getting in the communal bath.

—ROB GOSS
National Geographic contributor

breathtaking, especially from the **Suginoi Palace** (see Travelwise p. 379), a spa and hotel complex offering an astonishing variety of aquatic attractions for families. You need not be a guest to use the facilities.

Beppu is a great city for covered malls. These run halfway down the main street from the train station on your right. The main malls are festooned with colored paper lanterns and present the stress-free visitor—fresh from a long, relaxing soak—a striking array of restaurants and bars. The main shopping arcades, called **Ginza** and **Yayoi**, offer everything

from fancy souvenir shops to funky, old thrift stores.

Kannawa is celebrated for its eight **Kannawa Jigoku** (Kannawa Hells), where you can contemplate geysers, seething expanses of bubbling mud, and pools of steaming hot water dyed strange colors by minerals. The hells range from interesting geothermic displays to pure kitsch, including cramped crocodile farms, piranha tanks, petting zoos and massive souvenir stores. The best are the **Kamado Jigoku** (Oven Hell), with a variety of different pools, the bright blue **Umi Jigoku** (Sea Hell), and the red **Chi-no-Ike**, or "pond of blood." Going round the hells is a half-day excursion, best done by bus if you want to see them all.

If you find yourself suffering from *yu-atari* (hot-water fatigue), steaming, hissing, gurgling Kannawa is fascinating to wander. Endless miles of pipe, chimney, and arcane plumbing snake through narrow lanes, letting off a mist that cloaks the town and the various *ryokan, minshuku* (guesthouses), and homes that they serve.

An hour west of Beppu is the genteel resort of **Yufuin**. Set against Mount Yufu's stunning green grassy slopes, Yufuin's hot spring ryokan are smaller, quieter, and more traditional than the hot water megaplexes in Beppu. With annual movie and music festivals, Yufuin is one of the cultural hubs of Kyushu—and is in every way the antithesis of Beppu. Some of the baths were damaged in the 2016 Kumamoto earthquake, so it is best to check the state of repair before booking a ryokan. ∎

Beppu
🗺 313 D4

Visitor Information
✉ JR Beppu Station
☎ 0977/24-2838
🕐 8:30 a.m.– 5:30 p.m.
🚆 Train: From Hakata Station, Fukuoka, on JR Nippo line (2 hr. by express, 1.5 hr. by Shinkansen)
⛴ Overnight ferry from Osaka (12 hr.)

english.beppu-navi.jp

Ekimae Koto Onsen
✉ 13-14 Eki-mae
☎ 0977/21-0541
💲 $

Yufuin
🗺 313 C4

Visitor Information
✉ JR Yufuin Station
☎ 0977/84-2446
🕐 8:50 a.m.– 5:30 p.m.

www.yufuin.gr.jp

EXPERIENCE: Hot-Spring Heaven in an *Onsen*

The Japanese obsession with *onsen* (hot springs) goes back at least 1,400 years to the nation's earliest historical documents, and a dip in a bath is one of the experiences many travelers enjoy most here. For Japanese and foreigners alike, the bath is a chance to shed social barriers along with one's clothing, relax, and chat with old and newfound friends.

All but a few onsen deep in the countryside are sex segregated. The variety can be impressive: cloudy alkaline baths, tubs with aromatic herbs, scorching water straight from the source, booths with pulsing electric current running through their water to relax muscles, rocky outdoor baths in stunning gardens or edged in snow, infinity pools, and so on. There are usually a couple of saunas, too.

Visiting a bath is easy. Not everyone follows the rules exactly, but the onus is on visitors to make a good impression. Upon entering your part of the bath (see sidebar p. 25 for men's and women's symbols), take off your clothes and put them in a locker. Bathing suits are strictly not allowed, but you

can use the provided hand towels for scrubbing and modesty. Inside the bath, you'll find a row of showers and stools; take one that looks unoccupied and start scrubbing. Wash and rinse off thoroughly, then grab one of the buckets near the bath and pour a few buckets over yourself. Soap in the bath is really the only taboo for onsen, as the spa water is considered both clean and medicinal and shouldn't be contaminated.

Climbing in can be tricky: Some baths are volcano hot. Ease yourself in slowly, and avoid splashing others. If it is too hot, try another—there's usually a cooler one. Your modesty towel should stay out of the bath or folded on top of your head. If you start to overheat, take a plunge in the cold-water pool: Really,

it's exhilarating! A few rounds of hot and cold is sure to soften stiff muscles. After the bath, most people have a quick rinse under the shower and then dry off and dress in a *yukata* (light kimono) to meet friends or family in the lounge outside the baths.

If you are staying at a *ryokan* (traditional inn), it is customary to bathe before dinner, partly because the bath is less fun with a stomach full of food. Either way, don't soak too long, as the waters can be relaxing to the point of enervation.

SOME GREAT ONSEN:

- **Beppu Onsen (Kyushu, see pp. 320–321):** A huge variety of spas and strangely colored pools of boiling water
- **Dogo Onsen (Matsuyama, see pp. 299–300):** Steeped in history, the oldest bath in Japan
- **Kawayu Onsen (Tanabe, see p. 256):** Here the water bubbles up from under a river: Make your own pool in the riverbank.
- **Kinosaki Onsen (Toyooka, see p. 252):** Walk from bath to bath around the village and gorge on crabmeat.
- **Nyuto Onsen (Senboku, see p. 156):** Mixed baths for a hot-spring dip

A visitor enjoys the open-air hot springs at an Awanoyu onsen.

Kumamoto-ken

Kumamoto Prefecture lies on the west side of Kyushu, its geography dominated by the Aso-san caldera, the largest in the world. There's no escaping the mountain: Entire towns have taken root in the crater of this ancient—but still active—volcano. Kumamoto city, though modern and semi-industrial, has an excellent restored castle, Kumamoto-jo.

The imposing re-creation of Kumamoto-jo shows Japan's reverence for its past.

Although Kumamoto-ken has markedly fewer factories than Fukuoka-ken, it still suffered indiscriminate postwar industrialization. From an aesthetic viewpoint, development has proved more destructive than war in the prefectural capital, **Kumamoto.** Despite preserving few vestiges of the past, it's a pleasant city with a youthful feel (it has two of Kyushu's most important universities) and makes a perfect base for visits to other parts of Kyushu.

Kumamoto-jo is one of the city's two major sights and, though mainly a reproduction, is among Japan's finest castles. Completed in 1607, it was commissioned and designed by feudal lord Kato Kiyomasa. The walls of the castle form a perimeter of almost 8 miles (13 km) embracing 49 turrets; the garrison and private quarters took their water supply from 120 wells. Kato's skill as a military strategist was more than matched by his brilliance as an architect. The structural orientation ingeniously follows the topography of the land; the architectural feature of Japanese fortresses known as

Kumamoto
🅰 313 C4
Visitor Information
✉ JR Kumamoto Station
☎ 096/352-3743
🕐 8:30 a.m.–7 p.m.
🚆 Train: Kyushu Shinkansen from Hakata Station (40 min.); bus: from Fukuoka to Kotsu Center (2 hr.)

kumanago.jp

Kumamoto-jo (closed pending repairs)

- ✉ 1-1 Honmaru
- ☎ 096/352-5900
- 🕐 8:30 a.m.–5:30 p.m. April–Oct.; closes at 4:30 p.m. Nov.–Mar.
- 💲 $$
- 🚃 Tram: Kumamotojo-mae

Suizenji-koen

- ✉ 8-1 Suizenji-koen
- ☎ 096/383-0074
- 🕐 7:30 a.m.–6 p.m. Mar.–Oct.; 8:30 a.m.–5 p.m. Nov.–Feb.
- 💲 $

Aso-san

- 🅰 313 C4

Visitor Information

- ✉ Next to JR Aso Station
- ☎ 0967/34-1600
- 🕐 9 a.m.–5 p.m.

Aso Volcanic Museum (closed pending Mount Aso's stability)

- ✉ 1930-1 Akamizu, Aso-shi
- ☎ 0967/34-2111
- 💲 $$

musha-gaeshi (warrior-overturn), referring to the unclimbable concave shape of the massive walls supporting the keep, is regarded as reaching perfection in Kumamoto-jo, where some call it *nezumi-gaeshi*—"mouse-overturn."

Along with much of Kumamoto, the castle was damaged in a 2016 earthquake and is currently closed for repairs. See *kumanago .jp* for the latest information.

Suizenji-koen

Kumamoto's other main sight is Suizenji-koen, one of Japan's most celebrated gardens. Gentaku, a noted Buddhist monk from Kyoto, came to Kumamoto in 1632 at the behest of feudal lord Hosokawa Tadatoshi to build Suizen-ji, which included a magnificent garden. Upon Gentaku's demise, the temple was moved elsewhere, and the Hosokawas built a teahouse on the spot. Beautifully landscaped to evoke the sights most characteristic of each of the 53 stations of the old Tokaido trunk road between Edo and Kyoto, the garden features fountains and flowering shrubs, ponds studded with rocks suggesting islands, and miniature hills (one represents Fuji-san).

Mount Aso

Thirty miles (48 km) east of Kumamoto is **Aso-san,** created when the dome of a gigantic volcano collapsed during a cataclysmic eruption some 50,000 years ago. Aso-san actually embraces five cones, of which **Naka-dake** (5,223 feet/1,592 m) is the most active. The colossal caldera—believed to be the largest on Earth—is 11 miles (18 km) wide by 15 miles (25 km) long, covers an area of 98 square miles (255 sq km), and encompasses whole towns and villages.

The fertile volcanic soil has produced lush green meadows now used as pastureland for cattle and horses. The scenery in the vicinity is superb, with excellent views on the way to Naka-dake from Aso Station, especially that of lake-dotted **Kusasenri** meadow, with the intense green of **Mount Komezuka** (*komezuke* means "rice mound") rising out of it. The hill, actually a dormant volcano, gets its name from a myth about a god who scooped a chunk out of the top of a gigantic mound of rice to feed the starving population. Opposite it is the **Aso Volcanic Museum** (Aso Kazan Hakubutsu-kan), featuring a fascinating array of displays on the volcanology of Kyushu and other parts of the world.

Due to Kumamoto's 2016 earthquake, Naka-dake is currently off limits due to the possibility of further seismic activity and poor air quality. Ask at Aso Station about the latest conditions: If it is safe to venture out, there are fascinating trails around the crater edge with views down to clouds of steam billowing up from the pallid, evil-looking, gray-green lake 320 feet (100 m) below.

About 13 miles (20 km) northeast of Naka-dake, accessible by road from Aso Station, is the **Kikuchi Valley,** where the river has carved breathtaking gorges through a wooded landscape. ∎

Nagasaki-ken & Nagasaki

Occupying the northwestern corner of Kyushu, Nagasaki-ken contains some of Kyushu's cardinal historical and scenic sights. To make the most of both aspects in one go, you may want to begin in the east of the prefecture with a visit to the historical town of Shimabara, then hike around Unzen Volcanic Area, a UNESCO global geopark.

A night view of the port of Nagasaki from Mount Inasa

The prefecture's greatest draw is its capital, with its fascinating history of contacts with Europe. Nagasaki-ken includes Goto Archipelago off the west coast, famous refuge of "hidden Christians." In the east of Nagasaki-ken is the Shimabara Peninsula, noted both for the town of Shimabara on the Ariake Sea and for the scenic area around the Unzen-dake volcano.

Shimabara is an old castle town with a Christian twist, sitting at the foot of very active Unzen-dake. After the closure of the country to foreigners to limit Christian influence, a campaign of oppression was waged against the Japanese converts, particularly in Shimabara, where the European missionaries had made great inroads. The Christian *daimyo* was removed, and his replacement taxed the populace heavily, torturing those who could not pay and enslaving many to build **Shimabara-jo**. The Shimabara Rebellion boiled up in 1637, with 37,000 Christian peasants and samurai attacking Shimabara-jo. They failed to take the castle and retreated to the unoccupied Hara-jo, where they were besieged by a force three times larger for three months before being annihilated to the very last child. Shimabara-jo

Shimabara

🗺 313 B4

Visitor Information

✉ Shimabara ferry terminal

☎ 0957/62-3986

🕐 8:30 a.m.– 5:30 p.m.

🚆 Train: JR Nagasaki to Isahaya, transfer to Shimabara Railway to Shimabara Gaiko Station

⛴ Ferry: From Kumamoto (1 hr.), high-speed ferry (30 min.)

visit-nagasaki.com

Shimabara-jo

✉ 1-1183-1 Jonai

☎ 0957/62-4766

🕐 9 a.m.–5:30 p.m.

💲 $

🚃 Shimabara line: Shimabara

shimabarajou.com

Unzen-dake

🔺 313 B4

Visitor Information

✉ Unzen Tourist Association, 320 Unzen, Obama-cho, Unzen-shi (near Unzen Post Office)

☎ 0957/73-3434

🕐 9 a.m.–5 p.m.

🚃 Shimatetsu Bus from JR Isahaya to Unzen Office stop (80 min.)

unzen.org

Mount Unzen Disaster Memorial Hall

✉ 1-1 Heisei-machi

☎ 0957/65-5555

🕐 9 a.m.–6 p.m.

💲 $$

🚃 Bus: Arina-iriguchi-mae from Shimabara ferry terminal

www.udmh.or.jp

was demolished during the 1870s, though the walls and impressive original main gate remain. Rebuilt in 1964 with modern techniques (there now being a shortage of Christian slaves in the area), the keep houses a **museum** featuring ceramics, armor, and exhibits about the rebellion and the Christians in Kyushu. Northwest of the castle is the district of **Teppo-cho,** with its picturesque thatched and whitewashed **samurai houses** (two are open to the public). The stone channels that once served as the water supply, like the town's canals, are fed by mountain springs highly prized for their purity.

Other local springs are of the hot variety—the area surrounding the ferocious volcano **Unzen-dake** is hyperactively volcanic. The nearby town of Unzen has such a proliferation of volcanic "hells" and springs that the streets are festooned with pipes and plumbing, feeding the spas and hissing and bubbling with steam.

The magma percolating beneath Unzen-dake bubbled upward in a major eruption in 1792, triggering violent earthquakes that killed some 15,000 people; most of them were victims of 50-foot (15 m) tidal waves that thundered in from the sea. Today the most volatile cone of Unzen-dake is **Fugen-dake** (4,580 feet/1,396 m), which lies 5 miles (8 km) southwest of central Shimabara. Fugen-dake began to erupt again in November 1990. The lava dome collapsed the following month, leading to a lava explosion in

June 1991 that killed 43 people, including a group of French and American volcanologists. Intermittent eruptions continued until 1994, damaging or destroying some 2,000 buildings in the process. Some of the buried structures in the **Sembongi** district to the west of Shimabara city and along the **Mizunashi-gawa** ("waterless river") have been preserved as an unusual tourist attraction; only their roofs protruded from the mud and lava. The nearby **Mount Unzen Disaster Memorial Hall** commemorates the eruption and its devastation. As Japan's youngest mountain, the lava dome that blistered atop Fugen-dake has been called Heisei Shin-zan

INSIDER TIP:

When visiting Teppo-cho, look into the stone channels that snake through the town: You'll see some of the 1,500 carp that lazily swim along the streets.

—KENNY LING
National Geographic contributor

(Heisei New Mountain). The eruption was officially declared over in 1996; depending on the volcano's activity level, however, some hiking trails around Fugen-dake may be closed. Check with the visitor information centers in Nagasaki or Unzen before heading for the hills.

Statues line the Confucian shrine at Nagasaki.

Nagasaki City

As the historical point of entry for both European trade and Christianity in Japan, Nagasaki has a long and fascinating history. Many sights evoke the city's historical links with the rest of the world, despite the devastation of the atomic bombing in 1945.

On August 9, 1945, three days after the destruction of Hiroshima, the B-29 bomber *Bockscar* sighted Nagasaki through the clouds and dropped its lethal payload. The atomic bomb detonated above Urakami, a Catholic neighborhood, destroying its targeted arms factories, as well as the largest church in Asia, the Urakami Cathedral. Up to 75,000 people were killed instantly or died from their burns within days, and an equal number were irradiated and burned but survived.

The northern sector, home of the Christian community, was the most extensively destroyed. Some of the old buildings farther south were spared, and others were rebuilt. "Restoration of the city has been remarkable," declared a guidebook compiled only five years after the catastrophe, "and it appears to be almost as prosperous as before the war."

Today, unless you visit the Atomic Bomb Museum and Peace Park near the hypocenter of the blast, it is hard to imagine that the bombing ever happened, both for the lack of remaining damage and the tranquility of modern Nagasaki, surrounded by green, rolling hills and overlooking a deep bay. A visit to **Hypocenter Park** (see sidebar p. 329), which now stands on the site of the bomb blast, is a sobering and heart-wrenching experience.

South of the Peace Park is the **Nagasaki Atomic Bomb Museum** (Nagasaki Genbaku Shiryokan), which opened in 1996. Burned and twisted debris from the blast, along with horrific video presentations and translated accounts written by the children who lived through the blast, make this one of the most poignant and terrifying museums anywhere in the world.

The wall clock with its hands fused at 11:02 a.m.—the exact

Nagasaki
◭ 313 B4
Visitor Information
✉ JR Nagasaki Station
☎ 095/823-3631
🕐 8 a.m.–8 p.m.
🚆 Train: From Hakata Station, Fukuoka, to JR Nagasaki Station (2 hr.)
travel.at-nagasaki .jp/en

Hypocenter Park
🚆 Tram: Matsuyama-machi

Nagasaki Atomic Bomb Museum
✉ 7-8 Hirano-machi
☎ 095/844-1231
🕐 8:30 a.m.–5:30 p.m. Sept.–April; 8:30 a.m.–6:30 p.m. May–Aug.
💲 $
🚆 Tram: Hamaguchi-machi

Urakami Cathedral

☎ 095/844-1777

✉ 1-79 Motoomachi

🕑 9 a.m.–5 p.m.

🚋 Tram: Matsuyama-machi

Inasayama-koen

🕑 9 a.m.–10 p.m.

💲 $$$, park free; cable car access

🚋 Bus: Ropeway-mae, then cable car

moment when the bomb detonated on that day—is now a Nagasaki emblem. Historical and political arguments about the necessity of the bombings to prevent further casualties feel shallow once you've seen the grief it wrought: Over decades, many suffered radiation-related illness along with the stigma of being a "polluted" survivor.

The nearby **Nagasaki National Peace Memorial Hall for the Atomic Bomb Victims** (tel 095/814-0055, www.peace -nagasaki.go.jp, 8:30 a.m.–5:30 p.m.) enshrines the names of the 150,000 registered victims in a solemn, skylit hall. It's a quiet place to emotionally process the Bomb Museum's exhibits. Should you feel the desire to pray for the future of humanity, **Urakami Cathedral,** once the largest church in East Asia but almost

totally vaporized by the bomb, has been rebuilt and is five minutes north of the museums.

To get a sense of scale and see modern Nagasaki reborn, head to the top of 1,080-foot (330 m) **Inasayama-koen,** on the other side of the Urakami-gawa from the city. The peak is reached via cable car; the panorama over Nagasaki Harbor and the East China Sea from the observation platform is breathtaking, especially when the lights come on around the harbor.

Nagasaki's Central & Southern Sectors

The city's heart and most of its sights lie in the south. Just a short distance north of Nagasaki railway station is **26 Martyrs Memorial** (Nihon Niju-roku Seijin Junkyochi). The bronze bas-relief was erected in 1962, marking the passage of one

Hypocenter Park: Site of Nagasaki's atomic bomb obliteration

Hypocenter Park: Nagasaki's Ground Zero

In Hypocenter Park, a simple block of black marble marks the precise spot where the A-bomb exploded on August 19, 1945. The park also displays relics assembled from nearby, including all that remains of the original Urakami Cathedral: a section of brick wall and three blackened, eroded statues, one of them headless. To the north of Hypocenter Park is the **Peace Park** (Heiwa-koen), locus of several memorials donated to Nagasaki by various countries.

hundred years since Nagasaki's 26 Christian martyrs were canonized by Pope Pius IX.

Of particular interest is the adjacent museum, with exhibits relating to the history of Christianity in Japan. The country's "hidden Christians" concealed such items as religious scrolls and prayer books, as well as statuettes of the Virgin Mary disguised as the bodhisattva Kannon. The fate of the Nagasaki martyrs is thought to be connected to the *San Felipe*, a Spanish galleon wrecked on the Shikoku coast in 1596. After being rescued, its captain boasted about the might of Spain; her many overseas conquests, he claimed, had been launched by armies marching over ground prepared by Christian missionaries and their

converts. When this reached the ears of *daimyo* Toyotomi Hideyoshi (1536–1598), who was already growing suspicious of Christian designs, he had 26 Christians—including six Jesuit friars and three children—arrested in Kansai and forcibly marched all the way to Nagasaki in midwinter. There they were crucified on Nishi-zaka Hill on February 5, 1597, as a warning to others.

The curious **Fukusai-ji,** some 550 yards (500 m) southwest of the memorial, is one of four temples that were built by Chinese in the Ming-dynasty style in the 1620s; the original temple burned down after the atomic bombing. Although the turtle is a symbol of longevity in Japan as much as it is in China, that hardly justifies rebuilding Fukusai-ji to look like one, with a 60-foot (18 m) effigy of the Buddhist deity Kannon standing on its back. A bell sounds at 11:02 a.m. daily to commemorate the atomic bombing.

Opened in 2005, the **Nagasaki Museum of History and Culture** holds some 48,000 items detailing the city's role as Japan's sole window to the outside world. The theme here is "overseas exchange," focusing on trade with China, Korea, and the Netherlands, but another highlight is a reconstruction of the Edo-period Nagasaki Magistrate's Office featuring reenactments of trials on weekends.

Continuing east, you come to **Suwa-jinja,** originally built in 1629 by the feudal government to stem the growing influence of Christianity. Its 277 steps lead up to a grand

Peace Park
- 🚋 Tram: Matsuyama-machi

Fukusai-ji
- ✉ 2-56 Chikugo-machi
- ☎ 095/823-2663
- 🕐 8 a.m.–6 p.m.
- 💲 $
- 🚋 JR Nagasaki line: Nagasaki

Nagasaki Museum of History and Culture
- ✉ 1-1-1 Tateyama
- ☎ 095/818-8366
- 🕐 8:30 a.m.– 7 p.m., closed some 3rd Mon.
- 💲 $$
- 🚋 Tram: Sakura-machi

nmhc.jp

Suwa-jinja
- ✉ 18-15 Kaminishiyama-machi
- ☎ 095/824-0445
- 🕐 Open 24 hr.
- 🚋 Tram: Suwajinja-mae

The Silence of Japan's Christians

The release of Martin Scorsese's film *Silence*, based on Endo Shusaku's novel of the same name, has renewed interest in the persecution and stalwart faith of the Japanese Christians who worshipped in secret for two centuries.

Travelers interested in a Christian pilgrimage should start at the 26 Martyr's Memorial, Oura Church, and Urakami Cathedral in Nagasaki, then rent a car to Sotome, the village north of Nagasaki where many Christians hid and the basis for Tomogi village in the story. The area is dotted with churches and memorials to the secretive practices of the faithful.

Farther north, Hirado is notable as the first port open to foreign traders and missionaries; it is also home to St. Francis Xavier Memorial Church and a large Christian population. Adjacent Ikitsuki island has the excellent Shima no Yakata museum about the living tradition of the "hidden Christians" that endures throughout the Goto Archipelago to the west.

Shimabara's Christian population was nearly wiped out, but important sites remain. The boiling waters of Unzen hot spring's "hells" were used to torture missionaries and their flock, Shimabara-jo stands testament to Christian slavery, and the ruins of Hara-jo are evocative of those starved and slain here.

Sofuku-ji

- 7-5 Kajiya-machi
- 095/823-2645
- 8 a.m.–5 p.m.
- $
- Tram: Shokakujishita

Dejima

- 6-1 Dejima-machi
- 095/821-7200
- 8 a.m.–6 p.m.
- $$
- Tram: Dejima

www.city.nagasaki.lg.jp/dejima

bronze *torii* gateway in front of the shrine's main buildings, which date from the late 19th century. Nagasaki's most important and popular shrine, Suwa-jinja is the focus of the city's annual O-Kunchi Festival in October. Centering on a Dragon Dance, the festival parade reflects a strong Chinese influence.

South of Suwa-jinja, walk alongside the picturesque canal of the **Nakashima-gawa.** The street parallel to the canal on the east is Teramachi-dori. It contains a number of temples (hence the name) and is a pleasant area for strolling. The most famous of Nagasaki's four Chinese temples, **Sofuku-ji** to the southeast, was built by the Chinese monk Chonen in 1629 for the benefit of Nagasaki's large population of Chinese from Fujian. Displaying architecture of the late Ming period now rare in southern China itself, the Main Hall and Second Gate are National Treasures. The precinct features a

giant cauldron used to cook food for the starving during a famine in 1681.

West from Sofuku-ji toward the harbor is the onetime Dutch trading enclave of **Dejima,** a fan-shaped islet artificially fashioned from land reclaimed in Nagasaki Bay. Originally built to intern Portuguese traders and prevent the spread of Christianity, Dejima became the only permitted port of trade with the outside world after the Portuguese were driven out. Dutch traders from the East India Company dealing in books, sugar, pepper, and finery such as velvet and glass replaced the Portuguese missionaries, but contact between the island and the city was highly regulated to prevent the spread of Christianity. Subsequent land reclamation projects have made the restored "island" totally landlocked, save the narrow Nakashima-gawa running along its perimeter, but extensive work has added 16 restored buildings to the surviving

Protestant seminary, International Club, and stone warehouses. Most interesting perhaps is the Head Clerk's Quarters, which has displays on "Dutch Studies"—the Western science Japan received through imported Dutch books.

On Minami-yamate Hill, in the south of the city and with a spectacular view over the bay, **Glover Garden** (Guraba-en)—actually a sizable park—contains the earliest wooden Western-style buildings (dating from the 19th century) still standing in Japan. As such, it is probably Nagasaki's most popular tourist attraction. Originally sited

with verandas and shutters in typical Far Eastern colonial style, betraying the fact that their occupants had mainly been in China before coming to Japan. **Glover Mansion** (Kyu-Guraba Jutaku) is the only one that has always stood on this spot. It was built in 1863 for Thomas Glover (1838–1911), an enterprising Scotsman who arrived in Nagasaki in 1859 and spent the rest of his life in Japan. After running a coal mine, Glover built Japan's first modern shipyard (later operated by Mitsubishi). Also an arms dealer, he supplied weapons to the Satsuma clan,

Glover Garden

✉ 8-1 Minami Yamate-machi
☎ 095/822-8223
🕐 8 a.m.–6 p.m., until 9:30 p.m. in summer
💲 $$
🚃 Tram: Oura-Tenshudo-shita

glover-garden.jp

![The Glover Mansion, surrounded by the impressive Glover Garden]

The Glover Mansion, surrounded by the impressive Glover Garden

in other parts of the city, most of the houses were dismantled and reassembled here; among them is the **No. 2 Dock House** (Kyu-Mitsubishi Dai-ni Dokku Hausu), moved from the Mitsubishi Shipyard on the bay, and noteworthy **merchants' homes,** including the Walker, Ringer, and Alt houses. The buildings are largely of wood,

which overthrew the shogunate. Glover defied the ban on travel for Japanese, helping several young men escape to study in London; among them in 1862 was Ito Hirobumi, who later became Japan's first prime minister. Most importantly, Glover was involved in the establishment of Kirin, brewer of (probably!) Japan's

Confucian Shrine & Historical Museum of China

✉ 10-36 Oura-machi

☎ 095/824-4022

🕐 8:30 a.m.–5 p.m.

💲 $$

🚋 Tram: Oura-Tenshudo-shita

finest beer, although some in Sapporo might counter that claim.

The Japanese like to associate the Glover Mansion with Puccini's tragic opera *Madama Butterfly;* a marble relief of Puccini graces the house, and a statue of Japanese diva Miura Tamaki stands on the hill above it. In those days, temporary marriage contracts between foreigners and locals (usually geisha) legitimized relationships far too wittingly carnal to prompt a suicide. Glover's relationship with a local woman—unlike that of Lieutenant

INSIDER TIP:

If you're drinking a Kirin beer in Japan, raise a toast to the Scottish entrepreneur Thomas Glover: The famous moustache on the brand's mythical beast is said to resemble his.

—PERRIN LINDELAUF
National Geographic author

Pinkerton, the betrayer of the Nagasaki heroine of the opera—was permanent.

In the same area stands **Oura Catholic Church** (Oura Tenshu-do). Built by French priest Bernard Petitjean for the foreign community in 1865, this charming church commemorates Nagasaki's 26 Christian martyrs

Kirin Lager, as Thomas Glover would have liked it

and was the country's first in the Gothic style. It immediately attracted the hidden Christians, who came out for the first time in 200 years—albeit taking measures of extreme caution, for Japanese were forbidden to practice the religion until 1873. The meeting between the group and Father Petitjean is captured in a bronze bas-relief in the courtyard. Designated a National Treasure, the church is much admired for its wooden architecture and its fine stained-glass windows.

The **Confucian Shrine** (Koshi-byo), notable for its distinctive bright yellow roof tiles and rich red walls visible from the Dutch Slope, was originally built in 1893 by and for Nagasaki's Chinese community to honor the great sage Confucius. Torched in the conflagration that swept the city after the A-bomb, the shrine was rebuilt over an eight-year period and completed in 1967, then extensively refurbished in 1983.

Neither this history nor the marble statues of Confucius and his 72 disciples that stand around the courtyard make this shrine unique: Built and maintained by Chinese and kept under the jurisdiction of the Chinese embassy in Tokyo, Koshi-byo is officially a little corner of China.

The adjacent **Historical Museum of China** (Chugoku Rekidai Hakubutsukan) is part of the Koshi-byo complex. It is maintained by its counterpart in Beijing and may contain up to 80 national cultural treasures from China at any given time. ■

Yakushima

World Heritage–listed Yakushima island lies at the head of the Okinawan archipelago. Jutting abruptly from the sea, this mountainous island receives massive rainfall and is home to a lush semitropical forest, the innermost recesses of which have gone untouched by loggers and hold trees as old as Japan's recorded history. The verdant forest was the inspiration for animator Miyazaki Hayao's *Princess Mononoke* and the film's theme of nature's conflict with humanity.

The Jomon-sugi, Yakushima's oldest cryptomeria tree *(Cryptomeria japonica)*

Though the island is wooded, it is far from pristine, as centuries of forestry have shaped its history. The stone staircases used today by hikers were laid by Edo-period foresters who climbed deep into the mountains to fell trees or to harvest the strips of cedar bark used to roof Shinto shrines. Massive stumps from trees cut down centuries ago can still be seen here and there. It is the deepest part of the mountains, however, that remains largely as it has for millennia. Near the island's center lie several massive cedars, the goal points for most day trips. Each *yaku-sugi* (Yakushima cedar) is more than 1,000 years old, and the largest, the Jomon-sugi, named after

Japan's earliest historical period, has been roughly dated at more than 2,000 years old.

Getting to these ancient trees means a long day trip with a very early start; if you have more time, the three-day traverse of the island's main peaks is more pleasant and considerably quieter, as most visitors to Yakushima are package-tour day-hikers. The towns of Miyanoura and Onoaida Onsen are well equipped for hikers, with gear rental—especially rainwear—and guides available, although both may be difficult to come by during the Golden Week high season (first week of May). This season should be avoided as the narrow boardwalks become too crowded for most foreign nature lovers. ∎

Yakushima

⚠ 313 B1–C1

Visitor Information

✉ 823-1
Miyanoura, exit
to hydrofoil
terminal
building

☎ 0997/42-1019

🕐 9 a.m.–5:30 p.m.

Yakushima Airport

Visitor Information

✉ Outside the
airport

☎ 0997/49-4010

🕐 8:30 a.m.–6 p.m.

⛴ Hydrofoil from
Kagoshima
to Miyanoura
(100 min.); ferry
to Miyanoura
(4 hr.)

✈ Flights from
Kagoshima
(35 min.)

More Places to Visit on Kyushu

Pottery Towns of Saga-ken

Arita lies in a valley surrounded by hills that yield clay. The townscape is characterized by dozens of chimneys rising from its kilns. In addition to these, Arita has a cluster of substantial museums. **Kyushu Ceramic Museum** (Saga-kenritsu Kyushu Toji Bunkakan; *3100-1 Toshakuotsu, Aritamachi, tel 0955/ 43-3681, 9 a.m.–5 p.m., closed Mon.*) is highly recommended for anyone interested in the history and development of the craft over the island. Many kilns are open to the public; the most prestigious—**Kakiemon, Imaemon** (run by the descendants of the Nabeshima potters),

and **Iwao Taizan**—have museums containing fine collections of old Imari ware.

Nearby **Imari,** the site of what were called the "secret kilns" in the early days, is now occupied by **Nabeshima Hanyo-koen.** This is a kind of theme park, incorporating the ruins of the Nabeshima potteries and focusing on all there is to know about Imari pottery then and now, as well as on the working life of enslaved Korean potters. The Okawachicho area, the center of Imari's ceramic activities, still boasts some 20 kilns. Imari has a number of museums containing not only ceramic collections but also potters working on

Arita's Pottery History

Returning from ultimately futile attempts to conquer Korea in the 16th century, Toyotomi Hideyoshi's troops captured and enslaved thousands of Koreans, among them prized potters sent to work in Arita in northern Kyushu. Several, including the great Ri Sampei, later took Japanese citizenship. Nabeshima, feudal lords of the old province of Hizen, held their potters prisoner, which kept professional secrets from rivals; exclusive and reclusive, the Nabeshima potteries dominated the industry until the end of the feudal era. The first Arita ceramics are said to have been created by Ri Sampei in 1616, following his discovery in the local area of kaolin—the exceptionally light clay needed to produce the hardness and whiteness of porcelain.

In 1675 the Korean potters moved from Arita to Okawachiyama, a district of the nearby coastal town of Imari. The finished goods were exported from the port of Imari, which gave its name to this kind of pottery. The earliest variety of Imari ware was blue and white, but the Japanese ceramicist Sakaida Kakiemon

introduced new polychrome glazing techniques. Applied as an overglaze enamel, the brightly colored designs of Imari were inspired by Japanese screen paintings, textile design, and lacquerware. Imari ware was exported from Dejima (Nagasaki) by the Dutch East India Company and soon caught the eye of the West for its exquisite design and quality. Influenced by Chinese pottery, Imari in turn had an impact on ceramics in Holland (Delft), England, and Germany.

Imari's popularity declined during the 19th century, when the designs became overly ornate and were applied by transfer rather than hand-painting. Kakiemon porcelain, made by Sakaida's descendants and featuring delicate enamel painting on an immaculate white background, was considered the most refined. However, potteries in Okawachiyama and Arita continued to turn out traditional Imari designs, including hand-painted ones—as indeed they still do. Declared Intangible Cultural Assets by the government, the descendants of the Kakiemon and Nabeshima pottery families are still working today.

the premises, notably the **Imari and Arita Ceramic Industry Hall** (*Hei 221-2 Okawachi-cho, Imari-shi, tel 0955/22-6333*).

The other great Saga pottery town is **Karatsu,** 15 miles (25 km) due north of Imari. Originally based on Yi ware from Korea, Karatsu ware emerged as the tea ceremony gained popularity during the Momoyama period (1573–1603). Consisting of basic shapes and deliberately (if deceptively) rough-hewn, this type of ware was considered ideal for the tea ceremony. Still much sought after by tea lovers, Karatsu ware displays brown- and ocher-colored glazes sometimes decorated with geometric shapes, or plants and flowers executed with bold, simple brushstrokes. Kilns are open to the public; check times with the visitor information center.

INSIDER TIP:

Try the Japanese dessert *shirokuma* (literally "polar bear") in its birthplace of Kagoshima. It's made from shaved ice flavored with condensed milk, colorful agar cubes, fruits, and beans; it comes in sizes from large servings at restaurants to small cups from convenience stores.

—HIROMI ISHII
*National Geographic Japan
senior staff editor*

Like many former feudal towns, Karatsu rebuilt its vanished stronghold, **Karatsu-jo** (*8-1 Higashi Jonai, tel 0955/72-5697, $*), during the 1960s. Perched by the sea, the castle contains an interesting museum devoted to local archaeology and pottery. ▲ 313 B4–B5 **Visitor Information** ☎ Imari: 0955/23-3479; Karatsu: 0955/72-4963

Sakura-jima erupts near Kagoshima City.

Kagoshima City

With a pleasant climate and Mount Sakura-jima, its very own Vesuvius, smoking across the bay, vibrant Kagoshima is known as the "Naples of Japan." Of vital historical importance, Kagoshima saw the arrival of St. Francis Xavier and the Portuguese in the 16th century. It was also the domain of the Satsuma clan, instrumental in overthrowing the shogunate in 1867. The city's most famous hero is Saigo Takamori: Having successfully fought to oust the old regime, he later changed his mind and met his demise at Kumamoto-jo during the Satsuma Rebellion he instigated in 1877. Badly damaged in World War II, Kagoshima has few vestiges of the past. A couple of notable Western-style buildings from the 1860s stand in the north of town, and the **Museum of the Meiji Restoration** (Ishin Furusato-kan; *23-1 Kajiya-cho, Kagoshima-shi, tel 099/239-7700, 9 a.m.– 5 p.m., $*) has good exhibits on the revolution, but limited English signage.

Kagoshima is popular for its scenic views of Sakura-jima. Ferries run at 15-minute intervals; from the ferry terminal, you can board a bus to visit the volcano. If conditions near the summit are safe, Sakura-jima opens hiking trails that approach the crater, notably up to the Yunohira Observation Point. 313 C2 **Visitor Information** JR Kagoshimachuo Station 099/253-2500 (8 a.m.–8 p.m.)

Miyazaki

Mountainous Miyazaki-ken, 76 percent of which is forested, is refreshingly unspoiled. Attracting Japanese holidaymakers eager for a fix of tropicana with its avenues of palm trees, however, **Miyazaki** presents a rather different picture. Its huge Seagaia resort complex is famous for an enormous leisure facility incorporating golf courses, a spa and *onsen,* and luxury accommodations.

While **Miyazaki-jingu** is revered for its

link with Shinto creation myths, the region itself shows some of the earliest signs of habitation in Japan. Dating as far back as the fourth century, the 311 burial mounds at Saitobaro are one of Japan's most important archaeological sites.

Obi, near Nichinan city, is an old castle town with several old samurai and merchant houses. Its castle is partially restored as a museum depicting the lifestyle of Japan's last feudal lords.

Among Miyazaki's natural assets is **Kirishima-Yaku Parkland,** which includes Kirishima-yama, with 23 peaks. Here Japan's highest *onsen* resort soaks hikers' sore muscles in summer. One of the prefecture's many coastal resorts is **Aoshima,** known for its beaches—among the best for surfing in the country. 313 C3 **Visitor Information** JR Miyazaki Station 0985/22-6469

Shinto Creation Myths: Dirty Dancing 'til Dawn

Japan's oldest legends speak of a spat between godly siblings: Susano-o and Amaterasu. Fighting over the heavens, Susano-o went on a rampage when he lost; Amaterasu fled the chaos and hid in a cave, blocking it with a huge rock and shutting away the light of the sun from the world. All of the gods gathered and pleaded for her to come out, but to no avail. Finally, one deity decided to perform a bawdy dance, drawing hoots of laughter from the assembled gods and arousing the curiosity of Amaterasu, who came out and restored light to mankind. The caves where Amaterasu hid exist today at Amano Iwato-jinja in Takachiho, Miyazaki Prefecture. The goddess's cave can be seen across the river from within the shrine, and you can climb down into the cave where the gods gathered. Takachiho-jinja puts on night dances that reenact this story every Saturday through the winter, but don't expect any odd solar occurrences at the ribald dance moves.

Okinawa-ken, subtropical archipelago of Ryukyu-shoto with white sands, turquoise seas, and a unique culture

Okinawa & the Ryukyu Archipelago

Miyako Island, Okinawa

Okinawa & the Ryukyu Archipelago

Too far away to be on the itinerary of most visitors to Japan, Okinawa-ken is a destination worthy of consideration in its own right and a firm favorite with mainland Japanese sun-worshippers, water sports enthusiasts, and outdoor fanatics. History and culture make this Japan at its most un-Japanese; it is also Japan at its most exotic.

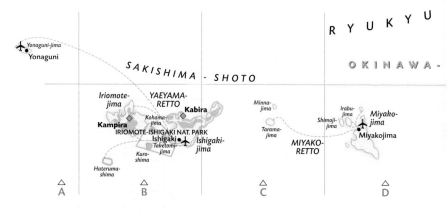

Basking in an annual mean temperature of 75°F (24°C) and lying at the same latitude as Miami and the Bahamas, Okinawa-ken is renowned for coral islands, year-round hibiscus flowers, and turquoise-blue seas. Forty-seven of its 160 or so islands, known as the Ryukyu-shoto, are inhabited. The largest is the main island of Okinawa Honto, which includes the prefectural capital of Naha. The main island saw the worst fighting during World War II and many memorials dot its southern end, commemorating the fallen.

Some 200 miles (320 km) southwest of Okinawa, the Miyako group centers on Miyako-jima, known for its spectacular beaches and the old town of Hirara. The Yaeyama Archipelago 60 miles (100 km) southwest includes Iriomote-jima, renowned for possessing Japan's only real jungle, and Yonaguni-jima, the nation's westernmost island, which lies only about 60 miles (100 km) east of Taiwan.

The Okinawans, primarily of Japanese origin, are thought to have migrated from the Japanese mainland. Virtually incomprehensible to other Japanese, their dialect is believed to be rooted in languages spoken in Japan more than a millennium ago. The Ryukyu islanders were seafarers and traders; a vital trading bridge between Japan and Asia from the 14th century onward, their kingdom reached its zenith in the 16th century, when it was invaded by the Japanese, then taxed, exploited, and controlled.

Following World War II, the U.S. military controlled the islands and returned them to the Japanese in 1972 on the condition that bases would remain. Fully 25,000 American service members live here, a source of controversy with locals. The vast amount of land that the bases take up, the noise from helicopters, and the sense of being colonized are the main complaints, but the bases also provide numerous jobs and an international atmosphere. Accordingly, the islands have a scintillating cultural diversity, the American presence mixed with historical influences from China,

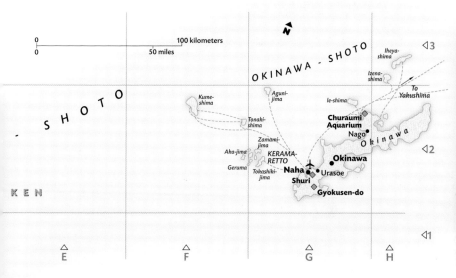

Area of map detail

Tokyo

pineapples, and fishing, Okinawa was long Japan's poorest prefecture, but today, tourism and the service industry make up 87 percent of GDP. Air and ferry services run between the islands and the mainland; all are interconnected by ferry and the larger islands by air. The islands are best seen from March through May. From June to October, typhoons typically hit Okinawa; although rarely lasting long, the storms may close airports. In the rainy season (tsuyu), from late May to June, expect downpours. ∎

Taiwan, and Indonesia. Traditional Okinawan textiles—the beautiful, brightly patterned *bingata* are the best known—are strikingly similar to the batik cloth of Java. The Indonesian connection is evident, too, in Okinawan music, which is based on a scale closer to the Javanese than the Japanese. Okinawa has several traditional dance forms; *eisa,* the most famous, is performed during the Okinawan equivalent of the Japanese O-Bon festival (see p. 280).

The local architecture blends Japanese with Ming-dynasty Chinese elements. The roofs of Shuri-jo in Naha and the ceramic dragons winding over them testify to this.

With an economy based on sugarcane,

NOT TO BE MISSED:

Completing your tour of Japan's castles at the exotic Shuri-jo   341–342

The tubing waves of Okinawa   342

Ishigaki's old villages and traditional crafts   348–349

Jungle kayaking and hiking on Iriomote-jima   349–350

Stargazing on Yonaguni-jima and Hateruma-jima   350

Naha

Naha, originally a trading port for the Ryukyu kingdom, benefited from trade and grew such that it was designated the capital of the Ryukyu Domain when the Japanese government dissolved the kingdom in 1872. Almost totally destroyed in 1945, the town recovered quickly during the U.S. occupation and is now a vibrant international city.

Shuri-jo's wall: The castle was designated a World Heritage site in 2000.

Naha

◭ 339 G2

Visitor Information

✉ Naha Airport

☏ 098/857-6884

🕓 9 a.m.–9 p.m.

okinawastory.jp

Tsuboya Pottery Museum

✉ 1-9-32 Tsuboya

☏ 098/862-3761

🕓 10 a.m.–6 p.m., closed Mon.

💲 $

🚉 Monorail: Makishi

Much of modern Naha's shape was made by the bulldozers of U.S. forces as they cut through the rubble from the "typhoon of steel" that was unleashed during the Battle of Okinawa. Running eastward from the town center to Makishi Station, **Kokusai-dori** (International Street) is the main artery. Once called Naha's "Miracle Mile" due to its rapid recovery after the war, the street is a dense jumble of department stores, hotels, boutiques, army-surplus stores, souvenir shops, restaurants, bars, *pachinko* parlors, and night clubs.

Halfway down Kokusai-dori the shopping options become more reminiscent of an Asian bazaar as covered arcades branch off to the south. Called **Ichiba-dori** and **Heiwa-dori,** these markets serve tourists and the locals with tropical fruit stands and goofy t-shirt shops among the clothing stores and housewares shops. Both lead to the colorful **Makishi Kosetsu Ichiba**—the Makishi food market. Vastly different from its typical mainland Japanese counterparts, the stores here stock cans of Spam, fluorescent tropical fish, and whole pig faces. It makes for fascinating browsing and a good introduction to the local cuisine, which heavily features pork and seafood. Southeast of the arcades is **Tsuboya,** a traditional Okinawan pottery district since the 17th century, where there are still some narrow lanes and older houses. Visit the potteries and kilns or **Tsuboya Pottery Museum.** Once purely utilitarian, Okinawan pottery consisted mainly of jars and pots; the repertoire has now been broadened to include attractive saké flasks and *shisa* (lion figurines).

For the full range of Okinawa's crafts, stop by the **Naha City Traditional Arts and Crafts Center** (Dento Kogeikan), which has displays on Okinawan ceramics and textiles, as well as hands-on workshops to make something in the local style, from blown glass to shisa statues. If you aren't up to trying your hand, you can still watch the pros plying their trades.

There is no shortage of action after nightfall in Naha. With all provinces of pleasure from restaurants to raunch, **Makishi** and **Maejima** districts boast a massive concentration of bars full of locals, American Marines and mainland tourists, all putting back copious amounts of Orion Beer and *awamori* (see p. 346). On a more sober note, traditional performing arts are presented weekly at the **Kenritsu Kyodo Theater** (Kenritsu Kyodo Gekijo), near Asahibashi Bridge.

Some 1.2 miles (2 km) beyond the city's eastern edge is **Shuri,** the old capital of the Ryukyu kingdom, famous for **Shuri-jo,** the region's prime tourist destination. The castle was used as the Japanese Army headquarters during World War II, and while you can still see the cave entrance to the former headquarters just below the main gates, the castle was bombed flat in the Battle of Okinawa in 1945. Afterwards, only

Naha City Traditional Arts and Crafts Center

- ✉ Tenbusu Naha 2F, 3-2-10 Makishi
- ☎ 098/868-7866
- 🕐 9 a.m.–6 p.m.
- 💲 $ (exhibits), $$$$ (craft experience)
- 🚉 Monorail: Makishi

kogeikan.jp

Shurji-jo

- ✉ 1-2 Kinjo-cho, Shuri
- ☎ 098/886-2020
- 🕐 8:30 a.m.–7 p.m. April–June, Oct.–Nov.; closes at 8 p.m. July–Sept.; closes at 6 p.m. Dec.–Mar.
- 💲 $$
- 🚉 Monorail: Shurijo

oki-park.jp/shurijo

NEED TO KNOW

Reaching Okinawa

A-Line Ferry (*aline-ferry.com*) connects Okinawa with the mainland by sea from Kobe, Osaka, and Kagoshima, but most visitors fly. ANA (*ana.co.jp*) and Japan's other airlines run flights from airports across the country, and major East Asian airports connect to Naha as well. Within the islands a mix of short-hop flights and high speed ferries link the islands together, though you'll need to fly to Ishigaki Airport to reach the southernmost Yaeyama Archipelago.

Getting Around

With Naha's short monorail the only rail service in Okinawa, you'll need a combination of buses, taxis, or rental bicycles to get around. Renting a car is more attractive here than anywhere else in Japan, particularly on smaller islands that are still too big to cycle. You'll need an international driver's license and a little Japanese ability to book a car (or some help from the locals).

The smallest reef islands, such as Taketomi-jima and Hateruma-jima, are pleasant to see by rental bicycle.

the massive stone walls, including the **Kankaimon gate,** were still standing, albeit heavily damaged. One gate of the former shrine on the compound remains intact, but everything else was reduced to rubble. The ornate Chinese-style **Shureimon** entry gate was reconstructed in 1958 and is now a symbol of Okinawa. One of the most ambitious restoration projects ever undertaken in Japan, Shuri-jo was completely rebuilt in 1992. Using surviving 18th-century plans and images from art pieces, restorers were able to reconstruct the main castle buildings as they appeared the 1700s, to the best of their knowledge. The main **Seiden Hall,** originally used for royal state ceremonies, is the most photographed building on Okinawa, but the whole compound is a masterpiece of restoration. Most interesting is the balance between the two buildings flanking the Seiden Hall. The **Hokuden Hall** on the left, done in Chinese style, was devoted to

judicial matters and housed agents of the Chinese government while Ryukyu was a vassal kingdom, whereas the **Nanden Hall** on the right, built in mainland Japanese style, was devoted to officers from Satsuma (Kagoshima Prefecture), who ruled Ryukyu from behind the titular king.

After the 1868 restoration of the Meiji Emperor (see p. 41), the new government decided to change Ryukyu's ambiguous status as a region under the control of Satsuma, to a prefecture directly subordinate to the throne. One king was plenty for the Meiji period, so Sho Tai, the last Okinawan king, was forced to abdicate and relocate to Tokyo, becoming a marquis in Japan's new peerage system. When he died in 1920, he was the last of the Sho line to be entombed at **Tamaudun,** the huge stone mausoleum near Shuji-jo. His great-great grandson, Sho Mamoru, and the rest of the former Okinawan nobility, still live in Tokyo. ■

EXPERIENCE: Surf's Up in Okinawa

Surfing is hugely popular with Okinawa's laid-back youth, and the islands offer a variety of beginner beaches and large tubing waves. The winter has the best swells, pushed south by storms on the mainland, but you'll need a 3-mm full-body wet suit to stay warm from November to April. Summer is less consistent but potentially more epic: Large Pacific typhoons batter the islands with week-long swells that cause massive waves and rare breaks deep within bays. No matter the season, surfing is limited to high tide

because the reefs run dry, killing the waves. Despite the lack of a soft, sandy bottom on Okinawa's beaches, there are plenty of easy, safe spots with predictable waves for beginners to learn. Yomitan village, just west of Okinawa city and the Kadena USAF base, has a good mix of beginner and advanced surf breaks. Contact **Dan Melhado** (happysurfingokinawa .com) for lessons or pro-surfer **Maki Hayato** (simplelife-adventures.com) for guided tours of the best local surf spots on Okinawa or the neighboring islands.

The Blue Zone of Okinawa

For nearly a millennium, the Pacific archipelago of Okinawa has maintained a reputation for nurturing extreme longevity. Reports from Chinese expeditions referred to these tiny islands as the land of the immortals. Despite the ensuing years of Chinese and then Japanese domination, a devastating world war, famines, and typhoons, Okinawa can still claim to be home to some of the world's longest-lived people.

In Okinawa, people enjoy what may be the world's highest life expectancy (in 2000 figures, this was 78 years for men and 86 years for women), the most years of healthy life (the Japanese have the greatest number of disability-free years), and one of the highest centenarian ratios (as high as 5 per 10,000). They suffer from the same diseases that kill Americans, but at much lower rates: a fifth the rate of cardiovascular disease, a fourth the rate of breast and prostate cancer, and a third the rate of dementia.

Over the past decade or so, National Geographic explorer Dan Buettner has concluded that many of the world's best practices in health and longevity are found in the Okinawan "Blue Zone"—his term for a region whose people live longer than most. He has interviewed numerous island centenarians and heard their stories. They all seemed to spend time outdoors each day, soaking up vitamin D from the sun, and all eat a lot vegetables. Many are prodigious gardeners, going into the fields every morning and returning with tasty greens and tubers in the afternoon. The islanders have also thrived on a staple food through the decades: the simple *imo*, or sweet potato. The tuber is incredibly healthy, extremely high in vitamins A and C, potassium, folic acid, fiber, and beta-carotene—an agent shown to have cancer-fighting properties.

The Okinawan elders all shared a sense of common purpose in life, with a strong connection to their ancestors, their children, and their community. So sunshine, spirituality, and sweet potatoes are all keys to a longer life. Other advice gleaned from the common practices of Okinawan centenarians include:

Eat more soy: Fermented soy foods lead to healthy intestines and offer good nutrition.

Plant a medicinal garden: Mugwort, ginger, and turmeric are health-boosting staples of an Okinawan garden.

Maintain a *moai*: This is the Okinawan tradition of maintaining a secure social network to share one's burdens in times of need.

Embrace an *ikigai*: This is the elders' term for their reason to get up in the morning. They have clear roles and feel cherished in old age.

Stay active: Okinawan elders are active walkers and gardeners. The idea of retirement never occurs to most Okinawans: To this day there is no word for it in their language.

Morning yoga helps this elderly Okinawan stay fit.

Okinawa Honto

The narrow main island *(honto)* of Okinawa is 84 miles (135 km) long. It still has unspoiled areas both inland and on the coast, but most are in the north, beyond the sleepy town of Nago. The central Motobu Peninsula has the excellent Churaumi Aquarium, whereas southern Okinawa, known as Nanbu, is dotted with monuments to the war dead.

Watching the whale sharks at the Okinawa Churaumi Aquarium

Underground Naval Headquarters

✉ 236 Azatomigusuku, Tomigusuku-shi

☎ 098/850-4055

🕐 8:30 a.m.–5 p.m.

💲 $

🚌 Bus 33, 46, or 101 from Naha terminal to Tomigusuku-joshi, Koen-mae

One such monument, the **Konpaku-no-To** on the south coast, is dedicated to the 35,000 war dead buried in a mass grave. About 2.5 miles (4 km) southwest of Naha, the **Underground Naval Headquarters** (Kyu Kaigun Shireibugo) was a stronghold honeycombed with almost a mile (1,500 m) of tunnels; 220 yards (200 m) of these are currently open to the public, along with the rooms they connected. Some of the walls are cratered and pock-marked—a gruesome reminder of the 4,000 members of the Japanese Navy who, spurning the disgrace of surrender, committed suicide here. More poignant still is **Himeyuri-no-To** *(671-1 Aza-Ihara, Itoman-shi, tel 098/997-2100, himeyuri.or.jp, 9 a.m.–5:30 p.m., $),* a monument and museum commemorating the 240 Okinawan schoolgirls and their teachers who had volunteered to nurse the wounded but were put to the dangerous work of fetching water and food for dying men in the caves where they hid from bombardment. When the U.S. military was nearly upon their hiding place, the girls were summarily dismissed and told to leave the shelter of the caves. Of the 240, all but 13 died. Many were cut down in the cross fire as they attempted to flee, but others took their own lives, unwilling to leave their wounded friends.

Farther south on the coast is **Mabuni Hill** (Mabuni-no-Oka), site of the Japanese Imperial Army's last stand on June 23, 1945. At the top of the hill is a monument to Lieutenant General Ushijima, who committed *seppuku* with his second in command in his operations hideout, a cave just below the cliff top. His decision to commit "honorable" suicide, rather than surrender in disgrace, led to thousands of unnecessary civilian deaths among the people of Okinawa as they had been ordered by the Japanese military to fight to the very last: "If you don't have a gun, use a bamboo spear, if you don't have a spear, use a rock. Each of you must kill ten Americans." This terrible consequence, along with the fact that hundreds of cornered civilians and soldiers jumped (or were forced to jump) to their deaths from the very cliff where his monument lies to avoid the shame of defeat or the supposed rape and murder that the Americans were about to perpetrate, raises questions as to why Ushijima receives any commemoration at all. The pretty view across the sea makes for troubling contrast with this dark history.

In addition to the hillside's forest of monuments and memorials, the **Peace Memorial Museum** (Heiwa Kinen Shiryokan) casts an objective eye on the lead up to the Battle of Okinawa, its horrific toll, and the difficult road to recovery. The exhibits are noteworthy for their exposition

on the struggle of peacetime and shed light on Okinawa's difficult relationship with both the Americans and the Japanese.

After all this, you may welcome some lighter entertainment in the form of **Okinawa World**. This Okinawan cultural theme park has artisans demonstrating crafts such as *bingata* textilemaking (see sidebar below) and a hyperactive display of *eisa* dancing. Underneath it is the **Gyokusendo limestone cave,** much visited for its thousands of stalagmites and stalactites. Spelunkers should inquire about the 2.5-hour tour off the walkways and deep into the cave system. The **Valley of Gangala** (*tel 098/948-4192, 10 a.m.–6 p.m., tours by reservation, $$$$),* just across the road, has a café in a huge cave and offers geography-themed walks through caves and along a valley formed where the cave system collapsed long ago.

Peace Memorial Museum

- ✉ 614-1 Mabuni, Itoman-shi
- ☎ 098/997-3844
- 🕐 9 a.m.–5 p.m.
- 💲 $
- 🚌 Bus 82 from Itoman bus terminal to Heiwankinendo-iriguchi

www.peace-museum .pref.okinawa.jp

Okinawa World

- ✉ 1336 Aza Maekawa, Tamagusuku, Nanjo-shi
- ☎ 098/949-7421
- 🕐 9 a.m.–5 p.m.
- 💲 $$$
- 🚌 Bus 54 or 83 from Naha terminal to Gyokusendo

gyokusendo.co.jp /okinawaworld

Okinawan Textiles

Depicting flowers, fish, birds, people, or festival scenes in vivid colors, *bingata* textiles rank among the finest in Japan. Bingata are hand-painted using specially prepared stencils and demand a lot of skill. The Ryukyus are known for textiles of other kinds, too. *Bashofu* is a lightweight fabric handwoven out of banana fibers in the north of Okinawa island; *kashuri* is a finely woven cloth made in the south. On Miyako-jima, the specialty is lightweight, indigo-dyed *jofu*. The *minsa* fabric of Yaeyama invariably shows a centipede woven in red against a dark background. Women made these for their fiancés as a sign of betrothal; the centipede symbolized eternal love.

Okinawa Churaumi Aquarium

✉ 424 Ishikawa, Motobu-cho, Kunigami-gun

☎ 098/048-3748

🕐 8:30 a.m.–6:30 p.m., closes 8:30 p.m. Mar.–Sept.

💲 $$$$

🚌 Bus YB from Naha airport or 65 from Nago terminal

churaumi.okinawa

Nakamura House

✉ 106 Azaooshiro Kitanakagusuku-son, Nakagami-gun

☎ 098/935-3500

🕐 9 a.m.–5 p.m.

💲 $

🚌 35 min. drive from Naha city

Ryukyu-mura Village

✉ 1130 Aza Yamada, Onna-son, Kunigami-gun

☎ 098/965-1234

🕐 8:30 a.m.–5:30 p.m.

💲 $$$

🚌 Bus 20 from Naha terminal

ryukyumura.co.jp

Sakiyama Awamori Distillery

✉ 751 Igei, Kincho, Kunigami-gun

☎ 098/968-2417

🕐 10 a.m.–5 p.m.

💲 Free tour, call ahead

🚌 Bus 77 from Naha terminal to Igei stop

The Motobu Peninsula on the north end of the island is notable for the **Ocean Expo Park,** which hosts attractions on the biology of the sea. Foremost is the **Okinawa Churaumi Aquarium,** a must-see on the main island. Here the largest tank holds 2 million gallons (7,500 cubic m) of water, big enough for whole schools of fish, manta rays, and three whale sharks, the world's largest species of fish. The dolphin show is a popular draw: Arrive early to secure a seat for the regularly scheduled performances. Also on the grounds is the **Oceanic Culture Museum** (oki-park.jp, $), which attempts to paint a picture of Ryukyu's early islander culture. Although there is little evidence of this older way of life to be found

INSIDER TIP:

Due to the lack of efficient public transit, many tourists opt to rent a compact car. It's quite reasonable for a group, about US$120 for a day of driving around the north end of the island.

—HANASHIRO MASAYO
Okinawa Guide, www.laternarius.net

in Okinawa, it is believed to have resembled cultures that still exist in parts of Polynesia.

Urasoe, the first capital of the Ryukyu kingdom, lies about 6 miles (10 km) north of Naha.

Joseki-koen contains the ruins of the first royal castle, and a short walk beyond it is a mausoleum built for kings of the 14th century. The ruins of another feudal castle stand nearby at **Kita Naka-Gusuku,** with fine views from its hilltop site. The area's main attraction is the **Nakamura House** (Nakamura-ke), just over half a mile (1 km) northeast, regarded as the finest example of aristocratic rural domestic architecture still standing in Okinawa.

Development has taken its toll on many venerable buildings in Okinawa, so fine farmhouses and other buildings representative of a past way of life were dismantled in other parts of the island and reassembled in an open-air museum. **Ryukyu-mura Village** has interesting exhibits of Okinawan culture and crafts, including demonstrations on traditional performing arts, music, and textile weaving. A 15-minute drive east takes you to the **Sakiyama Awamori Distillery,** one of the oldest producers of the local beverage. Awamori is native to Okinawa and is the strongest spirit in Japan, typically ranging between 30 and 43 percent alcohol (60–86 proof). It is made from Indica rice imported from Thailand and is distilled, making it more similar to a rice-based *shochu* than *saké,* which is fermented. Here the staff take visitors through the process of the initial fermentation, distillation, and aging in attractive clay pots. If you'd like to try some during your stay, a cocktail is an easy introduction, but locals drink it with ice and water. ∎

The Ryukyu Archipelago

It is in the farther-flung islands that Okinawa's subtropical paradise comes to the fore. The Kerama, Miyako, and Yaeyama island groups form a string leading southwest all the way to Taiwan and present a fascinating mix of reef-island and mountainous geography, with healthy reefs, vibrant semi-tropical jungles and dark, starry skies.

Miyako-jima Island coral and blue tang fish

You don't have to go too far from Okinawa to discover an island paradise. The spectacularly beautiful **Kerama Islands** are only 18 miles (30 km) offshore. Of the three main islands, **Tokashiki-jima** is the largest and most crowded during the holiday season due to easy access. Steeply rising from the sea, the island's winding roads and beautiful vantage points make for an excellent day-trip in a rented car. **Zamami-jima** and **Aka-jima** are both prized by divers and snorkelers; Furuzamami Beach on the former is one of the prettiest stretches of white sand in the area, with a coral reef just off-shore. Zamami has converted from whaling to whale-watching, a lucrative

pursuit that draws pod people to the island in winter. The inhabited islands are well endowed with hotels and *minshuku* (guesthouses), but they can get crowded. Ferries run regularly between the islands, so getting around is easy. From Zamami or Aka, you can visit the remoter island of **Geruma,** notable for the Kerama *shika*—a unique species of deer.

The **Miyako** group, eight islands boasting spectacular seascapes and coral reefs for diving and snorkeling, has few historical or cultural sights, except in the town of **Hirara** on the main island of **Miyako-jima.** Built low against the ground with thick surrounding walls of coral limestone,

Kerama Islands
 339 G2
Visitor Information
✉ Zamami Island
ferry terminal
☎ 098/987-2277
**zamamitouristinfo
.wordpress.com**

Miyako Islands
 338 C1–D1
Visitor Information
✉ Miyako Airport
☎ 0980/72-0899
🕐 9 a.m.–6 p.m.
**zamamitouristinfo
.wordpress.com**

Ishigaki-jima

▲ 338 B1

Visitor Information

✉ Ishigaki airport, or consult Hirata Kanko in the ferry terminal

☎ 0980/82-2809

🕓 7:30 a.m.–9 p.m.

yaeyama.or.jp

hirata-group.co.jp /english

the houses here have red-tiled roofs, a style that came to replace the thatch ubiquitous over the Ryukyu-shoto only within the 20th century. Other sights include **Nakasone Toimiya**—the ornate mausoleum of a local 15th-century military hero—and the curious **Jintoze-iseki** (Tax Stone). The stone stands 4.5 feet (1.4 m) high, and only those shorter than this were exempted from the taxes exacted by the ruling Satsuma clan of Kyushu.

Sports are popular on Miyako-jima: Several serious scuba diving enterprises operate here, and each April the isle hosts Japan's famous Strongman Challenge Triathlon.

Much less visited are Miyako's seven outlying islands, largely to the west, which are accessible by boat and possess beautiful beaches. Notable among them are **Shimoji-jima** and **Irabu-jima**, separated from each other by a narrow channel.

Okinawans reenact their original arrival on the archipelago.

INSIDER TIP:

Before each meal, many Okinawans say *"Hara hachi bu."* This means "Eat until you are 80 percent full," and could be one of the secrets to their amazing longevity.

—JUSTIN KAVANAGH
National Geographic Travel Books editor

Continuing southwest, you come to the **Yaeyama-shoto Islands. Ishigaki-jima** is the main transportation hub and municipal center for the Yaeyama group, but it has a handful of worthwhile sights, and Ishigaki city is a lively place with a good selection of restaurants and nightlife. **Kabira Bay** (Kabira-wan) in the northwest is a brilliant blue, scattered with little islands and is popular for glass-bottom boat tours because the current is too strong to swim safely. Nearby the **Ryukyu Pearl Company** *(ryukyu-shinju.co.jp)* explains the process whereby black pearls are cultivated from black-lipped oysters, pioneered here in 1953. Another artistic pioneer can be found at the **Ishigaki Pottery Studio** *(ishigaki-yaki.com)*, where potter Kaneko Haruhiko has struggled to achieve the striking and technically complex fusion of ceramics and glass in his dishes. The process, discovered by his father Kaneko Kyo-u, is unique and lends a transparent bright blue—the color of Ishigaki's sea—to the works.

Shamanism & the Sacred Spaces of *Utaki*

You won't find many Shinto shrines or Buddhist temples in Okinawa, despite the islands' long subjugation under the Japanese. Instead, most Okinawans follow a form of shamanism based around sacred places called *utaki*. These places could be a cluster of trees, a large rock, or even a symbolic gate, and they are scattered all across the islands.

Instead of male priests or monks, the utaki are attended to by female shamans, and many of the inner sanctums are off-limits to men. Ceremonies are conducted in the old Okinawan language, which is otherwise no longer used except for a number of vocabulary words sprinkled throughout the Okinawan dialect of Japanese.

One of the best glimpses of old Okinawa is at the **Ishigaki Yaima Village,** where old houses have been gathered in an open-air museum. Don't miss the traditional music performances held in one of the houses–you will get pulled into the dance, like it or not! Another fine aristocratic residence is the **Miyara Donchi,** built in the early 19th century and now a museum near the ferry terminal.

For a short hike, scenic **Omoto-dake** (1,726 feet/526 m), at the center of the island, is the highest point in Okinawa-ken.

Less than 15 minutes away by boat from Ishigaki-jima, **Taketomi-jima** (*painusima.com*) is a charming place, seemingly forgotten by the passage of time. **Taketomi village** occupies the bulk of the island with its low, garden-girdled houses, coral walls, and white sandy streets. You can see artisans making the textiles the island is known for at **Taketomi Folk Craft Museum.** The beaches on the west coast are the most popular: **Kondoi Beach** has floury soft sand and showers, making it popular with day-trippers. The **Hoshizuna-hama,** or Star-Sand Beach, just south is

made up of the star-shaped skeletons of tiny marine creatures.

Iriomote-jima, Japan's great tropical wilderness, has 80 miles (130 km) of coastline, mangrove swamps, and hills covered in dense, virgin jungle. This island also is the home of the Iriomote Wildcat, believed by some zoologists to be a living fossil. Experts reckon that only about 100 of the animals survive, so your chances of sighting one are slim. If you rent a car here, drive cautiously after dark as the cats often prowl the roadside for prey. Being struck by a car is the main culprit for the wildcat's decline, claiming two or three each year.

Though touted as wild and unexplored—so much so that the ferry staff keep an eye open for potential suicides coming from the mainland with little luggage to get lost in the jungle—Iriomote is crisscrossed with hiking trails. The best known path traverses the island diagonally from the northwest—but beware of leeches. The jungle can be very wet and tough going, so many tour companies offer kayaking tours up the rivers to see waterfalls, the most popular being the tall thin

Ishigaki Yaima Village
- ✉ 967-1 Najura
- ☎ 0980/82-8798
- 🕒 9 a.m.–5 p.m.
- 💲 $$

Miyara Donchi
- ✉ 178 Okawa
- ☎ 0980/82-2767
- 🕒 9 a.m.–5 p.m., closed Tues.
- 💲 $$

Taketomi Folk Craft Museum
- ✉ 381-4 Taketomi
- ☎ 0980/85-2302
- 🕒 9 a.m.–5 p.m.

Iriomote-jima
- 🅰 338 B1

Visitor Information
- ✉ Consult Hirata Kanko in the ferry terminal on Ishigaki-jima
- ☎ 0980/82-6711
- 🕒 7:30 a.m.–6:30 p.m.

town.taketomi.lg.jp

Yonaguni-jima

🗺 338 A2

Visitor Information

✉ Yonaguni airport

☎ 0980/87-2402

🕐 9 a.m.–7 p.m.

stream of **Pinaisara** (White Beard Falls). The current is lazy and the mangroves press close up against the boats. Mixed into the jungle are *sagaribana* (powder-puff trees), which open delicate pink flowers every night and drop the blossoms at dawn for two weeks at the beginning of July. Kayak tour operators such as **Osampo Kibun** (*iriomote-osanpo.com*) operate 4 a.m. tours to see the flowers at dawn. Large groups also take boat tours to **Kanbire Falls** on the Urauchi River. Iriomote, like the rest of Okinawa, has excellent beaches, particularly the long **Tsuki-ga-hama** (Moon Beach), which has soft sand and few visitors. For snorkeling, the hamlet of **Funauki** (*contact Funeya for tours, funauki.com*), accessible only by boat, has the healthiest coral reefs and excellent visibility.

INSIDER TIP:

Hateruma-jima is quiet, but the stars are so beautiful. Stay overnight and take a bicycle to Nishi Beach on the west coast. You can see the Southern Cross!

—YURIKA ITANI
Ishigaki guide

The final stop in the Ryukyu-shoto is **Yonaguni-jima,** an island 7 miles (11 km) long that lies just 60 miles (100 km) east of Taiwan. The island made international diving news in 1997 when the **Yonaguni Monument,** a strange

geological formation under the waters off-shore, was introduced in an English documentary. First discovered in 1987, the pyramidal sandstone structure was called "Japan's Atlantis" for its pillars, right angles, and wide, flat terraces. Detractors argue that such shapes could just as easily be part of the stone's natural splitting, but there's no denying that the site makes for a mysterious dive or glass-bottom boat ride.

After a day of diving with hammerhead sharks and ancient ruins, you may be up for a glass of the local awamori, strongest in Japan at 60 percent: Order it like a local by calling for "shima" (*shima-zaké,* or island saké) and you'll look cool until they are carrying you out of the bar. If you do sample it, don't worry about the size of the moths you might see flitting about—they'd look the same if you were sober; called *yonagunisan,* they are among the world's largest. Ultimately, Yonaguni's main attraction for domestic tourists is its role as the last outpost. The same applies to the isle of **Hateruma-jima,** south of Iriomote. Day-trippers like to visit this island's southernmost rock, **Sainantan-no-Hi,** a landmark designating the southernmost inhabited point in Japan. Both islands are so remote from the rest of Japan that light pollution is at a bare minimum and the skies are awash with stars. There's a small **Starry Sky Observation Tower** (*8 p.m.–10 p.m., $*) to get a better view, but it's better to lay claim to a quiet beach, kick back beneath the stars, and savor your own end of the Earth. ∎

Travelwise

SCMaglev and Railway Park,
Nagoya city, Aichi-ken

TRAVELWISE

PLANNING YOUR TRIP

When to Go

Japan has four distinct seasons, but spring and fall are the best times to visit, with the flowering cherries of spring and the autumnal reds of maple leaves constituting favorite postcard images. Rain is no stranger to either season, but fine spring weather really shows the country at its best.

Overall, the archipelago's climate ranges from Siberian (Hokkaido) to subtropical (Okinawa). There is also a short rainy season known as *tsuyu* lasting from early June to mid-July, after which hot winds from the tropical Pacific blow across Honshu, sending summer temperatures up to around 95°F (35°C) with humidity at a debilitating 80 percent plus. Summer temperatures in Kyushu and Okinawa are higher on average, but with less humidity the climate is more comfortable.

Despite the drawbacks of the Japanese summer, it can also be fun because of the large number of festivals. However, peak summer travel is marred by daunting crowds and higher prices; make reservations well ahead. In Northern Honshu (Tohoku) and Hokkaido, temperatures rarely go above 70°F (21°C) in late July. With the added attraction of its large wilderness, Hokkaido is an increasingly popular summer vacation destination.

November is the time to appreciate Japan's famous autumn colors. In early fall, from the start of September until around the end of October, the Pacific side of the country is prone to typhoons that sweep up from the tropics packing high winds and torrential rain. The Asian equivalent of the hurricane, they can occasionally cause disastrous flooding and mud slides.

Although it can get pretty cold at night, especially on high ground, winter is consistently fine and sunny on the Pacific coast. However, the area of Honshu bordering the Sea of Japan is one of the snowiest places in the world. It is also one of the rainiest: Average annual precipitation stands at 102 inches (265 cm)—about twice as much as Tokyo. Winter in northern Japan can be very cold, with ice floes sailing past the coast in Hokkaido's far north, where the sea can freeze for miles. Far from deterring visitors, such subarctic phenomena attract interest; hot springs are plentiful on Hokkaido, which also has some of the finest ski resorts in Japan.

What to Take

It doesn't rain so much in winter, but rainwear makes sense at any other time. Inexpensive umbrellas and plastic raincoats light enough to fold up and carry in a pocket or bag are sold everywhere.

Take account of heat and humidity when selecting summer clothing. A synthetic top or undershirt can ease the transition from hot streets to chilly AC. The Japanese are probably the best dressed people in the world; don't wander around urban centers in beachwear, although shorts are generally acceptable in the summer months. Coat-and-tie dress codes operate in some places, especially in expensive restaurants.

You will need strong, lightweight footwear. Consider shoes that you can slip out of easily when entering temples, *ryokan*, some restaurants, or private homes, but that are sturdy enough to handle uneven cobbled staircases or a hike to a hilltop temple. Be warned that the wooden floors of historic buildings such as castles can be bitterly cold in winter, so make sure you wear thick socks.

In summer, it can get cold at higher altitudes. Take a fleece jacket or lightweight parka. Winter may be sunny and mild in many places during the daytime, but you will still need warm clothing from December through March.

Insurance

Japan's medical standards are among the world's highest, but care is priced accordingly and fees are prohibitive. Make sure that medical coverage in your travel insurance is adequate. If your stay in Japan is extended, take out internationally recognized medical insurance before going.

Entry Formalities

Passports & Visas

Provided they have a valid passport, U.S. and Canadian citizens may remain in Japan for 90 days without a visa. U.K. citizens are also granted 90 days at time of landing, but can apply for an extension of up to six months. Japan has a bewildering array of visa exemption agreements with different countries. If you are in doubt, call a Japanese consulate before planning your trip.

Foreigners are required by law to carry their passports or alien registration cards, if required, at all times. Visitors are sometimes stopped by police (usually at night) and asked to produce their papers.

If you'd like to stay longer than the initial temporary visitor status, you'll have to leave and come back, the cheapest route being the ferry to Pusan from Osaka or Fukuoka. This is officially frowned upon, but if you spend a week away and can explain to immigration about your travel or international business plans, they'll usually allow it once. Needless to say, any mention of a job in Japan that you've been doing without a work visa will result in your being deported.

You are forbidden to work in Japan if your status is temporary visitor or tourist. If you do want to work, you must come in on a tourist visa and find a potential employer, or apply for work from abroad and process your work visa before you come, which is a less rushed and stressful process.

Customs

The standard allowances into Japan are 2 ounces (57 g) of perfume, gifts (duty-free items other than perfumes, spirits, and tobacco) up to a value of ¥200,000, and three 25-ounce (750 ml) bottles of spirits; to consume, purchase, or possess alcohol in Japan, you must be at least age 20. The tobacco allowance is 17.5 ounces (500 g, 400 cigarettes, or 100 cigars).

Immunizations

Japan requires no special immunizations, unless you arrive from an area in which diseases such as cholera or yellow fever are endemic, in which case you should possess a World Health Organization certificate of the appropriate vaccinations.

Pets

Pets may be brought to Japan provided they have health certificates. They must be examined by quarantine officers at the port of entry. Cats and dogs require certificates of vaccination against rabies. If you bring them from one of the designated rabies-free areas, or have all of your paperwork filled out correctly, the detention will take less than 12 hours; otherwise, pets are held in quarantine at the owner's expense, usually for at least two weeks. It can be difficult in Japan to find hotels, restaurants, or stores that accept pets.

HOW TO GET TO JAPAN

From the U.S., there are several flights daily to Japan both from the East Coast (average time 13 hours via the polar route) and West Coast (average time 10 hours via the Pacific route). The nonstop route from London to Tokyo takes around 12 hours.

Tokyo is served by Narita and Haneda airports, but there has been an increase in direct flights to other airports too. The largest is Kansai International Airport, the most convenient for Osaka, Kyoto, and Kobe. The Centrair (Central Japan International Airport) handles international flights for Nagoya, and its central location is worth considering while flight-shopping. There are direct flights to Fukuoka on Kyushu from Honolulu and Guam, but not from the U.S. mainland. There are no direct flights from the U.S. or Guam to Okinawa.

GETTING AROUND
From the Airports

Narita Airport, 41 miles (66 km) away from Tokyo, can be reached in several ways. A **taxi** journey costs more than $200, so the **Limousine Bus** is a better option: Most go to Tokyo City Air Terminal (TCAT), the central transfer junction for Haneda Airport, every 10–15 minutes, usually taking about 100 minutes. At TCAT, a fleet of taxis waits to take you to your hotel, or you can take the Hanzomon subway line.

The other way into town is by **train**, though it's less convenient if you have a lot of luggage. Tickets for the JR Narita Express (N'EX) are about $32, but it is faster than the bus, 53 minutes to Tokyo Station. The Keisei Skyliner to Ueno Station in north-central Tokyo is cheaper and slower if you don't have a JR pass.

There's a similar range of connections from Kansai International Airport to either Osaka or Kyoto;

the buses to the former take about an hour and to the latter 90–105 minutes. The JR HARUKA Express takes 50 minutes to Osaka and 75 minutes to Kyoto. If you have a rail pass coupon and want to take a JR train from Kansai International Airport, you can exchange it for the pass at the JR West information desk in the arrivals lobby.

Traveling in the Cities

Public transportation in Japanese cities is fast, efficient, and relatively cheap. With the traffic jams and difficult or expensive parking, the soundest advice is to forget about driving in the city unless you're planning an extended stay. GPS mapping is a great help in getting around Japan's big cities. You'll need a rental SIM (see p. 356) or regular Wi-Fi access for your smartphone. Augmented reality apps that translate words seen by the camera (e.g. Google Translate on iOS and Android) can help identify common signs and place-names.

Subways

Tokyo, Fukuoka, Kobe, Kyoto, Nagoya, Osaka, Sapporo, Sendai, and Yokohama all have subway systems. As with local line trains, you generally buy tickets from a machine. Some places have English-language maps inscribed with fare tariffs; most don't. When in doubt, pay the lowest fare and then pay the difference at your destination. This is often the best policy: In Tokyo, for instance, you might change between lines owned by different companies, and the pricing can be complicated. You can always ask the ticket office staff for assistance. Even easier: Buy and charge up an ICC transit card such as the Suica or ICOCA card and swipe it as you go through. Google Maps and HyperDia (www.hyperdia.com /en) have good way-finding.

Buses

In many cities, public transportation is provided solely by buses. Hakodate (Hokkaido), Hiroshima (Honshu), Matsuyama (Shikoku), and Nagasaki and Kumamoto (Kyushu) have streetcar systems. Not all buses or streetcars have destinations in Roman letters, so it's advisable to note the *kanji* or *hiragana* characters spelling out your destination on a piece of paper and look for it on the front of the vehicle before boarding.

In large cities you pay a flat fare on entering the bus, but in rural areas you take a ticket out of the automatic dispenser as you enter the bus or streetcar. The number on your ticket corresponds to the stop from which you boarded. Near the ceiling on the driver's left is an electric sign showing the stop number and the amount you must pay as you leave. Most buses show the next stop above this electric sign, usually in Japanese and English.

Taxis

Taxis are everywhere in urban Japan. Although prices vary in different areas, they are pricey. Taking a taxi at rush hour is never a good idea; if the cab gets caught in traffic, the extra time will be charged on the meter. There is a 20 percent surcharge for cabs summoned by phone, and the same applies to all taxis after 11 p.m.

Watch for the lights on the taxi roof: Yellow means that the cab is engaged, red that it is free, and green that a surcharge is operative. Whether inside or out of the taxi, don't even think of opening or closing the door—doors are automatically controlled by the driver. Japanese cabbies are polite and helpful, but a Japanese business card, or your destination written in Japanese, is advisable: Most cities are without street names, and the random numerical address system in suburban and residential areas is decipherable only to postal workers and police.

Traveling Around Japan

By Rail

The train is the most convenient and fastest way to travel in Japan; standards of punctuality, comfort, and cleanliness on Japanese rail services are legendary. But be warned: When changing trains, it can be a long way between platforms, there may be several staircases on the way, and few elevators. The golden rule is to travel light. Tickets can be purchased at all train stations.

The privatized **Japan Railways (JR)**, comprising six companies, runs major routes throughout the country, with other links—both express and local trains—provided by regional firms. It's possible to go virtually anywhere in Japan by train.

JR's premier service is the Shinkansen, the "bullet train," inaugurated for the 1964 Olympic Games. Long the world's fastest train, it currently vies for the record with France's TGV and China's new high-speed rail network. Tokaido (Tokyo–Osaka), Sanyo (Osaka–Hakata), and Tohoku (Tokyo–Hachinohe) are the main lines; new links include Hokuriku (Tokyo–Kanazawa) and Kyushu (Yatsushiro–Kagoshima). Trains are super express, express, and limited express—respectively called *Nozomi*, *Hikari*, and *Kodama* on the Tokaido and Sanyo lines. Expect impeccable service. Seat reservations are inexpensive, but book well over a month ahead for peak periods. To save money, go for the unreserved seat ticket and ride the slightly slower trains such as the Hikari or Kodama—you may need to stand during peak holidays though.

Rail Discounts

Children under 6 travel free by rail, and it's half price for those between 6 and 11; otherwise traveling by train—and by Shinkansen especially—can be very expensive. There are several different kinds of discount options available, notably the five-day **JR Youth 18 ticket** *(seishun juhachi kippu),* which costs around $100; contrary to the name, anyone can use this ticket pack, which allows five days, not necessarily contiguous, of unlimited local or express train travel during college vacation periods. The tickets can't be used for the Shinkansen, but regular express tends to be fairly fast.

By far the best deal is the **JR Rail Pass** *(japanrailpass.net /en),* available for 7 (US$280), 14 (US$450), or 21 (US$580) days (half price for children 6–11 years old). The pass entitles you to unlimited use of transportation in the JR system for the duration, including the Shinkansen (except for the ultrafast Nozomi), other JR trains, JR buses, and JR ferries. If you intend to make two or more intercity trips per week, you will save considerably, though the highway bus is still a cheaper option. Note that the pass must be purchased outside Japan from an authorized travel agent.

The pass must be validated within three months of the date of purchase, but the actual starting date is determined when you exchange the voucher issued by the travel agent for the actual rail pass in Japan. You can make seat reservations only after you have obtained your pass (obtainable at the JR Travel Service Center in any mainline train station—the options are listed on the back of the voucher). The rules governing the passes are strict. You cannot change the date once the pass is issued, and if you lose the pass, it will not be replaced. **JR West Rail Passes** or **JR Kyushu Rail Passes** also represent substantial savings; the **JR East Rail Pass** has a discount for those aged between 12 and 25. With the exception of JR West, these passes must also be purchased outside Japan. You are eligible for JR Passes only if you are entering Japan with temporary visitor status. You will need your passport bearing the relevant stamps when you exchange the voucher for the pass.

By Bus

Budget-conscious travelers often opt for the intercity bus services, a cheaper (though slower) alternative to the train. Fitted with reclining seats, night buses come in a variety of comfort levels, ranging from four-abreast cheapos to three-abreast super-recliners. Many bus companies provide AC outlets and Wi-Fi Internet access, but onboard toilets are not always available, in which case break stops are made every two hours. Tour buses abound in every major tourist center. They can make a good alternative to public buses if you are in a rush, but they are costly, and, unless stated otherwise, the tour will probably be conducted in Japanese.

By Air

All of Japan's prefectural capitals are connected by air; there are many options for reaching smaller cities, too. The main carriers are **All Nippon Airways (ANA)** and **Japan Airlines (JAL)** but since the deregulation of air transportation in 1986, the number of local carriers is ever increasing. In Tokyo, Narita Airport handles more international flights and Haneda Airport is more convenient for domestic flights. The Limousine Bus (see p. 353) shuttles between Haneda and Narita airports.

By Ferry

With an increasing number of tunnels and bridges, it's easy to forget that Japan is an island nation. But if you like older ways of traveling or are on a tight budget, the interisland ferry network is extensive. It's the best way to get to Sado Island and the most attractive means of traveling the Inland Sea. An overnight ferry to Hokkaido costs less than the train. JNTO (Japan National Tourism Organization) offices have information on routes, times, and costs (for JNTO centers, see p. 358).

Japanese ferries are fun: Passengers simply sprawl over large carpeted (or occasionally still tatami-matted) areas on the lower decks. Having removed your shoes, you select your spot and drop—to eat and drink, play cards, read, gossip, and eventually sleep. Cabins are available at extra cost.

By Car

Unless you are used to driving on the left-hand side of the road and can cope with some road signs in Japanese, you would be advised not to drive in Japan. That said, the car provides an alternative way to travel if you want to venture off the beaten path. The relatively high cost of highway tolls (Tokyo to Kyoto will set you back more than $120) and the price of gas may also deter you. You need a valid international driving permit plus your own license (and if you are staying on after the international driving license expires, you will need a Japanese one). The same pattern applies to motorcycles, although you may be required to take another test in Japan, especially for bikes of 750cc and up.

Car rental operations abound in Japan, with major international firms well represented. You may be able to reserve a car in Japan through a rental firm at home (try **Hertz**, hertz.com, or **National,** tel 800/227-7368). Large chains often allow you to leave a car at a different location than where you rented it for no extra cost—ask for *norisute* (drop-off) options.

The speed limits are 50 mph (80 kph) to 62 mph (100 kph) on highways, 37 mph (60 kph) on secondary roads, and 25 mph (40 kph) in towns. Although bilingual versions are becoming the norm, some signs may still be only in Japanese.

Cycling

Bicycle theft is probably the commonest of the few crimes you'll encounter in Japan, so if you cycle, make sure you always lock your bicycle. Provided you have a carrying bag (*rinko baggu*—available from cycling shops), you can take your bicycle on the train, though you may be asked to pay a small extra fee. This is a cycle-friendly country if you stay off the main roads; there's great cycling on well-maintained, winding tertiary highways. In Google Maps, skip the orange major highways and aim for the numbered yellow and white roads, which are the lesser used routes and typically run through high passes or along beautiful coast. Recommended areas are the foothills of the Japan Alps on Honshu, Kyushu, Shikoku, and the national park areas in Hokkaido. Many places have bicycles for rent; outlets are typically close to the train station or tourist center.

PRACTICAL ADVICE
Communications
Post Offices

Post offices and mailboxes are identified by a sign with a red or white "T" with a bar over the top. Main city and district post offices are open 9 a.m.–7 p.m. weekdays, 9 a.m.–3 p.m. Saturdays, and 9 a.m.–12:30 p.m. Sundays. Branch offices are open 9 a.m.–5 p.m. and closed weekends. Only larger post offices offer currency exchange and general delivery.

Telephones

Well maintained, though increasingly rare, Japan's pay phones almost always work. These accept both coins and prepaid telephone cards (terehon kado), which are widely sold in vending machines, station kiosks, and many other outlets. The cards come in denominations of ¥500, ¥1,000, ¥3,000, and ¥5,000.

Green phones take cards and coins but are mainly for domestic calls. Gray phones are both international and domestic and accept both coins and cards. The same applies to orange and green phones, which additionally accept international credit cards.

A discount of up to 40 percent operates between 11 p.m. and 8 a.m. You can make **operator-assisted international calls** by dialing 0051; the English-speaking operators can help make collect calls. Calls from pay phones will be cheaper than from hotel rooms.

To place an international call, dial 001-010 then the country code (1, in the case of the U.S.) and the rest of the number.

Most Japanese cell phones are compatible with W-CDMA and GSM, but Japan's network is entirely W-CDMA, so check your phone's compatibility before you come. If you have a carrier-unlocked LTE phone, you can rent a SIM card for your stay from Softbank (www.softbank-rental.jp/e) at the airport to avoid roaming charges; a smartphone's maps really come in handy. Alternately, b-mobile rents SIM cards with unlimited data for two-week periods (US$23).

English-language services (emergencies, general information, counseling) are available from Tokyo English Lifeline (TELL): 03/5774-0992, 9 a.m.–11 p.m., and Japan Helpline: 0570/000-911 (toll-free), 24 hours. In the event of an emergency, call 110 for police or 119 for fire or ambulance services. There is usually some English spoken.

Drinking Water

It is safe to drink water straight from the faucet anywhere in Japan, although it may taste chlorinated. Bottled water, imported and domestic, is widely available.

Electricity

Japan's electrical system is AC, running at 50 cycles in Tokyo and on the Pacific side, and at 60 cycles in western Japan. The voltage is 100V, unlike the 120V in North America and 220–240V in much of the rest of the world. Most modern electronics will function on this reduced voltage: Check the plugs for the "100–240V" label. Electronics bought in Japan and brought home will likely fry, however. Be sure to ask for the international model in large electronics stores, as these will work with higher voltages. You can always buy a voltage converter in Japan or back home.

Etiquette & Local Customs

There are only three serious faux-pas in Japan: soaping yourself in the bath; entering a home, temple, or shrine building without removing your shoes; and blowing your nose in public.

The word for foreigner, gaijin, a contraction of gaikoku-jin ("outside country-person"), is at the center of an ongoing political-correctness debate. Its use is widespread, and you may be addressed as gaijin-san or "Mr./Ms. Outsider" though long-term residents either find it offensive and discriminatory or have given up caring. The government is making efforts to shift back to gaikoku-jin, but either way the message is the same: If you are not Japanese, then you are an outsider. Japanese also discriminate among themselves, and relationships tend to be confined to the circles defining them: mostly kinship, education, or employment.

To most foreigners, Japanese behavior will appear strikingly formal. Harmony, achieved through conformity and consensus, is of the first importance; it dictates masking private cares with public smiles. Outspokenness is considered bad manners, and conversations find participants doing their utmost to agree. Decisions are reached through consensus; in corporate contexts, the process can take some time. Nodding means "I understand what you're saying," smiling is just polite—neither means yes.

The rules of etiquette tend to focus on specific group situations and do not always apply to the street, where men often spit or, late at night, urinate against the nearest wall. The Japanese can sometimes appear churlish. You might not get an apology from someone who collides with you on the street, but, if challenged, the embarrassed offender may be at a loss for words.

Yet if you address someone, the ice is usually broken immediately. Ask, and most people will go out of their way to help you. The Japanese won't expect you to be familiar with their complex etiquette. If you abide by the universal rules of kindness and consideration, you will get along fine in Japan.

How to Behave

The proper greeting on meeting or parting is a bow, and its degree (i.e., how low) and repetition are determined by the level of respect due to the recipient. For a foreigner, an exaggerated nod suffices; most Japanese are used to the idea of shaking hands with foreigners. Do not embrace; kissing is reserved for babies and lovers.

Introductions entail an exchange of names or business cards, and it's polite to look at them before putting them away carefully. Don't crush a business card or treat it casually—it represents the other person, who will take offense.

During business meetings, cards are placed on the table. Unless you are instructed otherwise, use of the family name is preferred and carries the suffix *san* (e.g., Yamada-san: Mr. or Ms. Yamada).

In Japan, gifts are less tokens of love or friendship than repayment for favors or a response in kind. If you are invited to a home, bring a present, typically a bottle of wine, or flowers; a small token from your country will also be appreciated. Avoid anything too extravagant—the recipient may feel obliged to repay you in kind. (See also sidebar p. 30 and Tipping, p. 358.)

Table Manners

As a foreigner, you will often be assumed to be incapable of using chopsticks. Use them if you can—but never leave them sticking in the bowl of food. Said to evoke the incense sticks burning in a bowl at a funeral, it's considered very bad manners.

Boiled rice, which is always served in its own bowl, is sacrosanct and should remain white. Placing items taken from the dishes on the table into it is acceptable for Chinese dishes, but sprinkling the rice with sauce is considered barbaric at any meal. Indeed, considering the delicate sweetness of Japanese glutinous short-grain rice, putting soy sauce on top is a culinary crime. The way to eat soup noodles is to raise them with your chopsticks and suck them up with a loud slurp. This cools the noodles and shows your appreciation.

Women pour drinks for men first. When your neighbor fills your glass, try to return the compliment. There may be a lot of raising or clinking of glasses, invariably accompanied with the word *kampai!*—cheers! (See also sidebar p. 25.)

Liquor Laws

You must be at least 20 years old to consume alcohol. It is legal to drink nearly everywhere (the street, the train, etc.), but drinking and driving is strictly punished.

Media

Newspapers

The *Japan Times* is the only English-first paper in Japan and it has long made effort to represent the diversity of its readers. The other main option is the *Japan News,* a translation of articles from the massive center-right *Yomiuri Shimbun* paper.

Radio

English-language programs are largely limited to the American Forces Network (AFN) Tokyo. There are some Japanese radio stations offering programs in overseas languages, such as Inter FM (Tokyo) and Cocolo FM (Osaka), but the best option is to access Internet stations from your laptop or smartphone.

Television

Japanese television has a terrible reputation. Still, the endless variety programs, samurai serials, soap operas, quiz shows, and ads provide insights into the country. NHK, the national network, has an international channel, NHK World, and many hotels provide CNN International or BBC News.

Video

The video system is NTSC, as in the United States, but Japan is DVD Region 2, so make sure any movies you buy are compatible with your player back home.

Money Matters

The Japanese currency is the yen. Bank notes come in denominations of ¥10,000, ¥5,000, ¥2,000, and ¥1,000; coins in ¥1 (aluminum), ¥5 (light copper, hole in center), ¥10 (copper), ¥50 (nickel, hole in center), ¥100 (nickel), and ¥500 (light copper).

National Holidays

January 1 New Year's Day—Gantan

January 1–3 New Year—Oshogatsu

January, 2nd Mon. Coming of Age Day—Seijin-no-Hi

February 11 National Foundation Day—Kenkoku Kinen-no-Hi

March 20 or 21 Vernal Equinox—Shunbun-no-hi

April 29 Greenery Day—Midori-no-Hi

May 3 Constitution Memorial Day—Kenpo Kinenbi

May 4 People's Holiday—Kokumin-no-Shukujitsu

May 5 Children's Day—Kodomo-no-Hi

July 20 Marine Day—Umi-no-Hi

September 15 Respect for the Aged Day—Keiro-no-Hi

September 23 Autumn Equinox—Shunbun-no-Hi

October, 2nd Mon. Health Sports Day—Taiiku-no-Hi

November 3 Culture Day—Bunka-no-Hi

November 23 Labor Thanksgiving Day—Kinro Kansha-no-Hi

December 23 Emperor's Birthday—Tenno Tanjobi

Opening Times

Banks: 9 a.m.–3 p.m. weekdays; closed weekends and holidays

Department stores: 10 a.m.–8 p.m. (closed one day a week)

Post offices: 9 a.m.–5 p.m. (see also Communications, p. 355)

Private offices: 9 a.m.–5 p.m. weekdays; some open 9 a.m.–noon on Saturdays

Public offices: 9 a.m.–5 p.m. weekdays; closed weekends

Restaurants: 11:30 a.m.–3 p.m.; 6–10 p.m.

Smoking

Smoking has declined with better health awareness, though the rates of 29.7 percent for men and 9.7 percent for women seem higher because of the prevalence of smoking in public. The trains are now nearly all 100 percent nonsmoking—there's usually one smoking car on long-distance express trains. Most restaurants and cafés have nonsmoking sections, but bars and clubs are smoky affairs. Many cities such as Kyoto have instituted no-smoking streets with $10 fines, but enforcement is unheard of. Most hotels have nonsmoking floors, but *ryokan* generally don't separate their rooms. The lack of furniture and the use of futon mattresses, which are easily washed, means that ryokan rooms rarely smell smoky.

Taxes & Surcharges

An 8 percent consumption tax is applicable to all goods and services; it is charged unless you purchase items tax free for export. The tax applies in restaurants and hotels. You can sometimes reduce the tax by asking hotels and *ryokan* to bill your meals and room separately. Service charges of between 10 and 20 percent are also added to your bill.

Tipping

In a word: don't; the practice is unknown in Japan and may cause offense. Expensive restaurants sometimes have a service fee tacked on though.

Toilets

Although the Western variety is prevalent, still fairly common in public places is the squat-toilet; the Japanese variant has a hood at one end and that's the way to face. Toilet technology is a science in Japan, however. The computerized Western-style "Washlet" toilet boasts a heated seat and incorporates a cleansing water jet and drier, technology to take your breath away—especially if you make a mistake over the water-temperature setting! Public toilets, especially in stations, don't have toilet paper: Either carry a pack of tissues or buy paper from the vending machine.

Travelers With Disabilities

For those with impaired sight, a strip of rubber indicates the edge of station platforms and musical signals give the all-clear at pedestrian crossings. Otherwise, this is not a great country for the disabled. International-class hotels have wheelchair access, but not the majority of *ryokan*. Access ramps are becoming more widespread, and staff will offer assistance in train and subway stations, but avoid rush hour.

Before you set off, get information from the Society for the Advancement of Travel for the Handicapped *(sath.org)*.

Visitor Information

The Japan National Tourism Organization operates TICs (Tourist Information Centers) in Tokyo *(1F Shin-Tokyo Bldg, 3-3-1 Marunouchi, Chiyoda-ku, tel 03/3201-3331)* and nationwide. Those outside Japan include:

JNTO Offices

United States
Suite 448, One Grand Central Place, 60 East 42nd St. New York, NY 10165
tel 212/757-5640

Suite 302 Little Tokyo Plaza 340 East 2nd St
Los Angeles, CA 90012
tel 213/623-1952

Canada
Suite 306, 481 University Ave., Toronto, ON M5G 2E9
tel 416/366-7140
United Kingdom
1F, 28 Lehman St.
London, E1 8ER
tel 020/7398-5670
Australia
Suite 1, Level 4, 56 Clarence St.

Sydney, NSW, 2000
tel 02/9279-2177

Websites

Japan Travel Updates (JNTO): www.jnto.go.jp
Japan News: the-japan-news.com
Japan Times online: japantimes.co.jp
Restaurant reviews and city guides: TripAdvisor: tripadvisor.com
Tabelog: tabelog.com
Metropolis: metropolis.co.jp

EMERGENCIES
Crime & Police

Japan's streets are among the safest in the world, even at night. Most metropolitan neighborhoods have a *koban,* a police kiosk manned by up to four police officers; this system partly explains the low crime rate. Murder and crimes of violence are reassuringly rare. However, alongside a recent increase in white-collar crime, the incidence of muggings and theft committed by young people is rising.

Rape is comparatively rare (though many cases are thought to go unreported), but secretive molesters on crowded trains are all too common, and foreign women are a typical target. The best defense is to go on the offense: A loud scream of *"chikan!"* (pervert) or grabbing the molester's hand and not letting go are effective strategies, as this crime proliferates due to the difficulty of discovering the culprit in a crowded train and the shame that Japanese women feel in crying out.

Caution and common sense are advisable around amusement districts when they empty in the wee hours. This said, honesty is one of Japan's greatest virtues, and travelers' tales of lost wallets being returned are plentiful.

Embassies & Consulates
United States
1-10-5 Akasaka, Minato-ku, Tokyo, tel 03/3224-5000

Australia
2-1-14 Mita, Minato-ku, Tokyo, tel 03/5232-4111

Canada
7-3-38 Akasaka, Minato-ku, Tokyo, tel 03/5412-6200

United Kingdom
1 Ichiban-cho, Chiyoda-ku, Tokyo, tel 03/5211-1100

Emergency Numbers
Call boxes all have an emergency red button—press this first.
Police: 110
Ambulance/Fire: 119

For credit card loss:
Amex: 1-800-528-4800
Visa: 00531-11-1555

Earthquakes
Japan lies in one of the most volcanically and seismically active areas in the world. If there's an earthquake, drop to your hands and knees and cover your head to protect against flying or falling debris. If outside, move away from buildings or power lines. In urban areas this may be impossible, so taking cover in a building is safer against falling glass.

Health
Travelers needn't be too concerned about contracting exotic diseases. The kind that you do have to worry about are much the same as at home. If you need to see a doctor—especially an English-speaker—the Tokyo Medical and Surgical Clinic (32 Shiba-koen Bldg. 2F, 3-4-30 Shiba-koen, Minato-ku, tel 03/3436-3028) is a good option, with a 24-hour emergency service.

Carry a sufficient supply of your own prescription drugs to cover your trip (and a letter from your physician for Customs). Make sure you know not just the brand name but the generic name, for the former is likely to be wholly different in Japan. You might find some imported drugs in the American Pharmacy in Tokyo, but don't count on it elsewhere. A lot of visitors complain about not being able to find over-the-counter drugs that are available back home, so bring them with you, too. You should be able to get equivalents in Japan that give the same results, though.

Birth control should also be brought from home: The Pill is hard to find (only legal in the last decade!), and sizing a Japanese condom can be a challenge without a few test boxes.

LANGUAGE GUIDE
Airport: *kuukoh*
Bank: *ginkoh*
Car: *kuruma*
Directions:
   Left: *hidari*/Right: *migi*
   Up: *ue*/Down: *shita*
   North: *kita*/South: *minami*
   East: *higashi*/West: *nishi*
Plane: *hikoki*
Post office: *yubin kyoku*
Restaurant: *resutoran*
Station: *eki*
Taxi: *takushi*
Temple: *tera/dera* or *-ji/-in*
Ticket: *kippu* (plane ticket: *kokuuken*)
Train: *densha*
Visitor (information) office: *kankoh annai-sho*
This: *kore*/that: *sore*/that (more distant, or not visible): *are*
I want to go to...: *...eh ikitai desu*
What time is it: *Nanji desuka?*
Hello (telephone): *moshi-moshi*
Is it far/near? *Toi/chikai desu-ka*
How much? *ikura desuka?*
No (contradiction): *iie* (usually followed with or completely replaced by *chigaimasu*: That's incorrect)
Won't do/don't do/stop it (including the "no!" against aggressive people): *dame*
Haven't/aren't any...: *...nai desu*
Do you speak English? *Eigo o hanasemasuka?*
I don't understand: *wakarimasen*
Where is (the tourist information center)? *(Kankoo annai-sho wa) doko desuka?*
I'm lost: *michi ni mayotta*
Do you take credit cards? *Kurejitto kaado tsukaemasu-ka?*
Do you have a room? *O heya aitemasu-ka?*
I'd like to make a reservation for ...(two people): *(Futari bun no)... yoyaku shitai no desu*
Expensive: *takai*
Cheap: *yasui*
Have you anything cheaper? *Mo chotto yasui no wa arimasen-ka?*
Is there any...? *...arimasu-ka?*
I want/would like...: *...ga hoshi desu*
Please show me...: *...misete kudasai*
Big: *ookii*
Little: *chiisai* (a little bit: *sukoshi*)
This is too big: *Chotto ookii sugimasu*
Help! *tasukete!*
Dangerous, look out: *abunai*
Call a doctor/police: *Issha/keisatsu o yonde kudasai*
I'm unwell: *byoki desu*

Numbers/quantity of things/number of people
One: *ichi/hitotsu/hitori*
Two: *ni/futatsu/futari*
Three: *san/mitsu/san nin*
Four: *shi* or *yon/yotsu/yon nin*
Five: *go/itsutsu/go nin*
Six: *roku/muttsu/roku nin*
Seven: *nana* or *shichi/nanatsu/shichi nin*
Eight: *hachi/yattsu/hachi nin*
Nine: *kyu/kokonotsu/kyu nin*
Ten: *jyu/to/jyu nin*

Hotels & Restaurants

Despite the seemingly high prices, accommodations in Japan are an excellent value, particularly in the low to mid-range. Since the economic heyday of the 1990s, budget-conscious lodging has also increased, so much of Japan outside pricey Tokyo offers rates equal to Europe. As the recent global proliferation of Japanese restaurants suggests, Japan is very much a food country. A bad meal is a rarity in Japan, where the native palate tends to be be discerning and standards of hygiene strict.

Accommodations

The Japan National Tourist Office (JNTO) regularly updates lists of accommodations that include the Japan Ryokan and Hotel Association (*ryokan.or.jp*), the Japanese Inn Group (JIG, *japaneseinngroup .com*) and Selected Onsen Ryokan (*selected-ryokan.com*). Other popular booking sites include Rakuten (*travel.rakuten.com*), JAPANiCAN (*japanican.com*), and Jalan (*jalan .net/en*). Major international hotel booking sites such as Trip Advisor can usually arrange for large hotels, but you'll likely need one of these Japanese sites to deal with little *ryokan*. Try to reserve special stays at least four months ahead. Note that at New Year's (Dec. 28–Jan. 4), many family-run ryokan close for family celebrations.

If you haven't made reservations, local visitor information centers can help. Staff at visitor information desks in mainline train stations will do the same, although they don't always speak English. Outside peak seasons (Golden Week, O-Bon, and New Year's), it's usually possible to find a mid-range business hotel without a reservation in midsize cities, though for the nicest ryokan or best budget accommodation, booking is advised.

All modern hotels and some ryokan offer air-conditioning and elevators. Smaller regional hotels, *minshuku* (see p. 361), and ryokan may not have elevators; you should check ahead. All hotels, most ryokan, and many minshuku provide TV in the rooms, and some offer English-language pay-per-view movies and cable TV.

Western-Style Hotels

International chains such as Holiday Inn, Hilton, Hyatt, and Meridien are well represented. Japanese chains also operate Western-style hotels, including JAL (Nikko Hotels), Dai-ichi, ANA, Prince, and Tokyu. Western-style hotels usually meet the highest international standards, although rooms tend to be small and prices may be based on occupancy, not the room itself. Many hotels also offer Japanese-style rooms, but it will be assumed that you want a Western one.

Hotels typically have a choice of bars and an array of restaurants, including Japanese, Western, and Chinese; the standards of cuisine are generally high.

Business Hotels

Bijinesu hoteru are a more economical Western-style option. Targeting business travelers, they usually have small single rooms with an adjoining bathroom. Don't expect room service, laundry, bellhops, or porters. You will be given towels and a *yukata* (cotton gown). A simple breakfast is usually included, but anything else, including canned drinks and beer, comes out of vending machines. If you are stuck for a room, business hotels are a cheap, clean, and convenient option. The Dormy Inn, Super Hotel, and Toyoko Inn chains all have hotels nationwide and are highly recommended, even if they are not particularly memorable.

Ryokan

Some *ryokan* have been operating for more than a century or have been converted from large ancestral residences; others are custom built. If you want a "real Japan" experience and a glimpse of a traditional Japanese home, these are the places to stay. The average ryokan is of modest size; charged mainly on a per-person basis, the prices range from astronomical heights (US$700 a head is not unknown) to very moderate. The rate normally includes an evening meal (often lavish and served in your room) and breakfast—both Japanese style. Some ryokan will reserve the room without meals.

There's usually someone who speaks a little English in JIG's 80 or so ryokan. Their rooms are small, basic, and spotless and they tend to fill quickly, so make reservations in advance. Unless you speak some Japanese, do not wander into a ryokan off the street; you might be turned away.

There are certain rules to bear in mind. When you enter, step out of your shoes, leave them in the entrance hall, and don the slippers provided. Use these in the corridors. You must remove them before stepping onto the tatami matting in your room as well as before entering the toilet, where you use the pairs of plastic or wooden sandals provided. Don't forget to take the sandals off again: Wandering the building in toilet slippers is bad form.

Your room contains no beds; the futon mattresses and bedding (stored in the closets) will be laid out for you by a maid. Although the mattress is placed directly on the floor, the tatami is springy enough to make this a much less spartan sleeping arrangement than it sounds. You will be given a cotton kimono that is both sleepwear and for wandering about the hotel. In winter, you'll get a warm gown to wear over it.

Bathrooms tend to be communal, and in many ryokan you will find thermal baths. Remember: You must soap and rinse thoroughly before entering the communal tub.

Dinner is served early; the latest will be about 8 p.m. Smaller, family-run ryokan often impose curfews. There may be no key to lock your door, but there is often a small safe. The incidence of theft in hotels is very low, though, so this isn't a major cause for worry.

Dotted about mountain, *onsen*, or seaside resorts, state-owned *kokumin shukusha* are run along exactly the same lines as ryokan, but without the attentive service. Room rates on average are about $60 a head, including two meals.

Minshuku

Minshuku, literally "people's lodging," are family businesses usually operating in a converted private home—as are many *ryokan*. There is little difference in price between minshuku and the more modest ryokan, which are run along almost identical lines. Meals in minshuku may be served in a dining area or family kitchen rather than in the room; some serve no meals at all. Many minshuku provide no towels, and some minshuku expect you to take your own bedding from the closets, put the sheets on, and take them off again and put the bedding away in the morning. Minshuku frequently close their doors at a fixed time at night.

Pension Hotels

Pronounced "pen-shon," this concept derives from the *pension* (full bed and board) formula in France. Usually frequented by young people, these are small Western-style hotels. Some are theme conceived and specialize in sports and pastimes; many cater to a largely female clientele.

Shukubo

Temples have traditionally offered lodgings to travelers, and many still do. The old concept of offering the lodging free in exchange for chores performed (e.g., sweeping, washing dishes, or gardening) sometimes still applies. You don't have to be a Buddhist to stay. Generally *shukubo* offer inexpensive accommodations, though some of the finer ones can be quite pricey. Some shukubo serve basic vegetarian food and impose a 9 p.m. curfew; others serve gourmet vegetarian cuisine and run their own bars. See the sidebar on page 257 for information about staying in a shukubo on Mount Koya.

Youth Hostels

Membership in the International Youth Hostel Association is not essential, though most hostels offer member discounts. They don't take children under four years, but adults of any age are welcome. Friendly, basic, and very clean, most are run like *minshuku* and in the Japanese style; the majority also close their doors at night. Dormitory beds cost less than $25, and single and double rooms are about $35 on average (without breakfast). Beware: Some youth hostels also maintain a teetotalist ethic sure to make some *gaijin* (foreigners) squirm.

Love Hotels

If it stands on the fringe of an amusement district looking like Cinderella's castle with a garish

neon sign, then it has to be a "love hotel." These accommodations are strictly for couples: Single people (and threesomes, probably!) will be turned away. Expect rotating beds, mirrored walls or ceilings, adult videos, and vending machines containing toys devised to tickle your fancy. Note that there are two prices: A "rest" is cheaper (from $30), but is usually limited to one or two hours; a "stay" is comparable to business hotel rates, although themed rooms are more expensive. The bed might look like a 1950s Cadillac in a Chinese restaurant, or the place could be decked out like a medieval torture chamber.

Capsule Hotels

The capsule hotel first appeared during the 1980s, the inebriated salaryman's dream come true: a cheap (under $40) alternative to an expensive taxi after the last train home. Reached by a ladder, the capsule is no larger than a shipboard berth (3 feet by 3 feet by 6 feet), though extremely comfortable and endowed with all kinds of amenities, including TV. The overall design is tellingly like a beehive. Some capsule hotels also feature saunas and public baths with spa pools. The majority are for men only. (See sidebar p. 71.)

Restaurants

Restaurants in big cities often have English menus, but places without English may have photo menus of the fare served. The windows of many Japanese restaurants also display disconcertingly realistic plastic models of the dishes served, so all you have to do is point. Unless you're undaunted at the prospect of a hefty check, avoid places that don't display models or menus with prices outside.

In most restaurants, a simple and often cheaper alternative

to ordering à la carte is to select *teishoku*—set meals. Served on a tray, these always include a small appetizer, rice, pickles, and a bowl of piping hot *miso-shiru* (fermented soy bean soup), the basic components of a standard Japanese meal. Low prices for set meals at lunchtime make some of the country's most expensive restaurants an affordable treat.

Sushi & Sashimi

Most restaurants specialize in a certain type of cuisine. Sushi restaurants serve nothing else, except perhaps sashimi—slices of raw fish picked up with chopsticks and dipped into soy sauce before eating. In the conveyor-belt style sushi restaurant, just take plates as they go by, or place an order from the touch-screen. In small sushi bars, talk to the chefs directly. In the absence of an English or picture menu, point to the fresh fish in the case along the counter. For *nigiri* sushi, larger-than-Western slices of raw fish are placed on a bite-size bed of rice. As *makizushi*, sushi filling is rolled together with rice in a sheet of dried seaweed. Sushi is eaten after a slight dip in soy spiced with *wasabi*, a fierce, bright green variety of horseradish relish. Other than cucumber or egg rolls, sushi restaurants don't serve the "vegetarian sushi" common in North America.

Vegetarian Food

Don't expect many Western-style vegetarian or vegan restaurants outside large cities, as there's limited understanding of what either diet entails. The majority of Japanese restaurants serve tofu (soybean curd), and some restaurants specialize in *tofu ryori*—cooking using tofu and other soybean-based products exclusively. Strict vegetarians and vegans should be aware that *dashi* (fish stock), unless stated as *konbu*

dashi (seaweed stock), is in nearly everything, including most styles of miso soup. *Shojin-ryori*, served in some temple restaurants, is a refined form of vegetarian cuisine. The best bet is to seek out foreign food: Increasingly common Indian restaurants nearly always serve standard veggie-friendly dishes.

Sukiyaki & Kaiseki Ryori

Succulent *sukiyaki* consists of choice slices of beef and vegetables cooked at the table in a sweet, soy-based stock pot. When cooked, the pieces are dipped into a sauce of soy and raw egg before eating. *Shabu-shabu* is thin slices of beef (or pork) with vegetables cooked in bubbling broth.

Kaiseki ryori stands at the summit of Japanese cuisine. It was developed in Kyoto and derived from the delicacies served during the tea ceremony. A succession of small dishes—usually seasonable vegetables and occasionally fish—made of the finest ingredients, *kaiseki* is presented with all the elegance of a fine art.

Noodles

Noodles are a Japanese staple. The most common are *soba,* made of buckwheat, and *udon,* a thick wheat noodle. Probably most popular of all is *ramen,* a soup-noodle formula of Chinese origin. In hot soup, chilled or fried (*yaki-soba, yaki-udon*), noodles are served ubiquitously in places ranging from upscale specialists to stand-up noodle joints. Soba restaurants also serve noodles cold (*zaru-soba*); dipped soy sauce with wasabi and spring onions, they make an ideal summer lunch.

Tempura & Tonkatsu

Tempura consists of shrimp, fish, and vegetables, individually deep-fried in light, crispy batter. Tempura is dipped into a small bowl of

PRICES

HOTELS

An indication of the cost of a double room in the high season is given by **$** signs.

$$$$$	Over $280
$$$$	$200–$280
$$$	$120–$200
$$	$80 $120
$	Under $80

RESTAURANTS

An indication of the cost of a three-course meal without drinks is given by **$** signs.

$$$$$	Over $80
$$$$	$50–$80
$$$	$35–$50
$$	$20–$35
$	Under $20

a sauce called *tsuyu* mixed with grated ginger and *daikon* (radish).

Tonkatsu consists of pork deep-fried in an egg-and-breadcrumb batter. This delicious dish finds several variants, including *ebi furai* (fried prawns) and *korokke* (potato croquettes). *Kushi-age,* originating in Osaka, is another delicious variant, consisting of a variety of skewered meat, fish, vegetables, and even cheese-based delicacies, dipped in batter and deep-fried.

Izakaya & Nomiya

Cheap savory dishes that go well with booze are popular nationwide. *Izakaya,* a kind of Japanese pub with a broader menu, serve easy-to-share dishes, such as the cheap, delicious *okonomi-yaki;* a savory cabbage pancake consisting of pieces of seafood or pork mixed with a batter consisting of egg, water, flour, and chopped cabbage, topped with a spicy-sweet sauce and mayonnaise.

A variant on the izakaya is the *nomiya:* Literally a drinking house, a nomiya serves cheap drinks and usually specializes in a certain dish, such as *yakitori,* grilled chicken skewers. Another popular nomiya dish is *oden*, a variety of items—including fishcakes, seafood, and eggs—in a piping hot fish stock.

International Cuisine

The Japanese passion for adopting and adapting applies very much to food. Coined during the late 19th century, the term *yoshoku-ya* (Western food restaurant) still applies to places serving Euro-Japanese hybrid food. The most refined recent examples of culinary hybridization are "nouvelle Japanese" and French food served *kaiseki* style. The love affair with French and Italian food is a long one; many of the chefs are foreigners, but increasing numbers of Japanese spend years studying in kitchens in France and Italy before opening restaurants in Japan. French cuisine got here first, but Italian currently has the lead; even the remotest rural coffee shops often produce a form of *spaghetti napolitano*.

Coffee shops are always good for a Western-style snack or *moningu-setto* (morning set)—breakfast. Unlike their big-city counterparts, however, coffee shops in smaller towns often don't open until midmorning. Many will serve lunchtime meals, though be prepared for strange hybrids such as Japanese-style "wafu-pizza" with seaweed, potato, and corn—not to mention Chinese-style ginger-pork, Italian spaghetti, noodles, *tonkatsu*, and potato salad—all on the same plate! Ubiquitous bakeries are usually a better bet for something edible and fast.

The oldest and most popular forms of non-Japanese Asian cuisine are Chinese and Korean. The past two decades have also seen a remarkable increase in authentic Indian and Thai restaurants in larger towns. Appetites for Indonesian and Malay food are escalating as well.

Listings

The hotels and restaurants listed here have been grouped first according to their region, city, and/or neighborhood then listed alphabetically by price category. For disabled access, it is recommended that you check with the establishment to verify the extent of their facilities. For further research, some of the Japanese food websites have new English translations. See Tabelog (*tabelog.com/en*), Gurunavi (*gurunavi.com*), and Hot Pepper (*www.hotpepper -gourmet.com/en*) for local listings beyond the somewhat touristy listings on Trip Advisor.

Listings & Abbreviations

MC = Mastercard, V = Visa

■ TOKYO

AKASAKA

🏨 ANA INTERCONTINENTAL TOKYO

$$$$$
1-12-33 AKASAKA, MINATO-KU
TEL 03/3505-1111
A favorite of foreign businesspeople, this stylish, recently refurbished 1980s hotel is close to Roppongi's nightlife. Highlights include a rooftop pool, the 36th-floor Manhattan Lounge, and excellent sushi and teppan-yaki restaurants.

ℹ️ 844 🚇 Subway: Tameike-sanno 🅿️ 🛗 🚭 Some floors ❄️ 🏊 🏋️ 📶 Free in some rooms 💳 All major cards

SOMETHING SPECIAL

🏨 OKURA TOKYO

$$$$$
2-10-4 TORANOMON, MINATO-KU
TEL 03/3582-0111
www.hotelokura.co.jp
Often cited in business pub-

lications as the finest hotel in Asia, the Okura has a reputation for comfort and service. The decor is understated, elegant 1950s modernism. The best rooms overlook a beautiful Japanese garden.

ℹ️ 381 🚇 Subway: Kamiyacho 🅿️ 🛗 🚭 Some floors 🏊 🏋️ 📶 Free 💳 All major cards

🏨 HILLTOP (YAMA-NO-UE)

$$$$
1-1 KANDA SURUGADAI, CHIYODA-KU
TEL 03/3293-2311
yamanoue-hotel.co.jp
Tokyo's oldest extant Western hotel, built in the 1930s, is a firm favorite with writers and academics, matching art deco styling with old-fashioned comforts and charm.

ℹ️ 35 🚇 Subway: Ochano-mizu, Jimbocho 🅿️ 🛗 📶 Free 💳 All major cards

SOMETHING SPECIAL

🍴 LA TOUR D'ARGENT

$$$$$
6F HOTEL NEW OTANI, 4-1 KIOI-CHO, CHIYODA-KU
TEL 03/3239-3111
The Tokyo branch of this Parisian temple of gastronomy offers superlative French cuisine in one of the city's most opulent settings. Jacket and tie. Reservations essential.

🪑 60 🚇 Subway: Akasaka-mitsuke; JR: Yotsuya 🅿️ 🕐 5:30 p.m.–8:30 p.m. (last reservation). Closed Mon. 🛗 🚭 💳 All major cards

🍴 NINJA AKASAKA

$$$$
1F AKASAKA TOKYU PLAZA, 2-14-3 NAGATA-CHO, CHIYODA-KU
TEL 03/5157-3936
ninjaakasaka.com
Pricey but fun, this ninja-themed restaurant is great for families. Your ninja

waiter leaps from a trapdoor on your arrival and guides you down secret passages to your table in a ninja village. The tasty dishes are presented with dramatic flair, and the magic show at your table is highly convincing.

🛏 143 🚇 Subway: Akasaka-mitsuke 🅿 🚭 None 🕐 5 p.m.–1 a.m., until 11 p.m. Sun. & holidays 💳 All major cards

🍴 ZAKURO
$$–$$$$$
2F AKASAKA BIZ TOWER, 5-3-1 AKASAKA, MINATO-KU
TEL 03/3582-6841
A great place to sample suki-yaki and shabu-shabu, though not the cheapest; you can also opt to have your meal made from Kobe beef. English menu and reasonable lunches.

🛏 143 🚇 Subway: Akasaka 🅿 🕐 11:30 a.m.–3 p.m., 5 p.m.–10 p.m. 🚭 Most seats 💳 All major cards

🍴 MOTI
$–$$$
3F KIMPA BLDG., 2-14-31 AKASAKA, MINATO-KU
TEL 03/3584-6640
This Indian restaurant is one that didn't make compromises to local taste and survived to open several branches. Great tandooris and curries.

🛏 55 🚇 Subway: Akasaka 🕐 11:30 a.m.–10 p.m. 🚭 All major cards

AOYAMA-SHIBUYA-HARAJUKU

🏨 CERULEAN TOWER TOKYU
$$$$$
26-1 SAKURAGAOKA-CHO, SHIBUYA-KU
TEL 03/3476-3000
ceruleantower-hotel.com
The city panoramas are superb, the location excellent, and a Noh theater and jazz club are bonuses. Spacious guest rooms include the

Japanese type, with cypress baths. The stylish lobby has a garden view.

ℹ 411 🚇 Subway/JR: Shibuya 🅿 🚭 🚭 Some floors 🛏 📺 🚭 Free 💳 All major cards

🏨 SHIBUYA EXCEL TOKYU
$$$$
1-12-2 DOGENZAKA, SHIBUYA-KU
TEL 03/5457-0109
www.tokyuhotelsjapan.com
Connected to JR Shibuya Station via footbridge and underground passage, the Excel is above the busy Mark City mall. The upper floors feature superb city views, and two are reserved for women only. Rooms here aren't exactly luxurious, but the location can't be beat.

ℹ 408 🚇 Subway/JR: Shibuya 🅿 🚭 🚭 All floors 🚭 Free 💳 All major cards

🍴 EL CASTELLANO
$$$
MARUSAN AOYAMA BLDG. 2F, 2-9-12 SHIBUYA, SHIBUYA-KU
TEL 03/3407-7197
This Spanish restaurant's genial owner is Castilian. His eatery is informal and high spirited, with authentic, delectable food. Wonderful paella and it's one of the only places in Japan serving rabbit. It can get crowded, so reserve a table. English menu.

🚇 Subway: Omotesando 🕐 6 p.m.–11 p.m. Closed Sun. 🅿 🚭 🚭 No credit cards

🍴 CRAYON HOUSE
$–$$
3-8-15 KITA-AOYAMA, MINATO-KU
TEL 03/3406-6308
www.crayonhouse.co.jp
A popular organic buffet restaurant that won't break the bank. The attached children's bookstore makes this a popular stop for families.

🛏 120 🚇 Subway: Omote-sando 🕐 11 a.m.–11 p.m., weekends & holidays opens 10:30 a.m. 🚭 🚭 All seats 💳 All major cards

GINZA

🏨 PENINSULA TOKYO
$$$$$
1-8-1 YURAKUCHO, CHIYODA-KU
TEL 03/6270-2888
tokyo.peninsula.com
For top-class luxury and service, try the Peninsula, opened in 2007. Steps from Ginza in the business district of Marunouchi, its spacious rooms have outstanding views overlooking the Imperial Palace gardens and moat.

ℹ 314 🚇 Subway: Hibiya, Yurakucho; JR: Tokyo 🅿 🚭 🚭 Some floors 🛏 📺 🚭 Free 💳 All major cards

🏨 🍴 MONTEREY LA SOEUR GINZA
$$$$
1-10-18 GINZA, CHUO-KU
TEL 03/3562-7111
www.hotelmonterey.co.jp
Built in 2000, this charming boutique hotel is popular for its rooms' striped curtains, carved headboards, and warm colors.

ℹ 141 🚇 Subway: Ginza Itchome 🅿 🚭 🚭 Some floors 🚭 Free 💳 All major cards

🏨 VILLA FONTAINE SHIODOME
$$$
SHIODOME SUMITOMO BLDG., HIGASHISHIMBASHI 1-9-2, MINATO-KU
TEL 03/3569-2220
hvf.jp
This business hotel has a dramatic, high atrium lobby and tasteful, minimalist rooms—some overlooking Hamarikyu Garden.

ℹ 492 🚇 Subway or Yurikamome line: Shiodome 🚭 🚭 Some floors 🚭 Free 💳 All major cards

---

🏨 Hotel 🍴 Restaurant ℹ No. of Guest Rooms 🚇 No. of Seats 🚇 Transportation 🅿 Parking 🕐 Hours

🍴 OMATSUYA

$$$$$

7F NISHI GOBANGAI BLDG.,
5-6-13 GINZA, CHUO-KU
TEL 03/3571-7053

This is about as refined as noodle cooking gets. In the evening, they grill meat, fish, and vegetables over charcoal at your table. English menu.

🍴 20 🚇 Subway: Ginza
🕐 5:30 p.m.–10:30 p.m.
Closed Sat., Sun., & holidays
🛗 🏧 All major cards

🍴 SUSHIKO

$$$$$

6-3-8 GINZA, CHUO-KU
TEL 03/3571-1968

The owner-chef of this small sushi parlor spurns displays of sectioned fish behind the counter, believing that it impairs freshness. Instead the fish is kept chilled out of sight, to be sliced when needed. Reservations recommended. English menu.

🍴 40 🚇 Subway: Ginza
🕐 11:30 a.m.–11:30 p.m.
🚭 Smoking only in private rooms 🏧 All major cards

ROPPONGI-AZABU

🏨 B ROPPONGI

$$$

3-9-8 ROPPONGI, MINATO-KU
TEL 03/5412-0451
theb-hotels.com

The b is as close to the madness of Roppongi's nightclubs as you'd want, yet quiet enough to permit sleep, particularly rooms at the back. The simple bright rooms are dominated by big beds.

ℹ️ 76 🚇 Subway: Roppongi
🅿️ 🛗 🚭 Some floors 📶 Free
🏧 All major cards

🏨 AJIA KAIKAN (HOTEL ASIA CENTER OF JAPAN)

$$

8-10-32 AKASAKA, MINATO-KU
TEL 03/3402-6111
asiacenter.or.jp

Rooms are basic and clean.

Singles are minute, twins and doubles adequate. For the central location and quality, rates are outstanding, so reserve well in advance. Canteen-style restaurant.

ℹ️ 175 🚇 Subway: Aoyama-ichome, Nogizaka 🛗
🚭 Some floors 🅿️ 📶 Free
🏧 All major cards

🍴 FUKUZUSHI

$$–$$$$$

5-7-8 ROPPONGI, MINATO-KU
TEL 03/3402-4116
roppongifukuzushi.com

This sushi restaurant, reputed as one of Tokyo's finest, serves exquisite fare in a minimalist modern setting. Dress shirts required for men. Reasonable lunch menu.

🍴 100 🚇 Subway: Roppongi
🕐 11:30 a.m.–2 p.m.,
6 p.m.–11 p.m. Closed Sun. & holidays 🚭 🏧 All major cards

🍴 KITCHEN FIVE

$$$$

4-2-15 NISHI-AZABU,
MINATO-KU
TEL 03/3409-8835

Everyone loves Kobayashi-san and her tiny counter restaurant, serving Mediterranean dishes such as moussaka gleaned from travels around Europe and Latin America. You may have to wait in line.

🍴 20 🚇 Subway: Roppongi
🕐 6 p.m.–11 p.m. Closed
Sun., Mon., Thurs., & holidays
🚭 All seats 🚫 No credit cards

🍴 TEMPURA FUKUSHIMA

$$$$

TANUKI BLDG. B1F, 4-10-12
ROPPONGI, MINATO-KU
TEL 03/3403-5507

Founded by the chef of the centuries-old Inagiku House in Ginza, this is a tempura paradigm (with kaiseki dishes, too). Everything reflects traditional Japanese taste—the decor, presentation, and, of course, food. English menu.

🍴 26 🚇 Subway: Roppongi 🕐 11:30 a.m.–2 p.m.,

5 p.m.–9 p.m. Closed Sun.
🚭 🏧 All major cards

🍴 GANCHAN

$$$

OKAUE BLDG. 1F, 6-8-23
ROPPONGI, MINATO-KU
TEL 03/3478-0092
gurunavi.com/en/g898300
/rst

The yakitori experience at its most relaxed and delicious. Boisterous, colorful, and tiny, Ganchan is a popular feeding station for the Roppongi clubbing crowd. English menu.

🍴 20 🚇 Subway: Roppongi
🕐 5 p.m.–3 a.m., 11 p.m. on
Sun. 🏧 All major cards

🍴 NANBANTEI

$$$

NANBAN BLDG. 1F, 4-5-6
ROPPONGI, MINATO-KU
TEL 03/3402-0606
nanbantei.com

Essentially *yakitori,* but a cut above the average— a specialty is meat dipped in miso sauce and grilled. The difference shows in *nanban yaki,* with succulent pieces of beef instead of chicken. English menu.

🍴 30 🚇 Subway: Roppongi
🕐 5:30 p.m.–11 p.m. Closed
Sun. 🏧 All major cards

SHINJUKU

🏨 🍴 PARK HYATT TOKYO

$$$$$

3-7-1-2 NISHI-SHINJUKU
TEL 03/5322-1234
tokyo.park.hyatt.com

Located in Kenzo Tange's Park Tower Building, the Park Hyatt is the ultimate luxury hotel. Plush and beautiful, its large rooms have stunning cityscapes from the windows and regal bathrooms. The four restaurants include the famed New York Grill (see p. 366).

ℹ️ 177 🚇 Subway: Shinjuku, Tochomae; JR: Shinjuku
🅿️ 🛗 🚭 Some floors 🏊 🏋️
📶 Free 🏧 All major cards

🛗 Elevator 🚭 Nonsmoking 🌀 Air-conditioning 🏊 Indoor Pool 🏊 Outdoor Pool 🏋️ Health Club 📶 Wi-Fi 🏧 Credit Cards

🏨 TOKYU STAY NISHI-SHINJUKU
$$
5-9-8 NISHI-SHINJUKU,
SHINJUKU-KU
TEL 03/3370-1090
tokyustay.co.jp
One of the new generation of weekly business hotels, Tokyu Stay offers great discounts on inexpensive rooms for longer reservations. Rooms are bright, and most are equipped with kitchenettes and washing machines.
🛏 148 🚇 Subway: Nishi Shinjuku Gochome; JR: Shinjuku 🍴 🅢 Some floors 🛜 Free 🅢 All major cards

SOMETHING SPECIAL

🍴 NEW YORK GRILL
$$$$$
52F PARK HYATT HOTEL,
3-7-1-2 NISHI-SHINJUKU
TEL 03/5323-3458
tokyo.park.hyatt.com
The Grill is one of Tokyo's prime locales for eating out in style. The food is American, including superlative steaks and seafood, in a modernist art deco setting with stunning cityscapes from the floor-to-ceiling windows. Reservations advised. English menu.
🪑 138 🚇 Subway: Shinjuku, Tochomae; JR: Shinjuku 🕐 11:30 a.m.–2:30 p.m., 5:30 p.m.–10 p.m. 🍴 🅢 Except the bar 🅢 All major cards

🍴 KAKIDEN
$$$–$$$$
YASUYO BLDG. 6-9F,
3-37-11 SHINJUKU
TEL 03/3352-5121
kakiden.com/english
The Tokyo branch of a venerable restaurant. Despite the modern building, the interior is traditional. Offers several set menus of refined kaiseki cuisine to suit your taste—and pocket. Reservations recommended

for Japanese-style rooms. English menu.
🪑 38 🚇 Subway/JR: Shinjuku 🕐 11 a.m.–10 p.m. 🍴 🅢 Except private rooms 🅢 All major cards

🍴 TSUKIJI EDOGIN
$$$
4-5-1 TSUKIJI, CHUO-KU
TEL 03/3543-4401
The fish is virtually ocean fresh at this venerable sushi restaurant close to Tsukiji market. It's packed at lunchtime. English menu.
🪑 140 🚇 Subway: Tsukiji, Higashi-Ginza 🕐 11:30 a.m.–9:30 p.m. 🅢 🅢 All major cards

🍴 TOKAIEN
$–$$$
1-6-3 KABUKI-CHO,
SHINJUKU-KU
TEL 03/3200-2934
A contender for the largest Korean *yakiniku* (grilled meat) restaurant in Japan, it covers nine floors offering different formulas: set meals, à la carte, all-you-can-eat, and private, sumptuous feasts.
🪑 12 🚇 Subway/JR: Shinjuku 🕐 11:30 a.m.–2 a.m. 🍴 🅢 All major cards

UENO/ASAKUSA

🏨 COCO GRAND UENO SHINOBAZU
$$$
2-12-14 UENO, TAITO-KU
TEL 03/5812-1155
cocogrand.co.jp/ueno shinobazu
This 2010 boutique hotel overlooks Shinobazu pond in Ueno Park. Rooms are on the small side, but stylish, and the staff helpful. The small spa is a great way to soak off muscles stiff from walking.
🛏 58 🚇 JR: Ueno 🍴 🅢 Some floors 🛜 Free 🅢 All major cards

🏨 SADACHIYO
🍴 **$$**
2-20-1 ASAKUSA, TAITO-KU
TEL 03/3842-6431
sadachiyo.co.jp
This friendly urban ryokan is a hit, with accents of the "real Japan." Rooms are beautifully designed in a modern, minimalist Japanese style with bath. Offers entertainments such as geisha-style dinners, sumo, and Sumida River boat trips. Meals not included. Dinner in the restaurant is excellent, but expensive.
🛏 20 🚇 Subway: Asakusa, Tawaramachi 🍴 🛜 Free 🅢 All major cards

🍴 WAENTAI KIKKO
$$–$$$$$
2-2-13 ASAKUSA, TAITO-KU
TEL 03/5828-8833
waentei-kikko.com
Just across from Senso-ji's bell tower, this restaurant's excellent lunch sets come with a performance of the *tsugaru-samisen* (traditional three-string lute) by the owner. The rustic style of the building is an excellent

complement to the perfor-
mance. English menu.
🚹 20 🚇 Subway: Asakusa
🕐 11:30 a.m.–2:30 p.m.,
5:30 p.m.–10 p.m. Closed
Wed. 🚫 Lunch only
🅰 All major cards

🍴 DAIKOKUYA
$$
1-38-10 ASAKUSA
TEL 03/3844-1111
tempura.co.jp
Serving tempura since
the late 19th century,
Daikokuya is in a traditional
building painted white.
What the food lacks in
refinement, it makes up for
with good, hearty flavor.
English menu.
🚹 300 🚇 Subway: Asakusa
🕐 11 a.m.–8:30 p.m.
🅰 No credit cards

■ EXCURSIONS FROM TOKYO

HAKONE & FUJI FIVE LAKES

SOMETHING SPECIAL
🏨 FUJIYA
🍴 $$$$
359 MIYANOSHITA, HAKONE-
MACHI, ASHIGARASHIMO-GUN
TEL 0460/82-2211
fujiyahotel.jp
One of Japan's most
famous, old, and charm-
ing hotels—a paragon of
Japanese-Eurasian style,
architecturally, conceptually,
and gastronomically. Stroll
in beautiful gardens with
views (and, hey, John and
Yoko used to stay here!).
English spoken. Good 1930s
Japanese deco-style res-
taurant serving a range of
meals from sandwiches to
opulent dinners ($–$$$$$).
🚹 146 🚇 Hakone Tozan;
Railway: Miyanoshita 🅿
🔄 🚫 All rooms 🅰 ❄
🛜 Free in lobby
🅰 All major cards

🏨 FUJI-VIEW
$$$
511 KATSUYAMA,
FUJI KAWAGUCHI-CHO,
MINAMI TSURU-GUN
TEL 0555/83-2211
fujiview.jp
A venerable hotel with a
lovely lakeside (Kawaguchi-
ko) location that's close to
Fuji-san. Has Western and
Japanese rooms. English-
speaking staff will help plan
your sightseeing.
🚹 79 🚇 Shuttle from Kawa-
guchiko Station 🅿
🔄 🚫 All rooms 🛜 Free
🅰 All major cards

🏨 ASHIWADA
$$
395 NAGAHAMA, FUJI
KAWAGUCHI-KO-MACHI,
MINAMITSURU-GUN,
YAMANASHI
TEL 0555/82-2321
asiwadahotel.co.jp
This concrete structure is a
bit of a blight on the lakeside,
but you won't notice once
inside. Many of the comfort-
able rooms (all with bath-
room) offer superb views of
Kawaguchi-ko. A Japanese
Inn Group (JIG) member, the
hotel is convenient for sight-
seeing and climbing Fuji-san.
🚹 40 🚇 Shuttle from
Kawaguchiko Station 🅿 🔄
🚫 Some rooms 🛜 Free
🅰 All major cards

🏨 FUJI-HAKONE GUESTHOUSE
$
912 SENGOKUHARA, HAKONE-
MACHI, KANAGAWA
TEL 0460/84-6577
fujihakone.com
A favorite on the Japanese
Inn Group circuit, this lies
in a wooded setting with
mountain views. The owners
speak English well and have a
reputation for being helpful;
a great choice if you intend
to go hiking. Communal bath
only with natural hot spring
water; breakfast only.
🚹 14 🚇 Hakone Tozan bus

for Togendai from Odawara
bus terminal (Senkyoro-mae
stop) 🅿 🚫 🛜 Free
🅰 All major cards

KAMAKURA

🍴 RAITEI
$–$$$$
3-1-1 KAMAKURA-YAMA
TEL 0467/32-5656
raitei.com
This restaurant is a highlight
of a trip to Kamakura. The
location is countrified, with
bamboo groves in the garden.
Choose cheap and varied
noodles or more expensive
kaiseki sets (must reserve in
advance). English menu.
🚹 60 🚇 JR: Kamakura
🕐 11 a.m.–5 p.m., kaiseki until
8 p.m. Closed major holidays.
🚫 🅰 All major cards

🍴 NAKAMURA-AN
$
1-7-6 KOMACHI
TEL 0467/25-3500
nakamura-an.com
At Kamakura's most famous
noodle place, favorites
include handmade soba
soup noodles with tempura
shrimp. English menu.
🚇 JR: Kamakura
🕐 11:30 a.m.–5 p.m.
Closed Irregularly 🚫
🅰 No credit cards

NIKKO

🏨 NIKKO KANAYA
🍴 HOTEL
$$$$
1300 KAMI-HATSUISHI-MACHI,
NIKKO-SHI, TOCHIGI
TEL 0288/54-0001
kanayahotel.co.jp
Opened by the Kanaya
family in 1873; current build-
ings and fixtures, including a
fireplace designed by Frank
Lloyd Wright, reflect the
Western-Japanese hybridiza-
tion popular in the early
20th century. Amenities in-
clude a Japanese garden and
a skating rink (winter only).
The wonderful columned

dining hall provides plenty of atmosphere; specialties include local rainbow trout (reservations advisable for weekends and holidays).

🛈 71 🚆 JR: Nikko
🅿 🍴 🏊 🛜 Free
🎴 All major cards

🏨 TURTLE INN

$

2-16 TAKUMI-CHO, NIKKO-SHI, TOCHIGI
TEL 0288/53-3168
turtle-nikko.com

A much-esteemed Japanese Inn Group member, this modern ryokan is close to the sights. The friendly, English-speaking owner will give you information about sightseeing and hiking. Both Japanese- and Western-style (with and without bath) rooms overlook the river. Order meals (which cost extra) in advance. There is a dining room, but guests can also dine in their rooms.

🛈 10; Hotori-an Annex 11
🚆 Bus from Tobu-Nikko or Nikko Station to Sogo Kaikan-mae stop 🈂 All rooms 🛜 Free
🎴 All major cards

🍴 MASUDA-YA

$$$

439-2 ISHIYA-MACHI, NIKKO-SHI, TOCHIGI
TEL 0288/54-2151

Built during the Taisho era (1912–1926), this venerable restaurant serves reasonably priced set meals known for incorporating *yuba* (the skin of soybean milk), a Nikko specialty once reserved for aristocrats and priests. Reservations advisable.

🍴 58 🚆 Tobu Nikko line: Tobu-Nikko ⏰ 11 a.m.– 2:30 p.m. Closed Thurs. April– Nov. Closed irregularly Dec.– Mar. 🈂 All 🎴 MC, V

YOKOHAMA

🍴 HEICHINRO

$$–$$$$

149 YAMASHITA-CHO, NAKA-KU
TEL 045/681-3001
heichin.com/en

They do dimsum (*yamucha* in Japanese) at lunchtime here and are recommended for their Cantonese cuisine. English menu.

🍴 684 🚆 Negishi line: Ishikawacho ⏰ 11 a.m.– 10 p.m. Closed 2nd & 4th Tues.
🍴 🈂 🎴 All major cards

🍴 SHIN-YOKOHAMA RAMEN MUSEUM

$

2-14-21 SHIN-YOKOHAMA, KOHOKU-KU
TEL 045/471-0503
raumen.co.jp

Come here to learn everything about Japan's favorite noodle of Chinese origin. This food theme park's mock-up of a 1950s Shitamachi (downtown) block has nine different ramen shops chosen from throughout the archipelago. English menu.

🍴 228 🚆 Train: Shin-Yokohama ⏰ 11 a.m.–10 p.m
🅿 🍴 🈂 A few smoking areas
🎴 No credit cards

⬛ HOKKAIDO

AKAN NATIONAL PARK

🏨 TSURUGA AKAN YUKU NO SATO

$$$

1-5-10 AKANKO ONSEN, AKAN-CHO, KUSHIRO-SHI
TEL 0154/67-4000
tsuruga.com

Yuku no Sato is one of the most luxurious ryokan on Lake Akan, with a host of baths, stunning rooms overlooking the lake, and a huge buffet restaurant.

🛈 233 🚆 10-min. walk from Akanko Onsen bus terminal
🅿 🍴 🈂 Some rooms
🛜 Free 🎴 All major cards

🏨 MINSHUKU KIRI

$

4-3-26 AKANKO ONSEN,
AKAN-CHO, KUSHIRO-SHI
TEL 0154/67-2755

Opposite the luxury Akan Grand Hotel is this popular, homey minshuku. Rooms are basic, clean, and Japanese style. Includes meals. Communal bathroom with spa water. No Internet.

🛈 7 🚆 10-min. walk from Akanko Onsen bus terminal
🅿 🎴 All major cards

DAISETSUZAN NATIONAL PARK

🏨 SOUNKYO MOUNTAIN VIEW HOTEL

$$$

SOUNKYO, KAMIKAWA-CHO, KAMIKAWA-GUN
TEL 0165/85-3011
hotel-taisetsu.com

This 1980s chalet-style hotel is a welcome change from concrete-blockhouse resort hotel architecture. It lies in a valley on the village outskirts. The best (i.e., higher) rooms offer good views of the gorge. Communal hot-spring bath. Meals included.

🛈 99 🚆 Sekihoku line: Kamikawa, then Dohoku Bus to Sounkyo stop 🅿 🍴
🛜 Free 🎴 All major cards

HAKODATE

🏨 HAKODATE KOKUSAI

$$$$

5-10 OTE-MACHI
TEL 0138/23-5151
hakodate-kokusai.jp

The city's best Western-style hotel consists of two adjacent buildings; the sleek new building has the more expensive rooms, with great views over the harbor.

🛈 305 🚆 JR: Hakodate 🅿
🍴 🈂 Some floors 🛜 Free
🎴 All major cards

🍴 HAKODATE BEER

$$

5-22 OTE-MACHI
TEL 0138/23-8000

This popular and crowded restaurant and microbrewery

is in a converted warehouse on the waterfront. You dine on Western and Japanese fare in a vast redbrick hall; copper vats behind glass produce the outstanding house brews. English menu.

🚋 Tram: Uoichiba-dori
🕐 11 a.m.–3 p.m., 5 p.m.–9:30 p.m. Closed Wed.
💳 All major cards

SAPPORO

🏨 🍴 SAPPORO GRAND HOTEL
$$$
KITA 1, NISHI 4, CHUO-KU
TEL 011/261-3311
grand1934.com
The city's longest established and most prestigious hotel (opened in 1934), a ten-minute walk south of the train station, embraces two newer buildings. Rooms are spacious and superbly appointed. Try **Le Grand Chef**, the hotel's plush French restaurant, for wonderful local ingredients (scallops, crab, duck, salmon, lamb, etc.).

ℹ️ 504 🚇 Subway: Odori; JR: Sapporo 🅿️ 🛗
📶 Some floors 💪 📶 Free
💳 All major cards

🏨 NAKAMURAYA RYOKAN
$$
KITA 3, NISHI 7, CHUO-KU
TEL 011/241-2111
nakamura-ya.com
A long-established Japanese Inn Group ryokan now housed in a modern building, this has good-size tatami rooms, all with bathrooms. The cuisine is based on local seafood.

ℹ️ 25 🚇 Subway/JR: Sapporo 🅿️ 📶 Free 💳 MC, V

🍴 HYOSETSU-NO-MON
$$$–$$$$$
MINAMI 5, NISHI 2, CHUO-KU
TEL 011/521-3046

King crab—and only king crab—is the stuff of this famous Sapporo institution, where it is served in various formats and prices on several floors. English menu.

🚋 400 🚇 JR: Susukino
🕐 11 a.m.–11 p.m. 🛗
💳 All major cards

SHIKOTSU-TOYA NATIONAL PARK

🏨 KASHOTEI HANAYA
$$$
134 NOBORIBETSUONSEN-CHO, NOBORIBETSU-SHI
TEL 0143/84-2521
kashoutei-hanaya.co.jp
A Japanese Inn Group member (mention you book), this is a very good value. Three Japanese rooms have bathrooms; there's a large public bathroom and outdoor baths—spa water, of course. Meals are extra, served in your room. English spoken.

ℹ️ 21 🚋 Bus from Noboribetsu Station 🅿️
📶 Free 💳 All major cards

🏨 TOYA SUN PALACE
$$
7-1 TOYA-KO ONSEN, SOBETSU-CHO, USU-GUN
TEL 0142/75-1111
toyasunpalace.co.jp
The largest and most famous of the Toya-ko lakeside resort hotels boasts thermal baths and swimming pools with waterslides for children. Staying at its similarly priced sister hotel, Toya Park Hotel Tensho (tel 0142/75-2445), entitles you to use the Sun Palace's bathing facilities, and vice versa.

ℹ️ 452 🚋 Donan bus: Higashimachi Terminal
🅿️ 🈂️ 📶 10 rooms
📶 Free 💳 All major cards

SHIRETOKO NATIONAL PARK

🏨 SHIRETOKO GRAND HOTEL KITAKOBUSHI
$$$
172 UTORO HIGASHI, SHARI-CHO, SHARI-GUN
TEL 0152/24-2021
shiretoko.co.jp
With fine views over the sea ice and rugged Shiretoko Peninsula, this hot spring hotel is the perfect place to relax after a day of natural adventure. The rooftop bath is particularly memorable.

ℹ️ 181 🚋 Bus: Utoro Terminal 🅿️ 🛗 💳 All 📶 Free
💳 All major cards

■ NORTHERN HONSHU (TOHOKU)

AKITA-KEN

🏨 TAMACHI BUKEYASHIKI
$$$
23 TAMACHISHIMO-CHO, KAKUNODATE
TEL 0187/52-1700
bukeyashiki.jp
An excellent fusion of Western and Japanese styles, the rooms combine the simple aesthetic of dark wood, whitewashed walls, and paper lamps with foreign comforts such as heated flooring and beds, rather than futons. Built in 1998, this boutique hotel strikes an excellent balance between hip and timelessly classic, with hospitable staff.

ℹ️ 12 🚇 JR: 15-min. walk from Kakunodate Station
🅿️ 💳 All rooms 📶 Free
💳 All major cards

🏨 TSURUNOYU ONSEN
$$$
50 KOKUYURIN SENDAT-SUIZAWA TAZAWA AZA, SENBOKU-SHI
TEL 0187/46-2139
tsurunoyu.com
The oldest ryokan in Nyuto

Onsen, Tsurunoyu has been a therapeutic retreat for 350 years. Notable for its milky-white waters, rustic thatched buildings, and mountain cuisine. The main outdoor bath is same-sex.

🚋 35 🚈 Akita Shinkansen: Tazawako Station, Ugo-Kotsu bus for Nyuto Onsen to Arupa Komakusa stop, then local pickup 🅿 ⬢ MC, V

🏨 AKITA CASTLE
$$
1-3-5 NAKA-DORI, AKITA-SHI
TEL 018/834-1141
castle-hotel.jp
This is a plush hotel with views of the park and moat surrounding Akita-jo's ruins.

🛏 150 🚈 JR: Akita ⬆
⬢ Some floors 📶 Free
⬢ All major cards

AOMORI-KEN

🏨 NEW CASTLE
$$
24-1 KAMISAYASHI-MACHI, HIROSAKI
TEL 0172/36-1211
Hirosaki's hotels conform to all the usual conveniences, comforts, and good service predominating in Japan. An added convenience is its proximity to Hirosaki Castle.

🛏 50 🚈 JR: Hirosaki 🅿 ⬆
📶 Free ⬢ All major cards

🏨 RICHMOND HOTEL AOMORI
$$
1-6-6 NAGASHIMA, AOMORI-SHI
TEL 017/732-7655
aomori.richmondhotel.jp
Built in 2009, this location pushes the boundaries of "business hotel" while keeping the price down. Rooms are decorated in tasteful dark hues and are considerably more spacious than those of a standard Tokyo business hotel.

🛏 175 🚈 JR: 15-min. walk from Aomori Station
🅿 ⬆ ⬢ Some floors
📶 Free ⬢ All major cards

🍴 JINTAKO
$$$$
1-6-16 YASUKATA, AOMORI-SHI
TEL 0177/22-7727
en-aomori.com/food-035.html
Here you can sample delicious local specialties such as scallops broiled in the shell and warming codfish stews. Make a night of it listening to the *samisen* played live in the rousing style.

🪑 24 🚈 JR: Aomori
🕐 6 p.m.–10:30 p.m. Closed 1st & 3rd Sun. ⬢ No credit cards

IWATE-KEN

🏨 METROPOLITAN MORIOKA
$$$
2-27 MORIOKA-EKIMAE-KITA-DORI (NEW WING), 1-44 MORIOKA-EKIMAE-DORI (MAIN WING), MORIOKA-SHI
TEL 019/625-1211
www.metro-morioka.co.jp
The Metropolitan's new wing is slightly more expensive than the nearby old wing. Rooms in the old wing are more basic, but in both places you get comfort and service.

🛏 121 (new wing), 190 (main wing) 🚈 JR: Morioka
🅿 ⬆ ⬢ Some floors 📶 Free
⬢ All major cards

🍴 AZUMAYA
$$
1-8-3 NAKA-NO-HASHI-DORI, MORIOKA-SHI
TEL 019/622-2252
wankosoba-azumaya.co.jp
This is the most famous place to eat local specialties. *Wanko soba* consists of soup noodles with fish, meat, and vegetable side dishes. The noodles are served in small bowls, and the idea is to stack up as many empty ones as you possibly can, outeating everyone else (don't worry, competitions are optional). *Reimen*, more popular in summer, are thin, translucent noodles served cold with various ingredients. English menu.

PRICES

HOTELS

An indication of the cost of a double room in the high season is given by $ signs.

$$$$$	Over $280
$$$$	$200–$280
$$$	$120–$200
$$	$80–$120
$	Under $80

RESTAURANTS

An indication of the cost of a three-course meal without drinks is given by $ signs.

$$$$$	Over $80
$$$$	$50–$80
$$$	$35–$50
$$	$20–$35
$	Under $20

🪑 100 🚈 JR: Morioka Station, then 10-min. taxi
🕐 11 a.m.–3 p.m., 5 p.m.–8 p.m. ⬢ All seats
⬢ All major cards

SENDAI & MATSUSHIMA

🏨 RICHMOND PREMIER SENDAI EKIMAE
$$$
5F SENDAI TOHO BLDG., 2-1-1 CHUO, AOBA-KU, SENDAI-SHI
TEL 022/716-2855
sendai-ekimae.richmondhotel.jp
Richmond Premier hotels are slightly more upscale from their standard business hotel line: This one sits moments away from Sendai Station, perfect for an early start or a late arrival. Rooms are larger than usual and tastefully but simply decorated.

🛏 184 🚈 JR: 3-min. walk from Sendai Station
⬆ ⬢ Some floors 📶 Free
⬢ All major cards

🏨 TAIKANSO
$$$
10-76 MATSUSHIMA AZA INUTA, MATSUSHIMA-MACHI,

MIYAGI-GUN
TEL 022/354-2161
taikanso.co.jp
If you're going to stay in Matsushima, why not do as the Japanese do and treat yourself to a palatial resort hotel like this? Spectacular views, a choice of Western or Japanese rooms (the most expensive look out over the bay), tantalizing food options, and onsen baths.
[i] 256 [F] Shuttle from JR Senseki line: Matsushimakaigan [car] [P] [elevator]
[wifi] In lobby [cards] All major cards

🍴 DONJIKI CHAYA
$
129 AZAMACHIUCHI, MATSU-SHIMA, MATSUSHIMA-CHO, MIYAGI-KEN
TEL 022/354-5855
Built in the late 1600s, this remains a charming and venerable noodle stop.
[clock] 35 [F] JR Senseki line: Matsushimakaigan [P]
[clock] 9 a.m.–5 p.m. Closed irregularly [cards] No credit cards

■ CENTRAL HONSHU (CHUBU)

KANAZAWA

Note that many restaurants in Kanazawa close their doors at 8 p.m. and sometimes even 7 p.m.

🏨 KANAZAWA NEW GRAND
$$
4-1 MINAMI-CHO
TEL 076/233-1311
newgrand-annex.com
In addition to a convenient location between Kenroku-en garden and the Nagamachi samurai district, the Grand offers great service, good views, fine cuisine in its four restaurants, and an English-speaking staff. The rooms are

plush and well appointed.
[i] 215 [F] Bus: Minami-cho stop [P] [elevator] [nonsmoking] Some floors [wifi] Free [cards] All major cards

🍴 KINOYA
$$$
5-7 SHOWA-MACHI, KANAZAWA-SHI, ISHIKAWA-KEN
TEL 076/221-8433
Depending on the season, saying *omakase* (it's up to the chef) could bring you little raw purple squid mixed with miso, cheesy *funazushi* (fermented fish), or a bowl of wriggling live minnows. The staff will help you with the menu if it's too extreme. The restaurant is just three blocks south of Kanazawa Station—look for the small playground out front.
[clock] 80 [F] Train: 5-min. walk from Kanazawa Station
[clock] 5 p.m.–11 p.m. Closed Sun. [nonsmoking] In private rooms
[cards] All major cards

🍴 MIYOSHIAN
$$–$$$$
1-11 KENROKU-MACHI
TEL 076/221-0127
Located in the Kenroku-en garden and more than 100 years old, this delightful restaurant is the place to try *Kaga ryori*. In winter it serves *jibuni*, duck stew; sashimi and eel on rice are on the menu in other seasons. Lunch sets (mainly bento boxes) are an outstanding value; a more expensive option is the Kaga ryori dinner, served kaiseki style. Dinner available by reservation only.
[clock] 80 [F] Bus 11 or 12 to Kenrokuenshita Kanazawajo 23 [clock] Closed Wed., irregularly [nonsmoking] All [cards] No credit cards

MATSUMOTO

🏨 BUENA VISTA
🍴 $$$$
1-2-1 HONJO
TEL 0263/37-0111

buena-vista.co.jp
At the smartest business hotel in town, the rooms are small but comfortable. One of the hotel's five restaurants, **Hanakirabe,** lets you sample most kinds of Japanese cuisine at a variety of counters.
[i] 190 [F] JR: Matsumoto [P] [elevator] [nonsmoking] Some floors [wifi] Free [cards] All major cards

🍴 HANATOBIRA
$$–$$$$
1-2-18 FUKASHI
TEL 0263/35-7632
Kajika, a local river fish, is one of the specialties. Pleasant traditional decor with black wood on white plaster. For lunch and dinner, different price and preparation offered.
[clock] 70 [clock] 11:30 a.m.–2 p.m., 5:30 p.m.–10 p.m. Closed Sun.
[F] JR: Matsumoto
[nonsmoking] Except private rooms
[cards] All major cards

NAGOYA

🏨 HILTON NAGOYA
$$$$
1-3-3 SAKAE, NAKA-KU
TEL 052/212-1111
hilton.com
This well-located, 28-story hotel has large rooms with king-size beds, Japanese design motifs, and Western comforts. Great cityscapes from rooms on upper floors. Amenities include a Japanese bath, gym, and tennis courts. Single rooms have double beds; couples can stay at the single rate during low season.
[i] 460 [F] Subway: Fushimi [P] [elevator] [nonsmoking] Some floors [indoor pool] [health club]
[wifi] Free [cards] All major cards

🏨 NAGOYA B'S HOTEL
$$
1-16-2 NISHIKI, NAKA-KU
TEL 052/220-3131
bs-hotel.co.jp
This older business hotel stands out for its efforts to provide unusual amenities,

including a public bath, treadmill room, relaxation room with board games, a large bank of free PCs, and a free Western breakfast. Some English spoken; very polite and welcoming.

🛈 387 🚇 Subway: Fushimi ⬆️⬇️ Some floors 📺 📶 Free ♿ All major cards

🍴 ATSUTA HORAIKEN HONTEN
$$$
503 GOUDO-CHO, ATSUTA-KU
TEL 052/671-8686
This well-known, 160-year-old restaurant south of Atsuta-jingu serves up *hitsumabushi*, Nagoya-style grilled eel. Guests divide the eel over rice into four, first eating a quarter plain, then with scallions and wasabi, then mixed with broth, and lastly in the way you liked best. Expect a wait of 30 minutes or try the branch next to the south gate of the shrine.

🪑 180 🚇 Subway: Temmacho 🕐 11:30 a.m.–2 p.m., 4:30 p.m.–8:30 p.m. Closed Wed., 2nd & 4th Thurs. 📶 ♿ All major cards

🍴 YABATON ESUKATEN
$
ESUKA UNDERGROUND SHOPPING CENTER, 6-9 TSUBAKI-CHO, NAKAMURA-KU, NAGOYA-SHI, AICHI-KEN
TEL 052/452-6500
english.yabaton.com
Nagoya is known for dishes flavored with red miso; Yabaton has made its name on huge, succulent *tonkatsu* (pork cutlets) slathered in this rich sauce, rather than the usual Japanese version of HP Sauce. Look for the pig character and the queue in the Esuka Mall.

🪑 49 🚇 JR: Nagoya 🕐 11 a.m.–10 p.m. 📶 All ♿ All major cards

TAKAYAMA

🏨 SUMIYOSHI RYOKAN
$$$
4-21 HONMACHI
TEL 0577/32-0228
sumiyoshi-ryokan.com
This quaint traditional inn overlooks the Miya-gawa riverbank, opposite one end of the morning market. Cozy, well-decorated rooms.

🛈 8 🚇 Train: 15-min. walk from Takayama Station 🅿️ 📶 Free ♿ No credit cards

🍴 FUNASAKA SHUZO
$$
105 KAMISANNO-MACHI
TEL 0577/32-0016
www.funasaka-shuzo.co.jp
One of several saké breweries in the traditional Sanmachi district, Funasaka stands out with its attached restaurant, serving soba, mountain vegetables, or Hida beef set meals as an excuse to try more of the local brew. Cross the Nakabashi bridge east from Takayama Jinya and turn north one block in from the Miya-gawa River.

🪑 80 🕐 11:30 a.m.–2:30 p.m., 5 p.m.–8 p.m. 🚇 Train: 15-min. walk from Takayama Station 📶 All ♿ No credit cards

🍴 SUZUYA
$$
24 HANAKAWA-MACHI
TEL 0577/32-2484
suzuyatakayama.ec-net.jp
South of Kokubunji St., Suzuya is an inexpensive place to try melt-in-the-mouth Hida beef and Takayama's specialty, *houba-miso*: vegetables (sometimes with beef) mixed with miso and grilled on a large magnolia leaf at the table.

🪑 60 🕐 11 a.m.–2 p.m., 5 p.m.–8 p.m. Closed some Tues. 🚇 Train: 10-min. walk from Takayama Station 🅿️ 📶 All at dinner ♿ All major cards

---

PRICES
HOTELS
An indication of the cost of a double room in the high season is given by **$** signs.

$$$$$	Over $280
$$$$	$200–$280
$$$	$120–$200
$$	$80–$120
$	Under $80

RESTAURANTS
An indication of the cost of a three-course meal without drinks is given by **$** signs.

$$$$$	Over $80
$$$$	$50–$80
$$$	$35–$50
$$	$20–$35
$	Under $20

YUZAWA ONSEN

🏨 TAKAHAN RYOKAN
$$$
923 YUZAWA, YUZAWA-MACHI
TEL 025/784-3333
takahan.co.jp
Eight hundred years old, this inn has been a family business since its founding, and it remains one of the most prestigious ryokan in Yuzawa Onsen. Yasunari Kawabata stayed here to pen his Nobel Prize–winning novel *Yukiguni*, and his room has been preserved as it was in 1934, though the current building dates from 1989. The meals and bath are excellent, and views stretch out across the snowy valley.

🛈 34 🚇 Shuttle bus available, call from Echigo-Yuzawa Station 🅿️ ⬆️⬇️ 📶 Free ♿ All major cards

🏛 KYOTO

ARASHIYAMA

🍴 KITCHO
$$$$$

---

58 SUSUKI-NO-BABA-CHO, TENRYU-JI, SAGA, UKYO-KU
TEL 075/881-1101
kitcho.com/kyoto/chef_en
Kitcho is often said to be the most expensive restaurant in Japan, but a meal here is an exquisite kaiseki experience: Wonderful food is served on priceless antique tableware in a beautiful sylvan setting in Arashiyama.

🛏 6 rooms 🚃 Keifuku Dentetsu Arashiyama line: Arashiyama 🕐 11:30 a.m.– 1 p.m., 5 p.m.–7 p.m. Closed Wed. 🃏 All major cards

🍴 UNAGI-YA HIROKAWA
$$–$$$
44-1 SAGATENRYUJI KITATSU-KURIMICHI-CHO, UKYO-KU
TEL 075/871-5226
unagi-hirokawa.jp
Directly facing the gates of Tenryu-ji in Arashiyama, this is Kyoto's preeminent *unagi* (eel) restaurant. The menu has several more expensive sets to splurge on for dinner, but the basic lunch set is very affordable and the eel is melt-in-your-mouth amazing.

🛏 50 🚃 JR: Saga-Arashiyama 🅿 🕐 11 a.m.–2:30 p.m., 5 p.m.–9 p.m. Closed Mon. 🃏 All major cards

CENTRAL KYOTO

SOMETHING SPECIAL

🏨 HIIRAGIYA
$$$$$
NAKAHAKUSANCHO, FUYACHO ANEKOJI-AGARU, NAKAGYO-KU
TEL 075/221-1136
hiiragiya.co.jp
A traditional ryokan that has accommodated Japanese royalty. The service is attentive, the tatami rooms beautifully appointed.

🛏 28 🚇 Tozai line: Kyoto Shiyakusho-mae 🅿 🚭 2 rooms 🛜 Free 🃏 All major cards

🏨 GRANVIA KYOTO
$$$–$$$$
JR KYOTO STATION,

KARASUMA CHUO-GUCHI, SHIOKOJI-SAGARU, KARASUMA DORI, SHIMOGYO-KU
TEL 075/344-8888
granviakyoto.com
The hotel's location is hard to beat for convenience for rail travelers. Since all the city's routes lead to and from here, there's no shortage of buses and taxis. Rooms are stylish, and there's a sky lounge with a view over the mountains.

🛏 535 🚃 JR: Kyoto Station 🚭 🚭 Some floors 🏊 🏊 🛜 Free 🃏 All major cards

🏨 SCREEN
$$$
640-1 SHIMOGORYOMAE-CHO, NAKAGYO-KU
TEL 075/252-1113
screen-hotel.jp
The rooms in this six-year-old boutique hotel were individually designed by architectural firms around the world in different styles, ranging from warm and intimate to cool, modern, and spacious. Online prices are significantly less than rack rates. Located just south of the southeast corner of Kyoto Imperial Palace.

🛏 13 🚃 Keihan line: Jingu-Marutamachi, then 5-min. walk 🚭 🚭 All rooms 🛜 Free 🃏 All major cards

🏨 YADOYA HIRAIWA
$
314 HAYAO-CHO, KAMINOKU-CHI-AGARU, NINOMIYACHO-DORI, SHIMOGYO-KU
TEL 075/351-6748
ryokan.or.jp/english/yado/main/58575
As a founding member of the Japanese Inn Group, this friendly little ryokan close to Kyoto Station is basic, clean, and an easy introduction to traditional inns. Family-size rooms are available, but bathrooms are shared in both the 100-year-old main building and the new annex.

🛏 12 🚃 15-min. walk from JR Kyoto Station 🚭 All rooms 🛜 Free 🃏 All major cards

🍴 TEMPURA YOSHIKAWA
$$$$$
OIKE-SAGARU, TOMINOKOJI-DORI, NAKAGYO-KU
TEL 075/221-5544
kyoto-yoshikawa.co.jp
Small restaurant in a delightful old ryokan in central Kyoto, serving great tempura and kaiseki. The price range is extreme, with kyo-kaiseki dinners in the tatami rooms upstairs costing nearly ten times more than a set lunch at the counter.

🛏 11 counter, some rooms 🚃 Keihan line: Sanjo 🕐 11 a.m.–1:30 p.m., 5 p.m.–8 p.m. Closed Sun. 🚭 All 🃏 All major cards

🍴 PIZZERIA NAPOLETANA DA YUKI
$$–$$$
36-3 OKAZAKI ENSHOJI-CHO, SAKYO-KU
TEL 075/761-6765
It's hard to go wrong with this popular pizzeria: The dishes are authentic, the service attentive, and the location central. It's along the canal just west of Heian-jingu's big *torii* gate. Calling ahead recommended. English menu.

🛏 18 🚃 Subway: Higashi-yama 🕐 Noon–2:30 p.m., 6 p.m.–10 p.m. Closed Mon. 🚭 All 🃏 No credit cards

🍴 MISOKA-AN KAWAMICHIYA
$
SANJO-AGARU, FUYA-CHO, NAKAGYO-KU
TEL 075/221-2525
kawamichiya.co.jp
They've been serving soba in this tiny building in central Kyoto forever. It even has an English menu. The specialty is *hokoro*—a satisfying soba pot stew for two containing tofu, chicken, and vegetables.

🛏 78 🚃 Subway: Kyoto Shiyakusho-mae 🕐 11 a.m.–8 p.m. Closed Thurs. 🚭 All major cards

EAST KYOTO

🏨 SEIKORO
$$$$$
TONYA-MACHI -DORI, GOJO-
SAGARU, HIGASHIYAMA-KU
TEL 075/561-0771
seikoro.com
This renowned ryokan in
eastern Kyoto was founded
in 1831. Its current buildings
(except a recent annex) date
from the late Meiji, with
warm low light, ancient
woodwork, and stunning
antiques. Prices include meals
and vary based on choice of
room (the best overlook the
garden) and set meal.
🛏 20 🚉 Keihan line:
Kiyomizu-Gojo 🅿 📶 Free
♿ All major cards

🏨 HYATT REGENCY KYOTO
$$$$
644-2 SANJUSANGENDO-
MAWARI, HIGASHIYAMA-KU
TEL 075/541-1234
kyoto.regency.hyatt.com
Don't let the unassuming
exterior fool you: The Hyatt
is one of Kyoto's finest
Western hotels. Recently
renovated, it is beautifully
decorated, with touches of
Japanese paper and kimonos
fabric throughout the rooms.
The staff is exceptionally
attentive, and the restaurants
are excellent.
🛏 187 🚉 Keihan line:
Shichijo 🅿 🔁 ♿ Some floors
📶 Free ♿ All major cards

🏨 YACHIYO
$$$$
34 FUKUJI-CHO, NANZEN-JI,
SAKYO-KU
TEL 075/771-4148
ryokan-yachiyo.com
Dark and romantic, Yachiyo
is very much the luxury
historic ryokan. The best
rooms in the oldest main
building surround a delightful
Japanese garden. Close to
East Kyoto's Nanzen-ji.
🛏 20 🚉 Tozai line: Keage
🅿 📶 Free ♿ All major cards

🏨 APA KYOTO GION HOTEL EXCELLENT
$$–$$$$
MINAMIGAWA, GION-MACHI,
HIGASHIYAMA-KU
TEL 075/551-2111
apahotel.com
In the geisha district and close
to the sights of east Kyoto,
this is an inexpensive option.
Rooms are cramped but
comfortable; ask for one with
a view of the old Gion houses.
🛏 154 🚉 Keihan line: Gion-
Shijo 🅿 🔁 ♿ Some floors
📶 Free ♿ All major cards

SOMETHING SPECIAL

🍴 HYOTEI
$$$$$
35 KUSAKAWA-CHO,
NANZEN-JI, SAKYO-KU
TEL 075/771-4116
hyotei.co.jp
In the late 17th century,
pilgrims and travelers used to
stop here for refreshment on
the way to Nanzen-ji. They
still do today. You can have
a kaiseki meal (reservations
required) in one of the small
garden teahouses, some of
which are as old as Hyotei
itself. The bento lunch boxes
are cheaper, but you eat
those in an ordinary (though
very pleasant) dining room.
🚉 Tozai line: Keage
🕐 Closed Thurs. ♿ All
♿ All major cards

🍴 JUNSEI
$$$–$$$$
60 KUSAKAWA-CHO,
NANZEN-JI, SAKYO-KU
TEL 075/761-2311
to-fu.co.jp
West of Nanzen-ji's main
gate, this tofu specialist is set
about a huge garden. One of
the buildings, originally one of
Kyoto's early Western medical
schools, is over 170 years old.
Lunches are great value; pricier
shabu-shabu and sukiyaki are
also available for dinner.
🪑 350 🚉 Tozai line: Keage
🕐 11 a.m.–9:30 p.m.
♿ ♿ All major cards

🍴 OMEN
$$
74 ISHIBASHI-CHO, JODOJI,
SAKYO-KU
TEL 075/771-8994
Just southwest of Ginkaku-ji
and the Path of Philosophy,
Omen serves soba (buck-
wheat noodles) and udon
(thick wheat noodles), either
in piping hot soup or cold
with dipping sauce, which
is a great way to cool off
on a hot day.
🪑 80 🚉 Bus 100 to
Ginkakuji-mae 🕐 11 a.m.–
9 p.m. Closed irregularly
🅿 ♿ All ♿ All major cards

KANSAI

KOBE

🍴 STEAKLAND KOBE-KAN
$$$$$
1F MIYASAKO BLDG., 1-8-2 KITA-
NAGASADORI, CHUO-KU
TEL 078/332-1653
This is one of the more
reasonably-priced and easy-
to-enter Kobe beef restaurants, but expect to wait in
line without reservations.

🏨 Hotel 🍴 Restaurant 🛏 No. of Guest Rooms 🪑 No. of Seats 🚉 Transportation 🅿 Parking 🕐 Hours

🛏 60 🚃 JR Tokaido line:
Kobe-sannomiya
🕐 11 a.m.–10 p.m.
💳 All major cards

NARA

🏨 NARA HOTEL
🍴 $$$$$
1096 TAKABATAKE-CHO
TEL 0742/26-3300
narahotel.co.jp
Built early last century and
blending Western and
Japanese architecture, the
historic building is famed
for its lovely dining hall. Like
the high-ceilinged Japanese
deco interior, the cuisine is a
hybrid: The menu typically
includes spaghetti and
sandwiches, along with more
refined meat and seafood
dishes, both Western and
Japanese. Dinner reservations
recommended.
🛏 127 🚃 Kintetsu Nara line:
Nara 🅿 🔁 💺 Some floors, all
floors in main building 🛜 Free
💳 All major cards

🏨 RYOKAN SEIKAN-SO
$
29 HIGASHI-KITSUJI-CHO
TEL 0742/22-2670
nara-ryokanseikanso.com
Many regard this 1916 ryokan in a former geisha house
as the jewel in the crown of
the Japanese Inn Group. Set
in a lovely garden, it's cen-
trally located near the main
sights, including Todai-ji,
Kofuku-ji, and Kasuga-jinga.
Run by a friendly couple
who speak English.
🛏 8 🚃 Kintetsu Nara line:
Nara 💺 All rooms 🅿 🛜 Free
💳 All major cards

🍴 HIYORI
$$$
26 NAKANOSHINYA-CHO
TEL 0742/24-1470
narakko.com/hiyori
This popular place about
10-minute walk straight
south of Sarusawa-ike pond
and Kofuku-ji serves Nara's
traditional vegetarian cuisine.

Look for the red lettering
on a steel sign in front of a
modern concrete building.
🛏 50 🚃 Kintetsu line: Nara
🕐 11:30 a.m.–2:30 p.m.,
5 p.m.–10 p.m. Closed Tues.
💺 All 💳 MC, V

OSAKA

🏨 GRANVIA OSAKA
$$$$$
3-1-1 UMEDA, KITA-KU
TEL 06/6344-1235
hotelgranviaosaka.jp
Right over Osaka Station
and with excellent city views
from the upper floors, the
Granvia Osaka is a cut above
most upscale business hotels.
Standard singles are small and
dark, but the twins are bright
and comfortable.
🛏 716 🚃 JR: Osaka 🔁
💺 Some floors 🛜 Free
💳 All major cards

🏨 SANSUIKAN
$$$
3-2-2 HARA, TAKATSUKI-SHI,
OSAKA-FU
TEL 072/687-4567
sansuikan.com
One of the few hot-spring
resorts close to Kyoto and
Osaka, Sansuikan pulls its
water up from beneath the
beautiful Settsukyo valley, a
popular swimming hole in
the summer. The baths, set
about with maples and massive boulders, are particularly
delightful in the autumn.
🛏 27 🚃 JR Kyoto line:
Takatsuki, then 15-min. taxi
🅿 🔁 🛜 Free 💳 All major
cards

🏨 SUNROUTE UMEDA
$$$
3-9-1 TOYOSAKI, KITA-KU
TEL 06/6373-1111
sunroute.jp
The Sunroute has stylishly
designed furniture and
rooms, both Western and
Japanese, and with its
convenient location, it's
one of the best values for
business hotels in town.

Umeda Station is within
easy walking distance.
🛏 217 🚃 Subway: Nakatsu
🅿 💺 Some floors 🛜 Free
💳 All major cards

🍴 FUJIYA 1935
$$$$$
2-4-14 YARIYAMACHI, CHUO-KU
TEL 06/6941-2483
fujiya1935.com
When you've tried all the
classics, splurge on this
Michelin three-star Spanish-
Japanese fusion restaurant.
Fujiya incorporates local,
seasonal ingredients such as
mountain vegetables and
Tajima beef into Spanish
dishes recreated in Japan's
subdued aesthetic. Have your
hotel make reservations.
🛏 20 🚃 Subway: Sakaisuji-
honmachi 🕐 Noon–1 p.m.,
6 p.m.–8 p.m. Closed Sun. &
1st Mon. 💺 All 💳 All major
cards

🍴 UOSHIN HONTEN
$$$
5-4 DOYAMA-CHO, KITA-KU
TEL 06/6313-0135
The sushi here is simply
gigantic, often with another
piece of fish piled on top,
and the staff blast new
customers with hearty cries
of "Irrashai!" (Welcome!). The
second branch just across the
arcade sells cheaper sets but
the flagship is all à la carte.
English menu.
🛏 40 🚃 Hankyu: Umeda
🕐 11 a.m.–midnight 💺 At
counter 💳 All major cards

🍴 ZA CHANKO!
$$$
1-14-23 DAIDO, TENNOJI-KU
TEL 06/6779-5446
Chanko nabe (hot pot) is
the traditional dish sumo
wrestlers eat to pack on the
pounds and fuel their train-
ing. Consisting of a hearty
stew of seafood, meatballs,
and vegetables, it isn't actu-
ally fattening—it's the beer
and rice that are to blame.

The restaurant is covered in sumo memorabilia, including huge handprints on the wall from famous wrestlers who ate here. Little English, but chanko nabe is the main thing on the menu.

🎫 60 🚇 Subway and JR: Tennoji 🕐 5 p.m.– 10:30 p.m. Closed Mon. 💳 All major cards

🍴 DARUMA TSUTENKAKU-TEN
$$
1-6-8 EBISUHIGASHI, NANIWA-KU
TEL 06/6643-1373

Don't be alarmed by the scary-looking picture of a cook shouting, "No double-dipping!": This *kushi-katsu* (fried skewers) restaurant, directly beneath Tsukenkaku Tower is friendly and used to foreigners. The dipping sauce is communal, so don't commit the above taboo. The deep-fried ginger and quail's eggs are great. Expect a line on weekends. English menu.

🛈 52 🚇 Subway: Ebisucho 🕐 11 a.m.–9 p.m. 💳 All major cards

🍴 HOUZENJI SANPEI
$$
1-7-9 DOTOMBORI, CHUO-KU
TEL 06/6211-0399

A great little *okonomiyaki* joint, Sanpei serves up Osaka's savory pancakes in the stylish Houzenji Yokocho alley a block south of the main drag of Dotombori.

🛈 26 🚇 Subway: Namba 🕐 5 p.m.–11 p.m., 11:30 a.m.– midnight weekends. Closed Tues. 💳 All major cards

WAKAYAMA

🏨 FUJIYA
$$$
1452 HONGUCHO KAWAYU, TANABE-SHI
TEL 0735/42-0007
fuziya.co.jp

This large ryokan in Kawayu Onsen sits on the Kumano-gawa: Hot water bubbles up from beneath the river, forming natural baths wherever one digs in the gravel bar.

🛈 31 🚇 Ryujin bus for Hongu-Taisha-mae to Fujiya-mae stop 🅂 🅿 🔁 📶 Free 💳 All major cards

🏨 RYOKAN KAMIGOTEN
$$$
42 RYUJIN, RYUJIN-MURA, TANABE-SHI
TEL 0739/79-0005
kamigoten.jp

Formerly the vacation villa of the feudal lord of Wakayama, this hot spring inn, perched alongside a narrow river valley, is under its 29th generation of ownership. The hot spring was opened to the public in 1871. Stay in the feudal lord's bedroom—complete with 340-year-old gold-dusted sliding doors and stunning murals—for less than a middling Tokyo business hotel. Excellent local mountain food served at dinner and breakfast.

🛈 10 🚇 Ryujin bus 80 min. from Kiitanabe Station or Koya-san 🅿 📶 Free in lobby 💳 No credit cards

■ WESTERN HONSHU (CHUGOKU)

HAGI

🏨 TOMOE RYOKAN
$$$$$
608-53 KOBOJI, HIJIWARA
TEL 0838/22-0150

Built of wood in 1926, it looks far older and is filled with antiques and scrolls. Beautiful rooms, some of which look out over a peaceful central garden, contain real antique features. Indeed, it's as close to the luxury traditional inn—with communal bath—as you can get for its very reasonable price (which includes two meals).

🛈 25 🚇 JR: Higashi Hagi 🅿 🅂 Some rooms 📶 Free in lounge 💳 All major cards

🏨 HAGI GRAND TENKU
$$
25 FURUHAGI-CHO
TEL 0838/25-1211

Convenient location between Higashi Hagi Station and the sights makes this popular with foreign visitors. It's considered the town's top Western-style hotel, although nearly half the rooms are Japanese. All are comfortable and above average in size.

🛈 183 🚇 JR San-in line: Higashi Hagi 🅿 🔁 🅂 Some rooms 📶 Free in lobby 💳 All major cards

HIROSHIMA & MIYAJIMA

🏨 IWASO RYOKAN
$$$$
MOMIJI-DANI, MIYAJIMA-CHO, HATSUKAISHI-SHI, HIROSHIMA-KEN
TEL 0829/44-2233
iwaso.com

Miyajima's first, best, and most beautiful ryokan is tucked up behind Itsukushima-jinja. The best rooms are in two old, exquisite individual cottages; more economical rooms are in the modern annex. Prices include two meals and vary according to room and dinner menu (both must be reserved in advance).

🛈 38 🚢 Ferry: Miyajima 🅿 📶 Free in some rooms, public areas 💳 All major cards

🍴 KAKIBUNE KANAWA
$$–$$$$
CHISAKI, 1 OTE-MACHI, NAKA-KU, HIROSHIMA-SHI
TEL: 082/241-7416
kanawa.co.jp

Hiroshima is famous for oysters farmed on thousands of rafts in the bay; this is *the* place to sample them. Actually a barge moored on the river at Heiwa Bridge (near Peace Park), it owes its distinguished reputation to the quality of its seafood, both cooked and raw. Jacket and tie. Reservations recommended. English menu.

🛏 84 🚃 Tram: Genbaku-Dome-Mae 🕐 11 a.m.–9 p.m. 🅢 🆔 All major cards

🍴 NIKUNOMASUI

$$
14-12 HATCHOBORI NAKA-KU
TEL 082/227-2983
Despite the humble appearance and the "Western Food" sign, this is a great spot for sukiyaki or shabu-shabu, at reasonable prices too.

🛏 100+ 🚃 Tram: Hatchobori 🕐 11 a.m.–9 p.m. Closed Wed. & 2nd Tues. 🅢 🆔 All major cards

🍴 OKONOMI MURA BUILDING

$
5-13 SHINTENCHI, NAKA-KU, HIROSHIMA-SHI
TEL 082/241-2210
okonomimura.jp
This cherished Hiroshima institution serves the city's specialty, Hiroshima-style *okonomi-yaki*. These "savory pancakes" are a mix of egg, cabbage noodles, and whatever topping you choose. The building is an entire "village" *(mura)* devoted to nothing else.

🚃 Tram: Hatchobori 🕐 Opens 11 a.m. 🛗 🆔 No credit cards

MATSUE

🏨 MINAMIKAN

$$$$$
14 SUETSUGU HON-MACHI
TEL 0852/21-5131
This modern and luxurious ryokan is Matsue's most

famous. Renowned for its outstanding cuisine, it's also a restaurant. It's very traditional with sublime service, natural hot-spring baths, a beautiful garden, and rooms facing Lake Shinji-ko.

🆔 14 🚃 JR: Matsue 🅿 🛗 Free 🆔 All major cards

OKAYAMA & KURASHIKI

🏨 RYOKAN KURASHIKI

🍴 **$$$$$**
4-1 HON-MACHI, KURASHIKI-SHI
TEL 086/422-0730
ryokan-kurashiki.jp
This is a 250-year-old merchant complex with a lovely inner garden right by the canal. Antiques furnish the dark, polished-wood rooms. Renowned for its service and cuisine, it's open also as a restaurant and a tearoom.

🆔 5 🚃 JR: Kurashiki 🅿 🛗 Free 🆔 All major cards

🏨 KURASHIKI KOKUSAI

$$$
1-1-44 CHUO, KURASHIKI-SHI
TEL 086/422-5141
kurashiki-kokusai-hotel.co.jp
Comfortable and good value, this is by far the area's most respected Western-style hotel. The best rooms have great views of old Kurashiki. The rooms are tastefully decorated, and the lobby exhibits 20th-century print master Munakata Shiko's largest work.

🆔 106 🚃 JR: Kurashiki 🛗 🅢 All rooms in main building 🛗 Free in lobby 🆔 All major cards

🏨 OKAYAMA PLAZA

$$$
2-3-12 HAMA, NAKA-KU
TEL 086/272-1201
This is an ideal hotel for both value and location close to the major sights. The comfortable rooms are larger

than the norm, the best with fine views over the castle.

🆔 79 🚃 JR: Okayama 🅿 🛗 🅢 All rooms 🛗 Free 🆔 All major cards

ONOMICHI & TOMONOURA

🏨 ONOFUNAYADO IROHA

$$$
670 TOMO, TOMO-CHO, FUKUYAMA-SHI
TEL 084/982-1920
www.vesta.dti.ne.jp/npo-tomo/iroha
This mid-19th-century merchant home was converted into a traditional inn in 2003 under the guidance of anime film director Hayao Miyazaki. Check out the creative lunch sets if you are in Tomonoura on a day trip.

🆔 3 🚢 1-min. walk from ferry terminal 🅿 🅢 All rooms 🛗 Free 🆔 No credit cards

🏨 ONOMICHI VIEW HOTEL SEIZAN

$
16-21 NISHI TSUCHIDO-CHO, ONOMICHI
TEL 0848/23-3313
onomichi-viewhotel.co.jp
Perched on a steep hill overlooking the station and the sea, this is a great budget pick with excellent views, a Thai restaurant and the defunct but striking "fake castle" Onomichi-jo right next door.

🆔 20 🚃 JR Sanyo line: Onomichi, then 10-min. taxi or 15-min. hike 🅿 🛗 🅢 Some floors 🛗 Free 🆔 All major cards

TSUWANO

🏨 KANKO WATAYA

$$$
82-3 USHIRODA-RO
TEL 0856/72-0333
The finest accommodation in Tsuwano, the Wataya has chic Western- and Japanese-style rooms and luxurious bathing facilities, including

baths that are partly outdoors. Meals are prepared with attention to detail—tofu is a specialty.

[i] 30 [🚆] JR: Tsuwano [P]
[💳] All major cards

🏨 MEIGETSU
🍴 $$$
665 USHIRODA-RO
TEL 08567/2-0685
With dark polished wood, spacious rooms, and a delightful central garden, this is probably Tsuwano's prettiest ryokan. It also has quite a reputation for local cuisine—mountain vegetable and river fish dishes—served in a large, traditional dining room. Communal bath.

[i] 13 [🚆] JR: Tsuwano [P]
[🛏] Some rooms [📶] Free
[💳] All major cards.

🍴 YUKI
$
RO 271-4, USHIRODA
TEL 0856/72-0162
The local specialties are carp, mountain vegetables, and *konyaku* (a kind of jelly made with potato flour). Sample them in this traditional eatery with a carp stream flowing through the dining room.

[🪑] 100 [🚆] JR Yamaguchi line: Tsuwano [P] [🕐] 11 a.m.–3 p.m. Closed Thurs.
[💳] No credit cards

■ SHIKOKU & THE SETO-NAIKAI

KOCHI

🏨 SANSUIEN
$$$
1-3-35 TAKAJOMACHI
TEL 088/822-0131
sansuien.co.jp
This modern Japanese onsen-hotel was built on the grounds of the villa of Kochi's last feudal lord, combining comfortable Japanese- and Western-style rooms with historical touches such as the original villa's

garden, great gate, and storehouse, now used to display historical artifacts.

[i] 150 [🚆] Tosaden Ino line: Kencho-mae [🚋]
[🛏] Some floors [📶] Free
[💳] All major cards

🏨 SEVEN DAYS HOTEL
$
2-13-17 HARIMAYA-CHO
TEL 088/884-7100
7dayshotel.com
This small business hotel, built in 2000, is a local favorite for its bright, tidy (but small) rooms and location central to Kochi's nightlife.

[i] 80 [🚆] JR: Kochi [P] [🚋]
[🛏] Some floors [📶] Free
[💳] All major cards

🍴 HIROME ICHIBA
$$
2-3-1 OBIYAMACHI
TEL 088/822-5287
This raucous collection of restaurants is nearly always packed with locals and visitors and is a great place to observe and taste bonito seared over a grass fire into *tataki-katsuo*. Friendly, communal seating makes it the place to grab a beer and squeeze into a long table with the locals. Located east of the castle on Ote-suji St.

[🚆] Tosaden Ino line: Ohashi-dori [P] [🕐] 8 a.m.–11 p.m.
[💳] No credit cards

MATSUYAMA & UCHIKO

🏨 FUNAYA
$$$$
1-33 DOGOYU-NO-MACHI, MATSUYAMA-SHI, EHIME-KEN
TEL 089/947-0278
dogo-funaya.co.jp
A luxurious ryokan with modern rooms and a history extending back to the 17th century. Many rooms look onto an exquisite garden. With indoor and outdoor public baths, sauna, spa pool, and outstanding food and service, this is the onsen elite.

[i] 58 [🚆] Iyo Tetsudo lines: Dogo Onsen [P] [🚋]
[🛏] Some rooms [♨] [📶] Free
[💳] All major cards

🏨 RYOKAN MATSUNOYA
🍴 $$$
1913 UCHIKO, UCHIKO-CHO, TEL 089/344-5000
The rooms are basic and very clean, but the accent here is on food. Reviewed in trendy Japanese travel magazines, this place has earned its reputation thanks to an inspired owner-chef, whose style subtly blends Japanese cuisine with Chinese and European elements. Communal bath.

[i] 9 [🚆] JR: Uchiko
[P] [📶] Free [💳] All major cards

🏨 MINSHUKU MIYOSHI
$
3-7-23 ISHITE, MATSUYAMA-SHI, EHIME-KEN
TEL 089/977-2581
Although the location behind a parking lot is a tad gloomy, this is an excellent value. It's just across the road from Ishitei-ji, Matsuyama's famous temple. Tatami-floored rooms are large, comfortable, and

spotless, with their own toilet. You can have a room with or without meals.

ℹ️ 6 🚋 Iyo Tetsudo lines: Dogo Onsen 🅿️ 📶 Free in lobby 💳 No credit cards

TAKAMATSU

🏨 DORMY INN
$$
1-10-10 KAWARAMACHI
TEL 087/832-5489
hotespa.net/hotels
/takamatsu
The rooftop public bath and eight-hour-stay rates make this business chain hotel stand out. Clean, small, and functional. Internet in all rooms.

ℹ️ 151 🚋 Kotoden lines: Kawaramachi 🔼 💳 Most floors 📶 Free 💳 All major cards

🍴 TE-UCHI UDON TSURUMARU
$
9-34 FURUBABACHO, TAKAMATSU
TEL 087/821-3780
There are countless *sanuki udon* restaurants in Takamatsu but this one stands out for its lively atmosphere and the hard-working noodle-makers, whom guests may watch behind the counter. It's four blocks north of Kawaramachi Station on Ferry Street. Look for the picture of a crane on the door-curtain. English picture menu.

🚋 Kotoden line: Kawaramachi ⏰ 8 p.m.–3 a.m. Closed Sun. 💳 No credit cards

◼️ KYUSHU

BEPPU

SOMETHING SPECIAL

🏨 SUGINOI
$$$
1 KANKAIJI
TEL 0977/24-1141
suginoi-hotel.com
Spa hotels are the Japanese

onsen enthusiast's idea of paradise. This one adjoins the Suginoi Palace, which provides every imaginable kind of spa bath and sauna as well as karaoke, restaurants and bars, an ice rink, a golfing range, shopping malls, an amusement park, a bowling alley, a new water park, and more. Rooms are surprisingly restrained, some with great bay views.

ℹ️ 641 🚋 Free shuttle from JR Beppu Station
🚭 All rooms 🏊 🏊 🏋️
Free 💳 All major cards

FUKUOKA-DAZAIFU-YANAGAWA

🏨 DAIMARU BESSO
$$$$
1-20-1 YU-MACHI, CHI-KUSHINO-SHI, FUKUOKA-KEN
TEL 092/924-3939
daimarubesso.com
First built during the 1860s and lying in an elegant garden, this is probably the most prestigious ryokan in Kyushu. All rooms have their own Japanese cypress-wood bath with spa water. Price includes two meals.

ℹ️ 41 🚋 JR: Futsukaic 🅿️ 🔼 📶 None 💳 All major cards

🏨 IL PALAZZO
$$$
3-13-1 HARUYOSHI, CHUO-KU, FUKUOKA-SHI
TEL 092/716-3333
ilpalazzo.jp
Emphasizing European-style elegance, this inspired blend of traditional Milanese urban architecture was designed by Italian architect Aldo Rossi. The hotel is notable for futuristic use of interior light and space, and for its comfort, service, and restaurants.

ℹ️ 62 🚋 Subway: Nakasu-kawabata; JR: Hakata
🅿️ 🔼 🚭 Some floors 📶 Free 💳 All major cards

🍴 YAMANAKA
$$$
2F SUNNY AKASAKA-TEN, 1-9-1 AKASAKA, CHUO-KU
TEL 092/716-2263
This is the place to try *motsu-nabe* (beef or pork intestines hot pot) and *mentaiko* (spiced cod roe). The hot pot is set on a hotplate in the center of your table and heaped with vegetables, which slowly cook down into the broth. Reasonable prices for a classy white marble decor. Reservations are recommended.

🪑 220 🚋 Kuko line: Akasaka ⏰ 5 p.m.–11:30 p.m. Closed Wed. 🔼 💳 No credit cards

🍴 IPPUDO TAO FUKUOKA
$
1-13-13 TENJIN, CHUO-KU, FUKUOKA-SHI
TEL 092/738-7061
Ippudo is a popular ramen chain, one of the few to make the leap abroad. This shop is conveniently located in the Tenjin shopping district; it serves up a traditional *tonkatsu* pork-bone soup, a white miso and garlic soup, and a special pig's head tonkatsu with caramelized onions.

🪑 26 🚋 Nanakuma line: Tenjinminami ⏰ 11 a.m.–midnight 🚭 All 💳 No credit cards

KAGOSHIMA

🏨 SHIROYAMA KANKO
$$$$$
41-1 SHIN-SHOIN-CHO
TEL 099/224-2211
shiroyama-g.co.jp
Hotel Shiroyama dominates the skyline over downtown Kagoshima, with excellent views of the city and Sakurajima. It's four restaurants, refined, stylish rooms, and hot-spring bath are sure to please.

ℹ️ 365 🚋 Shuttle bus from JR Kagoshimachuo Station
🅿️ 🔼 🚭 Some floors 📶 Free 💳 All major cards

🍴 KUMASOTEI
$$$
6-10 HIGASHI SENGOKU-CHO
TEL 099/222-6356
kumasotei.com
This huge restaurant is
the best place to sample
Kagoshima's regional cuisine,
Satsuma ryori (the province's
former name was Satsuma),
renowned by Japanese
gourmets.
ⓘ 300 🚉 JR: Kagoshima-
chuo 🕐 11 a.m.–2:30 p.m.,
5 p.m.–10 p.m. 🅿 🔁
🚬 Some rooms
💳 All major cards

KUMAMOTO

🏨 NEW OTANI KUMAMOTO
$$
1-13-1 KASUGA, NISHI-KU
TEL 096/326-1111
newotani-kumamoto.co.jp
Everything you'd expect
from the chain running one
of Tokyo's largest hotels.
Among the city's best
accommodations, with
spacious rooms featuring
the latest amenities.
ⓘ 123 🚉 JR: Kumamoto 🅿
🔁 🚬 Some floors 📶 Free
💳 All major cards

🍴 SENRI
$$$$
7-17 SUIZENJI-KOEN
TEL 096/381-1415
A great choice for Japanese
specialties, this restaurant
is located in Suizenji-koen
Park; its best tatami rooms
look over the famous garden.
Try *karashi renkon*—lotus
root stuffed with a savory
mixture of miso and mustard,
then sliced and deep-fried
in batter.
🪑 100 🚋 Tram: Suizenji
🅿 🕐 11 a.m.–2 p.m.,
5 p.m.–9 p.m. Closed Mon.
💳 No credit cards

NAGASAKI & UNZEN

🏨 UNZEN MIYAZAKI RYOKAN
$$$–$$$$$
320 UNZEN, OBAMA-CHO,
UNZEN-SHI
TEL 0957/73-3331
miyazaki-ryokan.co.jp
The rooms of this fine ryokan
may overlook the Unzen
"hells," but the hot-spring
baths are heavenly and the
service is impeccable. Be sure
to have a cup of tea over-
looking the hotel's garden,
with its own steaming pools.
ⓘ 96 🚉 Shuttle bus from
Nagasaki or Isahaya, by res-
ervation 🅿 🚬 None 📶 Free
💳 All major cards

🏨 BEST WESTERN PREMIER NAGASAKI
$$
2-26 TAKARA-MACHI,
NAGASAKI-SHI
TEL 095/821-1111
**bestwestern.co.jp/english
/nagasaki**
Many regard this as
Nagasaki's best hotel. The
ultramodern exterior and
lobby are almost belied by
the old-fashioned room comfort—where all amenities are
nonetheless cutting edge.
ⓘ 181 🚉 JR: Nagasaki
🅿 🔁 🚬 Some floors 📶 Free
💳 All major cards

🍴 SHIPPOKU HAMA KATSU
$$–$$$$
6-50 KAJIYA-MACHI,
NAGASAKI-SHI
TEL 095/826-8321
sippoku.jp
Shippoku cuisine—Nagasaki's
blend of Japanese, Chinese,
and European dishes—is typi-
cally served in huge courses for
four to five diners minimum.
Hama Katsu has a "mini" ship-
poku, great for couples or solo
foodies. Reservations recom-
mended for weekends.
🪑 160 🚋 Tram: Shianbashi
🕐 11:30 a.m.–10 p.m.
🔁 🚬 💳 All major cards

PRICES

HOTELS
An indication of the cost of
a double room in the high
season is given by **$** signs.

$$$$$	Over $280
$$$$	$200–$280
$$$	$120–$200
$$	$80–$120
$	Under $80

RESTAURANTS
An indication of the cost of
a three-course meal without
drinks is given by **$** signs.

$$$$$	Over $80
$$$$	$50–$80
$$$	$35–$50
$$	$20–$35
$	Under $20

🍴 SHIKAIRO
$–$$$$
4-5 MATSUGAE-CHO,
NAGASAKI-SHI
TEL 095/822-1296
Nagasaki's noodle special-
ties are *champon,* a hearty
Chinese-style noodle soup
with vegetables and meat or
seafood, and *sara udon,* udon
noodles stir-fried with similar
ingredients. This restaurant is
said to have invented these
dishes when it opened back
in 1899. There's a wealth
of Chinese dishes on an
English menu. Dinner
reservations necessary.
🪑 100 🚋 Tram: Oura
Tenshudo-shita 🕐 11:30 a.m.–
3 p.m., 5 p.m.–9 p.m.
Closed Irregularly 🔁 🚬 All
💳 All major cards

▮ OKINAWA & THE RYUKYU ARCHIPELAGO

OKINAWA HONTO

SOMETHING SPECIAL
🏨 HYAKUNA GARAN
$$$$$
1299-1 HYAKUNA YAMASHI-
TAHARA, TAMAGUSUKU-AZA,

NANJO-SHI
TEL 098/949-1011
hyakunagaran.com
Built in 2012, this superlative resort sits on a cape on the east coast of the Okinawa main island and feels worlds away from the rest of the island. The private rooftop baths are among the best bathing experiences to be had in the whole country.
🛏 17 🚕 Taxi: 30 min. from downtown Naha 🅿 ⬌ 🚭 All rooms 🛜 Free 💳 All major cards

🏨 DAIWA ROYNET NAHA KOKUSAI-DORI

$$
2-1-1 ASADO, NAHA-SHI
TEL 098/868-9055
daiwaroynet.jp
/naha-kokusaidori
It's hard to beat the location of this hotel, just steps away from Makishi monorail station, the eastern terminus of the main downtown drag, Kokusai-dori. Rooms are clean and serviceable, in the business hotel style, but the breakfast buffet has a great selection of local dishes.
🛏 261 🚈 Monorail: Makishi 🅿 ⬌ 🚭 Some floors 🛜 Free 💳 All major cards

🍴 ASHIBIUNA'A

$
2-13 SHURITONOKURA-CHO, NAHA-SHI
TEL 098/884-0035
The former home of the Takamiyagi clan, this traditional house has been converted into a popular restaurant below Shuri Castle. It serves typical Okinawan dishes, such as *tebichi* (boiled trotters) and *soki soba*, a thin, udon-like noodle topped with pork ribs.
🪑 70 🚶 5-min. walk from Shuri-jo 🅿 🕐 11 a.m.–3 p.m., 5 p.m.–11 p.m. 🚭 All seats 💳 All major cards

YAEYAMA ISLANDS

🏨 NIRAKANAI

$$$$
2-2 UEHARA, TAKETOMI-CHO
TEL 0980/85-7111
nirakanai-iriomotejima.jp
This eco-friendly resort strives to reduce its impact on the island and offers guests gift vouchers for more eco-friendly room options. The buffet is excellent and the resort faces the stunning Tsuki-ga-hama (Moon Beach).
🛏 140 🚌 Shuttle bus from Uehara port 🅿 ⬌ 🚭 All rooms 🏊 🛜 Free in lobby 💳 All major cards

🏨 GRANVIEW ISHIGAKI

$$–$$$
1 TONOSHIRO, ISHIGAKI-SHI
TEL 0980/82-6161
granview.co.jp
The Granview offers tidy, small rooms for travelers in transit to the far-flung islands of the Yaeyama Archipelago, just a minute's walk from the port.
🛏 85 🚶 1-min. walk from Ishigaki ferry terminal 🅿 🚭 Most floors 🛜 Free 💳 All major cards

🏨 IRIFUNE

$
59-6 AZA YONAGUNI, YONAGUNI-CHO
TEL 0980/87-2311
yonaguni.jp
This simple, tidy hotel caters to divers and runs tours to see the Yonaguni monument by glass-bottom boat as well. Two meals included.
🛏 11 🚌 Yonaguni Bus: Sonai stop (driver will take you here directly if requested) 🅿 🚭 Some rooms 🛜 Free 💳 No credit cards

🍴 KITCHEN INABA

$$$
742-6 UEHARA, TAKETOMI-CHO
TEL 0980/84-8164
kitcheninaba.com
Sanshin guitar performances by the owner are the big draw here, but the dishes are a mix of slightly upscale Okinawan favorites and Japanese-style pastas, at reasonable prices. Reservations recommended.
🪑 60 🚕 Taxi from Uehara port 🕐 11:30 a.m.–2:30 p.m., 6 p.m.–10:30 p.m. Closed Mon. 🚭 All seats 💳 No credit cards

🍴 USAGIYA

$$$
1-1 ISHIGAKI, ISHIGAKI-SHI
TEL 0980/88-5014
This Okinawan food *izakaya* puts on nightly live music (7 p.m.–8 p.m., 9 p.m.–10 p.m.), with local musicians playing the *sanshin* guitar and singing popular Okinawan tunes. Touristy, but with good food and a fun, lively atmosphere.
🪑 60 🚶 5-min. walk from Ishigaki ferry terminal 🕐 5 p.m.–midnight 🚭 All seats 💳 All major cards

🍴 NAKAMURA-YA

$
215 ISHIGAKI, ISHIGAKI-SHI
TEL 0980/87-5075
This friendly Japanese curry restaurant's dishes are much healthier than usual, with a variety of fresh ingredients. Picture menu.
🪑 27 🚶 15-min. walk N of Ishigaki ferry terminal 🅿 🕐 11:30 a.m.–2:30 p.m., dinner by reservation. Closed Wed. 🚭 All seats 💳 No credit cards

Shopping

The average Japanese city has a shopping precinct (shoten gai), an arcade (ahkaydo)—usually a street covered with a glass roof—a covered food market, and an underground mall, all around the main train station. In larger cities such as Tokyo, this pattern may be repeated in different districts. Both underground malls (chikagai) and shopping arcades are great for bargains, particularly photographic equipment, leather goods, and clothing. In many cities, you'll find some interesting junk shops and used clothing stores in arcades, but don't expect any great finds such as vintage kimonos and obi sashes.

Some stores offer goods tax free; however, this option applies only to electronic and computer goods, photographic equipment, and jewelry (containing precious metals or gems). Many cheapjack souvenir stores are emblazoned with the term "tax free," when in fact you will be paying regular prices for goods to which the concession doesn't apply. When purchasing tax free, you will need your passport; the store will give you a form to be given to Customs when leaving the country.

Antiques

Ceramics and tansu chests generally command high prices; although attractive and ubiquitous, ukiyo-e prints frequently sell more cheaply overseas. The number of flea markets is growing, although their prices are often only slightly less than in stores. However, they often present a variety of attractive, affordable items made between the 1890s and 1930s.

Clothing

If you are tall, you may have difficulty with clothing sizes in Japan. Always try on shoes or clothing before purchasing. Some garments carry the "F" (free size) label, but for Americans this is not always the one-size-fits-all guarantee it is for the Japanese.

The less expensive silk kimonos you find in large tourist outlets are probably made in China. The real thing, which ranges from seriously expensive to astronomical, can be made to measure in specialty stores. However, they

are heavy and impractical, and the large obi sash is restrictive. It's preferable to go for the more affordable cotton yukata; used either as sleepwear or in high summer, they come ready-made or made-to-order.

Department Stores

These are wonderful places to buy quality Japanese goods, including ceramics and lacquerware. Many of them have food halls in the basement with a fascinating selection of homegrown and imported goods. Chain stores such as Seibu, Isetan, Marui, and Matsuya have branches in major cities. The twice-yearly sales in these stores offer exceptional discounts. Lasting a week, sales usually start the second Friday in January and July. Prices on designer clothing, for instance, plummet by 50 percent on average.

Discount Stores

These appeared around Japan during the 1990s. Every town now has a hyaku-en kinitsu (¥100-only) outlet, with an astonishing array of goods (mainly made in China), including stationery, household goods, and novelties each costing around ¥100.

Electronics, Electrical Goods & Computer Stores

Discounts are available, but make sure that you get international models, so that the voltage back home doesn't fry the circuits. Also, ensure the device has an English-language setting.

Souvenirs

Most of the goods for sale at gift shops and souvenir stalls will be kitsch: hideous calendars, garish saké drinking sets, fluorescent paintings on velvet, key chains, cheap novelties, and so on. The most plentiful souvenirs are the edible kind; every region has its own specialties. In the cake and candy line, there are sembei (rice crackers) and mochi (a chewy sweet made with rice flour).

Traditional Arts & Crafts

These make the best buys in Japan. They include ceramics, textiles, paper and paperware (umbrellas, fans, hand-painted kites, stationery, etc.), dolls, wood and bamboo products, woodblock prints (antique and modern), cloisonné, and lacquerware. The crafts vary regionally, but craft shops, specialty stores, and department stores usually offer a range of goods from different parts of the country.

■ TOKYO

Tokyo is a paradise for shopaholics. The main shopping districts vary due to local consumer trends—Ginza is conservative and upscale, Shibuya a favorite with the young—or by specializing in certain kinds of goods. Akihabara is known for electronics, Harajuku for teen fashion, Kappabashi for catering supplies (including the incredible food models in restaurants), Jimbocho for books, and Kotto-dori in Aoyama for antiques. Nearby Omotesando is all expensive brand flamboyance.

Markets

The space underneath elevated train tracks has been used for covered markets or filled in with a miscellany of stores since World War II.

Ameyoko Ameya-yoko-cho, Ueno. Tokyo's most exciting street market (see pp. 92–93) is less touristy than the International Arcade.

AKIHABARA-KANDA

Akihabara's Denki Gai (Electric Town) is famous for sheer spectacle. Good for electronic and electrical goods.

Laox Computer-kan 1-2-9 Soto Kanda, Chiyoda-ku, tel 03/3253-7111. A computer superstore six stories high. If it isn't here, you probably won't find it in Japan.

Oya Shobo 1-1 Kanda Jimbocho, Chiyoda-ku, tel 03/3291-0062. This specialist in period maps and antique books also has a good selection of ukiyo-e prints.

Yodobashi Akiba 1-1 Kanda Hanaokacho, Chiyoda-ku, tel 03/5209-1010. On the east side of JR Akihabara Station, the area's latest electronics giant.

GINZA

Ginza is Tokyo's Fifth Avenue, with a great variety of shops and upscale department stores. More department stores are to be located just west of Ginza in Yurakucho.

Antique Mall Ginza 1-13-1 Ginza, Chuo-ku, tel 03/3535-2115, closed Wed. A fantastic emporium with around 300 stalls selling antiques, both Japanese and from around the world.

Kyukyodo 5-7-4 Ginza, Chuo-ku, tel 03/3571-4429. Sells incense, handmade paper, traditional stationery, brushes, and calligraphy requisites. Also stocks a marvelous selection of papercraft,

including boxes and miniature chests of drawers.

Mikimoto 4-5-5 Ginza, Chuo-ku, tel 03/3535-4611. Owned by the descendants of Mikimoto Kokichi, who invented the cultured pearl technique, this shop has branches nationwide.

Mitsukoshi 4-6-16 Ginza, Chuo-ku, tel 03/3562-1111. An elegant department store stocking the finest goods, both Japanese and imported, with prices to match.

Mujirushi Ryohin Yurakucho Branch 3-8-3 Infos Yurakucho Bldg., Marunouchi, Chiyoda-ku, tel 03/5208-8241. Muji sells high-quality generic goods with a simple Japanese aesthetic. The Yurakucho branch is its flagship, with every item on display, from cups to prefab houses.

Nihonshu Center 1-1-21 Nishi Shimbashi, Minato-ku, tel 03/3519-2091, closed Sat.–Sun. *Nihonshu* is the proper word for saké. You can sample some of 6,000 variations for a nominal fee.

Sakai Kokodo Gallery 1-2-14 Yurakucho, Chiyoda-ku, tel 03/3591-4678. Long-established dealer in woodblock prints, the range here goes from vintage rarities to modern reproductions.

Sony Showroom Sony Bldg., 5-3-1 Ginza, Chuo-ku, tel 03/3573-2371. This corner building at the main intersection is a Ginza landmark; all the latest audiovisual gadgetry and games technology are there for you to try out, as well as a multitude of audio, visual, and digital gizmos.

Yellow Submarine 1-15-4 Sotokanda, Chiyoda-ku, tel 03/5298-3123. Just south of the Radio Center on Chuo-dori, this multifloor shop sells anime figurines, cosplay costumes, and various collectibles.

ROPPONGI

Aoyama Book Center 1F Roppongi Denki Bldg., 6-1-20 Rop-

pongi, Minato-ku, tel 03/3479-0479. Book and magazine store emphasizing art, photography, and design, with a decent-size selection of books in English.

Axis Building 5-17-1 Roppongi, Minato-ku, tel 03/3587-2781. With stores variously devoted to furnishing and crafts (e.g., ceramics and textiles), this sleek building is the ideal place for an overview of the best of contemporary Japanese interior design.

Nuno Tokyo B1F Axis Bldg. (see above), tel 03/3582-7997. *Nuno* is Japanese for "textile" and also the name of a firm run by elite textile designer Reiko Sudo and colleagues, founded in 1983. Nuno fabrics meld the ancestral with the futuristic, the artisanal with the digital. The shop also sells clothes.

SHIBUYA

Daiso Harajuku Village 107, 1-19-24 Jingumae, Shibuya-ku, tel 03/5775-9641. Spawned by recession and still thriving, gaudy ¥100 *(hyaku-en)* stores are omnipresent in Tokyo and nationwide. Five floors of ¥100 kitchen and bathroom ware, accessories, toys, souvenirs, and gadgets you never knew you needed.

d47 8F Shibuya Hikarie, 2-21-1 Shibuya, Shibuya-ku, tel 03/6427-2301. This design-focused museum and store selects well-made items from all of Japan's 47 prefectures, highlighting the modern Japanese aesthetic.

Hysteric Glamour 6-23-2 Jingumae, Shibuya-ku, tel 03/3409-7227. Flagship store of a chain famed for ultrahip, grunge, and manga-inspired fashion. There are also two branches in LaForet (1-11-6 Jingumae, Shibuya-ku, tel 03/3475- 0411), a sleek Harajuku landmark with more than a hundred boutiques.

Issey Miyake 3-18-11 Minami Aoyama, Minato-ku, tel

03/3423-1407. Issey changed the face of world fashion in the 1980s with his revolutionary use of tailoring, fabrics, pleats, and plastics. Affordable or not, it's well worth a look.

Kiddyland 6-1-9 Jingu-mae, Shibuya-ku, tel 03/3409-3431. The ultimate store for toys, gadgets, gimmicks, models, etc.

Loft 21-1 Udagawa-cho, Shibuya-ku, tel 03/3462-3807. This "creative store" (a Seibu offshoot) features furnishings, fabrics, and endless supplies and materials for hobbies, arts, and crafts, places great emphasis on style.

Oriental Bazaar 5-9-13 Jingu-mae, Shibuya-ku, tel 03/3400-3933, closed Thurs. Though touristy, the best place for souvenirs: prints, ceramics, lacquerware, paperware, and lamps, as well as affordable antiques and vintage kimonos.

Parco 15-1 Udagawa-cho, Shibuya-ku, tel 03/3464-5111. Originally an offshoot of Seibu, this store launched the concept of the "fashion building"—several floors devoted solely to clothing, containing boutiques and sections operated by all the world's major designer brands.

Seibu 21-1 Udagawa-cho, Shibuya-ku, tel 03/3462-0111. The store had a seminal influence on fashion in Japan and remains outstanding for clothing, household goods, and gifts. Basement food hall.

Tokyu Hands 12-18 Udagawa-cho, Shibuya-ku, tel 03/5489-5111. A great handyman store, with several floors of tools, materials, and accessories required for arts, crafts, and hobbies.

SHINJUKU & IKEBUKURO

Shopping of all kinds at all prices—department stores, high-fashion outlets, general discount stores, and, most famously,

discount camera stores west of Shinjuku Station.

Japan Traditional Crafts Aoyama Square Akasaka Ouji Bldg., 8-1-22 Akasaka, Minato-ku, tel 03/5785-1001. The cream of Japanese traditional craftsmanship (ceramics, lacquerware, et al.) is not only exhibited here but also for sale.

Kinokuniya Bookstore 3-17-7 Shinjuku, tel 03/3354-0131. A Tokyo gem for foreign books, magazines, and paperbacks.

Map Camera 1-12-5 Nishi-Shinjuku, Shinjuku-ku, tel 03/3342-3381. Map Camera has an excellent selection of camera equipment. The used gear is typically in excellent condition.

Seibu 1-28-1 Minami Ikebukuro, Toshima-ku, tel 03/3981-0111. The original flagship store, and still Seibu's largest branch.

Shinjuku Marui Main Building 3-30-13 Shinjuku, tel 03/3354-0101. A comprehensive and trendy department store with two more branches nearby, Marui Annex and Marui Men.

Sunshine City 3-1 Higashi Ikebukuro, Toshima-ku, tel 03/3989-3331. One of Tokyo's tallest and largest buildings contains a branch of Mitsukoshi department store and a huge shopping mall.

Tobu 1-1-25 Nishi Ikebukuro, Toshima-ku, tel 03/3981-2211. The rival store to Seibu expanded during the mid-1990s, and here includes not only the colossal store itself but also the Tobu Museum of Art.

Yodobashi Camera Nishiguchi Honten, 1-11-1 Nishi Shinjuku, Shinjuku-ku, tel 03/3346-1010. Several floors of video, discount cameras and accessories, and general photographic items. There are often great bargains, but don't buy any digital or electronic goods without first checking on system compatibility.

UENO & ASAKUSA

Great for handmade traditional goods, including hardware and carpenter's tools, kimonos and accessories, fans, wooden combs, and paper lanterns.

Adachi-ya 2-22-12 Asakusa, Taito-ku, tel 03/3841-4915, closed Tues. Traditional working clothes, notably the blue denim *hanten* (or *happi* coat), the Edo-period townsman's garb still worn at festivals.

Hanato 2-25-6 Asakusa, Taito-ku, tel 03/3841-6411, closed Tues. An old-fashioned fireman's lantern bearing your name in *hiragana* characters? No problem: Hanato makes any kind of paper lantern (*chochin*) to order.

Kamata Hakensha 2-12-6 Matsugaya, Taito-ku, tel 03/3841-4205. The place to go for high quality Japanese knives in the Kappabashi area.

Kurodaya 1-2-5 Asakusa, Taito-ku, tel 03/3844-7511, closed Mon. Premier outlet for *washi* paper and papercraft, including kites and festival masks.

Matsuya 1-4-1 Hanakawado, Taito-ku, tel 03/3842-1111. There are often excellent craft exhibitions here, promoting ceramics, woodcraft, and lacquerware, with demonstrations by craftspeople from around Japan.

Sukeroku 2-3-1 Asakusa, Taito-ku, tel 03/3844-0577. This is the last store on the right as you walk up Nakamise to Senso-ji. It sells fine miniatures representing period people, houses, and shops, as well as other delightful statuettes.

■ CENTRAL HONSHU

KANAZAWA

Kanazawa has been a center for ceramics since feudal times and is known for *Ohi* and *Kutani* pottery. Devised for the tea ceremony, Ohi ware has beautiful warm-colored glazes; Kutani ware has ornate decoration in glowing colors. In the southwest of town is **Kutani Kosengama** *(Kosen Kutani Pottery Kiln, 5-3-3 Nomachi, tel 076/241-0902, by reservation).*

A major producer of gold leaf since ancient times, Kanazawa is also renowned for Kaga lacquer-ware *(Kaga maki-e)*, featuring intricate designs highlighted with gold and silver dust. The Japanese know the area most of all for *Kaga yuzen*—a distinctive dyeing and stenciling technique for silk kimono fabrics. Just north of the Kenroku-en garden, the **Ishikawa Bussankan** *(Ishikawa Prefectural Products Shop, 2-20 Kenroku-cho, tel 076/222-7788)* has all the specialties of the prefecture—arts, crafts, and edibles. Check the visitor information center for visits to other Kanazawa workshops.

NAGOYA

There are several department stores here, starting with **Meitetsu** at the train station, beneath which is a large underground shopping arcade. If you like junk shops and antiques, you should explore the Osu Arcade and vicinity. There's a weekend flea market at intervals at Osu Kannon Temple; check with the visitor information office.

Noritake has been famous for Western-style ceramics and chinaware for more than a century; you can visit the factory, the **Noritake Craft Center** *(3-1-36 Noritake Shinmachi, Nishi-ku, tel 052/561-7114)*, and try your hand at porcelain painting.

TAKAYAMA

There is plenty of local color in Takayama's morning street markets *(asa-ichi)*, which trade daily in local produce and flowers, as well as handicrafts. Both are open from 7 a.m. to noon, one at Jinya-mae near the historic government building and the other on the eastern bank of the Miya-gawa, across from Kajibashi Bridge. The old town center of Sanmachi Suji holds an antique market on the 7th of each month from May through October.

■ KANSAI

KYOTO

Kyoto's shopping is concentrated in the center of town, especially along Shijo-dori up to the intersection with Kawaramachi-dori. Shopping arcades sprawl beneath Kyoto Station and there's also a range of shops in the city's covered arcades: Shinkyogoku and Teramachi.

Kyoto's department stores have large selections of traditional local products and gifts. Among them are **Marui** *(68 Shin-machi, Shijo-dori, Shimogyo-ku, tel 075/257-0101)*, **Takashimaya** (see below), and **Daimaru** *(Shijo-dori, Shimogyo-ku, tel 075/211-8111)*. **Aritsugu** 219 Kajiya-cho, Go-komachi Nishi-iru, Nishikikoji-dri, Nakagyo-ku, tel 075/221-1091. This shop doesn't sell knives, it sells food lasers. The knife supplier for the Imperial family for centuries, Aritsugu has English-speaking staff to explain how to care for their carbon-steel blades. **Ippodo** 52 Tokiwagi-cho Teramachi-dori Nijo, Nakagyo-ku, tel 075/211-3421. Kyoto's most illustrious tea shop has English-speaking staff and can explain many aspects of *matcha* or *sencha*. Tea ceremony classes are also available. **Kasagen** 284 Kitagawa, Gion-machi, Higashiyama-ku, tel 075/561-2832, closed Wed. Has sold oiled paper umbrellas for well over a century.

Kyoto Handicraft Center 17 Shogoin, Entomi-cho, Sakyo-ku, tel 075/761-8001. Artisans and craftspeople work on the spot, and the full range of Kyoto crafts is on sale, from lacquer to textiles to ceramic knives. **Kyoto Tojiki Kaikan (Kyoto Ceramics Center;** closed Tues., Wed.) 583-1 Yugyomae-cho, Higashioji Gojo-agaru, Higashi-yamu-ku, tel 075/541-1102. Two floors filled with the works of members of the local potters' cooperative. **Miyawaki Baisen-an** 80-3 Daikoku-cho, Rokkaku-dori, Tom-inokoji Nishi-iru, Nakagyo-ku, tel 075/221-0181. This famous shop first started selling fans to geisha, actors, and the general public about 180 years ago. **Nishijin Orimono Textile Center** 414 Tatemonzenji-cho, Horikawa-Imadegawa Minami-iru, Kamigyo-ku, tel 075/451-9231. You can watch designers, dyers, and weavers at work on kimono silk of the highest quality; there's also a (pricey) sales area. **Sanko-sha** 79 Enoki-cho, Kitaga-wa-Nishi-iru, Nijo-Kawaramachi, Nakagyo-ku, tel 075/222-0390. This great calligraphy shop on Nijo-dori has a wide range of brushes and beautiful paper. **Takashimaya** 52 Shin-machi, Shijo-dori, Shimogyo-ku, tel 075/221-8811. Department store reputed to have the best selection of traditional gifts. **Tanakaya** Shijo-dori, Yanagino-banba-higashi-iru, Shimogyo-ku, tel 075/221-1959, closed Wed. A specialist in Japanese dolls, especially the local *kyo-ningyo*. Upstairs is a gallery of their antique counterparts. **Yamato Mingei-ten** Takoyakushi-agaru, Kawaramachi-dori, Nakagyo-ku, tel 075/221-2641, closed Tues. Good folk craft shop.

Entertainment & Festivals

Concentrated mainly in amusement districts, the array of entertainments in large Japanese cities is exhaustive. Even smaller towns have a district with bars, restaurants, discos, movie theaters—and more louche entertainments. Many visitors to Japan are attracted by the festivals taking place all over the country.

You'll find English-language listings in magazines such as *Tokyo Journal* and *Kansai Scene,* as well as on their websites. You can also check Tokyo and Kansai (Kyoto and Osaka) theater programs in the English-language newspapers (see p. 357). In other areas, you should pick up the local newsletters in visitor information centers.

Entertainment districts also present a substantial selection of live-music venues. Night clubs often bar men unaccompanied by women. Most places charge women lower rates; some have dress codes.

Tokyo, Kyoto, and other large cities feature traditional theater forms, including Kabuki and Noh. Elsewhere they are rare; you're more likely to see Western-style performing arts, notably world-class classical music.

To reserve tickets for shows, contact (or get someone to do it for you) the main booking agencies: **Ticket Pia** (*t.pia.jp*), **CN Playguide** (*cnplayguide.com*), and **eplus** (*eplus.jp*). Agencies also sell tickets for sports events.

▨ TOKYO

When going out on the town, choose between the entertainment districts of Shinjuku, Roppongi, and Shibuya, with plenty more alternatives in Aoyama, Ebisu, and Nishi-Azabu.

Bars & Clubs

The *Tokyo Journal* and *Metropolis* listings are excellent for bars and clubs. Fashions come and go at an alarming rate in Japan, so be aware that suggestions here may have lost favor or vanished by the time this book goes to press.

A971 9-7-2 Akasaka, Minato-ku, tel 03/5413-3210. Taking its name from the address, A971 is a hip bar nestled in the new Tokyo Midtown complex that attracts weekend party people.

Albatross 1-2-11 Nishi-Shinjuku, Shinjuku-ku, tel 03/3342-5758. Slightly more upscale than the surrounding bars of Omoideyo-kocho, Albatross is plastered with art and warm red decor.

Blue Note 6-3-16 Minami Aoyama, Minato-ku, tel 03/5485-0088. Like its New York counterpart, this is the place to catch the greatest names in jazz. Two sets nightly at 7 p.m. and 9:30 p.m.

Crocodile B1 New Sekiguchi Bldg., 6-18-8 Jingumae, Shibuya-ku, tel 03/3499-5205. Thirty years on, the Croc is still cool, still hip. An attractive bar and premier Tokyo "live house" popular with a mixed crowd of all ages.

Ginza Lion Ginza Lion Bldg. 1F, 7-9-20 Ginza, Chuo-ku, tel 03/3571-2590. Brewer Sapporo's massive beer hall was built in 1934, making it the oldest of its kind in Japan, and it retains its original decor, a sort of ersatz European but charming with the patina of age. The food is decent and the beer plentiful.

Legato 15F, E. Space Tower, 3-6 Maruyama-cho, Shibuya-ku, tel 03/5784-2121. This stylish Italian restaurant and bar decorated in low lights and burnished metal fixtures has an excellent view of Shibuya's shining nighttime cityscape. Drinks are pricey.

Muse B1, 4-1-1 Nishi-Azabu, Minato-ku, tel 03/5467-1188. A large warren of underground rooms, Muse has several different styles of music going at once, intimate nooks, and even dart boards.

Newlex Edo 5-5-1 Roppongi, Minato-ku, tel 03/3479-7477. Established in 1980, the Newlex is where international screen, stage, and rock celebrities visiting Tokyo wind up until the wee small hours—hosted by genial manager Bill Hersey.

Robot Restaurant 1-7-1 Kabuki-cho, Shinju-ku tel 03/3200-5500. Light-shows and sexy robot battles showcase "crazy Japan."

Womb 2-16 Maruyama-cho, Shibuya-ku. One of the hottest clubs in the international electronic scene, Womb is packed with young people on weekends.

For Children

Tokyo Disneyland
1-1 Mai-hama, Urayasu-shi, Chiba-ken, tel 045/330-5211, www.tokyodisneyresort.co.jp. A successful clone of its California parent and only a 15-minute train ride to Urayasu (from JR Tokyo Station on the JR Keiyo line to Maihama Station). Hours and prices vary seasonally.

Sumo

The nation's most important sumo tournaments take place at the **Kokugikan** (*National Sumo Hall; 1-3-28 Yokoami, Sumida-ku, tel 03/3623-5111*) from the 1st or 2nd Sunday to the 3rd or 4th Sunday in January and May and from the 2nd to 4th Sunday in September.

Theater

Tokyo has the largest number of playhouses staging traditional theater such as Kabuki and Noh (see pp. 53–54). Programs are seasonal; check for details in the English-language press or with the Japan National Tourist Office.

Kabukiza 4-12-15 Ginza, Chuo-ku, tel 03/3541-3131. Two Kabuki programs daily.
Kokuritsu Gekijo (National Theater) 4-1 Hayabusa-cho, Chiyoda-ku, tel 03/3265-7411. Sometimes presents Bunraku puppet theater; at other times, anything from Kabuki to works by contemporary composers.
Shinbashi Embujo 6-18-2 Ginza, Chuo-ku, tel 03/3541-2600. Mainly traditional fare, including Kabuki and seasonal dance presentations by the dwindling *shimabashi* geisha.
Takarazuka Theater 1-1-3 Yurakucho, Chiyoda-ku, tel 03/5251-2001. Tokyo branch of the all-female opera company: lavish revues, operettas, and musicals. Reserve ahead for a good seat.

◼ HOKKAIDO

SAPPORO

The action in Sapporo is concentrated in Susukino, where side streets present an unending array of bars and clubs. You can usually grab a beer from a vending machine and join in what seems like a party watching a ball game up on the giant TV screen over the area's main intersection.

500 Bar Minami 4, Nishi 2, Chuo-ku, tel 011/562-2556. All drinks at this chic chain are ¥500. The menu has it all, from cured ham to honey on toast.
Gaijin Bar 2F M's Space, Minami 2, Nishi 7, tel 011/272-1033, closed Sun. This is one of the city's top expat hangouts.

King Xmhu 424-10 Minami 7, Nishi 4, tel 011/252-9912. Pronounced "mu," the hottest dance spot features a colossal Aztec-style effigy of the king dominating the facade with glowing red eyes; a cadaverous interior matches it with glowing laser-eyed demon masks and trendy decor.

◼ CENTRAL HONSHU

KANAZAWA

A leading center for Noh drama for centuries. The place to see it is the **Ishikawa Prefectural Noh Theater** *(4-18-3 Ishibiki, tel 076/264-2598)*. Programs run every week during summer, but less regularly at other times. Check the visitor information center for schedules.

NAGOYA

Nagoya has a Noh theater and the Misono-za Kabuki theater, but programs are irregular. Check local listings available from the visitor information center. There is a concentration of bars and night spots in an energetic amusement district around Sakae 3-chome. **Sumo** is one of the highlights of the summer. Tournaments are held from the 1st to 3rd Sunday in July at the **Aichi-ken Taiiku-kan** *(Aichi Prefectural Gymnasium, 1-1 Ninomaru, Naka-ku, Nagoya, tel 052/971-2516)*.

◼ KYOTO
Bars & Clubs
Bungalow 15 Kashiwayacho, Shimogyo-ku, tel 075/256-8205. The craft beer scene in Japan has just started to take off and this "open" (it doesn't have first-floor walls) bar has a great selection of new domestic brews.

Metro Keihan Marutamachi Station, tel 075/752-4765. There are bigger clubs, but this is Kyoto's most interesting venue. It features big-name foreign DJs, art exhibits, fringe theater, and weird and wacky theme nights. This venue is small and gets crowded on weekends.
Sake Bar Yoramu 35-1 Matsuya-cho Nijo-dori, Higashinotoin Higashi-iru, Nakagyo-ku. Run by saké expert and Israeli expat Yoram, this is an excellent place to learn about Japan's rice wines.

Theater

Noh and Kabuki both originated in Kyoto. The same applies to geisha dance spectaculars; in addition to those mentioned below, others are also presented in the fall. Check for programs at the visitor information center.

Gion Corner 570-2 Minamigawa, Gion-machi, Higashiyama-ku, tel 075/561-1119. A small theater offering an eclectic digest of traditional entertainments, from Bunraku puppet drama excerpts to the tea ceremony.
Gion Kobu Kaburenjo 570-2 Minamigawa, Gion-machi, Higashiyama-ku, tel 075/541-3391. Next to Gion Corner (above), this theater has been putting on the *Miyako Odori* (Cherry Dance) of *maiko* (apprentice geisha) each April for almost 150 years.
Minamiza Shijo Ohashi Higashizume, Higashiyama-ku, tel 075/561-1155. This famous Kyoto landmark on the southern bank of the Kamo River is Japan's oldest Kabuki theater.
Pontocho Kaburenjo Theater Pontocho-dori, Sanjo Sagaru, Nakagyo-ku, tel 075/221-2025. Pontocho maiko and geisha present *Kamo-gawa Odori* (Kamo River Dance) spectaculars here twice a year—in May and mid-October to mid-November.

▦ KANSAI

OSAKA

Osaka rivals Tokyo as the nation's most hedonistic city; its entertainment district is Dotombori, just south of the center between Shinsaibashi and Namba Stations. Many expat-friendly dives lie north of Dotombori in hot and hip **Amerika Mura** (America Village), named for its many U.S.-style fashion outlets.

Drunk Bears 10-12 Chayamachi, Kita-ku. A Spanish/Italian cuisine pub, this is a popular spot for locals at the beginning of the night.

Owl Osaka 5-1 Kakuda-cho, Kita-ku. This huge club in Umeda plays mostly pop and has about 1,000 guests on weekends.

Suntory Yamazaki Distillery 5-2-1 Yamazaki, Shimamoto-cho, Mishima-gun. This award-winning distillery conducts tours and tasting, by reservation.

Sumo

Sumo tournaments are held in Osaka from the 2nd to 4th Sunday in March at the **Osaka Furitsu Taiiku Kaikan** *(3-4-36 Namba-Naka, Naniwa-ku, tel 06/6631-0121)*, near Namba subway station.

Theater

Check schedules either at the visitor information center or in publications such as *Kansai Time Out* magazine and *Meet Osaka.*

National Bunraku Theater of Japan 1-12-10 Nipponbashi, Chuo-ku, tel 06/6212-2531. Bunraku, the puppet theater form, originated in Osaka. It is worth going to see; performances have three-week runs in January, March, April, June to August, and November.

▦ KYUSHU

FUKUOKA

Nakasu amusement district, comprising restaurants, bars, nightclubs, theaters, and discos, is considered one of Japan's best. Tenjin, northwest of Nakasu, also has nightspots. Fukuoka is also a sumo city, hosting major tournaments from the 2nd to the 4th Sunday in November at the **Fukuoka Kokusai Center** *(2-2 Chikko-Hon-machi, Hakata-ku, Fukuoka-shi, tel 092/272-1111).*

FESTIVALS

The *matsuri* (festival) is where you'll find the "real Japan." Rituals and customs, food and drink, clothing and trappings, music and dance are all redolent of a cultural identity predating Western influence by centuries. Shinto festival parades always include *mikoshi*, the ornately decorated, gilded palanquins supported on long, thick wooden poles and carried around the streets by scores of chanting bearers. Each mikoshi was thought to be the means of conveyance for a deity; the object of the festival was to show the gods a good time.

Some matsuri are nostalgic pageants with parades of geisha or samurai warriors; others, especially Buddhist festivals such as O-Bon, commemorate the dead. Many festivals include markets selling food and sweets, good-luck charms, plants, and cheap toys. If you plan to attend a major festival, bear in mind that hotels in the area will be packed solid. There are many hundreds of festivals; those below are merely a few of the more important ones; confirm actual festival dates at local visitor centers.

COUNTRYWIDE

January

O-Shogatsu–New Year's Day (Dec 31–Jan 2). At midnight on New Year's Eve, people gather at temples to ring the bells. The next day, thousands pay their first visits to shrines in beautiful kimonos.
Seijin-no-Hi–Coming of Age Day (2nd Mon.). On this national holiday 20-year-olds dress in beautiful kimonos and visit shrines.

February

Setsubun–Parting of the Seasons (Feb. 3 or 4). Marks the last day of winter. Many shrines and temples host celebrations.

March

Hina Matsuri–Doll's Festival or Peach Blossom Festival (Mar. 3). A girls' festival: Dolls representing an imperial couple of ancient times, with attendant court, are displayed on specially erected shelves in homes (see sidebar p. 62).

April

Hanami–Flower viewing. Colleagues, friends, and families indulge in bibulous picnics beneath flowering cherry trees.
Hana Matsuri–Flower Festival (April 8). Celebrates Buddha's birthday in temples nationwide.

August

O-Bon–Festival of the Dead or Lantern Festival (mid-Aug.). Opens a season coinciding with the summer vacation. Events and festivals are held nationwide, notably *Bon odori* dancing, fireworks displays, and the charming custom of floating candles (each representing a soul) along rivers aboard little paper boats.

November

Shichi-go-san (Nov. 15). Children aged 7 *(shichi)*, 5 *(go)*, and 3 *(san)* don traditional finery for a ritual blessing at a Shinto shrine.

■ TOKYO

January

Dezome-shiki—New Year Firemen's Parade (Jan. 6). Attired in period garb, firemen parade along Harumi-dori on Tokyo Bay.

May

Sanja Matsuri (3rd Sat. in May). Crowds of people, many in period costume, throng the streets of Asakusa.

June

Sanno Matsuri (June 9–16). At Hie-jinja, mounted priests parade on Akasaka's main avenue in even-numbered years.

July

Fireworks (last Sat. in July). Held in Asakusa over Sumida-gawa, this is Japan's biggest display.

August

Typically held the second week of August and the end of December, **Comiket** is Japan's biggest celebration of manga and anime, with half a million people attending the 3-day convention devoted to independent manga artists.

November

Tori-no-Ichi—Rooster Fair (early to mid-Nov.). Night markets at Otori-jinja in Asakusa and Hanazono-jinja in Shinjuku. Ornately decorated *kumade* (rakes) are sold (to encourage the gods to help businesses rake in plenty of cash). A marvelous all-night street party, with stalls selling saké, noodles, and *yakitori* (skewered chicken).

December

Hagoita Ichi (Dec. 17–19). A festive all-night market at Senso-ji.

■ EXCURSIONS FROM TOKYO

April

Kamakura Matsuri (2nd to 3rd Sun. in April). Focuses on Tsurugaoka Hachiman-gu, and features dances and a parade of historical samurai figures, with a *yabusame* (archery on horseback) contest in samurai regalia.

May

Sennin Gyoretsu (May 17–18). The festival at Tosho-gu in Nikko culminates with a thousand men in samurai armor.

September

Yabusame (Sept. 16). Tsurugaoka Hachiman-gu, Kamakura. The most exciting demonstration of *yabusame* (archery on horseback).

October

Toshogu Matsuri (Oct. 17). Autumn Festival at Tosho-gu, Nikko, featuring a parade of mounted priests and samurai.

November

Daimyo Gyoretsu (Nov. 3). This costumed pageant evokes 17th-century processions of *daimyo* along the Tokaido Road in Hakone-Yumoto.

■ HOKKAIDO

February

Yuki Matsuri—Snow Festival (early Feb.). Intricate and ornate snow sculptures decorate the center of Sapporo.

■ NORTHERN HONSHU (TOHOKU)

February

Kamakura Matsuri (Feb. 15–16). This children's festival happens in several places, the most famous at Yokote, Akita-ken. It's named after the snow houses *(kamakura)* built for the event; children sit snugly in their candlelit igloos.

June

Chaguchagu Umako—Horse Festival (June 15). In Morioka, dealers and breeders parade horses to be blessed at Sozen-jinja.

August

Nebuta and **Neputa** (Aug. 2–7). These festivals, held at the same time in Aomori and Hirosaki, feature a spectacular parade of huge, beautifully painted, and ornate lanterns.

Kanto Matsuri (Aug. 3–6). Akita city. As the highlight of a rousing parade, men hold huge poles festooned with lanterns, balancing them on their hands, shoulders, chins, and foreheads.

December

Namahage (Dec. 31). Held on the Oga-hanto Peninsula in Akita-ken. Groups of bachelors don demon costumes and go from house to house bellowing, "Are there any rascals in here?" Residents entertain these *namahage* with rice cakes and saké.

■ CENTRAL HONSHU

March

Tagata Honen Matsuri—Bumper Harvest Festival (Mar. 15). The fertility shrine Tagata-jinja, near Inuyama, is renowned for this rousing and somewhat racy parade of huge wooden phalli.

April

Takayama Matsuri (April 14–15). This festival centers on Takayama's Hie-jinja. A splendid parade with 12 ornate *yatai*—wheeled juggernauts with performing *karakuri* automatons.

October

Takayama Hachimangu Matsuri (Oct. 9–10). Centered on Hachiman-gu, Takayama, this ancient festival is renowned for its beautiful floats and *mikoshi*.

■ KANSAI

January

Toka Ebisu (Jan. 9–11). At Imamiya Ebisu-jinja in Osaka, thousands pay their respects to Ebisu, a god of plenty and patron of businesspeople and fishermen. A parade of women in kimonos is carried aboard ornate palanquins.

Wakakusa Yamayaki (4th Sat. in Jan). The grass on Wakakusa-yama (in Nara-koen, Nara) is burned to commemorate the ending of rivalry between two temples in the tenth century.

February

Mantoro—Lantern Lighting Ceremony (Feb. 3 or 4 and Aug. 14–15, for the O-Bon season). This magical event takes place in Nara to usher in the spring. All 3,000 bronze and stone lanterns at Kasuga Taisha are lit.

March

Omizutori—Water-drawing Ceremony (Mar. 1–14). Performed annually at Todai-ji in Nara, since the ninth century. The climax is the 12th, when water is drawn from the Wakasa Well as bearers swing huge torches producing showers of sparks from the balcony of the Nigatsu-do hall.

May

Aoi Matsuri—Hollyhock Festival (May 15). Held at Shimo-gamo and Kami-gamo-jinja, Kyoto, with lavish costumes and pageantry. **Mifune Matsuri** (3rd Sun. in May). Poets, musicians, and dancers in period costume perform aboard boats on the Oi River at Arashiyama.

June

Takigi Noh (around June 1–2). A torchlit Noh performance, featuring some of the foremost protagonists of the art, in the open air at Heian-jinja.

Rice Planting Ceremony (June 14). Sumiyoshi-taisha in Osaka celebrates a rice planting ceremony led by 12 beauties.

July

Gion Matsuri (throughout July—night festival July 14–16, parade on July 17). This festival in Yasaka-jinja in Kyoto commemorates the end to a ninth-century plague and centers on the Yasaka in Kyoto.

August

Daimonji (Aug. 16). To guide the spirits of ancestors back to their resting places, huge Chinese characters cut into the mountainsides around Kyoto are lit on fire.

October

Jidai Matsuri—Eras Festival (Oct. 22). Heian Jingu, Kyoto. The highlight is a pageant celebrating the foundation of the city in 794.

December

Okera Mairi (Dec. 31). A huge bonfire is lit at midnight in Yasaka-jinja compound in Kyoto; everyone tries to take home kindling to start the first fire of the new year.

■ WESTERN HONSHU (CHUGOKU)

February

Eyo (3rd Sat. in Feb.). The most famous of the *hadaka matsuri* (naked festivals) held at several locations in Japan. Here, at Saidai-ji, Okayama-ken, youths wearing loincloths compete within the confined space of a temple tower to catch two wands, believed to bring a year's good luck, which are thrown down by priests.

June

Kangensai Music Festival (late July—early Aug.). Displays of ancient court dances and

music aboard ornate boats at Itsukushima-jinja, on Miyajima.

August

Peace Ceremony (Aug. 6). Held in Hiroshima. Prayers for the souls of the A-bomb victims.

October

Kenka Matsuri—Fighting Festival (Oct. 14–15). At Matsubara-jinja, Himeji, groups of bearers compete to lead the parade and be first at the shrine, each trying to topple their rivals' huge *mikoshi*.

■ SHIKOKU & THE SETO-NAIKAI

July

Warei Natsu Matsuri (July 23–24). Firework displays, torchlit parades, and bullfights on Uwajima.

August

Awa-odori (Aug. 12–15). Costumed and carousing citizens of Tokushima are joined by thousands of visitors to become the "dancing fools" in the city streets.

■ KYUSHU

May

Hakata Dontaku (May 3–4). A colorful street parade in Fukuoka with costumed revelers attired as gods and demons.

July

Hakata Gion Yamakasa (July 1–15). The climax on the last day consists of teams racing huge floats representing castles, dolls, etc., through Fukuoka's streets.

October

O-Kunchi (Oct. 7–9). Focused on Suwa-jinja shrine, Nagasaki. Highlights show strong Chinese influence (dragon dances), and some floats evoke historical contacts with Europe.

INDEX

ILLUSTRATIONS CREDITS

National Geographic
TRAVELER

Japan
FIFTH EDITION

Since 1888, the National Geographic Society has funded more than 12,000 research, exploration, and preservation projects around the world. National Geographic Partners distributes a portion of the funds it receives from your purchase to National Geographic Society to support programs including the conservation of animals and their habitats.

The information in this book has been carefully checked and to the best of our knowledge is accurate. However, details are subject to change, and the National Geographic publisher cannot be responsible for such changes, or for errors or omissions. Assessments of sites, hotels, and restaurants are based on the author's subjective opinions, which do not necessarily reflect the publisher's opinion.

National Geographic Partners
1145 17th Street NW
Washington, DC 20036-4688 USA

Become a member of National Geographic and activate your benefits today at natgeo.com/jointoday.

For information about special discounts for bulk purchases, please contact National Geographic Books Special Sales: specialsales@natgeo.com

For rights or permissions inquiries, please contact National Geographic Books Subsidiary Rights: bookrights@natgeo.com

Cutaway illustrations drawn by Maltings Partnership, Derby, England.

ISBN: 978-1-4262-1829-3

Printed in Hong Kong

17/THK/1